Applied Social Research

Tool for the Human Services

Fourth Edition

Duane R. Monette
Thomas J. Sullivan
Cornell R. DeJong

Northern Michigan University

Harcourt Brace College Publishers
Fort Worth   Philadelphia   San Diego   New York   Orlando   Austin   San Antonio
Toronto   Montreal   London   Sydney   Tokyo

Publisher	Earl McPeek
Acquisitions Editor	Brenda Weeks
Product Manager	Julie McBurney
Developmental Editor	Susan R. Petty
Project Editor	Angela Williams Urquhart
Production Managers	Cindy Young, Debra A. Jenkin
Art Director	Carol Kincaid

To My Mother,
Thanks for everything.
To Nancy,
Who accepted my fleeting presence.
To Susan,
From where the sun now stands, we shall commute no more forever.

Address for Editorial Correspondence
Harcourt Brace College Publishers, 301 Commerce Street, Suite 3700, Fort Worth, TX 76102

Address for Orders
Harcourt Brace & Company, 6277 Sea Harbor Drive, Orlando, FL 32887-6777; 1-800-782-4479

Web site address:
http://www.hbcollege.com

Harcourt Brace & Company will provide complimentary supplements or supplement packages to those adopters qualified under our adoption policy. Please contact your sales representative to learn how you qualify. If as an adopter or potential user you receive supplements you do not need, please return them to your sales representative or send them to:
ATTN: Returns Department
Troy Warehouse
165 South Lincoln Drive
Troy, MO 63379

ISBN: 0-03-019444-X

Library of Congress Catalogue Number: 97-75356

Printed in the United States of America

7 8 9 0 1 2 3 4 5 6   039   10 9 8 7 6 5 4 3 2 1

Preface

The social sciences and the human services confront an important challenge as the twentieth century ends and a new millennium begins. Human service programs in today's environment must demonstrate a need for their services, document the quality of services they deliver, and show evidence of the effectiveness of those services. These expectations mean that human service professionals must be well able to apply social science research methods to practice problems because it is those research methods that will provide convincing evidence of those needs, quality, and effectiveness.

Students new to the human service field are often unaware of the role of research in human service delivery. A common question that we hear from our own students is this: "I want a career where I can help people. Why do I need to study research methods?" We know that building a convincing case for the connection between research and practice in the human service curriculum cannot be done in a paragraph of an introduction, nor can it be accomplished in the first lecture of the semester. Sustaining student interest requires that the connection between research and practice be a constant theme throughout the textbook and the course. And so our goal, from the first edition through this fourth one, has been to present the methods of social science research within the context of human service practice. The importance of keeping this theme in mind was brought home in a story heard recently at a meeting of program evaluators one of us attended. Speaking on the importance of keeping the evaluation focused on priorities of the program managers, an evaluator began his presentation:

A guy is out for a Saturday afternoon drive in the country, and he happens upon a small airfield where a man is offering hot air balloon rides. It's a lovely day, so he decides to give it a try. Soon he's enjoying a tremendous view and the witty commentary of his guide. Suddenly, a dense fog rolls in out of nowhere. The wind begins to howl, and the balloon is buffeted about for what seems hours. Finally, the wind subsides, and a break appears in the clouds. The relieved pair look down and are ecstatic to see someone standing in a field immediately below them. The balloon pilot yells down, "Hey you! Down there! Where are we?"

The startled man on the ground looks up, pauses for a moment, and then shouts back, "You're up in the air!"

The pilot turns to his passenger. "You know what?" he says. "That guy down there has got to be a social researcher."

"What makes you say that?" inquired the passenger.

"Well," intones the pilot, "what he says is for sure right. But, it's absolutely useless!"

In revising this textbook for the fourth edition, we've tried to keep that friendly little jab in mind. Research is unquestionably a demanding subject, but consistently seeing the connections between research and human service practice can defuse a sense of drudgery and instill enthusiasm in its place. One of the most rewarding experiences we've enjoyed in writing this textbook or in teaching research has been to witness the apprehensions of a student dissipate with the discovery of new knowledge and the mastery of new ideas. It is our desire to emphasize the connections between research and practice and encourage more students to share that positive growth. Having engaged in both practice and research, we are convinced that each enterprise has much to offer the other, and we hope that the reader will share our enthusiasm for uncovering the parallels and linkages between research and practice.

We have retained the interdisciplinary cooperative effort of the earlier editions: Some authors are research methodologists, others have more experience with human service practice and program evaluation. However, our own professional lives reflect one of the major themes of this book in that each of us, in one way or another, has had one foot planted in the research world and the other in the world of practice delivery. We conceive of social research and human service practice as allies bound by common goals of advancing knowledge and creating a better world, goals that neither can achieve alone. As is the case with allies in any human enterprise, disputes, tensions, and disagreements occur between research-as-science and human-service-as-practice. But in the 20 years that we have worked on this book, we have been heartened by the many excellent examples of research and human service practice working together. In this fourth edition, we have incorporated recent data that show the growing diversity of ways in which research is being applied to practice and the increasingly extensive linkages between research and practice. Our goal, as with earlier editions, is to prepare a book that is useful to those in human service departments who integrate research into the student's practice education as well as to social scientists who emphasize the applied dimension of social science methods.

The special theme of this book, then, is that many parallels and links exist between social research and human service practice. We outline these ideas in the first chapter and then carry this theme through the remainder of the book. This textbook is primarily an introduction to social research as it relates to the human services. As such, we have presented all of the topics of scientific research important for such an introduction. But we have also offered a challenge—we hope that students will learn that social research has many parallels with human service practice. The challenge is also to recognize the ways in which the two can be

linked—by incorporating research activities into practice settings and by shaping practice settings into research opportunities.

Features

A number of special features in this book are designed to help develop an appreciation for social research and its importance to the human services.

Research in Practice: Each chapter includes boxed features titled "Research in Practice" in which we discuss some special examples where research and practice have been linked. In this way, we emphasize the theme of the book and encourage students to consider the many ways in which this linkage can be achieved.

Computers in Research: Recognizing that computers are an integral part of both research and human service practice, we have included in many chapters boxed features that present some application of computers in research. These inserts require no previous experience with or knowledge of computers, and they are intended to inform students of the general capabilities of software rather than to train them to use particular types of software.

Content on Women and Minorities: We have given additional recognition to the need for human service workers to be knowledgeable of the special needs and problems of women and minorities. To this end, we have addressed in most chapters some special considerations in research methods as they apply to these groups.

Exploring the Internet: We encourage students to go beyond the boundaries of what can be provided in a textbook by exploring additional resources available on the World Wide Web. The Internet has become an increasingly important adjunct to all kinds of research practice delivery tasks. In every chapter, a feature called "Exploring the Internet" suggests some specific Web sites that we personally have found to be valuable. Recognizing that this is a rapidly developing area, we have also included general suggestions for searching the World Wide Web for additional resources, including those that may very well be created after publication of this text. Also, a new appendix has been added to the textbook that provides the neophyte with basic instructions on how to use the Internet.

Grant Proposals and Writing: We have included a chapter on writing grant proposals and research reports. To be knowledgeable about research, students should understand how this process works because it is integral to the tasks of securing funding and communicating research findings.

For Further Reading: Each chapter includes a brief, annotated list of books that students will find useful for pursuing chapter topics in greater depth. An important consideration in choosing readings was that they further the overall theme of the book.

Exercises for Class Discussion: Each chapter ends with a set of exercises in which we present the student with some problem or setting in human service practice and ask questions that call for students to consider the parallels and linkages between research and practice. These exercises can be used as a context for class discussion, or they can serve as out-of-class assignments. Either way, students should find them challenging and stimulating.

Appendix on Library Usage: We have included an appendix in which we discuss how to use the library, focusing specifically on the special needs of students in the human services. Although many college students will be familiar with the library by the time they take a research course, some may find they have a weakness in this area that can be strengthened by studying the appendix. Even those familiar with the library will find some new and useful information about library resources relevant to the human services.

Instructor's Manual: A manual of test items and suggested lecture and class discussion topics is available from your local Harcourt representative or by contacting the Sociology Editor: Harcourt Brace College Publishers, 301 Commerce Street, Suite 3700, Fort Worth, TX 76102.

New to the Fourth Edition

Events have been unfolding rapidly in the social sciences and human services. Some of these changes are substantive—new research findings replacing earlier results and changing how we view such things as strategies to control domestic violence and sex stereotyping in children's books and textbooks. Other changes are methodological, such as a growing emphasis on qualitative research in the human services and new computer software that is revolutionizing the research process. These developments warrant a new edition of this book in order to ensure that both faculty and students have available the most current materials and information on the research process. The fourth edition has been thoroughly updated to reflect the most recent developments in the research field.

Among the major changes that were made in the fourth edition are the following:

• *Exploring the Internet*—The Internet, which was almost unheard of when we completed the previous edition, is now a major fixture of modern life. In recognition of the importance of this phenomenon, we have added a new section at the end of every chapter where the student will find guidance for harnessing the vast resources of the Internet for research and human service practice. We have personally investigated every Web site included in the Internet section and singled out ones that relate to the specific chapter at hand. Of course, the Internet is a rapidly changing resource, and there may be concern that sites we recommend today may be gone tomorrow. We address this in two ways: We emphasize major sites that should be accessible for some time in the future, and we place an emphasis on teaching *how* to use the Internet by using various search procedures. Using the same key concepts as search terms and applying similar search procedures should locate useful resources for several years. In addition, we have provided a new appendix that teaches the beginner how to use the Internet.

- *A new chapter on data analysis*—The increasing sophistication of personal computer software for data analysis has been a major impetus for revising our treatment of data analysis methods into two chapters of expanded coverage. Based on the assumption that many human service professionals will be collecting their own data in human service settings and processing that data on personal computers, Chapter 14 now provides much more detail on the process of transforming raw data into a useful computer file through data coding, data entry, data cleaning, and preparing new variables. Modern statistical software packages have impressive graphics capabilities, so we have also added a presentation on basic graphing procedures for displaying and analyzing data. Chapter 14 also includes discussion of bivariate and multivariate analysis through contingency tables and table elaboration that was in the previous edition. Chapter 15 is devoted to discussion of descriptive and inferential statistics found in the third edition, with the addition of a discussion on the normal distribution and the central limit theorem to help in understanding inferential statistics.
- Five new *Research in Practice* illustrations have been added to provide stimulating illustrations of the challenges of conducting research useful to human service practice. Also, a number of the Computers in Research features have been revised and updated.
- *Focus group content* has been added to Chapters 7 and 9. This research strategy is growing in popularity for program assessment, so we introduce students to it in the contexts of interviewing and observation.
- Finally, Appendix A on the use of the library required updating because of the ongoing revolution in information management. No longer simply a repository of books and journals, the library is being transformed into a center for in-

formation retrieval, and the appendix revision reflects this changing emphasis.

Acknowledgments

This book began as an idea born out of our own experience teaching research methods to future professionals in social work, criminal justice, education, health care, and other human service areas and being convinced that we could do better. Over the years, with each revision, we hope that we have come closer to the ideal of helping students to discover the linkages and parallels between practice and research. The students who have passed through our courses played a major role in shaping our thoughts and the content of this text. Their criticism, their frustration, their questioning, their desire to learn, have all motivated us to revise and improve with each edition. We owe them much. We also appreciate the many opportunities to participate in doing research on human service practice that have been extended by agencies throughout the Upper Peninsula of Michigan. Experience with these agencies has been a great teacher for us.

Many people at Northern Michigan University contributed to our ability to complete this project. Our department head, Richard Wright, made available to us whatever resources were at his disposal. Other colleagues—they know who they are—created an atmosphere that not only made this project possible, but highly rewarding. The University librarians have always come through for us with previous editions, and librarian Darlene Pierce was a great help on this one.

For their insightful comments and helpful suggestions, we wish to thank the following reviewers: Robert Freymeyer, Presbyterian College, Clinton, SC; Hugo Kamya, Boston College, Chestnut Hill, MA; James Petersen, Western Michigan University, Kalamazoo, MI; Howard Rebach, University of Maryland–Eastern Shore, Salisbury, MD; and Marvin Tossey, Salisbury State University, Salisbury, MD.

Once again, Harcourt Brace has been supportive in bringing this project to completion. We especially want to thank Susan Petty for helping us stay on task, for providing helpful suggestions, and for efficient project management. We would also like to thank the production team, Angela Williams Urquhart, Carol Kincaid, Debra Jenkin, and Cindy Young, for their help in speeding the manuscript through production.

Finally, we have dedicated this book to those crucial people who, just by being there, provide the support and motivation to see the project through to completion one more time. Doing a book is professionally rewarding, but there is no doubt, it does take time. A good many of the hours spent revising a manuscript were hours we took from them. We know we're indebted, and we know that interest on the debt is accruing rapidly. It looks like it could be our turn to cook for weeks to come. Anybody got a good recipe for lasagna?

Contents

Preface   iii

1 RESEARCH IN THE HUMAN SERVICES   1
Research in the Human Services   3
Goals of Research   3
Applications of Research   5
Special Issues: Research on Minorities and
   Women   8
Parallels Between Research and Practice   8
Steps in Conducting Research   8
Steps in Practice Intervention   10
The Plan of the Book   12
Main Points   13
Important Terms for Review   14
Exploring the Internet   15
For Further Reading   16
Exercises for Class Discussion   17

2 THE LOGIC OF SOCIAL RESEARCH   18
Sources of Knowledge   19
Tradition   19
Experience   20
Common Sense   21
Science   22
Scientific Practice   24
Theories in Research and Practice   25
What Is a Theory?   26
The Functions of Theories   28
Concepts and Hypotheses   30
Defining Concepts   30
Developing Hypotheses   31
Concepts and Operational Definitions Among
   Minority Populations   33
Deduction Versus Induction   34
Cause-and-Effect Relationships   34
Main Points   39
Important Terms for Review   39
Exploring the Internet   39
For Further Reading   41
Exercises for Class Discussion   42

3 ETHICAL ISSUES IN SOCIAL RESEARCH   44
**The Minority Experience: The Need for
   Ethical Standards**   46
Ethical Issues   50
Informed Consent   50
Confidentiality   53
Privacy   55
Physical or Mental Distress   56
Sponsored Research   56
Scientific Misconduct and Fraud   57
Scientific Advocacy   63
Protecting Vulnerable Clients   64
Withholding Treatment for Research Purposes   65
Codes of Ethics   67
Main Points   67
Important Terms for Review   68
Exploring the Internet   68
For Further Reading   68
Exercises for Class Discussion   69

4 ISSUES IN PROBLEM FORMULATION   71
Selecting a Research Problem   72
Personal Interest   72
Social Problems   73
Testing Theory   73
Prior Research   73
Program Evaluation   73
Human Service Practice   76
Minorities in Research: The Political Context of
   Problem Selection   77
Shaping and Refining the Problem   80
Conceptual Development   80
Review of Literature   81
Units of Analysis   83
Reactivity   86
Qualitative Versus Quantitative Research   86
Cross-Sectional Versus Longitudinal Research   87
Feasibility of a Research Project   90
Time Constraints   90
Financial Considerations   91
Anticipating and Avoiding Problems   93

Main Points   94
Important Terms for Review   94
Exploring the Internet   95
For Further Reading   95
Exercises for Class Discussion   96

5 THE PROCESS OF MEASUREMENT   98
Ways of Measuring   100
Levels of Measurement   101
 Nominal Measures   102
 Ordinal Measures   104
 Interval Measures   104
 Ratio Measures   105
 Discrete Versus Continuous Variables   106
Evaluating Measures   107
 Validity   107
 Reliability   111
 Measurement With Minority Populations   114
Errors in Measurement   115
 Random Errors   115
 Systematic Errors   116
Main Points   117
Important Terms for Review   120
Exploring the Internet   120
For Further Reading   121
Exercises for Class Discussion   121

6 SAMPLING   123
The Purpose of Sampling   124
Sampling Terminology   125
 Populations and Samples   125
 Sampling Frames   126
 A Classic Sampling Disaster   127
Probability Samples   128
 Simple Random Sampling   129
 Systematic Sampling   129
 Stratified Sampling   130
 Area Sampling   134
 Estimating Sample Size   136
Nonprobability Samples   140
 Availability Sampling   141
 Snowball Sampling   143
 Quota Sampling   143
 Purposive Sampling   144
 Dimensional Sampling   145
Sampling With Minority Populations   148
A Note on Sampling in Practice   149
Main Points   151
Important Terms for Review   152
Exploring the Internet   152

For Further Reading   153
Exercises for Class Discussion   153

7 SURVEY RESEARCH   155
Designing Questions   156
 Closed-Ended Versus Open-Ended
   Questions   156
 Wording of Questions   159
Questionnaires   161
 Structure and Design   161
 Response Rate   165
 Checking for Bias Due to Nonresponse   169
 An Assessment of Questionnaires   170
Interviews   170
 The Structure of Interviews   170
 Contacting Respondents   171
 Conducting an Interview   177
 Minorities and the Interview Relationship   179
 An Assessment of Interviews   180
Telephone Surveys   181
Focus Groups   184
**Practice and Research Interviews
   Compared   186**
Main Points   187
Important Terms for Review   187
Exploring the Internet   187
For Further Reading   190
Exercises for Class Discussion   191

8 ANALYSIS OF AVAILABLE DATA   193
Statistical Data   194
 Sources of Statistical Data   195
 Using Statistical Data   197
Content Analysis   201
 Coding Schemes   201
 Units of Analysis   204
Issues in Content Analysis   205
 Validity   205
 Reliability   206
 Level of Measurement   207
 Sampling   208
Assessment of Available Data Analysis   209
 Advantages   210
 Disadvantages   211
 Using Available Data in Research on
   Minorities   211
Main Points   213
Important Terms for Review   214
Exploring the Internet   214
For Further Reading   216
Exercises for Class Discussion   217

9 OBSERVATIONAL TECHNIQUES 218

Designs for Observation 220
Participant Observation 220
Unobtrusive Observation 227
Other Types of Observation 230

Issues in Observation 230
Recording Observations 231
Time Sampling 239
Validity and Reliability 240
Reactivity 242
Observational Research on Minority
  Populations 243

Assessment of Observational Techniques 244
Advantages 244
Disadvantages 244

Observation in Human Service Practice 245

Main Points 246

Important Terms for Review 247

Exploring the Internet 247

For Further Reading 248

Exercises for Class Discussion 250

10 EXPERIMENTAL RESEARCH 252

The Logic of Experimentation 254
Causation and Control 254
Matching and Randomization 256
Internal Validity 258

Experimental Designs 264
Preexperimental Designs 264
True Experimental Designs 265
Quasi-Experimental Designs 270

External Validity 275
Reactive Effects of Testing 275
Unrepresentative Samples 275
Reactive Settings 276
Multiple-Treatment Interference 277
The Importance of Replication 278
Lack of Minority Participation and Analysis 278

Assessment of Experiments 279
Advantages 279
Disadvantages 280

Main Points 281

Important Terms for Review 282

Exploring the Internet 282

For Further Reading 282

Exercises for Class Discussion 283

11 SINGLE-SUBJECT DESIGNS 285

The Cinical-Research Model 286

The Clinical-Research Process 288

Identify Problems 288
Establish Goals 288
Select a Single-Subject Design 289
Establish and Measure the Baseline 289
Introduce Treatment 294
Assess Treatment Effects 295

Types of Single-Subject Designs 297
Single-Treatment Designs 299
Specialized Designs 303

Generalizability of Single-Subject Designs 309

Assessment of the Clinical-Research Model 310
Advantages 310
Disadvantages 311

Main Points 311

Important Terms for Review 313

Exploring the Internet 314

For Further Reading 316

Exercises for Class Discussion 316

12 EVALUATION RESEARCH 318

What Is Evaluation Research? 319
Why Evaluate? 319
Evaluation Research and Basic Research 320
Types of Evaluation Research 321

Formative Evaluation Research 322

Summative Evaluation Research 323
Evaluability Assessment 324
Specification of Variables 325
Measuring Variables 327
The Evaluation of Minorities in Evaluation
  Research 328
Designs for Evaluation Research 328
Cost-Benefit Analysis 332
Cost-Effective Analysis 336

Barriers to the Use of Evaluation Research 337

Main Points 341

Important Terms for Review 341

Exploring the Internet 341

For Further Reading 342

Exercises for Class Discussion 343

13 SCALING 345

Advantages of Scaling 346

Developing Scales 347
Sources of Scale Items 348
Characteristics of Scale Items 348

Scaling Formats 350

Likert Scales   350
Thurstone Scales   353
Semantic Differential Scales   356
Guttman Scales   358
Multidimensional Scales   362
Scaling in the Human Services   363
Main Points   366
Important Terms for Review   366
Exploring the Internet   366
For Further Reading   367
Exercises for Class Discussion   368

14 DATA ANALYSIS I: DATA PREPARATION AND PRESENTATION   369
Preparation for Data Analysis   370
Coding Schemes   371
Preparing and Using a Codebook   375
Data Entry   376
Raw Data Entry   376
Data Cleaning   378
Creating New Variables   379
Data Distributions   379
Types of Data Distributions   380
Constructing Frequency Distributions   380
Graphical Display of Data Distributions   385
Bar Charts   385
Histograms and Frequency Polygons   387
Pie Charts   387
Contingency Tables   388
Bivariate Relationships   388
Multivariate Analysis   390
Main Points   397
Important Terms for Review   397
Exploring the Internet   398
For Further Reading   398
Exercises for Class Discussion   399

15 DATA ANALYSIS II: DESCRIPTIVE AND INFERENTIAL STATISTICS   400
Considerations in Choosing Statistics   401
Level of Measurement   401
Goals of the Data Analysis   403
Number of Variables   403
Properties of the Data   403
Audience   404
Descriptive Statistics   405
Measures of Central Tendency   405
Measures of Dispersion   406
Measures of Association   407
The Normal Distribution   411

Inferential Statistics   413
Probability Theory   413
Sampling Distributions   414
Statistical Hypothesis Testing   415
Statistical Procedures   417
Main Points   422
Important Terms for Review   424
Exploring the Internet   424
For Further Reading   424
Exercises for Class Discussion   425

16 WRITING FOR RESEARCH: GRANT PROPOSALS AND REPORT WRITING   427
The Grant-Funding Process   428
Federal Government Funding Sources   428
State Government Grants   429
Private Funding Sources   430
Learning About Funding Opportunities   434
Grant Proposal Planning   435
Proposal Development as a Process   435
Identifying the Topic   437
Needs Assessment   438
Specifying the Organization's Mission   438
Developing a Program   439
Targeting a Funding Source   440
Contacting and Visiting Funding Sources   441
Writing the Grant Proposal   443
Appearance and Writing Style   443
Components of the Proposal   444
Submitting the Proposal   447
Writing a Research Report   447
Consideration of the Audience   448
Organization of the Report   449
The Process of Writing   451
Main Points   452
Important Terms for Review   453
Exploring the Internet   453
For Further Reading   453
Exercises for Class Discussion   454

APPENDIX A   A GUIDE TO THE LIBRARY   456
Organization of the Library   457
Library Departments   457
Computers in Research: The Library   458
Accessing Library Materials   459
Books   459
The Classification System   459
The Public Catalog   461
Periodicals   462
Journals Important to the Human Services   463

Abstracts and Indexes   464
Reference Books for the Human Services   467
Government Documents   467
The *Monthly Catalog*   467
Subject Bibliographies and State Government
    Documents   470
Sources of Data in the Library   470
Government Sources   470
Nongovernment Sources   471
**Information Literacy and Critical Thinking
    Skills**   471
Exploring the Internet   472
For Further Reading   472

**APPENDIX B   GENERATING RANDOM
        NUMBERS   474**

**APPENDIX C   PROFESSIONAL CODES OF
        ETHICS   477**

**APPENDIX D   RESEARCH AND PRACTICE: THE
        WORLD WIDE WEB CONNECTION   483**
The Basics   484
Authors' Web Page   486
Internet Glossary   487

GLOSSARY   488

REFERENCES   496

NAME INDEX   514

SUBJECT INDEX   520

Research in Practice

1.1 Practice Effectiveness: "Scientific Practice" as a Challenge to the Human Services   **4**

1.2 Practice Effectiveness: The Social Agency as a Research Machine   **12**

2.1 Needs Assessment: Interviewing the Children of Lesbians   **26**

2.2 Practice Effectiveness: Social Theory and Burnout Among Social Workers   **36**

3.1 Practice Effectiveness: Sex Offenders as Participants   **58**

3.2 Program Evaluation: Vulnerable Clients at Risk   **60**

4.1 Needs Assessment: Reevaluating the Economic Consequences of Divorce   **74**

4.2 Behavior and Social Environments: Do Males and Females Have Different "Voices"?   **88**

5.1 Behavior and Social Environment: Problems of Measurement in Spouse Abuse Research   **102**

5.2 Assessment of Client Functioning: Valid and Reliable Practice Measurement   **117**

6.1 Program Evaluation: Sampling for Direct Observation of Seat Belt Use   **133**

6.2 Needs Assessment: Mental Health Among the Homeless   **146**

7.1 Needs Assessment: Response Bias in Human Service Research   **162**

7.2 Needs Assessment: Merging Quantitative and Qualitative Measures   **174**

8.1 Program Evaluation: Evaluating Family Preservation Services Through Agency Record Data   **198**

8.2 Needs Assessment: Hazards in Estimating the Crime Problem From Available Data   **202**

9.1 Program Evaluation: Participant Observation of a Token Economy Program Among Schizophrenics   **226**

9.2 Assessment of Client Functioning: Home Observation of Marital Conflicts   **236**

10.1 Program Evaluation: Meeting the Challenges to Experimentation in a Drug Prevention Program   **260**

10.2 Program Evaluation: Field Experiments on the Police Handling of Domestic Violence Cases   **268**

11.1 Assessment of Client Functioning: Rapid Assessment Instruments   **292**

11.2 Practice Effectiveness: A Multiple-Baseline Evaluation of Treating Panic Disorder   **304**

12.1 Program Evaluation: The Effectiveness of Financial Assistance in Reducing Recidivism **334**

12.2 Program Evaluation: Cost-Benefit Analysis of a Personnel Program **338**

13.1 Program Evaluation: Developing a Scale to Measure Client Satisfaction **354**

13.2 Client Functioning: Measurement for What? Benefits of Sequential Assessment **365**

14.1 Needs Assessment: Does Deer Hunting Really Prevent Domestic Violence? **392**

15.1 Program Evaluation: Designed for Failure: Statistical Power in Human Service Research **418**

Computers in Research

Chapter 1:   Information Technology in Human Services **14**

Chapter 2:   Using Agency Databases for Research: A Study of Leaving Welfare **40**

Chapter 5:   Enhancing Measurement Through Computer-Collected Data **118**

Chapter 6:   Software for Sampling **150**

Chapter 7:   Survey Design and Data Collection **188**

Chapter 8:   The Use of Computers in Content Analysis **214**

Chapter 9:   Collecting Observational Data by Computer **248**

Chapter 11: Computer-Aided Single-Subject Data Analysis **312**

Chapter 15: Statistical Software **422**

CHAPTER 1
Research in the Human Services

Research in the Human Services   3
Goals of Research   3
Applications of Research   5
Special Issues: Research on Minorities and Women   8

Parallels Between Research and Practice   8
Steps in Conducting Research   8
Steps in Practice Intervention   10

The Plan of the Book   12

Main Points   13

Important Terms for Review   14

Exploring the Internet   15

For Further Reading   16

Exercises for Class Discussion   17

This book is about the use of research in human services. The term **human services** refers to those professions with the primary goal of enhancing the relationship between people and societal institutions so that people may maximize their potential and alleviate distress. Among human service professionals are social workers, psychologists, counselors, probation officers, and daycare providers. Others who are not normally considered human service professionals, such as teachers and nurses, contribute to the delivery of human services as a part of their respective tasks. For all these groups, research is becoming increasingly essential to their delivery of human services. To illustrate how central research can be, consider the following actual case:

> Two months after giving birth to a baby boy, a young mother kills her infant son and disposes of the body by dumping it in the trash. Through a routine visit by a public health nurse, the tragedy is discovered. In the course of the investigation, it is learned that the mother had made threatening remarks about the child while still in the hospital. The local community is outraged. Why was the mother allowed to leave the hospital with the child? Why was there no police intervention? Where was the local community mental health agency? The various human service agencies of the community are called on to do something to make sure that similar events will not happen again.

Do something. But what? The human service professionals charged with taking action can first of all turn to research studies on the nature of child abuse and the effectiveness of child abuse programs in other communities. Second, they can use research to ascertain just how much abuse actually occurs in their community. The community response may be different if this event is an isolated one. In addition, research can help identify factors that can predict which families are most at risk for

some sort of family violence and assess the consequences of abuse in child development. Finally, once a plan is put into operation with the support of community funds, research can be conducted to assess whether the program is working properly.

Thus, numerous links exist between research and human service practice. Because research provides the means for understanding the problems with which professionals work and the means for evaluating change, practitioners in the human services are certain to encounter the need to understand, apply, and, in some cases, conduct research in carrying out the goals of their professions (Reinherz, Grob, and Berkman, 1983; O'Hare, 1991). Some would go farther and argue that the link between research and practice is even more intimate, namely, that there can be—and should be—a fruitful merger of the two. In fact, the notion that scientific research and human service practice are totally distinct enterprises is gradually disappearing (Barlow, Hayes, and Nelson, 1992; Ivanoff et al., 1987). Two reasons explain this.

First, strong parallels are now recognized between the conduct of research and the conduct of practice, and practitioners can benefit by incorporating into practice some of the techniques used in research. Both research and practice, for example, are based on observation, but the observations of practitioners are often unstructured and intuitive. Thus, practitioners can benefit from some of the techniques, discussed in Chapters 7 and 9, that researchers use to make structured observations.

A second reason for the changing views of research and practice is the realization that practice intervention, properly conducted, can provide scientifically valid knowledge about human behavior and the effectiveness of intervention. Practitioners, for example, can scientifically assess the effectiveness of their interventions if those interventions are organized in a manner known by researchers as "single-subject design," which parallels the scientific experiment. We discuss single-subject designs in Chapter 11. Some illustrations of how the tasks of research have been incorporated into the very definition of the human services are provided in Research in Practice 1.1.

The purpose of this book is to introduce students in the human services to social research logic, methods, and design. We do this by emphasizing the parallels and linkages between research and practice. Because research and practice are intertwined, human service professionals need training in the techniques of social research as much as they need to know about group processes or theories of personality. In some situations, human service providers will *consume social research* as they apply the findings of research to practice intervention. Therefore, they need to understand the logic of research and be able to assess research procedures critically to decide whether and in what fashion research findings can be introduced into practice. In other situations, human service workers may *conduct social research* as a part of their overall intervention strategy, so they need to know how to design and carry out scientifically valid research projects.

In this chapter, we discuss the goals of research in the human services and then illustrate five areas of human service activities in which research can make a contribution. Next, we draw some of the parallels between the steps in social research and the steps in the intervention process. Finally, we provide an overview of the plan of the book, including previews of later chapters.

Research in the Human Services
Goals of Research

The word "research" is applied to many activities: the student who browses in the library for a few hours; the social worker who, while visiting clients about other issues, makes a mental note of some of their social characteristics; the parole officer who routinely inquires, as a part of an intake interview, about a parolee's family life. All these people might claim to be doing "research." Yet the term, as it is commonly used in the social and behavioral sciences, has a considerably more precise meaning ac-

cording to which none of these activities would be considered scientific research. This is not to say that these activities are unimportant. They may have a variety of uses. However, social research has very specific goals that can be achieved only through utilizing the proper procedures.

Social research *is the systematic examination (or reexamination) of empirical data, collected by someone firsthand, concerning the social or psychological forces operating in a situation.* Three major elements characterize this definition. First, social research is *systematic.* That is, all aspects of the research process are carefully planned in advance, and nothing is done in a casual or haphazard fashion. The systematic nature of research is at the core of the scientific method, which is discussed in more detail in Chapter 2. Second, social research involves the collection of *empirical data*—that is, information or facts about the world based on sensory experiences. As such, it should not be confused with philosophizing or speculating, which lack the empirical base of research. Third, social research studies *social and psychological* factors that affect human behavior. Biological, physiological, nutritional, or other such factors would be a part of social research only to the extent that they affect, or are affected by, social and psychological factors.

Research in the human services generally focuses on one or more of the following goals: description, prediction, explanation, or evaluation. **Descriptive research** has as its goal *description,* or the attempt to discover facts or describe reality. Descriptive research, for example, might deal with such questions as: What are people's attitudes toward welfare? How widespread is child abuse? How many people avail themselves of the services of home health-care workers? Some descriptive research efforts are quite extensive. For example, the National Center for Health Statistics and the Centers for Disease Control collect voluminous amounts of data each year for purposes of describing the health status of Americans.

Predictive research focuses on *prediction,* or making projections about what may occur in the future or in other settings. Insurance companies, for example, make use of sophisticated actuarial

Research in Practice 1.1

Practice Effectiveness: "Scientific Practice" as a Challenge to the Human Services

Over two decades ago, the Health Research Group, one of Ralph Nader's public citizen organizations, aimed a challenge in the direction of the human services (Adams and Orgel, 1975). The group suggested that people seeking help from human service professionals should demand a written contract, at the outset of the relationship, that specified the conditions of the therapy, the goals of the intervention, and even the site at which the therapy would take place. They also suggested that the contract specify the character of the practitioner–client relationship, especially regarding the empirical evidence showing what kind of relationship would enhance the achievement of the client's goals. Underlying these recommendations was a demand for a high degree of *accountability* on the part of the helping professions. In a sense, the group was suggesting that clients have a right to demand that practitioners justify their actions and recommendations on specific and demonstrable

grounds. Though these demands for accountability are not new, they have become louder and broader in scope (*see* Sheafor, Horejsi, and Horejsi, 1997). And they even come from clients themselves. Some practitioners believe that clients would be upset if systematic evaluation procedures were used in treatment. Yet, research indicates that clients are overwhelmingly in favor of the use of systematic data collection procedures to assess treatment rather than relying merely on the opinions of practitioners (Campbell, 1988).

These demands for accountability have motivated human service professionals in fields such as psychology, social work, criminal justice, and nursing to begin defining the human services as a *scientific* discipline (Turnbull and Dietz-Uhler, 1995; Goldfried and Wolfe, 1996; Rosen, 1996). They now use such terms as "scientific practice," "scientist practitioner," and "research-based clinical services." In the field of community mental health,

---

schemes for predicting the risks involved in insuring people or property. Based on past descriptive research on deaths and injuries, they can project how long people with certain characteristics are likely to live or the degree of likelihood that they will suffer injuries. Such projections can also be made by the National Center for Health Statistics. For example, the NCHS can project that infants and children with particular social characteristics will have an increased likelihood of being undernourished or suffering from infectious or parasitic diseases. Armed with this information, it is possible to devise preventive health-care programs targeted at the high-risk groups.

Explanatory research involves *explanation*, or determining why or how something occurred. Explanatory research, for example, would go beyond describing rates of juvenile delinquency or even predicting who will engage in delinquent acts. Ex-

planatory research would focus on *why* certain people become delinquents. The goal of explanation may appear to be quite similar to that of prediction, but there is a difference: One can make predictions without an accompanying explanation. Insurance companies, for example, make actuarial predictions based on past statistical associations, often without knowing why those associations occurred.

Evaluation research focuses on *evaluation*, or the use of scientific research methods to plan intervention programs, to monitor the implementation of new programs and the operation of existing ones, and to determine how effectively programs or clinical practices achieve their goals. Evaluation research can also determine whether a program has unintended consequences that are either desirable or undesirable. In the past few decades, a vast array of social programs has emerged—relating to

Abraham Jeger and Robert Slotnick (1982) have developed what they call a "behavioral–ecological" approach to the delivery of mental health services. It represents a coalescence of "behavioral" approaches that derive from psychology and "ecological" approaches found in such disciplines as anthropology and sociology. More important, they view research as an integral part of the delivery system:

> The behavioral–ecological approach emphasizes incorporation of an evaluation design into all intervention programs. As such, it represents a merging of research and service, in contrast to traditional mental health models that tend to separate research and clinical practice. . . . A major characteristic of such evaluation is that program participants are involved in all phases of the evaluation process [Jeger and Slotnick, 1982, p. 13].

On a similar note, the social work profession has been challenged to begin training social work practitioners who

- use practice methods that are known *empirically* to be effective
- continuously *evaluate* the outcome of practice
- participate in the *discovery, testing,* and *reporting* of effective practice techniques
- use untested practice methods with great caution and only with adequate control and evaluation of the outcome
- *communicate* the results of evaluations to others

In fact, the Council on Social Work Education (1994) now calls for social work education to impart an understanding of and appreciation for the necessity of a scientific approach to knowledge building and practice, including the systematic evaluation of practice. The outcome, it is hoped, will be more effective, accountable, and creditable practitioners.

In each chapter, we will set aside separate space entitled "Research in Practice," where we will discuss particular instances where research and practice have been linked. In this fashion, students in the human services can gain a deeper understanding of the many ways in which this linkage might be achieved.

poverty, child development, crime, alcoholism, delinquency, and the like—that attempt to ameliorate undesirable social conditions. As competition for funds for such programs has increased, especially in the past decade, program directors are commonly required to justify and defend their programs in terms of cost effectiveness. Thus, evaluation research is now often an integral part of human service programs.

Applications of Research

Some social research is called **basic** (or **pure**) **research** in that its purpose is to advance our knowledge about human behavior with little concern for any immediate, practical benefits that might result. Many sociologists and psychologists conduct basic research. Research in the human services, however, is more likely to be **applied research**—research

designed with a practical outcome in mind and with the assumption that some group or society as a whole will gain specific benefits from the research. Thus, explaining juvenile delinquency is important to social workers, probation officers, and the police because it can lead to programs intended to alleviate delinquency in a community.

The focus of this book is on applied social research, especially the linkage of social research with the human services. Although we distinguish between basic and applied research, the line between the two is vague and, in fact, even pure research can have applications in the human service field. In order to organize our thinking about the applications of research to the human services, we find it useful to think in terms of five focal areas in which this linkage occurs: understanding human functioning in social environments, needs assessment, assessment of client functioning, program evaluation, and practice effectiveness evaluation. We do not claim that this is the only way to divide the human service field or that our list of areas is exhaustive. These five categories, however, serve as a helpful aid as we analyze the links between research and practice. We review each area briefly here. Then each "Research in Practice" insert in this and subsequent chapters emphasizes one of the focal areas.

Behavior and Social Environments

Human service providers do many things: link people to resources they can use, enhance people's coping abilities, improve the operation of social systems, and participate in the development of social policy, to name a few. All these activities rest on an understanding of the behavior of the people to whom services are provided and a comprehension of the social environment in which they function. Social research can provide much of this knowledge. An agency providing services to teenagers, for example, can turn to research on adolescents in American society for a better understanding of the problems facing their clients. One such area that has received considerable social research is the link between self-esteem and teenage pregnancy (Crockenberg and Soby, 1989). Although this research has typically been conducted without any particular practice intervention goals in mind, the results suggest that raising adolescent self-esteem may be one way to reduce rates of teenage pregnancy. The research shows that self-esteem does not seem to change the levels of sexual activity among teenagers, but it does document that teenagers with higher self-esteem—both males and females—are more likely to use contraceptives than are teenagers with low self-esteem. Knowledge of factors that influence adolescent behavior can provide practitioners with insights into how to shape effective intervention strategies to reduce teenage pregnancies. In other words, a wide range of behavioral research, much of it basic research, seems only indirectly linked to practice but can inform intervention. Human service providers need to be able to understand and assess this research in terms of whether it is sufficiently valid to incorporate into practice.

Although much research on human behavior and social environments is conducted by behavioral scientists, human service professionals themselves—therapists, social workers, nurses, and other practitioners—are increasingly doing research of this type.

Needs Assessment

Social research can also be used to make an accurate assessment of the need for various forms of service and suggest alternative strategies for meeting those needs (Rossi and Freeman, 1993; McKillip, 1987). The purpose of this research is to determine whether a problem exists, to indicate the severity of the problem, and to estimate the number and characteristics of people adversely affected by the problem. Needs assessment research is often highly descriptive rather than explanatory or predictive. One illustration of needs assessment research is a project that involved the cooperation of a mental health agency and a local university to collect data from a community about mental health needs and services (Witkin, 1984). Labeled a Community-Oriented Needs Assessment (CONA), it was based on questionnaires mailed to key informants, interviews of a random sample of community residents, and profiles based on demographic statistics. From it, the mental health agency received community input into client needs, service delivery planning, and evaluation. The data were used to help plan and implement programs and to support requests for additional funds from government and other funding agencies.

Assessment of Client Functioning

In the provision of human services, assessing the level of functioning of clients is often necessary. What kind of communication problems exist in a family? How capable is a teenage parent of dealing with the stresses of motherhood? How skilled is a person in negotiating a job interview? Though practitioners make such assessments often, the danger is that they will be made unsystematically. In the past 20 years, there has been extensive development of systematic and, in some cases, quantitative assessment tools that can be used for both research and practice tasks. As one example, Mary Lou Balassone (1991) has developed quantitative tools for assessing the degree to which youngsters are at risk of various problematic outcomes, such as dropping out of school or getting pregnant. She has detailed, in particular, how these tools could be used by social work practitioners to assess the degree of risk of inconsistent contraceptive use and failed pregnancy prevention among their clients. These assessments can be compared at different times to see if any change or improvement has occurred. Additional examples of such client assessment tools can be found in Sheafor, Horejsi, and Horejsi (1997).

Program Evaluation In the past few decades, we have seen the burgeoning of many large, ambitious, and expensive programs intended to cope with social problems and provide services to individuals. Along with the growth of these programs has emerged an increasing concern over their results: Do they achieve their intended goals? These programs are costly, and some evaluation is needed to assess whether resources are being used effectively. Equally important, a program that fails to achieve its goals leaves a problem unsolved or a service undelivered. *Program evaluation* is the use of scientific research techniques to assess the results of a program and evaluate whether the program as currently designed achieves its stated goals (Rutman, 1984). For example, one such evaluation project was part of an attempt in New York to replace foster care with a new method of providing services to children of families in need (Jones, 1985). The innovation was a response to a dramatic increase in the number of children in foster care and rapidly rising costs per child of providing that care. A program was developed around the idea that rather than using foster care, the family unit could be preserved by providing intensive services such as family casework, homemaker services, and vocational and referral services. In order to assess whether the program was effective, authorities provided some families with the intensive family services while other, comparable families were served as usual by the child welfare system (which, in most cases, meant foster care). The effectiveness of the program was then determined by comparing the two groups after 1 year in terms of the cost of providing ser-

vices to each group, the amount of services provided, and the level of functioning of parents and children. The results of the program indicated that it was a success by all criteria. In a 5-year follow-up, it was also found that the program led to fewer children going into foster care.

It is crucial that human service providers understand when program evaluation is called for and when it is possible to conduct an effective evaluation. In addition, many practitioners will likely find themselves participating in programs that will include evaluation as one of their goals.

Practice Effectiveness Evaluation Whereas program evaluation focuses on the assessment of entire programs, the concern of human service professionals is often considerably more specific— namely, "Is what I am doing right now with this particular client working?" For this reason, practitioners have often been disenchanted with the utility of evaluation research as a direct aid to helping clients. However, in recent years major advances have occurred in the ability of research to answer professionals' questions about the efficacy of intervention efforts on specific clients.

One form of such research is called *single-subject design,* in which clinicians devise a way to measure the occurrence of a problem and monitor the behavior of a client for a baseline period. Then intervention begins, and the behavior is again monitored. Comparison between the baseline and intervention periods permits the practitioner to make more accurate assessments of progress than the informal assessment on which human service professionals have traditionally relied. The procedures can be quite elaborate, but even a beginning staff member can readily apply the basic model. For example, an undergraduate student recently submitted a paper that described her work with a young mother who was trying to reduce the thumb-sucking behavior of her 6-year-old daughter. Adapting a measurement scheme reported in a professional journal, the student designed a monitoring system involving observation of the child by means of a small piece of litmus paper taped to the child's thumb. This procedure allowed the student to determine how much time the child actually spent thumb sucking and to specify the conditions under which the behavior occurred. A behavior modification procedure was implemented, and the amount of thumb sucking declined dramatically. (Single-subject research is discussed at length in Chapter 11.) Through such careful monitoring of behavior and measuring of intervention effects, human service workers can not only enhance their own effectiveness but also contribute to the development of an intervention technology that others can successfully apply.

Obvious similarities exist between program evaluation and practice effectiveness research. Both, for example, are concerned with the effectiveness of certain practices. The difference, however, is in the scope of the efforts. Program evaluation focuses on complete programs whereas practice effectiveness research emphasizes the assessment of some particular aspect of a practice situation in a way that will not necessarily affect the entire program.

Special Issues: Research on Minorities and Women

The human services devote special attention to the problems of minority groups, whether their minority status is a function of race, ethnicity, sex, or something else. The reason for this special attention is twofold: First, minorities tend to suffer disproportionately from the problems that human service workers attempt to alleviate; second, many social conditions affect minorities very negatively and limit their opportunities and achievements. Because of the position of minorities in American society, conducting research that produces accurate and complete data on them can be a challenge. In fact, in certain circumstances, the standard research methods used in human service research result in misleading and, in some cases, outright false conclusions regarding a minority.

This problem is sufficiently important to human service research that we devote special attention to it throughout the book. In each chapter where relevant, we point to particular ways in

which problems or biases in research on minorities can occur and strategies for overcoming them. The goal is to create a sensitivity to the fact that research methods can have built-in biases when focused on particular minority groups and that care must be exercised to detect and avoid this.

Parallels Between Research and Practice

Although scientific research is different in many respects from human service practice, important parallels exist between the two. In fact, researchers and practitioners use many of the same strategies in approaching their problems. After reviewing the steps in conducting research, we will point out parallels that can be found in practice.

Steps in Conducting Research

Although each research project is unique in some fashion, some general steps characterize virtually every project. The research process can be divided into six identifiable stages: problem formulation, research design development, data collection, data analysis, drawing conclusions, and public dissemination of the results.

Problem Formulation   The first step in conducting social research is to decide on the problem that will be researched. When first encountering the issue of problem formulation, students commonly question its importance. So many problems exist that it would appear to be a simple matter to select one on which to conduct research. However, such a casual view of scientific problem formulation is erroneous. For example, some problems about which we might desire answers are not scientific questions at all, and no amount of research will answer them. Other problems, though possibly interesting and intriguing, might prove impractical from a methodological, ethical, or financial standpoint.

Another element of problem formulation is to shape a concern into a specific researchable question. Such global concerns as "the state of the modern family" are far too broad to be considered research problems. They need to be narrowed down to specific problems for which empirical data can be gathered, such as: What is the divorce rate? How does it compare with the divorce rate of past years? Do children raised in single-parent families exhibit poorer social development than children raised in two-parent families? As the initial step in research, developing a researchable problem is highly important. In Chapter 4, we outline the many issues involved in this process.

Research Design Development Having successfully established a researchable problem, we next must develop a **research design,** a detailed plan outlining how observations will be made. The plan is followed by the researcher as the project is carried out. Research designs always address certain key issues, such as who will be studied, how these people will be selected, and what information will be gathered from or about them. In fact, the research design spells out in considerable detail what will occur in the following stages of the research process. Chapters 7 through 11 describe the different kinds of research designs and issues that must be considered in their development.

Data Collection A part of any research design is a description of what kinds of data will be collected and how this will be done. The data collected at this stage constitute the basic information from which conclusions will be drawn, so great care must be exercised. Two aspects of data collection, *pretests* and *pilot studies,* illustrate just how careful scientists are about this. The **pretest,** as the name implies, is a preliminary application of the data–gathering technique for the purpose of determining its adequacy. It certainly would be risky and unwise to jump prematurely into data gathering without first knowing that all the data collection procedures are sound. For example, if our study were a needs assessment of homemakers to deter-

mine how many would make use of occupational training services, we would choose a small group of homemakers and collect the same data from them that we plan to collect in the final project. It is, in a sense, a "trial run." And, unless we are very good or very lucky, some modifications in the data collection technique will likely be required based on the results of the pretest. After these modifications are made, the technique is pretested again. Additional pretests are always desirable after any modifications in the data-gathering technique in order to assess whether the modifications handle the problems encountered in the previous pretest.

In some cases, it may even be necessary to do a **pilot study,** which is a small-scale "trial run" of all the procedures planned for use in the main study. In addition to administering the data-gathering instrument, a pilot study might include such things as a test of the procedures for selecting the sample and an application of the statistical procedures to be used in the data analysis stage.

It is this kind of care in data collection that improves the validity of the data collected and bolsters our confidence in the conclusions drawn.

Data Analysis As with data collection, data analysis is spelled out in the research design, and it can be the most challenging and interesting aspect of a research project. It is challenging because data in raw form can be quite unrevealing. Data analysis is what unlocks the information hidden in the raw data and transforms it into something useful and meaningful. During data analysis, you learn whether your ideas are confirmed or refuted by empirical reality. During the course of data analysis, researchers often make use of statistical tools that can range from simple percentages to very complex statistical tests that require much training to understand and master. These statistics aid in communicating the findings of research to others. Once you learn the special language and interpretations of statistics, you can be more effective at communicating research findings in a clear, concise manner than when using conventional English. In Chapters 14 and 15, we review some of the basic data analysis and data manipulation techniques that are used in social research. We will see that modern data analysis is typically done with computers, so a research design must specify data collection procedures that are compatible with the computer hardware and software available.

Drawing Conclusions The next step in conducting social research is to draw some conclusions from the data analysis. The form this takes depends in part on the goals of the research project. A descriptive study, for example, would simply present what was found, possibly in a summarized form to make it more easily understood. Predictive and explanatory research, on the other hand, usually have hypotheses, or statements of what the researchers expect to find, stated before the data are collected. In this case, a major element of drawing conclusions is to assess how much support exists for the hypotheses. The support that data provide for hypotheses can range from strong to weak to none, and researchers have an obligation to those who might use their research to represent accurately the strength of their findings. Finally, in evaluation research, drawing conclusions usually involves making a judgment about the adequacy and effectiveness of programs and changes that might improve conditions.

Often, research discovers some things that do not relate directly to any specific hypothesis or things that are completely unanticipated. When drawing conclusions, the researchers should make note of the implications of any such findings that are of sufficient importance to warrant mention. When complete, the conclusions should clearly indicate what has been learned by conducting the research and the impact of this new knowledge.

Public Dissemination of Results Research findings are of little value if they remain the private property of the researchers who produce them. A crucial stage of social research is the public dissemination of the findings by publishing them in a book or professional journal or presenting them to a professional organization. This disseminates the newly created knowledge to those who can put

that knowledge to use or who can build on it in future research. In fact, public dissemination of knowledge is a major mechanism for scientific advancement. As we discuss further in Chapters 2 and 3, public dissemination makes it possible for others to reanalyze or replicate the research and to confirm the findings or identify cases of error-filled, biased, or fraudulent research.

Steps in Practice Intervention

Just as the research process can be organized as a series of steps, the process of human service practice is also often conceptualized as a series of stages (McMahon, 1990). In fact, the stages of practice closely parallel the steps in the research process (*see* Figure 1.1).

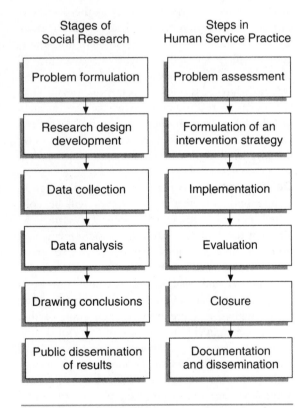

Stages of Social Research	Steps in Human Service Practice
Problem formulation	Problem assessment
Research design development	Formulation of an intervention strategy
Data collection	Implementation
Data analysis	Evaluation
Drawing conclusions	Closure
Public dissemination of results	Documentation and dissemination

Figure 1.1 Parallels Between Human Service Practice and Social Research

Problem Assessment In much the same way that social researchers must decide on the problem that will be researched, practitioners must specify the precise problem with which they are concerned, which factors might contribute to the problem, and which aspects of the problem will be given priority. In problem formulation, researchers make judgments concerning the feasibility of researching a particular phenomenon. Likewise, in problem assessment, practitioners must decide which behavioral systems are involved in a problem—individual, group, or societal—and whether effective intervention is possible.

Formulation of an Intervention Strategy
Just as researchers develop a research design, practitioners develop a strategy for intervention that will be effective in alleviating the problem specified in the assessment stage. Whereas researchers choose among a variety of research methods, practitioners choose among numerous intervention strategies, such as crisis intervention, behavior modification, or vocational training. Just as researchers may use more than one research technique over the course of a research project, so practitioners often use more than one intervention strategy in attacking a problem.

Implementation Following the development of the research design, researchers proceed to put it into practice. In similar fashion, practitioners implement the intervention strategies outlined in the preceding stage. Researchers' activities are normally limited to data collection, and they do not attempt to change the people they are studying. Practitioners, on the other hand, may collect data as a part of the implementation stage, but they are primarily concerned with the effectiveness of the intervention strategy in creating some change in clients or in the systems that affect them.

Evaluation Once researchers have collected their data, they analyze it in order to determine what their study has found. Similarly, practitioners evaluate the effectiveness of the intervention strategy implemented during the preceding stage. Were

the goals of the plan achieved? What were the costs of the strategy? Were any undesirable side effects brought about by the intervention? Which aspects of the intervention process seemed to be most important in producing the change that resulted?

Closure Termination of intervention is an important part of the helping process. The extent to which the intervention has been effective must be determined as well as the degree to which the goals of the intervention cannot be, and possibly never will be, achieved. Researchers may make suggestions for future research that might be helpful in further clarifying the relationships found in the study. Likewise, practitioners might suggest other sources of help that the client could use to cope with problems left unresolved by the intervention. In other words, for both researchers and practitioners, the conclusion is a time to review what has been accomplished and to look forward to directions and alternatives for the future.

Documentation and Dissemination We have made the point that both the process and the results of research must be carefully documented, and the same can be said for human service practice. At a minimum, this stage includes meeting agency requirements for record keeping and case documentation, such as preparing treatment plans and case closing reports. Although such agency-mandated reporting may serve a useful quality control function, practitioners also have a responsibility to share with others the knowledge gained from practice. This may take the form of case conferences within the agency, workshop presentations, or formal articles published in practice-related journals. As a consequence of subjecting practice to the scrutiny of supervisors and peers, deficits are identified, intervention techniques are refined, and advances are made in the delivery of human services.

By this point, you should be gaining an appreciation for the parallels and linkages between social research and human service practice. The parallels involve the similarities between the activities of

Research in Practice 1.2
Practice Effectiveness: The Social Agency as a Research Machine

A central point of this first chapter has been the importance of research skills for human service workers. For example, one study of social workers in agencies found that 73 percent had participated in a program evaluation, 66 percent had conducted a needs assessment, 36 percent had written a research grant proposal, and 35 percent had conducted a research project (Gentry, Connaway, and Morelock, 1984). In fact, the reciprocal relationship between practice and research is so central that suggestions have been made to reorganize human service delivery in such a way that it can make an even more valuable contribution to research. Along these lines, William Reid, a researcher and clinical practice theorist in social work, has suggested that social agencies can become "research machines" (Reid, 1978). Social agencies collect considerable amounts of data, in the form of case records, that are often a part of a computerized information system. These data are collected as a part of the everyday service delivery tasks of the agency, but they can also serve as data for research into many questions important to the agency.

If agencies are viewed not only as service delivery systems but also as "research machines," some reorganization could enhance their research potential. Reid suggests the following changes:

1. Build research questions into the routine collection of case information rather than simply attempt to devise research problems from the available data.

2. Devote special care and consideration to the selection and development of recording formats. Some data in agency records are ambiguous and organized in a haphazard fashion, but with attention, this problem can be reduced.
3. Structure practice in such a way that goals and targets are clear and the intervention is well specified. This contributes to the utility of case records for research.
4. Rely on multiple data sources. In addition to using the impressions of human service workers, consider using client questionnaires, direct observation of client behavior, and other methods to supplement the primary case record approach.

The extent to which the research potential of social agencies is realized in the future depends on human service professionals with a knowledge of, and interest in, research and a commitment to scientifically based practice. Human service agencies have been moving to implement these ideas. For example, systematic monitoring of child behavior is being used in residential facilities. Not only can such systems provide valuable feedback to practitioners on client progress, but also the data may have uses for research (Benbenishty, 1991). Both improved practice and increased knowledge of human behavior and the social environment can be fruits of the same endeavor. As you learn more about research in the human services, you will begin to grasp numerous ways in which Reid's suggestions can be applied.

researchers and those of practitioners. The linkages involve the contributions that research can make to practice endeavors, and vice versa. In fact, as pointed out in Research in Practice 1.2, there are ways in which these parallels and linkages can be made even more explicit and direct.

The Plan of the Book

This first chapter has discussed the extent to which research is fundamental to the delivery of human services. The remainder of the book discusses how research is applied to the human services. Chapters

2 through 6 present some of the important issues that underlie research, including the role of hypotheses and theories and ethical problems that researchers are likely to confront. We also address the issue of how to formulate a research problem and select a scientifically sound sample on which observations will be made.

With Chapter 7, we begin the first of five chapters on specific research methods. Chapter 7 covers *survey research,* which is a widely used data collection technique based on obtaining people's responses to questions. In Chapter 8, we discuss the use of *available data* in research. Though not as common as surveys, available data can be useful to human service researchers. The records kept by prisons, hospitals, or social service agencies, for example, would fall into the category of available data that could be used for research. Chapter 9 presents *observational methods,* which involve the observation of people's behavior. This is also a common research technique in the human services because human service practitioners typically make observations of clients in the course of intervention. In Chapter 10, we discuss *experiments,* which are research techniques designed to assess the effect of one factor on another. Although human service providers may only occasionally conduct conventional experiments, they are often in a position to carry out single-subject research, the topic of Chapter 11. *Single-subject research* involves assessing the impact of some factor on the feelings or actions of a client, and it derives its basic logic from the experimental designs discussed in Chapter 10.

The remaining five chapters focus on issues that may have to be addressed irrespective of which specific research method is used in a particular study. *Evaluation research,* discussed in Chapter 12, refers to assessing how well a particular program or practice achieves its goals. This has become an increasingly important element in the human services, and evaluation researchers often use some or all of the five research techniques discussed in the preceding five chapters. In Chapter 13, we analyze how to develop *scales,* which are a type of measuring device in which a single composite score is derived from a number of other scores that measure

something of interest. Chapters 14 and 15 offer an introduction to *data analysis,* or what to do with numerical data once they are collected. Chapter 16 is an introduction to the *grant-seeking process,* or how to find financial support for research, including how to write grant proposals and research reports.

Computers have now become an important tool in the research process. In fact, as one assessment concluded, "The entire research process . . . can now be directed and/or accomplished with available microcomputer software" (Carpenter, 1987, p. 529). In recognition of this, we have included in most chapters an insert titled "Computers in Research." Each insert describes a particular research use of the computer that is relevant to the topic of the chapter. In addition, a feature titled "Exploring the Internet" appears in each chapter; through exercises, this feature shows you how to use the Internet for a variety of research purposes.

The book ends with four appendices. The first is a guide to using the library for research in the human services. Effective use of library resources is an essential step in most research projects. The second appendix presents ways of generating and using tables of random numbers, which have many uses in research and are discussed in several chapters. The third appendix presents codes of ethics regarding research from two professional organizations. The fourth appendix is a short introduction to using the World Wide Web to help you with the Exploring the Internet feature.

Main Points

- The human services are those professions having the goal of enhancing the relations between people and societal institutions to enable people to maximize their potential and alleviate distress.
- Both research and practice are based on observation, but practice can benefit from adopting the techniques of scientific observation.
- Research has become a fundamental part of delivering human services.

COMPUTERS IN RESEARCH
Information Technology in the Human Services

The computer, probably more than any other single invention, stands as a symbol of technological progress at the end of the twentieth century. Computers have entered all areas of society, including the human services. A few decades ago, computer applications in the human services were limited to accounting and bureaucratic recordkeeping. In fact, the impersonality and quantification that seem associated with computers were viewed by many as antithetical to the personal and qualitative approach of human service practitioners. By the 1990s, however, computers, or what is broadly called information technologies (IT), have become an integral part of virtually all human service activities (Murphy and Pardeck, 1991; Phillips and Berman, 1995; Hughes and Fancett, 1996). This includes the Internet and World Wide Web, which have increasingly become resources for research by human service professionals. In recognition of this, we have added an appendix to this book (*see* Appendix D) that provides a brief introduction to using the Internet. We have also added to each chapter a section titled "Exploring the Internet." This feature follows the Computers in Research section or the Important Terms for Review at the end of each chapter and contains exercises for you to follow on how to use the Internet for research purposes related to a chapter.

The traditional use of computers in social research has been to assist in coding and analyzing data. In later chapters, we describe computer software that can run statistical tests, assist in interviewing respondents, help select a sample to use in data collection, and accomplish a host of other activities related directly to research fundamentals. However, computers today have many uses beyond these traditional ones. They can assist in the literature review process through computerized database searches available at most libraries (*see* Appendix A); they help in report preparation as word processors; and graphic display programs have become essential in producing charts and figures to communicate the findings of research.

Computers are also rapidly entering use for human service practice tasks, and, with creativity, these service-delivery applications can be harnessed to make applied research easier and more feasible. This service base also increases the possibilities for making use of research in practice. Our discussion of computer applications illustrates a

---

- A knowledge of research is necessary for both consumers of social research and those who produce it.
- Social research is a systematic examination of empirical data concerning social or psychological forces.
- Social research seeks to achieve the goals of description, prediction, explanation, and evaluation.
- The numerous links between social research and human service practice include understanding human functioning in social environments, needs assessment, assessment of client functioning, program evaluation, and practice effectiveness evaluation.

- Conducting accurate and unbiased research on members of minority groups confronts social researchers with special problems.
- Research and practice follow similar, parallel paths in approaching a problem.

Important Terms for Review

applied research
basic research
descriptive research
evaluation research
explanatory research
human services

central theme of this book: There are important linkages between social research and human service practice, and the imaginative application of computer technology is yet another way of forging this linkage.

For example, practitioners can perform assessments on a wide variety of problem areas by using such computer programs as Computer Assisted Social Services (CASS). CASS is a versatile program that can adapt to a variety of human service tasks. It uses structured forms, questionnaires, case notes, measurement or assessment scales, and tests or examinations (Hudson, 1996). CASS can provide clinicians with data to assist in diverse tasks from assessing marital interaction to making child placement decisions. Further information on CASS can be found on the publisher's Web page in the Internet (http://www.syspac.com/~walmyr/), and the actual CASS software can be downloaded from that site.

Although the use of computers in therapy is controversial, computers have been used creatively in several situations such as self-help therapies, biofeedback, and patient education. Clinical history-taking is another task to which the computer can readily be applied. For example, the Clinical Assessment System (CAS) starts with a computerized intake questionnaire and social history; it then has built-in clinical measurement scales

and inventories as well as features to monitor client progress and a host of other applications useful in service delivery settings (Nurius and Hudson, 1988). Computers are also being used in human service agencies for supervision tasks and training programs, and to create support networks. Good information about the uses of computers in human service research can be found in the journals *Computers in Human Services* and *Social Science Computer Review*. The first journal also has a site on the Internet (http://www.uta.edu/cussn/chs.html); another Internet site with information about computers in the human services is called Computers in Mental Health (http://www.ex.ac.uk/~mhbrisco/cimh/welcome.htm).

A Computers in Research section will be included in most chapters of this book. The goal is not to teach you *how* to use computer software because this depends on what kind of software and computers you have available at your school, home, or agency; instead, our purpose is to educate you regarding the range of computer uses in the field of social research today and to stimulate your thinking about ways of using this technology to link practice with research. This will enable you, when confronted with a research problem, to search for the computer tools that can assist in solving the problem.

pilot study
predictive research
pretest
pure research
research design
social research

Exploring the Internet

The Internet has rapidly become an indispensable resource for both human service practice and research. To encourage you to use this resource and to enrich your learning experience around research, each chapter of this textbook includes a

brief presentation on Internet resources. For an introduction to the Internet and an overview of its resources, refer to Appendix D at the end of this text.

The sheer volume of material available on the Internet makes it a powerful resource, but at the same time, it can seem overwhelming and chaotic. An important key to bringing order to the vast array of material is knowing where to look and how to search. An excellent starting point for exploring the Internet for research and practice is a Web site called *The Social Worker Networker* (http://pobox.com/~social.worker.networker). Although the title is "Social Worker Networker," this site is sufficiently broad-based that it can appeal to other human service professionals as well. For example, the site includes links to several Internet search engines that can help you locate resources on mental health, human services, criminal justice, education, and health care. In addition to search engines, there are directions for locating census data, chat channels, job opportunities, and legal information, and for accessing other sites on such topics as psychology, research, treatment, and welfare reform.

For a starter, we suggest that you explore some of the links to other sites by selecting the research and treatment links. Simply move the mouse pointer to "Professional Resources" and click the pointer. Then follow the directions to move to various sites. Remember, you can always return to the original Social Worker Networker site by using the "Back" option on the menu bar. Next, try using one or more of the search engines to which the Social Worker Networker has links. For example, use Yahoo to explore options under Health:Mental Health. Try entering search terms such as "sociology," "psychology," or "social science" in the search engine Alta Vista. We suggest that you print a copy of interesting sites that you locate, or record the Internet address, and share these with other students in the class. The class may wish to establish a discussion list on the university computer system to share information on research and practice topics as you discover them.

For Further Reading

Agnew, Neil M., and Sandra W. Pyke. *The Science Game: An Introduction to Research in the Behavioral Sciences,* 6th ed. Englewood Cliffs, N.J.: Prentice-Hall, 1994. Presented as a "consumer's guide" to the products of science, *The Science Game* is much more than that. It is a compact and highly readable introduction to the research craft.

Barlow, D. H., S. C. Hayes, and R. O. Nelson. *The Scientist-Practitioner: Research and Accountability in Clinical and Educational Settings.* Boston: Allyn & Bacon, 1992. This is an excellent book on the linkage of research and practice. Although it focuses on psychology, it will be of interest to any professional attempting to establish a scientist-practitioner model.

Burgess, Robert G. *Investigating Society.* New York: Longman, 1989. Giving us a somewhat different perspective on social research, this book presents the views of contributing British sociologists on a variety of research issues.

Finsterbusch, Kurt, and Annabelle Bender Motz. *Social Research for Policy Decisions.* Belmont, Calif.: Wadsworth, 1980. An excellent, brief book about research as it might be used by decision makers attempting to influence public policy.

Frost, Peter J., and Ralph E. Stablein, eds. *Doing Exemplary Research.* Newbury Park, Calif.: Sage, 1992. This is a collection of the reflections of several researchers about their research experiences. Among other things, it illustrates a wide array of research topics and approaches.

Hoover, Kenneth R. *The Elements of Social Scientific Thinking,* 5th ed. New York: St. Martin's, 1992. This book is an initiation to social science research intended for those who use the results of research or those just beginning as researchers. Through several editions it has remained to the point and up-to-date.

Kemeny, John G. *A Philosopher Looks at Science.* Princeton, N.J.: Van Nostrand, 1959. A discussion of the philosophical underpinnings of science and scientific research. To truly understand research, you need some knowledge of the basic logic of science, a field generally referred to as the "philosophy of science."

Rothman, Jack, and Edwin J. Thomas, eds. *Intervention Research: Design and Development for Human Service.* New York: Haworth, 1994. This book provides an extensive analysis of how research and practice activities can be fully integrated in order to enhance the effectiveness of practice intervention in the human services.

Social Work Research, 20 (June 1996) (special issue on the scientist-practitioner). All the articles in this volume of this very good research journal explore the issues surrounding empirical practice and the scientist-practitioner in the human services. It is a good supplement to the assessment in this chapter.

Stricker, George, and Robert H. Keisner, eds. *From Research to Clinical Practice: The Implications of Social and Developmental Research for Psychotherapy.* New York: Plenum, 1985. An excellent book of readings on the ways that research can be of value in human service practice. A number of authors address the issue of the tensions that can emerge between researchers and practitioners.

Sullivan, Thomas J. *Applied Sociology: Research and Critical Thinking.* Boston: Allyn and Bacon, 1992. This book provides a brief introduction to the manner in which social science research is conducted and suggests some of the many ways in which such research is applied to the human service field.

Exercises for Class Discussion

Use the case illustration presented below to do Exercise 1.1.

> While out of the office on a home call, a teacher's aide for the first grade at a rural school called the Intermediate School District office where you serve as a school social worker. In addition to identifying information, the secretary left you a message that contains the following details:
>
> "Janet has been absent from school for 8 days—illness, she says—and she is now back in school. Janet's mother and father are separating. The mother moved out; Janet, age 6, remained with the father. Now, the mother has returned, but the father moved out last week. Janet says that a 15-year-old girl is babysitting for her and her 2-year-old brother all the time. She hates the sitter. Her mother works at a local supermarket and hasn't responded to attendance letters. Janet is really upset and isn't doing schoolwork. She bursts into tears at the mention of her family. Janet's regular teacher is out for maternity leave."

The school district is asking you to look into Janet's situation.

1.1 We have emphasized the parallels between practice and research. With this in mind, do the following:

  a. Make a list of some problems in this referral that call for human service intervention. What additional information would you need in order to formulate an intervention plan?

  b. Make a list of research problems or questions that are suggested in this referral. How is this list similar to or different from your list of intervention problems?

1.2 Professional journals typically include a mixture of research articles, practice- and service-delivery descriptions, and policy issue discussions. Select recent issues of a major journal in your profession, such as *Social Work,* and identify those articles that qualify as research articles. Two or three students should independently review the same journal issue so that findings can be compared. What features distinguish a research article from other articles?

1.3 This chapter discusses several goals of research. For each of the research articles located for Exercise 1.2, determine whether it is primarily descriptive, predictive, explanatory, or evaluative. Explain why you classified each article as you did. If you are uncertain as to how an article should be classified, indicate why and state what additional information is needed to help you classify the study.

1.4 For each research study, state how it applies to human service practice in terms of the five focal areas discussed in the chapter.

CHAPTER 2

The Logic of
Social Research

Sources of Knowledge   19
Tradition   19
Experience   20
Common Sense   21
Science   22
Scientific Practice   24

Theories in Research and Practice   25
What Is a Theory?   26
The Functions of Theories   28

Concepts and Hypotheses   30
Defining Concepts   30
Developing Hypotheses   31
Concepts and Operational Definitions Among Minority Populations   33
Deduction Versus Induction   34

Cause-and-Effect Relationships   34

Main Points   39

Important Terms for Review   39

Exploring the Internet   39

For Further Reading   41

Exercises for Class Discussion   42

After dashing through the Looking-glass House in order to view its garden, Alice says:

> I should see the garden far better . . . if I could get to the top of that hill: and here's a path that leads straight to it—at least, no, it doesn't do *that* . . . but I suppose it will at last. But how curiously it twists! It's more like a corkscrew than a path! Well *this* turn goes to the hill, I suppose—no it doesn't! This goes straight back to the house! Well then, I'll try it the other way [Carroll, 1946, pp. 21–22].

Understanding the world—especially human behavior—sometimes bears a striking resemblance to Alice's convoluted and frustrating journey. People do what we least expect, without any apparent rhyme or reason. A prisoner on parole who appeared to be "making it on the outside" suddenly commits another offense and lands back in jail; a marriage of 25 years that seemed to be quite solid suddenly ends in divorce; a respected and successful business executive commits suicide. Human service providers, in particular, are familiar with experiences such as these, and the "path" to understanding seems to mirror Alice's "corkscrew."

Science, however, provides a method for mapping and understanding that corkscrew. In this chapter, we discuss the basic logic underlying scientific research, beginning with an assessment of how science differs from other ways of gaining knowledge. Then we analyze the importance of theories and their role in scientific research, drawing a parallel with the use of theories in human service practice. Following this, the role of concepts and hypotheses is discussed, showing how hypotheses serve to link theory and research. Finally, we analyze the nature of causality because research is, at its core, a search for cause-and-effect relationships among phenomena.

Sources of Knowledge

Human service practice is based on a knowledge of human behavior and the social environment. There are numerous ways of gaining such knowledge, but all sources of knowledge have their pitfalls. We argued in Chapter 1 that practice knowledge should be grounded in scientific research. This does not mean that science is infallible, but science does have advantages as a source of knowledge that make it superior to other ways of gaining knowledge.

To see why this is the case, we contrast science with three other common sources of knowledge: tradition, experience, and common sense. We then discuss how science can improve professional practice.

Tradition

Traditional knowledge is knowledge based on custom, habit, and repetition. It is founded on a belief in the sanctity of ancient wisdom and the ways of our forebears. People familiar with the musical *Fiddler on the Roof* will recall how the delightful character Tevye, a dairyman in the village of Anatevka, sang the praises of tradition:

> Because of our traditions, we've kept our balance for many, many years. Here in Anatevka we have traditions for everything—how to eat, how to sleep, how to wear clothes. . . . You may ask, how did this tradition start? I'll tell you—I don't know! But it's a tradition. Because of our traditions, everyone knows who he is and what God expects him to do. Tradition. Without our traditions, our lives would be as shaky as—as a fiddler on the roof! [Stein, 1964, pp. 1, 6]

For Tevye and the villagers of Anatevka, it is unimportant where traditions come from.

Traditions provide guidance; they offer "truth"; they are the final word. Tradition tells us that something is correct because it has always been done that way.

Traditional knowledge is widespread in all societies. Many people, for example, believe that the two-parent family is preferable to the single-parent family in that the former provides a more stable and effective socializing experience for children and reduces the likelihood of maladjustment. In some cases, these beliefs are grounded in religious traditions, whereas in other cases they are accepted because "everybody knows" how important two parents are to a child's development. In fact, some human service providers accept these beliefs about the traditional two-parent family despite the existence of considerable research suggesting that the two-parent family may *not* always be essential for high-quality adoption or foster care. For example, one review of research into this issue concluded, "In the studies reviewed here, single-parent families were found to be as nurturing and viable as dual-parent families. In fact, single-parent adoption emerged as a good plan for children" (Groze, 1991). Human service providers can be affected in other ways by traditional beliefs. For example, the works of a Sigmund Freud or an Erik Erikson might be accepted without question, and emphasis might be placed on remaining true to their words rather than assessing the accuracy or utility of their ideas.

Tradition can be an important source of knowledge, especially in such areas as moral judgments or value decisions, but it does have some major disadvantages. First, it is extremely resistant to change, even in those cases where change might be necessary because of the surfacing of new information or developments. Second, traditional knowledge easily confuses knowledge (an understanding of what *is*) with values (a preference for what *ought* to be). For many people, the traditional emphasis on the two-parent family is actually based on a value regarding the preferred family form rather than a knowledge of the effect such a family has on child development.

Experience

Experience as a source of knowledge refers to firsthand, personal observations of events. **Experiential knowledge** is based on the assumption that truth and understanding can be achieved through personal experience and that eyewitnessing events will lead to an accurate comprehension of those events.

Experience is a common source of knowledge for human service workers who have numerous opportunities to make firsthand observations of emotionally disturbed children, people with physical disabilities, foster children, and other service populations. From these contacts, practitioners can develop an understanding—not necessarily accurate—of what motivates their clients and what social or psychological processes have influenced them.

For example, a person working in a spouse-abuse shelter will have considerable contact with women who have been physically and psychologically abused by their husbands. Because of this, the person is likely to be sensitive to the harm that can come to women from their husbands. After seeing women who have been so abused, this worker may conclude that marital counseling with such spouses cannot work in a climate of violence and anger and may even be dangerous. In fact, social worker Liane Davis (1984) found that shelter workers were much less likely to recommend marital counseling than were family court judges. Family court judges did not have the powerful experience of seeing women when the effects of their abuse were most visible; moreover, they have a mandate to maintain the integrity of the family. For them, marital counseling seems both a feasible and an appropriate way to keep the family intact. So we see that the experiences of shelter workers and judges in different settings can lead them to perceive problems differently and assess solutions differently.

This experiential knowledge about family dynamics and abuse may be reinforced by traditional knowledge about the importance of family life. Armed with this knowledge, a practitioner might shape an intervention effort that focuses on individual counseling or marital counseling.

However, experiential knowledge should be relied on only with great caution because it has some severe limitations that can lead to erroneous conclusions. First, human perceptions are notoriously unreliable. Perception is affected by many factors, including the cultural background and the mood of the observer, the conditions under which something is observed, and the nature of what is being observed. Even under the best conditions, some misperception is likely, and thus, knowledge based on experience is often inaccurate.

Second, human knowledge and understanding do not result from direct perception but rather from *inferences* made from those perceptions. The conclusion that marital counseling doesn't work is an inference—it is not directly observed. All that has been observed is that these women have been battered by their husbands. There is no observation of the effectiveness of any type of counseling. (Later in this chapter, we discuss in more detail this problem of making inferences from observations when we address the issue of causality.)

Third, the very people in a position to experience something directly frequently have a vested interest in perceiving that thing in a certain way. Teachers, for example, observe that the students who do poorly are the ones who do not pay strict attention during class. However, teachers have a vested interest in showing that their teaching techniques are not the reason for poor performance among students. Teachers would probably be inclined to attribute students' failings to the students' lack of effort and attentiveness rather than to their own inadequacies as teachers.

A final limitation on experiential knowledge is that it is difficult to know if the people directly available to you are representative of all the people about whom you wish to draw conclusions. If they are not, any conclusions drawn from your observations may be in error. To use our earlier example, are the battered women who contact a spouse-abuse shelter representative of all battered women? If any differences influence the effectiveness of counseling in the shelter, then you cannot generalize conclusions from their outcomes in counseling to the experiences of all battered women. Battered women who go to a shelter may be more affluent or less isolated and might therefore evidence different outcomes in counseling than would less affluent or more isolated women.

Common Sense

The accumulation of knowledge from tradition and experience often blends to form what people call **common sense:** practical judgments based on the experiences, wisdoms, and prejudices of a people. People with common sense are presumed to be able to make sound decisions even though they lack any specialized training and knowledge. Yet, is common sense a very accurate source of knowledge? Consider the following contradictory examples. Common sense tells us that people with similar interests and inclinations will likely associate with one another. And when we see a youngster who smokes marijuana associating with others who do the same, we may sagely comment that "birds of a feather flock together." Then, we see an athletic woman become involved with a bookish, cerebral man, and we say "opposites attract."

In other words, common sense often explains everything—even when those explanations contradict one another. Not that common sense is unimportant or always useless. Common sense can be valuable and accurate, which is not surprising because people need sound information as a basis for interacting with others and functioning in society. However, common sense does not normally involve a rigorous and systematic attempt to distinguish reality from fiction. Rather, it tends to accept what "everyone knows" to be true and to reject contradictory information. Furthermore, common sense is often considered something people either have or don't have because it is not teachable. In fact, it is often contrasted with "book learning." This discourages people from critically assessing their commonsense knowledge and tempering it with knowledge acquired from other sources. For this reason, commonsense knowledge should be accepted and used cautiously. As a basis for human service practice, knowledge needs to be based on the rigorous and systematic methods used in scientific research. Common sense or a vague feeling of "helping" is not enough.

Science

Winston Churchill, prime minister of Britain during World War II, is reported to have said that democracy is an imperfect form of government but that it is far superior to all other forms of government. Many scientists have a similar view of science: They realize that it is imperfect and limited, but they also recognize that it is far superior to other sources of knowledge for gaining an understanding of the world. **Science** is a method of obtaining objective knowledge about the world through systematic observation. (The term "science" is also sometimes used to refer to the accumulated body of knowledge that results from scientific inquiry.) Science has five distinguishing characteristics that, taken together, set it apart from the other sources of knowledge.

First, science is *empirical,* which means simply that science is based on direct observation of the world. Science is not, as some people mistakenly believe, founded in theorizing, philosophizing, or speculating. Though scientists at times do all these things, they must eventually observe the world to see whether their theories or speculations agree with the facts. Because of this, the topics that can be subjected to scientific scrutiny are limited; any issue that cannot be resolved through observation is not within the scope of science. For example, the questions of whether God exists, or which values should underlie a human service profession, are not scientific issues because to determine their truth or falsity through observation is impossible. These are matters of faith or preference, not of science.

Second, science is *systematic,* meaning that the procedures used by scientists are organized, methodical, public, and recognized by other scientists. One dimension of the systematic nature of science is that scientists report in detail all the procedures used in coming to a conclusion. This enables other scientists to assess whether inferences and conclusions drawn are warranted given the observations

that were made. A second dimension of the systematic nature of science is *replication*—repeating studies numerous times to determine if the same results will be obtained. Scientists are very cautious about drawing hard-and-fast conclusions from a single observation or investigation. In fact, quite at variance with experiential knowledge, scientists assume that a single, direct observation is as likely to be incorrect as correct. Only repeated observations can reduce the chance of error and misinterpretation (Rosenthal, 1991).

Third, science is *the search for causes.* Scientists assume that there is order in the universe, that there are ascertainable reasons for the occurrence of all events, and that scientists can discover the orderly nature of the world. If we assume there is no order, no pattern, then there would be no need to search for it. We could write off events as due to chance or the intervention of some benevolent or malevolent otherworldly force that we can never understand.

Fourth, science is *provisional,* which means that scientific conclusions are always accepted as tentative and subject to question and possible refutation. There are no ultimate, untouchable, irrevocable truths in science. There are no scientists whose work is held in such esteem that it cannot be criticized or rejected. As philosopher Jacob Bronowski (1978, pp. 121–122) put it: "Science is not a finished enterprise. . . . The truth is [not] a thing, that you could find . . . the way you could find your hat or your umbrella." Science is a process of continuous movement toward a more accurate picture of the world, and scientists fully realize that we may never achieve the ultimate and final picture.

Finally, science is *objective,* which means that scientists attempt to remove their biases and values from their scientific research. This doesn't mean that scientists are devoid of values. Quite the contrary, they can be as passionate, concerned, and involved as any other group of citizens. They realize, however, that their values and biases can and probably will lead to erroneous scientific conclusions. To avoid this, science incorporates mechanisms to reduce the likelihood of biased observations becoming an accepted part of the body of scientific knowledge. For example, publicizing all research procedures enables others to assess whether the research was conducted in a way that justifies the conclusions reached. Furthermore, such detailed reporting permits replication, so that other researchers, with different values, can see if they come to the same conclusions regarding a set of observations.

Despite these checks, of course, values and biases will still be found in research. The very decision of what topics to investigate, for example, is often shaped by the researcher's values. One person studies family violence because a close friend was the victim of spouse abuse, and another person studies factors contributing to job satisfaction because of a personal belief that work is central to a person's identity. Values and biases also enter research through the interpretation of observations. For personal reasons, one researcher may want desperately to show that the criminal justice system rehabilitates (or does not rehabilitate). This may well influence how he or she goes about conducting research and interpreting the results. There are even a few cases, most common in biomedical research, of outright falsification of data to show a certain conclusion. The point is that values and biases commonly intrude on scientific research, but the overall scientific enterprise is organized to reduce their impact on the body of scientific knowledge.

The scientific method, then, with the characteristics just described, is viewed by scientists as preferable to other ways of gaining knowledge because it is more likely to lead to accurate knowledge of the world. To return to our earlier example of single-parent families and adoption, science views all knowledge regarding the family as provisional and open to question. And there have been many scientific investigations of the role of the family in these matters (*see* Larzelere and Patterson, 1990; Caplan, 1990; Register, 1991; Shireman and Johnson, 1986; and Zill and Nord, 1994). Child adjustment and development in intact families and single-parent families have been observed; comparisons have been made between children receiving group care and those in more traditional family settings; comparisons have been made between the family environments of delinquents, including delinquents who have not been brought before a juvenile court, and nondelinquents.

The conclusion from these various studies is that the traditional, intact family does not seem to play the indispensable role that much common-sense knowledge would accord it. Or at least the role of single-parent and two-parent families is more complicated than was once thought. For example, adoption by a single parent is not detrimental when compared with two-parent adoptive settings, and some children in need of foster care do quite well in group settings rather than a family. Divorce can have some negative consequences for children: Youngsters who experience divorce are more prone to delinquency and more likely to show a decline in school performance. The research on single-parent families also suggests, in a qualified way, that children are often worse off when raised by one parent than two. A recent summary of this research concludes:

> Growing up with only one biological parent frequently deprives children of important economic, parental, and community resources, and . . . these deprivations ultimately undermine their chances of future success. . . . While living with just one parent increases the risk of . . . negative outcomes, it is not the only, or even the major, cause of them. Growing up with a single parent is just one among many factors that put children at risk of failure [McLanahan and Sandefur, 1994, pp. 2–3].

Not all children in single-parent families will suffer the negative consequences because many factors influence a child's development. The researchers attribute the difficulties of children in single-parent families to three factors: low income, inadequate parental guidance, and less access to community resources. If a single parent can overcome these difficulties, then children can do quite well.

Finally, the research shows that it is not always the fact of divorce or single parenthood itself that produces the negative consequences. The poor parenting, conflict between parents, and economic difficulties that often precede or follow divorce contribute to the consequences (Amato, 1993; Amato and Rezac, 1994; Furstenberg and Teitler, 1994). Furthermore, children in one-parent families sometimes benefit from the experience (Amato, 1987; Goldscheider and Waite, 1991). For example, the single parent sometimes gives his or her teenage offspring more responsibility and a greater role in family decision making. Also, teenage boys in mother-only families do more household chores and develop more egalitarian sex-role attitudes than do boys *or* girls in two-parent homes; in addition, both boys and girls in single-parent homes may become more independent and resourceful. So, the commonsense or traditional view that the two-parent family is always superior to the single-parent setting is shown by research to be, at best, vastly oversimplified.

In this fashion, then, scientific knowledge overcomes many of the weaknesses of traditional, experiential, and commonsense knowledge. In particular, it enables us to accumulate accurate information despite the personal biases of individual researchers or practitioners. These positive attributes of science do not mean, however, that science is perfect. Scientists make errors. But, as Jacob Bronowski (1978, p. 122) so aptly put it, "Science is essentially a self-correcting activity." If proper scientific procedures are followed, today's errors will be corrected by researchers in the future, whose errors in turn will be corrected by yet further research.

Scientific Practice

We saw in Chapter 1 that there are parallels between the steps in the research process and the steps in practice intervention. Likewise, human service practice has characteristics, or at least it *should* have characteristics, that parallel those of science that were just described (Barlow, Hayes, and Nelson, 1992; Rosen, 1996). First of all, practice, like science, should be *empirical,* stressing problem assessment involving direct observation of client problems, actual counts of behaviors, and independent observations from multiple data sources. Such

data are less subject to distortion and bias than self-reports, speculations, and philosophizing. Second, practice, like research, should be *systematic.* To the extent that practice procedures are well organized, clearly specified, and made public, they can be replicated and tested by others. In this manner, ineffective procedures can be eliminated, and promising ones can be refined and improved. One of the recurring criticisms of many human service interventions is that the intervention itself is not well specified. Consequently, research evaluating the intervention cannot clearly indicate what did or did not work. Practice models also involve *causality* in terms of specifying a clear link between cause and effect or explicating why some proposed intervention should work with the particular problem that has been identified. Again, a criticism of human service projects in the past has been that many of them have consisted of a conglomeration of intervention efforts without a clearly articulated linkage between cause and effect.

Practice theory, like science, should be *provisional.* All practice models and techniques should be viewed as fair game for criticism and refutation. It is through such a process of testing and challenging existing practices that healthy growth can occur in practice methodology. Finally, human service professionals must deal with the problem of professional *objectivity.* The determination of the utility and effectiveness of practice procedures needs to be done under objective conditions. And just as the researcher must attempt to safeguard against the intrusion of values into the conduct of research, so practitioners must guard against the intrusion of values into practice. This issue of values and objectivity is a particularly difficult one for human service practitioners who often approach problems with a strong set of values, both personal and professional. Personally, practitioners may have strong feelings about such matters as abortion, alcohol use, or domestic violence that may clash with those of groups with whom they work. Furthermore, some human service providers are conventional and middle class in their personal lives, which may influence what they see as successful social functioning. In addition to these personal values, human service practice itself is heavily imbued with professional values. In fact, as one human service educator put it, "social work is among the most value-based of all professions. . . . Social work is deeply rooted in a fundamental set of values that ultimately shapes the profession's mission and its practitioners' priorities" (Reamer, 1995, p. 3). At times, these values may emphasize a conservatism or a pressure to preserve the status quo, while at other times the values may reflect a commitment to supporting vulnerable or oppressed populations. In either event, the recommendation that human service providers not let their values intrude into the provision of services to clients is a challenging one to satisfy. In fact, it is probably impossible to mount an effective change effort without some imposition of values, either implicit or explicit. Even more, there are therapeutic approaches, such as those of Carl Rogers, Albert Ellis, and Hobart Mowrer, that include as one of their goals the acceptance of new and more realistic values on the part of the client. In addition, many human services emphasize the value of alleviating deprivation and distress and of helping people achieve their aspirations.

As a means of controlling the imposition of practitioner values on clients, the human services emphasize the importance of client self-determination, the notion that individuals have the right to make choices about their lives freely. This can confront practitioners with a dilemma: What if self-determination leads to client choices that run counter to the practitioner's personal or professional values? For example, should practitioners work in a child welfare agency that makes abortion referrals if they are morally opposed to this procedure? But the issue need not be this dramatic and is often more subtle. Mental health has often been equated with a middle-class lifestyle. "Appropriate" behavior for women has been defined in terms of a male-dominated society, with one consequence being that there are now feminist therapists who target their services to clients with a feminist orientation.

So even though professional practice in the human services is clearly oriented toward the fulfillment of certain values, practicing in the profession requires that the worker establish checks on the intrusion of values into practice, much as the researcher does in the conduct of research. In later chapters, we will discuss research techniques that are less subject than others to biases in observation and measurement. Application of these principles in practice can also help restrict the unwanted intrusion of personal values into service delivery. Another way to control the influence of values is to do research on the role of values in practice and to design agency procedures that help provide services objectively. For example, Vannicelli and Hamilton (1984) conducted a study on sex-role values and bias among alcohol treatment personnel. Their results showed that clinicians perceived female clients as having poorer prognoses than males. Furthermore, presenting problems were perceived to be more important if they were "sex appropriate" than if they were not. So the clinicians viewed "typically" female problems in a male client as the least important. Armed with this knowledge, an agency can design procedures that will control the extent to which such biases might affect the equitable delivery of services to alcoholics.

As in research, the influence of values in the actual conduct of practice cannot be totally eliminated, but by relying on a practice approach that is empirically based, that employs procedures that have been supported by research, and that incorporates rigorous evaluation procedures, it is possible to sensitize professionals to the impact of their value positions and thus enhance the objectivity of service delivery. Research in Practice 2.1 offers an illustration of how this can be accomplished.

Theories in Research and Practice

"Theory" is a word that is misunderstood by many people. To the neophyte, theories are often associated with the abstract, the impractical, or the unreal. In actuality, nothing could be farther from the truth. In both research and practice settings, theories play a critical role in our understanding of reality and our ability to cope with problems. In fact, people commonly use theories in their daily lives

Research in Practice **2.1**
Needs Assessment: Interviewing the Children of Lesbians

The power and tenacity of stereotypes regarding gay men and lesbians is illustrated by the negative epithets in wide use in our society: fag, lesie, queer, butch, dyke, and the like. In part deriving from the Judeo-Christian values that pervade our culture, homosexuality is viewed by some as bizarre, evil, or a sign of psychological disturbance. In recent decades, a more accepting attitude toward homosexuality has emerged—at least in terms of reducing social and economic discrimination based on sexual orientation. There remains, however, at least one bastion of heterosexuality: the family. In the view of most people, the family should be a heterosexual couple (or single parent) and children. In fact, it was not until 1973 that a lesbian mother was awarded custody of her children after a divorce. The belief is still quite strong that a lesbian is unfit to be a mother and that children will be harmed if raised by a lesbian mother or lesbian couple.

Human service practitioners often deal with clients or situations that involve value-laden controversies such as this. The difficult problem is how to serve clients within the context of one's own personal and professional values. In some cases, it is possible to use scientific research to assess whether personal or professional values are *unreasonably* influencing the services provided to clients. This was

illustrated by a project at a child outreach program in a Massachusetts mental health center. Karen Lewis (1980), director of the program, saw several children in therapy whose mothers had recently made their lesbianism publicly known. In attempting to develop a knowledge base from which to establish a treatment strategy, she found very little literature on the children of lesbians. What she did find focused on the legal issues of whether lesbians should be permitted custody of their children or on what professionals *believed,* partly based on their own personal values, would be best for the children. No one had bothered to ask the clients—the children—about feelings, attitudes, and consequences of being raised by lesbian mothers.

Professional values dictate that intervention be based on what is in the best interests of the client. In determining what is best for the client, Lewis might have relied on traditional knowledge (for example, religious teachings or personal values regarding homosexuality, the family, and childrearing) or experiential knowledge (her contact with the few children of lesbian mothers who sought her services). Instead, she turned to scientific observation. She contacted lesbian mothers through a number of sources such as local gay newspapers. She eventually interviewed 21 children from eight families. The interviews were conducted with as

without recognizing it. First, then, we need to understand what theories are.

What Is a Theory?

A **theory** is a set of interrelated propositions or statements, organized into a deductive system, that offers an explanation of some phenomenon (Homans, 1964, p. 951). There are three key elements in this definition that are important to understanding theories. First, theories are made up of

propositions, which are statements about the relationship between some elements in the theory. For example, a proposition from the differential association theory of crime is that "a person becomes criminal because of an excess of definitions favorable to the violation of the law over definitions unfavorable to the violation of the law." Elements in this proposition include "criminal" and "definitions favorable to the violation of the law" (Sutherland, 1939). Behavior modification theory also contains numerous propositions, such as "behavior change

many of the children in each family as possible, and the mothers were not present. The interviews were not considered therapy sessions—the goal was to gain information about the adjustment problems of the children rather than to confront and solve those problems. Lewis is careful to point out that her sample is not representative of all children with lesbian mothers. These were for the most part upper-middle-class, educated women who were willing to make their sexual orientation public. What was learned from these children does not necessarily apply to all children of lesbian mothers.

Since Lewis's work of 20 years ago, a considerable body of research has accumulated on the development and experiences of the children of lesbians and gay men (Patterson, 1992; Golombok and Tasker, 1996). For the most part, this research does not support the negative developmental outcomes for the children that would be predicted by much traditional and experiential knowledge or some people's personal values. Although children with a gay parent do confront some developmental problems, the problems seem no more severe than the problems confronted by children of heterosexual parents. In fact, the developmental problems of the two groups of children are remarkably more similar than different. Of the children with gay parents, Lewis concludes:

> The children unanimously agreed that the breakup of their parents' marriage was far more upsetting than the subsequent disclo-

sure about their mother. . . . A heterosexual mother in remarrying confronts the same problems regarding the children's adjustment as a lesbian mother with a lover. . . . One striking point . . . was the children's desire to accept their mother's new lifestyle. Almost without exception, the children were proud of their mother for challenging society's rules and for standing up for what she believed. Problems between the mother and children seemed secondary to the children's respect for the difficult step she had taken [Lewis, 1980, pp. 199–203].

The work of Lewis illustrates the manner in which an objective science can work with a profession based on values to further the goals of the profession. Science cannot inform human service workers regarding what their personal values ought to be, but it can point to practice situations in which personal values seem to be unreasonably intruding on intervention decisions. Personal values might suggest that children should not live with a lesbian mother, but Lewis's data suggest that such living arrangements may not be detrimental to the children. Without such research, a greater danger may be that decisions based on personal values will parade as "what is in the client's best interest." So research can serve a watchdog function on the unwarranted intrusion of values into practice decisions.

can occur through a reorganization of the environmental cues that reward and punish behavior" (Sulzer-Azaroff and Mayer, 1991). The elements in this proposition include "behavior change," "environmental cues," and "reward and punish behavior."

A second important part of our definition of theory is that theories are *deductive* systems, meaning they move from general, abstract propositions to particular, testable statements. For a set of propositions to constitute a theory, deducing further relationships between the elements must be possible.

Differential association theory is again illustrative. As noted, this theory relates definitions favorable to the violation of the law with the greater likelihood of criminal behavior. This means that the theory is meant to apply to *all* specific types of crimes, such as robbery, larceny, or auto theft. So it would be logical to deduce from the theory that greater exposure to definitions favorable to the violation of the law would be associated with higher incidences of robbery, larceny, or auto theft. Theories are abstract because they have this deductive power:

The broader and more abstract the propositions and their related concepts are, the more numerous are the specific relationships that can be deduced from them.

The third key aspect of theories is that they provide *explanations* for the phenomena they address. Indeed, the ultimate purpose of a theory is to explain *why* something occurred. In differential association theory, the phenomenon to be explained is criminal behavior, and the explanation is that criminality is learned through much the same process as noncriminal behavior. It is the content of what is learned—definitions favorable to violation of the law—that makes the difference. Thus, differential association provides an explanation for the development of criminal behavior.

In comprehending theories and the role they play, it is helpful to realize that we all use "theories" in our everyday lives although we may not call them theories or be consciously aware of using them. Nonetheless, we base our decisions and behavior on our past experience and what we have learned from others. From these experiences, we generalize that certain physical, psychological, and social processes are operative and will continue to be important in the future with predictable consequences. This is our "commonsense theory" about how the world operates and forms the basis for our decisions. For example, most people have certain general notions—personal theories—about what causes poverty. Some personal theories emphasize poverty as an individual problem: People are poor because of their individual characteristics, such as laziness, low intelligence, poor education, or lack of marketable skills. Others' theories of poverty emphasize the structural features of the American economy that dictate that even in times of economic expansion some people will be left impoverished through no fault of their own. Which of these theories people identify with most closely will determine, in part, how they react to poor people and which public policy provisions toward poverty they support. Advocates of the individualistic theory might be hostile toward the poor and programs to aid them because they believe the poor are undeserving people suffering only from

their own shortcomings. Supporters of the structural theory may view the poor as victims and tend to be more benevolent toward them.

Personal theories, like these concerning poverty, may be extreme and misleading because they are based on casual observations, personal experience, or other information lacking the rigorous concern for accuracy of scientific investigations. Unlike commonsense theories, theories in research and practice are precise, detailed, and explicit. It is, however, important to recognize that a theory is always tentative in nature. That is, any theory is best viewed as a *possible* explanation for the phenomenon under investigation. By conducting research, scientists gather evidence that either supports or fails to support a theoretical explanation or practice intervention. No theory stands or falls on the basis of one trial. Theories are tested over a long period of time by many investigations. Only with the accumulation of research outcomes can we begin to have confidence concerning the validity of a theory.

The Functions of Theories

We have all heard the refrain "It's only a theory" or "That's your theory." Such phrases are often used in the context of deflating an argument that someone has put forth. Actually, these comments, though often intended in a disparaging sense, convey some truth regarding theories. In particular, they point out that theories are sometimes *untested* (but testable) assertions about reality, and that theories are not the end product of scientific investigation but rather are a part of the process of science. Theories are used for particular purposes in both research and practice settings. In fact, the same theories are often used in both research and practice because both researchers and practitioners turn to theories for similar reasons. We can identify two major functions of theories in research and practice.

Guide for Research and Practice   Theories serve to guide and direct research and practice. They focus attention on certain phenomena as being relevant to the issues of concern. If we were to dispense with theories altogether, as some would suggest, then what would we study? What data would be collected? What intervention strategy would be adopted? Theories aid us in finding answers to these questions.

Imagine that a counseling center is concerned with attacking the problem of teenage alcohol consumption in a particular high school and that the staff decides to study the problem. Where to begin? What variables are important? As a first step, it is essential to fall back on some theory related to these issues. We might, for example, use the theory of differential association, which posits that alcohol consumption results from attitudes and patterns of behavior that are learned in association with other people, particularly peers. In order to test this theory, we could determine whether alcohol consumption is more common when it is viewed as an acceptable form of behavior among peers. We are then in a position to collect data on attitudes toward alcohol and patterns of alcohol consumption in peer groups. If the theory is confirmed, then it supports the idea that effective intervention will need to focus on attitudes toward alcohol consumption in peer groups.

We could have selected quite a different theory regarding alcohol consumption. For example, some theories posit an inherited predisposition toward alcoholism. Other theories suggest that alcoholism results from a nutritional deficiency that is satiated by alcohol consumption. We do not presume to suggest which of these is the more accurate theory—future research will, one hopes, settle that issue. The same thing occurs in practice intervention. If a practitioner used crisis intervention theory to deal with the disruption caused by an alcoholic parent, the theory would direct attention to such factors as family coping strengths and emotional adaptation. Community organization practice theory, on the other hand, would focus on community resources available to recovering alcoholics and community services for families of alcoholics. The point is that the theories used by researchers and practitioners serve to guide their approaches and focus their attention on particular phenomena.

Integration of Multiple Observations Theories serve to integrate and explain the many observations made in diverse settings by researchers and practitioners. They tell us *why* something happened, and they enable us to link the outcomes of numerous studies and interventions made in a variety of settings. As long as the findings of these efforts remain individual and isolated, they are not particularly valuable to science. Recall that a single observation is viewed with considerable skepticism. Single research findings may be in error, they may be passed over and forgotten, or their broader implications may be missed entirely. Theories enable us to organize these dispersed findings into a larger explanatory scheme. For example, someone investigating problem pregnancies among teenagers might observe that the groups of teenagers among whom such pregnancies are common tend to view parenthood out of wedlock in a positive fashion. A familiarity with differential association theory would suggest that the social learning processes important in teenage drinking may also be relevant in problem pregnancies among teenagers. If this is the case, then practitioners working in one area may be able to borrow strategies for intervention from the other area. Thus, theories integrate the findings from independent research endeavors and provide implications for intervention strategies.

Theories, then, play an important part in both research and practice. But one point needs to be reiterated: The utility of theories must be based on their *demonstrated* effectiveness. Theories should never be allowed to become "sacred cows" whose use is based on tradition or custom. Authorities on human service practice report that the proliferation of theories in the social sciences and the human services has made using theory as a guide for practice a major challenge for today's practitioners. These theories differ widely in terms of what they specify as the cause of problems, the targets of change, and the most effective intervention techniques. Yet, when selecting among competing theories and integrating multiple theories into a change effort, most authorities would agree with this conclusion: "The most important criterion to consider is the extent to which a given theory has

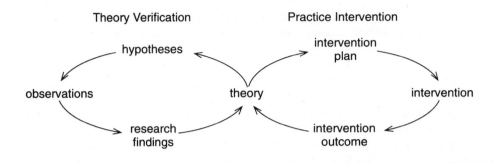

Figure 2.1   The Process of Theory Verification in Research Compared With Practice Intervention

been supported by empirical research" (Hepworth and Larsen, 1990, p. 18). In other words, has the intervention been shown to produce the desired results? In scientific research, this is called the **verification** of theories. Researchers approach the problem of verification by developing and testing hypotheses, which is our next topic. This process of verification is diagrammed in Figure 2.1, which also shows a parallel process as it occurs in human service practice.

Concepts and Hypotheses

Defining Concepts

An important part of theories are **concepts:** mental constructs or images developed to symbolize ideas, persons, things, or events. Concepts are the "elements" of theories discussed earlier; they are the building blocks that are interrelated in propositions that form the explanatory statements of a theory. Some of the concepts in behavior modification theory, for example, are reinforcement, conditioning, learning, and behavior change.

Concepts are similar in function to the words we use in everyday communication. The word "automobile," for example, is the agreed-on symbol for a particular object that is used as a mode of transportation. The symbol or word is not the object itself but rather something that stands for or represents that object. Scientific concepts, like words in everyday language, are also symbols that can refer to an extremely broad range of referents. They may refer to something fairly concrete like leadership or refer to something fairly concrete like leadership or

something highly abstract like reinforcement or cohesion.

Despite the similarities between scientific concepts and ordinary words, some differences are critical to the scientific endeavor. In particular, concepts used in scientific research must be defined very carefully. With the words we use for everyday communication, we can get along quite well with only a general idea of how these words are defined. In fact, whether most people could give a dictionary-perfect definition of even the most commonly used words is doubtful. Such imprecision in the use of scientific concepts, however, is totally inadequate. Scientists, widely scattered both geographically and temporally, carry on research that tests various aspects of theories. For these disconnected research projects to produce information of maximum utility, all the bits of knowledge need to be integrated into an explanatory scheme—a theory. This accumulation of knowledge is severely hampered—in fact, becomes practically impossible—if these isolated scientists use different definitions of the same concepts. For example, many studies of the relationship between reinforcement and learning have been conducted. If the results of different studies are to be comparable, the concepts of reinforcement and learning should be defined in the same way. Learning, for instance, can be defined in *behavioral* terms as the performance of a new behavior or in *cognitive* terms as the understanding of how a particular behavior might be performed. When defined in these two different ways, the concept refers to something quite different in the world, and results from two investigations using the different definitions would not be directly comparable. Perhaps, for example, behavioral learning occurs under quite different conditions than does cognitive learning.

Scientific analysis involves two types of definitions of concepts—each functioning at a different level of analysis and serving a different purpose. At the theoretical or abstract level, concepts are given **nominal definitions:** verbal definitions in which scientists agree that one set of words or symbols will be used to stand for another set of words or symbols. Nominal definitions are directly analogous to the dictionary definitions of ordinary words in which a phrase is designed to give meaning to the word or concept being defined (Cohen and Nagel, 1934). For example, a nominal definition of "poverty" might be a deficiency in resources to the extent that people are not able to maintain a lifestyle considered minimally acceptable in a particular society (Sullivan, 1997, p. 166).

An important step in moving from the abstract level of theory to the concrete level of research is to give concepts **operational definitions:** definitions that indicate the precise procedures, or operations, to be followed in measuring a concept. For example, one of the most widely used operational definitions of poverty was developed by Mollie Orshansky for the Social Security Administration (Ruggles, 1990). Her measure, still used by the government as a basis for policy decisions, is based on what it costs to purchase a low-budget, nutritious diet for a family. If we use United States Department of Agriculture figures, the poverty line is determined by the cost of food, the size of the family, the age and sex of the head of the household, and other factors. This operational definition of poverty actually yields a series of income cutoffs below which families are defined as poor. This is a precise definition that lists the exact operations (in this case, mathematical operations) to follow in defining poverty. Anyone using this definition will be measuring the same thing in the same way.

The process of moving from nominal to operational definitions can be complex because concepts are very general and abstract, and controversy often arises over exactly what they refer to. Some concepts that have been a part of the literature for

decades have yet to be operationalized in a way that is fully satisfactory. For example, "alcoholism" has proved extremely difficult to operationalize, especially establishing where alcoholism begins and social drinking leaves off (Schuckit, 1989). Owing to substantial individual and cultural differences, simple measures relying on amount and frequency of consumption are inadequate. Researchers have been forced to operationalize alcoholism on the basis of symptoms such as family or work problems, morning drinking, poor eating, and recurrent blackouts. Whereas symptom-based measures of alcoholism avoid the errors inherent in consumption measures, substantial controversy remains concerning which symptoms are the best indicators, how many symptoms must be evident, and how serious they must be before the label of "alcoholic" may be meaningfully applied.

Even the concept of poverty, which may seem straightforward and easy to operationalize, has proven controversial. There is, of course, the issue of where to set the income cutoffs. Orshansky's cutoffs are based on the assumption that the average American family spends one third of its income on food, and some critics have argued that this results in poverty thresholds that are too low. Furthermore, Orshansky's definition sets a fixed income level as the poverty level, and thus it is unaffected by changing levels of affluence within society as a whole. Some have argued for a "relative" definition of poverty that defines as poor those who earn one third or one half of the median family income (Bell, 1987). With such a definition, the poverty thresholds would automatically rise if the affluence of society as a whole increased. So it should be evident that operationalizing concepts can be difficult, complex, and sometimes controversial. The process of moving from the nominal to the operational level is called *measurement,* and it is treated extensively in Chapter 5.

Developing Hypotheses

A common strategy in scientific investigations is to move from a general theory to a specific, researchable problem. A part of this strategy is to develop

hypotheses, which are testable statements of presumed relationships between two or more concepts. Hypotheses state what we expect to find rather than what has already been determined to exist. A major purpose of developing hypotheses in research is to test the accuracy of a theory (*see* Figure 2.1). The concepts and propositions of which theories are composed are usually too broad and too abstract to be directly tested. Such concepts as *reinforcement* or *learning,* for example, need to be specified empirically through operational definitions before they are amenable to testing. Once operationally defined, these concepts are generally referred to as **variables,** or things that are capable of taking on more than one value. If hypotheses are supported, then this supplies evidence for the accuracy of the theory on which they are based.

In the construction of hypotheses, the relationship between variables is stated in one of two possible directions: a positive relationship or a negative (also called inverse) relationship. In a *positive relationship,* the values of the variables change in the *same* direction, both increasing or both decreasing. For example, we might hypothesize that the acceptance of the use of alcohol among an adolescent's peers will lead to increased likelihood that the adolescent will consume alcohol. In other words, as acceptance of the use of alcohol by one's peers increases, so does the adolescent's own use of alcohol. In a *negative* or *inverse relationship,* the values of variables change in *opposite* directions. We might hypothesize, for example, that, among adolescents, reduced parental supervision will lead to an increase in the likelihood of substance abuse. In this case, as the value of one variable (parental supervision) declines, the value of the other (substance abuse) is predicted to increase.

Useful guidelines to keep in mind for developing hypotheses include the following:

1. Testable statements are derived from abstract theories in a *deductive* process. Although generating hypotheses without deducing them from theories is possible, hypotheses are always linked to theories because the theories explain why things happen.

2. The *independent variable* is stated first in the hypothesis, followed by the *dependent variable.* The **independent variable** is the presumed active or causal variable—it is the one believed to be producing changes in the dependent variable. The **dependent variable** is the passive variable or the one that is affected. In the previous examples, peer acceptance of alcohol and parental supervision are the independent variables, and alcohol use and substance abuse are the dependent variables.

3. The independent and dependent variables need to be clearly specified. Great confusion can arise if the precise variables that a hypothesis contains are not made clear.

4. Hypotheses should be so stated that they can be verified or refuted. Otherwise, they are not hypotheses. Hypotheses, after all, are statements about which we can gather empirical evidence to determine whether they are correct or false. A common pitfall is to make statements that involve judgments or values rather than issues of empirical observation. For example, we might "hypothesize" that investigations should be increased to reduce the incidence of welfare fraud. On the surface, this statement might appear to be a hypothesis because it relates investigations and welfare fraud in a negative direction. But note that, as stated, it is not a testable hypothesis. The problem is the evaluative "should be." What should or should not be social policy has no place in hypotheses. However, the statement can be modified so that it qualifies as a testable hypothesis: Increased levels of investigation tend to reduce the incidence of welfare fraud. The hypothesis is now making an empirical assertion that can be checked against fact.

5. Developing hypotheses from theories is a *creative* process that depends in part on the insight of the investigator. Because hypotheses link theories to particular concrete settings, the researcher's insight is often the trigger to making such connections. In addition, researchers at times combine two or more theories to develop hypotheses that neither theory alone is capable of generating.

Concepts and Operational Definitions Among Minority Populations

When conducting research on minority populations, considerable opportunity for bias exists if concepts and operational definitions are not carefully developed. This has been a chronic problem with research on crime. For example, many people believe that nonwhites commit crimes at a higher rate than we would expect given their numbers in the population. Although this is partly true, it greatly oversimplifies a complex reality, and it reflects how crime is typically operationalized. Official crime statistics from the Federal Bureau of Investigation (1992) are an important source of data on crime. The FBI operationalizes some crimes as "offenses cleared by arrest" and others as "offenses known to the police." In other words, an occurrence is not officially considered a crime until it is "known to the police" or "cleared by arrest." These official crime statistics show that nonwhites commit more crimes proportionate to their numbers in the population than do whites. However, this is in part a function of how the official statistics operationalize the concept of crime. We know that nonwhites are more likely to be arrested for a given offense, suggesting that it may be arrest that is more common among them rather than the actual commission of crimes. It has been proposed that nonwhites are also more likely to commit highly visible crimes, such as armed robbery or assault, that are more frequently reported to the police and result in an arrest. Some suggest that whites, on the other hand, commit more "hidden" crimes, like embezzlement or fraud, that are less likely to come to the attention of the police. Research suggests that there may be no class difference in the amount of "hidden" crimes that are committed (Elliott and Huizinga, 1983). There are other ways to operationalize crime, such as through victimization studies (asking people if they have been a victim of a crime) and self-reports (having people anonymously report their own involvement in crime). Studies based on these operational definitions tend to show much smaller differences between white and nonwhite crime rates.

Another area where poorly constructed operational definitions have produced misleading conclusions is in the area of spouse abuse (Lockhart, 1985). Most studies have found rates of spouse abuse to be considerably higher among African Americans than among whites. Typically, these studies have used one of the following as an operational definition of the occurrence of wife abuse: a homicide involving a domestic killing, a battered woman seeking care in an emergency room or social service setting, a wife-abuse claim handled by a domestic court, or a domestic dispute call to a police department. It is well known, however, that African Americans are overrepresented among people who come to the attention of the police, emergency room personnel, or social service workers. Because they are generally overrepresented among these populations, they will appear to have higher rates of abuse than will whites when abuse is operationalized in this fashion. These problems can be reduced by selecting a sample of people from a community and having them answer questions about the amount of conflict and violence that occurs in their family. This avoids the biased effect of looking only at certain locales. The National Family Violence Resurvey, for example, employed a sampling strategy that selected about 6,000 cases representing all racial and ethnic groups (Straus and Gelles, 1988).

The Committee on the Status of Women in Sociology (1986) has indicated another area in which operational definitions have led to misleading results: studies of work and social contribution. Work is often operationalized in terms of paid employment, but this excludes many types of work, such as community service or home-based work, from consideration. With such an operational definition, if an employee of a carpet-cleaning firm shampoos the carpets in a home for a fee, that would be counted as "work," but if a woman does the same activity on her own time in her own home, it would not be classified as "work." Such an operationalization of work tends to underestimate the extent of productive activity engaged in by women because women are less likely than men to have paid employment.

So in developing operational definitions, care must be taken to assess whether they might lead to a distorted view of minorities. In some cases, this calls for careful consideration of what a concept is intended to mean. For example, is the focus of the research on "paid employment" or is it on "social contribution"? In other cases, it calls for careful assessment of whether a definition will lead to an inaccurate over- or underrepresentation of minorities.

Deduction Versus Induction

A comment should be made at this point about two forms of reasoning that are central to the scientific process: *deduction* and *induction*. We mentioned earlier that theories are deductive systems. This means that hypotheses can be logically derived from the propositions that make up a theory. So **deductive reasoning** involves deducing or inferring a conclusion from some premises or propositions. If the propositions—or the theory—are correct, then hypotheses logically derived from them will also be correct. In Figure 2.1, deduction involves moving from the level of theory to that of hypotheses or an intervention plan. Deductive reasoning is central to the scientific process.

However, it is inductive reasoning that enables us to assess the validity of the hypotheses and the theory. **Inductive reasoning** involves inferring something about a whole group or class of objects from our knowledge of one or a few members of that group or class. We test one or a few hypotheses derived from a theory and then infer something about the validity of the theory as a whole. Thus, inductive reasoning carries us from the observations or interventions in Figure 2.1 to some assessment regarding the validity of the theory. The logic of scientific analysis involves an interplay between deduction—deriving testable hypotheses—and induction—assessing theories based on tests of hypotheses derived from the theories.

At times, inductive research is conducted without benefit of prior deductive reasoning. This occurs in descriptive or exploratory research when no theory exists from which to deduce hypotheses. In the absence of theory, we begin by making observations and then developing some theoretical propositions that would be plausible given those observations. Practitioners, for example, may observe that clients with problem pregnancies tend to come from families with low socioeconomic status. Based on the assumption that the parent–child bond is weaker in low socioeconomic families and that such parents, therefore, have less control over their children, the practitioners could inductively conclude that a weak parent–child bond leads to an increased risk of unwanted pregnancy. In other words, the observations are used to infer a proposition regarding the causes of unwanted pregnancies. Inductive research of this sort can serve as a foundation for building a theory, and the theory in turn can serve as a source of testable hypotheses through deductive reasoning. Thus, induction and deduction are each key links in the chain of scientific reasoning, and they parallel the reasoning process that is found in practice intervention.

Research in Practice 2.2 offers an illustration of a research project that highlights many of the issues discussed in the previous two sections regarding the use of theories and hypotheses in research and the importance of inductive and deductive reasoning.

Cause-and-Effect Relationships

One of the more important, yet difficult, tasks in scientific research is the search for causes—the reasons *why* particular forms of behavior occur. Why do child abuse and spouse abuse occur? Why do some juveniles become delinquent whereas others present no behavior problems? Why do some people exhibit symptoms of mental illness whereas others appear psychologically stable? Discovering causal relationships is a difficult task because causality cannot be directly observed. Rather, it must be inferred from the observation of other factors. Because of this, the philosopher John Kemeny has labeled causality "the mysterious force" (1959, p. 49). We cannot see it, feel it, or hear it; but we often assume it is there and many scientists search for causality with hopefulness and tenacity. It is also a controversial task because some philosophers, notably Bertrand Russell (1953), have argued for excluding the notion of causality from scientific investigation altogether. These people would opt for restricting ourselves to description and the analysis of "associations" without the implication that a "mysterious force" called causality lurks behind the scene and orchestrates the actions of people and things. This controversy is long-standing, and we do not presume to resolve it here. Nonetheless, it is important to understand the criteria that need to be satisfied if one wants to infer that one event caused another.

By **causality,** we mean that some independent variable (X) is the factor, or one of several factors, whose change produces variation in a dependent variable (Y). As noted, causality can only be *inferred*. We can observe the relationships among things in the world, and from that we infer or deduce that changes in one factor are causing changes in another. However, it is always an inference. To infer the existence of a causal relationship, one must demonstrate the following:

1. A statistical association between the independent and dependent variables must exist.
2. The independent variable must occur prior in time to the dependent variable.
3. The relationship between independent and dependent variables must not be spurious; that is, the relationship must not disappear when the effects of other variables are taken into account.

We will consider each requirement of causal inference in the context of an issue that is much in the news today: the campaign to reduce cigarette smoking. Over the years, there have been reports in the media about the negative impact of cigarette smoking on people's health. Some have argued that making these reports public as a part of a health campaign can motivate people to quit. Table 2.1 presents hypothetical data seeming to show a link between reading such reports about smoking and actually quitting smoking: Fifty percent of those who read the reports quit smoking as compared to only 27 percent of those who do not read the reports. Finding such a statistical relationship satis-

Table 2.1 Effectiveness of Reading Media Reports on Smoking Cessation

		Person Reads Report	
		Yes	No
Person Quits Smoking	**Yes**	200 (50%)	135 (27%)
	No	200 (50%)	365 (73%)
	Totals	400 (100%)	500 (100%)

fies the first criterion for establishing a causal relationship.

The second requirement, that the independent variable occur prior in time to the dependent, is often not as easy to establish. A major factor in this is the nature of the study. Some research techniques, such as the experiment or participant observation, are inherently *longitudinal,* which means that the researcher is in a position to trace the development of behavior as it unfolds over time. In these cases, establishing the time sequence of events is generally simple. Questions of temporal order are more difficult to resolve when dealing with *cross-sectional* data, such as surveys, in which measurements of the independent and dependent variables occur at the same time. This is especially true if the question of temporal sequence is not addressed until after the data have been collected. It is sometimes possible to sort out the time sequence of variables in survey data by asking additional questions. However, if the necessary information is not gathered at the time of the survey, establishing the appropriate time order of the variables may be impossible—therefore the emphasis on the importance of carefully considering issues of data analysis when originally developing a research design.

The data in our illustration may suffer from this problem. One interpretation of the data is that reading reports is the independent variable that has an influence on whether people quit smoking, the dependent variable. For this interpretation to be correct, the reports would have to have been

Research in Practice 2.2
Practice Effectiveness: Social Theory and Burnout Among Social Workers

A SOCIAL WORKER: I began to despise everyone and could not conceal my contempt.

A PSYCHIATRIC NURSE: Sometimes you can't help but feel "Damn it, they want to be there, and they're fuckers, so let them stay there." You really put them down. . . .

A SOCIAL WORKER: I find myself caring less and possessing an extremely negative attitude. [Quoted in Maslach, 1979, p. 217]

These are hardly the caring, empathic reactions one would expect from human service workers. Yet these and similar negative attitudes toward clients are expressed at some point by many social workers, nurses, psychologists, and others. This problem—often referred to as "burnout"—is of considerable concern to human service professionals because it can impair their ability to deal with client problems. *Burnout* refers to a service worker's emotional disengagement from clients, dissatisfaction with his or her job, feelings of worthlessness, and physical and interpersonal problems (Arches, 1991). Commonsense approaches often focus on

the personal abilities of human service workers to explain why they suffer burnout: They lack sufficient emotional strength or distance from clients, or they overidentify or overempathize with their clients. Rather than relying on such intuition, scientific researchers turn to theories for direction in identifying variables that might play a part. One researcher, Joan Arches (1991), turned to *theories of organizational structure and change,* reasoning that recent developments in social service organizations might have an impact on burnout. The theories suggest that increasing bureaucratization and centralization in organizations can reduce workers' feelings of autonomy, and this in turn can contribute to the job dissatisfaction that is a part of burnout. Arches's research then provided evidence that this was the case, offering further verification for those organizational theories.

When social work researcher W. David Harrison (1980) approached these issues, he utilized a different theoretical approach. He turned to *role theory,* which views human behavior as resulting from conformity to expectations that are associated

---

publicized before the people quit smoking. If the respondents were not asked when they quit smoking, it would be impossible to say whether they quit smoking before or after reading the reports. Obviously, if they quit smoking before reading the reports, then such health campaigns could not have caused their quitting. In our example, without knowing the temporal sequence, one could argue logically for either factor being the cause of the other. Obviously, the health campaign could cause people to quit smoking if they become frightened by learning the dire consequences of their habit. However, it could also be that those who quit smoking are happy with and proud of their victory and enjoy reading reports on what could have happened to them had they not quit smoking. In this

second scenario, quitting smoking would be the independent variable that increases the likelihood that people will read reports about the health threat of smoking, the dependent variable.

The final criterion necessary for inferring causality is that the relationship between the independent and dependent variables not be *spurious* or disappear when the effects of other variables are considered. (The logic of causal and spurious relationships is compared in Figure 2.2.) This is often the most difficult of the three criteria to satisfy. In fact, one is never *totally* sure that some other variable—one you have not even considered—might not confound an apparent causal relationship. All that can be accomplished is to rule out as many extraneous variables as we can to the point

with particular roles. One of the tenets of role theory is that role expectations should be clear, unambiguous, and achievable. Furthermore, the various expectations associated with a role should not conflict with one another. Much previous research suggests that situations in which role expectations are conflicting, incompatible, or unclear lead to personal stress and dissatisfaction. *Role strain* refers to a felt difficulty in performing a role. The two types of role strain are role conflict and role ambiguity. *Role conflict* refers to a situation in which conflicting and incompatible demands are placed on a person in a role. *Role ambiguity* refers to a lack of clarity in terms of what is expected of a person in a particular role.

Harrison's research focused on child protective service (CPS) workers, and he found both role conflict and role ambiguity to be commonplace. Role conflict occurs because CPS workers must perform the role of advocate and enabler for the client while also representing the authority of law, often with involuntary clients. The expectations associated with the advocate-enabler role clash with those associated with the legal-representative role. Role ambiguity enters the picture for the CPS workers in terms of the lack of clarity regarding the ultimate goal of child protective services. The final step in Harrison's theoretical analysis was to hypothesize that role ambiguity and role conflict would be inversely related to job satisfaction and, therefore, positively related to burnout. Harrison then collected data to test this hypothesis, and the results showed that role strain, especially role ambiguity, produced job dissatisfaction and burnout.

Thus, the theoretical considerations of organizational theory and role theory do not point to excessive empathy or emotional weakness as the culprits in burnout among human service workers. Rather, it is the organizational and role structures that surround them that are important. These investigations illustrate the importance of grounding research in theory. It is theory that suggests which variables might be important and how they might relate to one another. It also shows how hypotheses can be developed through deductive reasoning. Once confirmed, Arches's and Harrison's hypotheses provided support, through inductive reasoning, for the organizational and role theory interpretations of burnout in the human services. Based on this slow, methodical accumulation of knowledge, we should eventually establish a solid foundation from which to develop programs to alleviate the problem of burnout among human service workers.

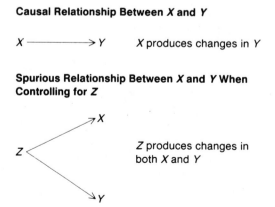

Causal Relationship Between *X* and *Y*

$X \longrightarrow Y$ *X* produces changes in *Y*

Spurious Relationship Between *X* and *Y* When Controlling for *Z*

Z produces changes in both *X* and *Y*

Figure 2.2   Causal and Spurious Relationships

where it is unlikely that a variable exists that could render a given relationship spurious or noncausal.

Considerable effort is expended during the design stage of research to control as many potentially troublesome extraneous variables as possible. Experiments, for example, are particularly good for avoiding spurious relationships owing to the high degree of control the experimental situation affords the researcher. Surveys, on the other hand, provide far less control, such that several variables capable of producing spuriousness will typically have to be considered during data analysis. Several statistical techniques exist to control extraneous variables when the data are analyzed.

Returning to our example of smoking cessation, suppose we had solved the time sequence problem and, thus, had satisfied the first two requirements for establishing a causal relationship. We would now begin to consider variables that might render the relationship spurious. One variable that might do this is the level of education of the people studied. (The logic of this is outlined in Figure 2.3.) Considerable research links education with health behavior: Generally, people with higher levels of education engage in more health-promoting activities such as quitting smoking or exercising. How do we determine whether the link between report reading and smoking cessation is spurious? We introduce the level of education as a control variable, which is illustrated with our hypothetical data in Table 2.2. We have divided the respondents in Table 2.1 into those with at least a high school education and those with less than a high school education. First, we can see by examining the row totals in each table that education is related to health behavior: Sixty percent of the better-educated group have quit smoking compared to only 19 percent of the less-educated group. However, we are really interested in what happens to the link between report reading and smoking cessation. Careful inspection of Table 2.2 will show that the relationship largely disappears: *Within each educational group,* the same percentage of people quit smoking among those who read the report as among those who did not. So it is educational level, not whether

Table 2.2   Effectiveness of Reading Media Reports on Smoking Cessation, Controlling for Education

Less Than High School Education

		Person Reads Report		
		Yes	**No**	**Totals**
Person Quits Smoking	**Yes**	20 (20%)	75 (19%)	95 (19%)
	No	80 (80%)	325 (81%)	405 (81%)
	Totals	100 (100%)	400 (100%)	500

High School Education or More

		Person Reads Report		
		Yes	**No**	**Totals**
Person Quits Smoking	**Yes**	180 (60%)	60 (60%)	240 (60%)
	No	120 (40%)	40 (40%)	160 (40%)
	Totals	300 (100%)	100 (100%)	400

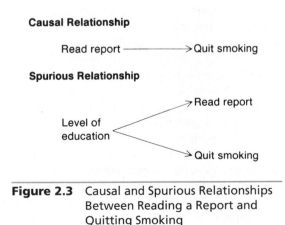

Causal Relationship

Read report ⟶ Quit smoking

Spurious Relationship

Level of education ⟶ Read report
Level of education ⟶ Quit smoking

Figure 2.3   Causal and Spurious Relationships Between Reading a Report and Quitting Smoking

one has read the report, that influences a person's likelihood of quitting smoking. Furthermore, in our hypothetical example, educational level also influences whether one reads the report: 300 out of 400, or 75 percent, of those with a high school education did so compared with only 100 of 500, or 20 percent, of the others. So, in our example, the link between reading the report and quitting smoking is spurious; it occurs only because each of those two variables is affected by the same third variable.

If we had found the link between report reading and smoking cessation to be nonspurious when we controlled for education, could we conclude that the relationship was causal? The answer is no. We could not come to that conclusion—at least not yet. All that would have been shown was that the relationship remained when *one* alternative explanation was ruled out. Any other variables that could render the relationship spurious would also have to be investigated and the relationship still hold before we could argue with any confidence that it was in fact causal. (More of the intricacies of this sort of analysis are addressed in Chapter 15).

We said at the outset that establishing the existence of causal relationships is difficult. From the preceding discussion, you should understand better why this is the case. Statistical relationships are easy to find but, on further investigation, all too frequently turn out to be spurious. The appropriate time sequence can also be problematic, especially with survey data. All in all, establishing causal relationships is a difficult but important and challenging task.

Main Points

- Science is one source of knowledge, along with tradition, experience, and common sense; but it is a superior source of objective and accurate knowledge about the world.
- The five key characteristics of science are that it is empirical, systematic, provisional, and objective, and that it searches for the causes of events.
- These crucial characteristics are also central features of scientifically based practice.
- Theories are sets of interrelated propositions in deductive systems that explain phenomena.
- Theories perform two major functions: They guide research and practice, and they integrate observations from research.
- Concepts are mental constructs that symbolize ideas, persons, things, or events and form the basis for propositions and theories.
- Concepts are given both nominal definitions, which explain their meaning, and operational definitions, which indicate how they are measured. Care must be taken in developing operational definitions in research on minorities to ensure that such definitions do not lead to a distorted view of these populations.
- Hypotheses are statements that predict relationships between two or more variables and are tested through research.

- Causality means that some independent variable produces variation in a dependent variable.
- To demonstrate a causal relationship one must establish a statistical association between two variables, show that the independent variable occurs temporally first, and demonstrate that the relationship is not spurious.
- Computerized databases developed by human service agencies as a part of their service-delivery tasks can be excellent sources of data for social research, and this research can also enhance practice.

Important Terms for Review

causality
common sense
concepts
deductive reasoning
dependent variable
experiential knowledge
hypotheses
independent variable
inductive reasoning
nominal definitions
operational definitions
propositions
science
theory
traditional knowledge
variables
verification

Exploring the Internet

The Computers in Research feature reports on research using a welfare agency database to assess the process of leaving welfare as one illustration of how research can inform practice. For an Internet resource on applying research to human service practice, we suggest you use one of the search engines, such as Yahoo or Lycos; search for phrases such as "children's mental health" or "evaluation

COMPUTERS IN RESEARCH
Using Agency Databases for Research: A Study of Leaving Welfare

A commonly held perception of welfare recipients is that, once on the rolls, they remain there for years as they develop a lifestyle of dependency. Is it true? If not, why does the perception persist? Creative research relying on a computerized database from the state of Wisconsin known as the CRN (Computer Reporting Network) suggests some answers (Rank, 1985). This research also illustrates the point made in the first chapter regarding how social agencies, especially with the assistance of computer technology, can be organized as "research machines." In addition, it illustrates how some of the elements of science, such as dependent variables and operational definitions, come into play in computer analysis.

In 1971, the Wisconsin Department of Health and Social Services initiated a project designed to produce a computer-based information system to handle the administration of AFDC, food stamps, and Medicaid. The system was headquartered in Madison with remote terminals linking county social service offices in a statewide network. By 1981, more than 99 percent of all cases in the state's 72 counties had been loaded onto the system. Data enter the system when a county worker fills out an application form that determines eligibility for AFDC, Medicaid, and food stamps. The information is keyed into a terminal at the local office and sent to the centralized computer; within minutes a case determination sheet is printed at the county office and all the information on each case is saved on the central computer file. This system greatly reduces processing errors and speeds up benefit determination. Although devised primarily to meet the data management demands of a complex welfare system, the CRN also provides an excellent source of data for research purposes, as illustrated by Mark Rank's (1985) study of how long people remain on welfare.

Rank used a 2-percent random sample of all cases in the CRN database that were participating in welfare as of September 30, 1980. Approximately 140,000 were eligible cases, resulting in a sample of 2,796. The cases were followed at 6-month intervals through September 1983 by matching the Social Security number of the head of household for each case in the sample against the entire CRN file at the end of each interval. Any cases in the sample that no longer appeared on the active CRN file had left welfare in Wisconsin. Although a study like this could have been done without computers, the collection and analysis of the data would have been far more costly and time consuming—probably prohibitively so.

The dependent variable in Rank's study was the length of time that people were on welfare. He had to determine an operational definition of that concept based on the information available in the

outcomes." A spot that we found from such a search was the Research and Training Center for Children's Mental Health, whose URL is http://lumpy.fmhi.usf.edu/CFSroot/rtc/rtchome.html. At that site, you can click on "publications" or "research and training center." Among the resources available at these locations are summaries of research projects related to children's mental health. The studies reviewed at this site provide excellent illustrations of efforts to scientifically evaluate a wide array of human service interventions devoted to the needs of children and youth. In this chapter, we discussed the development of hypotheses and introduced the ideas of operational definition, dependent variable, and independent variable. As a way of applying these concepts to actual research, select several of the evaluations reviewed at the Research and Training Center site. For each study

CRN. He used two operational definitions. First, he looked at recipients who entered welfare at the same time, referred to as a "case-opening cohort." Second, he looked at a cross section of recipients who were all on welfare on a given date, referred to as a "point-in-time cohort." With each method, he measured the average number of months until they left welfare ("exit time").

Contrary to popular belief, Rank found that most households who use welfare do so only briefly, typically for 1 to 2 years or less. Given this, why does the belief persist that welfare use equates with long-term dependency? At least part of the explanation may be found in the two different operational definitions: the case-opening cohort and the point-in-time cohort. When the study looked at a group of recipients who began using welfare at the same time (a case-opening cohort), the median exit time was 10.33 months. However, with a sample of people who happened to be on welfare at any given time (a point-in-time cohort), the median exit time was 20.58 months—twice as long.

A little thought reveals why these two different ways of measuring how long people stay on welfare come to strikingly different conclusions. To use a simplified example: Suppose 10 people get on welfare on January 1. A month later 5 people get off while a year later the other 5 are still on welfare. If we do a case-opening cohort study of those 10 people, our sample would consist of 5 people who got off welfare after a month and 5 who remained on for a year. However, if we did a point-in-time study at the end of the year, the sample would consist only of the 5 people who had been on welfare for a year. The latter sample would clearly show that people stay on welfare much longer than would the former sample. Now, reality is more complicated; people get on and off welfare constantly, but the impact is the same: Over time, any welfare caseload tends to have a larger proportion of people who have been on welfare longer. People who get off welfare quickly do not show up in a point-in-time study performed after they drop off welfare, while people who stay on welfare longer have a greater chance of showing up in such a study. Thus, point-in-time studies tend to "trap" proportionally more people who stay on longer than will cohort studies, and point-in-time studies have a bias toward showing people to be on welfare longer. So, point-in-time studies help to perpetuate the belief that people stay on welfare a long time. This comparison of point-in-time measures with case-opening measures illustrates the care necessary when developing operational definitions that do not provide a biased view of reality.

This study also illustrates how information collected by human service agencies as a part of service delivery can be computerized and used in research that can further enhance effective service delivery. Although this study focused on a statewide network, as personal computer technology advances, it is becoming feasible for small agencies to computerize their case record systems as well, making computer database research a potentially valuable tool for human service workers in a wide spectrum of settings.

---

that you select, identify one or more hypotheses that the study addressed. Determine if the review identifies how the dependent and independent variables were operationally defined. Finally, if the review describes how the independent and dependent variables are measured, state whether success in the program would be expected to show an inverse or direct relationship between the dependent and independent variables.

For Further Reading

Babbie, Earl R. *Observing Ourselves: Essays in Social Research.* Belmont, Calif.: Wadsworth, 1986. A thought-provoking anthology of essays concerning the fundamental issues in social science research, including determinism, objectivity, and causation, along with several more.

Glaser, Barney G., and Anselm L. Strauss. *The Discovery of Grounded Theory.* New York: Aldine, 1967. An excellent book about the virtues and procedures of developing theoretical propositions from data. This approach emphasizes qualitative research and induction.

Goldenberg, Sheldon. *Thinking Methodologically.* New York: HarperCollins, 1992. Although it contains additional topics, this book presents detailed and in-depth coverage of many of the issues that we touch upon in this chapter.

Hoover, Kenneth R. *The Elements of Social Scientific Thinking,* 5th ed. New York: St. Martin's, 1992. A brief and readable initiation into social science thinking and research. It is intended for those who use the results of research and those just getting into the field.

Kaplan, Abraham. *The Conduct of Inquiry.* New York: Harper & Row, 1963. A very good discussion of the logic of scientific analysis in the behavioral sciences. It covers such topics as concepts, theories, and values.

Merton, Robert K. *Social Theory and Social Structure,* 2nd ed. New York: Free Press, 1968. A classic statement by a sociologist of the relationship between theory and research.

Phillips, D. C. *Philosophy, Science, and Social Inquiry: Contemporary Methodological Controversies in Social Science and Related Applied Fields of Research.* Elmsford, N.Y.: Pergamon, 1987. An excellent philosophical analysis of issues in applied social research in such areas as social work and nursing. It addresses the issue of whether applied social research can or should emulate the positivist model found in the natural sciences.

Root, Michael. *Philosophy of Social Science: The Methods, Ideals, and Politics of Social Inquiry.* Oxford, U.K., and Cambridge, Mass.: Blackwell, 1993. This book provides an overview of the philosophical underpinnings of social science research. The author examines the position that social science should be objective and value free but concludes that this is not possible.

Sagan, Carl. *The Demon-Haunted World.* New York: Random House, 1996. In this controversial book, a noted astronomer and author makes the case that science is a kind of savior of humankind: It can save us from believing in the unproven. In making his argument for science, the author pillories many other ways of trying to understand the world, such as astrology, turning to psychics, mysticism, faith healing, and even conventional religion.

Exercises for Class Discussion

2.1 Many commonsense beliefs relate to child development, such as "spare the rod and spoil the child" or the belief that age-graded schools enhance learning. Through class discussion, develop a list of such "known" principles of child development. For each such principle, decide whether it is based on traditional knowledge, experiential knowledge, or a combination of these. How might you conduct systematic observations to determine the worth of these statements as scientific knowledge?

2.2 A mental health worker assigned to a large residential facility for senior citizens receives a request from staff members to "do something" about a new resident who is a 72-year-old woman. From the information provided, the woman has apparently been assigned to an eighth-floor room, but she refuses to take the elevator alone or if it is crowded. The woman becomes terrified of the enclosed space and uses the stairs unless she can ride the elevator with a staff member. The woman's husband died about 6 months ago, and she is now living alone for the first time.

a. Consider this case from the alternative theoretical positions of behavior modification versus traditional Freudian psychology. (You may substitute some other relevant theories of human behavior with which you are familiar.) What are some major theoretical concepts from each theory that apply to this case?

b. For the concepts that you identified in part a, use the illustrative case to develop operational definitions for each concept.

2.3 Using each theory from Exercise 2.2, construct a possible explanation for the woman's behavior. Now try to state your explanations in terms of testable hypotheses. Can you foresee any problems in assessing causality when testing these hypotheses? Compare the hypotheses you developed with those of other students in terms of the theory used, the concepts selected, and the variables identified. How are the concepts and variables that are derived from the same theory alike? How do they differ from those derived from the other theory?

2.4 We have made the point that the same theories can be useful to both practitioner and researcher. Using the hypotheses developed in Exercise 2.3, explain how they could be used either to help the worker change behavior or to conduct a study. How might the hypotheses need to be changed to be useful to both practice and research?

2.5 A clinician in a treatment program for woman batterers notices that about 75 percent of the individuals who are mandated by the court to participate in group therapy also have a history of substance abuse problems, such as arrests for drunk driving. Furthermore, a large proportion of the clients had been drinking prior to committing assault. Can the clinician conclude that substance abuse causes woman battering? Identify what conditions would need to be met in order to support this contention. Prepare a diagram involving a third variable that might show that the relation between substance abuse and woman battering is spurious.

CHAPTER 3

Ethical Issues in Social Research

The Minority Experience: The Need for Ethical Standards   46

Ethical Issues   50
  Informed Consent   50
  Confidentiality   53
  Privacy   55
  Physical or Mental Distress   56
  Sponsored Research   56
  Scientific Misconduct and Fraud   57
  Scientific Advocacy   63
  Protecting Vulnerable Clients   64
  Withholding Treatment for Research Purposes   65

Codes of Ethics   67

Main Points   67

Important Terms for Review   68

Exploring the Internet   68

For Further Reading   68

Exercises for Class Discussion   69

People are the subjects of social research, and, because people have rights and feelings, special considerations apply in social research that do not confront the chemist studying molecules or the physicist investigating gravity. Consider, for example, the area of substance-abuse control and treatment. In recent years, substantial controversy has arisen over the use of drug testing to deal with the problem. Some employers have instituted random drug testing of their employees as a condition of gaining employment or remaining employed. Some college athletes are randomly tested, as are prison inmates. In the context of social research, drug testing of a population would be a useful method for assessing the effectiveness of drug interdiction programs or substance-abuse counseling programs. To be most effective, such testing should be required of all people affected by a program. So if new security procedures to control the entrance of drugs into a prison are established, their effectiveness can be measured by random testing of a sample of inmates. Likewise, if a drug education program is established in a college, its effectiveness could be assessed by random testing of a sample of students at the college.

Would such involuntary drug testing of inmates or students be proper? This question can be answered only by referring to some cultural, professional, or personal values that help us decide what is right and proper behavior. There are three expressions of values with which most United States citizens and human service professionals would agree:

1. People have a right to privacy.
2. People have a right to self-determination.
3. One person should not do anything to intentionally harm another person.

Viewing drug testing in this context, some would argue that people's right to privacy precludes taking their bodily fluids against their will to find out something about them. Is such an invasion of the privacy of college students proper or acceptable? What about prison inmates? Involuntary testing of a whole population would also seem to violate self-determination: The subjects have no choice about participating in the research. Finally, because a person who tests positive for drugs might be subject to criminal prosecution or stigmatization, it raises the question of whether the research could bring harm to the person.

These are complicated issues that we grapple with in this chapter. We do not presume that our statement of values is the final word or that their application to particular cases is easy or straightforward. They do serve as a beginning, however, to the discussion of ethical issues in social research. **Ethics** is the study of what is proper and improper behavior, of moral duty and obligation (Reese and Fremouw, 1984). Moral principles can be grounded in philosophy, theology, or both. For social researchers, ethics involves the responsibilities that researchers bear toward those who participate in research, those who sponsor research, and those who are potential beneficiaries of research. It covers many specific issues. For example, is it ever permissible to harm people during the course of a research project? Should people who participate in a research project ever be deceived? Is it appropriate to suppress research findings that cast a sponsor's program in a negative light? Should researchers report to the police about crimes they uncover while conducting their research? The ethics of a given action depend on the standards used to assess the action, and those standards are grounded in human values. Because of this, there are few simple or final answers to ethical questions, and there are no scientific "tests" that can show us whether our actions are ethical. In fact, debate continues among scientists about ethical issues because such issues involve matters of judgment and assessment.

Our purpose in this chapter is to identify the basic ethical issues in social research and to suggest some strategies for making sure that ethical considerations are attended to in the conduct and use of research. We begin by considering efforts to codify ethical standards in recent decades. Then we review some of the core ethical dilemmas that researchers are likely to face. Finally, we discuss some ethical matters of special concern to researchers in the human services.

The Minority Experience: The Need for Ethical Standards

Ethical issues do not exist in a vacuum but rather within the context of a particular society and its historical development. Two events in the twentieth century—one abroad and the other in the United States—served as major catalysts for efforts to codify a set of ethical standards for research.

The first occurred in Europe during World War II: the heinous series of experiments conducted by the Nazis on Jews and others in concentration camps (Beauchamp et al., 1982). Prior to this, there had been no codification of scientific ethics, and researchers were left largely to their own devices in deciding how to conduct their studies. The revelation of the German atrocities, exposed during the Nuremberg trials in 1945 and 1946, shocked the sensibilities of the world and left an indelible imprint on research ethics. The cruelty of the experiments is almost inconceivable. Healthy people were intentionally infected with such serious diseases as spotted fever or malaria. Other people were used as subjects to test the effects of various poisons. Some had parts of their bodies frozen to test new treatments. Still others were purposely wounded to study new antibiotics and other treatments. Perhaps most evil of all were the excruciating decompression studies designed to test reactions to high-altitude flight (Katz, 1972). These gruesome experiments forcefully brought home exactly how far people would go in using research to further their own ends. They also brought home the vulnerability of minorities to exploitation in research, especially when the resources and authority of powerful groups support the research of people with few ethical standards. Public outrage afterward led to heightened concern for establishing codified standards for the ethical conduct of medical research on human subjects.

The second event that influenced the development of a codified set of ethical standards was an infamous study of syphilis conducted by the U.S. Public Health Service (PHS). The study began with black males from Tuskegee, Alabama, in 1932: 425 with syphilis and 200 without syphilis. All were poor and semiliterate. None was told he had syphilis. The intent was to observe the men over a span of years to learn how the disease progressed. When the study began, there was no cure for syphilis. Fifteen years later, penicillin was discovered to be an effective cure for this dreaded affliction. Despite this discovery, the PHS continued the syphilis study an additional 25 years, withholding treatment from all but those fortunate few who discovered its existence on their own and requested it. The justification for deceiving the men was that, because they were poor and semiliterate, they would in all likelihood not seek treatment even if they knew of it. The men were allowed to spread the disease to their wives and lovers. If syphilis is untreated, it can cause paralysis, insanity, blindness, and heart disease. Ultimately, it can be fatal. Many of the afflicted participants in the Tuskegee study suffered serious physical disorders or died as a result of not receiving treatment for the disease (Kimmel, 1988; Jones, 1992).

Most Americans today—and especially those in the human services—would agree that the actions of the PHS were repugnant, racist, and unethical in the extreme. When the study began, however—and even when effective treatment for syphilis became available—the subordinate position of blacks and poor people in American society resulted in their receiving fewer of the political, economic, and even medical rights that whites and the more affluent receive. It is unlikely that well-to-do whites would have been treated in the same arrogant fashion, and one would hope that no such debacle would be seriously contemplated today. Yet, we should keep in mind that the PHS study continued into the 1970s—an era we like to consider a more enlightened one regarding human rights—and ended only when it received public notoriety. This further documents the extent to which minorities (and others) can be at risk of dangerous and inhumane treatment by researchers who are not governed by clear and enforceable ethical standards.

So the immoral treatment of some minorities in research in this century, especially the Nazi and PHS episodes, brought home to people the need to codify standards for ethical conduct so that researchers would have guidelines available and research subjects would be afforded some protection. The first effort along these lines was the Nuremberg Code, developed in 1946 in direct response to the atrocities committed during World War II. The Nuremberg Code was limited to issues of ethics in medical research. In 1966, the United States Public Health Service established ethical regulations for medical research that emphasized the following: (1) Full disclosure of relevant information should be made to the participants, (2) the decision to participate must be completely voluntary, and (3) researchers must obtain documented, informed consent from participants (Reynolds, 1979; Gray, 1982). In 1974, the Department of Health, Education, and Welfare (DHEW, now the Department of Health and Human Services, or DHHS) decreed that the PHS guidelines would apply to social science research. Furthermore, DHEW recognized that codes of conduct alone would not ensure ethical research without some oversight procedures. To this end, DHEW required research institutions, such as universities, to establish institutional review boards, or IRBs, to review research proposals to ensure that the guidelines were followed. These DHHS regulations have been broadened so that they apply not only to those projects directly funded by that agency but also to any research carried on in organizations that obtain DHHS funding.

Reaction to the imposition of DHHS guidelines and the IRBs among social scientists has been somewhat hostile. A common feeling is that the risks to participants in most social science research are minimal and different from risks in medical research (Murray et al., 1980). Researchers see the major risk in social science research being a breach of confidentiality, not direct harm during the research process. Furthermore, researchers feel that the regulations obstruct important research, hinder response rates, and reduce the validity and generalizability of findings.

In response to these concerns, the Department of Health and Human Services, under a policy issued in 1981, exempted the following research methodologies from IRB review: evaluation of teaching procedures or courses, educational testing, survey or interview techniques, observation of public behavior, and documentary research (Huber, 1981). The only exceptions are research dealing with "sensitive" behavior, such as drug and alcohol use, illegal behavior, or sexual conduct. In assessing social science research not exempt from IRB review, the IRBs have tended to subscribe to a risk-benefit doctrine (Smith, 1981). This means that questionable practices, such as deception or disguised observation, may be utilized if the purpose of the study is viewed as sufficiently important to justify them.

Although the DHHS regulations exempt much social science research from IRB review, many universities and other research institutions require that *all* research projects be reviewed in order to determine whether they are legitimately exempt. Furthermore, it has become increasingly commonplace for private foundations to require IRB review as a prerequisite for funding (Ceci, Peters, and Plotkin, 1985). When planning research, an application to conduct the research should routinely be submitted to the appropriate IRB in order to determine whether the research is exempt and, if not exempt, gain permission to conduct the research. Figure 3.1 is an illustration of one such IRB application form. As you read the rest of this chapter, you will see that many of the ethical issues discussed are addressed in this application. Even if a project is exempt from IRB review, researchers are not exempt from ethical concerns. Whether one's research will be reviewed or not, one still has the responsibility of considering the impact of the research on those who participate and on those who might benefit from it. And, as we will see, ethical guidelines do not eliminate the controversy that surrounds ethical

The Northern Michigan University Human Subjects Research Review Committee approves/disapproves all requests to conduct research involving human subjects. In completing the following application, be advised that the persons reviewing it may be entirely unfamiliar with the field of study involved. Present the request in nontechnical terms understandable to the Committee. It is the investigators' responsibility to give information about research procedure that is most likely to entail risk but not to express judgment about the risk. Please submit a copy of your complete proposal and attach a curriculum vitae or biographical sketch if project is to be submitted to an outside funding source.

Principal Investigator or Project Director	Department	Date of Request

Type: [ ] New   [ ] Renewal   [ ] Continuation
If renewal or continuation, has procedure changed?   [ ] Yes   [ ] No

Project Title

Agency Submitting To	Date	Location of Project

1. General Purpose of Research:

2. Data Obtained By   [ ] Mail   [ ] Telephone   [ ] Interview   [ ] Observation
                           [ ] Experiment   [ ] Secondary Source   [ ] Other

3. Describe in nontechnical terms what will happen to subjects, with sufficient detail, so that the Committee can evaluate the risks if any to a subject. Do not merely list that the subject is under no risk. The Committee itself must have enough information about transactions with subjects to estimate the risks. Assurance from the investigator, no matter how strong, will not substitute for a description of the transaction between the investigator and subject. If a questionnaire is used, attach a copy.

[ ] Exempt   [ ] Not Exempt

When visual or auditory stimuli, chemical substances, or other measures might affect the health of subjects, it is suggested that the investigator attach a statement from a qualified person, or other appropriate documentation, evaluating the nature of any risk created. In questionable cases, the Committee will require such documentation.

(continued)

Figure 3.1   An Institutional Review Board (IRB) Application for Conducting Research on Human Subjects

Source   Northern Michigan University Human Subjects Research Review Committee, 1996. Reprinted with permission.

4. Give ages, sex, source, and number of subjects.

5. How will subjects be selected, enlisted or recruited?

6. How will subjects be informed of the procedures, intent of study and potential risks to them?

7. What steps will be taken to allow subjects to withdraw at any time without prejudice?

8. How will the subjects' privacy be maintained?

Attachments:

	Vitae or			
Complete	Biographical	Sample		
[ ] Proposal	[ ] Sketch	[ ] Questionnaire	[ ] Documentation	[ ] Other

===

In making this application, I certify that I have read and understand the "Rules Governing the Participation of Human Beings as Subjects in Research," and that I intend to comply with the letter and spirit of the University policy. Significant changes in the protocol will be submitted to the Committee for written approval prior to those changes being put into practice. Records will be kept of informed consent of the subjects for at least two (2) years after the subjects' participation.

_____   _____
Signature of Principal Investigator or Project Director   Date

===

[ ] Recommend Approval   [ ] Do Not Recommend Approval

_____   _____
Signature of Departmental/Collegial Committee Chair   Date

===

A. Exemption: [ ] Approved   [ ] Disapproved   (If disapproved, see B below.)

_____   _____
Director of Research Development   Date

===

B. This application has been reviewed and [ ] approved; [ ] disapproved by the Northern Michigan University Human Subjects Research Review Committee, or, deferred until adequate application has been made [ ].

Comments:

_____   _____
University Committee Representative   Date

===

issues—because guidelines need to be interpreted and applied to specific contexts. Much debate surrounds such interpretation and application.

The debate over the Nazi experiments is not over. Controversy persists in terms of whether the data from that research are valid and reliable, and, if so, whether those data should be used today (Moe, 1984; Schafer, 1986). Some have argued that use of the data is justified if they are scientifically valid and no other source of such data exists. If they are used, it is argued, one should feel compelled to express horror and regret at the manner of their collection. On the other side, some argue that our collective outrage at the treatment of minorities by the Nazis should be so great that use of the data is repulsive. In this view, refusing to use the data is a symbolic denunciation of such atrocities while using the data might be interpreted as an acceptance of their methods or at least a willingness to let the importance of the Holocaust diminish with the passage of time. Between these two extremes, some researchers argue that the data should be used only if some overriding need demands them and the objective of using them overrides our symbolic rejection of the manner in which they were collected. Recent assessments suggest that the data from the Nazi experiments are seriously flawed—and may even be fraudulent, in some cases—and therefore should not be used, regardless of the ethical issues surrounding how the data were obtained (Berger, 1994). This controversy shows how long-lasting and deeply rooted ethical issues in research can be.

We turn next to a consideration of the major ethical issues that should be assessed as a routine part of any research project.

Ethical Issues

Seven basic ethical issues arise in social science research: informed consent, confidentiality, privacy, physical or mental distress, problems in sponsored research, scientific misconduct or fraud, and scientific advocacy. The unique situation that confronts the human service researcher raises two additional considerations: protecting vulnerable clients and withholding treatment for research purposes.

Informed Consent

Informed consent refers to telling potential research participants about all aspects of the research that might reasonably influence their decision to participate. Very often people are asked to sign a *consent form,* which describes the elements of the research that might influence a person's decision to participate (*see* Figure 3.2). General agreement exists today on the desirability of informed consent in behavioral science research, primarily because in the United States, cultural values place great emphasis on freedom and self-determination. Whether the issue be whom to marry, what career to pursue, or whether to participate in a research project, we value the right of individuals to assess information and weigh alternatives before making their own judgments. To deceive potential research participants is to deny them the ability to determine their own destinies.

Although there is consensus about the general principle of informed consent, the debate regarding exactly how far researchers' obligations extend in this realm is a hot issue. At one extreme, researchers known as ethical "absolutists" argue that people should be *fully* informed of all aspects of the research in which they might play a part (Elms, 1982; Baumrind, 1985; Kimmel, 1988). Even when research is based on the public record, such as agency documents, or on observations of behavior in public, some absolutists argue that people about whom observations have been made should be informed of the research. Otherwise, they do not have the full right to decide whether to participate.

However, rigid adherence to the absolutist position makes social research much more difficult to conduct. First, such adherence rules out many practices that some researchers consider important or essential. Many experiments, for example, rely on some degree of deception, at least to the extent of not telling participants the true research hypotheses. The reason for this is that people might respond differently if they knew these hypotheses. However, all such studies would be unacceptable to the absolutists and could not be conducted. Disguised observation, in which people in public settings are not aware they are being observed, would also be

I, _____, in return for the opportunity of partici-
pating as a subject in a scientific research investigation and for other considerations, hereby authorize the
performance upon me of the following procedure:

_____

_____

_____

_____

_____

This consent I give voluntarily as the nature and purpose of the experimental procedure, the known dan-

gers and the possible risks and complications have been fully explained to me by _____.

I understand the potential benefits of the investigation to be _____

_____

_____

as well as the above procedure(s) to be used which may involve the following risks or discomforts: _____

_____

_____

I understand that, as a participant, my rights will not be jeopardized, that my privacy will be maintained
and that the data obtained in this study will be used in a manner to maintain confidentiality and personal rights.

I knowingly assume the risks involved, and I am aware that I may withdraw my consent and discontinue
participation at any time without penalty to myself.

I also am aware of the fact that in the event of physical injury or illness facilities and professional care
which are available will not be provided free of charge and that monetary compensation for such injuries or
illness will not be made.

Dated: _____   _____
                                           Signature

Dated: _____   _____
                                           Signature

Figure 3.2   Sample Consent Form for Adult Human Subjects in Research

Source   Northern Michigan University Human Subjects Research Review Committee, *Policies and Procedures,* December 20, 1982. Reprinted with permission.

disallowed by absolutists. No longer could researchers engage in such effective strategies as infiltrating organizations—unless, of course, they told all employees what they were doing. The net result would be to make social science research highly conservative and very limited. It would become the study of people who volunteer to be studied, and research shows that volunteers are different in many ways from people who do not volunteer. This would have the effect of seriously reducing the generalizability of research findings.

Second, the absolutist approach would call for obtaining informed consent in *all* research projects, and research has shown that obtaining *written* consent can reduce people's willingness to participate in research. One study found that formally requesting informed consent prior to conducting an interview reduced the rate of cooperation by 7 percent in comparison to cases in which a formal request was not made (Singer, VonThurn, and Miller, 1995). Because any reduction in response rate reduces the generalizability of the findings, as explained in Chapter 7, obtaining informed consent in survey research can have serious negative consequences in terms of the validity of the research.

Written informed consent probably reduces people's willingness to participate because it appears in the eyes of some respondents to contradict the researcher's assurance of confidentiality. One minute people are being told that their answers will remain confidential, and the next they are asked to sign a consent form! Even though signing a consent form need not impede the maintenance of confidentiality, it is not surprising that respondents may not view it that way. Anything that undermines respondents' beliefs in the confidentiality of the answers will reduce response rates. Signing the consent form may also affect the quality of the data obtained because those who do give their consent may be less candid in their responses than they otherwise would have been. It is ironic that an attempt to enhance one aspect of ethical research—informed consent—is potentially a threat to another aspect—confidentiality.

Because of these problems with the absolutist approach to informed consent, many researchers take a less extreme position. They argue, first of all, that people should be informed of factors that might reasonably be expected to influence their decision to participate, such as any harm that might occur or how much time and effort will be involved. However, they also use a risk-benefit approach: Questionable research strategies, such as deception, are appropriate if they are essential to conduct the research and will bring no harm to participants, and if the outcome of the research is sufficiently important to warrant it. It is ironic, but one study found evidence that the use of deception in small groups research may be increasing, despite its status as a questionable practice (Adair, Dushenko, and Lindsay, 1985). This review of major social psychology journals showed that the rate of use of deception increased from 14.3 percent in 1948 to 58.5 percent in 1979. Lively debate continues concerning the use of questionable practices and their routine approval by IRBs (*see* Baumrind, 1985).

A final issue regarding informed consent has to do with the possibility that a person might feel pressured to agree or might not understand precisely what he or she is agreeing to. After all, asking a person to participate in a study can involve social pressures not unlike those in other settings. We often feel pressured to help others when they ask our assistance, and some people find it difficult to say no to a face-to-face request. In addition, scientific researchers represent figures of some authority and status, and people are often disinclined to refuse their requests. In other cases, people may be momentarily confused about what is being asked of them. To resolve these problems, a study involving institutionalized elderly people used a two-step consent procedure (Ratzan, 1981). In the first step, people were told what their participation would involve, what risks were entailed, and that several days later they would be asked whether they were willing to participate. This was meant to reduce any immediate pressures to agree and to enable people to talk with others and clarify any confusing issues. The second step, occurring a few days later, involved obtaining the actual consent. In this study, all those who were asked refused to participate.

This was probably due to the fact that a part of the study involved having a needle inserted in a vein for 8 days straight in order to take blood samples. However, some of the people may have agreed to participate had they been asked to sign a consent form during the first interview. Yet, it is questionable whether consent obtained at that time would have been as "informed" and considered as it should be. The goal of obtaining informed consent is not to pressure people into participating in the research but rather to gain participation that is truly "informed."

Confidentiality

Another major ethical concern in scientific research is **confidentiality:** that particular information or responses not be publicly linked to any specific individual who participated in a study. Confidentiality was a major concern in the 1981 DHHS regulations. Participants in social research are commonly told that their responses will be confidential, and the overall record on this point has been very good. There have, however, been a few notable exceptions that show how confidentiality can be violated. Especially in observational and single-subject research, one must be careful to protect identities when presenting results. To do so, researchers make it a common practice in reporting research results to give fictitious names to people and places. This procedure works fairly well as long as researchers do not become so detailed in their descriptions of places, events, and people that the protection afforded by the fictitious names is undermined.

A now infamous example of this is *Small Town in Mass Society* by Arthur Vidich and Joseph Bensman. First published in 1958, this observational community study described the power relationships and local governmental operations in a small town the authors called "Springdale." The authors had assured all people they interviewed that confidentiality would be maintained. Even though no identities were, in fact, directly revealed, it was easy for the residents of the small community to recognize the people and events described in the highly detailed

report. Because the study was very critical of some residents of Springdale, these people—understandably—became outraged. Local newspapers vociferously attacked the researchers for betraying the community. The townspeople even held a Fourth of July parade that featured a full manure spreader carrying mired effigies of the authors (Whyte, 1958). In order to avoid such breaches of confidentiality, one must balance one's enthusiasm for producing a highly detailed account against the ethical obligation to protect fully the identities of those observed.

Single-subject research requires particular caution in this regard. As explained in Chapter 11, single-subject research involves observing the changes in feelings or behavior of an individual over a period of time. Furthermore, the clients in these studies often suffer from some condition, such as a mental disorder, that might lead to stigmatization should others find out about it. Therefore, great care must be taken to ensure that people's identities are not unintentionally revealed in the process of providing a description of the case. Researchers must often tread a fine line between providing sufficient case detail and minimizing the risk of identification of a client. Final reports should always be written with sensitivity to this issue.

Confidentiality can also be threatened when third parties, such as the people sponsoring the research or the courts, seek to identify research participants. Intrusion by a sponsor is relatively easy to avoid. When establishing a research agreement with a sponsoring agency or organization, one should make clear in the agreement that identities will not be revealed under any circumstances. If the sponsor objects, researchers should refuse to accept the agreement. We have more to say about sponsors and ethics later.

The courts pose another threat to confidentiality. Most communication that physicians, lawyers, and clergy have with their clients is protected from judicial subpoena. Social workers, in their clinical capacity, also are afforded such protection in many instances, although the degree of protection varies with agency settings and jurisdictions. Social researchers, however, do not have a clear protection of privileged communication with the people from whom they gather data (Reece and Siegal, 1986; Kimmel, 1988). Thus, courts may subpoena research data that reveal participants' identities, and failure to comply with such a subpoena renders researchers open to contempt of court charges. Actually, social science researchers have been treated very inconsistently by the courts in this regard, and this leaves their status unclear. In some civil cases, the courts have been reluctant to compel researchers to reveal information. In a civil suit in California, for example, the court refused to force a researcher to reveal the identities of respondents in confidential interviews (Smith, 1981).

In criminal cases, the courts have generally held that the right of the public to be protected from criminal activity supersedes any assurance of confidentiality in research. In one case, for example, the courts seemed to recognize that the confidentiality that a legitimate social researcher establishes in a relationship should be protected, if possible (Brajuha and Hallowell, 1986). In this case, the researcher had been making field observations in a restaurant when it was heavily damaged in a suspicious fire. Police wanted the researcher's field notes to determine whether any evidence of arson could be substantiated. One court quashed a subpoena for the field notes but another upheld it. Eventually a compromise was reached: The researcher's field notes were considered subject to subpoena, but the researcher was allowed to remove material that would have violated confidentiality.

In another recent case, a sociologist actually spent time in jail because he refused to give information in court that he believed violated his promise of confidentiality to his research subjects. Sociologist Rik Scarce conducted research on activists in the animal liberation movement in the early 1990s (Monaghan, 1993). A federal grand jury was investigating break-ins by such activists at university laboratories, and some of the activists in whom the grand jury was interested had been interviewed by Scarce as part of his research. He refused to answer certain questions about these activists put to him by the grand jury because he thought that it would violate the confidentiality he

had extended to the people he interviewed. He was jailed for 4 months on contempt of court charges. As these cases illustrate, the courts have generally held that confidential communication between a researcher and a research participant is not protected in criminal cases; however, the courts also recognize that the confidential relationship is an important and special one and that efforts should be made not to violate it.

Concern with possible subpoena of their research data has led some researchers to adopt elaborate measures to protect the data. For example, it is common to establish computer files with the data identified only by numbers rather than by names. Often, it is unnecessary to retain name identification for research purposes once the data have been collected. In such cases, the names should be destroyed. If name identification is required, say, because you want to interview the same people at a later time, the names should be stored in a separate computer file. This procedure reduces the possibility of unauthorized persons linking names with data.

One of the best means of securing confidentiality for sensitive research, such as that dealing with AIDS, substance abuse, or criminal behavior, is to use certificates of confidentiality, which were made available by the Public Health Service Act Amendments of 1974 (Melton and Gray, 1988). These certificates guarantee the confidentiality of identifying information associated with a research project, and they are intended to protect privacy against a wide array of legal actions, including those in federal, state, and local courts as well as in civil, criminal, legislative, and administrative proceedings. The Department of Health and Human Services awards certificates for research regardless of whether the research receives federal funding. However, the certificates are discretionary, so a researcher must make application to receive one. Some granting organizations, such as the Office of Assistance Programs in the Department of Justice, grant certificates to researchers to whom they are providing funds (Melton, 1990). Unfortunately, many researchers appear unaware of the availability of this procedure and have failed to take advantage of the protection that certificates afford.

Despite the fact that intrusion by the courts is a real danger with research on some topics, the reality is that court involvement is extremely rare. Though more than 200 cases have involved courts seeking journalists' information, in only a dozen or so cases have courts sought research data (Reynolds, 1979; Smith, 1981). Thus, the odds of a researcher's becoming embroiled in such a situation are remote. Nonetheless, researchers have an obligation to inform potential subjects accurately of any possible threats to confidentiality that might arise, including what would be likely to happen should their data be subpoenaed by the courts. The lengths to which investigators will go to protect confidentiality indicate the importance of this ethical issue. The bottom line is that no one should be threatened with harm to themselves or their reputation as a result of participating in a scientific study.

Privacy

The ethical issue of the right to privacy is related to confidentiality, but it also has some distinct elements. **Privacy** refers to the ability to control when and under what conditions others will have access to your beliefs, values, or behavior. Intrusions on our privacy have become endemic in modern society, and with the growth of social research in the past century the danger of even greater intrusion arises. Virtually any attempt to collect data from people raises the issue of privacy and confronts the investigator with the dilemma of whether threats to privacy are warranted by the research. A single, well-known illustration shows the complexity of this issue.

The sociologist Laud Humphreys (1970), in an effort to understand a particular type of sexual behavior, made observations of men having quick and impersonal sexual encounters in public restrooms. In order to gather his data without arousing suspicion, Humphreys played the role of the "watch queen," who keeps watch and warns participants of approaching police or "straight" males who might disrupt the activities. None of the men who went to the restrooms to engage in sex was aware that his behavior was being recorded by a researcher. Humphreys was heavily criticized for violating the privacy of these men engaging in highly stigmatized actions that, were they made public, might disrupt their family lives or threaten their jobs. Many sociologists believe that research on such sensitive topics is not merely a matter of confidentiality—that is, not letting people's identities become known. Rather, such data should not even be collected because these men were obviously trying to conceal their actions from prying eyes. Social science researchers, it is argued, should respect that privacy.

Humphreys defends his research on the grounds that the confidentiality of his subjects was maintained and the results of the study were of significant scientific value. In fact, no one else has formulated another method to study such sexual behavior. Humphreys discovered that the men who engage in this type of sexual activity are not unusual or deviant in the rest of their lives. In fact, they were, for the most part, normal, respectable citizens who had found a rather unusual sexual outlet. Humphreys believes that our greater understanding of what had been considered deviant sexual conduct justifies the threat to privacy these men experienced. In addition, the public setting in which they performed their acts, he argues, reduced their right to claim privacy.

As the Humphreys investigation shows, the right to privacy is often a difficult ethical issue to resolve. In fact, in some settings, people are fairly tolerant of invasions of privacy. A study of family interaction, for example, utilized videotape cameras installed in apartments to record all interchanges between family members (Ashcraft and Scheflen, 1976). Even though the families consented to the taping, the investigators, sensitive to the issue of privacy, offered the families the opportunity to review the tapes and edit out anything they wished. The assumption was that, despite agreeing to participate, family members might do something on the spur of the moment that they would prefer not be made public. Surprisingly, not one family exercised the option to edit the tapes.

Privacy can be ensured in a number of ways. One way, as illustrated in the preceding study, is to offer participants the opportunity to destroy any data they wish to remain private. A second—and very effective—means of ensuring privacy is to accord the participants **anonymity,** which means that *no one,* including the researcher, can link any data to a particular respondent. This can be accomplished by not including any identifying names or numbers with the data collected. When this is not possible, an alternative way to protect privacy is to destroy any such identifiers once the data have been put in a computer file.

Research in Practice 3.1 explores some of the difficulties surrounding issues of privacy, confidentiality, and informed consent, especially when the research topic is a sensitive one and there are demands on the researchers to ignore or violate the ethical safeguards.

Physical or Mental Distress

Researchers should avoid exposing participants to physical or mental distress or danger. If the potential for such distress exists in a research investigation, the participants should be fully informed, the potential research findings should be of sufficient importance that they warrant the risk, and no possibility should exist of achieving the results without the risk. People should never be exposed to situations that might cause serious or lasting harm.

Research in the human services rarely involves physical danger, but there are research settings in which psychological distress may be an element. Some studies, for example, have asked people to view such things as pornographic pictures, victims of automobile accidents, and the emaciated inmates of Nazi concentration camps. Certainly, these stimuli can induce powerful emotions, in some cases emotions that the participants had not expected that they would experience. A strong emotional reaction, especially an unexpected one, can be very distressful. In some studies, people have been given false feedback about themselves in order to see how they respond. People have been told, for example, that they failed an examination or that tests show that they have some negative personality characteristics. Any situation in which people might learn something about themselves of which they were unaware can be distressful. Even the minor deceptions that are a part of much research can be distressful to people who thought they could not be so easily deceived.

Assuming that the scientific benefits warrant the risk of distress and that the participants are fully informed, it is then the researcher's obligation to alleviate the impact of whatever distress does actually occur. This is most often accomplished through a *debriefing,* in which people's psychological and emotional reactions to the research are assessed (Smith and Richardson, 1983). Clinician-researchers should be especially adept at this stage in using their human service training to cope with people's reactions. Because the distress is usually mild and transitory, it can normally be dissipated quickly and with no permanent impact.

Sponsored Research

Because much social research is conducted under the auspices of a third-party sponsor, certain ethical considerations arise from that relationship. When research is sponsored, some type of research agreement, essentially a contract, is developed. Researchers and sponsors alike should exercise great care in drafting this agreement. The potential for ethical problems to arise later is reduced when the research agreement clearly specifies the rights and obligations of the parties involved. Three areas are of particular concern in sponsored research (Tripodi, 1974). First, it is common for sponsors to want to retain control over the release of the collected data. The precise conditions of release should be specified in the research agreement to avoid conflicts. One limitation that should not be tolerated, however, is the conditional publication of results—that is, agreeing to publish results only if they turn out a certain way (usually so they support the preconceived notions of the sponsor). Such conditional publication violates the integrity of the research process and the autonomy of the researcher (Wolfgang, 1981). If the researcher agrees to some other type of limitation on release, however, it must be honored. To do otherwise would be a breach of the agreement and therefore unethical.

The second major concern in sponsored research is the nature of the research project itself. The precise purpose and procedures of the study should be specified in the agreement. Ethical questions arise if the researcher heavily modifies the study to cover matters not in the agreement. Often, sponsors will allow researchers to use the data gathered for scientific purposes beyond the needs of the sponsor, but to agree to do a study that a sponsor wants and then change it for personal reasons so that it no longer meets the expectations of the sponsor is unethical.

A third area of ethical concern in sponsored research relates to the issue of informed consent, namely, revealing the sponsor's identity to participants. Although controversy exists in this regard, some researchers take the stance that truly informed consent can be given only if one knows who is sponsoring the study and for what purpose. Some people might object, for example, to providing data that would help a company better market a product, a political party present a candidate, or the government propagandize its citizens. In fact, studies show that people are less likely to participate in research they know to be sponsored by commercial organizations, which suggests that information about sponsorship can influence the decision of whether to participate (Bailey, 1987). Each researcher, then, must carefully consider whether to make the sponsorship of a research project explicit. At a minimum, to deceive people regarding the sponsorship of a study in order to gain their participation is certainly unethical.

Scientific Misconduct and Fraud

When a research project reaches the final stage— dissemination of results—the primary consideration regarding ethical conduct shifts from avoiding harming the participants in research to making sure the consumers of the research are not adversely affected. Results of a study are typically communicated in the form of a report to a sponsoring organization, a publication in a professional journal, or, possibly, a news release to the media. The preeminent ethical obligation in this regard is not to disclose inaccurate, deceptive, or fraudulent research results. To do so risks misleading scientists who depend on previous research to guide their work. Ethical violations concerning disclosure of results undermine the very nature of the scientific process that, as we have seen in Chapter 2, depends on building future knowledge on the foundation of existing knowledge. If we cannot depend on the accuracy of existing knowledge, then the scientific endeavor is threatened. In that case, the credibility of all research is damaged by such violations. Furthermore, deceptive or fraudulent disclosures of research results can cause human service practitioners to design useless—or even dangerous—interventions based on faulty studies.

Many ethical violations can occur in the process of reporting research (Morrison, 1990). **Fraud** is the deliberate falsification, misrepresentation, or plagiarizing of data, findings, or the ideas of others. This includes such things as falsifying data, embellishing research reports, reporting research that has not been conducted, or manipulating data in a deceptive way. **Misconduct** is a broader concept that includes not only fraud but also carelessness or bias in recording and reporting data, mishandling data, and incomplete reporting of results. Other questionable practices are irresponsible claims of authorship (listing coauthors who did not really make contributions to the research) and premature release of results to the public without peer review.

Estimates of the actual amount of scientific misconduct suggest that the problem is relatively small. One investigation found only 26 cases between 1980 and 1987 in which research fraud was either admitted by the researcher or proved by an investigating body; between 1988 and 1991, the National Science Foundation received only 99 allegations of scientific misconduct (Teich and Frankel, 1992). Of course, underreporting could hide a

Research in Practice 3.1
Practice Effectiveness: Sex Offenders as Participants

Social workers and other human service professionals emphasize the principles that all people have worth as human beings and that all are deserving of respect. However, when the service population consists of sex offenders, particularly child molesters, operationalizing those principles in research or practice presents major challenges. It is hard to imagine a service population that would raise more concern in the community and that would be more in need of ethical safeguards than child molesters. While researchers are seeking to assure the study participant of confidentiality, other interest groups in the community may well be actively seeking information about the participants. For example, federal legislation requiring notification of the residents when a sex offender is released into a community has recently become law. It was within such a context that the Center for Prevention of Child Molestation (CPCM) set out to conduct research on sex offenders (Jenkins–Hall and Osborn, 1994). The CPCM conducted a study on the effectiveness of two methods of community-based treatment for child molesters. The first approach treated deviant sexual arousal with behavior therapy, deviant cognitions with rational-emotive therapy, and recidivist tendencies with relapse prevention. This approach was compared to a second, more traditional treatment approach using only rational-emotive therapy. In the course of conducting the research, the researchers not only had to consider the rights of participants and the safety of staff, but they also had to contend with a letter-writing campaign against their project by the Church of Scientology and inquiries from members of Congress. How the research team dealt with these competing demands and designed ethical safeguards for this study provides direction for anyone undertaking socially sensitive research.

These researchers defined *socially sensitive research* as (1) studies for which there are potential negative social consequences for participants or for the class of individuals represented by the participants, or (2) studies about which the general public is uncertain, ambivalent, or strongly disapproving. In conducting research on sex offenders, Jenkins-Hall and Osborn identify three general areas of concern: (1) informed consent and voluntary participation, (2) confidentiality of data and privacy when interagency collaboration is required, and (3) duty to take proper care when a participant may pose a danger to himself or others. The researchers considered the risk of harm to the community to be the overriding concern for this project. Consequently, an extensive policy and procedures manual was developed to demonstrate that community safety and participant protection were assured.

Informed consent was considered so important by the researchers that they incorporated a multi-phase consent process that required participants to give consent at each stage of the process. All clients completed a general consent form that covered the basic requirements of the Department of Health and Human Services. Clients were informed that they would be protected by a federal confidentiality certificate. Prior to a comprehensive clinical assessment, the clients completed an evaluation consent form that spelled out the assessment process. Additional consent forms were completed in conjunction with each subsequent treatment component. These included: (1) a 20-week treatment phase in which one group received group and individual therapy while controls received only group treatment; (2) a reassessment; (3) a second treatment phase; (4) another reassessment; (5) a 6-month follow-up phase; and (6) a final assessment. Given the complexity of the intervention, this multi-phase consent process assured that participants understood the program and were freely consenting to participation throughout the project.

While certificates of confidentiality afforded some protection of participant privacy, other steps were also taken. The project was located in a public office building suite and was not identified as a sex offender treatment site. Each participant was given a six-digit ID number that appeared on all documents. Names and other identifying information were removed from all correspondence, consents, and records from referral sources. Staff addressed clients by first name only, and information was never released without signed waivers of confidentiality that specified what information could be released and to whom. Because the program involved the delivery of treatment services, the rights of the clients were protected by the provision of a client advocate who was a volunteer clinician and not affiliated with the project.

In applying the concept of being at risk of harm, the researchers addressed potential harm to the staff and members of the community as well as considering the rights of the participants. After all, these sex offenders might pose a threat to the safety of staff or to the safety of innocent community members. Several measures were employed to reduce such risks. One concern for the project was assuring quick detection of an impending relapse or actual re-offense. Researchers argue that the project had an ethical and, perhaps, a *legal* duty to protect potential victims. The project provided each participant with a 24-hour crisis call service as well as therapists to deal with minor crises, such as loss of employment or a breakup with a girlfriend. Over a 2-year period, three cases required involuntary commitment of participants due to suicidal ideation and psychotic decompensation. In several cases where the participant was exhibiting signs of a relapse, the participant was temporarily removed from the project and offered alternative treatment. If a participant who was at risk of relapse failed to follow the terms of a crisis intervention plan, the director of the project was notified

and authorities were alerted. Failure to comply would result in termination from the project.

To assure the safety of the staff, the program employed a variety of procedures. Staff were directed to have unlisted personal phone numbers, to never reveal home addresses, to never be alone with clients in the suite, and to never enter a room lockable from the inside with a client. Each office and work area contained a "panic button" that sounded an alarm in the office and at the university police office. Entry to the project was strictly controlled so that client interaction with other office building occupants was minimal. Clients were routinely debriefed after treatment sessions to assure that they would not leave the center in a distressed, agitated, or aroused state.

Dealing with opposition to the program by the public was another issue with ethical implications for the researchers. The researchers reported that the Church of Scientology objected to the exposure of clients to sexually explicit material on the grounds that it was inflaming the participants and increasing the likelihood of re-offense. The Scientologists undertook a national letter-writing campaign that led to requests for information from members of Congress and state legislators as well as from other researchers who had received the letters. Program team members developed a standard response package that was mailed to inquirers. The researchers also established a scientific advisory board composed of nationally known researchers to provide assistance in responding to issues that were raised.

A research program involving community treatment of sex offenders clearly presents researchers with more ethical challenges than most human service projects. The procedures described here enabled the researchers to successfully carry out a challenging project on a highly sensitive topic. The researchers argue that most of the procedures that they have employed could also be effective in conducting research on other groups who are feared or abhorred by the public, such as people judged not guilty by reason of insanity, people with AIDS, child abusers, or drug addicts.

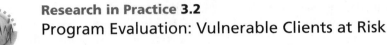

Research in Practice 3.2
Program Evaluation: Vulnerable Clients at Risk

Although science must be constantly vigilant against the danger of fraud, nowhere is this more true than in applied research, an area in which client treatment programs may be founded on the basis of research results. This hazard was graphically illustrated in the case of fraudulent research on the use of drugs to control the behavior of an extremely vulnerable population: severely retarded, hospitalized patients (Greenberg, 1987a, 1987b). This case is alarming not only because of the questioned authenticity of the research but also because it called into question, as the drama of the case unfolded, the adequacy of the institutionalized system of research safeguards for protecting society from fraudulent research.

The National Institute of Mental Health (NIMH) had been supporting the work of Dr. Stephen E. Breuning, who was a widely published psychologist and regarded as an expert in the control and treatment of the severely retarded. Based on his research, Dr. Breuning advocated the use of stimulants, such as dextroamphetamine, rather than neuroleptic drugs, such as thorazine, to control the behavior of the severely retarded. Not only would the former more effectively control behavioral problems, he claimed, but they would produce fewer side effects. Dr. Breuning's research and recommendations had been incorporated into many treatment programs. The NIMH report on Dr. Breuning's work stated, "There can be no question that States (e.g., Connecticut) have amended policies governing treatment practices in an effort to be consistent with what Dr. Breuning reports as scientific findings in his public addresses" (quoted in Greenberg, 1987a).

The possibility that the research was fraudulent came to light through the alert assessment of a for-mer colleague of Breuning who was involved in the study of the side effects of behavior-control drugs. Dr. Robert L. Sprague of the University of Illinois became suspicious because Breuning's results were simply too neat and without the variations in data typical of this kind of research. In 1983, Sprague contacted NIMH, informing them of his suspicions and urging them to investigate.

This request was the catalyst for a sequence of events that are as disturbing as the questioned research itself. Dr. Breuning was then working at the University of Pittsburgh, and NIMH reportedly asked the school to look into the charges. It did so, but the investigation stalled when Dr. Breuning suddenly resigned his position. Dr. Sprague continued to prod NIMH about the research, and finally, in early 1985, a panel of distinguished scientists was appointed to investigate the charges. The panel reported to NIMH in 1987 that Dr. Breuning had "knowingly, willfully, and repeatedly engaged in misleading and deceptive practices in reporting results of research" (quoted in Greenberg, 1987a). However, the concern in this case is much deeper than the apparent discovery of fraud. Because of the applied nature of the research, the disconcerting question is: What about the patients confined in institutions where treatment is based on Breuning's research? Apparently, NIMH has no procedures for notifying institutions that this research was under investigation and that there were serious questions about applications based on it. In addition, NIMH may have been reluctant to contact institutions because the investigation report had not been finalized and Dr. Breuning was denying the charges against him. There is no way as yet to determine whether these patients suffered any

larger problem. But even if the number of cases is small, any misconduct in research can still damage the credibility of all research and place human service clients—and, by extension, human service providers—at risk.

A recent example of a rather large-scale fraud involved research on the use of drugs to control the behavior of severely retarded children. Because this case illustrates how fraud can be detected as well as how it can impact on human service

harm or setbacks because of receiving treatments based on Dr. Breuning's recommendations or how many patients may have suffered.

Meanwhile, another disturbing event was the fact that Dr. Sprague, the researcher responsible for bringing the fraud to the attention of authorities in the first place, had his own NIMH grant canceled. He had been receiving funding for 18 years in support of his work on drug side effects. One explanation of the sudden funding cutoff was that officials at NIMH were getting back at him for embarrassing them with his dogged pursuit of the Breuning affair. This has not been proved but is consistent with experiences of other "whistle-blowers."

Eventually, in an unprecedented move, the U.S. government indicted Dr. Breuning on charges of falsifying data for his 1982 NIMH grant. The U.S. attorney in Baltimore was quoted as saying, "Let this investigation send a clear message to doctors and researchers who play fast and loose with their research that they will have to deal with the criminal justice system in addition to their peer review panels" ("Leading Researcher Indicted . . . ," 1988). Dr. Breuning subsequently pled guilty to two counts of making false statements on federal grant applications and was sentenced to 60 days in a halfway house, 250 hours of community service, and 5 years probation (Garfield and Welljams-Dorof, 1990).

This case highlights several disturbing issues in ethics, research, and human service practice. First, this research managed to pass through the filters of review panels and institutional procedures without question. How well can the institutionalized research system protect against fraudulent work? Second, when unethical practices are discovered, who bears the responsibility for alerting practitioners and the public to potential harmful implications? In manufacturing, the government can require product recalls, but how do we protect the public from implementation of fraudulent research? Third, how do we safeguard those who detect potential fraud? In many cases, the people most likely to discover it are colleagues, assistants, students, and others close to the research. To the extent that these people perceive disclosure as risking unpleasant consequences for themselves, they will be reluctant to come forward. And finally, the slow, plodding nature of the bureaucratic process raises the question of what can be done to efficiently process cases while at the same time protecting the rights of individuals accused of fraud.

A close study of the Breuning case suggests that the procedures of the scientific process do afford some protection against the widespread impact of fraudulent data on both science and practice. Based on the assumption that influential research will be widely cited in other research studies, an ingenious study used the *Science Citation Index* and the *Social Science Citation Index* to examine the number of citations made by other researchers to Breuning's 20 publications between 1980 and 1988 (Garfield and Welljams-Dorof, 1990). The 200 citations suggested that his work was influential. However, when the researchers evaluated who made the citations and the *context* of the citations to better understand the effects of the Breuning studies, things looked a little different. For example, of the 200 citations, 40 percent were self-citations by Breuning or his coauthors. In addition, following the publication of a critical review of Breuning's work, citations to his work by others declined sharply. Finally, of 38 studies judged to be materially affected by Breuning's publications, 21 led to negative conclusions, disagreeing with his findings or criticizing his methods. The authors conclude that the pattern of citations suggests that the process of scientific publication and critique is capable of purging science, to a degree, of fraudulent studies.

practice, it is discussed in detail in Research in Practice 3.2.

The issue of who has responsibility for detecting scientific misconduct is still very controversial (Teich and Frankel, 1992). For many years, government agencies that fund research pushed this responsibility onto the shoulders of the universities and other institutions where research was actually conducted. By the late 1980s, however, the National Institutes of Health and the Department of

Health and Human Services had both established their own offices to watch for misconduct. Yet, most scientists still consider protection against misconduct to be primarily a responsibility of the scientific community, which uses two major mechanisms to detect fraud: peer review and replication. There are, however, limitations to each of these, as illustrated by a case of fraud in medical research involving Dr. Robert Slutsky (Engler et al., 1987).

The prolific Dr. Slutsky had authored or coauthored 137 articles on cardiological and radiological research over a 7-year period. During an evaluation of his appointment as a researcher at a university, questions were raised about duplicate data in two of his papers. In the ensuing investigation, 12 articles were deemed fraudulent and 48 were considered questionable. In some cases, articles described experiments that had never been conducted. How is it that these articles eluded the net of peer review by respected medical journals? There seem to have been two problems. First, peer review of article submissions cannot detect plausible, internally consistent fabrications. Second, the sheer number of research articles submitted to publications for review requires a large number of qualified reviewers who understand both the methodology and the content of the article.

If peer review does not detect and deter fraud, then will replication solve the problem? It might, but the effectiveness of replication has been severely hobbled by the modern research system because research funds are not often appropriated for replication. Funding agencies prefer to fund research efforts delving into new areas. Furthermore, replication, where it does occur, tends to be reserved for projects that have produced unusual results. Fraudulent studies that enhance the prestige of researchers but that do not run counter to accepted findings in a field are not likely to arouse enough attention to warrant replication (Engler et al., 1987).

Beyond peer review and replication, there are several ways of reducing the chances of fraud or detecting it if it occurs. One is to supervise novice researchers until they demonstrate good practices and ethical conduct as well as technical compe-

tency. Second, organizations need to guard against overly prolific researchers. Senior researchers and coauthors should not simply allow their names to be associated with research reports without carefully examining the work. Third, journals can reduce fraud by requiring more complete data to be submitted to reviewers, even if they cannot be included in the published article. When fraud is detected, the journals have a responsibility to make the fraud public so that others will not unsuspectingly base research or treatments on the fraudulent material. Despite agreement on this responsibility, however, some question remains concerning the capacity or willingness of journals to deliver (Anderson, 1989). It seems that journals fear legal action against them by those accused of fraud, even when protected by the truth of factual statements. Legislation that would provide immunity for good faith reporting of scientific misconduct by academic institutions and scientific journals has been requested in order to bolster the watchdog function of journals. Fourth, professionals in the field can also help reduce fraud by considering it their ethical obligation to report suspected cases to appropriate authorities. Fifth, as the study on the impact of the Breuning case so forcefully demonstrates, consumers of research should make use of citation indexes and other resources before using research studies as guides in designing research or human service interventions. Tools such as the *Social Science Citation Index* can alert readers to retraction notices, reviews, editorials, and conflicting studies and thus help prevent the unknowing spread of false or erroneous studies. Finally, organizations can reduce fraud by establishing standards and developing facilities to retain data from research projects. Although cases of documented fraud may be rare, the costs of even those few can be high. Thousands of people unwittingly learn untruths. Economic resources may be wasted by basing policy decisions on false information. Social programs may be established or rescinded based on fraudulent data.

Though not as unethical as purposeful deception, careless errors in research have the same effect of creating misinformation. Social researchers owe the scientific community carefully conducted research that is as free of error as possible. As with frauds, errors are discovered and corrected through critical review of research and reanalysis of data or through replication. For example, Research in Practice 4.1 describes a study done in the 1980s that claimed to document substantial negative economic consequences of divorce for women and that was used as an important foundation for developing social policy. In part because these findings were somewhat at variance with the results of other studies, a reanalysis of the data was undertaken (Peterson, 1996). The reanalysis showed that the original conclusions were due in part to errors in the original analysis. The reanalysis showed that women suffer economically after divorce but not nearly as severely as the original analysis had suggested. Had the original research conclusions not been based on an inaccurate analysis, the subsequent policy development might have been different. Scientists are human, and human beings make mistakes. But, as researchers, we must maximize safeguards to keep mistakes to the absolute minimum.

Beyond the problems of fraud and carelessness, researchers also have an obligation to report their results thoroughly. Researchers must take care to ensure that what is reported does not give a distorted picture of the overall results. In addition, researchers should point out any limitations that might qualify the findings. Furthermore, some research in the human services is highly newsworthy, and this can create special ethical dilemmas. For example, a study of crime, poverty, and other problems in an urban public housing project in St. Louis in the 1960s found itself under intense scrutiny by the press (Rainwater and Pittman, 1967). Journalists exerted considerable pressure on the researchers, before their study was complete, to release their findings about the housing project and its problems. Fearing that premature disclosure of results might be inadvertently inaccurate or deceptive, the researchers chose to say absolutely nothing: "Ethically, we did not want to be in a position of asserting findings before we were really sure of what we knew" (Rainwater and Pittman, 1967, p. 359). In

addition to the timing of disseminating results, the researcher must be concerned with how the findings are applied to human service practice and policy decisions. The research projects on the effectiveness of arrest as a deterrent to wife abuse (*see* Chapter 10 for a detailed discussion) are an excellent example. A study conducted in Minneapolis has been singled out as a primary catalyst for widespread adoption of pro-arrest policies. Critics have argued that propaganda generated by some of the participating agencies was a key factor in the study's impact on policy, an impact which they say was unjustified by a single study (Binder and Meeker, 1988). Subsequent replications in several cities have failed to support the findings of the Minneapolis study and have underscored the call for caution in rushing to apply findings to practice (Sherman, 1992). This was not a case of publishing fraudulent results or misrepresenting data, but rather an issue of the researcher's role in applying research findings.

Scientific Advocacy

Scientific knowledge rarely remains the exclusive domain of the scientific community. It typically finds its way into public life in the form of inventions, technological developments, or social policy. This raises potential ethical dilemmas in terms of the role of researchers as advocates of particular uses of their research results. What responsibility, if any, do scientists have for overseeing the use to which their results are put? To what extent should scientists become advocates for applying knowledge in a particular way? Quite naturally, disagreements exist on how to resolve these issues. The controversy is compounded in the case of human service researchers because their research is normally initiated with some explicit clinical application in mind. The classic approach to these issues derives from the exhortations of the sociologist Max Weber that science should be "value-free" (Weber, 1946). Social scientists, according to Weber, should create knowledge, not apply it. They, therefore, have no special responsibility for the ultimate use to which that knowledge is put.

Furthermore, according to Weber, they are under no obligation to advocate particular uses of scientific knowledge. Indeed, advocacy is frowned on as threatening objectivity, which is a central concern of science. So while remaining value-free is difficult, many argue that abandoning the effort would be disastrous in that it would prevent us from acquiring an accurate body of knowledge about human social behavior and might threaten the researcher's credibility as a disinterested expert (Halfpenny, 1982; Gibbs, 1983; Gordon, 1988).

The opposite stance in this controversy was originally developed by Karl Marx (1964, orig. pub. 1848). Marx championed the cause of the poor and downtrodden, and he believed that social researchers should bring strong moral commitments to their work. They should strive to change unfair or immoral conditions. Following Marx, some researchers today believe that social research should be guided by personal and political values and should be directed toward alleviating social ills (Brunswick-Heinemann, 1981; Fay, 1987). Furthermore, scientists should advocate for uses of their research by others that would help accomplish those personal goals.

A compromise position on the value-free controversy was developed by sociologist Alvin Gouldner (1976). He pointed to the obvious, namely, that scientists have values just as do other human beings. Furthermore, he noted, those values can influence research in so many subtle ways that their effects can never be totally eliminated. Instead of denying or ignoring the existence or impact of these personal values, scientists need to be acutely aware of them and up-front about them in their research reports. Being thus forewarned, consumers of their research are then better able to assess whether the findings have been influenced by personal bias. In addition, Gouldner argued that social scientists have not only the right but also the duty to promote the constructive use of scientific knowledge (Becker, 1967; Gouldner, 1976). Because decisions will be made by someone concerning the use of scientific knowledge, scientists themselves are best equipped to make those judgments. As Gouldner states, technical competence would seem to provide a person with some warrant for making value judgments. People who take this position view the value-free stance as a potentially dangerous dereliction of a responsibility that accrues to scientists by virtue of their role in developing new knowledge and their expertise.

Clinician-researchers, in particular, may be attracted by this stance. Because their research is conducted, in part, to advance the practice goals of the profession, they would likely view it as one of their duties to ensure that any clinical application of the results be faithful to the outcome of the research. Thus, human service researchers are more likely than many other behavioral scientists to take a strong stand in favor of advocacy.

Nothing is wrong with researchers openly pressing for the application of scientific knowledge in ways they see as desirable so long as their advocacy is tempered with respect for objectivity. The danger of advocacy is that scientists can come to feel so strongly about issues they promote that it might hamper the objective collection and analysis of data.

Protecting Vulnerable Clients

Human service clients, because they are often involuntary recipients of services, may find themselves vulnerable to pressures to cooperate in research projects conducted by the organizations providing them with services. Such clients are likely to be sought out as research subjects because they are often viewed as deviant in some ways and, therefore, interesting to study or because they may be easier than other groups to locate and keep track of during a research project.

Welfare recipients, children in day care settings, patients in public mental hospitals, participants in job training programs, to name only a few, are likely candidates for participation in social research projects. In fact, it is common for operators of new or special programs to be required by their funding sources to do research on the effects of their programs as a requirement for receiving funds. Thus, people who obtain human services are likely to be solicited for research. Though such safeguards as codes of ethics and governmental regulations may serve as useful guides, special obligations fall on human service practitioners to safeguard their clients from unreasonable pressures to participate in research.

A crucial issue in this regard is the matter of voluntary and informed consent. Can clients actually give consent freely? This is one of the reasons that much research using prison inmates as subjects has been discontinued: It is debatable how free inmates really are to give consent. If participation in the research brings significant rewards in the form of separate living quarters or greater privacy, these rewards may be almost coercive in the spartan, degrading, and often dangerous world of the prison inmate. Although participation in the research is, on the face of it, voluntary, inmates may not seriously weigh the disadvantages or dangers of the research when participation is perceived as a means of avoiding assault or rape. Similar ethical questions arise with research on people with significant psychopathologies: If the psychopathology involves defective comprehension or impaired insight, then such people may be unable to give truly informed consent. Research on such a population would have to be approached very carefully: Such research could be justified only if it could not be done on a less vulnerable group. If the same research goals could be accomplished with a less vulnerable group, then that would be the route to go. If it were decided to do research on a group with significant psychopathology, then informed consent should be approached in ways that protect potential participants from even covert coercion; for example, consent could be sought by some party other than the researchers (to avoid the force of authority) or it could be sought in the presence of a relative, friend, or other advocate for the individual (to provide the social support for a refusal). If the psychopathology totally impairs the ability to consent, then most forms of research would be unethical unless it can be shown that either the patient or so-

ciety would benefit significantly and that the research could be done in no other way (Fulford and Howse, 1993).

The problem of voluntary consent may be somewhat more subtle among other recipients of human services. Though refusal to participate may not be linked to termination of benefits, clients may not be sure of this and may be disinclined to take the risk of finding out. For example, the reading level of AFDC clients is often less than that of the eighth grade, yet the reading level necessary to comprehend many welfare documents is above 13 years of education. Thus, it is not unreasonable to suspect that clients who are accustomed to being confused by welfare requirements might not aggressively seek to determine their right to refuse participation in a research project presented by official-looking people with official-looking forms. We are not suggesting that research never be conducted on prisoners or public welfare recipients. Rather, clinician-researchers need to exercise additional caution—and, in some cases, possibly forgo valuable research projects—in the interests of ensuring truly voluntary informed consent.

Withholding Treatment for Research Purposes

An issue of particular concern to human service providers is the research practice of withholding treatment from a control group in order to assess whether a given treatment is effective. The control group serves as a comparison group. If a group receiving the treatment shows more improvement than does the control group over a certain span of time, then we can feel justified in claiming that the treatment brought about the improvement. With no control group, when the treatment group shows improvement, we cannot say with confidence that the improvement was due to the treatment. It could be that the improvement would have occurred even in the absence of the treatment. The control group, which is comparable to the treatment group in all ways except that it does not receive the treatment, makes it possible to rule out this possibility. Control groups are thus very important to our ability to say whether an independent variable causes change in a dependent variable (*see* Chapters 2 and 10).

Presumably, research is being conducted on some treatment because the treatment is believed to be effective. And herein lies the ethical dilemma for some service providers who believe that it is unethical to withhold a treatment that might help people. They believe that it deprives people in the control group of the possibility of improvement. This is a serious problem that is not easy to resolve, but there are a number of issues to consider. First, we might ask whether it is ethical to proffer treatments that are untested. We pointed out in Chapter 1 that many contemporary approaches to human service professions explicitly caution against the use of treatments without proven effectiveness. Providing services is expensive and time consuming, and it also raises clients' expectations for improvement. Is it ethical to do this when there is no evidence to document that the treatment will be beneficial? We would not think of marketing drugs without a thorough test of their effects, both positive and negative. We should expect no less from the human services that we offer people.

There may be, in some cases, alternatives to withholding treatment. One alternative would be to offer the control group a treatment that is known to be effective and then see whether the new treatment provides more or less improvement. In this way, all clients are receiving a treatment that is either known to be, or suspected of being, effective. In the study of the effectiveness of suicide intervention programs, for example, one would certainly be reluctant to evaluate a new intervention by using a control group that received no intervention at all. One recent study of outpatient interventions targeting suicidal young adults used a randomized experiment in which subjects were assigned to either a new experimental treatment or a control group that received a treatment that had been commonly used for these interventions. Although both groups showed improvement, the experimental treatment was more effective in retain-

ing the highest risk participants (Rudd, Rajab, and Orman, 1996).

Another alternative to withholding treatment would be to delay giving the treatment to the control group for a period of time and make the comparisons between those receiving treatment and the control group over this time period. For example, in a study of two different approaches to controlling people's smoking, all participants in the study were told that, if they were randomly placed in the group that would not receive treatment, they would receive treatment when the study was over and would receive the treatment the study showed to be most effective (Coelho, 1983). This resolves the ethical problem by ensuring that all participants will receive treatment *at some point*. In fact, clients often confront a delay in receiving services when the resources of an agency are taxed.

In cases without such alternatives, however, clinician-researchers must use the risk-benefit approach: Does the benefit to be gained from the research outweigh the risks of withholding treatment from the people in the control group? If we were studying people at high risk of suicide, we would be cautious about withholding treatment. In the treatment of nonassertiveness, on the other hand, we might decide that a delay of a few weeks in treatment would not be terribly detrimental, and whatever damage occurred could be undone once treatment was initiated. As with so many other ethical issues, this is ultimately a judgmental one over which clinician-researchers will continue to agonize.

The ethical issues involved in withholding treatment can also arise in a more subtle fashion, namely, the extent to which research activities might interfere with the delivery of services to clients. Research activities might include, for example, administering questionnaires, making observations in clients' homes, or gathering data from agency records. If these activities take much of a client's time, the client may be reluctant to ask for services or cooperate with treatment. Likewise, the time necessary to interview a client for purposes of data collection might reduce the amount of time available to provide treatment. Given that a major concern of practitioners is to provide services, they would have to weigh the costs of any interference with service delivery against the benefits of conducting research. And they would also need to consider the costs of *not* carrying out the research in their assessment of whether the interference is unethically impairing service delivery.

Codes of Ethics

A point that has been emphasized in this chapter is that ethical judgments are difficult and often controversial because they involve interpretation and assessment. Most professional organizations establish written codes of ethics to serve as guides for their members to follow. Though these codes by no means settle all debate, they do stand as a foundation from which professionals can begin to formulate ethical decisions. Appendix C includes those parts of the codes of ethics of the National Association of Social Workers and the American Sociological Association that relate to the conduct of research. The codes of ethics of other human service professions would be similar to these.

Main Points

- What is ethical in research practice is based on human values and varies as those values change.
- The mistreatment of minority peoples in research has been a major impetus to the development of ethical standards for research in the United States and abroad.
- Social research is typically evaluated in terms of risks versus benefits, with "questionable practices" being allowed if the research promises sufficient benefits.
- Informed consent refers to telling potential research participants about all aspects of the pending research before they agree to participate.

- Rigid adherence to the doctrine of informed consent can limit social research by eliminating some useful research methods and forcing the study of only those persons who volunteer.
- Confidentiality means that the researcher will not publicly identify individual participants and their responses or actions.
- Intrusion by third parties, such as courts of law, can occasionally be a threat to the guarantee of confidentiality.
- Privacy refers to the ability to control when and under what conditions others will have access to your beliefs, values, or behavior.
- Exposing subjects to physical or mental distress should be kept to a minimum and should never be done without fully informed consent. Subjects should be thoroughly debriefed at the conclusion of the research.
- When conducting research for a sponsor, many ethical difficulties can be avoided by a detailed research agreement that covers such things as the purpose and nature of the research, rights of publication, and revealing to participants the sponsor of the research.
- Researchers have an obligation to report their results fully and honestly and to avoid any kind of scientific misconduct or fraud.
- Replication is a major tool of science for correcting research errors and fraudulent reports.
- It is the researcher's own decision regarding the degree to which he or she will become an advocate; however, caution is required so that objectivity is not undermined.
- Because of their disadvantaged status, human service clients are often vulnerable to coercion to participate in research projects and, therefore, require special protection.
- Withholding treatment from control groups raises an ethical dilemma, but it is often justified when testing unproved approaches.
- Most professional organizations have established codes of ethics that provide useful guidelines for making ethical decisions.

Important Terms for Review

anonymity
confidentiality
ethics
fraud (scientific)
informed consent
misconduct (scientific)
privacy

Exploring the Internet

The Internet offers several resources that will expand your understanding of ethical issues in research. First, it's always a good idea to use one or more of the available search engines, such as Magellan, Lycos, Yahoo, or AltaVista. Searching for keywords—such as ethics and science, research fraud, IRB, informed consent, and human subjects—will lead you to a variety of research ethics-related sites. An excellent site for a multitude of social science topics, including ethics, is Craig McKie's Web site entitled Research Engines for the Social Sciences (http://www.carleton.ca/~cmckie/research.html). One specific site to investigate is Ethics in Science (http://www.chem.vt.edu/ethics/ethics.html). This site provides links to a wide array of ethics-related sources. Although many of the links focus on the physical and natural sciences, a number of them do apply to the social sciences and human services. For example, there is a thought-provoking essay related to applied research entitled "Bad Science" by D. H. Garrison, Jr., a forensic scientist with the Grand Rapids, Michigan, police department. Another promising entry to ethics material is Walter W. Stewart's Page on Scientific Misconduct (http://www.nyx.net/~wstewart/home.html). As you investigate ethics-related sites, here are two specific ideas to pursue:

First, in the discussion of the minority experience, institutional review boards were introduced as one approach to protecting human subjects. By using either Ethics in Science or one of the search engines, check out some of the university-related

sites. Typically, these sites will be labeled "guidelines for researchers" or "policies and procedures." Such sites will provide the policies and procedures used by universities to assure compliance with DHHS regulations for human subject protection, including institutional review board procedures. Presently, Cornell University and Brown University have comprehensive Web sites devoted to this topic. Compare several sites. Review your own university's home page and ascertain if your school has a comparable policy statement available.

Second, the codes of ethics of several human service and social science organizations are available at their Web sites. The National Association of Social Workers (NASW) revised its code in 1996. The text of this code is available at http://www.ssc.msu.edu/~sw/nasweth.html. The American Sociological Association (ASA) Code of Ethics can be located at the ASA Web site (http://www.asanet.org) by selecting "Code of Ethics" from the menu choices on the ASA home page. Because such codes are revised periodically, the Internet is an excellent way of keeping abreast of the latest version. Depending on the particular organization, research may be the primary focus of the code of ethics or the code may focus on both research and practice issues, as in the case of the NASW code. You can also search the Internet for the Web sites of other research organizations, such as the American Psychological Association, the Society for Applied Sociology, and the American Association of Public Opinion Research. Compare the ethical concerns and focuses of each of these organizations with those of the NASW and the ASA.

For Further Reading

Beauchamp, Tom L., et al., eds. *Ethical Issues in Social Science Research.* Baltimore: Johns Hopkins University Press, 1982. A volume of readings that covers the range of ethical issues one is likely to face in human service research.

Caplan, A. L., ed. *When Medicine Went Mad.* Totowa, N.J.: Humana Press, 1992. This volume contains articles relating to the research conducted by the Nazis during World War II. Although it deals with an extreme situation that many hope will never occur again, it does provide an illustration of what can happen when science "goes mad."

Corey, Gerald, Marianne Schneider Corey, and Patrick Callanan. *Issues and Ethics in the Helping Professions.* Pacific Grove, Calif.: Brooks/Cole, 1993. This is a comprehensive review of ethical issues in the many realms of human service practice. Given the linkage between research and practice, the analysis of practice ethics is relevant to clinician-researchers in the human services.

Crossen, Cynthia. *Tainted Truth: The Manipulation of Fact in America.* New York: Simon & Schuster, 1994. An enlightened book by a journalist about the many frauds that can be perpetrated by scientists. The author shows how frauds can be artfully crafted and how they can adversely affect us all.

Faden, Ruth R., and Tom L. Beauchamp. *A History and Theory of Informed Consent.* New York: Oxford University Press, 1986. A detailed examination of the moral, legal, and historical foundations of informed consent and its impact on research today.

Gubrium, Jaber F., and David Silverman, eds. *The Politics of Field Research.* Newbury Park, Calif.: Sage, 1989. This collection of articles by experienced researchers focuses on the special ethical issues surrounding the conduct of field research.

Homan, Roger. *The Ethics of Social Research.* London: Longman, 1991. This book provides a general overview of ethical issues in social science and human service research and some ways of resolving ethical dilemmas.

Kimmel, Allan J. *Ethics and Values in Applied Social Research.* Beverly Hills, Calif.: Sage, 1988. An excellent overview of the ethical dilemmas that confront applied researchers.

LaFollette, Marcel C. *Stealing Into Print: Fraud, Plagiarism, and Misconduct in Scientific Publishing.* Berkeley: University of California Press, 1992. This book focuses on the impact of scientific misconduct and fraud on the practices and policies of the journals that disseminate the results of scientific research. It provides a good analysis of why such misconduct and fraud occurs and of how the system can be changed to detect and prevent it.

Lee, Raymond. *Doing Research on Sensitive Topics.* Newbury Park, Calif.: Sage, 1993. Ethical issues become especially important and complicated when doing research on sensitive topics, and this author suggests ethical guidelines for navigating in such treacherous waters.

Miller, Arthur G. *The Obedience Experiments: A Case Study of Controversy in Social Science.* New York: Praeger, 1986. An exhaustive discussion of the controversial Milgram experiments on obedience to authority and their ethical implications, especially in terms of the psychological harm done to the participants. Other experiments involving deception and stressful conditions are also presented.

Reamer, Frederic G. *Ethical Dilemmas in Social Service.* New York: Columbia University Press, 1990. This book presents an in-depth look at ethical issues relating to both social work practice and research.

Sieber, Joan E. *Planning Ethically Responsible Research: A Guide for Students and Internal Review Boards.* Newbury Park, Calif.: Sage, 1992. This short volume offers a lot of practical information on how to translate ethical principles and federal regulations into valid applied research methods.

Exercises for Class Discussion

3.1 A student majoring in criminal justice needs to do a research project as a course requirement. He is working part-time as an undercover store detective in a large discount department store. His idea is to do observational research on the shoplifting behavior that he encounters as a part of his job. In addition, he has access to store records on suspects apprehended for shoplifting in the past. He also plans to interview a sample of shoppers about shoplifting without disclosing that he is also a store detective.

   Discuss how the issues of informed consent, confidentiality, and disclosure of results apply to this case.

3.2 What recommendations could you make to the student in Exercise 3.1 to safeguard the ethical standards for research in this case? Consider each of the ethical issues discussed in this chapter. Do you think the study could be done ethically at all? Support your conclusion.

3.3 Suppose that you are working in an alcoholism treatment unit, and a proposal is made to initiate a new treatment program that looks promising but is largely untested. Under what conditions do you think it would be acceptable to utilize a control group as a comparison group that does not receive any treatment? Under what conditions would it be ethically unacceptable? How might you avoid some of the ethical dilemmas that come from withholding treatment but still have some form of control group to use for comparison?

3.4 Consider the codes of ethics presented in Appendix C. What changes in the codes would

you recommend making in order to improve them? Why do you think these would be improvements?

3.5 Invite a representative of the institutional review board at your college or university to address your class on the kinds of ethical issues that arise in research done by faculty or students at the university. Explore with this person the safeguards that can be built into research designs to protect against such ethical problems.

CHAPTER 4

Issues in Problem Formulation

Selecting a Research Problem   72
  Personal Interest   72
  Social Problems   73
  Testing Theory   73
  Prior Research   73
  Program Evaluation   73
  Human Service Practice   76
  Minorities in Research: The Political Context of Problem Selection   77

Shaping and Refining the Problem   80
  Conceptual Development   80
  Review of the Literature   81
  Units of Analysis   83
  Reactivity   86
  Qualitative Versus Quantitative Research   86
  Cross-Sectional Versus Longitudinal Research   87

Feasibility of a Research Project   90
  Time Constraints   90
  Financial Considerations   91
  Anticipating and Avoiding Problems   93

Main Points   94

Important Terms for Review   94

Exploring the Internet   95

For Further Reading   95

Exercises for Class Discussion   96

Suppose you were required, as many students in courses on social research are, to design and conduct a research project. Our experience teaching research courses in the social sciences and human services is that some students respond to this assignment by drawing a total blank. Other students grasp eagerly onto a topic, such as "the cause of drug addiction," and rush off with total confidence that they are about to solve this enduring problem. In each case, the student is having difficulty adequately formulating a research problem. In the first case, the difficulty is in locating a problem to investigate, whereas in the second, it is in formulating a problem sufficiently specific that it is amenable to scientific research. We assure you that this problem is not unique to students. Every researcher must grapple with the issue of problem formulation. Because it is the initial step and provides the basis for the complete research project, problem formulation is of crucial importance. Many potentially serious difficulties can be avoided—or at least minimized—by careful problem formulation. In this chapter, we present the major issues to be considered in problem formulation, beginning with how to select a problem on which to conduct research. Then we analyze how to refine the research question so that it can be answered through research. Finally, factors relating to the feasibility of research are discussed.

Selecting a Research Problem

The first hurdle confronting a researcher is to select an appropriate topic for scientific investigation. Actually, this is not as difficult as it may first appear because the social world around us is teeming with unanswered questions. Selecting a problem calls for some creativity and imagination, but there are also a number of places to which you can turn for inspiration. We will discuss the more common sources of research problems.

Personal Interest

Research topics are often selected because a researcher has an interest in some aspect of human behavior, possibly owing to some personal experience. One social scientist, for example, conducted research on battered women and women's shelters in part because of her own earlier experience of being abused by her husband; another researcher, who had grown up in the only African American family in a small rural town, later did research on prejudice, discrimination, and the experience of minorities (Higgins and Johnson, 1988). Research sometimes focuses on behavior that is unique or bizarre and thus compelling to some. Examples of such research abound, including studies of people's behavior in bars (Cavan, 1966) and nudist colonies (Weinberg, 1968), pool hustlers (Polsky, 1967), juvenile gangs (Horowitz, 1987), striptease dancers (Dressel and Petersen, 1982), and even serial murderers (Holmes and DeBurger, 1988).

Researchers who select topics out of personal interest must be careful to demonstrate the scientific worth of their projects. Recall from Chapter 1 that the goals of scientific research are to describe, explain, predict, and evaluate. The purpose of research is to advance our knowledge, not just satisfy personal curiosity. In his study of strippers, for example, sociologist James Skipper (1979) was interested in learning about how people adapt to a job that many people consider deviant. Such a focus placed his research firmly in an established area of study and amplified its scientific contribution. A researcher who chooses a topic based on personal interest—especially if it deals with some unusual or bizarre aspect of human behavior—should be prepared for the possibility that others will fail to see the worth of that research. Even though Skipper, as noted, established a scientific rationale for his study of strippers, he and his associates were subjected to much abuse by those who failed to appreciate its scientific value.

Social Problems

In selecting a topic for research, you often need look no farther than the daily newspaper, where you can read about the many social problems that our society faces. Problems such as crime, delinquency, poverty, pollution, overpopulation, drug abuse, alcoholism, mental illness, sexual deviance, discrimination, and political oppression have all been popular sources of topics for social research. The Society for the Study of Social Problems—a professional organization to which many social scientists and human service providers belong—publishes a journal titled *Social Problems,* whose sole purpose is to communicate the results of scientific investigations into current social problems.

Within each of these general categories of social problems, a range of issues can be studied. Many studies, for example, focus on the sources of a problem. Others are concerned with the consequences these problems have for individuals or for society. Still others deal with the outcomes of social programs and other intervention efforts intended to ameliorate these problems. People in the human services, who are routinely involved with many of these problems, can find opportunities for research that are directly related to their professional activities.

Testing Theory

Some research problems are selected on the basis of their use in testing and verifying a particular theory. We noted in Chapter 2 that theoretical concerns should be at issue to some degree in all research. At a minimum, nearly all research has some implications for existing theory. Certain research topics, however, are selected specifically for the purpose of testing some aspect of a given theory. Many theories relevant to the human services have not been thoroughly tested. In some cases, this means we do not know how valid the theories are, whereas in other cases it means that we do not know how wide the range of human behavior is to which the theory can be applied.

Prior Research

One of the most fruitful sources of research problems is prior research because the findings of all research projects have limitations. Though some questions are answered, others always remain. In addition, new questions may be raised by the findings. It is, in fact, common for investigators to conclude research reports with a discussion of the weaknesses and limitations of the research, including suggestions for future research that follow from the findings that have been presented. Focusing on these unanswered questions or expanding on previous research is a good way to find research problems.

Prior research can also lead to new research problems if we have reason to question the findings of the original research. Research in Practice 4.1 provides an example of this. As emphasized in Chapter 2, it is imperative that we not complacently accept research findings, especially when conclusions are based on a single study, because there are numerous opportunities for error or biases to influence results. If we have reason to suspect research findings, we have a ready-made problem on which to conduct research ourselves. One of our students, in fact, found his problem in just this way when faced with the course assignment of conducting a research project. The student had read a research article suggesting a number of differences between the social settings in which marijuana is used and those in which alcohol is used. The student disagreed, partly because of his own experiences, believing that the social environments in which the two substances were used were quite similar. He designed a study that allowed him to determine whether his hypotheses—or those presumably verified by the previous investigation—would better predict what he would observe. As it turned out, many of his hypotheses were supported by his findings.

Program Evaluation

Program evaluation focuses on assessing the effectiveness or efficiency of some program or practice.

Research in Practice **4.1**
Needs Assessment: Reevaluating the Economic Consequences of Divorce

A particularly controversial policy issue in recent years involves the large proportion of American marriages that end in divorce. Widespread concern has been voiced over deleterious consequences that ensue for individuals, families, and society at large, and various remedies have been proposed. A policy innovation that was intended to correct injustice in the divorce process and that became widely adopted during the 1970s, was "no-fault" divorce, so called because it did not require either partner to be found legally at fault for the deterioration of the marriage. It was supposed to reduce the contentiousness and cost associated with bitter divorce battles. Just how well women and children were fairing under the new divorce codes was the subject of a study by Lenore Weitzman, who analyzed data on 228 cases drawn from the Los Angeles County Court docket in 1977. Only one member of each couple was interviewed, with equal numbers (114) of men and women in the final sample. The shocking conclusion was that, in the first year following divorce, the average standard of living of women who divorced declined by 73 percent while men's standard of living actually rose by 42 percent (Weitzman, 1985). Published in book form as *The Divorce Revolution: The Unexpected Social and Economic Consequences for Women and Children in America,* the study became widely used in policy debates. The study was reviewed in at least 22 social science journals, 12 law reviews, and 10 national magazines. The book received the American Sociological Association's 1986 Book Award for "Distinguished Contribution to Scholarship." From 1986 to 1993 it was cited in 348 social science articles and in more than 250 law review articles. *The Divorce Revolution* was cited by at least 24 legal cases in state appellate and supreme courts and even once by the U.S. Supreme Court. The impact of the study was eloquently summed up as follows:

> Perhaps no one person did more to fuel the attack on divorce-law reform in the backlash decade than sociologist Lenore Weitzman, whose 1985 book, *The Divorce Revolution: The Unexpected Social and Economic Consequences for Women and Children in America,* supplied the numbers quoted by everyone assailing the new laws. From Phyllis Schlafly to Betty Friedan, from the *National Review* to the "CBS Evening News," Weitzman's "devastating" statistics were invoked as proof that women who sought freedom from unhappy marriages were making a big financial mistake: They would wind up poorer under the new laws—worse off than if they had divorced under the older, more "protective," system or if they had simply stayed married. [Faludi, 1991, p.19]

When research findings are extreme, as these are, and when they are so influential in social policy debates, the research is often replicated by other researchers to ensure that the results are not due to some bias or error in the research. Such replications involve using prior research as the source of the research problem, as was the case of the Weitzman results on divorce. In fact, in the decade after the Weitzman research results were reported, many replications of it were conducted, often based on much broader-based national samples. One of the better examples of such studies is based on longitudinal data from the Panel Study on Income Dynamics. This study, based on a large, representative sample, found that the economic status of women fell by about 30 percent in the first year after divorce, not 73 percent as reported by Weitzman (Duncan and Hoffman, 1985). Similarly, other studies also showed that disparities existed between the financial experiences of women and men after divorce. However, these replications also consistently showed a much smaller disparity than had Weitzman: Women's standard of living declined by 13 percent to 35 percent (depending on the particular study) while men's standard of living increased by 11 percent to 13 percent. As noted in Chapter 2, replications of this sort are one of the self-correcting mechanisms in science for rooting out error and providing the most accurate findings.

When replications produce results that are widely at variance with the original research, an effort is sometimes made to reanalyze the original data in order to determine the source of the disparity, and so it was in the case of the Weitzman data (Peterson, 1996). However, the task of reanalysis proved difficult from the beginning. First of all, Weitzman was reluctant to turn over the data for reanalysis. She alleged that there were errors in the master computer file that she wanted to correct first (Weitzman, 1996). In the course of various moves between universities, the original, cleaned, master data file had disappeared. What data did remain had been cobbled together from various subanalyses and were likely to contain many errors. Eventually, the data were deposited in a university data archive, a common practice with data sets after the original researcher is done with them. However, it was only after the National Science Foundation, which had funded the original research, threatened to withhold future grant money from Weitzman that she reluctantly allowed other researchers access to the data.

Having obtained the data, social scientist Richard Peterson still faced a number of challenges. One was detecting and eliminating, or at least reducing, the errors in the data file. By painstaking comparison of computer files with paper records, he was able to prepare a final computer file that was suitable for analysis. In the process of so doing, he detected errors in important income variables for 27 of the 228 cases. There were also questions about how certain concepts were measured. One criticism that Peterson made of the original measures is that new spouses, cohabitators, and other adults were included in calculation of economic need, but not included in calculation of income. Another challenge was creating measures to replicate those used in the original analysis. Peterson's task was complicated by the fact that the original researcher had not thoroughly documented how a number of measurement problems had been handled. Consequently he could

not be certain that he was duplicating Weitzman's procedures exactly. Without such duplication, the researcher would be prevented from pinpointing where errors occurred in the original study. In order to compensate for lack of documentation on the original procedures, the new study also included reanalyses using a variety of reasonable alternative approaches in an effort to discover how the estimates of a 73-percent decline in women's standard of living and a 42-percent increase for men might have been obtained. Peterson's final conclusion was that errors in the original analysis of the data were responsible for the results. Based on the corrected data files, his analysis showed that women's standard of living declined by 27 percent while men's increased by 10 percent. Even with testing various alternative assumptions, the results came out about the same. The results of the reanalysis are generally consistent with those of other studies that have looked at the consequences of divorce.

We can draw a number of lessons from examining the reanalysis of *The Divorce Revolution* data. First, in spite of the wide difference in findings, both the original analysis by Weitzman and the reanalysis by Peterson found a significant gender gap in the economic consequences of divorce, that this gap produces hardships for many divorced women and children, and that legal reforms and public policy must address the hardships. Second, the errors in the original research underscore the need to scrupulously check analysis to prevent errors in the first place, particularly when a study has the potential to influence policy decisions. This study had been widely used and was playing a key role in policy decisions about no-fault divorce; therefore, it was especially crucial that the analysis be correct. The experience also reinforces the importance of carefully and fully documenting the procedures that one uses in the course of conducting a study. Had the original data set been safely retained and had the analysis procedures been fully documented, then carrying out replication of this important study could more readily have been completed. Had the data been immediately accessible, the errors could have been detected more quickly and the impact of the study on policy decisions

continued on next page

lessened. Third, Peterson's work also clearly illustrates the value of replication to science, especially applied research. Simply because a study is published in a respectable journal and widely cited by researchers and policymakers does not prove that it is completely accurate, and certainly no single study is the definitive answer. Erroneous results are still possible; replication with other samples and direct reanalysis of questionable studies are the best ways to correct such flaws. In this case, the replications by other scholars with other data raised suspicion about the original analysis, and the reanalysis of the actual data confirmed those suspicions. The self-correcting process of science did occur, albeit in a more ponderous than exemplary fashion given the problems that we have described.

Finally, the experience of attempting to replicate this study illustrates how knowledge development is fostered through replication. Not only did the results lead to the conclusion that error caused the extreme findings in the original study, but because the corrected results are consistent with the general body of scientific investigation, policymakers can now be more confident in estimates of the actual impact of divorce on women and children. Evaluating the effects of current legal and policy changes can proceed with more confidence in our understanding of what the real financial consequences of divorce have been in the past and what differences new policies have on those consequences.

As noted in Chapter 1, evaluation, in the form of program evaluation and practice effectiveness evaluation, has become an increasingly important activity of human service professionals. Agencies or organizations that fund the human services today typically demand that evaluation research be conducted if funding is to be granted or continued. Such research, developed for practical reasons, can take many forms. A social agency, for example, may require some needs assessment research to gather information about its clients if it is to efficiently deliver services to them. Or a practitioner may need to know which intervention strategy—group work, psychotherapy, behavior therapy, or some other—will be most effective with a particular problem. Prison officials need to know which criminal offenders are the riskiest to parole. Home health-care workers need information about how to ensure that people will take medications as prescribed. In all these cases, the practical information required by an agency or practitioner determines the focus of the research effort.

The ability to find problems in practice settings that could be the focus of program evaluation research is limited only by the creativity and imagination of the practitioner. This was brought home to us by two of our students in a social research

course. They were doing a field placement in a community mental health clinic while taking the research course, so they decided to search for some problem at the clinic to serve as the focus of their research paper. They noticed that one problem the clinic faced was the failure of clients to show up for appointments. In addition to creating difficulties in achieving effective intervention, this also resulted in an inefficient use of staff resources because counselors were left idle by missed appointments. The students designed a very simple investigation in which some clients were given a "reminder" phone call a day or so before their appointment and other clients were not contacted, as had been previous practice. The researchers' concern was to establish whether the "reminder" phone call increased the rate at which people showed up for their appointments. After implementing this procedure for a while, the students concluded that the phone call did help and would be a useful and efficient addition to the functioning of the agency.

Human Service Practice

The linkage between human service practice and evaluation research is obvious, but service delivery can serve as the catalyst for basic research as well. In the course of working in human service programs, practitioners are confronted daily with social problems and human diversity as they interact with clients who are struggling with their life problems. Often the behavior encountered by human service workers is unusual, even dramatic, and it stimulates questions about human behavior and society. The protective service worker who faces child abuse and neglect may derive research questions about parent–child bonding or human development. Hospice staff may generate questions about the dying process and grieving. Although answers to these questions may have practice implications, research that addresses issues such as these also has important implications for social science theory.

It is not only the behavior or characteristics of clients that generate research questions in practice settings; the mode and process of human service practice itself may even be the topic of research. For example, the mechanisms by which some human service agencies differentially allocate services according to social class or race might be a research issue. In fact, many of the major theoretical advances in our understanding of human behavior and social environments have been generated from the study of the human service delivery system. The classic studies by Glaser and Strauss concerning death and social worth, for instance, were based on observations of hospital patient care (Glaser and Strauss, 1965). More recently, controversy has surfaced in the human services over what appears to be the intergenerational transmission of family violence, suggesting that experiencing or observing violence in childhood results in using violence as a parent or spouse. Not only does research into this issue have practical implications for intervention programs, but it is also directly relevant to developing our understanding of learning, human development, the family, and society as well (Burgess and Youngblade, 1988).

Minorities in Research: The Political Context of Problem Selection

From the preceding discussion on how to select a research problem, one could get the impression that

the problem selection process is largely a matter of personal preference. Guided by personal interest or experience, the prospective researcher identifies a worthy problem and sallies forth in the pursuit of knowledge. But problem selection, like most other types of human activity, cannot be explained solely in such individual terms. In fact, if you were to ask students in research courses why they chose the term paper topics they did, you might find that, in addition to personal interest, theoretical orientation, or practice interest, their choices were governed by such factors as these: "My instructor had a data set available on this problem"; "I got financial aid to work as a research assistant"; or "I knew my prof was interested in this topic, so I hoped studying it might help me get a better grade." In other words, issues of political efficacy can influence problem selection.

In the world of professional research, the situation is not unlike that of the student. However, the stakes are much higher, and the consequences are much greater. Although the number of problems to be studied may be infinite, the resources society can allocate to research them are not. Research is a major societal enterprise in which universities, governmental organizations, private research corporations, and independent researchers compete with each other for limited resources. At the same time, there are forces working in society to make sure that the concerns of vested interest groups receive attention from the research community. Thus, problem selection is very much a political issue, and the problems that affect minorities and other groups with little clout may not receive the research attention they deserve.

Consider the example of spouse abuse. Men have been assaulting their wives since long before there was social research. Prior to the 1970s, however, one would have been hard pressed to find much research on the topic. Today the social science and human service literature is replete with studies on the topic. What explains the change? Certainly, there is no single answer, but a major factor has been the women's movement. Before the 1960s, women as a group had considerably less political power than they do today, and the special problems of this minority often received little research attention. Woman battering is now an important issue to the women's movement, and this politically powerful group has been able to translate its concerns into public policy. Partly because of its pressure, the government has allocated money specifically for domestic violence research. In addition, with the changing roles of women in society, more women in the past three decades have chosen to pursue careers as researchers in the social sciences. One consequence of more women in research positions is that, given the role of personal interest in the selection of research topics, they are more likely to identify woman battering as a problem warranting research investigation. As the topic gained more prominence in the social science and human service fields, editors of journals became more receptive to publishing research articles on the topic. And all these factors, over time, had a snowball effect. Researchers seeking problems to study were attracted to the area by the availability of funds, the potential for publication, and the desire to contribute knowledge to an area of public concern.

So one major factor influencing the allocation of research funds is the existence of a powerful, articulate, and effective interest group that can push for research on a particular problem (Strickland, 1972; Lally, 1977). Other factors include the following:

- support for research by influentials at the national policy-making levels
- definition of a condition as a social problem by national influentials
- public awareness of and concern about the condition
- the severity, extent, and economic costs of the condition
- the amount of publicity about the condition
- the amount of support for research on the condition in the major funding agencies

On this last point, it is important to recognize that major agencies of the government, such as the Department of Health and Human Services and the National Science Foundation, dispense millions of dollars for research each year. Support of congressional leaders and key personnel in these major departments is essential for problem areas to be deemed worthy of financial backing for research. Typically, funding sources publish "Requests for Proposals" (RFPs), which outline the organization's funding priorities and requirements. Researchers are invited to submit proposals for competitive consideration with other researchers. Proposals may be for millions of research dollars, and the competition for funding is as intense and high-pressure as any big business deal.

Given that the political process plays a major role in determining which problems are sufficiently important to warrant research attention, it is not surprising that those people who lack access to social power in our society are also those whose interests are least likely to be served by the research conducted. Children, for example, are among the least powerful groups in our society, and where their interests conflict with those of adults, the children are typically the losers. Child abuse has been around for centuries, but it was not until recently that the research and practice communities began to pay attention to the needs of abused children (Radbill, 1980; Gelles, 1987). As another example, problem pregnancies have traditionally been viewed as a "female" problem despite the fact that it doesn't take a researcher to surmise that a male was involved somewhere. Only recently, possibly because more women are now conducting research, have researchers begun to use the couple as the unit of analysis rather than the teenage mother when studying problem pregnancies (Brown, 1983).

One recent and particularly disturbing case where minority status influenced funding was with Acquired Immune Deficiency Syndrome, or AIDS, research. AIDS has become a huge health problem. By the mid-1990s, over 200,000 people in the United States had AIDS and close to 1 million were infected with the HIV virus; 40,000 new infections occur each year (Kolata, 1995; Rosenberg, 1995). This will translate into massive health-care costs as these people develop full-blown AIDS. AIDS is now the leading cause of death among young adults. In the early years of the spread of AIDS, a substantial portion of the people contracting the virus were men who had sex with other men. This has changed: Currently, three quarters of the people newly infected with the HIV virus are drug addicts, either heroin addicts who share infected needles or crack addicts who have unprotected sex with multiple partners. However, in the earlier years, AIDS was associated in many people's minds with two groups of people—homosexuals and IV drug users—who were seen as marginal and highly stigmatized by many Americans, especially those in positions of power. In fact, AIDS was widely defined for a number of years as a "gay disease" and, thus, something that most Americans need not worry about. The attitude of many could be summed up by the comment of a person who was later to be a staff member at the White House: "Those poor homosexuals. They have declared war on nature, and nature is exacting an awful retribution" (quoted in Shilts, 1987, p. 311). As long as AIDS was defined as a disease of "those deviants," funds for research on the cause and prevention of AIDS were slow in coming.

There were other reasons for the delayed response to the AIDS crisis beyond the marginality and stigma suffered by the early victims (Shilts, 1987). One was the policy of the Reagan administration, which entered office in 1981, to emphasize smaller government and austerity in social and health programs. The first AIDS victims in the United States appeared in 1980. The competition for government funds in the early 1980s was fierce, and AIDS researchers typically lost out in the battle, partly because those suffering from AIDS had less clout in the policy process than did other groups competing for dwindling funds. Yet another reason the battle against AIDS was slow to start had to do with urban politics. New York City had the largest number of AIDS cases in the early 1980s, yet New York Mayor Edward Koch refused to do anything about it for a number of years, apparently because of the belief that support for gay causes would link him with the gay rights movement and hurt his chances for reelection.

In short, society's response to the minority status of those afflicted with AIDS, along with other political factors, contributed to a significant delay in attacking the problem. It wasn't until AIDS began to threaten the supply of blood available for blood transfusions, and the fear arose that AIDS was entering the heterosexual population, that considerable research support was forthcoming. Even though gays have become a fairly powerful minority group in some cities—as a group, they are well educated and affluent—they did not have clout in the domains where decisions were made about the funding of research.

Most of those afflicted with AIDS in the United States have been men, so most research on AIDS has been on men. However, more women are becoming HIV-infected, and heterosexual transmission of AIDS has been growing rapidly, from less than 100 new cases in 1985 to over 600 new cases per year by 1989 (Centers for Disease Control, 1990). The failure to include women in the research on AIDS has also created some problems (Mitchell et al., 1992). To be HIV-infected means that a person has the AIDS virus but has not yet developed the symptoms of the diseases that one will get as the virus destroys the immune system. A diagnosis of AIDS is made when enough of those symptoms appear. The Centers for Disease Control has developed a classification system for these symptoms that is used by many agencies to determine if a person has AIDS and is thus eligible for various reimbursements, benefits, or entrance into experimental treatment programs. With early AIDS sufferers being overwhelmingly male, this classification system was based primarily on their symptom experience. The AIDS-defining conditions in men are things like Kaposi's sarcoma and *pneumocystis carinii* pneumonia; however, the first symptoms of AIDS in women appear to be such conditions as pelvic inflammatory disease and abnormal PAP smears. So women whose immune systems were being destroyed by the AIDS virus often found themselves not diagnosed with AIDS, and thus not eligible for a variety of benefits and programs, because their diseases were different from those of men. It was not until women's groups lobbied for more research on women's experiences with AIDS that a broadening of the symptoms that would be considered "getting AIDS" began to occur.

The selection of research problems is thus a highly political process. Although powerful interest groups will always play a role in this process, researchers need to avoid the perceptual blinders that often hinder the ability of the powerful to see which problems are sufficiently important or serious to warrant attention. Human service professionals can play an important role in the political issues surrounding problem selection whether they actually conduct research or not. In the course of practice, human service providers deal directly with the poor, those labeled as deviant, minorities, and the powerless. This puts these providers in a position to serve as advocates for the inclusion on the societal research agenda of problems relevant to their clientele.

We have discussed numerous sources of research topics for practitioner-researchers. Although we have discussed them separately, choice of a research topic is often influenced by more than one of these factors at the same time. Finding a research topic, however, is only the first step in problem formulation. The next step is to shape it into a problem that can be solved through empirical research.

Shaping and Refining the Problem

As we mentioned, one frustrating trap in which novice researchers often become ensnarled is choosing a topic that is so broad and encompassing that, by itself, it offers little guidance in terms of how to proceed. Finding the "causes of juvenile delinquency" or the "weaknesses of the modern family" sounds intriguing, but these topics provide little direction concerning specifically *where* to begin to look. The next step in the research process, then, is to begin translating a general topical interest into a precise, researchable problem. The scope of the problem needs to be narrowed to manageable proportions. One investigation is unlikely to

uncover "the causes of juvenile delinquency," but it might provide some insight regarding the influence of particular variables on the emergence of particular delinquencies. Refining, narrowing, and focusing a research problem do not occur at once but rather form a continuous process involving a number of procedures. We now discuss some of the major influences on this shaping process.

Conceptual Development

In Chapter 2, we discussed the role of theories and hypotheses in the research process, pointing out that concepts are one of the central components of theories. In the refining of a research problem, one of the key steps is *conceptual development:* identifying and properly defining the concepts that will be the focus of the study. In exploratory studies, of course, we are entering areas where there is little conceptual development, and a major purpose of the research itself may be to identify and define concepts. In cases where there is existing theory and research to rely on, however, some conceptual development occurs as a part of formulating a research problem. One part of this process, already discussed in Chapter 2, is to clearly define the meaning of concepts. Another part of the process is to narrow the focus of the concept so that it encompasses something that is feasible to research in a single study. Practitioners in a youth home, for example, with an interest in juvenile delinquency might ask themselves: Are we interested in all forms of delinquent behavior or only in some types? In reality, the concept of delinquency is an extremely broad category that includes all actions by juveniles that violate criminal or juvenile codes. There is no reason to assume that *all* types of delinquency can be explained on the basis of a *single cause*. The focus of the research, therefore, might be narrowed so that it includes only certain behaviors, such as violence or truancy. The goal of this specification process, then, is to make clear *exactly* what the focus of the research effort is to be.

Once key concepts have been clearly defined, the next consideration is their measurability. Only concepts that are in some way measurable can be used in the research process. Eventually, of course, concepts will have to be operationalized, as is pointed out in Chapter 2, so any that are not readily measurable will have to be dropped. Measuring concepts can sometimes be difficult, as we note in more detail in Chapter 5. In fact, theories at times include concepts that are difficult to operationalize. Theorists are sometimes criticized for this practice, although the criticism is misdirected. Theorists, of necessity, must be free to create and utilize whatever concepts are deemed necessary without regard to their immediate measurability. To do otherwise would limit theoretical development to those concepts that we currently have the skill to measure (Shearing, 1973; Denzin, 1989). Theorists' use of concepts that are not immediately measurable allows for theoretical advances, but it also presents researchers with the task of creating ways to measure the concepts. However, if concepts in a proposed study cannot be measured, then some modification in the project—and possibly in the theory—will be necessary. This process of refining and developing concepts as a part of the research process illustrates a point made in Chapter 2 regarding the interplay between theory and research: Theories provide concepts and hypotheses for research while research modifies theories through conceptual development.

Review of the Literature

With concepts clarified and deemed measurable, we are ready to conduct a review of previous research that relates to our research problem. This "review of the literature" is a necessary and important part of the research process. We do it in order to familiarize ourselves with the current state of knowledge regarding our research problem and to learn how others have delineated similar problems. Unless we are planning a replication, it is unlikely that we will formulate our problem precisely like any one of these previous studies. Rather, we are likely to pick up ideas from several that can be integrated to improve our own. Through reviewing the relevant literature, we can further narrow the focus of the research project and ensure that we do

not unnecessarily duplicate what others have already done. Researchers will undoubtedly find that pitfalls can be avoided by learning from others' experiences. It may be, for example, that one or more specific approaches to a topic have proved unproductive. That is, several studies have failed to find significant results or strong relationships. Unless there is good reason to believe that there were methodological weaknesses in these earlier studies, using the same approach is likely to lead once again to failure. Research is likely to be more productive if it focuses on studies that have achieved some positive results.

A thorough literature review calls for familiarity with basic library utilization skills, including how to locate books, professional journals, and public documents. To help with this important aspect of doing research, we have included Appendix A in this book on the use of the library. This appendix shows you how to find the books, journals, government documents, and other sources in which the reports of research are found. Even those with some experience using the library will likely find some helpful new information in this appendix.

In a literature review, a systematic search is conducted of each research report for certain kinds of information. First, the reviewer pays attention to *theoretical and conceptual issues:* What concepts and theories are used, how well developed are they, and have they been subject to empirical test before? If the theories and concepts are well developed, they can serve as an important guide in designing the planned research and explaining the relationships between variables. If they are not well developed, one will have to rely more on personal insight and creativity. In this case, researchers sometimes consider doing exploratory research, which may involve loosely structured interviews and less quantitative measuring devices, as a way of advancing conceptual and theoretical development.

A second component of a literature review is the *research hypotheses,* including identification of the *independent and dependent variables.* Are the hypotheses clearly stated and testable? Are they related to the variables and hypotheses being considered in the planned study? Existing research can provide some fairly specific direction in terms of already-tested relationships between independent and dependent variables.

A third focus of a literature review should be the *operational definitions* that have been used in previous research. As noted, successful operationalization of concepts is often difficult. Previous work in this area is invaluable in finding workable measures for concepts. Measures used in the past may require modification to meet current needs, of course, but making these modifications is likely to be easier than developing completely new measures, which is a difficult and time-consuming process.

The literature review will also inform us about a fourth important element of research—the most appropriate *research technique* for a particular research problem. Successful approaches by others should be noted, and unsuccessful ones should be avoided. It is of the utmost importance that the problem determine the research technique used, and not the other way around. A variety of data-gathering techniques exists because no one method is always best. As will be noted in subsequent chapters, each technique has its strengths and weaknesses, and each is suitable for answering some questions but not others.

A fifth element obtained from a literature review is the *sampling strategy*. Previous research can be useful in determining the sampling strategy that should be used and in avoiding sampling problems encountered by others. Suppose, for example, that the study we propose calls for the use of mailed questionnaires. An ever-present problem with mailed questionnaires is making sure that a sufficient number of people complete and return them. It would be useful for us to know what the experience of other investigators has been with people like those we plan to survey. Not all groups respond to mailed questionnaires with the same degree of enthusiasm. If the group we are proposing to sample has exhibited notoriously low return rates in the previous studies, we have to plan accordingly. We would likely increase the number of questionnaires mailed and would certainly use all available means of obtaining the highest response rate possi-

ble. Or, if very low return rates are anticipated, we may want to search for another group to study or even consider whether this particular project is feasible given the anticipated low return rate.

A sixth element of a literature review is the *statistical techniques* used. In Chapters 5, 14, and 15, we discuss issues relating to appropriate use of statistics. In a literature review, one must be aware of whether the appropriate procedures were used, if any inappropriate ones were used, and what constraints the concepts, variables, and hypotheses placed on the kind of statistics that would be appropriate.

Finally, a literature review would note the *findings and conclusions* of the study. Which hypotheses were confirmed, and what guidelines for future research were presented? One aspect of the findings to watch for is the *effect size,* which refers to how big an effect an independent variable has on a dependent variable. Although we discuss this concept more in Chapter 15, you need to assess whether a dependent variable is affected in only a small, although measurable, way or whether the impact is dramatic (Gibbs, 1991).

A thorough literature review would involve evaluating and comparing many research reports, identifying where they used similar procedures and reached similar outcomes, and where there were discrepancies between studies. This can be a complicated process, especially when there may be hundreds of studies involved. It is sometimes helpful to produce a summary table to make comparisons. An example of such a table, comparing studies on the relationship between self-esteem and teenage pregnancies, is presented in Table 4.1. Studies that show an association are in the top half of the table, while those showing self-esteem as not related to pregnancy are in the bottom half. Notice that this table cites each separate study in the left-hand column, including a notation as to whether it was a longitudinal study. The next column provides information about the sample used, while the third column indicates which scale was used to measure self-esteem. The right-hand column indicates, for those studies showing an association, the direction of the relationship. In this case, the relationships are all negative, indicating that teenagers with high

Table 4.1   A Summary Table of a Literature Review of the Association Between Self-Esteem and Teenage Pregnancy

	Sample	Self-Esteem Scale	Association[a]
Self-Esteem Related to Teenage Pregnancy			
Barth, Schinke, and Maxwell, 1983	117 nonwhite females, 68 white females; 11–21 years old	Rosenberg Self-Esteem Scale	Negative
Kaplan, Smith, and Pokorny, 1979 (longitudinal)	410 females	Self-Derogation Scale	Negative
Robbins, Kaplan, and Martin, 1985 (longitudinal)	2,158 males and females; white, black, and Hispanic	Self-Derogation Scale	Negative, for females only
Werner and Smith, 1977 (longitudinal)	614 males and females; 18 years old	California Personality Inventory	Negative
Self-Esteem Not Related to Teenage Pregnancy			
Brunswick, 1971	196 black females; 12–17 years old	Rosenberg Self-Esteem Scale (subset)	
Streetman, 1987	93 nonwhite females; 14–19 years old	Coopersmith Self-Esteem Inventory; Rosenberg Self-Esteem Scale	
Vernon, Green, and Frothingham, 1983 (longitudinal)	745 black females, 22 other nonwhite females, 91 white females; 13–19 years old	Coopersmith Self-Esteem Inventory	

[a]A negative association indicates that low self-esteem is associated with a greater risk of becoming pregnant during adolescence.

Source   Adapted from Susan B. Crockenberg and Barbara A. Soby, "Self-Esteem and Teenage Pregnancy," in *The Social Importance of Self-Esteem,* edited by Andrew M. Mecca, Neil J. Smelser, and John Vasconcellos (Berkeley: University of California Press, 1989), p. 148.

self-esteem are less likely to get pregnant. A systematic literature review of this sort provides the most useful information from previous studies. One can see at a glance how many studies came to similar conclusions and how commonly certain measuring devices were used. The ability to compile and summarize succinctly the features of studies in this fashion is essential to formulating a research problem and refining it into a research question that can be empirically investigated.

Units of Analysis

An important element in the process of shaping and refining a research problem is the decision re-

garding the unit of analysis to be investigated. **Units of analysis** are the specific objects or elements whose characteristics we wish to describe or explain and about which data will be collected. Although there are many units of analysis, five commonly used in human service research are individuals, groups, organizations, programs, and social artifacts (*see* Table 4.2). (There are different units of analysis used in studying documents, and these are discussed in Chapter 8.)

Much social research focuses on the *individual* as the unit of analysis. The typical survey, for example, obtains information from individuals about their attitudes or behavior. Anytime we define our population of inquiry with reference to some

Table 4.2   Possible Units of Analysis in Research on Juvenile Delinquency

Unit of Analysis	Example	Appropriate Variables	Research Problem
Individuals	Adolescents arrested for larceny	Age, sex, prior arrests	Do males receive different penalties from females for similar offenses?
Groups	Delinquent gangs	Size, norms on drug usage	Are gangs involved in drug trafficking more violent than other gangs?
Organizations	Adolescent treatment agencies	Size, auspices, funding level	Do private agencies serve fewer minority and lower-class delinquents than public agencies?
Programs	Delinquency prevention programs	Theoretical model, type of host setting	What services are most frequently included in prevention programs?
Social artifacts	Transcripts of adjudication hearings	Number of references to victim injury	To what extent does the level of violence in the offense affect the kind of penalty imposed?

personal status, we are operating at the individual level of analysis. For example, unwed mothers, welfare recipients, mental patients, retarded children, and similar categories all identify individuals with reference to a status they occupy.

If we identify our unit of analysis as individuals, it is important to recognize that the entire analysis will remain at that level. For the sake of describing large numbers of individuals, it is necessary to utilize summarizing statistics such as averages. We might, for example, as a part of a study of unwed mothers, note that their average age when giving birth was 16.8 years. Aggregating data in this fashion in no way changes the unit of analysis. Our data are still being collected about individuals.

Social scientists sometimes focus on social *groups* as their unit of analysis and collect data on some group characteristic or behavior. Some groups are made up of individuals who share some social relationship with the other group members. For example, in families, peer groups, occupational groups, or juvenile gangs, the members have some sense of membership or belonging to the group. If we study families in terms of whether they are intact or not, we are investigating the characteristics

of a group—the family—not of individuals. Other groups of interest to social scientists are merely aggregates of individuals with no necessary sense of membership, such as census tracts, cities, states, or members of a particular social class. For example, we might study the relationship between poverty and delinquency by comparing rates of delinquency in census tracts with low income and those with high income. In this case, we have collected data regarding the characteristics of census tracts rather than individuals.

Social scientists also deal with *organizations* as the unit of analysis. Formal organizations are deliberately constructed groups organized for the achievement of some specific goals. Examples of formal organizations include corporations, schools, prisons, unions, government bureaus, and human service agencies. For example, our experience may lead us to suspect that organizations providing substance abuse services can more effectively serve their clients if they have a more open and democratic communication structure in contrast to a closed and rigidly stratified one. If we compared the success rates of organizations with different communication structures, our study would be utilizing organizations, not individuals or groups, as the unit of analysis. Although individuals may experience success at overcoming substance abuse, only organizations can have a *success rate.*

Research in the human services can also focus on *programs* as the basic unit of analysis. The program may provide services for individuals, and it may exist as part of an organization, but it is still a separate unit of analysis about which data can be collected. Like organizations, programs can have success rates or be assessed in terms of overall costs. For example, one research project investigated 456 delinquency prevention programs across the nation, looking for whether there were different types of human services delivered to minorities as opposed to whites (Hawkins and Salisbury, 1983). Among other things, the researchers found that whites were more likely to receive such services as family training and training in affective skills, whereas blacks received remedial and employment services. Programs might cut across a number of different organizations, such as social service agencies, in which case the unit being observed is the effectiveness of the combination of services provided by these organizations.

Finally, in fairly rare instances, the unit of analysis may be *social artifacts,* which are simply any material products produced by people. Examples are virtually endless: newspapers, buildings, movies, books, magazines, automobiles, songs, graffiti, and so on. Of all the units of analysis, social artifacts are the least frequent focus of human service research, but as reflections of people and the society that produces them, analysis of social artifacts can be useful. Books and magazines, for example, can be used as artifacts in the assessment of sex-role stereotyping. Children's books have been attacked for allegedly reinforcing traditional sex roles through their presentations of men and women (Peterson and Lack, 1990; Purcell and Stewart, 1990). Any kind of legal or administrative statute can also be an artifact worthy of study. One effort, for instance, used the state juvenile codes as the independent variable in a study of whether legal statutes made a difference in how the courts handled the cases of juveniles (Grichting, 1979).

Clearly specifying the unit of analysis in research is very important in order to avoid a serious problem: an illegitimate shift in the analysis from one unit to another. Careless jumping from one level to another can result in drawing erroneous conclusions. An example of this type of error is called the **ecological fallacy:** inferring something about individuals based on data collected about groups (Robinson, 1950). Suppose, for example, a study found that census tracts with high rates of teenage drug abuse also had a large percentage of single-parent families. We might be tempted to conclude that single-parent families are a factor promoting teenage drug abuse. Such a conclusion, however, represents an illegitimate shift in the unit of analysis. The data have been collected about census tracts, which are at the group level. The conclusion drawn, however, is at the individual level, namely, that teenage drug abusers live in single-parent families. The data do *not* show this. They only show the association of two rates—substance abuse and single parenthood—in census tracts. It is, of course, possible that relationships found at the group level will hold at the individual level, but they may not. It is always an empirical question whether relationships found at one level of analysis will hold up at other levels. In our hypothetical study, it may be that some other characteristic of census tracts leads to both high rates of drug abuse *and* single-parent families. The error comes in the automatic assumption that correlations at the group level necessarily reflect relationships at the individual level. A clear awareness of the unit of analysis with which we are dealing can help ensure that we do not make such illegitimate shifts.

A final point needs to be made about the unit of analysis in contrast to the source of data. The unit of analysis refers to the element *about which* data are collected and inferences made, but it is not necessarily the source *from which* data are collected. A common example is the U.S. Census, which reports data on *households.* We speak of household size and income, but households don't fill out questionnaires; people do. In this case, individuals, such as the heads of households, are the *source* of the data, but the household is the unit of analysis *about which* data are collected. When the unit of analysis is something other than the individual, attention must be paid to the source of the data because this might introduce bias into the data analysis. For example, when the household is the unit of analysis, data are often collected from one member of the household. In single-parent families, which are headed primarily by women, we would be gathering data mostly from women. In two-parent families we would be obtaining data from both men and women since either could be the head of the household, and in some cases men might be the majority of those from whom data are collected. If men tend to give answers to some questions that are different from those women give, there could be a sex bias in the results even though our unit of analysis was not linked to sex. A difference that we attribute to single-parent as compared to two-parent families may be due to the fact that the former involves mostly women answering questions, whereas the latter involves more men.

Reactivity

Another consideration in refining a research problem is the issue of reactivity. The term **reactivity** refers to the fact that people can react to being studied and may behave differently from when they don't think they are being studied. In other words, the data collected from people who know they are the object of study might be different from data collected from the same people if they did not know. So a reactive research technique changes the very thing that is being studied. Suppose, for example, that you are a parent. A researcher enters your home and sets up videotaping equipment to observe your interactions with your children. Would you behave in the same way that you would if the observer were not present? You might, but most people would feel strong pressures to be "on their toes" and present themselves as "good" parents. You might be more forgiving of your child, for instance, or give fewer negative sanctions.

Reactivity in research can take many forms, and it is a problem for virtually all sciences. However, it is especially acute in social research because human beings are so self-conscious and aware of what is happening to them. Refining a research problem and choosing a research design are done with an eye toward reducing as much as possible the extensiveness of reactivity. We consider this in assessing the various research strategies in later chapters.

Qualitative Versus Quantitative Research

Another aspect of refining a research problem is to decide whether to use one of two broad categories of research: qualitative or quantitative. **Qualitative research** basically involves data in the form of words, pictures, descriptions, or narratives. **Quantitative research** uses numbers, counts, and measures of things (Berg, 1995; Wakefield, 1995). The decision as to which general orientation to follow in a given research project depends primarily on two factors: the state of our knowledge on a particular research topic, and the individual researcher's position regarding the nature of human social behavior. When knowledge is sketchy or when there is little theoretical understanding of a phenomenon, it may be impossible to develop precise hypotheses or operational definitions. In such cases, researchers often turn to qualitative research because it can be more exploratory in nature. The research can be very descriptive, possibly resulting in the formulation of hypotheses rather than the verification of them. When there is enough previous research on a topic, it may be more feasible to precisely state concepts, variables, and hypotheses. It also may be possible to develop quantifiable operational definitions of what you are interested in, which then allows research to take on a more quantitative nature.

The second consideration in choosing between quantitative and qualitative research stems from a more fundamental controversy over the nature of human social behavior. It is a complicated issue we discuss in more detail in Chapter 9, but it basically involves debate over whether the human experience can be meaningfully reduced to numbers and measures. Some social scientists argue that the human experience has a subjective dimension to it—the very personal meanings and feelings that people have about themselves and what they do. These meanings or feelings cannot be captured very well through numbers or measures. They are better captured through narrative descriptions of people going about their daily routines or through lengthy and broad-ranging interviews with them. These techniques are better able to capture the very critical subjective meanings that are an essential element of understanding human behavior. Quantitative research, on the other hand, provides us with much more precise statements about human behavior.

The line between qualitative and quantitative approaches is not always completely clear, and the choice between the two can be difficult. Many research projects incorporate both approaches in order to gain the most benefit. Research in Practice 4.2 presents some additional elaboration on this issue. In later chapters, we discuss additional considerations relevant to this choice between quantitative and qualitative research.

Cross-Sectional Versus Longitudinal Research

In addition to deciding on the unit of analysis to be investigated, refining a research problem also requires a decision about the time dimension. The basic issue involved is whether you want a single "snapshot" in time of some phenomenon or an ongoing series of photographs over time. The former is called **cross-sectional research,** and it focuses on a cross section of a population at one point in time. Many surveys, for example, are cross-sectional in nature.

Although all the data in cross-sectional research are collected at one time, such studies can nonetheless be used to investigate the development of some phenomenon over time. For example, to study the developmental problems of children of alcoholic parents, one could select groups of children of varying ages, say, one group at age 5, another at 10, and a third group at age 15. By observing differ-

ences in developmental problems among these groups, we may infer that a single youngster would experience changes as he or she grew up similar to the differences observed among these three groups. Yet, one of the major weaknesses of such cross-sectional studies is that we have not actually observed the changes an individual goes through; rather, we have observed three different groups of individuals at one point in time. Differences among these groups may reflect something other than the developmental changes that individuals experience. Because of this disadvantage, researchers sometimes resort to the other way of handling the time issue: longitudinal studies.

Longitudinal research involves gathering data over an extended period, which might span months, years, or, in a few cases, decades. One type of longitudinal approach is the **panel study,** in which the same people are studied at different times. This allows us to observe the actual changes that these individuals go through over time. For example, a study of the social, psychological, and familial characteristics that influence whether drug addicts can successfully remain free of drugs followed the same 354 narcotics addicts for over 24 years, collecting data on their family experiences, employment records, and a host of other factors (Bailey et al., 1994). Another longitudinal approach is the **trend study,** in which different people are observed at different times. Public opinion polling and research on political attitudes are often trend studies.

The decision whether to use a longitudinal or cross-sectional approach is typically determined both by the nature of the research problem and by practical considerations. Longitudinal studies, especially panel studies, have the advantage of providing the most accurate information regarding changes over time. A research question regarding such changes, then, would probably benefit from this approach. A disadvantage of panel studies is that they can be reactive: People's responses or behavior at one time may be influenced by the fact that they have been observed earlier. For example, a person who stated opposition to abortion in one survey may be inclined to respond the same way 6 months

Research in Practice **4.2**
Behavior and Social Environments: Do Males and Females Have Different "Voices"?

We have analyzed some of the explicit elements that feed into the shaping and refining of research problems, such as conceptual development and the avoidance of reactivity. However, there may be much more subtle and unnoticed influences on problem development. Feminists have brought attention to one such area that has generated considerable controversy today in the human services, both in research and in practice: Are males and females socialized to perceive the world and acquire knowledge in fundamentally different ways? There is great debate over this issue, with strong advocates supporting each side. At the heart of the debate are fundamentally different ways of knowing the world, and these differences could translate into quite different approaches to problem formulation in research (Nielson, 1989).

In Chapter 2, we discussed the characteristics of science and emphasized the importance of objectivity. However, there are critics who claim that our knowledge of the world is always subjective and relative because knowledge is interpreted through a filter of human perceptions and meanings (Heineman, 1981). Nothing has meaning for human beings until we attach some social importance to it, and this makes all knowledge subjective. Because of our biology, socialization, and experiences, people attach a variety of meanings to knowledge and events, and we are often unaware of these influences. One important influence, it is argued, is our socialization as males and females and possibly even biological differences (Davis, 1986; Ivanoff, Robinson, and Blythe, 1987).

The basic argument is that, because of differences between the sexes, there is a male model of knowledge development and a female one, and that the two are, to an extent, alien to each other. In developing some of these ideas, Carol Gilligan (1982) used the term "voice" to mean modes of thinking about the world and tried to describe the differences between male and female "voices." Women emphasize the importance of relationships and the danger of being separated from others. Women see connectedness between people and feel obliged to protect and nurture those to whom they feel connected. This leads to a concern about the needs of others, but the needs of self and others exist primarily in the context of their relationships with other people. So women's voices focus on the individual embedded in a social network. This emphasis on connectedness and relationships means that problems and people are inextricably intertwined. Neither problems nor the people they affect can be fully understood if they are separated from one another.

By contrast, men's voices speak of separation and autonomy. They emphasize independence and, to an extent, alienation in the sense that people can be abstracted from their relationships, from their context, and even from their own uniqueness. For men, the separate individual has some meaning and importance, and possibly even more value than a person encumbered by relationships and connections. In this view, these abstracted individuals can all be treated the same, ignoring the unique needs or contexts of each person. To this extent, men's voices are abstract and formal. People and their problems can be separated.

A concrete example of this difference is supplied by Gilligan from her work on moral development. A boy and a girl, both age 11, were asked to evaluate a dilemma faced by "Heinz," who is confronted with choosing between stealing a drug that he cannot afford in order to keep his wife alive or obeying the law and letting her die without the drug. According to Gilligan, the boy's conclusion is that Heinz should steal the drug because a life is more valuable than property. For him, it's fundamentally a math problem: weigh the alternatives and take the highest value. In contrast, the girl sees a more complex problem. She responds, "I think there might be other ways besides stealing it, like if he could borrow the money or make a loan or something. . . . If he stole the drug, he might save his wife then, but if he did, he might have to go to jail, and then his wife might get sicker again, and he couldn't get more of the drug" (Gilligan, 1982, p. 28). In contrast to the boy's math problem perspective, the girl sees the moral problem in the context of "a narrative of relationships that extend over time" (Gilligan, 1982, p. 28).

Proponents of the male–female distinction argue that these male and female voices are fundamentally contrasting ways of perceiving and developing knowledge about the world. As for shaping research problems, the male voice will tend toward a research problem where separation predominates: The researcher extracts data from the "subject" or "respondent" and any personal relationship (or connectedness) between them is avoided in the interests of objectivity. All contact except that necessary to collect data is avoided. A more quantitative approach is preferred, with standardized measuring instruments and procedures used on the assumption that all people can be treated alike and this will produce the most valid and objective data. A number of procedures commonly used in research can be seen as efforts to strip away the context from the individual: placing them in laboratory settings, using random assignment to conditions, using aggregate responses from large-scale surveys, and isolating variables for study. All these procedures assume that the context in which a person lives is merely interfering "noise" and that more meaningful information can be gotten without it. Through quantification, the male voice minimizes the uniqueness and subjectivity of experiences by providing summary responses of the aggregate; so the fact that Jane Doe got pregnant at age 13 under a certain set of unique and meaningful circumstances gets lost when we conclude that the average teenage pregnancy in a high school occurs at age 14.7 years.

The key in the development of a research problem for the female voice is connectedness: Researcher and respondent are tied together in a relationship that influences the data that are produced. "Objectivity," in the traditional sense, is impossible because the meaning and importance of data relate to specific individuals and their relationships with one another. The researcher and subject are seen as partners in the relationship of producing research. Subjects are seen more as collaborators. "Female"-oriented researchers also disdain the notion of the objective, impartial researcher in favor of involvement with the topics of their research. "Thus, the researcher and subject can work in different ways to explore a 'truth' that they mutually create and define" (Davis, 1986, p. 38). Research questions will be developed in the direction of emphasizing connectedness: keeping people in their social contexts and studying the complexity of the whole. In short, more qualitative approaches are preferred. People can be studied in their homes or where they work and play. Some research methods, such as participant observation, as discussed in Chapter 9, are better suited to emphasizing this connectedness. Female perspective research also emphasizes in-depth interviews, where people have an opportunity to express the fullness and complexity of their lives in their own words.

Obviously, it is possible for men to speak with a female voice and women with a male voice. The point is that people's experiences can lead to fundamentally different ways of perceiving the world. In fact, some critics would argue that researchers in the social sciences and human services, whether male or female, tend to be trained in graduate school with a male voice because that is what has dominated over the years among graduate faculty. Yet, neither voice is inherently superior. Each is a valid way of gaining knowledge about the world. However, researchers need to be clear, as they shape a research problem and choose a research methodology, about which voice would best serve the research goals. In some cases, the most solid foundation of knowledge would be to use both voices. No single research method is complete or totally objective. They all involve a perspective that has some limitations. It is especially dangerous to assume that a single research method can provide all answers about a problem.

later so as not to appear inconsistent or vacillating even if those attitudes had changed in the interim. Another disadvantage of panel studies is that people who participated early in a panel study may not want to, or be unable to, participate later. People die, move away, become uninterested, or in other ways become unavailable as panel studies progress. This loss of participants can adversely affect the validity of the research findings. The disadvantages of all longitudinal studies are that they can be difficult and expensive to conduct, especially if they span a long period of time.

Cross-sectional research is cheaper and faster to conduct, and one need not worry about the loss of participants. However, cross-sectional research may not provide the most useful data for some research questions. Thus, the decision on the issue of time dimension should be based on considerations of both the nature of the research problem and practical issues. There are times, of course, when practical feasibility plays a large part in the decision. We end this chapter with a discussion of factors related to the feasibility of research.

Feasibility of a Research Project

By the time researchers have selected, shaped, and refined a research problem, the problem should be sufficiently clear that a consideration of practical issues involving the feasibility of the project is in order. Practical considerations of what can reasonably be accomplished given the time and resources available can force researchers, sometimes painfully, to reduce the scale of a project. A careful and honest appraisal of the time and money required to accomplish a project will be useful in determining the feasibility of the project as envisioned and reveal if a change in goals is called for. In making a feasibility assessment, one should keep in mind a couple of axioms that apply to research projects: "Anything that can go wrong will," and "Everything will take longer than possibly imagined."

The practical aspects of a project's feasibility center primarily on two related concerns: time and money (Kelly and McGrath, 1988).

Time Constraints

In developing a research project, one of the major considerations is whether there will be sufficient time to complete adequately what you hope to do. In later chapters, as we consider specific research techniques, we will see how different techniques vary in terms of how much time they take. Here, we want to mention some of the major factors related to time considerations. One factor concerns the population that is the focus of the research. If that population has characteristics that are fairly widespread, then a sufficient number of people will be readily available from which to collect data. If we were studying the differing attitudes of men and women toward work-release programs for prison inmates, we could select a sample of men and women from whatever city or state we happened to be in. If, however, our study focuses on people with special characteristics that are somewhat rare, problems may arise. In general, the smaller the number of people who have the characteristics needed for inclusion in a study, the more difficult and time consuming it will be to contact a sufficiently large number necessary to make scientifically valid conclusions. For example, a study of incestuous fathers, even in a large city, may encounter problems obtaining enough cases because relatively few such people will be openly known.

A second problem relating to time constraints involves the proper development of measuring devices. All techniques used for gathering data should be tested before the actual study is conducted, and this can be very time consuming. A pretest, as we saw in Chapter 1, refers to the preliminary application of the data-gathering techniques for purposes of assessing their adequacy. A pilot study is a small-scale "trial run" of all the procedures planned for use in the main study. In some studies, several pretests may need to be conducted as data collection devices are modified based on the results of previous pretests. All in all, a lot of time can be consumed in such refining of data-gathering procedures.

A third major factor related to time considerations is the amount of time required for actual data collection, which can range from a few hours for a questionnaire administered to a group of "captive" students to the years that are necessary in many longitudinal studies. Because the amount of time required for data collection is so variable, it should be given close scrutiny when addressing the question of the feasibility of a particular research design.

A fourth consideration related to the time issue is the amount of time necessary to complete the analysis of the data. In general, the less structured the data, the more time will be required for analysis. The field notes that serve as the data for some observational studies, for example, can be very time consuming to analyze (*see* Chapter 9). Likewise, the videotapes collected during an experiment or during single-subject research may take many viewings before they are adequately understood (*see* Chapters 10 and 11). However, highly structured data in quantified form can also be time consuming to analyze, as we see in Chapters 14 and 15. Although computers can manipulate the data rapidly, it takes considerable time to prepare the data for entry into the computer, and the amount of time needed increases as the number of cases increases. So, as with the time required for data collection, the time needed for analysis should be carefully considered owing to wide variation in the amount that may be necessary.

The fifth area in which time becomes a factor is writing the report itself. The amount of time this consumes depends on the length and complexity of the report and the skills of the investigator. Each researcher is in the best position, based on past writing experiences, to assess the amount of time he or she will require. As a final reminder, it will likely take longer than you expect.

Financial Considerations

The financial expenditures associated with a research project are another constraint on feasibility. Good research is not always expensive. In many instances, students and human service practitioners are able to get by with only modest costs because data are easy to obtain, analysis procedures are simple, and the labor is voluntary or provided at no

additional charge. But even small projects are likely to require money for long-distance telephone calls, typing and duplicating questionnaires, and other services that can quickly stress the tight resources of a small human service agency. At the other extreme, it is not unusual for the price tag of major research and demonstration projects in the human services to run into six figures. For example, in 1990 the National Institute of Justice announced five grants, ranging from $300,000 to $400,000 each, awarded to cooperating teams of police departments and research agencies for the development and evaluation of computerized drug information systems to combat drug use (Uchida, 1990). Table 4.3 shows the budget for a modest research project at our university and indicates some of the general expenditure categories that should be considered in assessing the feasibility of any project.

The salaries of those who conduct the study are potentially the most expensive item, especially for studies that require large interviewer staffs. Not only must the interviewers' wages be paid, but transportation costs and living expenses, which can be sizable, must also be covered. Interviewers may also require hours of training time before they can begin to collect data. If respondents are not available, callbacks may be necessary, which further increases the cost of each interview. To get the work done in a timely fashion and to ensure reliability, investigators may need to hire individuals or contract with an organization to code the raw data into an analyzable format.

Computer expenses can also be formidable. In some settings, particularly for data analysis on large mainframe computers, cost is determined by the amount of computer time used to run the data analysis. Formerly, data analysis comprised the bulk of computer costs, but today computers are also used for questionnaire design, project management, data collection, literature searches, and report preparation. These tasks are commonly performed on personal computers. A significant cost here is for the software packages that actually perform the procedures in addition to the cost of the computer itself and peripherals like printers, scanners, and modems.

Table 4.3 A Budget for a Study of Interventions to Improve the Health of School-Age Children

Category	Subtotal	Total	Percent of Total[a]
	Budget		
Salaries/Wages		14,400	46.8
Principal Invest.	6,000		
Graduate Asst.	7,000		
Clerical Asst.	1,400		
Fringe Benefits		2,346	7.6
Travel		1,800	5.8
Present initial results at a regional conf.	800		
Present final results at a national conf.	1,000		
Supplies/Materials		2,500	8.1
Produce surveys, copyright fees	2,000		
Prizes for survey participants	180		
Paper, postage, envelopes, etc.	320		
Other Expenses		2,100	6.8
Indirect Costs		7,837	25.3
46.8% of wages, salaries and fringe benefits			
Total Research Project Funding		$30,983	

[a]Totals to more than 100% because of rounding.

Source Director, Office of Research and Development, Northern Michigan University.

Another major cost consideration is expenditures for office supplies and equipment. Under this category are such items as paper, envelopes, postage, tape, printing, and the like. Paper products might seem inexpensive at first glance, but given the large samples used for some surveys, the cost can be substantial. For example, we recently conducted a survey of approximately 500 potential students for a graduate program in social work. Each person received a large envelope containing a letter of introduction, a professionally printed four-page questionnaire, and a postage-paid return envelope.

In addition, all members of the sample received a reminder letter urging them to respond, and about 250 nonrespondents received a second questionnaire. Cost for printing, envelopes, and postage exceeded $1,250. Different kinds of studies present different cost issues. For example, studies based on direct observation of behavior may necessitate high-cost equipment items such as video cameras, recorders, and videotape. Unless these are already available, substantial outlays will be needed.

Providing incentives to ensure cooperation of people in the study may also be a cost factor. This may range from giving stickers or balloons to schoolchildren for completing a questionnaire to paying respondents in recognition of the large time commitment required for a longitudinal study. A study evaluating the effectiveness of advocacy services to women who were leaving their abusive partners illustrates participant incentive costs. Women were interviewed before the program and at 5, 10, and 20 weeks following the program. Not only was it difficult to maintain contact with this highly mobile population, but completing a survey form was very likely a low priority for them, given the stress and disruption in their lives. In order to encourage the women to participate, the 46 participants were paid $10, $20, $30, and $40, respectively, for the four interviews for a total cost of $4,600 (Sullivan, 1991). Payment of subjects is more likely to be an issue in experiments that require more time investment and greater commitment from participants than is usually required in most surveys or observational studies.

Dissemination of research findings also generates costs. Besides the additional printing and office supplies for preparing reports, this may include travel to professional meetings to present papers. In the case of program evaluation studies, it may also entail hosting workshops or conferences with sponsors and other interested parties to ensure that the findings are incorporated into the policy and intervention planning process.

Finally, some costs associated with a research project are difficult to specify. Where research is being conducted under the auspices of a university, a human service agency, or a research center, some organizational resources will partially or indirectly support the research. For example, money will be spent to heat and light the building where the research project is housed, but this cost is difficult to assess precisely. A major factor in awarding a research project to a particular organization may be the fact that it has an extensive research library, sophisticated computer facilities, or an extensive laboratory for conducting research. The organization maintains these facilities for general use, not just for a particular research project, and it is difficult to ascertain how much of the overall cost of supporting the facilities should be assigned to a given project. Consequently, the concept of "indirect cost," typically a percentage of the total grant request, is employed to cover these real but hard-to-specify costs. Each organization negotiates its rate with the federal government on the basis of the facilities and equipment that the organization has for research. The amount charged to indirect costs varies from 15 percent to well in excess of 100 percent of the basic grant.

Anticipating and Avoiding Problems

Problems related to time and financial considerations arise during virtually all research projects, but their impact on the outcome of the research can be minimized if they can be anticipated as much as possible, especially during the planning stage when the details of the project are easier to change. A number of things can be done to anticipate problems. First, learn as much as possible from the experiences of others. One way to do this is through the studies consulted during the review of the literature. We mentioned earlier that noting problems these other researchers encountered is one focus of this review. Personal advice from experienced researchers who might be available for consultation can also be solicited. A knowledgeable researcher may be able to identify potential trouble spots in your plans and suggest modifications to avoid them.

Second, obtain whatever permissions or consents may be needed early in the planning stages of the project. Depending on the people you wish to study, it may be necessary to obtain permission

from them officially to collect data. For example, some studies are aimed at school-age children and seek to gather data while the children are in school. School administrators, to protect students from undue harassment and themselves from parental complaints, are frequently cool to allowing researchers into their schools. It may take considerable time to persuade whatever authorities are involved to grant the permissions you need—if they are granted at all. It is certainly wise to obtain any needed permissions before expending effort on other phases of the project, which might be wasted if permissions cannot be obtained.

The final—and perhaps most important—suggestion for avoiding problems is to conduct a pilot study. As noted, a pilot study is a preliminary run-through on a small scale of all the procedures planned for the main study. For surveys, a small part of the sample, say 20 people, should be contacted and interviewed. The data should be analyzed as they will be in the complete project. In experiments, the researcher should run a few groups through all procedures, looking for any unexpected reactions from participants. Observational researchers should visit the observation sites and make observations as planned for the larger study. The focus is again on problems that might force modifications in research plans. Any problems that surface during the pilot study can then be dealt with before the main project is launched.

Given all the pitfalls that a project might encounter, it is quite possible that at some point you may conclude that the project is not feasible as planned. Before throwing up your hands and calling it quits, however, you should give careful consideration to possible modifications in the project that would enhance its feasibility. If inadequate time or money is the problem, perhaps the project can be scaled down. It might be possible to reduce the sample size or reduce the number of hypotheses tested to make the project manageable. If interviewing were originally planned, consider a mailed questionnaire or even a telephone survey as cost-cutting and time-reducing measures. If the problem is with procedures, such as may occur in an experiment, consider how they might be changed so that the project can proceed. For example, in an experiment conducted by one of the authors and two associates, a problem surfaced concerning a negative reaction to one of our experimental procedures (Norland et al., 1976). The reaction was so severe among some participants that for a while it appeared we would have to give up the project on ethical grounds. After considerable thought and some trial and error, however, it was found that the negative reactions could be eliminated by more thorough debriefing of the subjects after they had participated in the experiment. The point is that a project should not be abandoned until all efforts to make it feasible have been investigated.

Main Points

▪ Suitable topics for research may be obtained from a variety of sources, including personal interest, social problems, theory testing, prior research, program evaluation, and human service practice.

▪ Problem selection is also influenced by political factors, which means that powerful interest groups encourage the expenditure of research resources on issues that are of interest to them and that may not serve the interests of less-advantaged and minority groups.

▪ After a general topic for research is selected, it must be narrowed and focused into a precise, researchable problem.

▪ An important part of refining a research problem is conceptual development: identifying and defining the concepts that will be the focus of the study.

▪ Reviewing previous research related to the selected topic is a crucial step in problem development and preparing to conduct a research project.

▪ The nature of the research problem should dictate the choice of the specific research technique employed; do not attempt to make the problem fit a particular method of data gathering.

▪ The units of analysis must be clearly specified and may be either individuals, groups, organizations, programs, or social artifacts.

▪ Continual awareness of the operative unit of analysis is necessary to avoid errors such as the ecological fallacy: inferring something about individuals from data collected about groups.

▪ Reactivity refers to the fact that people may behave differently when being observed than when they are not being watched, and the effects of reactivity must be considered when shaping a research problem.

▪ Qualitative research is a research method that emphasizes the description of how the world is experienced by people; it relies on data in the form of words, pictures, descriptions, and narratives. Quantitative research uses numbers, counts, and measures to assess statistical relationships between variables.

▪ Cross-sectional research is based on data collected at one point in time, making accurate conclusions about trends or behavioral changes difficult. Longitudinal studies are based on data collected over a period of time and are particularly useful for studying trends or behavioral changes.

▪ Once a proposed research problem is fully refined, the practical feasibility of the project should be realistically assessed.

▪ Data analysis, including how to prepare a data set for computer analysis, must be considered when shaping a research problem in order to ensure that appropriate data are available to answer all research questions.

Important Terms for Review

cross-sectional research
ecological fallacy
longitudinal research
panel study
qualitative research
quantitative research
reactivity
trend study
units of analysis

Exploring the Internet

The Internet can be a valuable resource throughout the problem formulation process, from selecting a problem through shaping and refining the problem to ascertaining the feasibility of the project. When selecting a problem based on personal interest, a social problem, or testing a theory, it can be worthwhile to begin by using some of the search engines on the Web to locate information on that general topic. For example, if you were interested in conducting research on such topics as self-esteem, drug use, or depression, you could use such search engines as Magellan, Infoseek, Excite, Lycos, or Yahoo to locate a wide array of sites devoted to those topics. An initial perusal of such sites can help identify important issues for developing the research problem, such as: How is the concept defined? Does there appear to be consensus on what the concept is? What controversies or issues are being debated about the topic? Exploring such questions can help you focus on potentially interesting research problems. You may also find organizations and resources that may be useful in later steps in the research process, such as measurement tools. Select a topic that you think might be interesting to research and explore some of the Web sites that the search engine locates.

The Internet can prove extremely useful in discovering prior research. Many Web sites consist of bibliographies or include bibliographies as a special section. One example is the National Criminal Justice Reference Service. Access this site at http://www.ncjrs.org/homepage.htm and select "victims" from the home page. This will lead to a diverse listing of sources on victims of crime. Select one of the victim categories, such as "domestic violence," and peruse some of the available sources. Note that Web sites such as this also contain links to other sites that may be specifically devoted to your topic of interest. For example, the domestic violence page includes a link to the Minnesota Higher Education Center Against Violence and Abuse (http://www.umn.edu/mincava/arts.htm). Here you will find several current scholarly papers and guides to other sources. Other sites provide searchable databases. For example, the National Clearinghouse for Alcohol and Drug Information (http://www.health.org/dbases.htm) provides immediate access to a wealth of articles related to substance abuse. Try out this site by entering a combination of terms such as "alcohol" and "violence." By beginning with a basic search engine, such as Lycos, and using a general term, such as "crime," "health," or "education," you can locate a major center or clearinghouse for that topic as illustrated for domestic violence and alcohol. These sites will then lead you to the specific articles and bibliographies.

For those seeking to develop research questions around program evaluation, the Internet can be an excellent source. Sites associated with organizations that sponsor program evaluations often include descriptions of previous evaluations, projects that are currently under way, and information on future funding opportunities. As an example, explore "Research and Evaluation" from the Justice Information Center home page (http://www.ncjrs.org/homepage.htm).

We noted that human service practice itself serves as the stimulus for many research projects. Internet sites devoted to human service professions can help you identify a wide range of practice issues in need of scientific study. For an illustration, check out the Social Worker Networker site at http://pobox.com/~social.worker.networker. One of the options available at this site is "Professional Resources" and then "Treatment Modalities." Select these options and review some of the sources included there. Can you identify some practice-related research questions related to the issues presented in these sources?

For Further Reading

Berg, Bruce L. *Qualitative Research Methods for the Social Sciences.* 2nd ed. Boston: Allyn & Bacon, 1995. Although this book focuses primarily on how to conduct good qualitative research, it also contains a good comparison of qualitative and quantitative research and assesses when each is the most appropriate design.

Bransford, John D., and Barry S. Stein. *The Ideal Problem Solver: A Guide for Improving Thinking, Learning, and Creativity,* 2nd ed. New York: Freeman, 1995. Sound thinking combined with creativity are clearly important to formulating research problems. This guide assists you in improving thought processes, drawing logical deductions, enhancing creativity, and even improving your communication skills.

Gross, Ronald. *The Independent Scholar's Handbook.* Berkeley, Calif.: Ten Speed Press, 1993. This book contains many examples of how successful scholars developed personal hunches and notions into serious research inquiries. It is also filled with practical advice about such things as obtaining resources and communicating with other researchers who share similar research interests.

Higgins, P. C., and J. M. Johnson. *Personal Sociology.* New York: Praeger, 1988. This book includes many illustrations of how personal life events and experiences shaped the research interests of a variety of sociologists.

Hunt, Morton. *Profiles of Social Research: The Scientific Study of Human Interactions.* New York: Basic Books, 1985. As its title implies, this book presents a series of descriptions of major research projects. Follow these projects from inception to completion and see successful social scientists at work.

Journals in the Human Services. An excellent source for research ideas and for well-formulated research problems is the many journals that publish research relevant to the human services. Numerous journals are listed in Appendix A of this book.

Menard, Scott. *Longitudinal Research.* Newbury Park, Calif.: Sage, 1991. This book provides a readable overview of both longitudinal and cross-sectional research. It discusses when each is an appropriate design and some of the problems confronted in doing good longitudinal research.

Reinharz, Shulamit. *Feminist Methods in Social Research.* New York: Oxford University Press, 1992. This book is a massive compilation of examples of all types of research conducted by researchers identified as feminists. Anyone interested in conducting research from this perspective is well advised to consult this impressive work.

Exercises for Class Discussion

In working through the exercises in this chapter, we suggest that you review Appendix A, which covers the basic issues involved in conducting research in the library. We have also found it helpful for students in our research classes to schedule a 1- or 2-hour workshop with the reference personnel in the library. This helps familiarize students with the materials available in their library, especially human service resource material.

4.1 Following are several broad topic areas that are relevant to the human services. Select one that has the greatest personal appeal to you. Identify why this topic interests you. How do your selection and the reasons for it compare with those of other students?

a. child abuse

b. nursing home care of the elderly

c. emotionally disturbed children

d. victims of crime

e. violence in the family

f. alcoholism

g. discrimination against minorities

h. adaptation to stress

i. community living for the developmentally disabled

j. effects of unemployment

4.2 Use your library resources to locate at least five research studies published in the professional literature on the topic you selected. Your search efforts should include, but need not be limited to, the following: *Social Science Index, Social Work Abstracts, Monthly Catalog of Government Publications,* and the library public catalog. Be prepared to discuss with the class how you located your studies.

4.3 For each research study you locate, do the following:

a. Indicate which factors seemed to influence the selection of topic in this study (that is, personal interest, social problems, theory testing, program evaluation, prior research, or practice experience).

b. What was the unit of analysis for each study? Was it the same as, or different from, the source of the data? If different, indicate the source. Can you think of any reasons for selecting a different unit of analysis?

c. What was the *specific* problem that the study addressed? From the presentation of the study, what factors influenced the final, actual problem formulation? In particular, were there issues of cost, time, or feasibility that necessitated a modification of the problem from what was initially proposed?

d. Chapter 3 presented a discussion of ethical issues in research. What ethical issues confronted the researchers in studying each problem? Did a concern for ethics impact on what specific research problem emerged from an interest in studying the general topic?

4.4 We have made the point that problem selection in research is a social process in which power, interest groups, and other factors play significant roles. One practice issue that has received considerable attention in recent years is the placement of minority children, especially Native American children, in white foster and adoptive homes.

a. Have one group of students imagine that they are members of an adoptive/foster parent association that has been asked to provide suggestions to the Department of Health and Human Services for research priorities. What research problems would this group want to have studied?

b. Have a second group of students imagine that they are tribal leaders representing Native Amer-ican interests. What priorities would they have and what questions might this group suggest? Contrast the problems suggested by each group.

CHAPTER 5

The Process of Measurement

Ways of Measuring   100

Levels of Measurement   101
  Nominal Measures   102
  Ordinal Measures   104
  Interval Measures   104
  Ratio Measures   105
  Discrete Versus Continuous Variables   106

Evaluating Measures   107
  Validity   107
  Reliability   111
  Measurement With Minority Populations   114

Errors in Measurement   115
  Random Errors   115
  Systematic Errors   116

Main Points   117

Important Terms for Review   120

Exploring the Internet   120

For Further Reading   121

Exercises for Class Discussion   121

A crisis counselor working with a mental health agency receives a call from the county jail. The deputy there is concerned about an inmate whom he describes as severely depressed. The counselor responds by asking a number of questions such as the following: Has the inmate been eating his meals? Is he sleeping too much or too little? Is his affect flat when he responds to questions? Has he made any remarks about committing suicide? By asking these questions, the counselor is attempting to make an initial assessment of the severity of the inmate's depression. Later, the counselor may interview the inmate directly, request psychological testing, or refer him to a psychiatrist for further evaluation. Assessments such as these are analogous to a process in research called *measurement*. Just as the clinician just mentioned used a variety of observations by the deputy as indicators of the inmate's condition, so researchers use various observations as indicators of the concepts of interest in a research project. **Measurement** refers to the process of describing abstract concepts in terms or specific indicators by the assignment of numbers or other symbols to these indicants in accordance with rules. At the very minimum, we must have some means of determining whether a variable is either present or absent, just as the counselor needs to know whether or not the inmate is eating. In many cases,

however, measurement is more complex and involves assessing how much or to what degree a variable is present. This is illustrated by the counselor's asking how much the inmate is sleeping, "amount of sleep" being a variable that can take on many values.

Measurement is a part of the process of moving from the abstract or theoretical level to the concrete. Recall from Chapter 2 that scientific concepts have two types of definitions—nominal and operational. Before research can proceed, nominal definitions have to be translated into operational ones. The operational definitions indicate the exact procedures, or operations, that will be used to measure the concepts. Measurement is essentially the process of operationalizing concepts. Figure 5.1 illustrates the place of measurement in the research process. Measurement will be a topic of interest throughout this book.

In this chapter, we discuss the general issues that relate to all measurement, beginning with some of the different ways in which measurements can be made. We then analyze how measurements can be made at different levels, and examine their effects on the mathematical operations that can be performed on them. Finally, we present ways of evaluating measures and determining the errors that can occur in the measurement process.

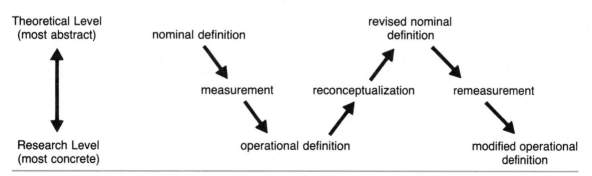

Figure 5.1 The Measurement Process

Ways of Measuring

The concepts and variables that are the focus of both research and practice cannot normally be directly observed. Such things as poverty, social class, mental retardation, and the like cannot be seen but only inferred from something else. Take something as seemingly obvious as child abuse. Can you directly observe child abuse? Not really. What you directly observe is a bruise on a child's back, an infant's broken leg, or a father slapping his daughter. Even the slap may not relate to child abuse because parents sometimes slap their children without its being a case of child abuse. However, all these things—the bruise, the broken leg, the slap—may be used as *indicators* of child abuse. In research and in practice, an **indicator** is an observation that is assumed to be evidence of the attributes or properties of some phenomenon. What we observe are the indicators of a variable, not the actual properties of the variable itself. Emergency room personnel may take a child's broken leg as an indicator of child abuse even though they have not observed the actual abuse.

Child abuse represents a good illustration of the difficulties of moving from nominal to operational definitions with variables involving social and psychological events. At the nominal level, we might define child abuse as an occurrence in which a parent or caretaker injures a child, not by accident but in anger or with deliberate intent (Gelles, 1987; Korbin, 1987). But what indicators would we use to operationalize this definition? Some things would obviously seem to indicate child abuse, such as a cigarette burn on a child's buttock. What about a bruise on the arm? There are subcultures in our own society that view hitting children, even to the point of bruising, as an appropriate way to train or discipline a child. Furthermore, some people would argue that a serious psychological disorder suffered by a child is an indicator of child abuse because it shows the parents did not provide the proper love and affection for stable development. In short, one of the problems in operationalizing child abuse, as is true with many other variables in human service research, is that its definition is culture-bound and

involves subjective judgments. This illustrates the importance of good conceptual development and precise nominal definitions for research. It also shows how the theoretical and research levels can mutually influence one another: As nominal definitions are shaped into operational ones, difficulties that arise often lead to a reconceptualization, or change in the nominal definition at the theoretical level (*see* Figure 5.1). Research in Practice 5.1 describes a research project in the human services that involved some fairly complex measurement problems and shows how theoretical considerations can play a substantial role in operationalizing concepts.

The example of child abuse also illustrates another point, namely, that there can be more than one indicator of a variable. The term **item** is used to refer to a single indicator of a variable. Items can take numerous forms, such as an answer to a question or an observation of some behavior or characteristic. Asking a person her age or noting her sex, for example, would both produce "items" of measurement. In many cases, however, operationalizing variables involves combining a number of items into a composite score called an **index** or **scale.** (Although scales involve more rigor in their construction than do indexes, for our purposes we can use the terms interchangeably.) Attitude scales, for example, commonly involve asking people a series of questions, or items, and then summarizing their responses into a single score that represents their attitude on an issue. A major reason for using scales or indexes rather than single items is that they enable us to measure variables in a more precise and usually more accurate fashion. To illustrate the value of scales over items, consider your grade in this course. In all likelihood, your final grade will be an index, or composite score, of your answers to many questions on many tests throughout the semester. Would you prefer that your final grade be determined by a one-item measure? Probably not, because it would not measure the full range of what you learned in the course. Furthermore, an error on that question would indicate that you had not learned much in the course even if the error were due to ill health or personal problems on the day of the exam. For these reasons, then, multiple-item measures are usually preferred to single-item indicators. In this chapter, we discuss general issues related to measurement, and then in Chapter 13 we return to the issue of constructing indexes and scales.

We began this discussion by noting that variables are abstract and cannot normally be directly observed. Actually, variables differ in their degree of abstraction, and this affects the ease with which we can accomplish measurement. In general, the more abstract the variable, the more difficult it is to measure. For example, a study of child abuse might include the variable "number of children in family," on the theoretical presumption that large families create more stress for parents and are, therefore, more likely to precipitate abusive attacks on children. This is a rather easy variable to measure because the concepts "children" and "family" have readily identifiable empirical referents, and they are relatively easy and unambiguous to observe and count. Suppose, however, that the child abuse study also included as a dependent variable "positiveness of a child's self-concept." "Self-concept" is a difficult notion to measure because it can take many different forms. Although we have narrowed it to the "positive–negative" dimension, it is still more difficult to measure than "number of children in family" because a whole variety of questions could be asked to explore how positively people feel about themselves. Self-concept can also be measured by behaviors on the theoretical presumption that people who feel positively about themselves behave differently from those who do not. The point is that with highly abstract concepts there is usually no single empirical indicator that is clearly and obviously preferable to others as a measure of the concept.

We have emphasized the point that measurement involves the transition from the abstract conceptual level to the concrete and observable, and this is what most typically occurs in research. However, exploratory studies can involve measurement in the opposite direction: First, we observe empirical indicators and then formulate theoretical concepts that those indicators presumably represent. In

Chapter 2, we called this "inductive reasoning." In a sense, you might think of Sigmund Freud or Jean Piaget as having done this when they developed their theories of personality and cognitive development, respectively. Piaget, for example, observed the behavior of children for many years as he gradually developed his theory of the stages of cognitive development, including concepts like egocentrism, object permanence, and reversibility (Ginsburg and Opper, 1988). Piaget recognized that what he observed could be understood only if placed in a more abstract theoretical context. In a sense, he had measured something before he knew what it was he had measured. Once his theories began to develop, he then tested them deductively by developing new concepts and hypotheses and formulating different measuring devices. The point is that whether one shifts from the abstract to the concrete, or vice versa, the logic is the same, involving the relationship between theoretical concepts and empirical indicators.

A major problem in most measurement has to do with which indicators are to be used in a particular research project. This depends in part, of course, on theoretical concerns, but there are other matters to be considered. One such matter has to do with whether a particular measure permits one to perform mathematical operations on it, and we turn to this issue next.

Levels of Measurement

We have seen that there are numerous ways of measuring phenomena, such as by asking questions or noting observations. Measures also differ from one another in terms of what is called their **level of measurement,** or the rules that define permissible mathematical operations that can be performed on a set of numbers produced by a measure. There are four levels of measurement: nominal, ordinal, interval, and ratio. If we keep in mind that variables are things that can take on different values, measurement basically involves assessing the value, or category into which a particular entity falls. Measuring age, for example, is the

Research in Practice 5.1
Behavior and Social Environment: Problems of Measurement in Spouse Abuse Research

A major problem today—and one that calls for the skilled intervention of human service professionals—is spouse abuse. And recent studies of spouse abuse illustrate some of the problems of measurement in social research. One study hypothesized that *status inconsistency* and *status incompatibility* might increase the risk of spouse abuse for a couple (Hornung, McCullough, and Sugimoto, 1981). Thus, the hypotheses to be tested in this research contained at least three highly abstract concepts: status inconsistency, status incompatibility, and spouse abuse. First, it was necessary to define the concept of "spouse." Even though its definition would seem obvious, men and women today often live together without being married, and these women are also at risk of being abused by their partners. In order to focus the study on all women who might be battered by their intimates, the researchers wanted to include these cohabiting couples. So the data were collected in interviews with women, and women were considered eligible for the study if they were at least 18 years old and were either married at the time of the interview or had lived with a male partner within the preceding 12 months.

Next, the investigators needed measures of their independent variables, status inconsistency and status incompatibility. Status inconsistency refers to possessing status characteristics that are not consistent with one another, as when a highly educated person has a low-status occupation. To operationalize this concept, the investigators compared people in terms of occupation and educa-

tion. The U.S. Census Bureau makes available an occupational index that can be used to measure a person's occupational status. Educational status was measured by asking people how many years of school they had completed. However, what the researchers were really interested in was the *consistency* of these two statuses for each person in their study. When was a person's education "inconsistent" with his or her occupation? For guidance in measuring consistency, the researchers relied on a theoretical assumption, namely, that *most* people have levels of education that are consistent with the job they hold. People were divided into occupational groups of roughly equal status, using the Census Bureau's index. Within each occupational category, people were ranked according to their level of education. Then the middle 70 percent of the people in each occupational category were assumed to have educations consistent with their job. The 15 percent with the lowest levels of education in each occupational category were defined as status inconsistent-low in terms of education, the 15 percent with the highest levels of education as status inconsistent-high.

This operational definition of status inconsistency, only one of several used in this study, illustrates the complexity that can be involved in measuring social variables. It also illustrates how operational definitions are influenced by theoretical considerations, such as the assumption that most people will have consistent status characteristics. Status incompatibility was measured in much the same way although now it involved comparing

process of placing each person into a particular age category.

Nominal Measures

Nominal measures classify observations into mutually exclusive categories. They represent

nominal variables at the theoretical level. Variables such as sex, ethnicity, religion, or political party preference are examples. Thus, we might classify people according to their religious affiliation by placing them into one of five categories: Protestant, Catholic, Jewish, other, or no religious affiliation. These are mutually exclusive categories

the status characteristics of the husband with those of the wife. Again, the theoretical assumption that guided this measurement process was that *atypical* combinations of husband's and wife's status characteristics would be perceived and experienced as incompatible and thus stressful. Consistency in this regard does not mean that husband and wife have the same status, only that the status differences between them be typical and commonly found.

Next, the researchers turned their attention to the problem of measuring spouse abuse, and they followed one of the principles we describe in this chapter: They borrowed and modified a measurement device that another researcher had used successfully and had already tested. Murray Straus had developed the Conflict Tactics (CT) scale (Straus and Gelles, 1990). This instrument includes items that measure different types of abuse: psychological abuse (e.g., "Did or said something to spite the other person"); violent aggression (e.g., "Pushed, grabbed, or shoved the other one"); and severely violent aggression (e.g., "Beat up the other one"). With people's responses to these items, the researchers could compare levels of abuse among couples at varying levels of status inconsistency and status incompatibility. They found that both were associated with increased risk of spouse abuse, both psychological and physical. Some types of inconsistency had a greater impact. A couple with a husband who was underachieving, in terms of his occupation, was, for example, at very high risk of abuse. An overachieving husband, on the other hand, seemed to buffer the couple against abuse.

Although the CT scale was a valid way to measure spouse abuse for Hornung et al., it has been criticized on a number of grounds: It measures only conflict-related violence, it measures a limited set of violent acts, it equates acts that differ greatly in severity, it ignores the context in which the violence occurs, and it ignores who initiates the violence. Because of these weaknesses, the CT scale can be misleading when used for some types of research, especially comparisons of the levels of abuse perpetrated by women as opposed to men. A number of investigations using the CT scale have reported that women abuse men about as much as, and maybe more than, men abuse women (McNeely and Robinson-Simpson, 1987). The problem, however, is that the CT scale measures *actions,* such as hitting or shoving, but it ignores *motivations* and *effects* (Saunders, 1988). Women may hit men as much as men hit women, but the women's actions are more likely to be self-defensive rather than aggressive. They hit in order to ward off the assaults of men. In terms of effects, men's attacks are far more serious and injurious, largely due to their greater physical size and strength. Taking motivations and effects into account in measuring spouse abuse, one researcher and therapist concluded that "husband assault is not a major social problem because few males are injured by female violence. Wife assault, on the other hand, does produce serious injuries and physical risk" (Dutton, 1995, p. 45). Despite these criticisms, the Conflict Tactics scale is probably the most widely used measure of intrafamily violence. In fact, the CT scale has been revised recently to address, among other things, the criticism related to degree of injury; this revision is discussed in more detail in Research in Practice 7.1.

This discussion illustrates some of the complex considerations that need to be taken into account in finding appropriate measures for social and psychological variables.

because membership in one precludes membership in another. For purposes of data analysis, we might assign numbers to represent each of the categories. We could label Protestant as 1, Catholic as 2, Jewish as 3, other as 4, and none as 5. It is important to recognize, however, that the assignment of numbers is purely arbitrary; the numbers comprising a nominal measure have none of the properties, such as ranking, ordering, and magnitude, that we usually associate with numbers. None of the usual arithmetic operations, such as adding, subtracting, multiplying, or dividing, can legitimately be performed on numbers comprising a nominal scale. The reason for this is that the numbers in a nominal scale are merely symbols or labels used to identify a category of the nominal variable. Protestant could have been labeled as 2 as easily as 1.

Ordinal Measures

When variables can be conceptualized as having an inherent order at the theoretical level, we have an ordinal variable and, when operationalized, an **ordinal measure.** Ordinal measures are considered of a higher level than nominal because, in addition to being mutually exclusive, the categories have a fixed order. Socioeconomic status, for example, constitutes an ordinal variable, and measures of socioeconomic status are ordinal scales. Table 5.1 illustrates how socioeconomic status might be divided into ordinal categories. With ordinal measurement, we can speak of a given category as ranking higher or lower than some other category; lower-upper class, for example, is higher than middle class but not as high as upper-upper class. It is important to recognize that ordinal measurement does not assume that the categories are equally spaced. For example, the distance between lower-upper and upper-upper is not necessarily the same as between lower-middle and middle even though in both cases the classes are one rank apart. This lack of equal spacing means that the numbers assigned to ordinal categories do not have the numerical properties necessary for arithmetic operations. Like nominal scales, ordinal scales cannot be

Table 5.1   Ordinal Ranking of Socioeconomic Status

Category	Rank
Upper-upper	7
Lower-upper	6
Upper-middle	5
Middle	4
Lower-middle	3
Upper-lower	2
Lower-lower	1

added, subtracted, multiplied, or divided. The only characteristic they have that nominal scales do not is the fixed order of the categories.

Interval Measures

The next highest level of measurement is called *interval.* **Interval measures** share the characteristics of ordinal scales—mutually exclusive categories and an inherent order—but also have equal spacing between the categories. Equal spacing comes about because some specific unit of measurement, such as the degrees of a temperature scale, is a part of the measure. Each of these units is considered to have a certain value, making for the equal spacing characteristic of an interval scale. We would have an interval scale if the difference between, say, scores of 30 and 40 was the same as the difference between scores of 70 and 80. A 10-point difference is a 10-point difference regardless of where on the scale it occurs.

The common temperature scales, Fahrenheit and Celsius, are true interval scales. Both of these temperature scales have, as units of measurement, degrees and the equal spacing characteristic of interval scales. A difference of 10 degrees is always the same, no matter where it occurs on the scale. These temperature scales illustrate another characteristic of true interval scales: The point on the scale labeled zero is arbitrarily selected. Neither 0°C nor 0°F is absolute zero, the complete absence of heat. Because the zero point is arbitrary in true interval scales, we cannot make statements concerning ratios. That is, we cannot say that a given score is twice or three times as high as some other score. For example, a temperature of 80°F is not twice as hot as a temperature of 40°F. Despite not having this ratio characteristic, interval scales have numbers with all the other arithmetic properties. If we have achieved interval level measurement, we can legitimately perform all the common arithmetic operations on the numbers.

Considerable controversy exists over which measures used in behavioral science research are true interval measures, with only a few measures clearly of interval level. One, for example, that is relevant to the human services is intelligence, as measured by IQ tests. With IQ tests, there are specific units of measurement—points on the IQ scale—and each point on the scale is mutually exclusive. Furthermore, the distance between IQs of 80 and 90 is equivalent to the distance between IQs of 110 and 120. However, there is no absolute zero point on an IQ scale, so we cannot say that a person with an IQ of 150 is twice as intelligent as a person with an IQ of 75. As with temperature scales, the IQ scale is in part an arbitrary construction that allows us to make some comparisons but not others. Beyond a few measures such as intelligence, however, the debate ensues. Some researchers would argue, for example, that attitude scales can be treated as interval scales (Kenny, 1986). The questions that make up attitude scales commonly involve choosing one of five responses: strongly agree, agree, uncertain, disagree, or strongly disagree. The argument is that people see the difference between "strongly agree" and "agree" as roughly equivalent to the distance between "disagree" and "strongly disagree." This perceived equidistance, some argue, makes it possible to treat these scales as interval level. Other researchers would argue that there is no logical or empirical reason to assume that such perceived equidistance exists and, therefore, that attitude scales should always be considered ordinal measures rather than interval measures.

We will not presume to settle this debate here. Rather, we raise the issue because level of measurement influences which statistical procedures can be used at the data analysis stage of research. This matter is discussed in Chapters 14 and 15. You should be sensitive to the issue of levels of measurement when utilizing research. The results of research in which a statistical procedure inappropriate for a given level of measurement has been used should be viewed with caution.

Ratio Measures

The highest level of measurement is *ratio*. **Ratio measures** have all the characteristics of interval measures, but the zero point is absolute and mean-

ingful rather than arbitrary. As the name implies, with ratio measures we can make statements to the effect that some score is a given ratio of another score. For example, one ratio variable with which human service workers are likely to deal is income. With income, we have the dollar as the unit of measurement. Also, as many are all too well aware, there is such a thing as no income at all, so the zero point is absolute. Because it is absolute, it is perfectly legitimate to make the kinds of statements about income that are commonly made: An income of $20,000 is twice as much as $10,000, but only one third as much as $60,000. (Recognize, of course, that income is a ratio measure only as an indicator of the *amount* of money available to a person; if income is used as a measure of a person's *social status*, for example, then a difference between $110,000 and $120,000 does not necessarily represent a shift in status equivalent to that between $10,000 and $20,000.) Given that ratio scales have all the characteristics of interval scales, we can, of course, perform all arithmetic operations on them.

The characteristics of the four levels of measurement are summarized in Table 5.2. Keep in mind that, although researchers have no control over the nature of a variable, they do have some control over how they will define variables, at both the nominal and operational levels, and this affects the level of measurement. It is sometimes possible to change the level of measurement of a variable by redefining it at the nominal or operational level. This is important because researchers generally strive for the highest level of measurement possible. They do this because higher levels of measurement generally enable us to measure variables more precisely and use more powerful statistical procedures (*see* Chapters 14 and 15). It is also desirable to measure at the highest possible level of measurement because it gives the researcher the most options: The level of measurement can be reduced during the data analysis, but it cannot be increased. Thus, choosing a level of measurement that is too low introduces a permanent limitation into the data analysis.

It is important to recognize, however, that the primary determinant of the level of measurement is

Table 5.2   The Characteristics of the Four Levels of Measurement

Level of Measurement	Characteristics of Categories			
	Mutually Exclusive	**Possesses a Fixed Order**	**Equal Spacing Between Ranks**[a]	**A True Zero Point**[a, b]
Nominal	y			
Ordinal	y	y		
Interval	y	y	y	
Ratio	y	y	y	y

y = possesses that characteristic
[a]Permits standard mathematical operations of addition, subtraction, multiplication, and division.
[b]Permits statements about proportions and ratios.

the nature of the variable being measured. The major concern is to have an accurate measure of a variable (a topic discussed at length in the next section). Religious affiliation, for example, is a nominal variable because that is the nature of the theoretical concept "religious affiliation." There is no way to treat religious affiliation as anything other than merely nominal classification. It is sometimes possible, however, by changing the theoretical variable somewhat, to open up higher levels of measurement. If, instead of religious *affiliation,* we were to measure *religiosity,* or the strength of religious beliefs, we would have a variable that could be conceptualized and measured as ordinal and perhaps even interval. People could easily be ranked, on the basis of certain responses, into ordered categories of greater or lesser religiosity. It should be clear from this example that the theoretical nature of the variable plays a large part in determining the level of measurement. This illustrates once again the constant interplay between theoretical and research levels (*see* Figure 5.1). The decision regarding level of measurement at the research level might affect the conceptualization of variables at the theoretical level.

It should be noted, finally, that there is nothing inherently undesirable about nominal variables. It would be quite wrong to get the impression that variables capable of being measured at higher levels are always better than nominal variables. The first consideration should be to select variables on theo-

retical grounds and not on the basis of their possible level of measurement. Thus, if a research study is really concerned with religious affiliation and not religiosity, the nominal measure is the correct one to use, and not a measure of religiosity even though it is ordinal or possibly interval. On the other hand, researchers do strive for more accurate and powerful measurement. Other things being equal, a researcher having two measures available, one ordinal and the other interval, would generally prefer the interval measure.

Discrete Versus Continuous Variables

In addition to considering the level of measurement of a variable, researchers also distinguish between variables that are *discrete* or *continuous*. **Discrete variables** are variables with a finite number of distinct and separate values. A perusal of a typical client fact sheet from a human service agency will reveal many examples of discrete variables, such as sex, race, household size, number of days absent, or number of arrests. Household size is a discrete variable because households can be measured only in a discrete set of units, such as having one member, two members, and so on. No meaningful measurement values lie between these distinct and separate values. **Continuous variables** are variables that, at least theoretically, can take on an infinite number of values. Age is a continuous variable because it can be measured by an infinite array of values. We normally measure age in terms of years, but theoretically we could measure it in terms of months, weeks, days, minutes, seconds, or even nanoseconds! There is no theoretical limit to how precise the measurement of age might be. For most social science purposes, the measurement of age in terms of years is quite satisfactory, but age is nonetheless a continuous variable.

Nominal variables are, by definition, discrete in that they consist of mutually exclusive or discrete categories. Ordinal variables are also discrete. The mutually exclusive categories of an ordinal variable may be ranked from low to high, but there cannot be a partial rank. For example, in a study of the military, rank might be ordered 1 = private, 2 = corporal, and so on, but it would be nonsensical to speak of a rank of 1.3. In some cases, interval and ratio variables may be discrete. For example, family size or number of arrests can only be whole numbers, or discrete intervals. (We can summarize discrete interval and ratio data by saying, for example, that the average family size is 1.8 people, but this is a summary statistic, not a measurement of a particular household.) Many variables at the interval and ratio level are continuous, at least at the theoretical level. A researcher may settle for discrete indicators because the study does not demand greater precision or because there are no existing tools that can measure the continuous variable with sufficient reliability. In some cases, there is debate among researchers over whether a particular variable is discrete or continuous in nature. For example, we used social class as an illustration of an ordinal variable, suggesting that there are several distinct classes. Others argue that social class is inherently a continuous interval variable and that we only treat it as ordinal because of the lack of instruments that would permit researchers to reliably measure it as a true continuous, interval variable (Borgatta and Bohrnstedt, 1981).

It is important to recognize that a variable is continuous or discrete by its very nature and the researcher cannot change that. It is possible to measure a continuous variable by specifying a number of discrete categories, as is typically done with age, but this does not change the nature of the variable itself. Whether variables are discrete or continuous may influence how they are used in data analysis. For example, in setting up categories for a frequency distribution on household size, which is a discrete variable, intervals of 1, 2, 3, and so on would be used instead of .4–1.7, 1.8–2.3, or 2.4–3.8. Sometimes discrete data are treated as continuous in order to use statistical models, but care must be taken to assure that the results will be meaningful. Knowing the level of measurement and whether variables are discrete or continuous has implications for selecting the best procedures for analyzing the data.

Evaluating Measures

We have seen that there are normally a number of indicators, sometimes a large number and at different levels of measurement, that can be used to measure a variable. How do we choose the best of these measures to use in a particular study? A number of factors come into play in making this decision, including matters of feasibility discussed in Chapter 4. Here we want to discuss two additional and very important considerations in this regard: the validity and reliability of measures.

Validity

Validity refers to the accuracy of a measure: Does it accurately measure the variable that it is intended to measure? If we were developing a measure of self-concept, a major concern would be whether our measuring device measures the concept as it is theoretically defined. There must be a fairly clear and logical relationship between the way a variable is nominally defined and the way it is operationalized. For example, if we propose to measure self-concept on the basis of how stylishly people dress, we would probably have an invalid measure. Many factors influence the way people are dressed at any given time. The slight possibility that one of these factors might have something to do with self-concept would not be sufficient to make the suggested measure valid. The validity of measures is very difficult to demonstrate with any finality. However, several approaches to the question of validity exist, and they can offer evidence regarding the validity of a measure.

Face validity involves assessing whether a logical relationship exists between the variable and the proposed measure. It essentially amounts to a rather commonsense comparison of what comprises the measure and the theoretical definition of the variable: Does it seem logical to use this measure to reflect that variable? We might measure child abuse in terms of the reports made by physicians or emergency room personnel of injuries suffered by children. Although this is not a perfect measure because health personnel might be wrong, it does seem logical that an injury reported by such people might reflect actual abuse.

No matter how carefully done, face validity clearly is subjective in nature. All we have is logic and common sense as arguments for the validity of a measure. This serves to make face validity the weakest demonstration of validity, and it should usually be considered no more than a starting point. All measures must pass the test of face validity. If they do, we should attempt one of the more stringent methods of assessing validity.

An extension of face validity is called **content validity** or **sampling validity.** It has to do with whether a measuring device covers the full range of meanings or forms that would be included in a variable that is being measured. In other words, a valid measuring device would provide an adequate, or representative, *sample* of all *content,* or elements, or instances of the phenomenon being measured. For example, if one were measuring general self-esteem, it would be important to recognize that self-esteem can relate to many realms of people's lives, such as at work, at school, or in the family. Self-esteem might get expressed or come into play in all those settings. A valid measure of self-esteem would take that variability into account. If a measure of self-esteem consisted of a series of statements to which people expressed degrees of agreement, then a valid measure would include statements that relate to those many settings in which self-esteem might be expressed. If all the statements in the measuring device had to do, say, with school, then it would be a less valid measure of general self-esteem.

Content validity is a more extensive assessment of validity than is face validity because it involves a detailed analysis of the breadth of the concept being measured and how it relates to the measuring device. Content validity involves two distinct steps: (1) determining the full range or domain of the content of a variable, and (2) determining whether all those domains are represented among the items that constitute the measuring device. It is still a somewhat subjective assessment, however, in that someone has to judge what the full domain of the variable is and whether a particular aspect of a concept has been adequately represented in the measuring device. There are no agreed-upon criteria that can be applied to determine whether a measure has content validity. It is ultimately a judgment, albeit a more carefully considered judgment than with face validity.

One way to strengthen confidence in face or content validity is to gather the opinions of other investigators, especially those knowledgeable about the variables involved, regarding whether particular operational definitions seem to be logical measures of the variables. This extension of face or content validity, sometimes referred to as *jury opinion,* is still subjective, of course. However, because there are more people to serve as a check on bias or misinterpretation, jury opinion is superior to using individual tests of face or content validity.

Criterion validity refers to establishing validity by showing a correlation between a measurement device and some other criterion or standard that we know or believe accurately measures the variable under consideration. Or we might correlate the results of the measuring device with some properties or characteristics of the variable the measuring device is intended to measure. For example, a scale intended to measure risk of suicide should correlate with the occurrence of self-destructive behavior if it is to be considered valid. The key to criterion validity is to find a criterion variable against which to compare the results of our measuring device.

Criterion validity moves away from the subjective assessments of face validity and provides more objective evidence of validity. One type of criterion validity is **concurrent validity,** in which the instrument being evaluated is compared to some already existing criterion, such as the results of another measuring device. (Presumably, any other measuring devices used in this assessment have already been tested for validity.) Lawrence Shulman (1978), for example, used a form of concurrent validity to test an instrument intended to measure the practice skills of human service practitioners. The instrument consisted of questions on a questionnaire, in which clients rated the skills of practitioners. Shulman reasoned that more skilled practitioners would be viewed as more helpful by clients and would have more satisfied clients. Thus, he looked for correlations between how positively clients rated a practitioner's skills and the perceived helpfulness of practitioners or satisfaction of clients. These correlations offered evidence for the validity of the measure of practitioners' skills.

Numerous existing measures can be used to establish the concurrent validity of a newly developed measure. (The following are only some of the compilations of such measures available in the social sciences and the human services: Bonjean et al., 1967; Lake et al., 1973; Magura and Moses, 1986; Fredman and Sherman, 1987; Miller, 1991; Robinson, Shaver, and Wrightsman, 1991; Fischer and Corcoran, 1994; Bloom, Fischer, and Orme, 1995; Schutte and Malouff, 1995; McDowell and Newell, 1996.) More measures can be found in research articles in professional journals. In addition, the Consulting Psychologists Press and other organizations publish catalogs of the measures they make available to measure and assess a wide array of skills, behaviors, attitudes, and other variables. (This also suggests, as pointed out in Chapter 4, that a thorough review of existing literature should be undertaken before going through all the work of creating a new measure. An existing measure may be found that meets one's needs and that has already demonstrated adequate validity and reliability.) Should a suitable measure for comparison be found, it is a matter of applying both measures to

the same sample and comparing the results. If a substantial correlation is found between the measures, we have reason to believe that our measure has concurrent validity. As a matter of convention, a correlation of $r = .50$ is considered the minimum required for establishing concurrent validity.

The inherent weakness of concurrent validity is the validity of the existing measure that is used for comparison. All we can conclude is that our measure is about as valid as the other one. If the measure we select for comparison is not valid, the fact that ours correlates with it hardly makes our measure valid. For this reason, only those measures established by research to be valid should be used for comparison purposes in concurrent validity.

A second form of criterion validity is **predictive validity,** in which an instrument is used to predict some future state of affairs. In this case, the "criterion" used to assess the instrument is certain future events. The Scholastic Aptitude Test (SAT), for example, can be subjected to predictive validity by comparing performance on the test with how people perform in college. If people who score high on the SAT do better in college than do low-scorers, then the SAT is presumably a valid measure of "scholastic aptitude." Some measures are created for the specific purpose of predicting a given behavior, and these measures are obvious candidates for assessment by predictive validity. For example, attempts have been made to develop a measure that can predict which convicted criminals are likely to revert to high involvement with crime when released from prison (Chaiken and Chaiken, 1984). These predictions are based on information about the number and types of crimes people commit, the age at which they commit their first crime, and involvement with hard drugs. Ultimately, a measure such as this is validated by its ability to make accurate predictions about who actually experiences high crime involvement after release.

Because this may require numerous applications and many years, the scales can be initially assessed for validity on their ability to differentiate between high and low crime involvement among current criminals. It is expected that if a measure can make this differentiation, it can also predict future involvement in crime. This variation on predictive validity is called the *known groups* approach to validity. If it is known that certain groups are likely to differ substantially on a given variable, a measure's ability to discriminate between these groups can be used as an indicator of validity. Suppose, for example, we were working on a measure of prejudice. We might apply the measure to a group of ministers, who we would expect to be low in prejudice, and to people affiliated with the group Aryan Nation, who we would expect to be high in prejudice. If these groups differed significantly in how they responded to the instrument, then we would have reason to believe that the measure is valid. If it failed to show a substantial difference, we would certainly have doubt about its validity.

Despite the apparent potential of the known groups approach, it does have its limitations. Frequently, there are no groups known to differ on the variable we are attempting to measure. In fact, the purpose of developing a measure is often to allow the identification of groups who do differ on some variable. The upshot of this is that the known groups technique cannot always be used. When it is used, it has a further limitation, namely, that it cannot tell us whether a measure can make finer distinctions between less extreme groups than those used in the validation. It may be, for example, that the measure of prejudice just described shows the members of Aryan Nation to be high in prejudice and the ministers low. With a broader sample, though, the measure may show that *only* the Aryan Nation members score high and *everyone else,* not just ministers, scores low. Thus, the measure can distinguish between groups only in a very crude fashion.

Construct validity, the most complex of the types of validity we discuss here, involves relating an instrument to an overall theoretical framework in order to determine whether the instrument is correlated with all the concepts and propositions that comprise the theory (Cronbach and Meehl, 1955). In this case, instruments are not assessed in terms of how they relate to one criterion but rather to the numerous criteria derivable from

some theory. For example, if we develop a new measure of socioeconomic status (SES), we can assess construct validity by showing that the new measure predicts accurately the many hypotheses that can be derived from a theory of occupational attainment. In the theory, there would be numerous propositions relating occupational attainment and SES to a variety of other concepts. If some or all of the predicted relationships are not found, then we may question the validity of the new measuring instrument. (Of course, it may be that the theory itself is flawed, and this possibility must always be considered in assessing construct validity.)

There are some very complex forms of construct validity. One is the **multitrait–multimethod approach** (Campbell and Fiske, 1959). This is based on two ideas. The first is that two instruments that are valid measures of the same concept should correlate rather highly with each other even though they are different instruments. Second, two instruments, although similar to each other, should not correlate highly if they measure different concepts. You can readily imagine that this approach to validity involves the simultaneous assessment of numerous instruments (multimethod) and numerous concepts (multitrait) through the computation of intercorrelations. This technique was used to assess the validity of children's self-reports about their negative emotions, such as aggressiveness and depression (Wolfe et al., 1987). The point is that assessing construct validity can become highly complex, but the complexity offers greater evidence of the validity of the measures.

The types of validity we have discussed—face, content, criterion, and construct—involve a progression in which each builds on the previous one. Each requires more information than prior ones, but it also provides a better assessment of validity. Unfortunately, many studies limit their assessment to content validity, with its heavy reliance on the subjective judgments of individuals or juries. Although sometimes this is necessary, measures that have been subjected only to content validity should be used with caution.

Reliability

In addition to validity, measures are also evaluated in terms of their **reliability,** which refers to a measure's ability to yield consistent results each time it is applied. In other words, reliable measures do not fluctuate except because of variations in the variable being measured. An illustration of reliability can be found at most any carnival. At carnivals, there is usually a booth with a person guessing people's weight within a certain range of accuracy, say, plus or minus 3 pounds. The customer essentially bets that the carny's ability to guess weights is sufficiently unreliable, that his or her estimate will fall outside the prescribed range, and that the customer will win a prize. A weight scale, of course, is a reliable indicator of a person's weight because it will record roughly the same weight each time the same person stands on it, and a scale is provided by the carny to assess his or her guess of the customer's weight. Despite the fact that carnies who operate such booths become quite good at guessing weights, they do occasionally give the wrong weight. The unreliability of the guesses is mainly due to the carny's being influenced by aspects of the customer other than actual weight, such as loose clothing that obscures the customer's physique.

In general, a valid measure is a reliable one. So if we were certain of the validity of a measure, we would not need to concern ourselves with its reliability. However, evidence of validity is always less than perfect, and that is why we turn to other ways of evaluating measures, including reliability. Reliability gives us more evidence for validity since a reliable measure may be a valid one. Fortunately, reliability can be demonstrated in a more straightforward manner than validity. Many specific techniques exist for estimating the reliability of a measure, but they are all based on one of two principles: stability or equivalence. *Stability* is the idea that a reliable measure should not change from one application to the next, assuming the concept being measured has not changed. *Equivalence* is the idea that all items that make up a measuring instru-

ment should be measuring the same thing and thus be consistent with one another. The first technique for estimating reliability, test–retest reliability, is based on the stability approach. The others discussed use the equivalence principle.

Test–Retest The first and most generally applicable assessment of reliability is called test–retest. As the name implies, this technique involves applying a measure to a sample of people and then, somewhat later, applying the same measure to the same people again. After the retest, we have two scores on the same measure for each person, as illustrated in Table 5.3. These two sets of scores are then correlated by using an appropriate statistical measure of association (*see* Chapter 15). Because the association in test–retest reliability involves scores obtained from two identical questionnaires, we fully expect a high degree of association. As a matter of convention, a correlation coefficient of .80 or better is normally necessary for a measure to be considered reliable. In Table 5.3, the *r* means that the particular statistic used was Pearson's correlation coefficient, and the value of .98 indicates that the measurement instrument is highly reliable according to the test–retest method.

Table 5.3 Hypothetical Test–Retest Data

Subjects	Initial Test	Retest
1	12	15
2	15	20
3	22	30
4	38	35
5	40	35
6	40	38
7	40	41
8	60	55
9	70	65
10	75	77

$r = .98$

Lawrence Shulman (1978), in addition to subjecting his measure of practice skills to the tests of validity mentioned earlier, also tested its reliability. He did so by sending versions of the questionnaire to a set of clients and then sending an identical questionnaire 2 weeks later to the same clients. This provided him with a test–retest assessment of reliability, and he obtained a correlation coefficient of .75. When a reliability coefficient is close to the conventional level, such as this is, the researcher must make a judgment about whether to assume the instrument is reliable (and the low coefficient is due to factors other than the unreliability of the instrument) or to rework the instrument in order to obtain higher levels of association.

In actual practice, the test–retest method cannot be used quite as simply as suggested because exposing people to the same measure twice creates a problem known as *multiple-testing effects* (Campbell and Stanley, 1963). Whenever a measure is applied to a group of people a second time, people may not react to it the same as they did the first. They may, for example, recall their previous answers, and this could influence their second response. People might respond as they recall doing the first time to maintain consistency or purposely change responses for the sake of variety. Either case can have a confounding effect on testing reliability. If people strive for consistency, their efforts can mask actual unreliability in the instrument. If they purposely change responses, they can make a reliable measure appear unreliable.

A solution to this dilemma is to divide the test group randomly into two groups: an experimental group that is tested twice and a control group that is tested only once. Table 5.4 illustrates the design for such an experiment. Ideally, the measure will yield consistent results in all three testing sessions, and, if it does, we have solid reason to believe the measure is reliable. On the other hand, substantial differences among the groups may indicate unreliability. If, for example, the experimental group shows consistency in both responses to the measurement instrument, but the control group differs, the measure may be unreliable, and the consistency of the experimental group might result from the

Table 5.4   Design for Test–Retest

	Initial Test	Retest
Experimental group	Yes	Yes
Control group	No	Yes

multiple-testing effects. On the other hand, if the experimental group yields inconsistent results, but the control group is similar to the results of the experimental group's initial test, this outcome could also be due to multiple-testing effects and result from the experimental group's purposely changing their answers during the retest. Despite the inconsistency in the experimental group, the measure still might be reliable if this outcome is observed. Finally, the results of all three testing sessions may be inconsistent. Such an outcome would suggest that the measure is not reliable. If either of the outcomes that leaves the reliability of the measure in doubt occurs, a second test–retest experiment should be conducted with the hope of obtaining clearer results. If the same result occurs, the instrument needs to be redesigned.

The test–retest method of assessing reliability has both advantages and disadvantages. Its major advantage is that it can be used with many measures, which is not true of alternative tests of reliability. However, its disadvantage is that it is slow and cumbersome to use, with its required two testing sessions and the desirability of having a control group. In addition, as we have seen, the outcome may not be clear, leading to the necessity of repeating the whole procedure. Finally, the test–retest method cannot be used on measures of variables whose value might have changed in the interval between tests. For example, people's attitudes can change for reasons that have nothing to do with the testing, and a measure of attitudes might appear unreliable when it is not.

Multiple Forms   If our measuring device is a multiple-item scale, as is often the case, we can approach the question of reliability through the technique of *multiple forms*. When developing the scale, we create two separate but equivalent versions made up of different items, such as different questions. These two forms are administered successively to the same people at a single testing session. The results from each form are correlated with each other, as was done in test–retest, using an appropriate statistical measure of association, with the same convention of $r = .80$ required for establishing reliability. If the correlation between the two forms is sufficiently high, we can assume that each scale is reliable.

The advantage of multiple forms is that only one testing session is required and no control group is needed. This may be a significant advantage if either multiple-testing sessions or using a control group is impractical. In addition, one need not worry about changes in a variable over time because both forms are administered at the same time.

The multiple forms technique relies on the two forms' appearing to the respondents as though they were only one long measure so that the respondents will not realize that they are really taking the same test twice. This necessity of deluding people points to one of the disadvantages of multiple forms. To maintain the equivalence of the forms, the items in the two forms will likely be quite similar—so similar that people may realize that they are responding to essentially the same items twice. If this occurs, it raises the specter of multiple-testing effects and casts doubt on the accuracy of the reliability test. Another disadvantage of multiple forms is the difficulty of developing two measures with different items that are really equivalent. If we obtain inconsistent results from the two forms, it may be due to differences in the *forms* rather than the unreliability of either one. In a way, it is questionable whether multiple forms really test reliability and not just our ability to create equivalent versions of the measure.

Split-Half Approach In the *split-half approach* to reliability, the test group responds to the complete measuring instrument. The responses to the instrument are then randomly divided into halves. Each half is then treated as though it were a separate

scale, and the two halves are correlated by using an appropriate measure of association. Once again, a coefficient of $r = .80$ is needed to demonstrate reliability. Shulman, in his study of practice skills mentioned earlier, utilized a split-half reliability test on his instrument in addition to the test–retest method. He divided each respondent's answers to his questions about practitioners' skills into two roughly equivalent sets, correlated the two sets of answers, and found a correlation (following a correction, to be mentioned shortly) of .79. This is an improvement over the reliability he found with the test–retest method and comes very close to the conventional level of .80.

One complication in using the split-half reliability test is that the correlation coefficient may understate the reliability of the measure because, other things being equal, a longer measuring scale is more reliable than a shorter one. Because the split-half approach divides the scale in two, each half is shorter than the whole scale and will appear less reliable than the whole scale. To correct for this, the correlation coefficient is adjusted by applying the *Spearman-Brown formula*, which was the correction used by Shulman:

$$r = \frac{2r_i}{1 + r_i}$$

where:

  r_i = uncorrected correlation coefficient

  r = corrected correlation coefficient (reliability coefficient)

To illustrate the effect of the Spearman-Brown formula, suppose we have a 20-item scale with a correlation between the two halves of $r_i = .70$, which is smaller than the minimum needed to demonstrate reliability. The Spearman-Brown formula corrects as follows:

$$r = \frac{(2)(.70)}{1 + .70} = \frac{1.40}{1.70} = .82$$

It can be seen that the Spearman-Brown formula has a substantial effect, increasing the uncorrected coefficient from well below .80 to just over it. If we had obtained these results with an actual scale, we would conclude that its reliability was now adequate.

Using the split-half technique requires that two preconditions be met that can limit its applicability. First, all the items in the scale must be measuring the same variable. If the scale in question is a jumble of items measuring several different variables, it would be meaningless to divide it and compare the halves. Second, the scale must contain a sufficient number of items so that, when it is divided, the halves do not become too short to be considered scales in themselves. A suggested minimum is 8 to 10 items per half (Goode and Hatt, 1952, p. 236). As many measures are shorter than these minimums, it may not be possible to assess their reliability with the split-half technique.

Randomly dividing the items in a scale into halves could result in many different arrangements of items. For a 20-item scale, for example, there are 184,756 possible arrangements of the items into two halves. Thus, there are conceivably 184,756 different possible tests of reliability that could be made when using the split-half technique, and each would yield a slightly different correlation between the halves. Which should be used to assess reliability? The most popular approach to this problem is to use *Cronbach's alpha,* which may be thought of as the average of all possible split-half correlations. Theoretically, the scale is divided into all possible configurations of two halves; a correlation is computed for each possibility, and the average of those correlations is computed to derive alpha (Cronbach, 1951). The computation of alpha is complicated and beyond the scope of this book, but many common statistical packages will compute Cronbach's alpha as well as other complex reliability tests. All that is required to run the procedure is that the researcher prepare a data set comprised of the responses by each respondent to the items of the measurement scale.

The split-half reliability test has several advantages. It requires only one testing session, and no control group is required. It also gives the clearest indication of reliability. For these reasons, it is the preferred method of assessing reliability when it can be used. The only disadvantage, as we noted, is that it cannot always be used. A lesson should be learned, however, from Shulman's approach: It is preferable to use more than one test, if possible, in assessing both reliability and validity. The issues are sufficiently important that the expenditure of time is justified.

Measurement With Minority Populations

The validity and reliability of measuring instruments is often first assessed by applying them to white, non-Hispanic respondents because such people are often the most accessible to researchers. However, it should almost never be assumed that such assessments can be generalized to minority populations (Becerra and Zambrana, 1985; Tran and Williams, 1994). The unique cultural characteristics and attitudes of minorities are, typically, not considered in the development of such instruments. For some minorities, such as Asians and Hispanics, language differences mean that an English-language interview would have some respondents answering in a second language. It cannot be assumed that such a respondent will understand words and phrases as well as, or in the same way as, a person for whom English is his or her first language. In addition, there may be concepts in English that do not have a precise equivalent in another language.

Measuring instruments, therefore, usually need to be refined if they are to be valid and reliable measures among minorities. A study of mental health among Native Americans, for example, had to drop the word "blue" as a descriptor of depression because that word had no equivalent meaning among the Native Americans (Manson, 1986). Researchers also had to add a category of "traditional healer" to a list of professionals to whom one might turn for help. A study of Eskimos found that, because of the cultural context, the same question could be used but had to be interpreted differently. Because Eskimo culture emphasizes tolerance and endurance, Eskimos are less likely than Anglo-

Americans to give in to pain by staying off work. A positive response from an Eskimo to a question like "Does sickness often keep you from doing your work?" is thus considered a much more potent indicator of distress than the same answer by Anglo-Americans.

These illustrations should make clear that measurement in social research must be culture sensitive. When conducting research on a group with a culture different from that of the researchers, there are a number of things that researchers can do to produce more valid and reliable measurement instruments (Marin and Marin, 1991; Tran and Williams, 1994):

1. Researchers can immerse themselves in the culture of the group to be studied, experiencing the daily activities of life and the cultural products as the "natives" do.
2. Researchers should use key informants, people who participate routinely in the culture of the group to be studied, to help develop and assess the measurement instruments.
3. When translating an instrument from English into another language, researchers should use the most effective translation methods, usually "double translation" (translate from English into the target language and then translate by an independent person back into English to check for errors or inconsistencies).
4. After developing or translating measurement instruments for use with minority populations, the instruments should be tested for validity and reliability on the population intended.

Errors in Measurement

The range of precision in measurement is quite broad: from the cook who measures in terms of pinches, dashes, and smidgens to the physicist who measures in tiny angstrom units (0.003937 millionths of an inch). No matter whether measurement is crude or precise, it is important to recognize that *all* measurement involves some component of error. There is no such thing as an exact measurement. Although some measurement devices in the social sciences are fairly precise, others contain substantial error components. The major reason for this error is that most of our measures deal with abstract and shifting phenomena, such as attitudes, values, or opinions, which are difficult to measure with a high degree of precision. The large error component in many of our measurements means that researchers must be concerned with the different types and sources of error so they can be kept to a minimum.

Random Errors

In measurement, researchers confront two basic types of error: *random* and *systematic*. **Random errors** are those that are neither consistent nor patterned; the error is as likely to be in one direction as another. They are essentially chance errors that in the long run tend to cancel themselves out. For example, a respondent may misread or mismark an item on a questionnaire; a counselor may misunderstand and thus record incorrectly something said during an interview; or a computer operator may enter incorrect data into a computerized data file. All these are random sources of error and can occur at virtually every point in a research project. Cognizant of the numerous sources of random error, researchers take steps to minimize them. Careful wording of questions, convenient response formats, and "cleaning" of computerized data are some of the things that can be done to keep random error down. Despite all efforts, however, the final data may contain some component of random error.

Because of their unpatterned nature, it is assumed that random errors tend to cancel each other out. For example, the careless computer operator mentioned earlier would be just as likely to enter a score lower than the actual one as to enter a higher score. The net effect is that the random errors, at least in part, offset each other. The major problem with random error is that it weakens the precision with which a researcher can measure variables, and this can reduce the ability to detect a relationship between variables when in fact one is present. For example, consider a hypothetical study on the relationship between empathy on the part of human service workers and client satisfaction with treatment. Let's assume that higher levels of client satisfaction actually are associated with higher levels of empathy. For such a study, measurements would be taken of the level of empathy that a worker expressed and of client satisfaction. Suppose five client interviews by each of five workers—a total sample of 25 cases—are monitored for level of worker empathy and client satisfaction. To the extent that random error is present in our measures, some interviews will be scored too high and some too low, even though the overall mean empathy and satisfaction scores can be expected to be quite close to the true averages. However, in terms of individual cases, random measurement will produce some empathy scores that are erroneously low for their associated satisfaction scores. Conversely, random error will produce some empathy scores that are high for their associated satisfaction scores. Thus, the random error will tend to mask the true correlation between empathy and satisfaction. Despite the fact that worker empathy and client satisfaction really are correlated, if there is too much of this type of random measurement error, it will result in concluding that the relationship between the variables does not exist.

Fortunately, researchers can combat random error with a variety of strategies. One is to increase sample size. Instead of using 5 workers and 5 interviews per worker, the researcher might use 10 workers and 10 interviews per worker for a total sample of 100. A second strategy is to increase the "dose" or contrast between levels of the independent variable. For example, workers used in the study might be selected according to their empathy skills in order to assure that there will be some cases with low expression of empathy and some with high expression. Finally, the researcher might be able to increase the number of items on the measurement scales or in other ways refine the tools to be more precise. Although such strategies can reduce the impact of random error, the same cannot be said for systematic error.

Systematic Errors

Systematic error is error that is consistent and patterned. Unlike random errors, systematic errors may not cancel themselves out. If there is a consistent over- or understatement of the value of a given variable, then the errors will accumulate. For example, it is well known that systematic error occurs when measuring crime with official reports of crimes known to the police; the Uniform Crime Reports (UCR) of the Federal Bureau of Investigation counts only crimes that are reported to the police. The Department of Justice supplements these statistics with the National Crime Survey (NCS), which measures the number of people who claim to be the victims of crime. Comparisons of these two measures consistently reveal a substantial amount of "hidden" crime: crimes reported by victims but never brought to the attention of the police. For example, NCS data indicate that approximately two thirds of all personal and household crimes are not reported to the police (Reid, 1991). So there is a very large systematic error when measuring the amount of crime the way the UCR does because of the underreporting of most crimes (see Research in Practice 8.2 for a more detailed discussion of this issue).

Systematic errors are more troublesome to researchers than random errors because they are more likely to lead to false conclusions. For example, official juvenile delinquency statistics consistently show higher rates of delinquency among children of lower socioeconomic status families. Self-report studies of delinquency involvement suggest, however, that the official data systematically overstate the relationship between delinquency and socioeconomic status (Binder, Geis, and Bruce, 1988). It should be easy to see how the systematic error in delinquency data could lead to erroneous conclusions as to possible causes of delinquency as well as to inappropriate prevention or treatment strategies.

Researchers deal with error, both random and systematic, by eliminating as much of it as they can and accepting what remains as inevitable. Because systematic error is potentially the most damaging,

Research in Practice **5.2**
Assessment of Client Functioning: Valid and Reliable Practice Measurement

At the beginning of this chapter, we emphasized the point that practitioners as well as researchers engage in a process of measurement, although for different purposes. We have discussed the evaluation of measurement primarily as it applies to research settings. Yet, practitioners need to be equally concerned about such measurement issues to ensure that instruments used in practice are valid and reliable. This problem was brought to light dramatically by a now well-known study conducted by D. L. Rosenhan (1973).

Rosenhan was concerned with the ability of mental health practitioners to diagnose, or measure accurately, the presence of various mental disorders in people. To evaluate these abilities, he and a few other people attempted to gain admission to mental hospitals as patients. All these people, whom Rosenhan called "pseudopatients," had been given a variety of psychological tests and judged to have no serious mental disorders. Yet, every pseudopatient gained entrance to the hospital he or she approached, and with surprising ease! All were diagnosed as schizophrenic based on their intake interview, in which they claimed they heard voices saying things like "thud" and "hollow." All were later released as "schizophrenia in remission."

It seems clear that the assessment tools used by these mental health practitioners were not completely valid measures of psychological disorder. (The diagnostic tool used here was the *Diagnostic and Statistical Manual,* or DSM, of the American Psychiatric Association.) It is possible, of course, that the psychological tests Rosenhan administered to the pseudopatients were invalid and the pseudopatients (including Rosenhan) were, in fact, schizophrenic. Yet, we know from a host of research studies that the reliability of psychiatric diagnoses is highly variable (Kirk and Kutchins, 1992). In some cases, diagnoses vary little from one practitioner to another, whereas in other settings there is great variation. The reliability of psychiatric diagnoses is affected by the nature of the disorder, the skill of the practitioner, and the circumstances under which assessments are made as well as by the kinds of efforts that are made to reach agreement. This fluctuation in reliability certainly suggests that the assessments made by practitioners at the hospitals were unreliable and may very well have been invalid also.

The point is that practitioners need to be concerned with measurement issues as much as do researchers. Problems of validity, reliability, and error can result in ineffective and possibly harmful practice intervention. By observing how researchers deal with such problems, practitioners can learn systematic ways of evaluating measurement instruments.

In addition, measures developed for practice are often used to measure the independent or dependent variable in research. Research on mental illness, for example, sometimes uses the DSM as a measurement tool for assessing the extent and type of mental illness. Corcoran and Fischer (1987) describe a host of practice measures that can be very useful in research. They also assess what reliability and validity information exists about each measure.

---

reducing that type of error to the minimum is of greater concern. In the chapters that follow, where we present specific measurement techniques, procedures for reducing error are a major focus.

In Research in Practice 5.2, we suggest ways in which concerns about measurement—problems of reliability, validity, and error—have direct parallels in practice intervention.

Main Points

- Measurement is the process of describing abstract concepts in terms of specific indicators by assigning numbers or other symbols to them.
- An indicator is an observation that is assumed to be evidence of the attributes or properties of some phenomenon.

COMPUTERS IN RESEARCH
Enhancing Measurement Through Computer-Collected Data

Marshall McLuhan, noted authority on mass media, made the statement "the medium is the message" to explain how the development of electronic media revolutionized life in our society. He argued that the electronic age created a new environment in which the media are not merely a passive vehicle that simply transmits reality; instead, the electronic media shape and change the reality that we confront (McLuhan, 1965). In terms of the impact of the computer age on research measurement, we can paraphrase McLuhan to say that the medium is the measurement. The computer has revolutionized how data are collected. In the process, it has helped to reduce measurement error through systematizing data collection and helping researchers to evaluate the reliability and validity of the data that are collected. In keeping with McLuhan's point, however, the computer not only helps researchers do traditional measurement better, it also enables them to measure social phenomena in ways that were heretofore impossible. The computer has created a new environment for measurement. We can illustrate this with two developments: computer-assisted survey research and continuous audience response technology.

Computer-assisted survey research (CASR) involves substitution of a computer for some portion of a personal interview (Witt and Bernstein, 1992; Buetow et al., 1996). In some cases, respondents receive all interview instructions via a computer terminal and enter their responses to questions that appear on the monitor. In one variation, interviewers bring a portable computer to the interview site, read questions from it, and enter the responses. For some panel research projects, computers are placed right in the home. In some cases, respondents who provide data for an entire project get to keep the computers. Games and other software are included as inducements to log in. A central computer polls the panel respondents. An interesting variation on this is "disk-by-mail."

In certain situations, where the population of interest has access to computers, sending respondents the survey on computer disk is not merely a gimmick; users of this approach report as much as a 50 percent response rate improvement over mailed questionnaires.

Using computers in place of interviewers is advocated for many reasons other than reducing the amount of repetitive work associated with large-scale surveys. One argument is that the computer helps eliminate inter-interviewer variation because it presents exactly the same instrument to each respondent in exactly the same way. The computer can also handle complex question branching, in which each question asked is dependent on earlier answers given by respondents. Several studies conclude that computerized interviews compare very favorably to in-person interviews: They reduce coding error, assure anonymity, and help reduce interviewer bias and intimidation of respondents.

Not only can the computer collect survey data as well as or better than personal interviewers, but researchers are also finding ways to access information not attainable through personal interviews. Researchers have discovered that the computer can monitor response delay, or the duration between when the question is asked and when the response is entered. Response delay has been associated with faking answers, presumably because it takes longer to think up a falsehood than to give the correct response. The computer can monitor response delay times and compare them to norms that have been developed for those questions. If a respondent's response delays are outside the normalized range for certain questions, the computerized interview can automatically branch to probe questions (Hanney, 1989; George and Skinner, 1990). Thus, the measurement process itself is being measured and serves as a guide to determining what questions need to be asked.

Computerization of measurement is not restricted to the traditionally quantitative fields such as survey research. Continuous audience response technology (CART), another example of the innovative application of computerization to measurement, is being applied to the qualitative research methodology known as focus group research (Krueger, 1994). In a focus group, discussed in more detail in Chapter 7, a small group of participants is brought together to discuss an issue, such as their reactions to a political campaign, under the direction of a focus group leader. A positive feature of focus group research is that it permits the researcher to obtain rich, qualitative data in greater depth than is possible with basic survey techniques. A criticism of the technique, however, has been that the group atmosphere, while stimulating discussion, tends to bias individual responses due to group effects such as "group think," where an outspoken "opinion leader" may attempt to dominate the group and less assertive members conform to the opinions that emerge in the group.

CART utilizes a similar group format for presenting data to participants, but the computerization of data collection adds a new dimension to the group process while helping to control negative processes. The method represents a merger of microcomputer and video technology that permits subjects to respond to a variety of continuous stimuli. For example, respondents may view political speeches, commercials, or other video material. However, unlike traditional focus groups, participants anonymously enter their reactions to the presented material on a continuous basis via a dial or a handheld keypad, moving a slide, or pressing a button on an individual response device. Individual responses are immediately analyzed and summarized in the form of a moving graph that is overlaid on the stimulus tape. Subjects can be shown parts of the tape with the group data and asked to discuss reasons for their responses. A researcher, physically separated from the group, has information about individual responses. This individual communicates with the moderator via a wireless communication device, providing information about large deviations and aiding in directing the session and debriefing.

Computer technology's capacity to rapidly analyze and display results to the group adds a new dimension to focus group research. In effect, the computerization of data collection itself becomes a stimulus to which participants respond. For example, if the responses show that men and women are differing in reaction to a portion of the stimulus tape, the group leader can replay that portion of the tape, display group and individual responses to participants, and probe members about why they or the group responded as they did. In a traditional focus group, the moderator would not even be aware of the gender split during the session itself, much less be able to present it in the form of a graph and use it for discussion.

The use of CART has implications for validity and reliability of focus group research. In a CART session, group members have anonymity of response by means of using their keypads. The capacity to continuously monitor all participants helps reduce the effect of outspoken or dominating members. The group moderator, linked to the control room, can be instantly aware of actual group opinions and use this knowledge to direct discussion. In effect, CART permits the researcher to mitigate many of the negative aspects of the group environment. Furthermore, the permanent videotape account with the quantitative overlays serves as an enduring record of the session. This allows multiple independent judgments of the same events and variables as a way of evaluating reliability. To date, CART has been primarily used for commercial and political issue analysis. For example, one group of researchers used CART to study voter reaction to California Proposition 103, an initiative passed by California voters in 1988 to limit car insurance rates (Javidi et al., 1991). However, the method has potential for many human service issues as well, such as understanding public attitudes toward welfare reform or studying community reactions to the location of correctional facilities.

■ The four levels of measurement are nominal, ordinal, interval, and ratio.

■ The level of measurement achieved with a given variable is determined by the nature of the variable itself and by the way it is measured.

■ Discrete variables have a limited number of distinct and separate values.

■ Continuous variables theoretically have an infinite number of possible values.

■ Validity refers to a measure's ability to measure accurately the variable it is intended to measure.

■ Face validity, content or sampling validity, jury opinion, criterion validity, and construct validity are techniques of assessing the validity of measures.

■ Reliability refers to a measure's ability to yield consistent results each time it is applied.

■ Test–retest, multiple forms, and split-half are techniques for assessing the reliability of measures.

■ Measurement in social research must be culture sensitive; it should never be assumed that a measurement instrument that is valid and reliable for majority group populations will be so for minorities.

■ Random errors are those that are neither consistent nor patterned and can reduce the precision with which variables are measured.

■ Systematic errors are consistent and patterned and, unless noted, can potentially lead to erroneous conclusions.

■ A part of the measurement process is to use computer capabilities in the collection and analysis of data.

Important Terms for Review

concurrent validity
construct validity
content validity
continuous variables
criterion validity
discrete variables
face validity
index

indicator
interval measures
item
level of measurement
measurement
multitrait-multimethod approach to validity
nominal measures
ordinal measures
predictive validity
random errors
ratio measures
reliability
sampling validity
scale
systematic errors
validity

Exploring the Internet

In this chapter, we have emphasized the importance of good measurement to the research process. Locating the best available measurement tools and designing measurement strategies are two functions with which the Internet can be of great help to researchers. Many sites can help you find existing measurement tools, such as scales and indexes. An excellent example is the Center for Mental Health Services Research Measures Collection maintained by the George Warren Brown School of Social Work at Washington University. This extensive collection of measurement instruments includes measures for client satisfaction, mental health status, stress, service utilization, substance abuse, and many more topics. We suggest that you access this site (http://www.gwbssw.wustl.edu/~cmhsr/measure. html) and examine a few of the available scales that are suitable for an issue of interest for you. Another site worth visiting is the WALMYR Publishing Company home page (http://www.syspac.com/~ walmyr/). This site includes information on the CASS system, mentioned in Chapter 1, and permits you to access and download the system as well as examine specific scales and measurement tools. We suggest that you review the list of scales and examine the complete details on the CASS program.

Another approach to finding Internet resources on measurement would be to use a search engine and search for terms such as "measurement group" or "social work measurement." The former term produced the Web site of The Measurement Group, which is a private consulting firm that focuses on evaluation research and policy development primarily in the health area. At this location, you will find much information about measurement with standardized tests and instruments as well as links to numerous Web sites, journals, and professional associations relevant to measurement issues.

For Further Reading

Blythe, Betty J., and Tony Tripodi. *Measurement in Direct Practice.* Newbury Park, Calif.: Sage, 1989. This book looks at measurement issues from the standpoint of day-to-day efforts to apply successful interventions to help clients. It should be particularly useful for those who are currently in or those planning to enter direct practice.

Burgess, Robert G., ed. *Key Variables in Social Investigation.* London: Routledge & Kegan Paul, 1986. This collection of essays is unusual in that it focuses on 10 of the most commonly used social science variables, analyzing their underlying concepts and how they have been operationalized.

Geismar, Ludwig L., and Michael Camasso. *The Family Functioning Scale: A Guide to Research and Practice.* New York: Springer, 1993. This book provides an excellent illustration of measurement in both research and practice as it explores how a family functioning scale was developed for use in both realms. It is a good example of both the parallels and linkages between research and practice.

Hindelang, Michael J., Travis Hirschi, and Joseph G. Weis. *Measuring Delinquency.* Beverly Hills, Calif.: Sage, 1980. A good description of the development of a measuring device related to a human service issue. The volume covers all the issues related to problems of measurement.

Kirk, Jerome, and Marc L. Miller. *Reliability and Validity in Qualitative Research.* Beverly Hills, Calif.: Sage, 1986. This work presents the measurement issues of reliability and validity as they apply to qualitative research

such as field research (*see* Chapter 9). Unfortunately, reliability and validity are often only presented in the context of quantitative research.

Martin, Lawrence L., and Peter M. Kettner. *Measuring the Performance of Human Service Programs.* Thousand Oaks, Calif.: Sage, 1996. This short book explains in detail how to measure and assess human service programs, especially with outcome measures. It includes such measures as levels of functioning scales and client satisfaction.

Miller, Delbert C. *Handbook of Research Design and Social Measurement,* 5th ed. Newbury Park, Calif.: Sage, 1991. A good resource work for scales and indexes focusing on specific human service concerns.

Price, James L. *Handbook of Organizational Measurement.* Marshfield, Mass.: Pitman, 1986. Using concepts that are a part of organizational theory, this book illustrates how to link concepts with indicators.

Exercises for Class Discussion

5.1 Here is an interesting way to illustrate measurement issues. Imagine a new student at your college is blind. He is trying to become independent of others and asks some students to help him measure the distance to such places as the nearest drinking fountain, the restroom, and the student lounge. To help this student, select a destination that is at least 50 feet from the classroom and preferably around a corner or two. Have four or five students independently count the number of steps to the destination and write their count on the board. Compare the counts. How does this exercise illustrate the definition of measurement presented in this chapter? Given the responses of the volunteers, would the blind student be able to find the destination? Was this a valid and reliable measurement procedure?

5.2 Are there modifications that you could make in the "rules" of measurement presented in Exercise 5.1 that would improve the validity and reliability of the measure?

5.3 The following list contains variables that researchers and practitioners in the human services commonly encounter:
race
income
health
drug use

school achievement
number of arrests
depression
marital satisfaction
employment status
assertiveness
parenting skill
client satisfaction

Which level of measurement is applicable to each of these variables? Which of these variables are discrete and which continuous? Which of these variables could be measured at more than one level of measurement? Which level would be best?

5.4 Working independently or in teams of two or three students, locate in your library some studies that have used one of the variables from the list in Exercise 5.3. Describe how the variable was operationalized in each study. Do you see any weaknesses in using this operational definition given the nominal definition of the variable? What problems might there be in obtaining valid and reliable measures of these variables based on the studies that you have reviewed?

CHAPTER 6
Sampling

The Purpose of Sampling   124

Sampling Terminology   125
Populations and Samples   125
Sampling Frames   126
A Classic Sampling Disaster   127

Probability Samples   128
Simple Random Sampling   129
Systematic Sampling   129
Stratified Sampling   130
Area Sampling   134
Estimating Sample Size   136

Nonprobability Samples   140
Availability Sampling   141
Snowball Sampling   143
Quota Sampling   143
Purposive Sampling   144
Dimensional Sampling   145

Sampling With Minority Populations   148

A Note on Sampling in Practice   149

Main Points   151

Important Terms for Review   152

Exploring the Internet   152

For Further Reading   153

Exercises for Class Discussion   153

A number of correctional systems have established programs that use behavior modification techniques to shape inmate behavior, rewarding sought-after behavior and withholding privileges from inmates who are recalcitrant or hostile. Each inmate who is placed in such a program becomes, in a sense, a test of the hypotheses about behavior change derived from behavioral theory. What can we conclude, however, if one inmate's behavior changes in a way that supports these hypotheses? Will the program work with other inmates? This is the issue at the core of this chapter: Can knowledge gained from one or a few cases be considered knowledge about a whole group of people? The answer to this question depends on whether the inmate is *representative* of some larger group, of which the inmate is a "sample." Does he or she represent all inmates? Only inmates in a particular prison? Just inmates who have committed certain offenses? Or is this inmate not representative of any larger group? These issues are at the center of the problem of *sampling,* or selecting a few cases out of some larger grouping for study. All of us have had experience with sampling. Cautiously tasting a spoonful of soup is a process of sampling to see how hot it is, and taking a bite of a new brand of pizza is sampling to see if we like it. All sampling involves attempting to make a judgment about a whole something—a bowl of soup, a brand of pizza, or an inmate population—based on an analysis of a part of the whole. Scientific sampling, however, is considerably more careful and systematic than casual, everyday sampling. In this chapter, we discuss the fundamentals of sampling along with the benefits and disadvantages of various sampling techniques.

The Purpose of Sampling

When the subject of sampling is first encountered, a not uncommon question is: Why bother? Why not just study the whole group? A major reason for studying samples rather than the whole group is that the whole group is sometimes so large it is not feasible to study it. For example, human service workers might be interested in learning about welfare recipients, the mentally ill, prison inmates, or some other rather large group of people. It would be difficult—and often impossible—to study all members of these groups. Sampling allows us to study a workable number of cases from the large group to derive findings that are relevant for all members of the group.

A second reason for sampling is that, as surprising as it may seem, information based on carefully drawn samples can be better than information from an entire group. This is especially true when the group being studied is extremely large. For example, a census of all residents of the United States is taken at the beginning of each decade. Despite the vast resources the federal government puts into the census, substantial undercounts and other errors occur. In fact, after both the 1980 and the 1990 censuses, numerous cities filed lawsuits complaining of alleged undercounts. Between the decennial censuses, the Census Bureau conducts *sample* surveys to update population statistics and collect data on other matters. The quality of the data gathered by these sample surveys is actually superior to that of the census itself. The reason for this is that, with only a few thousand people to contact, the task is more manageable: Better-trained interviewers can be used, greater control can be exercised over the interviewers, and fewer hard-to-find respondents are involved. In fact, the Bureau of the Census even conducts a sample survey after each census as a check on the accuracy of that census. Indeed, were it not a constitutional requirement, the complete census might well be dropped and replaced by sample surveys.

Much research, then, is based on samples of people. Samples make possible a glimpse at the behavior and attitudes of whole groups of people, and the validity and accuracy of research results depend heavily on how samples are drawn. An improperly drawn sample renders the data collected virtually useless. An important consideration regarding samples is how *representative* they are of the population from which they are drawn. A **representative sample** is one that accurately reflects the distribution of relevant variables in the target population. In a sense, the sample should be considered a small reproduction of the population. Imagine, for example, that you were interested in the success of unmarried teenage mothers in raising their children, your goal being to improve the provision of services to these adolescents. Your sample should reflect the relevant characteristics of unmarried teenage mothers in your community. Such characteristics might include age, years of education, and socioeconomic status. To be representative, the sample would have to contain the same proportion of unmarried teenage mothers at each age level, educational level, and socioeconomic status that exists in the community. In short, a representative sample should have all the same characteristics as the population. The representative character of samples allows the conclusions based on them to be legitimately generalized to the populations from which they are drawn. As we will see later in this chapter, nonrepresentative samples can be useful for some research purposes, but researchers must always assess the representativeness of their samples in order to make accurate conclusions. Before comparing the various techniques for drawing samples, we will define some of the major terms used in the field of sampling.

Sampling Terminology

Populations and Samples

A sample is drawn from a **population,** which refers to all possible cases of what we are interested in studying. In the human services, the target population is often people who have some particular characteristic in common, such as all Americans, all eligible voters, all school-age children, and so on. A population need not, however, be composed of people. Recall from Chapter 4 that the unit of analysis can be something other than individuals,

such as groups or programs. Then, the target population will be all possible cases of whatever our unit of analysis is. A **sample** consists of one or more elements selected from a population. The manner in which the elements are selected for the sample has enormous implications for the scientific utility of the research based on that sample. To select a good sample, you need to define clearly the population from which the sample is to be drawn. Failure to define the population clearly can make generalizing from the sample observations highly ambiguous and result in drawing inaccurate conclusions.

The definition of a population should specify four things: content, units, extent, and time (Kish, 1965, p. 7). These can be illustrated by the sample used by James Greenley and Richard Schoenherr (1981) to study the effects of agency characteristics on the delivery of social services. First, the *content* of the population refers to the particular characteristic that the members of the population have in common. For Greenley and Schoenherr, the characteristic held in common by the members of their population was that they were health or social service agencies. Second, the *unit* indicates the unit of analysis, which in our illustration is organizations rather than individuals or groups. Although Greenley and Schoenherr collected data from practitioners and clients in the organizations, their focus was on comparing the performance of agencies. Third, the *extent* of the population refers to its spacial or geographic coverage. For practical reasons, Greenley and Schoenherr limited the extent of their population to health and social agencies serving one county in Wisconsin. It would not have been financially feasible for them to define the extent of their population as all agencies in Wisconsin or the United States. Finally, the *time* factor refers to the temporal period during which a unit would have to possess the appropriate characteristic in order to qualify for the sample. Greenley and Schoenherr conducted a cross-sectional study, and only agencies that were in operation at the time they collected their data qualified. A longitudinal study might include agencies that came into existence during the course of the study.

So with these four factors clearly defined, a population will normally be adequately delimited, and what is called a *sampling frame* can be constructed.

Sampling Frames

A **sampling frame** is a listing of all the elements in a population. In many studies, the actual sample is drawn from this listing. The adequacy of the sampling frame is crucial in determining the quality of the sample drawn from it. Of major importance is the degree to which the sampling frame includes *all* members of the population. Although there is an endless number of possible sampling frames depending on the research problem, a few illustrations will describe some of the intricacies of developing good sampling frames.

In human service research, some of the most adequate sampling frames consist of lists of members of organizations. If we wanted, for example, to expand the study of the impact of behavior modification on inmates mentioned at the beginning of this chapter, we could draw a larger sample of inmates in that prison. The sampling frame would be quite straightforward, consisting of all inmates currently listed as residents of that institution. Given the care with which correctional facilities maintain accurate records of inmates, the sampling frame would undoubtedly be complete and accurate. Other examples of sampling frames based on organizational affiliation would be the membership rosters of professional groups, such as the National Association of Social Workers, the American Psychological Association, or the American Society of Criminology. These lists would not be quite as accurate as the inmate roster because people who had very recently joined the organization might not appear on the official list; also, clerical errors might lead to a few missing names. These few errors, however, would have little effect on the adequacy of the sampling frame.

When using organizational lists as a sampling frame, caution must be exercised regarding what is defined as the population and about whom generalizations are made. The population consists of the sampling frame, and legitimate generalizations can be made only about the sampling frame. Many social workers, for example, do not belong to the Na-tional Association of Social Workers (NASW). Thus, a sample taken from the NASW membership roster represents only NASW members and not all social workers. In the use of organizational lists as sampling frames, then, it is important to assess carefully whom the list includes and whom it excludes. Sometimes research focuses on a theoretical concept that is operationalized in terms of an organizational list that does not include all actual instances of what is intended by the concept. For example, a study of poverty could operationalize the concept "poor" as those receiving welfare payments. Yet, many people with little or no income do not receive welfare. In this case, the sampling frame would not completely reflect the population intended by the theoretical concept.

Some research focuses on populations that are quite large, such as residents of a city or state. This is particularly true of needs assessment research and, oftentimes, of evaluation research. To develop sampling frames for these populations, three listings are commonly used: telephone numbers, utility subscribers, or city directories (Lavrakas, 1987). A listing of telephone numbers in an area can be found in telephone books, but telephone books have a number of problems when used as sampling frames. Even today some people do not have telephone service, and others have unlisted numbers. The number of households that lack telephone service has diminished over the past few decades. As recently as 1970, 13 percent of American households were without telephone service; today, probably no more than 6 percent lack such service (U.S. Bureau of the Census, 1991). Those without telephones, however, are concentrated among the poor, those living in rural areas, and transient groups, such as the young. So for a research project in which these groups are important, sampling based on telephone books could be very unrepresentative. As for unlisted numbers, the extent varies from one locale to another, but it could be as much as 50 percent in some areas. Because of these problems with the listings in telephone books, they are typically not used, at least by themselves, for drawing samples. Instead, there are other techniques, such as *random digit dialing* (or RDD), that can assure that every household with telephone service has an equal chance of appearing in the sample. With RDD, telephone numbers are selected for the sample by using a table of random numbers or having a computer generate random telephone numbers (*see* Appendix B). (If the researcher knows the telephone prefixes of the areas to be sampled, then only the last four numbers need be randomly chosen.) Because the phone numbers are randomly determined, RDD gives all telephone numbers an equal chance of being selected, regardless of whether they are listed in the directory, and therefore removes the problem of unlisted numbers. Random digit dialing, of course, does nothing about noncoverage due to the lack of telephone service in some households.

Another population listing that can be used for sampling is a list of customers from the local electric utility. Though some households do not have telephone service, relatively few lack electricity, and the problem of noncoverage is, therefore, less significant. Utility listings do, however, have their own problems that must be handled in order to draw a satisfactory sample. The major problem comes from multiple-family dwellings, which often have utilities listed only in the name of the owner rather than all the individual residents. Multiple-family dwellings are more likely to be inhabited by the young, the old, and the unmarried. Unless the utility listings are supplemented, samples will systematically underrepresent people in these groups. This problem can be overcome by visiting the dwellings and adding the residents to the list of utility subscribers, but this is a very time-consuming task. Beyond the problem of multiple dwellings, the old, the poor, and those living in rural areas are more likely to be without utilities and thus not appear in the sampling frame.

As a source of population listings, city directories are quite useful. City directories can be found in most libraries, and they are generally divided into four sections. The first is a listing of commercial firms and is analogous to the yellow pages of the telephone book. The second section is an alphabetical listing of residents together with their addresses, phone numbers, and the head of household's occupation. This section of the directory is useful if the research problem calls for a sample of people or households with particular occupational characteristics. Next comes an alphabetical listing of streets and addresses with residents' names. For sampling purposes, this is often the most useful section of the directory. The other sections can become outdated, but the address listing will exclude only new construction. The last section is a listing of telephone numbers in numerical order, together with the name of the person to whom the number is assigned. The accuracy of city directories is quite high, certainly as good a sampling frame as a researcher could compile starting from scratch (Sudman, 1976). In addition, city directories are the least likely to exclude people with low incomes.

A Classic Sampling Disaster

Some disastrous mistakes have occurred in sampling in past investigations, often because of inadequate sampling frames. These mistakes result in special chagrin when the investigator makes some precise—and easily refutable—predictions based on the sample. A classic example of this was the attempt by *Literary Digest* magazine to predict the outcome of the 1936 presidential race between Alfred Landon and Franklin Roosevelt. In election predicting, the target population is all likely voters. The *Literary Digest,* however, did not utilize a sampling frame that listed all likely voters. Rather, they drew their sample from lists of automobile owners and from telephone directories. On the basis of their sample results, Landon was predicted to win by a substantial margin. But, of course, Roosevelt won the election easily. Why the error in prediction? This question continues to generate debate in the professional literature, but the evidence points to two possible factors, each serious by itself but deadly in combination (Bryson, 1976; Squire, 1988; Cahalan, 1989). The first problem was a flawed sampling frame. In 1936, the Great Depression was at its peak, and a substantial proportion of eligible voters, especially the poorer ones, did not own cars or have telephones. In short, the sample was drawn from an inadequate sampling frame and did not represent the target population. Because the poor are more likely to vote Democratic, most of the eligible voters excluded from the sampling frame—and thus having no chance to be in the sample—voted for the Democratic candidate, Roosevelt. The second problem in the *Literary Digest* poll was a poor response rate. Although employing a massive sample size, the pollsters used a mailed survey and the percentage of respondents who returned the surveys was very low, about 23 percent. An independent follow-up investigation in a city where half the voters voted for Roosevelt and half for Landon found that only 15 percent of the Roosevelt supporters returned their surveys, whereas 33 percent of the Landon supporters did (Cahalan, 1989). So if there was a bias in the sampling frame against Roosevelt supporters, it was compounded by the nonresponse bias: Landon supporters were much more likely to return their surveys to the *Literary Digest*. The result was the magazine's embarrassingly inaccurate prediction. Although the *Literary Digest* was a popular and respected magazine before the election, it never recovered from its prediction and went out of business a short time later.

For many human service projects, adequate sampling frames can be constructed from existing listings (such as those already mentioned) that are available or can readily be created. Still, caution in using such lists must be exercised because they may inadvertently exclude some people. In fact, human service research may be especially vulnerable to this because we often study populations that are difficult to enumerate. For example, undocumented aliens are by definition not listed anywhere. We know they comprise a large segment of the population in such urban centers as Los Angeles, but a study of the poor in these areas that relied on a city directory would obviously miss large numbers of such people. Early studies of gay men also fell prey to this problem (Hooker, 1957; Bell and Weinberg, 1978). In some of these studies, the sampling frame was homosexuals who were listed as patients by therapists who were participating in the research. The studies concluded that homosexuality was associated with personality disturbance. Yet, it does not take great insight to recognize that many gay men—those feeling no need to see a therapist—

were not listed in the sampling frames, and the samples were thus strongly biased toward finding personality disorders among gays.

So sampling frames need to be assessed carefully to ensure that they include all elements of the population of interest. The remainder of this chapter is a discussion of the different ways in which samples can be selected. First, we discuss probability samples, for which we are most likely to have a sampling frame from which to draw the sample. Probability samples are often used in such human service research as needs assessment and evaluation research. Then we discuss nonprobability samples, which are often used in such research as assessing client functioning and evaluating the effectiveness of intervention strategies.

Probability Samples

With luck, almost any sampling procedure could produce a representative sample. But that is little comfort to a researcher who wants to be as certain as possible that his or her sample is representative. Techniques that make use of probability theory can both greatly reduce the chances of getting a nonrepresentative sample and, what is more important, permit the researcher to estimate precisely the likelihood that a sample differs from the true population by a given amount. In these samples, known as **probability samples,** each element in the population has some chance of being included in the sample, and the investigator can determine the chances or probability of each element's being included (Scheaffer, Mendenhall, and Ott, 1996). In their simpler versions, probability sampling techniques ensure that each element has an *equal* chance of being included. In more elaborate versions, the researcher takes advantage of knowledge about the population to select elements with differing probabilities. The key point is that, whether the probabilities are equal or different, each element's probability of being included in a probability sample is nonzero and known. Furthermore, probability sampling enables us to calculate **sampling error,** which is an estimate of the extent to which the values of the sample differ from those of the population from which it was drawn. Next we discuss the major types of probability samples, followed by an analysis of how to estimate the sample size needed to produce a given amount of sampling error.

Simple Random Sampling

The simplest technique for drawing probability samples is **simple random sampling** (SRS), in which each element in the population has an equal probability of being chosen for the sample. Simple random sampling treats the target population as a unitary whole. One begins with a sampling frame containing a list of the entire population or as complete a list as can be obtained. The elements in the sampling frame are then numbered sequentially, and elements are selected from the list by using a procedure known to be random. If the sampling frame is computerized, random selection can be accomplished by merely programming the computer to select randomly a sample of whatever size is desired.

If one is drawing the sample by hand, a common method of ensuring random selection is to use a table of random numbers, which consists of digits from zero to nine that are equally represented and have no pattern or order to them. Appendix B contains an illustration of a table of random numbers, and using one to draw a simple random sample from a sampling frame is a straightforward procedure. First, we note the size of the population. This will determine how many of the random digits we need when selecting each element. For example, if the population did not exceed 9,999 elements, we would use four columns of random digits for each of the selections from the sampling frame. If the population exceeded 9,999 elements, but not 99,999, we would take random digits five columns at a time.

The second step is to select a starting point in the table of random numbers. It is important that one not always start from the same place in the table, such as the upper left corner. If that were done, every sample, assuming the same number of digits were used, would select the same elements from the population. That would, of course, violate the randomness we seek to achieve. This problem can be easily avoided by merely starting in the table at some point that is itself randomly determined (close your eyes and point).

Assuming a population smaller than 9,999, we would proceed through the table from the randomly selected starting point, taking each set of four digits that is a part of the sampling frame until we had reached the desired sample size. (If the sampling frame contains 2,000 elements, we just ignore any number between 2,001 and 9,999 that appears on the random number list.) This list of random numbers is then used to identify the elements to be included in the sample. If one of the random numbers is 426, for example, then the 426th element in the sampling frame would become a part of the sample.

Although simple random samples have the desirable feature of giving each element in the sampling frame an equal chance of appearing in the sample, they are often impractical. A major reason for this is the cost. Imagine doing a research project that calls for a national sample of 2,000 households. Even if one could obtain such a sample using SRS, which is unlikely, it would be prohibitively expensive to send interviewers all over the country to obtain the data. Furthermore, alternatives to SRS may be more efficient in terms of providing a high degree of representativeness with a smaller sample. Simple random sampling is normally limited to fairly small-scale projects dealing with populations of modest size for which adequate sampling frames can be obtained. The importance of simple random sampling lies not in its wide application. Rather, simple random sampling is the basic sampling procedure on which statistical theory is based, and it is the standard against which other sampling procedures are measured.

Systematic Sampling

A variation on simple random sampling is called **systematic sampling,** which involves taking every kth element listed in a sampling frame.

Systematic sampling uses the table of random numbers to determine a random starting point in the sampling frame. From that random start, we select every *k*th element into the sample. The value of *k* is called the *sampling interval,* and it is determined by dividing the population size by the desired sample size. For example, if we wanted a sample of 100 from a population of 1,000, the sampling interval would be 10. From the random starting point, we would select every 10th element from the sampling frame for the sample. (If the starting point is in the middle of the list, we proceed to the end, jump to the beginning, and end up at the middle again.)

In actual practice, dividing the population by the sample size will usually not produce a whole number. The decimal should be rounded upward to the next largest whole number. This will provide a sampling interval that will take us completely through the sampling frame. If we rounded downward, the sampling interval would be slightly too narrow, and we would reach the desired sample size before we had exhausted the sampling frame. This would mean that those elements farthest from the starting point would have no chance of being selected.

Systematic sampling is commonly used when samples are drawn by hand rather than by computer. The only advantage of systematic sampling over SRS is in clerical efficiency. In SRS, the random numbers will select elements that are scattered throughout the sampling frame. It is time-consuming to search all over the sampling frame to identify the elements that correspond with the random numbers. In systematic sampling, we proceed in an orderly fashion through the sampling frame from the random starting point.

Unfortunately, systematic sampling can produce biased samples, although this is rare. The difficulty occurs when the sampling frame consists of a population list that has a cyclical or recurring pattern, called *periodicity.* If the sampling interval happens to be the same as that of the cycle in the list, it is possible to draw a seriously biased sample. For example, suppose we were sampling households in a large apartment building. The apartments are listed in the sampling frame by floor and apartment number (2A, 2B, 2C, 2D, 2E, 2F, 3A, 3B, and so on). Further, suppose that, on each floor, apartment F is a corner apartment with an extra bedroom and correspondingly higher rent than the other apartments on the floor. If we had a sampling interval of 3 and randomly chose to begin counting with apartment 2D, every F apartment would appear in the sample, which would mean that the sample is biased in favor of the more expensive apartments and thus the more affluent residents of the apartment building. So when using systematic sampling techniques, the sampling frame needs to be carefully assessed for any cyclical pattern that might confound the sample, and the list should be rearranged to eliminate the pattern. Alternatively, SRS could be used instead of systematic sampling.

Stratified Sampling

With simple random and systematic sampling methods, the target population is treated as a unitary whole when sampling from it. **Stratified sampling** changes this by dividing the population into smaller subgroups, called *strata,* prior to drawing the sample, and then separate random samples are drawn from each of the strata.

Reduction in Sampling Error   One of the major reasons for using a stratified sample is that stratifying has the effect of reducing sampling error for a given sample size to a level lower than that of an SRS of the same size. This is so because of a very simple principle: the more homogeneous a population on the variables being studied, the smaller the sample size needed to represent it accurately. Stratifying makes each subsample more homogeneous by eliminating the variation on the variable that is used for stratifying. Perhaps a gastronomic example will help illustrate this point. Imagine two large commercial-size cans of nuts, one labeled peanuts and the other labeled mixed nuts. Because the can of peanuts is highly homogeneous, only a small handful from it would give a fairly accurate indication of the remainder of its contents. The can of mixed nuts, however, is quite heterogeneous, containing several kinds of nuts in different proportions. A small handful of nuts from the top of the can could not be relied on to represent the contents of the entire can. If, however, the mixed nuts were stratified by type of nut into homogeneous piles, a few nuts from each pile could constitute a representative sample of the entire can.

Although stratifying does reduce sampling error, it is important to recognize that the effects are modest. One should expect approximately 10 percent to 20 percent or less reduction in comparison to an SRS of equal size (Sudman, 1976; Henry, 1990). Essentially, the decision to stratify depends on two issues: the difficulty of stratifying and the cost of each additional element in the sample. It can be difficult to stratify a sample on a particular variable if it is hard to get access to data on that variable. For example, it would be relatively easy to stratify a sample of university students according to class level because universities typically include class status as part of a database on all registered students. In contrast, it would be difficult to stratify the same sample on the basis of whether they had been victims of sexual abuse during childhood because these data are not readily available and getting it would require a major study in itself. So stratification requires either that the sampling frame include information on the stratification variable or that the stratification variable be easily determined. The latter situation may be illustrated by telephone surveys and stratification by gender of respondent. Telephone interviewers can simply ask to speak to the man of the house to obtain the male stratum and request to speak to the woman of the house for the female stratum. If no one of the desired gender is available, the household is dropped and another is substituted. The process may require some extra phone calls, but the time and cost of doing this can pay for itself in the quality of the sample. As for the effect of cost issues on the decision of whether to stratify, if the cost of obtaining data on each case is high, as in an interview survey, stratifying to minimize sample size is probably warranted. If each case is inexpensive, however, stratifying to reduce cost may not be worth the effort unless it can be easily accomplished.

Proportionate Sampling When stratification is used for reducing sampling error, *proportionate* stratified sampling is normally used, in which the size of the sample taken from each stratum is proportionate to the stratum's presence in the population. Consider a sample of the undergraduates at your college or university. Although students differ on many characteristics, an obvious one is their class standing in school. Any representative sample of the student body should reflect the relative proportions of the various classes as they exist in the college as a whole. If we drew an SRS, the sample size would have to be quite large in order for the sample to reflect accurately the distribution of class levels. Small samples would have a greater likelihood of being disproportionate. If we stratify on class level, however, the sample can easily be made to match the actual class distribution regardless of sample size. Table 6.1 contains the hypothetical class distribution of a university student body. If one wished a sample of 200 students with these proportions of students accurately represented, stratifying could easily accomplish it. One would begin by developing a sampling frame with the students grouped according to class level. Separate SRSs would then be drawn from each of the four class strata in numbers proportionate to their presence in the population: 70 freshmen, 50 sophomores, 40 juniors, and 40 seniors.

In actual practice, it is normal to stratify on more than one variable. In the case of a student population, one might wish to stratify on sex as well as class level. That would double the number

Table 6.1 Hypothetical Proportionate Stratified Sample of University Students

Proportion in University		Stratified Sample of 200	
Seniors	20%	Seniors	40
Juniors	20%	Juniors	40
Sophomores	25%	Sophomores	50
Freshmen	35%	Freshmen	70
	100%		200

Research in Practice 6.1
Program Evaluation: Sampling for Direct Observation of Seat Belt Use

During the 1960s, seat belts were mandated as standard equipment in all passenger cars. Millions of drivers, however, remained unimpressed by the belts and merely sat on them. There was talk of passive restraints and other mechanisms to ensure that people used their seat belts. Eventually, a compromise emerged between the automakers and the federal regulators in the form of an agreement that if a majority of the states passed mandatory seat belt use laws and if the compliance rate was high enough, then there would be no passive restraints required in new cars. This created the impetus for states to pass legislation requiring the use of seat belts by drivers and passengers. Do the laws work? Do people wear their seat belts in states that require them? To answer this question through observation has required the development of some creative sampling procedures.

One approach might be to take a random sample of driver's license holders and conduct a survey of seat belt use. Unfortunately, this is precisely the type of question that is likely to evoke a socially desirable response rather than an accurate one. Everyone knows they should wear their seat belts, so a survey is likely to produce results indicating substantially higher levels of belt use than is actually the case. Faced with the undesirability of a sur-

vey, researchers at the University of Michigan Transportation Research Institute turned to direct observation of drivers and passengers to accurately determine levels of seat belt use (Wagenaar and Wiviott, 1986). But direct observation had its own problems. Early on, it was determined that to reliably code the desired information about each vehicle, enough time was required that the vehicle had to be stopped, at least briefly. This requirement greatly affected both the sampling and observational procedures.

Because the major purpose of the study was to estimate seat belt use rates for the state of Michigan, a representative sample was crucial. Given the requirements for observation, the researchers needed a representative sample of places where vehicles would be temporarily stopped. They solved their unique sampling problem by selecting a sample of intersections controlled by automatic traffic signals. The signals held the traffic long enough for accurate observations to be made and were located in places with sufficient traffic to keep the observers efficiently busy. Specifically, 240 intersections were selected using a multistaged stratified probability sampling procedure. First, the researchers identified all counties in Michigan that had at least three intersections controlled by elec-

---

of separate subsamples from four to eight: senior men, senior women, junior men, and so on. Even though stratifying on appropriate variables always improves a sample, it should be used judiciously. Stratifying on a few variables provides nearly as much benefit as stratifying on many. Because the number of subsamples increases geometrically as the number of stratified variables and their number of categories increases, attempting to stratify on too many variables can excessively complicate sampling without offering substantially increased benefits in terms of reduction in sampling error.

Disproportionate Sampling   In addition to reducing error, stratified samples are used to enable one to make comparisons among various subgroups in the population when one or more of the subgroups are relatively uncommon. For example, suppose we were interested in comparing two-parent families receiving AFDC with other AFDC families. If two-parent families comprise only about 2 percent of families on the AFDC rolls, a large SRS of 500 AFDC families would be expected to contain only 10 such families. This number would be far too small to make meaningful statistical

tronic signals. They discovered that 20 of Michigan's 83 counties did not meet this criterion, so those were grouped with adjacent counties to form 63 counties or county groups.

The 63 areas were then grouped into 7 regions, which became strata for a stratified sample, with a separate sample drawn from each region. Given the great differences in population density, from high in the southeastern part of the state to very low in the north and northwest, a disproportionate sample was drawn to ensure some inclusion of the low population density areas. This was important as one might hypothesize that population density could be related to seat belt use rates. The counties and county groups in the 7 regions constituted the primary sampling units (PSUs). Sixty PSUs were selected, resulting in 32 of the county and county groups being included in the sample.

For the next stage, a complete list of all intersections equipped with electronic signals in the selected counties and county groups was constructed to serve as a sampling frame. From this sampling frame, the final sample of intersections was randomly selected for a total of 240 observation sites.

Sampling considerations did not end with the final sample of intersections. Because the goal was to estimate seat belt use at *all times* on Michigan roads, time sampling (discussed in more detail in Chapter 9) became important. Unfortunately, the researchers could not meet this ambitious goal because accurate observations could not be made during the night. Therefore, observations and conclusions were restricted to daylight hours. During the daytime, however, observations were distributed throughout the daylight hours and across all days of the week. The resulting observations of the sample of intersections, days of the week, and times of day could be expected to reasonably approximate the seat belt use rates for the population of Michigan motorists.

Care to know what the researchers found out? Well, actually three observational studies were conducted, one prior to passage of a mandatory seat belt use law, one shortly after such a law was passed, and a third approximately 2 years after the law went into effect. (This is called a time series design and is discussed in more detail in Chapter 10). Results of the first survey revealed a relatively low level of seat belt use, 19.8 percent. After the law went into effect, use rose to 58.4 percent, clearly indicating that mandatory seat belt laws are effective in encouraging belt use. The last survey showed that the effectiveness of belt laws does wear off to some extent after the publicity dies down and some people revert to their old habits. Two years after the law was passed, the seat belt use rate was down to 46.6 percent, still more than double the rate prior to the legal mandate. So can motorists be coerced into doing what is good for them against their will? Apparently, over the long run, about half can be. The other half, rebels to the end, will be saved only by passive restraints or their own dumb luck.

comparisons. Stratifying in this case would allow us to draw a larger sample of two-parent families to provide enough cases for reliable comparisons to be made. This is called *disproportionate* stratified sampling because the strata are not sampled proportionately to their presence in the population. This type of sample is different from most probability samples where representativeness is achieved by giving every element in the population an equal chance of appearing in the sample. With a disproportionate stratified sample, each element of a stratum has an equal chance of appearing in the sample of that stratum, but the elements in some strata have a better chance of appearing in the overall sample than do the elements of other strata.

So far, we have said nothing about the selection of variables on which to stratify. This depends on the reason for stratifying. If stratifying is being done to ensure sufficient numbers of cases for analysis in all groups of interest, as in the example of two-parent AFDC families, then stratifying would be done on the variable that has a category with a small proportion of cases in it. This would often be an independent variable and would involve disproportionate stratified sampling. On the other hand, if the goal of stratifying is to reduce sampling error, as is the case in proportionate stratified sampling, then variables other than the independent variable may be used. Stratifying has an effect in reducing sampling error only when the stratification variables are related to the dependent variables under study. So variables should be selected that are known or suspected of having an impact on the dependent variables. For example, a study of the impact of religiosity on delinquency might stratify on socioeconomic status because this variable has been shown to be related to delinquency involvement. Stratifying on a frivolous variable, such as eye color, would probably gain us nothing, for it is unlikely to be related to delinquency involvement. It is worth noting, however, that stratifying never hurts a sample. The worst that can happen is that the stratified sample will have about the same sampling error as an equivalent-size SRS, and our stratifying efforts will have gone for naught. Research in Practice 6.1 illustrates a fairly complex use of a stratified sample.

Area Sampling

Area sampling (also called **cluster** or **multistage sampling**) is a procedure in which the final units to be included in the sample are obtained by first sampling among larger units, called *clusters,* in which the smaller sampling units are contained. A series of sampling stages are involved, working down from larger clusters to smaller ones. Imagine, for example, that we wanted to conduct a needs assessment survey to determine the extent and distribution of preschool children with educational deficiencies in a large urban area. Simple random and systematic samples would be out of the question because there would likely be no sampling frame that would list all such children. We could turn to area sampling, which is a technique that enables us to draw a probability sample without having a complete list of all elements in the population. The ultimate unit of analysis in this needs assessment would be households because children live in

households and we can create a sampling frame of households. We get there in the following way (*see* Figure 6.1). First, we would take a simple random sample from among all census tracts in the urban area. The Census Bureau divides urban areas into a number of census tracts, which are areas of approximately 4,000 people. At the second stage, we would list all the city blocks in each census tract in our sample and then select a simple random sample from among those city blocks. In the final stage, we would list the households on each city block in our sample and select a simple random sample of households on that list. With this procedure, we have what is called an *area probability sample* of households in that urban area. (Public opinion polling agencies, such as Roper, typically use area sampling, or a variant of it.) Each household in the sample is interviewed regarding educational deficiencies among children in the household. If we were sampling an entire state or the whole country, there would be even more stages of sampling, starting with even larger areas, but eventually working down to the household or individual level, whichever is our unit of analysis.

A number of factors can complicate area sampling. For example, selected blocks often contain vastly different numbers of people—from high-density, inner-city areas to the low-density suburbs. The number of blocks and the number of households per block selected into the sample must be adjusted to take into account the differing population densities. Another complication involves the estimation of sampling error. With the simpler sampling techniques, there are fairly straightforward formulas for estimating sampling error. With area sampling, however, the many stages of sampling involved make error estimation exceedingly complex. It can be done, however, and those interested in the procedures are advised to see Kish (1965) or Scheaffer, Mendenhall, and Ott (1996).

Error estimation is quite important for area samples because they are subject to greater error than other probability samples. The reason is that some error is introduced at each stage of sampling. The more stages involved, the more the sampling error accumulates. Other factors affecting sampling

Step 1:
Take a random sample of census tracts in an
urban area (the shaded tracts are those sampled).

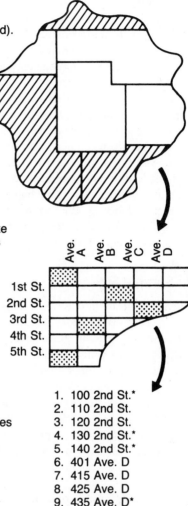

Step 2:
Identify city blocks in each census tract, and take
a random sample from a list of those city blocks
(the shaded blocks are those sampled).

Step 3:
Using a table of random numbers, select a
sample of five households from each city block
sampled in each census tract sampled (addresses
with an asterisk are those sampled).

1. 100 2nd St.*
2. 110 2nd St.
3. 120 2nd St.
4. 130 2nd St.*
5. 140 2nd St.*
6. 401 Ave. D
7. 415 Ave. D
8. 425 Ave. D
9. 435 Ave. D*
10. 201 3rd St.
11. 205 3rd St.
12. 209 3rd St.
13. 213 3rd St.*
14. 217 3rd St.
15. 400 Ave. C
16. 410 Ave. C
17. 420 Ave. C
18. 430 Ave. C

Figure 6.1   Drawing an Area Probability Sample

error are the size of the areas initially selected and their degree of homogeneity. The larger the initial areas and the greater their homogeneity, the greater the sampling error. This may seem odd because, with stratified sampling, greater homogeneity leads to less error. Remember, however, that with stratified sampling, we select a sample from *each stratum*. With area sampling, we draw samples only from *a few areas*. If the few areas in a sample are very homogeneous in comparison to the others, they will be unrepresentative. Small and more numerous, heterogeneous clusters lead to more representative area samples. Despite the complexity, area sampling allows highly accurate probability samples to be drawn from populations that, because of their size or geographical spread, could not otherwise be sampled.

Estimating Sample Size

As we have seen, a key issue in selecting a sample is that it *represent* the population from which it was drawn. People sometimes assume that a larger sample is more representative than a smaller one, and thus one should go for the largest sample possible. Actually, deciding on an appropriate sample size is far more complicated than this. Five factors influence the sample size that a researcher will choose: the research hypotheses, the level of precision, the homogeneity of the population, the sampling fraction, and the sampling technique used.

Research Hypotheses   One concern in establishing desired sample size is that we have a sufficient number of cases to examine our research hypotheses. Consider a hypothetical study in which we have three variables containing three values each. For an adequate test of the hypotheses, we need a cross-tabulation of these three variables, and this would require a 3 × 3 × 3 table, or 27 cells. If our sample were small, many cells would have few or no cases in them, and we could not test the hypotheses. Johann Galtung (1967, p. 60) has suggested that there should be from 10 to 20 cases in each cell in order to provide an adequate test of hypotheses. Disproportionate stratified sampling could be used here to ensure an adequate number

of cases in each cell. When that is not possible, Galtung suggests the following formula to determine sample size:

$$r^n \times 20 = \text{sample size}$$

where *r* refers to the number of values on each variable, and *n* refers to the number of variables. Thus, for our hypothetical study:

$$r^n \times 20 = 3^3 \times 20 = 540$$

So we would need a sample of 540 in order to feel reasonably assured of having a sufficient number of cases in each cell. The formula works only if, as in our example, all variables have the same number of values. Furthermore, this technique does not guarantee an adequate number of cases in each cell. If some combination of variables is very rare in the population, then we may still find few cases in our sample.

Statistical procedures are often used in testing hypotheses, and most such procedures require some minimum number of cases in order to give accurate results. What is the smallest legitimate sample size? This depends, of course, on the number of variables and the values they can take, but generally 30 cases is considered the bare minimum, and some researchers conservatively set 100 as the smallest legitimate sample size (Champion, 1981; Bailey, 1987). Anything smaller begins to raise questions about whether statistical procedures can be properly applied.

Precision   Another factor influencing sample size is the level of precision, or the amount of sampling error, a researcher is willing to accept. Recall that sampling error refers to the difference between a sample value of some variable and the population value of the same variable. Suppose the average age of all teenagers in a city is 15.4 years. If we draw a sample of 200 teenagers and calculate an average age of 15.1 years, then our sample statistic is close to the population value, but there is an error of 0.3 years. Recall, however, that the ultimate reason for collecting data from samples is to draw conclusions regarding the population from which those samples were drawn. We have data from a sample, such as the average age of a group of teenagers, but *we do* *not have those same data for the population as a whole.* If we did, there would be no need to study the sample because we already would know what we want to know about the population. If we do not know what the population value is, how can we assess the difference between our sample value and the population value? We do it in terms of the likelihood or probability that our sample value differs by a certain amount from the population value. (Probability theory is discussed in more detail in Chapter 15.) This is done by establishing a confidence interval, or a range in which we are fairly certain that the population value lies. We can illustrate this without showing the actual computations. If we draw a sample with a mean age of 15.1 years and establish a confidence interval of ±1.2 years, we are fairly certain that the mean age in the population is between 13.9 and 16.3 years of age. Probability theory also enables us to be precise about how certain we are. For example, we might be 95 percent certain, which is called the confidence level. (The computation of confidence levels is beyond the intent of this book.) Technically, this means that, if we draw a large number of random samples from our population and compute a mean age for each of those samples, 95 percent of those means would have confidence intervals that include the population mean and 5 percent would not. What is the actual population mean? We don't know because we have not collected data from the whole population. We have data from only one sample, but we can conclude that we are 95 percent sure that the population mean lies within the confidence interval of that sample.

Precision is directly related to sample size: Larger samples are more precise than smaller ones. Thus, probability theory enables us to calculate the sample size that would be required to achieve a given level of precision. Table 6.2 does this for simple random samples taken from populations of various sizes. As an example of how to read the table, a sample size of 1,023 would give you a 95 percent chance to obtain a sampling error of 3 percent or less with a population of 25,000 elements and a relatively heterogeneous population (50/50 split identifies a heterogeneous population and an 80/20

split is a homogeneous population). Or, in other words, a 95 percent chance exists that the population value is within 3 percent of (above or below) the sample estimate. Again, to be technical, it means that if we draw many random samples and determine a confidence interval of 3 percent for each, 95 percent of those confidence intervals will include the population value. The table shows that sample size must increase when, other things being equal, you want less sampling error (that is, more precision) or the population size is larger or the population is more heterogeneous.

In actuality, of course, only one sample would be drawn; probability theory tells us the chance we run of a single sample's having a given level of error. There is a chance—5 times out of 100—that the sample will have an error level greater than 3 percent. In fact, there is a chance, albeit a very minuscule one, that the sample will have a very large error level. This is a part of the nature of sampling: Because we are selecting a segment of a population, there is always a chance that the sample will be very unrepresentative of the population. The goal of good sampling techniques is to reduce the likelihood of that error. (Furthermore, one goal of replication in science, as discussed in Chapter 2, is to protect against the possibility that the findings of a single study are based on a sample that unknowingly contains a large error.)

If the 95 percent confidence level is not satisfactory for your purposes, you can raise the odds to the 99 percent level by increasing the sample size (this is *not* shown in Table 6.2). In this case, only 1 out of 100 samples is likely to have an error level greater than 3 percent. However, a sample size large enough for this confidence level might be very expensive and time-consuming to gather data from. For this reason, professional pollsters are normally satisfied with a sample size that will enable them to achieve an error level in the 2 percent to 4 percent range. Likewise, most scientific researchers are forced to accept higher levels of error—often as much as 5 percent to 6 percent with a 95 percent confidence level. At the other end of the spectrum, exploratory studies can provide useful data even though they incorporate considerably

Table 6.2 Calculating Sample Size Based on Confidence Level, Sampling Error, Population Heterogeneity, and Population Size

	Sample size for the 95 percent confidence level					
	±3% Sampling Error		±5% Sampling Error		±10% Sampling Error	
Population Size	50/50 Split	80/20 Split	50/50 Split	80/20 Split	50/50 Split	80/20 Split
100	92	87	80	71	49	38
250	203	183	152	124	70	49
500	341	289	217	165	81	55
750	441	358	254	185	85	57
1.000	516	406	278	198	88	58
2,500	748	537	333	224	93	60
5,000	880	601	357	234	94	61
10,000	964	639	370	240	95	61
25,000	1,023	665	378	234	96	61
50,000	1,045	674	381	245	96	61
100,000	1,056	678	383	245	96	61
1,000,000	1,066	682	384	246	96	61
100,000,000	1,067	683	384	246	96	61

How to read this table: For a population with 250 members whom we expect to be about evenly split on the characteristic in which we are interested, we need a sample of 152 to make estimates with a sampling error of no more than ±5 percent, at the 95 percent confidence level. A "50/50 split" means the population is relatively varied. An "80/20 split" means it is less varied; most people have a certain characteristic, a few do not. Unless we know the split ahead of time, it is best to be conservative and use 50/50.

Numbers in the table refer to completed, usable questionnaires needed for various levels of sampling error. Starting sample size should allow for ineligibles and nonrespondents. Note that when the population is small, little is gained by sampling, especially if the need for precision is great.

Source Reprinted with permission from Priscilla Salant and Don A. Dillman, *How to Conduct Your Own Survey* (New York: John Wiley and Sons, 1994), p. 55. Used with permission.

more imprecision and sampling error. So the issue of sample size and error is influenced in part by the goals of the research project.

Population Homogeneity The third factor impacting on sample size is the variability of the population to be sampled. As we have noted, a large sample is more essential for a heterogeneous population than for a homogeneous one. Unfortunately, researchers may know little about the homogeneity of their target population. Accurate estimates of population variability can often be made only *after*

the sample is drawn and data are collected and at least partially analyzed. On the surface, this would appear to preclude estimating sample size in advance. In fact, however, probability theory still allows sample size to be estimated by simply assuming maximum variability in the population. In Table 6.2, the assumption of "50/50 split" means that maximum variability is assumed. Such estimates are, of course, conservative. This means that the sample size estimates will be larger than needed for a given level of precision if the actual variability in the population is less than assumed.

Sampling Fraction A fourth factor influencing sample size is the *sampling fraction,* or the number of elements in the sample relative to the number of elements in the population (or n/N, where n = estimated sample size ignoring sampling fraction and N = population size). With large populations, the sampling fraction can be ignored because the sample will constitute only a tiny fraction of the population. In Table 6.2, for example, a population of 10,000 calls for a sample size of only 370 (5 percent sampling error and 50/50 split), which is less than 4 percent of the population. For such samples, the research hypotheses, sampling error, and population homogeneity would be sufficient to determine sample size. With smaller populations, however, a sample that meets these criteria may constitute a relatively large fraction of the whole population and, in fact, may be larger than it needs to be (Moser and Kalton, 1972). This is so because a sample that constitutes a large fraction of the population will contain less sampling error than if the sample were a small fraction. In such cases, the sample size can be adjusted by the following formula:

$$n' = n/[1 + (n/N)]$$

where:

n' = adjusted sample size
n = estimated sample size ignoring the sampling fraction
N = population size

As a rule of thumb, this correction formula should be used if the sampling fraction is more than 5 percent. For example, suppose that a community action agency is conducting a needs assessment survey for an Indian tribal organization with 3,000 tribal members. On the basis of the research hypothesis, sampling error, and population variance on key variables, it is estimated that a sample of 600 is needed. The sampling fraction, then, is n/N = 600/3,000 = 0.2, or 20 percent. As this is well over 5 percent, we apply the correction:

$$n' = 600/[1 + (600/3,000)]$$
$$n' = 600/1.20$$
$$n' = 500$$

Thus, instead of a sample of 600, only 500 are needed to achieve the same level of precision. At costs that often exceed $50 per interview, the savings of this adjustment could be significant.

Sampling Technique The final factor influencing sample size is the sampling technique employed. The estimates discussed thus far are for simple random samples. More complex sampling procedures change the estimates of sample size. Area sampling, for example, tends to increase sampling error in comparison with SRS. A rough estimate of sample sizes for area samples can be obtained by simply increasing the suggested sizes in Table 6.2 by one half (Backstrom and Hursh, 1981). That estimate will be crude and probably conservative, but it is simple to obtain. Stratified sampling, on the other hand, tends to reduce sampling error and decrease required sample size. Estimating sample sizes for stratified samples is relatively complex. Readers interested in this are advised to consult Kish (1965) or Scheaffer, Mendenhall, and Ott (1996).

In an assessment of the implications of scientific work for clinical application, the issue of precision in sampling comes to the fore. Practitioners need to exercise judgment regarding how scientifically sound the research is and whether it is sufficiently valid to be introduced into practice. As we have emphasized, single studies should be viewed with caution, irrespective of how low the sampling error is. As numerous studies begin to accumulate, it is necessary to assess them in terms of how much error can be expected, given the sample size and the sampling technique. If the sampling errors appear to be quite low, then a few replications might confirm that the findings from these samples reflect the state of the actual population. With large sampling errors, however, the probability that the samples do not represent the population is increased. In such cases, confidence in the outcomes would be established only if a *number* of studies arrive at the same conclusions. More studies mean that more samples were drawn, which in turn reduces the likelihood that *all* the samples contain large sampling errors.

Nonprobability Samples

Probability samples are not required or even appropriate for all studies. Some research situations call for **nonprobability samples,** samples in which the investigator does not know the probability of each population element's being included in the sample. Although nonprobability samples can be very useful, they do have some important limitations. First, without the use of probability in the selection of elements for the sample, no real claim of representativeness can be made. There is simply no way of knowing precisely what population, if any, a nonprobability sample represents. This question of representativeness greatly limits the ability to generalize findings beyond the level of the sample cases.

A second limitation is that the degree of sampling error remains unknown and unknowable. With no clear population being represented by the sample, there is nothing with which to compare it. The lack of probability in the selection of cases means that the techniques employed for estimating sampling error with probability samples are not appropriate. This also means that the techniques for estimating sample size are also not applicable to nonprobability samples. The only factor impacting on sample size for nonprobability samples is that sufficient cases be selected to allow the types of data analysis that are planned.

A final limitation of nonprobability samples involves statistical tests of significance. These commonly used statistics, to be discussed in Chapter 15, indicate to the researcher whether relationships found in sample data are sufficiently strong to be generalizable to the whole population. All these statistical tests, however, are based on various laws of probability and assume that a random process is utilized in selecting sample elements. Because nonprobability samples violate the basic assumption of these tests, they should not be used on data derived from such samples.

Despite these limitations, nonprobability samples have their uses. For example, they are especially useful when the goal of research is to see whether there is a relationship between independent and dependent variables and there is no intent to generalize the results from the sample to a larger population. This is sometimes the case, for instance, in experimental research. However, when generalizing sample results to a population is a major goal of the research, then nonprobability samples must be used with care because they can produce very misleading results. A television program titled *America On The Line,* broadcast by CBS News in 1992, provides an interesting illustration of this. It was the night of President Bush's State of the Union address and, after the speech, CBS conducted a call-in poll where viewers could respond to questions via touch-tone telephone to a computerized system capable of handling tens of thousands of phone calls at a time. This resulted in a very large sample of over 300,000 respondents. At the same time, CBS also conducted a survey of a scientifically based probability sample of 1,200 people and asked respondents the same questions that viewers responded to during the call-in. As can be seen from Table 6.3, responses from the callers were substantially more negative toward the Bush administration than were those from respondents in the scientific survey. For example, the call-in respondents were much more likely to feel that they were worse off now than 4 years ago and to be worried about losing their jobs. Given the sample size of the scientific survey, we know that the probable margin of error was 3 percent, meaning that any difference between call-in responses and survey responses greater than that is probably not due to chance. Many of the differences are far greater than 3 percent, so an obvious question becomes: Why?

Several factors probably combined to skew the call-in responses toward the negative. First, only those viewers with touch-tone phones could participate in the call-in. Although widely available, this service is least available in rural areas where President Bush tended to have stronger support. Another factor was that, as people called in their opinions, the program continued, showing mostly short reports emphasizing how bad the economy was and how people were hurting across the country. These clearly negative images, presented as people were calling in, could have skewed their responses. Additionally, it is well known that people

Table 6.3 A Comparison of a Nonprobability and a Probability Sample

Question	Viewer Call-In (314,786)		CBS Formal Poll (1,234)
Are you better off now than 4 years ago?	29%	better off	24%
	54%	worse off	32%
	17%	the same	44%
Are you worried about job loss this year?	64%	yes	48%
	36%	no	52%
Would you pay more taxes for free health care?	58%	yes	46%
	42%	no	53%
Does the president understand the middle class?	30%	yes	43%
	70%	no	57%
Are the media exaggerating how bad economic conditions are?	39%	yes	35%
	51%	no	64%
Future of America's children?	21%	will be better	24%
	57%	will be worse	36%
	22%	about the same	39%

Source From CBS news release, January 29, 1992.

who are angry or upset are more likely to take some action than those who are more content. This effect was exaggerated in this case by the fact that the computerized answering system was immediately overwhelmed by calls and bogged down to the point where only the most persistent callers got through. Because such persistence is associated with being dissatisfied, this factor tended to bias the call-in poll against the president. So we see that, for a variety of reasons, the results of the call-in produced a distorted view of people's opinions on the night of the president's speech. The poll may have appeared "high-tech," but it suffered from problems similar to the 1936 *Literary Digest* poll. Even though the sampling frame of CBS viewers was large and national in scope, it was not representative of the U.S. citizenry. Even though hundreds of thousands responded, nonresponse was more likely

among those who approved of the president so that the final results were even more biased.

The knowledge about sampling that you have gained from your study of research methods should make you highly critical of any attempt to draw conclusions about actual population values from nonprobability samples similar to the CBS call-in. The huge sample sizes may tempt some to believe the results, but as we have demonstrated it is not the size of the sample that makes for accurate results. Far more important are the procedures used for selecting elements into the sample. We now discuss the most widely used types of nonprobability samples.

Availability Sampling

Availability sampling (also called **convenience** or **accidental sampling**) involves taking whichever elements are readily available to the researcher. These samples are especially popular and appropriate for research in which it is very difficult or impossible to develop a complete sampling frame. Sometimes it is too costly to do so, whereas in other cases it is impossible to identify all the elements of a population. Helen Mendes (1976), for example, used an availability sample in her study of single fathers. Because it would be practically impossible to develop a sampling frame of all single fathers, she turned to teachers, physicians, social workers, and self-help groups for assistance. She asked these people to refer single fathers to her. The limitation on generalizability, however, seriously reduces the utility of findings based on availability samples. It would be impossible for Mendes to argue, for example, that the single fathers she studied were representative of all single fathers. It may well be that only fathers with certain characteristics were likely to become a part of her sample.

Availability samples are often used in experimental or quasi-experimental research. This is because it can be difficult to get a representative sample of people to participate in an experiment—especially one that is lengthy and time-consuming. For example, Ronald Feldman and Timothy Caplinger (1977) were interested in factors that bring about behavior change in young boys who had exhibited highly visible antisocial behavior. Their research design was a field experiment calling for the youngsters participating in the study to meet periodically in groups over an 8-month period. Groups met an average of 22.2 times for 2 to 3 hours each. Most youngsters could be expected to refuse such a commitment of time and energy. Had the investigators attempted to draw a probability sample from the community, they probably would have had such a high refusal rate that the representativeness of their sample would have been questionable. They would have expended considerable resources and still had, in effect, a nonprobability sample. So they resorted to an availability sample. To locate boys who had exhibited antisocial behavior, they sought referrals from numerous sources: mental health centers, juvenile courts, and the like. In order to have a comparison group of boys who had not been identified as antisocial, they sought volunteers from a large community center association. Given the purpose of experimentation, representative samples are less important. Experiments serve to determine *if* cause-and-effect relationships can be found. The issue of how generalizable those relationships are becomes important only after the relationships have been established.

Availability sampling is probably one of the more common forms of sampling used in human service research, both because it is less expensive than many other methods and because it is often impossible to develop an exhaustive sampling frame. For example, in all issues of the *Journal of Social Service Research* from 1980 through 1984, at least 52 of the 76 research articles could be classified as reporting some form of availability sample. You can readily grasp the problems of trying to develop a sampling frame in the following studies:

- The evaluation of interviewer competence: Graduate students in an advanced social work methods course constituted the sample.
- The effect of using videotapes in training: The sample consisted of 55 non-MSW social workers in a public welfare agency.
- Techniques of assertion training: The sample contained people who responded to posters or advertisements in the local media.
- The assessment of sexual dysfunction: The sample was 190 couples who applied for treatment at a sex therapy clinic during a 2-year period.
- The patterns of utilization of a prenatal clinic: The sample was 185 women who sought prenatal services at a clinic.

An exhaustive sampling frame that would make possible the selection of a probability sample in each of these studies might be, respectively, as follows:

- all interviewers
- all non-MSW social workers in public welfare agencies
- all people
- all couples with some sexual dysfunction
- all pregnant women

Clearly, such probability sampling is beyond the realm of most investigators. Availability samples, though less desirable, make it possible for scientific investigation to move forward in those cases where probability sampling is impossible or prohibitively costly.

Snowball Sampling

When a snowball is rolled along in wet, sticky snow, it picks up more snow, becoming larger and larger. This is analogous to what happens with **snowball sampling:** We start with a few cases of the type we wish to study and have them lead us to more cases, who, in turn, are expected to lead us to still more cases, and so on. Like the rolling snowball, the snowball sample builds up as we continue adding cases. Because snowball sampling depends on the sampled cases being knowledgeable of other relevant cases, the technique is especially useful for sampling subcultures where the members routinely interact with one another. Snowball sampling can also be useful in the investigation of sensitive topics, such as child abuse or drug use, where the perpetrators or the victims might be hesitant to identify themselves if approached by a stranger, such as a researcher, but might be open to an approach by someone who they know shares their experience or deviant status (Gelles, 1978).

Snowball sampling allows the researcher to accomplish what Norman Denzin (1989) calls *interactive* sampling—that is, the sampling of persons who interact with one another. Probability samples are all noninteractive because knowing someone who has been selected for the sample does not change the probability of being selected. Interactive sampling is often theoretically relevant because many social science theories stress the impact of one's associates on one's behavior. In order to study these associational influences, researchers often combine snowball sampling with a probability sample. For example, Albert Reiss and Lewis Rhodes (1967), in a study of associational influences on delinquency, drew a probability sample of 378 boys between the ages of 12 and 16. They then had the members of this sample indicate their two best friends. By correlating various characteristics of the juveniles and their friends, the researchers were able to study how friendship patterns affect delinquency.

This interactive element, however, also points to one of the drawbacks of snowball sampling: Though it taps people who are involved in social networks, it misses people who may be isolated from such networks. Thus, a snowball sample of drug users would be limited to those users who are a part of some social network, but would ignore those who use drugs in an individual and isolated fashion. It may well be that drug users involved in a social network differ from isolated users in significant ways. Care must be taken in making generalizations from snowball samples to ensure that we generalize only to those people who are like those in our sample.

Quota Sampling

Quota sampling involves dividing a population into various categories and setting quotas on the number of elements to be selected from each category. Once the quota is reached, no more elements from that category are put in the sample. Quota sampling is like stratified sampling in that both divide a population into categories, and then samples are taken from the categories, but quota sampling is a nonprobability technique, often depending on availability to determine precisely which elements will be in the sample. Quota sampling was at one time the method of choice among many professional pollsters. Problems deriving from efforts to predict the very close 1948 presidential election caused pollsters to turn away from quota sampling and embrace the newly developed probability sampling techniques. With its fall from grace among pollsters, quota sampling also declined in popularity among researchers. Presently, use of quota sampling is best restricted to those situations in which its advantages clearly outweigh its considerable disadvantages. For example, quota sampling might be used to study crowd behavior, where it is not possible to establish a sampling frame given the unstable nature of the phenomenon. Quota sampling might be justified for a researcher who is studying reaction to disasters such as a flood or tornado, where the need for immediate reaction is critical and takes precedence over sample representativeness.

Quotas are normally established for several variables. Typically included among these variables are common demographic characteristics such as age, sex, race, socioeconomic status, and education. In addition, it is common to include one or more quotas directly related to the research topic. For example, a study of political behavior would likely include a quota on political party affiliation to ensure that the sample mirrored the population on the central variable in the study.

In quota sampling, interviewers do the actual selection of respondents. Armed with the preestablished quotas, interviewers begin interviewing people until they have their quotas on each variable filled. The fact that quota sampling utilizes interviewers to do the actual selection of cases is one of its major shortcomings. Despite the quotas, much bias can enter quota sampling owing to interviewer behavior. Some people simply look more approachable than others, and interviewers naturally gravitate toward the former. Interviewers are also not stupid. They realize that certain areas of major cities are less than safe places to go around asking questions of strangers. Protecting their personal safety by avoiding these areas can introduce obvious bias into the resulting sample. The reluctance to interview certain potential respondents was graphically stated by Robert Rygor of the Census Bureau while speaking of the 1980 census: "Any outlandish person was theoretically supposed to be approached. But imagine a person lying on the ground with wine all over and urine and a fly on his nose and asking if he had been counted" (Magnet, 1981). Whether based on reality or prejudicial bias, such feelings on the part of interviewers will influence sample selection.

Because of the potential for large biases to enter quota samples, the technique is considered unreliable. Its major positive attributes, however, are that it is cheaper and faster than probability sampling. At times, these advantages can be sufficient to make quota sampling the logical choice. For exam-

ple, if we wanted a rapid assessment of people's reactions to some event that had just occurred, quota sampling would probably be the best approach.

Purposive Sampling

In the sampling procedures discussed thus far, one major concern has been to select a sample that is representative of, and will enable generalizations to, a larger population. However, generalizability is only one goal, albeit an important one, of scientific research. In some studies, the issue of *control* may take on considerable importance and dictate a slightly different sampling procedure. In some investigations, control takes the form of choosing a sample that specifically *excludes* certain types of people because their presence might confuse the research findings. For example, if one were conducting an exploratory study of a psychotherapeutic model of treatment, it might be desirable to choose people for the sample from among those who would be "ideal" candidates for psychotherapy. Because psychotherapy is based on talking about yourself and gaining insight into feelings, "ideal" candidates for psychotherapy are people with good verbal skills and the ability to explore and express inner feelings. Because well-educated, middle-class people are more likely to have these characteristics, they might be chosen for the sample.

This is called **purposive** (or **judgmental**) **sampling:** The investigators use their judgment and prior knowledge to choose people for the sample who would best serve the purposes of the study. Lest you think this is "stacking the deck" in your favor, consider the illustration given earlier. The basic research question is whether this type of psychotherapy can work at all. If we selected a random sample, we would have variation based on age, sex, education, socioeconomic status, and a host of other variables that are not of direct interest in this study but that might influence receptiveness to psychotherapy. Certainly, in a truly random sample, the effects of this variation would be washed out. The sample, however, would have to be so large that it would not be feasible to do psychotherapy on that many people. So rather than use some other sampling technique, we choose a group that is homogeneous in terms of the factors that are likely to influence receptiveness to psychotherapy. This enables us to see whether psychotherapy works better than some other form of therapy. If it does not work with this "ideal" group, then we can probably forget the idea. If it does work, then we can generalize *only to this group.* Further research would be required among other groups to see how extensively the results could be generalized.

In a study of social supports among elderly women, Gertrude Goldberg and her colleagues (1986) used a purposive sample. Their basic interest was to investigate the sources of support among women who face old age with neither a spouse nor a child to provide them with support. For this exploratory study, they selected a sample of women who were single or widowed, childless, and not working full-time. Because the sources of support for women who are married or have children have been studied extensively, there was no need to repeat this. This enabled the researchers to look directly at such questions as whether kin and friends provide different kinds of support for these childless, spouseless women and whether widowed or divorced women have social supports that are different from those of women who never married.

Dimensional Sampling

It is often expeditious, if not essential, that small samples be used. Small samples can be very use-ful, but considerable care must be exercised in drawing the sample. (The smallest sample size, of course, is the single case, which is discussed in Chapter 11.) **Dimensional sampling** is a sampling technique for selecting small samples in a way that enhances their representativeness (Arnold, 1970). There are basically two steps to dimensional sampling: First, specify all the dimensions or variables that are important, and second, choose a sample that includes at least one case representing each possible combination of dimensions. We can illustrate this with a study of the effectiveness of various institutional approaches to the control of juvenile delinquency (Street, Vinter, and Perrow, 1966). The population consisted of all institutions for delinquents. To draw a random sample of all those institutions, however, would have called for a sample size that would tax the resources of most investigators. As an alternative, the researchers used a dimensional sample. The first step was to spell out the conceptual dimensions that were important. In terms of juvenile institutions, this investigation considered three dimensions, each containing two values as illustrated in Table 6.4: organizational goals (custodial or rehabilitative), organizational control (public or private), and organizational size (large or small). The second step was to select at least one case to represent each of the eight possibilities that resulted.

Dimensional sampling has a number of advantages that can make it an attractive alternative in some situations. First, it is faster and less expensive than studying large samples. Second, it is valuable in exploratory studies where there is little theoretical development to support a large-scale study.

Table 6.4 An Illustration of Institutional Dimensions for a Dimensional Sample

	Custodial Goals		Rehabilitative Goals	
	Public	**Private**	**Public**	**Private**
Large Size				
Small Size				

Research in Practice 6.2
Needs Assessment: Mental Health Among the Homeless

With the implementation of the mental health policy known as "deinstitutionalization" over the past three decades, many people with mental disorders are outside of mental institutions rather than in them. Linked with this development has been a growth in concern over the number of homeless people in the United States. In fact, the rise in homelessness has been tied to mental health policies through the belief that many of the homeless are those with moderate-to-severe emotional disorders who in the past would have been institutionalized. Instead, many presume, these people have been released from the mental health system (or never placed there in the first place) even though they lack the financial or personal resources to maintain a home to live in. Needs assessment research has produced varying estimates of the percent of mentally ill among the homeless, from a low of 25 percent in a New York study to a high of 90 percent in a Boston investigation (New York Office of Mental Health, 1982; Bassuk, 1984). From the perspective of mental health planners and policymakers, such widely varying estimates offer little assistance in assessing how adequately the system meets the needs of the homeless and mentally ill or what policies could overcome the shortcomings in service delivery.

For many obvious and some not so obvious reasons, homelessness is an extremely difficult phenomenon to study. A major problem in studying it is sampling, and this accounts in part for the widely varying conclusions that different studies have come to (Burnam and Koegel, 1988). Clearly, conventional probability samples are out of the question because it would be impossible to de-velop a complete sampling frame of all homeless people in a community. Most studies of the homeless have been limited to collecting data at one type of location, such as at shelters for the homeless, in one city. Mental health researchers in Ohio (Roth et al., 1985) developed a creative sampling procedure to try to overcome these problems. First, they found that the concept of "homelessness" was too simple to reflect the complexities of life for people without permanent residences. They developed an operational definition that classified people into four types or levels of homelessness:

1. Those with no shelter at all to spend the night in
2. People living in public or private shelters or missions
3. People living in cheap hotels or motels for 45 days or less
4. Other unique situations, such as living with friends, in a tent city, or in jail

Persons were classified into these categories based on where they had slept the night before the interview. (If the person became homeless on the day of the interview, then placement was based on where he or she intended to sleep during the coming night.) This illustrates once again the importance of conceptual development and the reconceptualization that often occurs in the process of operationalizing concepts (*see* Figure 5.1).

The goal of the sampling technique used in the Ohio study was to establish the highest probability that the sample was representative of the homeless in Ohio, including both urban and nonurban homeless. To achieve this, researchers

Third, dimensional sampling provides more detailed knowledge of each case than is likely to be gained from a large sample. With a large sample, data collection will necessarily be more cursory and focused (which is justified if previous research has narrowed the focus of what variables are important).

Despite their limitations, nonprobability samples can be valuable tools in the conduct of human

used a combination of stratified, purposive, and random sampling techniques. The state was stratified into five geographic regions, and four counties were selected from each region, one being the major urban center in the region. In addition, two rural counties and one mixed type were selected from each region through a random process. Through this method, the researchers increased the likelihood that their sample would be representative of the homeless in Ohio.

To further ensure that sufficient data were collected from the different types of homeless people, the sample in each county was stratified according to type of homelessness as spelled out in the operational definitions. Then, equal numbers of each type of homeless person were interviewed in each county. Because of the small number of homeless in rural and mixed counties, all homeless persons identified in these counties were interviewed to ensure that there was a sufficient number of cases for data analysis in each county. In urban counties, purposive processes were used to develop sampling frames that listed sites at which homeless people of each type could be found, and sites were randomly selected for interviewing from these lists. At the sites themselves, the interviewers were trained to use random techniques, when possible, to select specific individuals to interview. For example, at shelters they interviewed the person at every tenth sleeping location. Had the interviewers selected whom they wished to interview at these sites, they might be inclined to interview people who looked least dangerous, most approachable, or most articulate, and this would have biased the sample.

A research team in Chicago used an additional sampling technique to reduce bias in the sampling of homeless people (Rossi et al., 1987). They began with a list of census blocks in the city and asked police and others in a position to know which blocks would have many homeless and which only

a few. They then stratified blocks by the number of homeless, choosing a larger random sample among blocks believed to contain many homeless. Then the interviewers, accompanied by off-duty police officers, looked for homeless people to interview in all the nondwelling places on the sampled blocks to which they could gain access between midnight and 6 A.M., including hallways, roofs, abandoned buildings, and parked cars. This strategy is obviously far more likely to produce a sample that is representative of all homeless people than are the many studies that limit their sampling to people in shelters.

To assess the mental status of the homeless, the Ohio researchers used an existing scale known as the Psychiatric Status Schedule, or PSS (Spitzer, Endicott, and Cohen, 1970). After analyzing the data, the researchers concluded that "about 31 percent of the respondent group presented problems or symptoms that possibly required a mental health service" (Bean, Stefl, and Howe, 1987, p. 414). Because some people having symptoms detected by the PSS do not require treatment, the actual number of homeless needing mental health intervention in Ohio is probably somewhat less. This figure of 31 percent is at considerable variance with assessments of the problem in the popular literature, which typically reports much higher levels.

These studies, of course, are not free of sampling problems. For example, the use of a police escort in the Chicago study may have caused many homeless people, understandably suspicious of someone seeking them out and possibly waking them up in the night, to flee, and this could have introduced a bias into the sample (Burnam and Koegel, 1988). Yet, the sampling procedures used in these needs assessments give us much more confidence that the results are accurate than does the more limited sampling typically done.

service research. However, two points need to be reiterated. First, some research uses both probability and nonprobability samples in a single research project, and we have given some illustrations of this. The point is that the two types of samples

should not be considered competitors for our attention. Second, findings based on nonprobability samples should be viewed as suggestive rather than conclusive, and opportunities to retest hypotheses using probability samples should be sought.

Research in Practice 6.2 illustrates how a complex research problem might call for the use of several sampling techniques as discussed in this chapter for a single research study.

Sampling With Minority Populations

The key to selecting scientifically valid samples is to ensure their representativeness so that valid generalizations can be made. Accomplishing this can be an especially difficult challenge when research is conducted on racial or ethnic minorities. One problem is that some minorities have "rare event" status—that is, they constitute a relatively small percentage of our populace. African Americans, for example, constitute approximately 12 percent, Hispanics around 7 percent (slightly higher if those in the country illegally are counted), Native Americans maybe 3 percent (U.S. Bureau of the Census, 1991). This means that a representative sample of 1,500 Americans would, if it included the proper proportions of minorities, contain 180 African Americans, 105 Hispanics, and 45 Native Americans. These numbers are too small for most data analysis purposes. The Native Americans, especially, are so few that any analysis that breaks the sample down into subgroups would result in meaninglessly small numbers in each subgroup. Furthermore, these small numbers mean that the error rate will be much higher for the minorities than for nonminority groups because small samples are less reliable and have more error (A. W. Smith, 1987). These small sample sizes make it difficult to assess differences of opinion or behavior within a minority group, and thus it is easy to falsely conclude that the group is homogeneous. As a consequence, we know little about gender, social class, regional, or religious differences among members of particular minorities. The outcome, according to one researcher, is "little more than a form of stereotyping, an *underestimation* of the variability of opinions among blacks. This leads to an *overestimation* of the contribution of race, per se, to black–white differences" in attitude and behavior (A. W. Smith, 1987,

p. 445). The Committee on the Status of Women in Sociology (1986) makes the same recommendations regarding gender: "Research should include sufficiently large subsamples of male and female subjects to allow meaningful analysis of subgroups."

Some minorities have "rare event" status in another way that can cause problems in sampling. Because of substantial residential segregation of minorities in the United States, minorities who live in largely white areas are relatively small in number and can be easily missed by chance even in a well-chosen, representative sample. The result is a sample of minorities that is biased: It includes minorities living in largely minority communities but not minorities living elsewhere. Because minorities living in different communities probably vary in terms of attitudes and behavior, such a biased sample would give a deceptively homogeneous picture of the minority.

So efforts must be made in sampling to ensure that those "rare events" have a chance to be selected for the sample. In some cases, this can be done with disproportionate sampling, in which some individuals or households have a greater probability of appearing in the sample than do other individuals or households. Another way to avoid some of these problems is to use both probability and nonprobability sampling techniques when studying minorities. Some researchers suggest that purposive, dimensional, and snowball sampling can be effectively combined with some type of probability sample to ensure effective coverage of a minority population (Becerra and Zambrana, 1985). A dimensional sample of Hispanics, for example, might specify a series of dimensions that would all have to be covered by the sample. Thus, you might specify that certain age cohorts of Hispanic women (20–30 years of age, 31–40, and 41 and older) would have to be included in the sample, or some minimum number of single-parent and two-parent Hispanic families would have to be included. This would ensure that there were sufficient people with certain characteristics in the sample for valid data analysis. Another study of mental health among Asian immigrants used the snowball technique to ensure a complete sampling frame (Kuo and Tsai,

1986). Part of the sampling frame was developed by using local telephone directories and gathering names from ethnic and community organizations. However, given the dispersion of Asian Americans in the Seattle area where this study was done, researchers also used the snowball technique.

A Note on Sampling in Practice

Human service practitioners do not routinely engage in sampling procedures like those used for research purposes. Yet, there are parallels between what occurs in practice and in research along these lines, and some of the principles of sampling discussed in this chapter can be applied to providing client services. The assessments and actions of practitioners are typically guided by the needs and characteristics of a particular client. However, to what extent are judgments about one client based on experiences with other clients? The issue being raised here, of course, is that of *generalizability*. As human beings, we constantly dip into our own fund of experience to help us cope with situations that we confront. Practitioners use their past experience with clients—sometimes very effectively—to grapple with problems of other clients. The critical judgment that needs to be made in this regard is whether it is legitimate to generalize those past outcomes to current situations.

In practice settings, you will not likely be dealing with probability samples. Irrespective of whether one's clients are welfare recipients, elderly people receiving nursing home care, child abusers, or individuals with problem pregnancies, you have no way of knowing whether *all* people with such characteristics had a chance to be in your "sample" (that is, be one of your clients) or how great that chance was. For all practical purposes, then, you will be dealing with nonprobability samples, with all the limitations that they entail. In most cases, you will have an availability sample—those people who happened to come to your attention because they are your clients. This means that you need to show caution in making generalizations from your observations. This is, however, no reason for despair.

Remember that many scientific investigations are based on availability samples. One simply needs to recognize their limitations and use care in generalizing.

If your main concern is to generalize to other clients with similar problems, then a reasonable assumption is that the clients you see are representative of others with similar problems who seek the aid of a practitioner. Whatever propels people to see a practitioner is likely to be operative on many, if not all, of your clients. However, if your research interest concerns all people experiencing a certain type of problem, then agency clients would not be an appropriate sample. Agencies intentionally and unintentionally screen their prospective clients; thus, many people who could use services are not included in a sample of agency clients. The well-known study by Robert Scott (1975) on agencies serving the blind is a classic example. Scott found that these agencies concentrated their efforts on young, trainable clientele even though most blind people are elderly or have multiple handicaps. If workers in such an agency assumed that the agency clientele represented all blind people, they would have a distorted perspective on the actual blind population.

There are, of course, ways of checking on such distortions. For example, you can compare notes with other practitioners. Do they find the same kinds of things among their clients? If so, that is support for your assumption that your clients are representative of all people with similar problems. You might also consider utilizing, at least in an informal fashion, other sampling techniques. For example, you could adopt a snowball technique by asking your clients to recommend someone they know who has a similar problem but is not receiving any services. Especially with people whose problems may be of a "sensitive" nature, this snowball approach is a mode of entry with a considerable likelihood of success. Another sampling technique that might be effective in practice is purposive sampling. For example, in dealing with unplanned pregnancies among teenagers, suppose that all your clients are members of ethnic minorities. It might occur to you that your clients' behavior, such as

COMPUTERS IN RESEARCH
Software for Sampling

One question that haunts any researcher embarking on a research project is: How big a sample do I need? Unfortunately, the only concise answer to this question is the frustrating reply: It depends. It depends on many things, as is evident from the five key factors detailed in this chapter. Although understanding these factors conceptually helps one understand what influences sample size, the researcher needs a number, not a general explanation. Because an appropriately sized sample is so important to research and because the problem of selecting a sample is one that readily lends itself to computerization, several software options are available to assist the researcher with sampling decisions.

One such software program is Design Power, available from Scientific Software. This program helps researchers estimate several related factors in research planning. One is the design power or ability to detect an effect of an independent variable (*see* Research in Practice 15.1). Essentially, the program can tell the researcher how big a difference must occur between experimental and control conditions in order to conclude that a statistically significant difference exists. For example, imagine that an experimental treatment actually raises the reading scores of a group by 10 points on average. With a weak design, statistical results might lead

the researcher to conclude that the difference is simply a chance variation and not a real difference. The researcher enters information about the study, such as the proposed sample size and the desired level of statistical significance, and the program reports how big an effect must occur to reject the hypothesis that the change occurred by chance. Conversely, when the researcher specifies the power of the test, the program can specify how big a sample is necessary for an effect of a given size to be statistically significant.

The program operates through a series of menus that guide the user through making choices in the program. The researcher need only select the menu option for sample size and complete a limited number of information entries requested by the program, and the program will designate the sample size needed without requiring the user to provide complex formulas or large amounts of data.

Another sampling aid is the program Ex-Sample. This program also helps determine sample size by using information supplied by the researcher, such as anticipated data analysis procedures, time, money, projected response rate, and so on. Besides generating a recommended sample size, this program leads the researcher through a structured decision-making system that reduces the possibility

hostility toward practitioners, could either be due to the crisis of the pregnancy or to the animosity of a minority member toward the welfare bureaucracy. Your problem is that you have a sample that is homogeneous with respect to two variables that may be important: They all have problem pregnancies and they are all members of an ethnic minority. To get around this problem, you might begin to choose a purposive sample in which the problem pregnancies occur among nonminority teenagers. In this way, you would be in a better position to determine the source of the hostility.

In some ways, dimensional sampling might be the most feasible one for practitioners. In our previous illustration, for example, there are two variables—race and pregnancy status—with two values each—white versus nonwhite and pregnant versus not pregnant. Thus, there are four possible cells in the analysis. If for some reason, such as past experience, you believe that these two variables interrelate in important ways in determining such factors as clients' hostility or adjustment, you could make sure that you had at least one client in each of those four cells. In this way, you would be able

that some important considerations will be left out of the sampling decision.

In addition to sample size estimation, computers are also used to select the sample. One sampling frame that has been rejuvenated thanks to computerization is the telephone directory. In addition to the limitations covered in the discussion on sampling frames, telephone directories are physically cumbersome to work with. Furthermore, for anything other than a local survey, research would require amassing a large number of directories, certainly an impractical approach to selecting a national sample. However, these problems are being overcome with the new mass storage capacity available for personal computers, particularly with the development of CD-ROM. The CD disc has the capacity to store vast amounts of data, such as encyclopedias, abstracts, and guides to professional literature. For survey research, Silverplatter, Inc., offers PhoneDisc USA Residential, a two-disc set containing 90 million names from 4,000 phone books (Garson, 1991). The capacity to rapidly search the database and to apply various selection criteria make this kind of product a valuable sampling tool for many kinds of survey research. In addition to the United States database, similar products are available for Canada and European countries. Regular updates are available, in some cases as frequently as monthly, to assure that the sampling frame is current.

As we have seen, instead of relying on directories to supply the sample, many surveys use random digit dialing. The convenience of random digit dialing is not limited to large-scale survey organizations with mainframe computers. One option has been for agencies to purchase telephone samples from outside organizations. Software is now available, however, for agencies to do the job themselves on microcomputers. One such program is The Survey Sampler, from Creative Research Systems. To use the system, the researcher must specify the area codes and three-digit prefixes to be included, and the percentages that these prefixes should represent in the sample. It is also possible to specify blocks of numbers that you do not want included. Telephone companies may be able to identify unassigned numbers to avoid a high frequency of nonworking numbers. The program will also eliminate numbers ending in a specified number of zeros, because these are often nonresidential numbers.

Because of the proliferation and frequent modification of computer products that are available for social research purposes, several professional publications regularly report on new developments. The journal *Social Science Computer Review* contains a section called "News and Notes" that alerts readers to new developments in the field of computers, as well as publishes feature articles on computer applications. Popular publications such as *Byte, PC Week, PC World,* and *PC Connection* often provide articles evaluating software, including survey, sampling, and statistical software products.

to make some preliminary judgments regarding the importance of these two factors.

In summary, every client you encounter is part of a sample, and they are all a part of the larger population of clients that are of interest to you as a practitioner. In Chapter 11, we discuss single-subject designs and the ways in which considerable scientific knowledge can be gained from studying changes in behavior of a single person. For now, however, it is important to have an awareness of how scientific sampling procedures can aid in assessing the validity of what is learned from a client.

Once again, we can see that the gap between scientific research and human service practice is not nearly as large as is often assumed. They are both linked in a common endeavor—to gain useful knowledge of human behavior.

Main Points

■ A population consists of all possible cases of whatever one is interested in studying.

- A sample is composed of one or more elements selected from a population.
- A sampling frame is a list of the population elements used to draw some types of probability samples.
- The representativeness of a sample is its most important characteristic, referring to the degree to which the sample reflects the population from which it was drawn.
- Sampling error is the difference between sample values and true population values.
- Probability sampling techniques are the best for obtaining representative samples.
- The key characteristic of probability sampling is that every element in the population has a known chance of being selected into the sample.
- Simple random, systematic, stratified, and area samples are all types of probability samples.
- Nonprobability samples do not assure each population element a known chance of being selected into the sample and, therefore, lack the degree of representativeness of probability samples.
- Availability, snowball, quota, purposive, and dimensional samples are all types of nonprobability samples.
- Data based on properly drawn probability samples are reliable and generalizable within known limits of error to the sampled populations.
- In studies of racial and other minorities, care must be taken to ensure that sampling procedures do not result in unrepresentative samples, especially given the "rare event" status of many minorities.
- Computer software is available to assist in such sampling tasks as selecting a sample size and selecting the sample itself through random digit dialing.

Important Terms for Review

accidental sampling
area sampling
availability sampling
cluster sampling
convenience sampling
dimensional sampling
judgmental sampling
multistage sampling
nonprobability samples
population
probability samples
purposive sampling
quota sampling
representative samples
sample
sampling error
sampling frame
simple random sampling
snowball sampling
stratified sampling
systematic sampling

Exploring the Internet

In this chapter, we have discussed many of the technical aspects of sampling. To expand your knowledge about sampling and how it is actually used in research, we recommend that you explore Internet sites that are affiliated with some of the major survey research endeavors that are widely used to produce social science research data. The following sites include information about the sampling process used in their survey. Once you have accessed the main site, look for highlighted text about sampling procedures.

The General Social Survey (GSS) site can be found at http://www.icpsr.umich.edu/GSS/home.htm. This site has its own search capacity, which makes locating material of interest fairly easy. Entering the term "sampling" in the search engine will lead to a variety of pages dealing with sampling. Currently, extensive sampling information is available in the site's appendix A, "Sampling and Weighting." This appendix is located at http://www.icpsr.umich.edu/GSS/append/apdx_a.htm. From this site, you can learn how the GSS sample is actually selected, how the procedure has changed over time, and what controversies have arisen over the sampling system modifications. In the discussion of sampling, presented on the GSS site, you will find a discussion of primary sampling units (PSU). Selecting the highlighted text "PSU" will lead you to a U.S. map that displays the location of PSUs for the NORC General Social Survey. Currently, the map is located at http://www.icpsr.umich.edu/GSS/images/pas100.jpg.

The Crime Victimization Survey is another major survey conducted in the United States. You can learn about the sampling for this survey by going to the Bureau of Justice Statistics home page located at http://www.ojp.usdoj.gov/bjs/welcome.html. This site will refer you to other pages that describe sampling issues with the Crime Victimization Survey. The page located at http://www.ojp.usdoj.gov/pub/bjs/ascii/ncsrqa.txt provides not only a description of the sampling procedure, but information on a variety of research issues involved in obtaining estimates of crime from talking to victims.

The Bureau of Labor Statistics and the Census Bureau cooperate in providing the Current Population Survey (CPS). To learn more about how sampling is done for this key survey, visit the CPS Web site at http://www.bls.census.gov/cps/cpsmain.htm. In addition to the information available here, more specific data on the Basic Monthly Survey can be accessed from the main CPS site or by going directly to http://www.bls.census.gov/cps/bsampdes.htm.

For Further Reading

Epstein, Irwin, and Tony Tripodi. *Research Techniques for Program Planning, Monitoring, and Evaluation.* New York: Columbia University Press, 1977. This book contains a chapter on sampling considerations when assessing the performance of agency workers, along with other brief discussions of sampling.

Henry, Gary T. *Practical Sampling.* Newbury Park, Calif.: Sage, 1990. This concise book is a handy guide to basic issues related to sampling. It also includes some interesting examples of research projects and the sampling procedures that were used in them.

Hess, Irene. *Sampling for Social Research Surveys, 1947–1980.* Ann Arbor: University of Michigan Institute for Social Research, 1985. Sometimes a good example can enhance the understanding of complex subjects, and that is what Hess provides in her historical review of survey sampling. In addition, further discussion of many sampling issues is provided.

Kish, Leslie. *Survey Sampling.* New York: Wiley, 1965. Considered the mainstay regarding sampling issues in social research, this book assumes that the reader has an elementary understanding of statistics.

Scheaffer, Richard L., William Mendenhall, and Lyman Ott. *Elementary Survey Sampling,* 5th ed. Belmont, Calif.: Wadsworth, 1996. As the name implies, this book is meant as an introductory text on the design and analysis of sample surveys. Limited to coverage of probability sampling techniques, it provides the information necessary to successfully complete a sample survey.

Stuart, Alan. *The Ideas of Sampling,* 3rd ed. New York: Oxford University Press, 1987. This book is another good review of sampling strategies that can be used in many human service settings.

Sudman, Seymour. *Applied Sampling.* New York: Academic Press, 1976. This book, along with the Kish work, will tell you almost all you need to know about sampling.

Wainer, Howard. *Drawing Inferences From Self-Selected Surveys.* New York: Springer-Verlag, 1986. This book focuses on the issue of self-selection into samples and the problems this can create in terms of making inferences from samples to populations.

Exercises for Class Discussion

A student is doing an internship with the Metropolis Senior Citizens Service Center (MSCSC), where she has been asked to help do a needs assessment. MSCSC is a publicly funded agency that is supposed to serve all residents of Metropolis who are 60 years of age or older. Spouses of such individuals are also eligible to receive services if they are at least 50 years old. As a part of the internship, the director wants the student to conduct interviews with all senior citizens in this city of 25,000 inhabitants. The student, having taken a research methods course, knows that this would be time-consuming and inefficient as well as unnecessary.

She suggests that selecting a probability sample and conducting careful interviews with those people selected will yield better information with less interviewing time. The director tells her to develop a plan to convince the agency board how this might be done.

6.1 What is the population for this project? Try to define the population as specifically as possible.

6.2 Three sampling frames that might be used are (a) the city directory, (b) the local telephone book, or (c) a Social Security Administration listing of recipients of benefits for the county. What might be the advantages and disadvantages of each? Can you think of any other sampling frames that might be useful for this project?

6.3 Could you use a random digit dialing method to sample this population? Indicate reasons for and against using such a technique.

6.4 A staff member at the agency suggests dispensing with the sampling and just running a series of public service announcements on the local radio station and in the newspaper in which senior citi-

zens are urged to call the agency to express their concerns. Those people who call in could be interviewed, and these interviews would constitute the "needs assessment." What kind of sampling process is being suggested? What are its advantages and disadvantages?

6.5 The elderly who reside in nursing homes make up a group of special interest to the center although they represent only 1.5 percent of the eligible residents. Describe how sampling procedures could address the problem of including a representative group of nursing home elderly in the sample.

6.6 Use your local city directory to compile a simple random sample of 25 households, using the street address portion of the directory.

6.7 In the previous exercises, options included random digit dialing, the city directory, the telephone book, Social Security recipients, and respondents to radio announcements. Evaluate each of these options in terms of potential for underrepresenting minorities in the sample. Which method would be best?

CHAPTER 7
Survey Research

Designing Questions   156
Closed-Ended Versus Open-Ended Questions   156
Wording of Questions   159

Questionnaires   161
Structure and Design   161
Response Rate   165
Checking for Bias Due to Nonresponse   169
An Assessment of Questionnaires   170

Interviews   170
The Structure of Interviews   170
Contacting Respondents   171
Conducting an Interview   177
Minorities and the Interview Relationship   179
An Assessment of Interviews   180

Telephone Surveys   181

Focus Groups   184

Practice and Research Interviews Compared   186

Main Points   187

Important Terms for Review   187

Exploring the Internet   187

For Further Reading   190

Exercises for Class Discussion   191

A **survey** is a data collection technique in which information is gathered from individuals, called *respondents,* by having them respond to questions. It is probably the most widely used research method in social science research. One of the earliest large-scale surveys in the human service field was a needs assessment survey in Pittsburgh in 1907 that focused on the extent of problems accompanying industrialization, like poor living conditions and industrial accidents. In the 1995 volume of *Social Service Review,* 50 percent of the articles relied on survey research as a method of data collection. Likewise, in the 1995 volume of the *Journal of Health and Social Behavior,* 84 percent of the articles were based, at least in part, on survey data. In the human services, surveys have been used to investigate the functioning of clients, the effectiveness of practitioners, and the operation of human service agencies. In fact, surveys have been used to study all five of the human service focal areas discussed in Chapter 1. This illustrates a major attraction of surveys—their flexibility. Surveys can be used for all types of studies—exploratory, descriptive, explanatory, and evaluative.

The many techniques available for conducting a survey make it a versatile tool. However, all surveys share certain characteristics. First, surveys typically involve collecting data from large samples of people; therefore, they are ideal for obtaining data representative of populations too large to be dealt with by other methods. Indeed, the generalizability of survey findings is another major attraction of the method. Second, all surveys involve presenting respondents with a series of questions to be answered. These questions may tap matters of fact, attitudes and opinions, or future expectations. The questions may be simple single-item measures or complex multiple-item scales. In whatever form, however, survey data are basically what people say to the investigator in response to a question.

Data can be collected in survey research in two basic ways: with *questionnaires* or with *interviews.* A **questionnaire** contains written questions that people respond to directly on the questionnaire form itself, without the aid of an interviewer. A questionnaire can be handed directly to a respondent, or it can be mailed to the members of a sample, who then fill it out on their own and mail it back to the researcher. An **interview** involves an interviewer reading questions to respondents and recording their answers. Interviews can be conducted either in person or over the telephone. Some survey research uses both questionnaire and interview techniques, with respondents filling in some answers themselves and being asked other questions by interviewers. Because both questionnaires and interviews involve asking people to respond to questions, a problem central to both is what type of question is to be asked. We discuss this issue first and then analyze the elements of questionnaires and interviews separately. An important point to emphasize about surveys is that they only measure what people *say* about their thoughts, feelings, and behaviors. Surveys do not measure those thoughts, feelings, and behaviors directly. For example, if people tell us in a survey that they do not take drugs, we have not measured actual drug-taking behavior but only people's reports about that behavior. This is very important in terms of the conclusions that can be drawn: We can conclude that people report not taking drugs, but we cannot conclude that people do not take drugs. This latter would be an inference we draw from what people say. So surveys always involve data on what people say about what they do, not what they actually do.

Designing Questions

Closed-Ended Versus Open-Ended Questions

Two basic types of questions can be used in questionnaires and interviews: closed-ended or open-ended. **Closed-ended questions** are those that provide respondents with a fixed set of alternatives from which they are to choose. The response formats of multiple-item scales, for example, are all closed-ended, as are multiple-choice examination questions, with which you are undoubtedly familiar. **Open-ended questions** are questions to which the respondents write their own responses, much as you do for an essay-type examination question.

The proper use of open-ended and closed-ended questions is important for the quality of data generated as well as for the ease of handling the data. Theoretical considerations play an important part in the decision about which type of question to use. In general, closed-ended questions should be used when all the possible, theoretically relevant responses to a question can be determined in advance and the number of possible responses is limited. For example, a question relating to marital status would almost certainly be treated as a closed-ended question. A known and limited number of answers are possible: married, single, divorced, separated, or widowed. In research today, people are commonly offered another alternative in answering this question, namely, "living together," or cohabitating. Although cohabitation is not legally a "marital" status, it helps to reflect more accurately the living arrangements available to people today. Another obvious closed-ended question is about sexual status. To leave such questions open-ended runs the risk that some respondent will either purposefully or inadvertently answer in a way that provides meaningless data. Putting "sex" with a blank after it, for example, is an open invitation for some character with an overinflated sense of comedic skills to write "yes" rather than the information wanted.

Open-ended questions, on the other hand, would be appropriate in an exploratory study in which the lack of theoretical development suggests that we should place few restrictions on people's answers. In addition, when researchers cannot predict all the possible answers to a question in advance or when too many possible answers exist to list them all practically, then closed-ended questions

are not appropriate. Suppose we wanted to know the reasons why people moved to their current residence. So many possible reasons exist that such a question would have to be treated as open-ended. If interested in the county and state in which our respondents reside, we could generate a complete list of all the possibilities and thus create a closed-ended question. But the list would consume so much space on the questionnaire that it would be excessively cumbersome, especially considering that respondents should be able to answer this question correctly in its open-ended form.

Some questions lend themselves to a combination of both formats. Religious affiliation is a question usually handled in this way. Although there are a great many religions, there are some to which only a few respondents will belong. Thus, religions with large memberships can be listed in closed-ended fashion with a category "other," where a person can write the name of a religion not found on the list (*see* question 4, Table 7.1). Any question with a similar pattern of responses—numerous possibilities, but a few popular ones—can be efficiently handled in this way. The combined format maintains the convenience of closed-ended questions for most of the respondents but also allows those with less common responses to express them.

When the option of "other" is used in a closed-ended question, it is a good idea to request respondents to write in their response by indicating "please specify." These answers can then be coded into whatever response categories seem appropriate for data analysis. However, the opportunity to specify an alternative should be offered even if, for purposes of data analysis, the written responses will not be used. This is done because respondents who hold uncommon views or memberships may be proud of them and desirous of expressing them on the questionnaire. In addition, well-educated professionals tend to react against completely closed-ended questions as too simple, especially when the questions deal with complicated professional matters (Sudman, 1985). The opportunity to provide a written response to a question will be more satisfying to such respondents, and they will be more likely to complete the questionnaire.

Table 7.1   Formatting Questions for a Questionnaire

Please indicate your response to the following questions by placing an *X* in the appropriate box.

1. Which of the following best describes where you live?
   - ☒ In a large city (100,000 population or more)
   - ☐ In a suburb near a large city
   - ☐ In a middle-sized city or small town (under 100,000 population) but not a suburb of a large city
   - ☐ Open country (but not on a farm)
   - ☐ On a farm

2. Have you ever shoplifted an item with a value of $10 or more?
   - ☐ Yes
   - ☐ No

   > *If Yes:* How many times have you taken such items?
   > - ☐ Once
   > - ☐ 2 to 5 times
   > - ☐ 6 to 10 times
   > - ☐ More than 10 times

3. Have you purchased a *new* automobile between 1995 and the present?
   - ☐ Yes
   - ☐ No (*If No,* please skip to Section C, question1.)

4. Please indicate the religion to which you belong:
   - ☐ Protestant
   - ☐ Catholic
   - ☐ Jewish
   - ☐ Other. Please specify. _____

Another factor in choosing between open- and closed-ended questions is the ease with which each can be handled at the data analysis stage. Open-ended questions can sometimes be quite difficult to work with. One difficulty is that poor handwriting or the failure of respondents to be clear in their answers can result in data that cannot be analyzed (Rea and Parker, 1992). Commonly, some responses to open-ended questions just do not make sense, so they end up being dropped from analysis. In addition, open-ended questions are more complicated to analyze by computer because a respondent's answers must first be coded into a limited set of categories, and this coding is time-consuming and can introduce error (*see* Chapter 14).

Another related difficulty with open-ended questions is that some respondents are likely to give more than one answer to a question. For example, in a study of substance abuse, people might be asked why they use or do not use alcoholic beverages. As a response to this question, a researcher might receive the following: "I quit drinking because booze was too expensive and my wife was getting angry at me for getting drunk." How should this response be categorized? Should the person be counted as quitting because of the expense or because of marital problems created by drinking? It may be, of course, that both factors were important in the decision to quit. Data analysis problems such as this are usually handled in one of two ways. First, all the individual's responses can be accepted as data. This, however, creates difficulties in data analysis; some people may give more reasons than others because they are talkative rather than because there are actually more reasons for their behavior. A second way of handling multiple responses is to assume that each respondent's *first* answer is the most important one and consider it to be the only response. This assumption, of course, may not always be valid, but it does solve the dilemma in a systematic fashion.

The decision about whether to use open- or closed-ended questions is complex, often requiring considerable experience with survey methods to assess. An important issue, it can have substantial effects on the type and quality of the data that are collected, as was illustrated in a survey of attitudes about social problems confronting the United States. The Institute for Social Research at the University of Michigan asked a sample of people open-ended and closed-ended versions of essentially the same questions (Schuman and Presser, 1979). The two versions elicited quite different responses. For example, with the closed-ended version, 35 percent of the respondents indicated that crime and violence were important social problems, compared to only 15.7 percent in the open-ended version. With a number of other issues, people responding to the closed-ended questions were more likely to indicate that particular issues were problems. One reason that the type of question has such an effect on the data is that the list of alternatives in the closed-ended questions tends to serve as a "reminder" to the respondent of issues that might be problems. Without the stimulus of the list, some respondents would not even think of some of those issues. A second reason is that people tend to choose from the list provided in closed-ended questions rather than writing in their own answers even when provided with an "other" category.

It is possible, in some cases, to gain the benefits of both open- and closed-ended questions by using an open-ended format in a pretest or pilot study and then, based on the results, designing closed-ended questions for the actual survey. See Sudman and Bradburn (1982) for further discussion of open- versus closed-ended questions in surveys.

Wording of Questions

Because the questions that make up a survey are the basic data-gathering devices, they need to be worded with great care. Especially with questionnaires that allow no opportunity to clarify ques-

tions for the respondent, ambiguity in questions can be a source of substantial trouble. We will review some of the major issues in developing good survey questions (Sudman and Bradburn, 1982). (In Chapter 13, we discuss some problems of question construction having to do specifically with questions that are part of multiple-item scales.)

The wording of questions should be subject, whenever possible, to empirical assessment to determine whether particular wording might be leading to unnoticed bias. Words, after all, have connotative meanings (that is, emotional or evaluative associations) that the researcher may not be aware of but that may influence respondents' answers to questions. In a study of people's attitudes about social welfare policy in the United States, for example, survey respondents were asked whether they believed we should spend more money on welfare or less (T. W. Smith, 1987). However, they were asked the question in three slightly different ways. One group was asked about whether we were spending too much or too little on "welfare," a second was asked about spending too much or too little on "assistance for the poor," while a third was asked about money for "caring for the poor." At first glance, all three questions would seem to have much the same meaning. Yet, people's responses to them suggested something quite different. Basically, people responded much more negatively to the question with the word "welfare" in it, indicating much less willingness to spend more money on "welfare" than they were to "assist the poor." For example, 64.7 percent of the respondents indicated that too little was being spent on "assistance to the poor" while only 19.3 percent said we were spending too little on "welfare." This is a very dramatic difference in opinion, due to what might seem, at a glance, to be a minor difference in wording. Although the study didn't investigate why these differing responses occurred, it seems plausible that the word "welfare" had connotative meanings for many people that involve images of laziness, waste, fraud, bureaucracy, or the poor as disreputable. "Assisting the poor," on the other hand, is more likely to be associated with giving and Judeo-Christian charitableness. These connotations lead to very different responses. In many cases, the only way to assess such differences is to compare people's responses with different versions of the same question during a pretest.

In general, questions should be stated in the present tense. An exception would be specialized questions that focus on past experiences or future expectations. In these situations, the appropriate tense would be used. Of major importance is that tenses are not carelessly mixed. Failure to maintain consistent tense of questions can lead to an understandable confusion on the part of respondents and, therefore, more measurement error.

Questions should be simple and direct, expressing only one idea. Complex statements expressing more than one idea should be avoided. For example, a statement that reads, "The city needs more housing for the elderly and property taxes should be raised to finance it," is not good because it is possible that some respondents might agree with the first part but disagree with the second. Statements such as this should be broken up into two separate statements, each expressing a single idea.

Statements that seem crystal clear to a researcher may prove unclear to many respondents. One common error is to overestimate the reading ability of the average respondent. American newspaper editor and critic H. L. Mencken is credited with this observation: "No one ever went broke underestimating the intelligence of the American public." Though this comment is perhaps overstated and slightly cynical, the wise researcher will keep it in mind when writing questions. This is especially true in the human services, where respondents of interest may have poor reading and writing skills. Accordingly, the researcher should avoid the use of technical terms. For example, it would not be advisable to include a statement that reads, "The current stratification system in the United States is too rigid." "Stratification" is a technical term in the social sciences that many people outside the field may not understand in the same sense that social scientists do.

Another practice to avoid is reference to things that are not clearly definable or that depend on the respondent's interpretation. For example, "Children who get into trouble typically have had a bad home life" would be an undesirable statement because there are two sources of vagueness. The word "trouble" is unclear. What kind of trouble? Is it trouble with the law, trouble at school, trouble with parents, or what? The other problem is "bad home life." What constitutes a "bad home life" depends on the respondent's interpretation.

Finally, for the majority of questions designed for the general public, slang terminology should never be used. Slang usage tends to arise in the context of particular groups and subcultures. Slang terms may have a precise meaning within those groups, but confuse people outside those groups. Occasionally, however, the target population for a survey will be more specialized than the general population, and the use of their "in-group" jargon may be appropriate. It would demonstrate to the respondents that the researcher cared enough to "learn their language" and could increase rapport, resulting in better responses. Having decided to use slang, however, the burden is on the researcher to be certain the slang is used correctly.

Once a survey instrument is developed, it must be pretested to see if questions are clearly and properly understood and are unbiased. Pretesting can be done by having people respond to the questionnaire or interview and then reviewing it with them to find any problems. The way in which a group responds to the questions themselves can also point to trouble. For example, if many respondents leave a particular answer blank, then there may be a problem with the question. Once the instrument is pretested, modifications should be made where called for, and it should be pretested again. Any change in the questionnaire requires more pretesting. Once it is pretested with no changes called for, it is ready to be used in research.

One of the critical decisions to be made in survey research—and it is a complex decision—is whether to collect data through questionnaires or interviews. We discuss both types of surveys with an eye on the criteria to be used in assessing which is more appropriate for a particular research project.

Questionnaires

Questionnaires are designed so that they can be answered without assistance. Of course, if a researcher hands a questionnaire to the respondent, as is sometimes done, the respondent then has the opportunity to ask the researcher to clarify anything that is ambiguous. A good questionnaire, however, should not rely on such assistance. In fact, questionnaires are often mailed to respondents, who thereby have no opportunity to ask questions. In other cases, questionnaires are administered to many people simultaneously in a classroom, auditorium, or agency setting. Such modes of administration make questionnaires quicker and less expensive than most interviews. But it also places a burden on researchers to design questionnaires so that they can be properly completed without assistance (Dillman, 1991).

Structure and Design

Directions   One of the simplest, but also most important, tasks of questionnaire construction is the inclusion of precise directions for respondents. Good directions can go a long way toward improving the quality of data generated by questionnaires. If you want respondents to put an X in a box corresponding to their answer, tell them precisely that. Questionnaires often contain questions requiring different ways of answering. At each place in the questionnaire where the format changes, additional directions should be included.

Order of Questions   An element of questionnaire construction that takes careful consideration is the proper ordering of questions. Careless ordering can lead to undesirable consequences, such as a reduced response rate or biased responses to questions. Generally, questions asked early in the questionnaire should not bias answers to those questions that come later. For example, if we asked several factual questions regarding poverty and the conditions of the poor and later asked a question concerning which social problems people consider to

be serious, more will likely include poverty than would otherwise have done so. These potentially biasing effects can sometimes be avoided by placing opinion questions first when a questionnaire contains both factual and opinion questions.

Ordering of questions can also increase a respondent's interest in answering a questionnaire—this is especially helpful for boosting response rates on mailed questionnaires. Questions dealing with particularly intriguing issues should be asked first. The idea is to interest the recipients enough to get them to start answering. Once they have started, they are more likely to complete the entire questionnaire. If the questionnaire does not deal with any topics that are obviously more interesting than others, then opinion questions should be placed first. People like to express their opinions and, for the reasons mentioned earlier, opinion questions should be first anyway. A pitfall definitely to be avoided is beginning a questionnaire with the standard demographic questions of age, sex, income, and the like. People are so accustomed to those questions that they may be disinclined to answer them again and may promptly file the questionnaire in the nearest wastebasket.

Question Formats   All our efforts at careful wording and ordering of the questions will be for naught unless the questions are presented in a manner that facilitates responding to them. The goal is to make responding to the questions as straightforward and convenient as possible and to reduce the amount of data lost because of uninterpretable responses.

When presenting response alternatives for closed-ended questions, best results are obtained by having respondents indicate their selection by placing an X in a box corresponding to that alternative, as illustrated in question 1 of Table 7.1. This format is preferable to open blanks and check marks (✔) because it is too easy for respondents to get sloppy and place check marks *between* alternatives, rendering their responses unclear and therefore useless as data. Boxes force respondents to give unambiguous responses. Though this may seem a minor point, we can attest from our own experience in

Research in Practice 7.1

Needs Assessment: Response Bias in Human Service Research

The phone rings. You answer it, and a complete stranger wants to know, "How many times in the past 12 months have you used a knife on or fired a gun at your spouse?" Would you answer that question? Imagine that you actually had committed one of those acts. Would you answer truthfully? Social researchers, whether doing basic research on social behavior or attempting to determine the need for social intervention programs in applied research, are faced with the challenge of getting survey respondents not only to answer such questions but also to provide complete and accurate answers. Murray Straus, in discussing difficulties in measuring family violence, asked the rhetorical question, "Assuming they can remember, why would people tell the truth about deviant, illegal, or embarrassing behavior?" (Straus, 1990).

We must keep in mind, after all, that survey data involve what people *say* about their feelings, their beliefs, or their behaviors. When we ask people what they have done, the data we obtain is what they *say* about their behavior, not the actual behavior itself. So a key issue in surveys is whether people's responses are accurate reflections of their actual feelings, beliefs, or behaviors. One source of distortion in surveys is **response bias,** the tendency for people's answers to questions to be influenced by things other than their true feelings, beliefs, and behaviors. It can result in a patterned overestimation or underestimation of variables in a survey. Some common causes of response bias are inaccurate recall, conscious or unconscious distortion, and differential interpretation of the questions and terms. In the latter case, some people who have slapped a spouse would answer "No" to the question, "Have you ever abused your spouse?" because slapping would not fit their definition of abuse. Another source of response bias is people's tendency to give socially acceptable answers to survey questions. It is very socially unacceptable to admit using a knife or gun on your spouse, and people may answer this question in the negative, even if they have done so, in order to avoid appearing socially unacceptable to an interviewer.

Although response bias is a potential problem for all survey research, human service needs assessment especially requires attention to the problem because of the sensitive topics with which it is often concerned. For example, studies of mental health have commonly found that women report more psychiatric symptoms than do men (Gallagher, 1987). From this it might be concluded that women are less mentally healthy than men and, at a more general level, that one's gender has an impact on one's mental health. Critics respond that women may report more symptoms because it is more socially acceptable for women in our society to "complain," show weakness, and the like. In other words, the actual rates of mental illness might be similar for both sexes, but women simply report more symptoms than do men. The relationship between an independent variable (gender) and a dependent variable (mental health status) may be an artifact due to response bias: People are answering questions in terms of the social acceptability of their responses rather than in terms of their actual feelings.

Recall from Chapter 5 that bias involves systematic, rather than random, error. Although both types of error are of concern, bias due to systematic error is of greater concern because its magnitude is unknown and cannot be as easily estimated the way random error can. While random error can be reduced by such straightforward techniques as increasing sample size, coping with systematic error is more complex, involving basically two strategies: improving the survey techniques and estimating the extent of the bias (Moser and Kalton, 1972). One example of how improved survey techniques can reduce response bias is represented by the instruments known as the Conflict Tactics (CT) scales and a recent revision referred to as CTS2.

The original CT scales present the respondent with a series of questions that ask how often a person has engaged in certain behaviors, such as insulting or swearing at a spouse, slapping a spouse, or using a knife or gun on a spouse (*see* Table 7.2). In spite of the extreme social undesirability associated with such behaviors, most people answer the items and many respondents *do* report such socially unacceptable behaviors. A number of elements were included in the design of the original CT in an effort to minimize response bias due to the so-cially sensitive nature of the topic. First, the questions about violent acts were presented in the context of disagreements and conflicts, which appear more neutral and less judgmental than abuse and violence. Second, the items of the CT were arranged in a hierarchical order, beginning with statements about positive ways of dealing with conflict and gradually increasing the level of coerciveness and social disapproval through items about slapping and, finally, use of a weapon. The rationale for this design was that people would feel less

Table 7.2 The Conflict Tactics (CT) Scale

No matter how well a couple get along, there are times when they disagree, get annoyed with the other person, or just have spats or fights because they're in a bad mood or tired or for some other reason. They also use many different ways of trying to settle their differences. I'm going to read some things that you and your (spouse/partner) might do when you have an argument. I would like you to tell me how many times (Once, Twice, 3–5 times, 6–10 times, 11–20 times, or more than 20 times) in the past 12 months you (READ ITEM)

| | **035. Respondent In Past Year** | | | | | | |
	1—Once 2—Twice 3—3–5 Times 4—6–10 Times 5—11–20 Times 6—More than 20 0—Never (don't read)						
A. Discussed an issue calmly	1	2	3	4	5	6	0
B. Got information to back up your/his/her side of things	1	2	3	4	5	6	0
C. Brought in, or tried to bring in, someone to help settle things	1	2	3	4	5	6	0
D. Insulted or swore at him/her/you	1	2	3	4	5	6	0
E. Sulked or refused to talk about an issue	1	2	3	4	5	6	0
F. Stomped out of the room or house or yard	1	2	3	4	5	6	0
G. Cried	1	2	3	4	5	6	0
H. Did or said something to spite him/her/you	1	2	3	4	5	6	0
I. Threatened to hit or throw something at him/her/you	1	2	3	4	5	6	0
J. Threw or smashed or hit or kicked something	1	2	3	4	5	6	0
K. Threw something *at* him/her/you	1	2	3	4	5	6	0
L. Pushed, grabbed, or shoved him/her/you	1	2	3	4	5	6	0
M. Slapped him/her/you	1	2	3	4	5	6	0
N. Kicked, bit, or hit him/her/you with a fist	1	2	3	4	5	6	0
O. Hit or tried to hit him/her/you with something	1	2	3	4	5	6	0
P. Beat him/her/you up	1	2	3	4	5	6	0
Q. Choked him/her/you	1	2	3	4	5	6	0
R. *Threatened* him/her/you with a knife or gun	1	2	3	4	5	6	0
S. Used a knife or fired a gun	1	2	3	4	5	6	0

Source Adapted from Murray A. Straus, "Measuring Intrafamily Conflict and Violence: The Conflict Tactics (CT) Scales," in *Physical Violence in American Families,* edited by Murray A. Straus and Richard J. Gelles (New Brunswick: Transaction Publishers, 1990). Not copyrighted, but contact author for information on use.

continued on next page

reticent about divulging acts of violence if they had been given the chance to show that such acts were "the last straw" after attempting other means of conflict resolution. Third, the process for administration of the CT called for a careful ordering of the relationships about which the instrument inquired. Parent–child conflict was to be covered first because it is socially more acceptable to have conflicts with children and to use physical force to resolve them. Next, the interviewer was to inquire about child–child conflict and, finally, about spousal conflict. It was expected that by the time the respondent got to questions about spousal conflict, the sensitive items would be familiar, and the shock or edge would have been removed from discussing such behaviors as choking, beating up, or using a weapon on a family member. Although the techniques might not eliminate response bias, it was hoped that they would reduce it considerably and increase the accuracy of the data.

Straus and his colleagues had employed the hierarchical pattern of question ordering because qualitative research conducted during the design phase of the original CT had indicated that such a pattern created a context that supported disclosure of violent acts. However, when the Conflict Tactics instrument was recently revised (Straus et al., 1996), the researchers discarded the hierarchical pattern for CTS2 and opted for an interspersed pattern instead. The new instrument has positive items, such as "I said I was sure we could work out a problem," followed by such items as "My partner needed to see a doctor because of a fight with me." The reasons for making the change illustrate the challenging nature of survey instrument design. First of all, the scale designers report that a number of researchers had used only the physical violence items of the scale and had still obtained meaningful results, thus calling into question the necessity of permitting respondents to legitimize violence through hierarchical ordering of items. A second reason for changing the item order was that, although the hierarchical ordering may have created a supportive atmosphere, it opened the door for another bias problem known as "response set," wherein a respondent may blindly answer "never" to every item once items began referring to violent acts. Interspersing sensitive items with positive ones encourages participants to think more carefully about each item. The researchers also reported that the hierarchical pattern produced a negative reaction for some respondents who were nonviolent. For example, parents who had already made it quite clear that they did not employ even mild forms of physical discipline such as spanking were annoyed by subsequently being asked if they ever beat up their child, used a knife, or used a gun. Based on such experience with the CT, the researchers recommended an interspersed item ordering be used in CTS2. However, it should be noted that even in the revised version, the idea of beginning with socially approved behaviors has not been entirely abandoned. The first few items are positive responses to conflict. Physically assaultive behaviors such as "I twisted my partner's arm" do not appear until about the 10th

administering questionnaires that it makes an important difference.

Some questions on a questionnaire may apply to only some respondents and not others. These questions are normally handled by what are called *contingency questions:* Depending on the response to one question, the next question may or may not be relevant to that respondent. The question format must clearly guide respondents to the next relevant question for them. A good way to accomplish this is to set off the contingency questions from the main questions, as illustrated in question 2 of Table 7.1. This reduces the likelihood that questions will be missed by respondents. A different contingency situation arises with sections of a questionnaire that may not apply to some respondents. You need to provide instructions to skip to the next relevant question, as illustrated in question 3 of Table 7.1. By sectioning the questionnaire on the basis of contingency questions such as this, the respondent can be guided through even the most complex questionnaire. The resulting path that an actual

item. Of course, whether a hierarchical pattern or an interspersed ordering of items really produces the least bias and generates the best data is a research question in itself, and the scale designers are planning a randomized experiment in which one group receives items in a hierarchical pattern and the other group receives an interspersed-item version.

Another technique that helps to reduce response bias is called "funneling." A researcher might ask respondents first about conflict in their city, then about conflict in their local community and among neighbors, and finally about conflict in their own family. Moser and Kalton (1972) suggest phrasing questions so that respondents can answer in the third person. For example, "Many men have hit their wives at one time or another. I wonder if you know under what circumstances it happens?" This can be followed with a direct question asking if the respondent has done it.

Response bias can also be reduced by using more anonymous techniques of interviewing. For example, administering questionnaires by computer rather than by mailed questionnaire generates responses that are less socially desirable and more extreme (Kiesler and Sproull, 1986). The anonymity and impersonal nature of interacting with a machine rather than a human interviewer may reduce respondents' concerns about how their responses appear to others. For example, a study of tobacco, alcohol, marijuana, and cocaine use showed that people were more willing to admit using these substances and to admit higher levels of

use when interviewed over the phone rather than in person (Aquilino and LoSciuto, 1990).

No matter how carefully a survey is administered and how well response bias is reduced, the only way one can know the extent of the problem is to estimate its effect by using a known comparison standard or by comparing survey data to data gathered by some other approach. For example, in measuring the degree of response bias to questions about number of arrests, a sample of respondents for whom arrest records are available might be used. Comparing the number of reported arrests to the actual number would enable a researcher to make an estimate of the amount of underreporting. The problems of bias are not limited to stigmatized behaviors such as crime. For example, nutritional researchers at the U.S. Department of Agriculture have been conducting a research program during the past 14 years that suggests that Americans underreport the amount of food they eat by about 18 percent (Mertz et al., 1991). At first glance this may not appear to be a serious issue, but such underreporting may have significant policy implications because food consumption studies are used to determine the nutritional status of a population, to estimate risk for certain diseases in a group, and for other health policy purposes.

The work by Straus and the studies by Mertz and colleagues illustrate two different approaches to coping with response bias: the use of proper survey techniques and the use of comparison groups.

respondent follows through the questionnaire is referred to as the *skip pattern*. As is true of many aspects of instrument design, it is important to evaluate the skip pattern by pretesting the questionnaire to be sure that all appropriate sections are completed and that frustration to the respondent is minimized.

The proper design of survey instruments is very important to collecting valid data. Research in Practice 7.1 explores some more elements of proper survey design.

Response Rate

A major problem in many research endeavors is to gain people's cooperation so that they will provide whatever data are needed. In surveys, this cooperation is measured by the **response rate,** or the proportion of a sample that completes and returns a questionnaire or agrees to be interviewed. With interviews, response rates are often very high—in the area of 90 percent—largely because people are reluctant to refuse a face-to-face request for cooperation. In fact, with interviews, the largest nonresponse factor is the inability of the interviewers to locate respondents. With mailed questionnaires, however, this personal pressure is absent, and people feel freer to refuse (Bridge, 1974). This can result in many *nonreturns,* or people who refuse to complete and return a questionnaire. Response rates with questionnaires, especially mailed ones, vary considerably, from an unacceptably low 20 percent to levels that rival those of interviews.

Why is a low response rate of such concern? This has to do with the issue of the representativeness of a sample, discussed in Chapter 6. If we selected a representative sample and obtained a perfect 100 percent response, we would have confidence in the representativeness of the sample data. However, as the response rate drops below 100 percent, the sample may become less and less representative. Those who refuse to cooperate may differ from those who return the questionnaire in some systematic ways that affect the results of the research. In other words, any response rate less than 100 percent may result in a biased sample. Of course, a perfect response rate is rarely achieved, but the closer the response rate is to that level, the

more likely that the data are representative. A number of things can be done to improve response rates. Most of these apply only to questionnaires, but a few can also be used to increase response rates in interviews.

The Cover Letter   A properly constructed cover letter can help increase the response rate. A **cover letter** is a letter that accompanies a questionnaire and serves to introduce and explain it to the recipient. Because, with mailed questionnaires, the cover letter is the researcher's only medium for communicating with the recipient, it must be carefully drafted to include information recipients will want to know and to encourage them to complete the questionnaire (*see* Table 7.3).

Prominent in the cover letter should be the sponsor of the research project. Recipients are understandably interested in who is seeking the information they are asked to provide, and research clearly indicates that the sponsoring organization influences the response rate (Goyder, 1985; Rea and Parker, 1992). The highest response rates are for questionnaires sponsored by government agencies. University-sponsored research generates somewhat lower response rates, and commercially sponsored

Table 7.3   Items to Be Included in the Cover Letter of a Questionnaire or the Introduction to an Interview

Item	Cover Letter	Interview Introduction
1. Sponsor of the research	yes	yes
2. Address/phone number of the researcher	yes	if required
3. How the respondent was selected	yes	yes
4. Who else was selected	yes	yes
5. The purpose of the research	yes	yes
6. Who will utilize or benefit from the research	yes	yes
7. An appeal for the person's cooperation	yes	yes
8. How long it will take the respondent to complete the survey	yes	yes
9. Payment	if given	if given
10. Anonymity/confidentiality	if given	if given
11. Deadline for return	yes	not applicable

research produces the lowest of all. Apparently, if the research is at all associated with a government agency, stressing that in the cover letter may have a beneficial effect on the response rate. The response rates of particular groups can be increased if the research is sponsored or endorsed by an organization that people in the group believe has legitimacy. For example, response rates of professionals can be increased if the research is linked to relevant professional organizations, such as the National Association of Social Workers, the American Nurses Association, or the National Education Association (Sudman, 1985).

The address and telephone number of the researcher should appear prominently on the cover letter. In fact, using letterhead stationery for the cover letter is a good idea. Especially if the sponsor of the research is not well known, some recipients may desire further information before they decide to participate. Although relatively few respondents will ask for more information, including the address and telephone number gives the cover letter a completely open and aboveboard appearance that may further the general cooperation of recipients.

The cover letter should also inform the respondent how people were selected to receive the questionnaire. It is not necessary to go into great detail on this matter, but people receiving an unanticipated questionnaire are quite naturally curious about how they were chosen to be a part of a study. A brief statement that they were randomly selected or selected by computer (if this is the case) should suffice.

Recipients will also want to know the purpose of the research. Again, without going into great detail, the cover letter should explain such things as why the research is being conducted, why and by whom it is considered important, and the potential benefits anticipated from the study. Investigations have clearly shown that the response rate can be significantly increased if the importance of the research, as perceived by the respondent, is emphasized. This part of the cover letter must be worded very carefully, however, so that it does not sensitize respondents in such a way that their answers to questions are affected. Sensitizing effects can be minimized by keeping the description of the purpose very general—certainly, do not suggest what any of the research hypotheses might be. Regarding the importance of the data and anticipated benefits, the researcher should resist the temptation of hyperbole and instead make honest, straightforward statements. Exaggerated claims about "solving a significant social problem" or "alleviating the problems of the poor" are likely to be seen as precisely what they are.

The preceding information provides a foundation for the single most important component of the cover letter, a direct appeal for the recipient's cooperation. General statements about the importance of the research are no substitute for a more personal appeal to the recipient as to why he or she should take time to complete the questionnaire. Respondents must believe that their responses are very important to the outcome (as, in reality, they are). A statement to the effect that "your views are important to us" is a good approach. It emphasizes the importance of each individual respondent and emphasizes that the questionnaire will allow the expression of opinions, which people like.

The cover letter should indicate that the respondent will remain anonymous or that the data will be treated as confidential, whichever will be the case. "Anonymous" means that *no one,* including the researcher, can link a particular respondent's name to his or her questionnaire. "Confidentiality" means that, even though the researcher can match respondents to their questionnaires, the information will be treated collectively, and no individuals will be publicly linked to their responses.

With mailed questionnaires, two techniques assure anonymity (Sudman, 1985). Best is to keep the questionnaire itself completely anonymous, with no identifying numbers or symbols, providing the respondent with a separate postcard, including the respondent's name, to be mailed at the same time the completed questionnaire is mailed. This way, the researcher knows who has responded and need not send reminders to respond; and no one can link a respondent's name with a particular questionnaire. A second way to ensure anonymity is to attach to the questionnaire a cover sheet with an identifying number and assure the respondents that the cover sheet will be removed and destroyed once the receipt of the questionnaire has been recorded. This second procedure provides less assurance to the respondent because an unethical researcher might retain the link between questionnaires and their identification numbers. The first procedure, however, is more expensive because of the additional postcard mailing, so the second procedure may be preferred in questionnaires that do not deal with highly sensitive issues that would make respondents very concerned about anonymity. If the material is not very sensitive, assurances of confidentiality can be adequate to ensure a good return rate. No evidence indicates that assuring anonymity rather than confidentiality will increase the response rate in nonsensitive surveys (Moser and Kalton, 1972).

Finally, the cover letter should include a deadline for returning the questionnaire, calculated to take into account mailing time and a few days to complete the questionnaire. The rationale for a fairly tight deadline is that it will encourage the recipient to complete the questionnaire soon after it is received and not set it aside where it can be forgotten or misplaced.

Payment   Response rates can also be increased by offering a small payment as a part of the appeal for cooperation. Research indicates that, like most things, a recipient's cooperation can be bought—and not at a high price. One study reported that a 25-cent incentive added almost 10 percent to the response rate, and $1 added another 10 percent (James and Bolstein, 1990). By offering recipients $1, the researcher with a bountiful treasury could increase the response rate to approximately 20 percent more than what it would be with no payment. For the payments to have their greatest effect, they should be included with the initial mailing and not promised on return of the questionnaire. One study found that including the payment with the questionnaire boosted the return rate by 12 percent over promising payment on return of the questionnaire (Berry and Kanouse, 1987). However, such payments are not always feasible because even small payments can add substantial costs to a survey with a large sample.

Response rates are also affected by mailing procedures. It almost goes without saying that a stamped, self-addressed envelope should be supplied for returning the questionnaire, making things as convenient as possible for the respondent. The type of postage utilized also affects the response rate, with stamps bringing about 4 percent higher return than bulk-printed postage (Scott, 1961). Presumably, the stamp makes the questionnaire appear more personal and less like unimportant junk mail. A regular stamped envelope also substantially increases the response rate in comparison with a business reply envelope (Armstrong and Luck, 1987).

Follow-Ups   The most important procedural matter affecting response rates is the use of follow-up letters. A substantial percentage of nonrespondents to the initial mailing will respond to follow-up letters. With two follow-ups, 15 to 20 percent increases over the initial return can be achieved (James and Bolstein, 1990). Such follow-ups are clearly essential, and they can be done by telephone, if budget permits and speed is important. With aggressive follow-ups, the difference in response rates between mailed questionnaires and interviews declines substantially (Goyder, 1985).

In general, two follow-ups should be used. When response to the initial mailing drops off, follow-up letters should be sent to the nonrespondents encouraging them to return the questionnaire. The follow-up letter should include a restatement of the points in the original cover letter with an additional appeal for their cooperation. When response to the first follow-up declines, a second follow-up is then sent to the remaining nonrespondents, including another copy of the questionnaire because people may have misplaced the original. After two follow-ups, the remaining nonrespondents are a pretty intransigent lot, and additional follow-ups will generate relatively few further responses.

Length and Appearance   Two other factors that affect the rate of response to a mailed questionnaire are the length of the questionnaire and its appearance. As length increases, the response rate declines. However, no hard-and-fast rule governs the length of mailed questionnaires. Much depends on the intelligence and literacy of the respondents, the degree of interest in the topic of the questionnaire, and other such matters. However, it is probably a good idea to keep the questionnaire less than five pages long, requiring no more than 30 minutes to fill out. Great care must be taken to remove any extraneous questions or any questions that are not essential to the hypotheses under investigation (Epstein and Tripodi, 1977). Although keeping the questionnaire less than five pages is a general guide, this should not be achieved by cramming so much material onto each page that the respondent has difficulty using the instrument—the appearance of the questionnaire can also be important in generating a high response rate. As discussed earlier, the use of boxed response choices and smooth transitions through contingency questions help make completing the questionnaire easier and more enjoyable for the respondent, which in turn increases the probability that it will be returned.

Other Influences on Response Rate Many other factors can work to lower response rates. In telephone surveys, for example, the voice and manner of the interviewer can have an important effect (Oksenberg, Coleman, and Cannell, 1986). Interviewers with higher-pitched, louder voices and clear and distinct pronunciation have lower refusal rates. The same is true for interviewers who sound more competent and upbeat toward the respondent. Reminders of confidentiality can also affect the response rate (Frey, 1986). People who are reminded of the confidentiality of the information partway through the interview are more likely to refuse to respond to some of the remaining questions than are people who do not receive such a reminder. It may be that the reminder works to undo whatever rapport the interviewer has already built up with the respondent.

A survey following all the suggested procedures should yield an acceptably high response rate. Specialized populations may, of course, produce either higher or lower rates. Because so many variables are involved, only rough guidelines can be offered for evaluating response rates with mailed questionnaires. Babbie (1995) suggests that a 50 percent rate is adequate for analysis. Rates in the 60 percent range are considered good, and anything more than 70 percent is very good. A properly conducted general population survey should have little trouble surpassing the minimum needed for analysis and would be expected to do even better.

Checking for Bias Due to Nonresponse

Even if a relatively high rate of response is obtained, possible bias due to nonresponse should be investigated by determining the extent to which respondents differ from nonrespondents (Groves, 1989; Miller, 1991; Rea and Parker, 1992). One common way of doing this is to compare the characteristics of the respondents with the characteristics of the population from which they were selected. If a database on the population exists, this job can be simplified. For example, if you are studying a representative sample of welfare recipients in a community, the Department of Social Services is likely to have data on age, sex, marital status, level of education, and other characteristics for all the welfare recipients in the community. You can compare your respondents with this database on the characteristics for which data have already been collected. A second approach to assessing bias resulting from nonresponse is to locate a subsample of nonrespondents and interview them. In this way, the responses to the questionnaire by a representative sample of nonrespondents can be compared with those of the respondents. This is the preferred method because the direction and the extent of bias that are due to nonresponse can be directly measured. It is, however, the most costly and time-consuming approach.

Any check for bias due to nonresponse, of course, informs us only about those characteristics on which we make comparisons. It does not prove that the respondents are representative of the whole sample on any other variables—including those that might be of considerable importance to the study. In short, though we can gather some information regarding such bias, in most cases it is not possible to *prove* that bias due to nonresponse does not exist.

An Assessment of Questionnaires

Advantages   As a technique of survey research, questionnaires have a number of desirable features. First, they can be used to gather data far more inexpensively and quickly than interviews. Only a month to 6 weeks is needed for mailed questionnaires, whereas obtaining the same data by personal interviews would likely take several months—at a minimum. Mailed questionnaires also save the expense of interviewers, interviewer travel, and other such costs.

Second, mailed questionnaires enable the researcher to collect data from a sample that is geographically dispersed. It costs no more to mail a questionnaire across the country than across a city. Costs of interviewer travel rise enormously as distance increases, making interviewing over wide geographic areas expensive.

Third, with questions of a personal or sensitive nature, mailed questionnaires may provide more accurate answers than interviews. People may be more likely to respond honestly to such questions when they are not face-to-face with a person they perceive as possibly making judgments about them. Some evidence indicates, for example, that questions about premarital sex are answered more honestly in a questionnaire than an interview (Knudsen, Pope, and Irish, 1967). However, this does not appear to be true for all topics, so the choice of questionnaire versus interview on these grounds would depend on the subject of the research (Moser and Kalton, 1972).

Finally, mailed questionnaires eliminate the problem of interviewer bias. Interviewer bias occurs when an interviewer influences a person's response to a question through what the interviewer says, his or her tone of voice, or demeanor. Because no interviewer is present when the person fills out the questionnaire, it is not possible for an interviewer to bias the respondent's answers in a particular direction (Cannell and Kahn, 1968).

Disadvantages   Despite their many advantages, mailed questionnaires have important limitations that may make them less desirable for some research efforts (Moser and Kalton, 1972).

First, mailed questionnaires require a minimal degree of literacy and facility in English that some respondents do not possess. Substantial nonresponse is, of course, likely with such people. With most general population surveys, the nonresponse due to illiteracy will not seriously bias the results. Self-administered questionnaires are more successful among people who are better educated, motivated to respond, and involved in issues and organizations. However, some groups of interest to human service practitioners often do not possess these characteristics. If the survey is aimed at a special population in which less than average literacy is suspected, personal interviews are a better choice.

Second, the questions must all be sufficiently simple to be comprehended on the basis of printed instructions. Third, there is no opportunity to probe for more information or evaluate the nonverbal behavior of the respondents. The answers they mark on the questionnaire form are final. Fourth, there is no assurance that the person who should answer the questionnaire is the one who actually does so. Fifth, responses cannot be considered independent, for the respondent can read through the entire questionnaire before completing it. Finally, all mailed questionnaires face the problem of nonresponse bias.

Interviews

In an interview, the investigator or an assistant reads the questions directly to the respondents and records their answers. Interviews offer the investigator a degree of flexibility that is not available with questionnaires. One area of increased flexibility relates to the degree of structure built into an interview.

The Structure of Interviews

The element of structure in interviews refers to the degree of freedom the interviewer has in conducting the interview and respondents have in answering questions. Interviews are usually classified in terms of three levels of structure: (1) the *unstandard-*

ized, (2) the *nonschedule-standardized,* and (3) the *schedule-standardized.*

The *unstandardized* interview has the least structure. All the interviewer typically will have for guidance is a general topic area, as illustrated in Figure 7.1. By developing his or her own questions and probes as the interview progresses, the interviewer explores the topic with the respondent. The approach is called "unstandardized" because different questions will be asked by each interviewer and different information obtained from each respondent. There is a heavy reliance on the skills of the interviewer to ask good questions and to keep the interview going, and this can only be done if experienced interviewers are available. This unstructured approach makes unstandardized interviewing especially appropriate for exploratory research. In Figure 7.1, for example, the interviewer is guided only by the general topic of parent–child conflicts. The example also illustrates the suitability of this style of interviewing for exploratory research as the interviewer is directed to search for as many areas of conflict as can be found.

Nonschedule-standardized interviews add more structure, with the topic narrower and specific questions asked of all respondents. However, the interview remains fairly conversational, and the interviewer is free to probe, rephrase questions, or take the questions in whatever order best fits that particular interview. Note in Figure 7.1 that specific questions are of the open-ended type, allowing the respondent full freedom of expression. As in the case of the unstandardized form, success with this type of interview requires an experienced interviewer.

The *schedule-standardized interview* is the most structured type. An **interview schedule** is used, which contains specific instructions for the interviewer, specific questions in a fixed order, and transition phrases for the interviewer to use. Sometimes the schedule also contains acceptable rephrasings for questions and a selection of stock probes. Schedule-standardized interviews are fairly rigid, with neither interviewer nor respondent allowed to depart from the structure of the schedule. Although some questions may be open-ended, most will

likely be closed-ended. In fact, some schedule-standardized interviews are very similar to a questionnaire except that the interviewer asks the questions rather than having the respondent read them. Note, in Figure 7.1, the use of cards with response alternatives that are handed to the respondent. This is a popular way of supplying respondents with a complex set of closed-ended alternatives. Note also the precise directions for the interviewer as well as verbatim phrases to be read to the respondent. Schedule-standardized interviews can be coducted by relatively untrained, part-time interviewers because nearly everything they need to say is contained in the schedule. This makes schedule-standardized interviews the preferred choice for studies with large sample sizes requiring many interviewers. The structure of these interviews also ensures that all respondents are presented with the same questions in the same order. This heightens reliability and makes schedule-standardized interviews popular for rigorous hypothesis testing. Research in Practice 7.2 explores some further advantages of having more or less structure in an interview.

Contacting Respondents

As with mailed questionnaires, interviewers face the problem of contacting respondents and eliciting their cooperation. Many interviews are conducted in the homes of the respondents, and locating and traveling to their homes are two of the more troublesome and costly aspects of interviewing. It has been estimated that as much as 40 percent of a typical interviewer's time is spent traveling (Sudman, 1965). Because so much time and cost are involved and because high response rates are desirable, substantial efforts are directed at minimizing the rate of refusal. The way prospective respondents are first contacted has substantial impact on the refusal rate.

Two approaches to contacting respondents that might appear logical to the neophyte researcher, in fact, have an effect opposite of that desired. It might seem that *telephoning* to set up an appointment for the interview would be a good idea. In reality, it greatly increases the rate of refusal. In one experiment, for example, the part of the sample that was

The Unstandardized Interview

Instructions to the interviewer: Discover the kinds of conflicts that the child has had with the parents. Conflicts should include disagreements, tensions due to past, present, or potential disagreements, outright arguments and physical conflicts. Be alert for as many categories and examples of conflicts and tensions as possible.

The Nonschedule-Standardized Interview

Instructions to the interviewer: Your task is to discover as many specific kinds of conflicts and tensions between child and parent as possible. The more *concrete* and detailed the account of each type of conflict the better. Although there are 12 areas of possible conflict which we want to explore (listed in question 3 below), you should not mention any area until after you have asked the first two questions in the order indicated. The first question takes an indirect approach, giving you time to build up rapport with the respondent and to demonstrate a nonjudgmental attitude toward teenagers who have conflicts with their parents.

1. What sorts of problems do teenagers you know have in getting along with their parents?
   (Possible probes: Do they always agree with their parents? Do any of your friends have "problem parents"? What other kinds of disagreements do they have?)
2. What sorts of disagreements do you have with your parents?
   (Possible probes: Do they cause you any problems? In what ways do they try to restrict you? Do you always agree with them on everything? Do they like the same things you do? Do they try to get you to do some things you don't like? Do they ever bore you? Make you mad? Do they understand you? etc.)
3. Have you ever had any disagreements with either of your parents over:
   a. Using the family car
   b. Friends of the same sex
   c. Dating
   d. School (homework, grades, activities)
   e. Religion (church, beliefs, etc.)
   f. Political views
   g. Working for pay outside the home
   h. Allowances
   i. Smoking
   j. Drinking
   k. Eating habits
   l. Household chores

(continued on next page)

Figure 7.1 Examples of Various Interview Structures

telephoned had nearly *triple* the rate of refusal of those contacted in person (Brunner and Carroll, 1967). Apparently, it is much easier to refuse over the relatively impersonal medium of the telephone than in a face-to-face encounter with an interviewer. *Sending people a letter* asking them to participate in an interview has much the same effect (Cartwright and Tucker, 1967). The letter seems to give people sufficient time before the interviewer arrives to develop reasons why they do not want to cooperate. Those first contacted in person, on the other hand, have only those excuses they can muster on the spur of the moment. Clearly, then, the lowest refusal rates are obtained by contacting interviewees in person.

Additional factors can affect the refusal rate (Gorden, 1987). For example, information regarding the research project should blanket the total survey population through the news media. The purpose of this is to demonstrate general community acceptance of the project. The information provided should be essentially the same as that of a cover letter for a mailed questionnaire, with a few differences (*see* Table 7.3). Pictures of the interviewers and mention of any props they will be carrying such as clipboards or zipper cases should be included. This information assists people in identifying interviewers and reducing possible confusion with salespeople or bill collectors. In fact, it is a good idea to equip the interviewers with identifi-

The Schedule-Standardized Interview

Interviewer's explanation to the teenage respondent: We are interested in the kinds of problems teenagers have with their parents. We need to know how many teenagers have which kinds of conflicts with their parents and whether they are just mild disagreements or serious fights. We have a checklist here of some of the kinds of things that happen. Would you think about your own situation and put a check to show which conflicts you, personally, have had and about how often they have happened. Be sure to put a check in every row. If you have never had such a conflict then put the check in the first column where it says "never."

(Hand him the first card dealing with conflicts over the use of the automobile, saying, "If you don't under-stand any of those things listed or have some other things you would like to mention about how you disagree with your parents over the automobile let me know and we'll talk about it.") (When the respondent finishes checking all rows, hand him card number 2, saying, "Here is a list of types of conflicts teenagers have with their parents over their friends of the same sex. Do the same with this as you did with the last list.")

Automobile	Never	Only Once	More Than Once	Many Times
1. Wanting to learn to drive				
2. Getting a driver's license				
3. Wanting to use the family car				
4. What you use the car for				
5. The way you drive it				
6. Using it too much				
7. Keeping the car clean				
8. Putting gas or oil in the car				
9. Repairing the car				
10. Driving someone else's car				
11. Wanting to own a car				
12. The way you drive your own car				
13. What you use your car for				
14. Other				

Source From Raymond L. Gorden, *Interviewing Strategy, Techniques, and Tactics,* 4th ed. Copyright © 1987 by the Dorsey Press. Reprinted by permission of the author.

cation badges or something else that is easily recognizable so that interviewers are not mistaken for others who go door-to-door. When the interviewers go into the field, they should take along copies of the news coverage. If they encounter an interviewee who has not seen the media coverage, the clippings can be shown during the initial contact.

The timing of the initial contact also affects the refusal rate. It is preferable to contact interviewees at a time convenient for them to complete the interview without the need for a second call. De-pending on the nature of the sample, predicting availability may be fairly easy or virtually impossible. For example, if the information required can be obtained from any household member, almost any reasonable time of day will do. On the other hand, if specific individuals must be contacted, timing becomes more critical. If the breadwinner in a household must be interviewed, for example, then contacts should probably be made at night or on weekends unless knowledge of the person's occupation suggests a different time of greater

Research in Practice 7.2
Needs Assessment: Merging Quantitative and Qualitative Measures

It is probably a common misconception that survey research is necessarily quantitative in nature. Certainly survey results presented in the popular media support such a view. Virtually every edition of the evening news presents the results from one or more surveys indicating that a certain percentage of respondents hold a given opinion or plan to vote for a particular candidate, or offering other information that is basically quantitative or reduced to numbers. Especially in the case of face-to-face interviewing, however, survey research is not necessarily limited to quantitative analysis. In fact, as we note in the discussion of Figure 7.1, interviews may run the gamut from being totally quantitative in the highly structured type, to being fully qualitative in the least structured variety, as well as any combination in-between. This flexibility has led some researchers to combine both quantitative and qualitative measures in individual studies to obtain the benefits of each approach.

Two studies of homeless families, headed by females, can serve to illustrate such a merging of interview styles. Shirley Thrasher and Carol Mowbray (1995) interviewed 15 homeless families from three shelters. Their focus was primarily on the experiences of the mothers and their efforts to take care of their children. The other study, conducted by Elizabeth Timberlake (1994), was based on interviews with 200 families, not in shelters, and focused predominantly on the experiences of the homeless children. In both studies, the researchers used structured interview questions to provide quantitative demographic information about the homeless families. This was done to get an idea about who comprises the ranks of homeless families. For example, Timberlake found the ethnic composition of her sample to be 40 percent African American, 35 percent Caucasian, and 21 percent Hispanic, leaving 4 percent unclassified. She also found that the average length of time of homelessness, at the time of the interviews, was 7.7 months with a range of 1.2 to 19.8 months. The other study noted that at the time of their interviews, all the women were unemployed.

As interesting as these numbers might be, the researchers in both studies wanted to get at the more personal meaning of, and feelings associated with, being homeless. For this, they turned to the unstructured parts of the interviews (sometimes called *ethnographic interviews*) designed to get the homeless to tell their stories in their own words. The goal of both studies was to assess the needs of the homeless families in order to develop new programs to assist them or to modify existing programs to better fit their needs. The researchers felt that the best way to accomplish this goal was to get the story of being homeless, in as pure a form as possible, from the people who lived it, without any distortion by the researchers' preconceived notions. The open-ended questions that Timberlake asked the homeless children illustrate this unstructured approach: "Tell me about not having a place to live." "What is it like?" "What do you do?" "How do you feel?" "How do you handle being homeless?" "Are there things that you do or say?" The questions asked of the homeless mothers by Thrasher and Mowbray were remarkably similar. In both studies probes were used as needed to elicit greater response and to clarify vague responses.

An example from Thrasher and Mowbray will illustrate how responses to open-ended questions provide insight into what the respondent is experiencing. The researchers found that a common experience of the women in the shelters was that before coming to the shelter, they had bounced around among friends and relatives, experiencing a series of short-term and unstable living arrangements. The researchers present the following quote from 19-year-old "Nancy":

I went from friend to friend before going back to my mother and her boyfriend. And all my friends they live with their parents, and so you know, I could only stay like a night, maybe two nights before I had to leave. So, the only thing I could do was to come here to the shelter and so that's what I did. After all, there is only so many friends. I went to live once with my grandmother for a week who lives in a senior citizens' high riser. But they don't allow anyone to stay there longer than a

week as a visitor. So, I had to move on. I finally went to my social worker and told her I don't have any place to stay. She put me in a motel first because there was no opening in the shelter. Then, I came here.

As this example illustrates, there is no substitute for hearing the plight of these people in their

Table 7.4   Meaning of Homelessness

	Complaints About Deprivation (*N* = 2,835, 71.8% of total items)	Statements About Restoration (*N* = 1,111, 27.2% of total items)
	(*n* = 1,215, 72.8% of deprivation complaints)	(*n* = 455, 27.2% of restoration statements)
Separation/Loss (***N*** = **1,669, 42.3%** of total items)	They take away your home. They make you move all the time. My friends are all gone. My dog is gone. I got no room. I can't do nothing. I got no privacy. I'm scared I'll get left. We got no privacy. We have to move a lot.	Mama stays with us. We got our car. We got our place to sleep. I got my doll/ball/favorite toy. I still got my clothes. I still got my school.
	(*n* = 945, 67.5% of deprivation complaints)	(*n* = 455, 32.5% of restoration statements)
Caretaking/Nurturance (***N*** = **1,400, 35.5%** of total items)	We got no food. We got nothing left. We got no place to sleep. We got no clothes. We have nothing. Mama lost her job. Daddy left us. Mama's boyfriend left us.	We sleep in the car. We get food at the Kitchen. Mama works. Mama stands in line to get money. I look after Mama 'cause she cries. I help out a lot. Mama gets us food. I get us money and food sometimes.
	(*n* = 675, 77.1% of deprivation complaints)	(*n* = 201, 22.9% of restoration statements)
Security/Protection (***N*** = **876, 22.2%** of total items)	No place is safe. Weird things happen. It's too noisy and crowded. People get cut/shot/killed. People steal your stuff. Too many people tell you what to do.	We're safe in the car. Daddy protects us. John/Bill/Tom protects us. We get away from druggies/drunks.

Source   Adapted from Elizabeth M. Timberlake, "Children With No Place to Call Home: Survival in Cars and on the Streets," *Child and Adolescent Social Work Journal,* Vol. 4 (1994), p. 268. Used with permission.

(continued on next page)

own words to help us, who are not homeless, to gain some understanding of what it is like not to have a stable place to call home.

In part, because of her much larger sample, Timberlake did not tape-record her interviews, so no verbatim transcripts were made. Instead, she took field notes that summarized the responses of the homeless children. This resulted in a different approach to analysis because she did not have the long narratives that Thrasher and Mowbray had. Instead, she had a large number of summarized statements from her notes. She ended up doing a more quantitative analysis by categorizing the statements made by the respondents. Upon analyzing the responses, Timberlake found that they clustered around three themes: separation/loss, caretaking/nurturance, and security/protection. Within each theme were statements along two dimensions of the theme, which Timberlake refers to as "deprivation" and "restoration." Essentially these are, respectively, the negative statements about what is bad about being homeless and the positive statements about what the children still have and how they cope. As can be seen from Table 7.4, Timberlake tabulated the number of each kind of statement. It seems rather telling about the devastation of homelessness on the children that there were approximately three times as many "deprivation" statements as there were "restoration" statements. It is important to note that these categories and themes were not used by the respondents themselves, but were created by Timberlake in an effort to extract theoretical meaning from the narratives. Another researcher analyzing the same data, but with a different theoretical focus, might very well create different categories. Some critics of this sort of quantifying of narrative data suggest that there is a danger of the researcher imposing too much of himself or herself into the analysis.

Neither of these illustrative studies used an interview format that would be suitable for interviewing a large, randomly selected sample of homeless people with the purpose of estimating the demographic characteristics of the entire homeless population. Imagine trying to organize and summarize data from several thousand interviews such as those conducted by Thrasher and Mowbray! To reasonably accomplish such a population estimate, a schedule-standardized interview format, producing quantitative data, would be far more appropriate. However, if the goal of the research project is to gain an understanding of the personal experiences and reactions to being homeless, as it was in the two studies just discussed, then presenting results in the respondents' own words is more effective.

The Timberlake study develops the concepts of deprivation and restoration, which were, essentially, "discovered" in her data. Although more abstract and removed from the respondents than direct quotations, the statements in Table 7.4 nevertheless communicate a sense of the personal meaning of homelessness while also providing quantitative summary data. If one were to design a schedule-standardized survey project to do a population description of the homeless, studies such as the two discussed here would be invaluable for determining what concepts to measure and for developing the quantitative indicators that such a study would demand.

These two studies illustrate that both qualitative and quantitative approaches are essential to social research. Depending on the particular goals of the research, one approach or the other may be most appropriate, and, in some cases, a blend of both quantitative and qualitative approaches may be used in the same project to obtain the desired results.

availability. Whatever time the interviewer makes the initial contact, it still may not be convenient for the respondent, especially if the interview is lengthy. If the respondent is pressed for time, it is better to use the initial contact to establish rapport and set another time for the interview, even though

callbacks are costly. This is certainly preferable to the rushed interview that results in inferior data.

When the interviewer and potential respondent first meet, the interviewer should include certain points of information in the introduction. One suggestion is the following (Smith, 1981):

Good day. I am from the Public Opinion Survey Unit of the University of Missouri (shows official identification). We are doing a survey at this time on how people feel about police–community relationships. This study is being done throughout the state, and the results will be used by local and state governments. The addresses at which we interview are chosen entirely by chance, and the interview only takes 45 minutes. All information is entirely confidential, of course.

Respondents will be looking for much the same basic information as with mailed questionnaires. As the preceding example illustrates, respondents should also be informed of the approximate length of the interview. After giving the introduction, the interviewer should be prepared to elaborate on any points the interviewee questions. Care must be exercised, however, when discussing the purpose of the survey to avoid biasing responses.

Conducting an Interview

A large-scale survey with an adequate budget will often turn to private research agencies to train interviewers and conduct interviews. Smaller research projects, however, may not be able to afford this and will have to train and coordinate their own team of interviewers, possibly with the researchers themselves doing some of the interviewing. It is important, therefore, to know how to conduct an interview properly.

The Interview as a Social Relationship   The interview is a social relationship designed to exchange information between respondent and interviewer. The quantity and quality of information exchanged depend on how astute and creative the interviewer is at understanding and managing that relationship (Bradburn and Sudman, 1979; Fowler and Mangione, 1990). Human service workers are generally knowledgeable regarding the properties and processes of social interaction, and in fact much human service practice is founded on the establishment of social relationships with clients. However, a few elements of the research interview are worth emphasizing because they have direct implications for conducting the interview.

The research interview is a secondary relationship in which the interviewer has a practical, utilitarian goal. It is easy, especially for an inexperienced interviewer, to be drawn into a more casual or personal interchange with the respondent. Especially with a friendly, outgoing respondent, the conversation could drift off to sports, politics, or children. That, however, is not the purpose of the interview. The goal is not to make friends or give the respondent a sympathetic ear but rather to collect complete and unbiased data following the interview schedule.

We all recognize the powerful impact that first impressions can have on our perceptions of other people. This is especially true in interview situations, where the interviewer and respondent are likely to be total strangers. The first things that impact a respondent are the physical and social characteristics of the interviewer. Therefore, considerable care needs to be taken to ensure that the first contact enhances the likelihood of cooperation by the respondent (Warwick and Lininger, 1975). Most research suggests that interviewers are more successful if they have social characteristics similar to those of their respondents. Thus, characteristics such as socioeconomic status, age, sex, race, and ethnicity might influence the success of the interview—especially if the subject matter of the interview relates to one of these topics. In addition, the personal demeanor of the interviewer plays an important role, and interviewers should be neat, clean, and businesslike, but friendly.

After initial pleasantries have been exchanged, the interviewer should begin the interview. The interviewee may be a bit apprehensive during the initial stages of an interview. In recognition of this, the interview should begin with fairly simple, nonthreatening questions. If a schedule is used, it should be designed to begin with these kinds of questions. The demographic questions that are reserved until the later stages of a mailed questionnaire are good to begin an interview. Respondents' familiarity with these questions makes them non-threatening and a good means of reducing tension in the respondent.

Probes If an interview schedule is used, the interview will progress in accordance with the schedule. As needed, the interviewer will use **probes,** or follow-up questions, that are intended to elicit clearer and more complete responses. In some cases, suggestions for probes will be contained in the interview schedule. In less structured interviews, however, interviewers must be prepared to develop and use their own probes. Probes can take the form of a pause in conversation that encourages the respondent to elaborate. Or a probe could be an explicit request to clarify or elaborate on something. A major concern with any probe is that it not bias the respondent's answer by suggesting how he or she should answer (Fowler and Mangione, 1990).

Recording Responses A central task of interviewers, of course, is to record the responses of respondents. The four most common ways are: classifying responses into predetermined categories, summarizing the "high points" of what is said, taking verbatim notes, or recording the interview with a tape recorder or videotape machine.

Recording responses is generally easiest when an interview schedule is used. Because closed-ended questions are typical of such schedules, responses can simply be classified into the predetermined alternatives. This simplicity of recording is another factor making schedule-standardized interviews suitable for use with relatively untrained interviewers as no special recording skills are required.

With nonschedule interviewing, the questions are likely to be open-ended and the responses longer. Often all that need be recorded are the key points that the respondent makes. The interviewer condenses and summarizes what the respondent says. This requires an experienced interviewer familiar with the research questions who can accurately identify what should be recorded and do so

without injecting his or her own interpretation, which would bias the summary.

Sometimes it may be desirable that everything the respondent says be recorded verbatim in order to avoid the possible biasing effect of summarizing responses. If the anticipated responses are reasonably short, competent interviewers can take verbatim notes. Special skills such as shorthand, however, may be necessary. If the responses are lengthy, verbatim note taking can cause difficulties such as leading the interviewer to fail to monitor the respondent or to be unprepared to probe when necessary. It can also damage rapport by making it appear that the interviewer is ignoring the respondent. Problems such as this can be eliminated by recording the interviews. This, however, increases the costs substantially. Though individual cassettes and recorders are not very expensive, the number needed for a large-scale survey would certainly drive costs up considerably. The really big cost comes, however, when transcribing the tapes. Vast amounts of secretarial time are required for this (Gorden, 1987).

The fear of some researchers that tape recorders will increase the refusal rate appears unwarranted (Gorden, 1987). If the use of the recorder is explained as a routine procedure that aids in recording complete and accurate responses, few respondents object. You should avoid asking the respondents if they mind if you record the interview. The question itself implies legitimate reasons for objecting and almost invites the respondent to object. The interviewer should assume that the tape recorder will be accepted unless the respondent raises the issue.

Controlling Interviewers Once interviewers go into the field, the quality of the resulting data is heavily dependent on them. It is a naive researcher indeed who assumes that, without supervision, they will all do their job properly, especially when part-time interviewers who have little commitment to the research project are used. Proper supervision begins during interviewer training. The importance of contacting the right respondents and meticulously following established procedures should be stressed. Interviewers should be informed that their work will be carefully checked, and failure to follow procedures will not be tolerated.

One particularly serious problem with hiring people to conduct interviews is a practice variously known as "curbing," "curbstoning," or "shade-treeing." These terms refer to interviewers' filling in the responses themselves without contacting respondents (Frey, 1989). In large-scale surveys, this can be a real problem. For example, a New York City reporter serving as a census enumerator for the 1980 census observed for 8 days in a row as a carload of census takers "parked . . . turned the radio on, and boogied—just had a good time—talked—took drugs—ate—slept—and basically just loafed" while falsely filling in census forms (Magnet, 1981). Fortunately, with projects of a smaller scale than the census, curbing can be controlled with adequate supervision. Completed interviews should be scrutinized for any evidence of falsification. Spot checks can be made to see if interviewers are where they are supposed to be at any given time, and respondents can be telephoned to see if they have, in fact, been interviewed.

Minorities and the Interview Relationship

Many interviewers in survey research are white, middle-class women with white-collar occupations (Alreck and Settle, 1985). Many respondents in surveys have different characteristics than these. Does it make a difference in terms of the quantity or quality of data collected in surveys when interviewer and interviewee have different characteristics? It appears to. In survey research, three elements interact to affect the quality of the data collected: the minority status of the interviewer, the minority status of the respondent, and the minority content of the survey instrument. The interrelationships among these elements need to be considered carefully to ensure that the least amount of bias enters the data collection process.

As we have emphasized, an interview is a social relationship in which interviewer and respondent have cultural and subcultural expectations for appropriate behavior. One set of expectations that comes into play in this regard is the social desirability of respondents' answers to questions. Substantial research documents a tendency for people to choose more desirable or socially acceptable answers to questions in surveys (DeMaio, 1984). This stems in part from the desire to appear sensible, reasonable, and pleasant to the interviewer. In all of our contacts with people, including an interview relationship, people typically prefer to please someone rather than offend or alienate. In cases in which interviewer and respondent are from different racial, ethnic, or sexual groups, respondents tend to give answers they perceive to be more desirable, or at least less offensive, to the interviewer; this is especially true when the content of the questions is related to racial, ethnic, or sexual issues. A second set of expectations that comes into play and affects responses in interviews is the social distance between interviewer and respondent, or how much they differ from each other on important social dimensions such as age or minority status. Generally, the less social distance between people, the more freely, openly, and honestly they will talk. Racial, sexual, and ethnic differences often indicate a degree of social distance.

The impact of cross-race interviewing has been studied extensively with African American and white respondents (Bradburn and Sudman, 1979; Schaeffer, 1980; Cotter, Cohen, and Coulter, 1982; Bachman and O'Malley, 1984; Anderson, Silver, and Abramson, 1988). African American respondents, for example, express more warmth and closeness for whites when interviewed by a white person and are less likely to express dissatisfaction or resentment over discrimination or inequities against African Americans. White respondents tend to express more "pro-black" attitudes when interviewed by an African American than by a white. This race-of-interviewer effect can be quite large and occurs fairly consistently, but it seems to play a part mostly when questions involve race or other sensitive topics. Nonracial or nonsensitive items seem not to be affected.

The impact of ethnicity on interviews has been studied much less, probably because the ethnicity of both interviewer and respondent is not as readily apparent in most cases as is race, which is very visibly signified by skin color. One study used both Jewish and non-Jewish interviewers asking questions about the extent of Jewish influence in the United States (Hyman, 1954). Respondents were much more willing to say that Jews had too much influence when they were being interviewed by a non-Jew. Gender also has an effect on interviews. Women are much more likely to report honestly about things like rape, battering, sexual behavior, and male–female relationships in general when they are interviewed by a woman instead of a man (Eichler, 1988; Reinharz, 1992).

Some researchers recommend routinely matching interviewer and respondent for race, ethnicity, or gender in interviews on racial or sensitive topics, and this is generally sound advice. Sometimes, however, a little more thought is called for. The problem is that we are not always sure in which direction bias might occur. If white respondents give different answers to white as opposed to black interviewers, which of their answers most accurately reflect their attitudes? For the most part, we aren't sure. It is generally assumed that the same-race interviewer will gather more accurate data (Fowler and Mangione, 1990). A more conservative assumption is that the truth falls somewhere between the data that the two interviewers collect.

When minorities speak a language different from that of the dominant group, the quality of data collected can be affected if the interview is conducted in the dominant group's language (Marin and Marin, 1991). For example, a study of Native American children in Canada found that these children expressed a strong white bias in racial preferences when the study was conducted in English; the bias declined significantly when the children's native Ojibwa language was used (Annis and Corenblum, 1986). This impact of language should not be surprising, considering that language is not solely a mechanism for communication; it also reflects cultural values, norms, and a way of life. So when interviewing groups where a language other than English is widely used, it would

be appropriate to consider conducting interviews in that other language.

An Assessment of Interviews

Advantages   First, interviews can help to *motivate* respondents to give more accurate and complete information. There is little motivation for respondents to be especially accurate or complete when responding to a mailed questionnaire. They can hurry through it if they want to. The control afforded by an interviewer encourages better responses. This becomes especially important as the information sought becomes more complex.

Second, interviewing affords an opportunity to *explain* questions that respondents may not otherwise understand. Again, if the information sought is complex, this can be of great importance, and the literacy problem that was a limitation of mailed questionnaires is virtually eliminated. Even lack of facility in English can be handled by using multilingual interviewers. (When we conducted a needs assessment survey in some rural parts of Upper Michigan some years ago, we employed one interviewer who was fluent in Finnish because a number of people in the area spoke Finnish but little or no English.)

Third, the presence of an interviewer allows *control* over factors uncontrollable with mailed questionnaires. For example, the interviewer can ensure that the proper person responds to the questions and that questions are responded to in sequence. Furthermore, the interviewer can arrange for the interview to be conducted such that the respondent does not consult with, or is not influenced by, other people before responding.

Fourth, interviewing is a more *flexible* form of data collection than questionnaires. The style of interviewing can be tailored to the needs of the study. A free, conversational style, with much probing, can be adopted in an exploratory study. In a more developed study, a highly structured approach can be utilized. This flexibility makes interviewing suitable for a far broader range of research situations than are mailed questionnaires.

Finally, the interviewer can add *observational information* to the responses of the respondent. What was the respondent's attitude toward the interview? Was it essentially cooperative, indifferent, or hostile? Did the respondent appear to the fabricating answers? Did he or she react emotionally to some questions? This additional information helps to better evaluate the responses given, especially when the subject matter is highly personal or controversial (Gorden, 1987).

Disadvantages Some disadvantages associated with personal interviews may lead the researcher to choose another data collection technique.

The first disadvantage is *cost*. Interviewers must be hired, trained, and equipped; and their travel must be paid for. All of these together can be very expensive.

The second limitation is *time*. Traveling to respondents' homes requires much time and limits each interviewer to only a few interviews each day. If particular individuals must be contacted, several time-consuming callbacks may be needed to complete many of the interviews. Considerable time is also required for start-up operations, such as developing questions, designing schedules, and training interviewers.

A third limitation of interviews is the problem of interviewer bias. Especially in unstructured interviews, interviewers may misinterpret or misrecord something because of their own personal feelings about the topic. Furthermore, just as the respondent is affected by the interviewer's characteristics, so the interviewer is similarly affected by the characteristics of the respondent. Sex, age, race, social class, and a host of other factors may subtly shape the way in which the interviewer asks questions and interprets the words of respondents.

A fourth limitation of interviews, especially with less structured interviews, is the possibility of significant but unnoticed variation in wording from one interview to the next or among interviewers. We know that variations in wording can produce variations in response, and the more freedom interviewers have in this regard, the more of a problem it is. Wording variation can affect both reliability and validity (*see* Chapter 5).

Telephone Surveys

Face-to-face interviews tend to be a considerably more expensive means of gathering data in comparison to mailed questionnaires or telephone surveys (Rea and Parker, 1992). As Table 7.5 shows, face-to-face interviews can be more than twice as expensive as a survey done over the phone or through the mail. The table shows that, with face-to-face interviews, there are substantially higher costs for such things as locating residents, contacting respondents, conducting interviews, traveling, and training interviewers. With mail or telephone surveys, there is no travel time and fewer interviewers are needed; in addition, fewer supervisory personnel are needed. Although such costs as telephone charges are higher in telephone surveys, they are far outweighed by the other savings. The cost advantage of the less expensive types of surveys makes feasible research that otherwise would be prohibitively expensive.

The speed with which a telephone survey can be completed also makes it preferable at times. If we wanted people's reactions to some event, for example, or repeated measures of public opinion, which can change rapidly, the speed of telephone surveys makes them preferable in these circumstances.

Certain areas of the country and many major cities contain substantial numbers of non-English-speaking people. These people are difficult to accommodate with mailed questionnaires and personal interviews unless we know ahead of time what language a respondent speaks. Non-English-speaking people can be handled fairly easily with telephone surveys, however. All that is needed are a few multilingual interviewers. (Spanish-speakers account for the vast majority of non-English-speaking persons in the United States.) If an interviewer contacts a non-English-speaking respondent, that respondent can be conveniently transferred to an interviewer conversant in the respondent's

Table 7.5   Cost Comparison of Telephone, Mail, and Face-to-Face Surveys, With a Sample Size of 520

A. Mail Survey

	Total Cost (dollars)		Total Cost (dollars)
Prepare for survey		Postage for return envelopes, 960 @ $.52 each	500
Purchase sample list in machine-readable form	375	Sign letters, stamp envelopes	100
Load database of names and addresses	17	Prepare mail-out packets	118
Graphic design for questionnaire cover (hire out)	100	Third mail-out (960)	
Print questionnaires: 4 sheets, legal-size, folded, 1,350 @ $.15 each (includes paper) (hire out)	203	Prestamped postcards, 4 bunches of 250 @ $.19 each	190
		Address postcards	25
Telephone	100	Print message and sign postcards	50
Supplies		Process, precode, edit 390 returned questionnaires, 10 min each	546
Mail-out envelopes, 2,310 @ $.05 each, with return address	116	Fourth mail-out (475)	
Return envelopes, 1,350 @ $.05 each, pre-addressed but no return address	68	Print cover letter	25
		Address envelopes	25
Letterhead for cover letters, 2,310 @ $.05 each	116	Sign letters, stamp envelopes	25
Miscellaneous	200	Prepare mail-out packets	168
First mail-out (960)		Postage for mail-out, 475 @ $.52 each	247
Print advance-notice letter	25	Postage for return envelopes, 475 @ $.52 each	247
Address envelopes	25		
Sign letters, stamp envelopes	50	Process, precode, edit 185 returned questionnaires, 10 min each	260
Postage for mail-out, 960 @ $.29 each	278		
Prepare mail-out packets	134	**Total, excluding professional time**	**4,883**
Second mail-out (960)		Professional time (120 hrs @ $35,000 annual salary plus 20% fringe benefits)	2,423
Print cover letter	25		
Address envelopes	25	**Total, including professional time**	**7,306**
Postage for mail-out, 960 @ $.52 each	500		

(continued on next page)

language. Though multilingual interviewers can be and are used in personal interviews, this is far less efficient, probably involving at least one callback so that an interviewer with the needed language facility can be sent out. A final advantage of telephone interviews is that supervision of the interviewers is far easier. The problem of curbing is eliminated be- cause supervisors can monitor the interviews any time they wish. This makes it easy to ensure that specified procedures are followed and that any problems that might arise are quickly discovered and corrected.

Despite these considerable advantages, tele- phone surveys have several limitations that may

Table 7.5 *Continued*

B. Telephone Survey	Total Cost (dollars)	C. Face-to-Face Survey	Total Cost (dollars)
Prepare for survey		Prepare for survey	
Use add-a-digit calling based on systematic, random sampling from directory	84	Purchase map for area frame	200
		Print interviewer manuals	29
Print interviewer manuals	37	Print questionnaires (690)	379
Print questionnaires (940)	84	Train interviewers (20-hour training session)	1,134
Train interviewers (12-hour training session)	700	Miscellaneous supplies	25
Miscellaneous supplies	25	Conduct the survey	
Conduct the survey		Locate residences; contact respondents; conduct interviews; field edit questionnaires; 3.5 completed interviews per 8-hour day	9,655
Contact and interview respondents; edit questionnaires; 50 minutes per completed questionnaire	2,786	Travel cost ($8.50 per completed interview; interviewers use own car)	4,420
Telephone charges	3,203	Office edit and general clerical	
Total, excluding professional time	**6,919**	(6 completed questionnaires per hour)	728
Professional time (120 hrs @ $35,000 annual salary plus 20% fringe benefits)	2,423	**Total, excluding professional time**	**16,570**
Total, including professional time	**9,342**	Professional time (160 hrs @ $35,000 annual salary plus 20% fringe benefits)	3,231
		Total, including professional time	**19,801**

Source Adapted from Priscilla Salant and Don A. Dillman, *How to Conduct Your Own Survey* (New York: John Wiley and Sons, 1994), pp. 46–49. Used with permission.

make the method unsuitable for many research purposes. First, they must be quite short in duration. Normally, the maximum length is about 20 minutes, with most being even shorter. This is in sharp contrast to personal interviews, which can extend to an hour or more. The time limitation obviously restricts the volume of information that can be obtained and the depth to which issues can be explored. Telephone surveys work best when the information desired is fairly simple and the questions are uncomplicated.

A second limitation stems from telephone communication's being only voice-to-voice. Lack

of visual contact eliminates several desirable features characteristic of personal interviews. The interviewer is unable to supplement responses with observational information, and it is harder to probe effectively without seeing the respondent. Furthermore, the use of cards with response alternatives or other visual stimuli is precluded. The inability to present complex sets of response alternatives in this format can make it difficult to ask some questions that are important.

Finally, as noted in Chapter 6, surveys based on samples drawn from telephone directories may have considerable noncoverage because some people are without telephones and others have unlisted numbers. Although modern telephone sampling techniques, such as random digit dialing, eliminate the problem of unlisted numbers, the approximately 6 percent of households without telephones remain unreachable, and they are concentrated among the poor and transient segments of the population. So some sampling bias remains even if random digit dialing is used. Because some human service clients are heavily concentrated in the population groups with lower rates of telephone service, special caution should be exercised before deciding on a telephone survey.

Focus Groups

Research situations arise in which the standardization found in most surveys and interviews is not appropriate and researchers need more flexibility in how they elicit responses to questions. One area where this is likely to be true is exploratory research. Here, research questions cannot be formulated into precise hypotheses, and our knowledge of some phenomenon is too sketchy to allow precise measurement of variables. It is also true in research on very personal and subjective experiences that are unlikely to be adequately tapped by asking the same structured questions of everyone.

In such research situations, a flexible strategy for gathering data is the **focus group,** or **group depth interview** (Krueger, 1994; Morgan, 1994). As the name implies, it is *an interview with a whole group of people at the same time.* Focus groups were originally used as a preliminary step in the research process to generate quantitative hypotheses and develop questionnaire items, and they are still used this way. Survey researchers, for example, sometimes use focus groups as a tool for developing questionnaires and interview schedules. However, focus groups are now also used in applied research as a strategy for collecting data in their own right, especially when researchers are seeking people's subjective reactions and the many levels of meaning that are important to people's behavior. Today, tens

of millions of dollars are spent each year on focus groups in applied research, marketing research, and political campaigns. One example of this is a study of the barriers women confront in obtaining medical care to detect and treat cervical cancer, a potentially fatal ailment that can be readily detected and treated if women obtain Pap smears on a regular basis and return for follow-up care when necessary. The researchers decided that a focus group "would allow free expression of thoughts and feelings about cancer and related issues" and would be the most effective mechanism to probe women's motivations for not seeking appropriate medical care (Dignan et al., 1990, p. 370).

A focus group usually consists of at least one moderator and up to 10 respondents and lasts for up to 3 hours. The moderator will have an interview guide that outlines the main topics of inquiry and the order in which they will be covered and may have a variety of props, such as audiovisual cues, to prompt discussion and elicit reactions. The members of focus groups are selected on the basis of their usefulness in providing the data called for in the research. The women for the study on cervical cancer, for example, were chosen, among other things, because they had had some previous experience with cancer. Focus group membership is not normally based on probability samples, which Chapter 6 points out as the most likely to be representative samples. This can therefore throw the generalizability of focus group results into question. However, in exploratory research, such generalizability is not as critically important as it is in other research. In addition, most focus group research enhances its representativeness and generalizability by collecting data from more than one focus group. The cervical cancer study involved four separate focus groups of 10 to 12 women, and some research projects use 20 or more focus groups.

The moderator's job in a focus group is to initiate discussion and facilitate the flow of responses. Following an outline of topics to be covered, the moderator would ask questions, probe areas that are not clear, and pursue lines of inquiry that seem fruitful. However, a focus group is not just 10 in-depth interviews. Rather, the moderator uses a knowledge of group dynamics to elicit data that might not have been obtained in an in-depth interview. For example, a status structure emerges in all groups, including focus groups; some people become leaders and others followers. The moderator will use this group dynamic by encouraging the emergence of leaders and using them to elicit responses, reactions, or information from other group members. Group members will often respond to other group members differently than they respond to the researcher/moderator. People in a focus group will make side comments to one another—obviously not possible in a one-person interview—and the moderator will make note of these comments and possibly encourage group members to elaborate on them. In fact, in a well-run focus group, the members may interact among themselves as much as with the group moderator. In a standard interview, the stimulus for people's responses is the interviewer's questions; by contrast, focus group interviews provide a second stimulus for people's responses—the group experience itself.

Group moderators will also direct the group discussion, usually from more general topics in the beginning to more specific issues toward the end (Krueger, 1994). For example, in the focus group study of cervical cancer, the moderators began with questions about general life concerns and the perceived value of health and ended with specific questions about cancer, cancer screening, and Pap smears. The general questions provide a foundation and a context without which the women might not be as willing or as able to come up with useful answers to the more specific questions. Group moderators take great care in developing these sequences of questions. The moderator also must observe the characteristics of the participants in the group to ensure the most effective participation by all members. For example, a "rambler" who talks a lot but doesn't say much that is useful needs to be constrained while "shy ones" who tend to say little need to be encouraged to express themselves. In short, being a moderator of a focus group is a complex job that calls for an understanding of group dynamics as well as skills in understanding and working with people.

During a focus group, there is too much happening too fast to engage in any useful data analysis. The focus group is to produce the data, which is preserved on videotape or a tape recording for later analysis. During the analysis, the researcher makes field notes from the recordings and then prepares a report summarizing the findings and presenting conclusions and implications. Data from a focus group are usually presented in one of the following three forms (Krueger, 1994). In the *raw data format,* the researcher presents all the comments made by the group participants about particular issues. This provides the complete range of opinions that were expressed in the group. Little interpretation is offered by the researcher, unless some nonverbal interaction needs to be interpreted or some nuance of meaning clarified that could only be grasped in context. The second format for presentation is the *descriptive approach,* in which the researchers summarize in narrative form the kinds of opinions expressed in the group, with some quotes from group members as illustrations. This calls for more summary on the part of the researcher but also enables the researcher to cast the results in a way that best conveys the meaning communicated in the group session. The third format is the *interpretive model,* which expands on the descriptive approach by providing more interpretation. The researcher can provide his or her own interpretations of the group's mood, feelings, and reactions to questions. This may include the moderator's impression of the motivations and unexpressed desires of members of the group. The raw data model is the quickest manner of reporting results, but the interpretive model provides the greatest depth of information from the group sessions. Of course, the interpretive approach, because it does involve interpretation, is more likely to exhibit some bias or error.

Focus groups have major advantages over more structured, single-person interviews: The former are more flexible, cost less, and can provide quick results. In addition, focus groups have the advantage of using the interaction between people to stimulate ideas and encourage group members to participate. In fact, focus groups, when run properly, have very high levels of participation and thus elicit reactions that might not have been obtained in a one-on-one interview setting. Unfortunately, focus groups also have disadvantages: The results are less generalizable to a larger population, and the data are more difficult and subjective to analyze. Focus groups are also less likely than interviews to produce quantitative data; in fact, focus group data may more closely resemble the field notes produced in field research discussed in Chapter 9.

Practice and Research Interviews Compared

The interview is undoubtedly the most commonly employed technique in human service practice. Therefore, it is natural for students in the human services to wonder how research interviewing compares with practice interviewing. The fundamental difference is the *purpose* of the interview. Practice interviews are conducted for the purpose of helping a client, while research interviews are designed to gain knowledge about a problem or population under study. Whereas the practitioner seeks to understand the client as an individual and often uses the interview as a means of effecting change, the researcher uses the data collected on individuals to describe the characteristics of, and variations in, a population. To the practitioner, the individual client system is central. To the researcher, the respondent is merely the unit of analysis; the characteristics and variability of the population are of primary concern.

The difference in purpose is the basis for differences between practice and research interviewing. Whereas *respondents* are selected to represent a population, *clients* are accepted because they have individual needs that the agency is designed to serve. Research interviews are typically brief, often single encounters, whereas practice relationships may be intensive, long-term relationships. Clients (or the client's needs) often determine the topic and focus of a practice interview, whereas the content of the research interview is predetermined by the nature of the research project. The ideal research interview presents each respondent with exactly the same stimulus in order to obtain validly comparable responses. The ideal practice interview provides the client with a unique situation that maximizes the potential to help that individual.

An emphasis on differences between the two forms of interviewing, however, should not obscure many of the similarities. Both require that the interviewer make clear the general purpose of the interview. Both require keen observational skills and disciplined use of self according to the purpose of the interview. This last point is crucial to answering another question about interviewing: Do practitioners make good research interviewers? The answer depends on the nature of the particular interview task and the capacity of the interviewer to perform that particular task. Some situations may best be served by interviewers who display warmth, patience, compassion, tolerance, and sincerity, whereas other situations would require interviewers who are reserved and controlled and who bring an atmosphere of objective, detached sensitivity to the interview (Kadushin, 1972). Some researchers have found that using verbal reinforcement—both positive comments to complete responses and negative feedback to inadequate responses—resulted in obtaining more complete information from respondents (Vinokur, Oksenberg, and Cannell, 1979). Although successful in terms of amount of information gained, such techniques might be foreign to the style of interviewing that a practitioner uses. Thus, for the structured, highly controlled interview, the practitioner who is used to improvising questions and demonstrating willingness to help may be a poor choice of interviewer. In other situations, in which in-depth, unstructured exploratory interviews are needed, the practitioner's skills might be ideal. Again, the purpose of the interview and the nature of the task determine the compatibility of human service skills with the research interview.

Main Points

- Surveys are of two general types: (1) questionnaires completed directly by respondents and (2) interviews with the questions read and responses recorded by an interviewer.
- Closed-ended questions provide a fixed set of response alternatives from which respondents choose.
- Open-ended questions provide no response alternatives, leaving respondents complete freedom of expression.
- Once developed, survey instruments should be pretested to see if questions are clearly understood and unbiased; when changes are made in the instrument, it should be pretested again.
- Clear directions must be provided on questionnaires to indicate what respondents are to do and to guide them through the questionnaire.
- Questions should be ordered so that early questions maximize the response rate but do not affect the responses to later questions.
- Obtaining a high response rate, the percentage of surveys actually completed, is very important for representativeness in survey research.
- Central to efforts to maximize the response rate with the mailed questionnaire are the cover letter, the use of payments and follow-up letters, and the length and appearance of the questionnaire.
- Interviews are classified by their degree of structure as unstandardized, nonschedule-standardized, or schedule-standardized.
- Probes are used to elicit clearer and more complete responses during interviews.
- Telephone surveys offer significant time and cost savings compared with interviews or mailed questionnaires and are a suitable alternative in many cases.
- Computer software now enables telephone surveyors to input responses directly into a computer file as well as check for errors or inconsistencies in the data.

Important Terms for Review

closed-ended questions
cover letter
focus group
group depth interview
interview
interview schedule
open-ended questions
probes
questionnaire
response bias
response rate
survey

Exploring the Internet

A rich variety of resources awaits anyone who seeks information about survey research on the Internet, from a basic introduction to surveys for the neophyte to highly technical details of interest mainly to the professional survey researcher. There are home pages for the major surveys conducted by thoe government as well as pages for university and private survey companies. A good beginning point is the American Statistical Association Research Methods Section at http://www.minority.unc.edu/~kalsbeek/asa/srms.html. This site provides access to a basic overview of survey research, including ethics, a discussion of privacy issues, and information on how to plan a survey. The material complements the general discussion of surveys presented in this chapter.

One of the more enlightening opportunities available through the Internet is that of examining questions that are used in actual surveys. Not only will you become more familiar with major survey projects around the world, but you can learn a great deal about how good survey questions are designed. Depending on the source, you may be able to use or adapt questions from these surveys for use in a survey instrument that you are designing.

COMPUTERS IN RESEARCH
Survey Design and Data Collection

A popular truism about the computer is, "garbage in; garbage out." For the researcher, it is a fact that the quality of the research produced can be no better than the quality of the data used to do the analysis; and in survey research, the computer is rapidly becoming an essential tool in the effort to elicit valid and reliable data from respondents and to accurately record these data for analysis.

Probably the most intensive application of computer technology to survey research is computer-assisted telephone interviewing, or CATI (Groves et al., 1988; Buetow et al., 1996). With CATI, the interview is conducted over the telephone as the interviewer reads questions from a computer monitor (instead of a clipboard) and records responses directly into the computer via the keyboard instead of using a paper form. Superficially, CATI replaces the paper-and-pencil format of interviewing with a monitor-and-keyboard arrangement, but the differences are much more significant. Some of the special techniques that are possible with CATI include personalizing the wording of questions based on answers to previous questions and automatic branching for contingency questions. For example, in a study on sibling relations, if a respondent reported that she has a son named David who is 14 and another named Peter who is 11, the computer can automatically insert the name "David" into questions to refer to the older child. If one subset of questions concerns same-sex siblings, and a different set addresses boy–girl relations, the computer will automatically select the former subset and skip the latter. These features speed up the interview and improve accuracy because the interviewer can concentrate fully on the questions at hand instead of searching through pages of items that do not apply. The CATI program may also include enforced probing when respondents give incomplete answers, editing of responses, and automatic call scheduling.

In computer terminology, such programs are "interactive," that is, the interview schedule changes and presents customized instructions for the interviewer depending on the responses that are recorded. Although these CATI features are common for large-scale survey organizations with custom software such as the U.S. Bureau of the Census, a variety of microcomputer software now makes the technology feasible for smaller organizations that need to do frequent surveys.

Computer-assisted interviewing involves two steps. The first is designing a computer program application that contains the interview schedule. To accomplish this task, the researcher can turn to specialized software for designing data collection programs such as the Viking Forms Manager program, which is available for a variety of mini- and microcomputers and is designed to permit nonprogrammers to develop the interactive screen formats that make CATI effective.

The second step is conducting the interviews. The interactive forms are used by means of a companion software program, the Viking Data Entry System, to collect and enter the data from respondents into a data file for analysis.

Besides customizing questions and utilizing branching routines, the program helps prevent errors from entering the data during the collection phase. For example, with a question that requires numeric data such as "How old are you?" the program can require that only numeric characters be entered. If the interviewer accidentally hits an alphanumeric character, the program responds with an error message and requires the interviewer to reenter the response. Range checks can also be used to catch errors. Assuming one is interviewing adults, the age range might be set to 18–99. Any response outside that range would result in an error message or a request to recheck the entry.

Data entry can be simplified by prerecording responses to which most people will give the same answer. For example, when asking about health status, very few respondents may have had heart attacks. A "No" response can be prerecorded for this item so that data need be changed only for those few individuals who respond "Yes."

The interview schedule can be further refined to warn of logical inconsistencies. If a respondent lists three family members as being employed during the year, an error message would result if the interviewer attempts to enter zero annual income for one of those persons at a later point in the survey. The program will also catch errors such as a February 29 birthday in a non-leap year.

In some situations, the order in which questions are asked can affect the responses in a survey. Because of this, it is common to administer scale items in a random order in a questionnaire. Some software now includes a special feature to take the principle of randomized question ordering a step farther. In administering a scale, it will randomly order the items separately for each respondent to eliminate possible bias due to question order.

A special problem in survey research is coping with open-ended or narrative responses. Even here, computer software is available to aid in survey research. The Survey System is a microcomputer application designed with the survey researcher in mind. In addition to many of the features already described, it has available a special component known as the Verbatim Module. It will search for key words in the narrative responses and even accept approximate spelling of names or key words. The program will then generate reports that display narrative responses.

Although telephone interviewing is undoubtedly the most intensive application of computerized interviewing, it is not the only application. Respondent-completed questionnaires can also be computerized in some situations. Hudson (1988) describes the use of his Clinical Assessment System by clients in social work settings. When clients come to the agency for their appointments, they can use a computer to complete various assessment instruments. Personal interviews can also be adapted to computerized interviewing. With the advent of truly portable personal computers with high memory capacity, questionnaires developed with the help of programs like the Viking Form Manager can be taken into the field. Probably the ultimate application of this concept is the survey research package INTERV, which uses a design called "tele-interviewing" for panel studies. With tele-interviewing, inexpensive microcomputers are placed in the sampled homes. Respondents get to keep them if they stay in the panel for the duration of the study. Games and other software are provided to the respondents in each panel period as an additional incentive to stay with the study. A central computer polls the panel respondents, who record data on the computers in their homes ("News and Notes," 1987).

Of course, any organization contemplating the expense of computerized interviewing must ask the question: Is it worth it? Two recent evaluations suggest that CATI clearly has some advantages over traditional methods but is not without problems (Catlin and Ingram, 1988; Weeks, 1988). The costs of the two approaches proved to be about equal. However, CATI had a lower overall response rate because CATI interviews took longer, especially when conducted by interviewers who were unfamiliar with the procedure. However, as the interviewers gained practice, interview time was cut dramatically. Another problem was computer downtime. Monday through Wednesday were the most productive interviewing days. If the computer system happened to be inoperable during that time, there was no way to make up the difference later in the week. CATI had its greatest benefit in reducing the error rate. It was 50 percent less overall with CATI, and 60 percent less in the portion of the questionnaire that required complex branching. The researchers concluded that studies that require complex branching would benefit the most from CATI. With the rapid development of microcomputer capacity and the development of more sophisticated software, the computer is expected to play an expanded role in the conduct of survey research.

One of the best sites for examining questions is the Institute for Research in Social Science (IRSS) located at http://www.unc.edu/depts/irss/. IRSS provides a data archive that includes a public opinion poll question database. A search engine at this site enables the user to locate questions on almost any topic imaginable. The search engine is easy to use. If you are constructing a survey instrument, it would be worthwhile to examine questions in the database that relate to variables to be used in your survey or questionnaire. We suggest that you try the search engine by entering a topic of interest to you, such as domestic violence, health care, or poverty. Determine if the questions are open-ended or closed-ended. Examine how the questions are worded and consider how you might improve them or adapt them to a project of interest to you. Another site that provides similar details on the General Social Survey is http://www.icpsr.umich.edu/gss/. This site also provides a search engine and permits you to examine questions used in the General Social Survey.

In addition to examining specific questions, it is also possible to download and read entire questionnaires and survey instruments. One site that offers this capability is the Centre for Applied Social Surveys in England (http://www.scpr.ac.uk/cass/). It provides short courses in survey methods and is developing a survey question bank for use by social scientists and social researchers in the academic world, government, market research, and the independent and voluntary sectors. In order to read the questionnaires, you will need to either already have or download an Acrobat Reader program (it can be downloaded from this site). By reviewing a survey instrument, you can explore how the instrument is structured, the ordering of questions, skip patterns, and other features that enhance the quality of the research instrument.

Finally, for locating information about any aspect of survey research, an excellent resource is the Survey Research Center at Princeton University, whose Web site address is http://www.princeton.edu/~abelson/index.html. This site includes links to most major organizations involved in survey research throughout the world.

For Further Reading

Cormier, William H., and L. Sherilyn Cormier. *Interviewing Strategies for Helpers,* 3rd ed. Monterey, Calif.: Brooks/Cole, 1991. The four major stages of the helping process—relationship assessment, goal setting, strategy selection and implementation, and evaluation-termination—are presented with an eye toward tactics for improving each stage through improved interviewing skills. Not just for social workers, this book is a "must read" for anyone in the helping professions, including counseling.

Gorden, Raymond. *Basic Interviewing Skills.* Itasca, Ill.: Peacock, 1992. A very useful "how-to" book on interviewing, it covers everything from how to develop questions, to how to motivate good responses, to how to evaluate respondents' nonverbal behavior.

Rosenberg, M. *The Logic of Survey Analysis.* New York: Basic Books, 1968. A presentation of the logic of surveys, understanding relationships between variables, and analyzing the findings of surveys that requires very little statistical background to comprehend.

Salant, Priscilla, and Don Dillman. *Conducting Surveys: A Step-by-Step Guide to Getting the Information You Need.* New York: Wiley, 1994. As the title states, this is a very useful guide to all the steps in conducting sound survey research.

Schuman, Howard, and Stanley Presser. *Questions and Answers in Attitude Surveys: Experiments on Question Form, Wording, and Content.* Thousand Oaks, Calif.: Sage, 1996. This is a comprehensive handbook on the rules, problems, and pitfalls of designing questions for surveys. It goes far beyond what this chapter is able to cover on this important topic.

Schwarz, N., and S. Sudman, eds. *Answering Questions: Methodology for Determining Cognitive and Communicative Processes in Survey Research.* San Francisco: Jossey-Bass, 1996. This collection discusses the methods involved in observation and/or taping and the subsequent coding and analysis of interviews; explores how to obtain, code, and analyze verbal protocols from respondents; and examines other survey techniques, including sorting tasks and response latency measures.

Stewart, David W., and Prem N. Shamdasni. *Focus Groups: Theory and Practice.* Newbury Park, Calif.: Sage, 1990. This book presents a thorough discussion of the role that focus groups can play in survey as well as other types of research. It presents detailed coverage of the design and conduct of focus groups as well as techniques for analyzing the data generated from them.

Sudman, S., N. Bradburn, and N. Schwarz. *Thinking About Answers: The Application of Cognitive Processes to Survey Methodology.* San Francisco: Jossey-Bass, 1996. An exploration of what answers mean in relation to how people understand the world around them and communicate with one another. The authors present the survey as a social conversation and investigate and document the meanings of the answers respondents give.

Weisberg, Herbert F., Jon A. Krosnick, and Bruce D. Bowen. *An Introduction to Survey Research, Polling, and Data Analysis.* Thousand Oaks, Calif.: Sage, 1996. This is a comprehensive guide to conducting surveys and large-scale public opinion polls, and it also provides the reader with a cautious approach toward the interpretation of survey results.

Weiss, Robert S. *Learning From Strangers: The Art and Method of Qualitative Interview Studies.* New York: Free Press, 1993. This is the definitive work on qualitative research interviewing. Weiss provides examples and running commentary on how social interaction during interviews either inhibits or promotes trust and alliance. Used as a reference, handbook, or text, this book is appropriate for novices and professionals.

Wentland, Ellen J., and Kent W. Smith. *Survey Responses: An Evaluation of Their Validity.* San Diego, Calif.: Academic Press, 1993. This is a comprehensive assessment of the issue of whether survey research produces accurate data about people's feelings, attitudes, and behaviors.

Exercises for Class Discussion

The state Health and Human Services Department has recently released a controversial study that concludes that the state is able to provide better quality foster care for less cost than private agencies can provide under a "purchase of services" contract. The private agencies are outraged and point out some serious flaws in the study. For example, the state study was done by people who might lose their jobs if the state contracts out for services. Furthermore, the study compared a state program in an urban area with a rural private agency program. To resolve these concerns, the independent research firm where you are employed has been asked to conduct a survey that will generate results that are representative of the entire state.

The following exercises explore some of the tasks and decisions you would face in undertaking such a survey.

7.1 Would you use mailed questionnaires, telephone surveys, or personal interviews with: (a) foster parents, (b) adolescents in care, (c) line workers? Defend your choices. What additional information would help you make these decisions?

7.2 If your organization decides to send a mailed questionnaire to foster parents, what things could you suggest to improve the response rate?

7.3 One of the topics to cover with foster parents would be their satisfaction with the services provided by the foster care worker. Write a closed-ended question and an open-ended question to deal with this topic. Which type of question would, in your opinion, be best?

7.4 For interviewing the foster children, would you think a nonstandardized, a nonschedule-standardized, or a schedule-standardized format would be best? Why?

7.5 You are given the task of selecting the interviewers to conduct face-to-face interviews with the adolescents. You are given the following options: Department of Health and Human Services workers, interviewers from a political polling organization who are mostly middle-aged women, or teenagers between 16 and 19 who are eligible for a state-sponsored summer jobs program. Which group would you pick and why? What would be the advantages and disadvantages associated with each of these groups as interviewers?

7.6 Approximately 30 percent of the young people in foster care are known to be African Americans and another 15 percent are Hispanic. What differences does the racial composition of the population make in terms of the way you would suggest doing the study?

7.7 As a way of experiencing the importance of question ordering in survey research, student volunteers can role-play a simulated interview on conflict tactics. Conduct one simulation using the CT scale as presented in this chapter. Conduct a second simulated interview using the scale in *reverse* order. Have the participants discuss how they felt about responding to the items about violent behavior.

7.8 A study in Chapter 6 describes a sample of homeless people. In some cases, the homeless people were found as they slept in doorways or abandoned buildings during the night. Is it ethical for an interviewer to intrude on the homeless in this fashion? We would not intrude on the sleep of suburbanites by phoning them in the middle of the night. The homeless, of course, are in public areas. Nonetheless, discuss the extent to which this is an unacceptable invasion of their privacy.

CHAPTER 8

Analysis of
Available Data

Statistical Data   194
  Sources of Statistical Data   195
  Using Statistical Data   197
Content Analysis   201
  Coding Schemes   201
  Units of Analysis   204
Issues in Content Analysis   205
  Validity   205
  Reliability   206
  Level of Measurement   207
  Sampling   208
Assessment of Available Data Analysis   209
  Advantages   210
  Disadvantages   211
  Using Available Data in Research on Minorities   211
Main Points   213
Important Terms for Review   214
Exploring the Internet   214
For Further Reading   216
Exercises for Class Discussion   217

Normally, researchers prefer to organize and direct the collection of the data themselves. This enables them to tailor the nature and form of the data collected to the research hypotheses and the state of knowledge in the field (*see* Chapter 4). In some cases, however, collecting their own data may be far too costly and time-consuming. In other cases, it may simply be impractical or unnecessary to do so. Consider, for example, a study by Deborah Wingard (1987) of the characteristics of adopted children and their parents in California. Wingard could have gotten a list of the children and their parents from agencies and then conducted mailed questionnaires or interviews. As we saw in Chapter 7, however, the former suffer from nonresponse problems, and the latter are expensive. Furthermore, as a routine part of service delivery, adoption agencies gather information about the characteristics of children and both their birth and adoptive parents. So, in this case, data collection by Wingard was unnecessary because the data to test the hypotheses already existed in an agency computerized information file.

Data of this type are referred to as **available data:** observations collected by someone other than the investigator for purposes that differ from the investigator's but that nonetheless are available to be analyzed. A vast array of this type of data is available for scientific analysis. In some cases, it takes the form of *statistical data,* or quantified observations of some element of human behavior. Large amounts of statistical data, for example, are collected by the various branches of government and provide quantified information about crime, health, birth rates, death rates, and the like. *Documents* are another form of available data and refer, in their broadest sense, to any form of communication that is nonquantitative in format. They include such things as books, magazines, letters, memoranda, diaries, and other media of communication such as radio, television, movies, and plays. Documents can also make up a part of records main-

tained by various institutions, such as military records, police records, court records, social work case records, and agency records. Some such records, of course, include statistical data as well as information in nonstatistical form.

Available data are a rich source of data for human service research, and they are sometimes used in conjunction with data collected from other sources, such as surveys. Furthermore, available data can often be treated as if they were data the researchers had collected themselves. Wingard, for example, could work with the agency data much as if they were survey data that she had collected. There are, however, some situations in which available data present researchers with some new problems, and these problems are the topic of this chapter. We first review sources of available statistical data and problems associated with their use. Then we discuss content analysis, a mechanism for analyzing the nonstatistical data in documents. Finally, we weigh the advantages and disadvantages of using available data.

Statistical Data

Human service professionals often complain about the mountains of paperwork associated with the procedures of trying to help people. But the facts and figures generated by these procedures can be a rich source of data for research. Unfortunately, the statistical data available to human service agencies often are overlooked or are found to be deficient in some critical respects. An important contribution that the research-knowledgeable human service professional can make to both practice and research is to help develop data collection procedures that generate useful statistical data. This is a major theme of Research in Practice 1.2, in which the social agency is described as a "research machine." To make such a contribution, human service professionals must have an understanding of how available statistical data are used in research and what qualities enhance the usefulness of available data for research.

Sources of Statistical Data

Statistical data are collected for many reasons, and much of these data are available to human service researchers. First of all, some statistical data are collected as part of many research projects. Many research organizations, such as the Institute for Social Research at the University of Michigan or the Institute for Research on Poverty at the University of Wisconsin, collect large amounts of very useful data that may be reanalyzed by others with different research questions in mind. In this way, data collected for one project may be reanalyzed by a number of different people in the years that follow. This reanalysis of data collected for some other research project is called **secondary analysis.** In fact, some research organizations, such as universities or government agencies, have organized a national system of **data archives,** which are essentially libraries that lend or sell data sets much as libraries or bookstores lend or sell books. Among the better known are the Inter-university Consortium of Political and Social Research (ICPSR) at the University of Michigan, the Roper Center at the University of Connecticut, the National Institute of Child Health and Human Development, and the National Institute of Justice (Sieber, 1991; ICPSR, 1996). Also, some private organizations have created data archives in specialized areas. The Sociometrics Corporation, for example, offers numerous data sets from studies focusing on adolescent pregnancy issues. Many individual researchers also make data sets available to those with legitimate secondary uses of the data (Verdonik and Sherrod, 1984; Young, Savola, and Phelps, 1991). Some funders of research, such as the National Science Foundation, now require, as a stipulation for receiving research funds, that the data eventually be delivered to a public data archive. Fienberg, Martin, and Straf (1985) list more than 50 major data archives in the social sciences. Data collected for research purposes and made available for secondary analysis tend to be of fairly high quality because they were collected by professional researchers. Nonetheless, such data still suffer from some of the problems to be discussed shortly.

A second source of statistical data is the federal, state, and local human service agencies that collect data for either administrative purposes or for purposes of client service. Community mental health centers, Head Start programs, departments of social services, and health and educational institutions are repositories of vast amounts of available data. Figure 8.1 illustrates some of the data regarding clients that are routinely collected by human service agencies. This form, used by the Department of Social Services (DSS) in Michigan (now called the Family Independence Agency) is completed for each suspected case of child abuse or neglect that is referred to DSS. The upper part of the form provides space for various specific bits of information on cases to be recorded, while the lower half provides a convenient coding scheme to ease the entry of information. Some of these data are in quantitative form (such as the age of the client, the number of prior referrals, and the number of days the client is in foster care), and these variables are amenable to statistical manipulation. Agencies collect such data for many reasons that may have nothing to do with their eventual research purposes. Sometimes agencies are simply required by law to collect such information, which is then stored in data banks and may be available to researchers. The authors combined the data on these forms with data from other organizational records in a study to assess the impact of a school social work program on the referral of cases of child abuse and neglect. Unfortunately, data from human service agencies are often not efficiently cataloged and indexed and therefore may be difficult for investigators to locate and use. Such data have, nonetheless, grown to voluminous proportions during the past two decades. This has occurred because human service agencies have increasingly been required to engage in needs assessment, planning, accountability, and evaluation. In addition, the strides made in computer technology,

MANAGEMENT INFORMATION REPORT
Michigan Department of Social Services
CHILDRENS PROTECTIVE SERVICES

1. Primary Recipient Name			Date Received
2. Case Number		3. Referral Date	Reason Issued
4. County / District / Unit / Worker	5. Referral Number		Transaction Number
6. Action	7. Referral Source	8. No. Prior Ref.	9. Hours to First Contact	10. Date Invest. Comp.	11. Living Arr - Invest	12. ADC Status

ADDRESS OF PRIMARY RECIPIENT

13. In Care Of

Comments:

18. Document Number

14. Number and Street

15. City   16. State   17. Zip Code

19. Recipient Update Action	20. NAME (Last, First, Middle Initial)	21. PSMIS CLIENT IDENTIFIER	22. BIRTH DATE	23. Sex	24. Race	25. Role	26. Abuse	27. Neglect	28. Living Arrangement At Closing

CLOSING DATA (Also Complete Item 28)

29. Close Date	30. Closing Code	If Item 30 = 6, Complete Item 31	31. Court Involvement/ Disposition	If Item 31 = 1, Complete Item 32	32. Non-Court Disposition	33. Greatest No. Days In Temp. Foster Care	34. Reason in Foster Care Over 21 Days	35. Reason Case Open Over 6 Months

Signature of Worker   Date

DSS-2070 (4-78)   CENTRAL OFFICE

---

6. ACTION
1 = Investigation
2 = Close
3 = Invest/Close
4 = Change/Update

7. REFERRAL SOURCE
Mandated
01 = Pvt. Physician
02 = Hosp./Clinic Phys.
03 = Coroner/Med. Examiner
04 = Dentist
05 = Audiologist
06 = Nurse (Not school)
11 = School Nurse
12 = Teacher
13 = School Administrator
14 = School Counselor
21 = Law Enforcement
31 = Child Care Provider
41 = Hosp./Clinic Soc. Wkr.
42 = DSS Facil. Soc. Wkr.
43 = DMH Facil. Soc. Wkr.
44 = Other Pub. Soc. Wkr.
45 = Pvt. Agy. Soc. Wkr.
46 = Court Soc. Wkr.
47 = Other Soc. Wkr.

Non-Mandated
51 = Hosp./Clinic Personnel
52 = DSS Facil. Personnel
53 = DMH Facil. Personnel
54 = Other Pub. Soc. Agy. Pers.
55 = Pvt. Soc. Agy. Pers.
56 = Court Personnel
57 = Other School Pers.
61 = Victim
62 = Relative
63 = Sibling
64 = Parent/Sub in Home
65 = Parent/Sub Out of Home
66 = Anonymous
67 = Friend/Neighbor
68 = Other

11. LIVING ARR. AT INVESTIGATION
01 = Own Home
02 = Foster, Shelter, Group Home
03 = Shelter Facility
04 = DSS Facility
05 = DMH Facility
06 = Court Facility
07 = Pvt. Facility
08 = Resid. Ed. Facility
09 = Other Child Care Inst.
10 = Other Out of Home
11 = Mult. Plcmts.

12. ADC STATUS
1 = ADC
2 = GA
3 = ADC & GA
4 = None

19. RECIPIENT UPDATE
1 = Update Existing Recipient
2 = Add New Recipient
3 = Delete Recipient

23. SEX
M = Male
F = Female

24. RACE
Migrant
A = Caucasian
B = Negro
C = Indian
D = Other
E = Unknown
F = Sp. Surname

Non-Migrant
1 = Caucasian
2 = Negro
3 = Indian
4 = Other
5 = Unknown
6 = Sp. Surname

25. ROLE
11 = Victim
21 = Perp-Parent in Home
22 = Perp-Sibling
23 = Perp-Other Relat.
24 = Perp-Other Household Memb.
25 = Perp-Day Care
26 = Perp-Fost. Parent
27 = Perp-Inst. Staff
28 = Perp-Parent Out of Home
29 = Perp-Other
31 = Uninvolv. - Parent
32 = Uninvolv. - Sibling
33 = Uninvolv. - Other

26. ABUSE (Victim only)
1 = Physical Injury
2 = Congen. Drug Addict
3 = Rape
4 = Incest
5 = Molestation
6 = Exploitation
7 = Unnatural Acts

27. NEGLECT (Victim only)
1 = Physical
2 = Social
3 = Abandonment
4 = Inapp. Use of Funds
5 = Unlicensed Home/ Improp. Guardianship

28. LIVING ARR. AT CLOSE (Victim and uninvolved siblings only)
1 = In Home
2 = Out of Home

30. CLOSING CODE
1 = Unable to Locate
2 = No Evidence
3 = Not Sufficient
4 = Other Agency Contact
5 = Invest. Only
6 = Services Provided

31. COURT INVOLVEMENT/DISPOSITION
1 = No Court
2 = Accept PS Recom - Adjudication and Disposition
3 = Accept PS Recom - Adjudication Only
4 = Not Accept PS Recommendation
5 = Court - Other

32. NON-COURT DISPOSITION
1 = Satisfact. - No Referral
2 = Satisfact. - Refer to DSS
3 = Satisfact. - Refer Comm. Agency
4 = Unsatisf. Family Resp. - Court Not Feasible
5 = Unsatisf. - Comm. Agency Not Avail; PS Not App.
6 = Unsatisfact. - Refer to DSS
7 = Other

34. REASON FOSTER CARE OVER 21 DAYS
1 = Pending Court
2 = Other

35. REASON OPEN OVER 6 MO.
1 = Await Court Action
2 = Protective Payment
3 = Court Ward in Home
4 = Still Danger
5 = New Danger
6 = Other

DSS-2070 (4-78) (Back)

Figure 8.1 An Example of a Client Information Form Used in a Human Service Agency

along with the widespread use of management information systems in social agencies, have contributed to the growth and increased availability of data produced by social agencies (Hoshino and Lynch, 1981). Research in Practice 8.1 gives further illustrations of agency records serving as a source of research data.

A third source of statistical data is the organizations and government agencies that collect data as a public service or to serve as a basis for social policy decisions. Such agencies as the Federal Bureau of Investigation and the National Center for Health Statistics, for example, collect vast amounts of data, as do state and local governments. The U.S. Bureau of the Census also collects enormous amounts of data to be used for establishing and changing the boundaries of political districts and allocating government funds that are based on population size. Often data from this source can be used in conjunction with other types of data—from questionnaires, for example, or from agency records—to test hypotheses. One study of caseworker accuracy hypothesized that caseworker errors might be influenced by the political and economic characteristics of the local community (Piliavin, Masters, and Corbett, 1977). Data were based on interviews, questionnaires, and other sources. In addition, the political and economic characteristics of each community were measured with data from the Bureau of the Census regarding the percentage of poor people in the county, how the county voted in the most recent gubernatorial election, and the percentage of poor families that were headed by women. Thus, data from multiple sources can be combined to measure variables and test hypotheses in a single study.

Data collected by private organizations are distributed less widely than government statistics and for that reason may be more difficult to locate. Professional associations, such as the American Medical Association, the American Bar Association, and the National Association of Social Workers, produce statistics relating to their membership and issues of concern to their members. Additionally, statistical data are produced by research institutes and commercial polling firms.

Using Statistical Data

When using available statistical data, remember that most such data were not collected for research purposes—or at least not for the specific research questions for which you now intend to use them. They were collected to meet the needs of whatever agency, organization, or researcher originally collected them, and you are limited by the form in which the data were collected. This leads to some special problems that call for caution.

Missing Data   For a variety of reasons, a data set may not include complete data for every person studied or may fail to collect data from the entire population or sample of interest. For example, a person may refuse to answer certain questions, which results in a gap in his or her data set. Or data may not be collected in a particular neighborhood because it is considered too dangerous for interviewers to enter. Such gaps in a data set are referred to as **missing data** and are found to some degree in practically all studies. The problem when using available data files is that you have no control over this failure to collect a complete set of data. Missing data result in incomplete coverage, which, if extensive, can throw into question the representativeness of the data. Furthermore, because statistical procedures are based on the assumption of complete data, missing data can result in misleading statistical conclusions. As we dig back into data from the past, it is not uncommon to find data for whole periods of time missing. This can occur for many reasons, such as data destroyed by fires, lost data, changes in policy, and the like. Finding data that cover only a portion of one's target population is also quite common. For example, the researchers in a study of marriage rates among older Americans in the United States were forced to do without data from three states—Arizona, New Mexico, and Oklahoma—because those states did not maintain central marriage files (Treas and VanHilst, 1976). Given the high concentration of retirees in Arizona, however, it is possible that

Research in Practice 8.1
Program Evaluation: Evaluating Family Preservation Services Through Agency Record Data

When child abuse or neglect occur, the result is often removal of the child from the parental home and placement in foster care. But such placements are far from ideal and are intended as only temporary solutions. Also, such placement in and of itself does not solve the problem of family dysfunction that produced the abuse. Furthermore, the high cost of such placement, estimated to be more than $7,000 for an average stay of about 19 months, has given policymakers and practitioners strong incentives to seek alternatives (Behavioral Science Institute, 1987).

One promising alternative to traditional, expensive out-of-home placement is Intensive Family Preservation. These services are typically provided to families at imminent risk of having a child removed from the home. The home is often used as the primary site of service delivery instead of an agency or institution, and the family, rather than only a parent or the child, is considered the client. The premise of such programs is that treating the family within its own environment permits dealing with the family-interaction problems that may precipitate abuse and neglect. Such programs also try not only to keep the family together but also to improve family relations. Doing so may include around-the-clock availability of family service workers using a wide range of skills and resources, such as teaching positive child-rearing skills, finding housing, advocating with a landlord to fix the heat, and showing parents how to repair a broken window. Unlike traditional programs, family preservation programs are short-term and labor intensive. Workers in

the program discussed here typically carried only two to five cases, and cases were intended to be open for only about 3 months.

With any such radical departure from traditional service delivery, evaluation is crucial to ensure that the programs do what they claim; a growing body of evaluative literature suggests the programs are beneficial (Wells and Biegel, 1991). A common feature of Family Preservation Services evaluation studies is that they rely extensively on available data gathered from human service agency records. Interviews with service providers and questionnaires sent to clients may be used, but the extensive data required to trace the delivery of services and to evaluate outcomes necessitates using data generated by the program itself. For example, Marianne Berry (1992) evaluated the In-Home Family Care Program by examining the characteristics of families and services that contributed to family preservation, including the match of services to the needs of the clients. Program success was measured by skill-gains among families as well as by avoiding the placement of a child outside the home. She studied a sample of about 400 families in the program in the San Francisco area from 1985 to 1987. All families had at least one child at risk of imminent placement and received intensive services. Although some data came from interviewing caseworkers about their knowledge of child placements in their caseloads, the project relied heavily upon Department of Social Services (DSS) shelter and foster care logs as well as standard follow-up forms. These records provided demographic data on client families, as well as information on amounts and kinds of services provided,

the exclusion of data from that state might have affected their results. When working with data that suffer from noncoverage, one should assess the implications that noncoverage has for the results of the research.

Inductive Versus Deductive Analysis   In research investigations in which data are collected firsthand, a deductive approach is commonly used. That is, hypotheses are deduced from a theory, variables in the hypotheses are operationally defined,

location of contacts, and other agencies participating in the contacts.

The study found that 88 percent of the families receiving services avoided having a child removed from the home for the year after receiving the services. Cases received an average of 67 hours of service. And, supporting one of the innovative features of Intensive Family Preservation, researchers found that the location where services are delivered makes a difference: No families experienced a child placed outside the home when more than half of the service time was spent in the home. Conversely, in those families where more than half of service time was in the agency, 28 percent had a child placed outside the home. Furthermore, the service log provided a clue as to what services made a difference in treatment success. Families that remained intact had received more supplemental parenting, teaching of family care, and medical help. Finally, the In-Home Family Care Program cost averaged about $2,700 per family compared to the California foster care rate of $7,400 for 16 months during the time of the study.

Although the available data of the Department of Social Services provided a rich source of information for the project, those data were not without problems. For example, the most commonly reported service provided, case planning, was described by the author as a catchall category without much meaning. However, the vagueness of the category was considered an administrative problem, too, and it has since been changed by DSS to reflect more specific services.

Another study examined five home-based programs across several states (Nelson, 1991). The focus of this study was the criticism that the only families kept together by family preservation programs are those families with few problems to begin with. Data were obtained for this study by having trained case readers, mostly graduate and undergraduate social work students, extract the data from case records. One portion of the data collection task consisted of applying the Child Well-Being Scales to the case record data (Magura and Moses, 1986). These scales are designed to rate problem levels based on assessments by the actual human service practitioner. Because of the lack of detail in the case records, case readers could only assess whether a particular problem was found in a case, rather than specifying the extent of the problem—as can be done when practitioners themselves complete the scales. So, although it was possible to use the scales, the researchers had to settle for less precision in measurement due to the necessity of using available data. Missing data is another problem common to studies based on available data. The researchers in this study reported that the proportion of missing data was comparable on most subscales to that found by Magura and Moses relying on direct data collection from workers.

The study concluded that the family-based service sample had a consistent pattern of more problems than the comparison child welfare-based sample. Thus, the study does not support the criticism that family-based service success is an artifact of selecting families with few problems. These two program evaluations illustrate some of the advantages and challenges of using available data from the records of social service agencies. Existing agency records eliminated the need for extensive interviewing and duplication of efforts. The agency logs proved to be a good supplemental data source in the first study, and the second study was able to rely entirely on existing data files. The potential for conducting sound evaluation studies underscores the need for human service agencies to provide good documentation of services, not only for administrative purposes, but also with an eye toward applied research on program effectiveness.

and data are collected based on these operational definitions. In short, research moves from the abstract to the concrete: The kind of data collected is determined by the theory and hypotheses being tested (*see* Chapter 2). In the analysis of available data, however, such a deductive approach is often impossible because the data necessary to measure the variables derived from a theory may not have been included when the original data were collected. For example, a theory regarding caseworker effectiveness with clients might include the variable of the intensity of the casework relationship. Although intensity of relationship is a crucial concept in interpersonal helping, it is unfortunately not the type of variable that is included in routine agency data collection procedures. In circumstances such as this, it is not possible to operationalize the variable in the way most appropriate to the theory. If this difficulty is encountered, a compromise is often made. As shown in Chapter 5, the measurement process often calls for modifying nominal and operational definitions (*see* Figure 5.1). Operational definitions and, in some cases, hypotheses are revised so that they can be tested with the data available (*see* Figure 8.2). In the example of caseworker effectiveness, we might measure intensity of relationship by looking at the amount of time a worker spends with a given client over the course of treatment, the frequency of contacts, or the duration of contacts. Although none of these variables may be the best measure of "intensity of relationship," each is readily derived from the worker time sheets that are mandatory in many agencies. Total contact time, frequency of contact, duration of contact, or some combination of these may be used even though they are not thoroughly accurate measures of the variable of interest.

In other words, we have modified our research to fit the data. When this occurs, research takes on a somewhat inductive character. In inductive research, we move from the concrete to the abstract: Starting with data collected, we develop hypotheses and theories to explain what we find in the data. The situation we have described is actually some-

where in limbo between induction and deduction. We have begun with theories and hypotheses, but we have also been forced to let the available data influence how we test the hypotheses. This is a frequent problem in the analysis of available statistical data and has led some to argue that available data are most appropriately used in purely inductive research that has an exploratory purpose (Hoshino and Lynch, 1981). Although this caution is well taken, there are many areas in which available data can be used in deductive research, provided that care is exercised in how extensively hypotheses and operational definitions are changed to fit the data. The major danger when extensive changes are made is one that has been discussed in relation to other data collection techniques: validity.

Validity   Validity refers to whether a measurement instrument actually measures what it is intended to measure (*see* Chapter 5). Many data in existing statistical files can be considered valid indicators of certain things that they directly describe. The age, sex, and racial profiles of clients, along with the amounts of different kinds of services provided, would be examples of these. However, validity problems frequently arise in three areas.

First, many elements of agency operation—such as achievement of goals, success of programs, or satisfaction of clients—may not be measured directly by any data normally collected by an agency. To study these, one would have to search for indirect measures among the agency data that might enable one to infer such things as goal achieve-

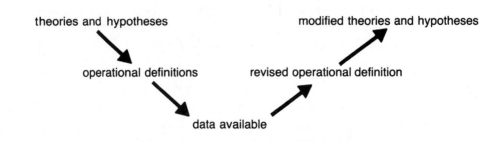

Figure 8.2   The Measurement Process With Available Statistical Data

ment, success, or satisfaction. These situations create the same kinds of validity problems that confront researchers using other methods except that, when available data are used, validity problems cannot be considered and resolved *before* the data are collected. Because the data have already been collected, the problems are entrenched.

A second area in which validity problems frequently arise is data analysis that becomes inductive, as we have just discussed—that is, when operational definitions are changed so that variables can be measured with the data available. The more the definitions are changed, the more the validity of the measures is called into question. The operational definitions may be changed so drastically that they no longer measure the theoretical concepts they were first intended to measure.

Finally, validity questions arise when procedures used in gathering data by an agency or organization have changed over the years. Changing modes of collecting data, such as dropping some questions or developing new definitions of something, are quite common in any agency or organization. These procedural changes can, however, affect the comparability of data collected at various times and the validity of using the same operational definitions. An example of this can be found in crime statistics. Data from the Uniform Crime Reports (UCR), compiled by the Federal Bureau of Investigation (FBI), are commonly used as a measure of the volume of crimes in the United States. Research in Practice 8.2 explores some of the problems that can arise when using this particular set of available data.

The amount of available statistical data from various sources is likely to grow astronomically in the future. In addition, the increasing availability and sophistication of computer technology, along with the growing expertise of human service workers in using computers, are likely to make these data more readily available for research (Murphy and Pardeck, 1991; Brent and Anderson, 1990; Parker et al., 1987). Such data represent vast, but currently much underutilized, sources for research. When contemplating a research project, you would be wise to consider whether there are some available data that might serve as a legitimate source of information.

Content Analysis

Whenever activity is recorded in some document—whether a book, diary, case record, film, or tape recording—it is amenable to scientific analysis. Although the data discussed in the previous section were already quantified when made available for research, the documents now being considered have basically *qualitative* data that must be quantified. **Content analysis** refers to a method of transforming the symbolic content of a document, such as words or other images, from a qualitative, unsystematic form into a quantitative, systematic form (Krippendorff, 1980; Weber, 1990; Gottschalk, 1995). Audrey Smith (1982) and Paula Allen-Meares (1984) discuss some of the many uses of content analysis in human service research and practice. Content analysis is a form of coding, a practice we discuss as a way of transforming data used in some surveys and observational research in Chapters 7 and 9. **Coding** refers to categorizing behaviors or elements into a limited number of categories. In surveys and observational research, coding is performed on data that are collected first-hand by the investigator for particular research purposes. In content analysis, coding is performed on documents that are produced for purposes other than research and then made available for research purposes. In both survey data coding and content analysis, categories and coding schemes are developed in order to quantify verbal or symbolic content.

Coding Schemes

A major step in content analysis is to develop a coding scheme that can be used in analyzing the documents at hand. Coding schemes in content analysis, like those in coding observed behavior, can be quite variable, and their exact form depends on the documents being studied and the hypotheses being tested in the research project.

Research in Practice 8.2
Needs Assessment: Hazards in Estimating the Crime Problem From Available Data

Combating crime is a key objective for many human service programs, whether it be running a neighborhood watch to increase safety for the elderly, providing late-night basketball for inner-city youths, offering treatment groups for offenders, providing rape crisis counseling for victims, or monitoring ex-felons on parole. Whenever an organization embarks on an effort to design and implement a program such as one of these, the planning process commonly requires that the program planners demonstrate the need for the program by documenting the seriousness of the crime problem in a community. It is unlikely that most human service organizations have either the resources or capacity to gather crime data for themselves, so using available data may be an appealing alternative. As we note in this chapter, one of the advantages to conducting research using available data is that they are available and somebody else paid to collect them. It is, however, very important when using available data to make serious inquiries about exactly how the data were collected and how the numbers were produced. The human service agency that would use available crime data faces several possible pitfalls. One of the most widely used sources of crime data is produced by the Federal Bureau of Investigation and is called the Uniform Crime Reports (UCR). It is published annually and is available in practically every library. Some parts of it are now also available on the Internet(http://www.crime.orgorhttp://www.fbi.og).

On the surface it might seem that data produced by an agency of the federal government, with all its authority and resources, would be reliable, and within limitations it is. But it is those limitations that can cause problems if they are not understood. One of the most basic questions people have about crime is: How much crime exists? Even this apparently simple question is not well answered by UCR data. In order for an event to be recorded as a crime in the UCR, it must come to the attention of some police officials. In a minority of cases, police chance across a crime event taking place and so it gets officially recorded. Most often, however, police must rely on citizens who are victimized by crime to report it to them, and herein lies one of the problems with UCR data. A large percentage of even serious crimes are never reported to the police. A recent estimate made by Lisa Bastion (1995) of the Bureau of Justice Statistics suggests that only around 40 percent of serious crimes are reported to the police and make their way into the UCR data. Clearly this reporting gap causes the UCR data to significantly understate the true impact of criminal activity in the United States.

You may be wondering how such an estimate of unreported crime can be made. Another measure of criminal activity is the National Crime Survey (NCS). This survey is conducted every year on a representative sample of over 100,000 citizens, inquiring if they have been victims of crimes. The disparity between the NCS data and the UCR data provides an indicator of the amount of crime that goes unreported by the UCR and thus gives a clearer picture of actual criminal activity.

Another possible pitfall awaiting the user of UCR data is the fact that reporting to the FBI is voluntary on the part of local law enforcement agencies. This fact leads to a number of possible misinterpretations of the data. For example, one

Existing Coding Schemes In some cases, it is possible to find existing coding schemes that can be used for content analysis. For example, the coding categories developed by Bales (1950) for the analysis of interaction in small groups have been widely used in research and can be applied to documents if they suit the purpose of the study (*see* Chapter 9). Another example of a general scheme is one commonly used for categorizing themes in fiction and drama. The basic themes

could not compare different regions or localities and conclude with any certainty which area had the higher or lower crime rate. Any differences noted might be real or they might be merely differences in the willingness of officials to report to the FBI. A related problem confronts anyone interested in longitudinal analysis. Over the long history of the UCR, the percentage of police agencies that report their numbers has steadily increased. This, of course, means that any comparison over time has a built-in problem. Even if crime has not increased, it will appear to have increased over time due to the higher rate of reporting in more recent years.

Yet another problem stems from the fact that during the first several decades of the UCR, crime rates were computed not from updated population estimates, but from the most recent census count. As the census is conducted only once every 10 years, this meant that the basis for computing the crime rates stayed the same for a decade until the numbers from a new census became available. But, of course, a population does not remain stagnant and then suddenly appear to explode every 10 years. The population steadily increases from year to year, meaning that there are more people to commit crimes and to become crime victims. Using the same census number to compute crime rates meant that there were bound to be apparent increases in crime from year to year. Then, when a new census number was used, there would appear to be a substantial drop in crime. Obviously this "drop" was not due to a real decline in criminal activity, but rather to the census number used to compute the crime rate catching up with the population increase. Although this is no longer a problem with UCR data because yearly population estimates, which are quite accurate, are now used in computing the crime rates, it typifies the kind of traps that may await the unsuspecting researcher using other people's data.

Finally, when working with data that have been collected over a long period of time, such as the UCR, an important question is: Have definitions or categorizations changed over time that would hamper making meaningful comparisons? Again, the UCR is illustrative. According to Barlow (1996), during the history of the UCR the FBI's classification system for counting crime has changed several times. In fact, in 1979 the FBI added an additional crime, arson, to the crimes that makeup what is known as the "crime index." These are the crimes that are tracked and used to compute the general crime rate. In addition to arson, the index crimes are homicide, aggravated assault, sexual assault, robbery, burglary, larceny, and auto theft. Naturally, when the crime of arson was added to the index, it made it appear that crime had suddenly and dramatically increased when, of course, the change in the numbers was primarily caused by a change in measurement.

As we have illustrated with the UCR data, a researcher utilizing available data must be very careful not to fall into possible traps that may be hidden in the data. These risks do not mean that available data should always be avoided, but, rather, that they should be used with caution. For example, the UCR data are not without value, as they reflect changes in people's willingness to report crime to the police. In recent years UCR data have shown a marked increase in the number of reported rapes, while the NCS data show no such increase (Perkins and Klaus, 1996). This difference is evidence of increased willingness of victims to report the crime to the police. Changed women's roles in society together with greater sensitivity on the part of authorities in handling rape cases are probably responsible for the higher reporting rate. So we see that despite its limitations and potential for misinterpretation, the UCR data do have their uses.

are these: (1) love, (2) morality, (3) idealism, (4) power, (5) outcast, (6) career, and (7) no agreement (McGranahan and Wayne, 1948). There are also categories for classifying endings, temporal settings, spacial settings, and patterns of love in the

love theme. In the human services, coding schemes have been developed to analyze the content of a clinician's responses to patients in interviews. In a study of the impact of a clinician's responses on whether clients continued with treatment, a coding system utilizing three categories was developed:

1. Substantive congruent responses: clinician responses that referred to the client's immediately preceding response or contained some elements of that response
2. Nonsubstantive congruent responses: clinician responses, such as "I see" or "Yes," that indicate that the clinician is aware of and paying attention to the client's verbalizations
3. Incongruent responses: clinician responses that appear unrelated to what the client has said

Others interested in similar aspects of the practitioner–client interview might be able to utilize the same coding scheme.

In conducting content analysis, then, one will find it beneficial to search for an existing coding scheme that might be applicable to the research problem at hand. Not only does the use of an existing coding scheme result in considerable savings for the researcher in terms of time, energy, and money, but it also serves to make the research project comparable with other studies that have also used the same coding system.

Coding schemes can be found in the many journals that report research relevant to the human services or in books, such as Holsti's (1969) or Krippendorff's (1980), that are devoted to the study of content analysis.

Characteristics Like categories in any measurement process, those used in content analysis should be exhaustive and mutually exclusive. Categories are *exhaustive* when a category is available for every relevant element in the documents. If there are only a few possibilities and they can be clearly defined, an exhaustive set of categories will not be difficult to develop. If what we are trying to measure is rather open-ended with many possibilities, however, developing an exhaustive set of categories may well be difficult. For example, presidential speeches have been analyzed in terms of the values expressed. Obviously, there are so many values that an exhaustive list is unlikely to be developed. One such list contained 14 value categories, which un-

doubtedly cover the most important or commonly mentioned values (Prothro, 1956). It is doubtful whether even that many categories are really exhaustive, however. If it is impossible to be exhaustive, then the most common or most important categories are used, and a residual category ("others") is made available for those items that do not fit any of the other categories.

Coding categories should also be *mutually exclusive,* which means that each coded item can fall into one—and only one—category. This requirement forces one to have precise definitions for each category so that there is no ambiguity concerning which items it includes and which it does not. Failure to meet this requirement can totally befuddle the measurement process because items will be placed every which way by coders confused with overlapping categories. Lack of mutual exclusiveness will likely show up in low levels of reliability as the coders disagree on the placement of items into categories.

Units of Analysis

With the categories established, the next research decision concerns precisely what aspects of the documents will be recorded. Generally, there are four units of analysis: a word, a theme, a major character, or a sentence or paragraph. (The units of analysis commonly found in research other than content analysis are discussed in Chapter 4.) An often convenient unit of analysis is a *single word.* Coding the presence of certain words in documents can be accomplished easily and with a high degree of reliability. If a single word qualifies as a valid indicator of what you wish to measure, it is a good choice for the unit of analysis. For example, as a part of their study of colonial families, Herman Lantz and his colleagues (1968) counted the frequency with which the word "power" was associated with men or women in colonial magazines. In this context, the single word was used as a measure of the perceived distribution of power between men and women during colonial times. When using single words as the unit of analysis, it is often helpful to make use of a context unit, which is the context in which a single word is found. The words surrounding the word used as the unit of analysis modify it and further explain its meaning. This contextual information is taken into account when coding the unit of analysis. For example, in the study just mentioned, the investigators needed to know whether the word "power" referred to men or to women. The context surrounding the word supplied this crucial information. The amount of context needed to explain the use of a given word adequately is, of course, variable.

The *theme* as a unit of analysis refers to the major subject matter of a document or part of a document. An entire document can be characterized as having a primary theme. Novels, for example, can be described as mysteries, science fiction, historical, and so on. In a study of the images of women during World War II and their treatment by government propaganda agencies, one researcher analyzed themes relating to the role of women in the work force found in fiction pieces in two magazines that were popular during the war, *Saturday Evening Post* and *True Story* (Honey, 1984). Themes can, however, be difficult to delineate. The overall theme may or may not be clear, or there may be multiple themes. Coder reliability is likely to be lower than when easily identifiable words are the unit of analysis.

A third unit of analysis in documents is the *main character.* The use of this unit of analysis is, of course, limited to documents that have a cast of characters, such as plays, novels, movies, or television programs. A study of children's television programs, for example, used the major dramatic character as the unit of analysis. The study, funded by the Ford and Carnegie foundations, found that only 16 percent of the major characters were women and "females were portrayed as married, less active, and with lower self-esteem" (Corry, 1982).

The fourth unit of analysis is a *sentence* or *paragraph.* The study described earlier regarding congruency in clinician–client interaction used a similar unit of analysis: *Each clinician response, preceded and followed by a client comment, was considered the unit to be coded as congruent or incongruent.* A paragraph

or even a single sentence, however, often contains more than one idea, and this may make these larger units more difficult to classify while maintaining mutually exclusive categories and intercoder reliability. Indeed, reliability may well be lower than with the word or main character units. Yet, the larger units are often more theoretically relevant in the human services. In clinician–client interaction, for example, it would make little conceptual sense to characterize an interchange as congruent on the basis of one word. Meaning in social interaction normally arises from a whole block of words or sentences. So, as we emphasized when discussing units of analysis in Chapter 4, the primary consideration in selecting a unit of analysis is theoretical: which unit seems to be preferable given theoretical and conceptual considerations.

Issues in Content Analysis

When developing coding categories for content analysis, researchers confront several issues. Remember that content analysis is a form of measurement—measurement of aspects of a document's contents. As such, we encounter the familiar concerns regarding validity and reliability, along with problems of choosing a level of measurement and a sample (*see* Chapters 5 and 6).

Validity

In content analysis, validity refers to whether the categories we develop and the aspects of the content coded are meaningful indicators of what we intend to measure. Developing coding schemes that are valid indicators can be a challenging task. Anne Fortune (1979), for example, reported on an effort to study communication patterns between social workers and their clients in which recordings of interviews were content analyzed. The goal of the research was to discover which interview techniques used by practitioners would bring about cognitive and affective change in clients. Fortune was concerned, in particular, with how techniques varied when clients were adults rather than children. First, a typology of communication techniques was developed based on William Reid's work on task-centered casework. As there are many ways to execute a particular verbal technique in a therapeutic setting, it was impossible to base the content analysis on a single word or phrase. Instead, coders were provided with a description of each technique and examples of the verbal forms that each technique might take. For example, the communication technique of "exploration" was described as "communication intended to elicit information, including questions and restatements or 'echoes' of client's communications." Examples of this technique provided to the coders were such phrases as "What class was that?" and "You said your son misbehaved. . . . " The communication technique of "direction" was exemplified by "I think the first step would be to talk this over with your daughter" (Fortune, 1979, p. 391). By the provision of specific examples of how to code comments, it was hoped that the resulting coding would have greater validity than if coders were left on their own.

Depending on the nature of the research and the documents to be analyzed, any of the methods of assessing validity discussed in Chapter 5 may be applicable. The logical approaches of content validity and jury opinion are the most generally used assessments of validity in content analysis, although criterion validity is sometimes used. For example, in a content analysis of suicide notes, an attempt was made to identify aspects of the content of real suicide notes that would differentiate them from simulated ones written by people who had not attempted suicide (Ogilvie, Stone, and Shneidman, 1966). The researchers compared half of the genuine notes with half of the simulated ones and found that genuine notes made more references to concrete things and greater use of the word "love." The simulated notes, on the other hand, contained more references to the thought processes that went into the decision to kill oneself. Using these observations to predict which of the remaining notes were genuine, the researchers were able to do so at a 94 percent level of accuracy. The ability to predict

at such a level suggests that the content aspects of the notes they discovered were valid indicators of genuine suicide notes.

Researchers must be able to argue convincingly that indicators are valid if scientific outcomes are to be accepted. Though most content analyses do not go beyond content validity or jury opinion, it is important to remember that these are the weakest demonstrations of validity. Whenever possible, more rigorous tests should be attempted.

Reliability

Reliability refers to the ability of a measure to yield consistent results each time it is used. In content analysis, reliability relates to the ability of coders to apply consistently the coding scheme that has been developed. The question is: Can several workers code the documents according to the coding scheme and obtain consistent results? Reliability in content analysis depends on many factors, including the skill of the coders, the nature of the categories, the rules guiding the use of the categories, and the degree of clarity or ambiguity in the documents (Holsti, 1969; Weber, 1990; Scott, 1990). The clarity of the documents in any given study is largely fixed, so our discussion of control over reliability is limited to the coders and the categories utilized.

First, reliability can be enhanced by a thorough training of the coders and by practice in applying the coding scheme. Coders who continually deviate from the others in their coding during this practice period should not be relied on as coders. One must be cautious, however, about eliminating coders without assessing whether their deviation indicates poor performance or an ambiguous coding scheme.

Second, the nature of the categories to be applied to the document is also important for reliability. The simpler and more objective the categories, the higher the reliability will be. Vaguely defined categories or those requiring substantial interpretation will decrease reliability because they create greater opportunity for disagreement among the coders.

Measuring reliability in content analysis is much the same as measuring reliability when coding observed behavior (*see* Chapter 9). One simple way to do this is to calculate the percent of judgments on which coders agree out of the total number of judgments that they must make:

$$\text{percent of agreement} = \frac{2 \times \text{no. of agreements}}{\begin{array}{c}\text{total no. of observations}\\\text{recorded by both}\\\text{observers}\end{array}}$$

This measure of intercoder reliability, however, does not take into account the extent to which intercoder agreement can occur by chance. Paula Allen-Meares (1984) presents other ways of measuring intercoder reliability. Accepted levels of reliability are 75 percent agreement between coders or better. Well-trained coders using well-constructed coding schemes should achieve better than an 85 percent agreement.

A certain tension exists between validity and reliability in content analysis. The simplest coding schemes—such as those employing word frequency counts—produce the highest reliability because they are very easy to apply in a consistent manner. As noted, however, word frequency counts may not validly measure what we want to measure. Sacrificing some degree of reliability for the sake of validity may be necessary. Researchers often end up performing a balancing act between the dual requirements of validity and reliability.

Level of Measurement

Like other methods of collecting data, content analysis involves a decision about the level of measurement to be used (*see* Chapter 5). The level of measurement achieved depends on the variable being measured and on the process used to measure it. The variable being measured puts an upper limit on the level of measurement that can be reached. For example, if we rate main characters in a book according to marital status, the highest level of measurement would be nominal because marital status is a nominal variable. No amount of measurement finesse can change this once the key variables have been selected. However, researchers have some control over the level of measurement depending on the process used to measure the variables. The important factor is how the unit of analysis is quantified in the coding process. Coding systems in content analysis generally fall into one of four categories: (1) presence or absence of an element, (2) frequency of occurrence of an element, (3) amount of space devoted to an element, and (4) intensity of expression.

The simplest rating system is to indicate merely *the presence or absence of an element* in a document. For example, we might rate interviews as to whether the clinician mentions certain subjects, such as sexual behavior or parent–child relationships. This simple system would yield nominal data and convey a minimum of information about content. Several important questions would remain unanswered. We would not know whether the subject was addressed in a positive or negative light nor how the client reacted. Also unknown would be how much time was devoted to that subject or how frequently it was repeated. Consideration of these factors would make the study more informative.

Frequency counts are very common methods of rating. We simply count how often an element appears. For example, Jack Levin and James Spates (1970) sought to compare the dominant values expressed in middle-class publications with those in the so-called underground press. The investigators rated the frequency with which statements of various values appeared in the two types of publications. On the basis of the frequency counts, the study concluded that the underground press emphasized values related to self-expression, whereas the middle-class publications stressed values related to various types of personal achievement. Frequency counts reveal more information about the document than does the simple present-or-absent approach. They also open the way for more sophisticated statistical analysis because they can, with the appropriate theoretical concepts, achieve an interval or ratio level of measurement.

Coding systems based on *amount of space devoted to an element* have proved useful for analyzing the mass media. In newspapers or magazines, the normal approach is to measure column inches. The equivalent for films or television would be time. For example, for a study of the contribution of social work writers to the development of professional knowledge, Merlin Taber and Iris Shapiro (1965) counted the number of column inches in selected social work journals that were devoted to a discussion of different types of knowledge, such as theoretical versus empirical knowledge. We could measure the amount of space devoted to a topic, such as family violence or the problems of lesbian mothers, over the years in order to assess the impact of popular trends or political events on professional concern about various issues. The major attraction of space/time measures is their ease of use. The amount of space devoted to a given topic can be measured far more rapidly than word frequency counts or even whether key words are present or absent. As each document takes only a short time to analyze, space/time measures allow a larger sample size, possibly leading to greater representativeness. Space/time measures also can yield interval or ratio level measurement with theoretical concepts that are amenable to such a level of measurement.

Unfortunately, space/time measures are still somewhat crude. Other than the volume of space devoted to the particular topic in question, they reveal nothing further about the content. For example, time measures applied to the network news could tell us which types of news are allotted the most coverage, but nothing about more subtle issues such as whether the news coverage was biased. As Ole Holsti (1969, p. 121) notes, "A one-to-one relationship between the amount of space devoted to a subject and the manner in which it is treated cannot be assumed."

The most complex rating systems involve a *measure of intensity*—the forcefulness of expression in the documents. However, developing intensity measures is difficult. Intensity of expression can be quite subtle and dependent on many aspects of word usage. This makes it extremely difficult to clearly specify the conditions for coding content elements. The coders will have to make many judgments before deciding how to categorize the content, and this leads to disagreements and low reliability.

Developing intensity measures that will produce reliable results is quite similar to constructing measurement scales. We could, for example, have coders rate documents along a scale (as in the semantic differential or the Likert scales discussed in detail in Chapter 13). Newspaper editorials dealing with public assistance programs might be rated as (1) very unfavorable, (2) unfavorable, (3) neutral, (4) favorable, or (5) very favorable. The options for intensity scales are nearly endless given the vast variety of intensity questions that can arise concerning the contents of documents. Despite their complexity, intensity measures are the most revealing concerning a document's contents.

Sampling

In document analysis, the number of documents is often too vast for all to be analyzed, and it is then necessary to take a sample from a group of documents. For example, we might wish to study the extent to which concern for child abuse has changed among human service providers between the 1950s and the 1990s. We could do this by studying the extent of coverage of the topic in human service journals during those years. Considering the number of journals and thousands of pages involved, sampling would clearly be necessary to make such a project feasible. As with other types of sampling, a critical issue is representativeness. In order to generalize the findings of our document analysis, the sampling procedure must be likely to yield a representative sample, which is often difficult to achieve with documents. One problem is that the elements of the population of documents may not be equal. In studying child abuse, for example, some journals would be more likely to publish articles on that topic than would others. Such journals as *Child Welfare* or the *Journal of Interpersonal Violence,* for example, would be more likely to receive and publish an article on child abuse. A more general journal, like *Social Service Review,* would include a much smaller proportion of articles dealing with child abuse. Likewise, a journal specializing in a different area, such as the *Journal of Gerontology,* would probably publish few if any articles on child abuse. A random sample of all human service journals, then, might include only a few of those most likely to publish articles on this topic. Therefore, the sample would be dominated by journals having a small likelihood of publishing family violence articles, making it more difficult to measure changes in practitioner concern for family violence. This problem could be solved by choosing our sample from among those journals specializing in areas related to family violence. Or we could stratify the journals by type and then select a stratified random sample, taking disproportionately more journals that are likely to publish articles on family violence (*see* Chapter 6).

A second issue in sampling documents is the difficulty in defining the population of documents. For example, for a study of the changing image of the social work profession, James Billups and Maria Julia (1987) conducted a content analysis of advertisements for job vacancies in social work positions. Because such ads are published in many different places—in local, state, and national publications—defining that population of documents would have been difficult. To get around this problem, they limited themselves to advertisements in national publications on the grounds that they would be most likely to reflect national trends in the changing image of social work. At a national level, most ads were placed in *Social Casework* in 1960 and 1970 and in the *NASW News* in 1980. In order to assess trends over time, it was not necessary to sample documents from each year. Instead, the researchers took a random sample of 10 percent of the ads appearing in these journals in 1960, 1970, and 1980, which covered the period in which they were interested. The changing trends in practice that Billups and Julia found in their content analysis research reflected what had been discovered in other research: The distinction between casework and group practice had become less important over time, and social workers, especially those with graduate degrees, were more likely to find supervisory or administrative positions.

Assuming that the population to be sampled can be adequately defined, the normal procedures of sampling discussed in Chapter 6 can be applied to documents. Of those, simple random sampling is probably most common and most generally applicable (Scott, 1990). As we have seen, however, stratified sampling may be required to avoid bias when sampling from a population of unequal elements. Systematic sampling should be approached cautiously as it is easy to be trapped by *periodicity* in documents. Periodicity is the problem in which elements with certain characteristics occur at patterned intervals throughout the sampling frame. For example, the size and content of newspapers vary substantially with the days of the week. If the sampling interval were seven or a multiple of seven, a systematic sample would include only papers published on the same day of the week and could be very biased depending on the aspects of content under study.

Sampling documents often involves multistage sampling. As in all multistage sampling, we start with large units and work down through a series of sampling stages to smaller and smaller units. Levin and Spates's (1970) sample of the underground press illustrates multistage sampling. The first stage was selecting a sample of publications from the membership of the Underground Press Syndicate. This was done by choosing the top five in terms of circulation. The second stage involved randomly selecting a single issue of each publication for every other month from September 1967 through August 1968. This produced 6 sample issues of each of the five publications for a total of 30 issues. The final stage was to select every other nonfiction article appearing in the sample issues for analysis. The resulting sample contained 316 articles to represent the underground press.

Assessment of Available Data Analysis

Like other research techniques, the use of available data has both advantages and disadvantages. A consideration of these will assist in determining when such analysis is the most appropriate choice, as well as in pointing out some potential problems associated with its use.

Advantages

Lower Costs   Document analysis can be one of the least costly forms of research, and using available statistical data can help reduce the costs of a research project. The major expense of data gathering is borne by the producers of the documents and statistics rather than by the researcher. The sheer volume of data collected by the U.S. Bureau of the Census, the National Association of Social Workers, or the many local and state social agencies is so massive that only the best-endowed research projects could possibly duplicate their data collection efforts. In the study of caseworker accuracy that used the political and economic characteristics of the community as one of its independent variables, for example, the costs of the investigation would have escalated tremendously if the researchers were forced to collect these data themselves (Piliavin, Masters, and Corbett, 1977). Fortunately, they were able to use Census Bureau data, which is virtually cost-free. Document analysis can become expensive if the documents of interest are widely scattered and difficult to obtain or if very large samples are employed. Also, the more complex the coding process, the more expensive the study will become. Overall, however, available data offer an opportunity to conduct valuable research at reasonable cost.

Nonreactivity   Like simple observation and unobtrusive measures, available data are nonreactive (*see* Chapters 4 and 9). Unlike the case of surveys or experiments, in which the participants are aware that they are being studied, producers of documents do not normally anticipate a researcher coming along at some later date to analyze those documents. The contents of the documents are, therefore, unaffected by the researcher's activities. This does not mean, of course, that those producing the documents are not reacting to some elements that might result in biased documents. For example, police officers might be more likely to record an instance of physical or verbal assault in an arrest report when the suspect is nonwhite than when the suspect is white, thus generating data that make nonwhites appear more abusive and introducing bias into arrest records. In addition, people who compile documents may be reacting to how people other than researchers, such as a supervisor or politician, may respond to their document. Likewise, the preparation of a document might be shaped by the preparer's hope for a "place in history." Despite all this, researchers are not a source of reactivity with available data.

Inaccessible Subjects   Properly cared for, documents can survive far longer than the people who produce them. Document analysis allows us to study the ways of society long ago and the behavior of people who are long dead. Several of the examples cited in this chapter illustrate the use of document analysis for this purpose. The Lantz and colleagues (1968) study of the colonial family and the study of suicide notes by Ogilvie, Stone, and Shneidman (1966) dealt with the behavior of persons quite inaccessible by research techniques other than document analysis.

Longitudinal Analysis   Many statistical data and documents are collected routinely over a period of years—even centuries. This contrasts sharply with the typical "one-shot," cross-sectional survey data. With such longitudinal data, trend analysis—looking for changing patterns over time—can be accomplished. For example, a longitudinal analysis of available data was used in an evaluation of the progress of African Americans in the United States since the 1950s by Reynolds Farley (1984). Using census data from the 1950s, 1960s, and 1970s, Farley compared the position of African Americans relative to whites over three decades. He found mixed results. The census data revealed that African Americans as a whole had made substantial gains in the quality of employment, family earnings, and educational attainment. Other indicators were less encouraging, however, showing little or no improvement. In the areas of residential integration, unemployment rate, and school integration, African Americans' position relative to whites had not improved during 30 years. In general, Farley's analysis reveals that although African Americans have experienced significant gains in some areas, substantial gaps remain and appear quite persistent. This type of research is obviously valuable in putting today's conditions into a historical perspective, and just as obviously this type of longitudinal analysis of *past* trends can be done only through the analysis of available data. Existing statistical data often lend themselves to the kind of time series analysis described in Chapter 10. In fact, the illustration of the multiple time series analysis by Kohfeld and Leip (1991) in that chapter utilized existing data on traffic accidents in California that were alcohol-related.

Sample Size   Many types of documents are abundant. As mentioned when discussing sampling, a researcher is likely to confront far more documents than can be analyzed, rather than too few. This means that large samples can be employed to increase one's confidence in the results. The low cost associated with document analysis also contributes to the researcher's ability to use substantial sample sizes without encountering prohibitive costs.

Disadvantages

Variable Quality   Because documents are produced for purposes other than research, their quality for research purposes is quite variable. Unless the limitations of the documents are known, as with crime statistics, researchers may have little idea of the conditions under which the data were collected or the amount of attention to quality that went into them. Researchers should, of course, investigate the issue of quality when possible so that any deficiencies in the data are discovered. When this cannot be done, we simply have to draw conclusions cautiously.

Incompleteness   Documents, especially those of a historical nature, are frequently incomplete. Gaps of weeks, months, or even years are not uncommon. In addition, data may be missing in available statistics. The effect of these gaps on a study is often impossible to know except that confidence in the findings is reduced. Incompleteness is simply a common characteristic plaguing available data that researchers have to work around if they can.

Lack of Comparability Over Time   Even though documents are commonly used in longitudinal analysis, this can be problematic. Things can change over time that create statistical artifacts in the data and render comparisons useless. We illustrated this with crime statistics, where changes in how the data are collected by the FBI can make it misleading to compare crime statistics over long periods of time. Researchers need to be careful of similar kinds of changes in other data.

Bias   Because documents are produced for purposes other than research, there is no assurance that they are objective. Data from private sources, for example, may be intentionally slanted to present a particular viewpoint. A researcher blindly accepting these data could be walking into a trap. Nonstatistical documents may suffer from biased presentation as well. A good example is the corporate annual reports to stockholders, which are filled with glowing praise for management, impressive color photographs, and bright prospects for the future, with anything negative presented in the most favorable light or camouflaged in legalese.

Sampling Bias   Bias may creep into otherwise objective data during the sampling process. As we noted, sampling documents is often difficult owing to unequal population elements and hard-to-define populations. We also commented that document sampling is frequently complex, requiring several stages. If errors or bad decisions are made in the sampling process, it is quite possible to end up with a highly biased sample that will produce misleading results.

Using Available Data in Research on Minorities

When studying emotionally charged topics such as racism or sexism, reactivity can be a very serious problem because people may be inclined to disguise their true feelings or motives if these might result in disapproval. People may deny feelings of prejudice toward minorities or women, when asked by a survey researcher about such feelings, even though they may feel some prejudice and it influences their behavior. However, one of the major benefits of available data is that they are often less reactive than other data used to study behavior. Therefore, it may be the preferred research method, or a valued adjunct to other research methods, when studying such emotion-laden topics. Consider, for example, some of the uses to which available data have been put in the study of racism and sexism.

The records of agencies and organizations often contain evidence of sexism despite the denial of those who run the organizations. David Fanshel (1976) studied sex differences in salaries and in representation in leadership positions in social work by using a membership survey conducted by the National Association of Social Workers (NASW) and data routinely collected with the application for membership to the NASW. He found that the status of women in social work is quite different from that of men. First, men were more heavily concentrated in administrative positions, whereas women were more common in casework positions. Second, men earned substantially higher salaries than did women, even among those who entered the profession at the same time. Third, single women and previously married women without children were most likely to be in administrative positions, while married women with children were least likely to be administrators.

Such evidence of sexism would be more difficult to detect if agency directors had been asked directly about their promotion or salary policies. It is often less reactive and more valid to measure the consequences of organizational decisions. Another way to detect the persistence of prejudices and stereotypes is to study the portrayal of people in various cultural productions, such as books, magazines, or movies. During the 1970s, a study by the Michigan Women's Commission revealed that boys far outnumbered girls in schoolbooks and adult males outnumbered adult females (Michigan

Women's Commission, 1974). In addition, many elementary schoolbooks portrayed men as capable of performing many more jobs than women: Men appeared in 213 different occupations, while women were pictured in only 39. The women were typically portrayed in stereotypically female occupations, such as nurse or secretary, and they were frequently portrayed as working only if they were unmarried (Fisher, 1974).

But haven't there been changes in all of this in the past 20 to 25 years? Not as much as you might think. Things have improved, especially when efforts are made to produce materials that are nonsexist in their presentation. However, stereotyping persists. More recent studies of children's picture books, for example, found that more women are portrayed than in the past but still fewer than men (only one third of the illustrations are of women), almost no women are portrayed as working outside the home, women are still shown in fewer occupations than men, and women are portrayed as less brave and adventurous and more helpless (Williams et al., 1987; Peterson and Lach, 1990; Purcell and Stewart, 1990). Another study of newspaper photographs found that men appear in these photos far more frequently than women and that men are typically pictured in professional roles while women are in domestic roles (Luebke, 1989). Even college textbooks are not immune to these influences. Studies of the pictorial content of texts for college-level psychology and sociology courses found that women are shown less often than men and are portrayed more passively and negatively than men (Ferree and Hall, 1990; Peterson and Kroner, 1992). For example, the psychology texts portray women as the victims of mental disorders and the clients in therapy, while men are pictured as the therapists. These are examples of how cultural products, like books or newspapers, can serve as available data to detect sex-role stereotyping that might not have been detected by other research methods.

Some differences in the portrayal of men and women in cultural products can be very subtle. In a creative series of studies involving an intriguing application of available data, Dane Archer and colleagues (1983) measured the amount of space in photographs devoted to people's faces. They divided the distance from the top of the head to the bottom of the chin by the distance from the top of the head to the lowest point of the body visible in the depiction. The result is a proportion with an upper limit of 1.00 (face fills entire picture) that indicates the degree to which the face is prominent in the picture. The first application of this measure was on 1,750 photographs drawn from *Time, Newsweek,* and *Ms.* magazines, and from the *San Francisco Chronicle* and the *Santa Cruz Sentinel.* Before even measuring the photos, the researchers discovered an interesting finding: More than 60 percent of the photos were of men! When they applied their facial prominence indicator, they found another difference between the sexes: The average "face-ism" value was .67 for men and .45 for women, indicating that the pictures of males tended to feature the face more prominently, whereas pictures of women featured more of the body; and more recent studies show that this tendency persisted into the 1980s (Nigro et al., 1988). A subsequent study by Archer and colleagues found that this pattern held across pictures in publications from 11 other countries. Applying the indicator to paintings going back as far as 600 years showed that the pattern they had found had a long history and the difference seemed to be increasing. Just how deeply ingrained this tendency is was illustrated in another part of the study in which subjects were instructed to draw a picture of a man or a woman. Consistently, and regardless of the sex of the subject, the subjects drew men with faces more prominent than for women.

What is the significance of this face-ism? It may represent another mechanism for perpetuating stereotypes about the sexes. The researchers followed up their available data study of the existence of face-ism by collecting data regarding its consequences. They printed up two sets of pictures of the same individuals, varying only in facial prominence. Subjects then rated the people in the pictures on a variety of characteristics. Sure enough, those depicted with more prominent faces were rated more intelligent, more ambitious, and as having a better physical appearance. In other words,

the faces of men are more prominently displayed in the pictures we are surrounded with every day, and a more prominent facial display leads people unwittingly to the perception of the person as more intelligent and ambitious. The authors conclude that this face-ism could contribute to unconscious stereotyping of women as less intelligent and capable and could contribute to discrimination against women. They suggest that face-ism may contribute to another stereotype: "that essential aspects of personal identity are thought to be centered in different anatomic locations in men and women. Men are represented by their heads and faces; women are represented using more of their bodies" (Archer et al., 1983, p. 733).

Main Points

- Available data include both statistical data collected by others and documents, which include any form of communication.
- Content analysis quantifies and organizes the qualitative and unsystematic information contained in documents.
- Content analysis is essentially a form of measurement making the issues of validity and reliability paramount.
- Document analysis will normally include some form of sampling procedure, which must be performed carefully for the sake of representativeness.
- Document analysis offers the advantages of low cost, nonreactivity, ability to study otherwise inaccessible subjects, easy longitudinal analysis, and often large samples.
- Problems in using available data include the variable quality of the data, incomplete data, changes in data over time, possible bias in data, and possible sampling bias.
- The analysis of available data is often less reactive than other research methods, and this can make it very useful in the study of emotionally charged topics such as racism and sexism, where people may be inclined to hide their true feelings and emotions.

COMPUTERS IN RESEARCH
The Use of Computers in Content Analysis

When available data are in a quantitative form, such as a data set from previous research found in data archives, then the use of computers to analyze the data is straightforward: Computers perform the statistical analysis on the data. However, when the available data take a more qualitative form, such as the text of a magazine article, the written comments on a case file, or a videotape, the manner in which computers would be used to analyze the data is less obvious. Yet, as early as the 1960s, computer programs existed that could perform content analysis on texts. Since then, advances in computer hardware and software, artificial intelligence, and optical scanning technologies have expanded substantially the kinds of tasks that computers can do in content analysis (Bainbridge et al., 1994; Evans, 1996).

To illustrate what content analysis software can do these days, let's look at a qualitative study of eating disorders among people referred to an addiction treatment center. The data in this study might consist of open-ended interviews with the clients, client social histories and treatment plans, and chart logs taken from client records. There might also be videotapes of meetings where the staff discusses cases. Many of these documents would be in narrative form, and the first step would be to enter them into a computer as text files. (Of course, many social agencies already store records as computer files, so that step is already done.) Content analysis software can then search through the text identifying and counting the appearance of certain words or phrases (Kelle, 1995; Weitzman and Miles, 1995; Evans, 1996). In addition, researchers can create their own coding scheme and code a text. To do this, the researcher displays the text on the screen and selects a portion of interest, much like one might highlight printed text with a marker pen. A section of text describing the way a mother disapproved of her daughter's behavior could be selected and marked with a code for "Mother disapproval of daughter behavior." Most content analysis software programs can store the codes for a given case in a special file called an "index card." When done coding the material for one case, the index card computer file contains all the codes that the researcher used for all the materials pertaining to that individual. Thus, the computer program follows a logical procedure that is much like the traditional practice of manually preparing note cards for cross-referencing cases. To help with coding, the program provides a code list, which contains all the codes used thus far for all cases in the study.

Important Terms for Review

available data
coding
content analysis
data archives
missing data
secondary analysis

Exploring the Internet

We identified three major sources of available statistical data in this chapter: research organizations; federal, state, and local human service organizations; and organizations that collect data as a public service or as a basis for policy decisions. Each of these three general types of data sources may be

To begin analyzing the data, the researcher uses the search function of the program. In this hypothetical study, one might begin by locating all cases that contain the codes "Mother pressured" or "Father pressured." This process is similar to conducting a computerized literature search by entering combinations of key words. By using these codes joined by the key term "OR," a subset of all cases where parental pressure was indicated can be identified. This group of files could then be saved for further analysis. Having selected a subset of cases based on one or more codes, the program can produce a report with whatever information the researcher wishes: the individual's name, the name given to various codes, the frequency of use of various codes, and which source material the data were taken from.

Some content analysis software can test hypotheses by performing searches for all cases containing particular combinations of codes. Suppose our hypothesis was that "mothers who are critical of their daughter's body image will have a negative effect on their daughter's self-image." The software could search for all cases that include the codes "Mother critical of daughter's body image," "Mother–daughter relationship strained," and "Daughter experiencing weight loss." To each of those cases, it then adds the code "Mother negative influence on daughter self-image," indicating that these cases confirm the hypothesis. Only cases meeting all three conditions would have the new code added to their files. In a similar way, codes can be constructed for other code combinations of interest.

Some content analysis software can perform statistical analyses of the frequency of occurrence of various codes and display the data in graphical form. In addition, beyond merely automating content analysis procedures, some programs provide important advances in the validation, reliability, and generalizability of qualitative data analysis. For example, an independent researcher can code the same data with the codes already developed and stored and thus determine interrater reliability. To assess validity, an independent researcher might code the same material blindly, that is, without benefit of the existing coding scheme, to determine if the second coder develops the same or similar meanings as the first.

Advanced content analysis software can also analyze whether two words tend to be used together, how far apart from one another they tend to be used, whether words used in a text tend to be positively or negatively evaluated, and whether certain words tend to be associated with certain other words. All these new technologies do not relieve the researcher entirely from the hard work of content analysis, which is time-consuming even with computer assistance. However, the new technologies do make possible longer and more sophisticated analyses of the meanings of documents than are possible without computer assistance.

found on the Internet. First, explore the site of the Inter-university Consortium of Political and Social Research. The ICPSR home page is located at http://www.icpsr.umich.edu/. This site provides links to the National Archive of Criminal Justice Data (NACJD). Established in 1978 under the auspices of the Inter-university Consortium for Political and Social Research (ICPSR) and the Bureau of Justice Statistics (BJS), U.S. Department of Justice, the NACJD currently holds over 500 data collections relating to criminal justice. This Web site provides browsing and downloading access to most of the data and documentation.

The site also provides a link to the National Archive of Computerized Data on Aging (NACDA), which is funded by the National Institute on Aging. NACDA's mission is to advance research on aging by helping researchers to profit from the under-exploited potential of a broad range of data sets. NACDA acquires and preserves data relevant to gerontological research, processes them as needed to promote effective research use, disseminates them to researchers, and facilitates their use. By preserving and making available the U.S.'s largest library of electronic data on aging, NACDA offers opportunities for secondary analysis on major issues of scientific and policy relevance.

To learn more about the ICPSR, we suggest that you select "Description" for an overview and then try "F.A.Q." (Frequently Asked Questions), from the menu options on the "Contents" page, for more detailed information. Next, select the "Archives" page and use the search engine to locate studies that relate to a topic of interest to you. For example, you might enter "domestic violence" or "poverty"; the archive search function returns a descriptive listing of data sets that include a focus on that concept.

Julian Faraway of the University of Michigan maintains an extensive list of data sources at http://www.stat.lsa.umich.edu/~faraway/data.html. Exploring just a few of the many sites listed here will give you a sense of the wide array of data sites. Some of the better sites are the Roper Center, the Gallup Organization, the U.S. Census Bureau, and Statistics Canada.

Not only can you locate data sets via the Internet, but you can also actually use available data at some sites. The U.S. Census Web site includes a page called "Just for Fun." It includes a map program that permits you to generate statistical data on demographic variables from each state and county. Another excellent site for using available data is the Crime Statistics site located at http://www.crime.org/. In addition to learning more about crime data at this site, you can be linked to the U.S. Census site where you can use the "Create a Theme" program to compute various statistics including crime rates. We suggest first exploring the Crime Statistics information entitled "Where Can I Get the Data to Calculate My Own U.S. Crime Rates?" This will help you through the process of calculating a rate by identifying variables that you might use and explaining the steps to follow. We suggest you try calculating a statistic such as the number of serious crimes known to the police for your state.

A recently established Web site is very useful for those interested in issues related to content analysis research. Called "Content Analysis: Resources for Making Child's Play of Sophisticated Content Analyses," its Internet address is http://www.gsu.edu/~wwwcom/content.html. It includes buttons that can lead you to summaries of recent publications on content analysis, analyses of software used for content analysis, and links to related Internet sites. You might explore this Web site by identifying materials found at the site that have been discussed in this chapter.

For Further Reading

Davies, James A., and Tom W. Smith. *The NORC General Social Survey: A Users Guide.* Newbury Park, Calif.: Sage, 1994. This book describes a body of available statistical data based on surveys conducted since the 1970s. It includes data on a wide range of topics of interest to people in the social sciences and human services.

Jacob, H. *Using Published Data: Errors and Remedies.* Beverly Hills, Calif.: Sage, 1984. An excellent guide to the problems and pitfalls of using existing data sets. The book focuses primarily on issues of validity and reliability.

Price, J. *Handbook of Organizational Measurement.* Marshfield, Mass.: Pitman, 1986. This volume describes a diversity of ways of measuring organizational variables, many of which are based on available data.

Rutman, L., ed. *Evaluation Research Methods,* 2nd ed. Beverly Hills, Calif.: Sage, 1984. Although devoted to evaluation in general, it also contains an excellent discussion of how to make agency information systems of maximum utility for research purposes.

Stewart, David W., and Michael A. Kamins. *Secondary Research: Information Sources and Methods.* Thousand Oaks, Calif.: Sage, 1993. This useful guide to the many sources of data that are available for secondary analysis also reviews some of the methodological issues that are important to consider in doing such data analysis.

Webb, J., D. Campbell, R. Schwartz, L. Sechrest, and J. Grove. *Nonreactive Measures in Social Research,* 2nd ed.

Chicago: Rand McNally, 1981. A discussion of the advantages and problems in the use of nonreactive measures, with two chapters devoted to archival records.

Weber, R. P. *Basic Content Analysis,* 2nd ed. Thousand Oaks, Calif.: Sage, 1990. This is a basic introduction to the procedures used in conducting content analysis research.

Exercises for Class Discussion

8.1 A valuable source of available data is agency records. If you are in a field placement, an internship, or doing volunteer work in a human service agency, ask the agency to provide sample copies of required and routine data collected on clients. Of course, you should be certain to obtain the forms and reports in a way that will not infringe on client or service-user confidentiality.

  a. Compare the types of information gathered in the agency with which you are affiliated to that gathered by other students in other agencies. Can you think of some specific research questions you could explore with these data? Can you suggest some changes in agency data-gathering procedures that might produce more data for research at little additional effort?

  b. What steps are required in order to obtain existing data on clients so as to meet ethical safeguards for confidentiality?

8.2 A researcher is interested in studying the impact of changing economic conditions on the retention of minority students in college. The researcher's hypothesis is that an economic recession will have a greater negative effect on the retention and graduation of minorities than on nonminority students.

  Using your own institution as the site for the project, what sources of data, already available in some data bank in your institution, might be used in such a study? What problems do you envision with these data in terms of sampling, unit of analysis, and levels of measurement?

8.3 A concern of human service professionals is the negative portrayal of public welfare service users in the media. Is the image of welfare recipients really negative? Has there been a trend toward improvement? Does the image portrayed improve or deteriorate in conjunction with changes in the national economy? These are questions that might be approached through a content analysis of the news media. Develop a research project that could be conducted in your community that would utilize content analysis to answer these questions.

  a. Suggest what elements you think the population being studied contains.

  b. Identify some sampling issues the researcher would confront.

  c. What different problems are involved in answering the second and third questions posed in the above paragraph in contrast to the first question about negative image?

  d. Assume the research is confined to daily newspapers. Suggest some possibilities for the unit of analysis.

  e. How could operational definitions of "negative image" and "welfare recipient" be developed?

CHAPTER 9

Observational Techniques

Designs for Observation 220
Participant Observation   220
Unobtrusive Observation   227
Other Types of Observation   230

Issues in Observation 230
Recording Observations   231
Time Sampling   239
Validity and Reliability   240
Reactivity   242
Observational Research on Minority Populations   243

Assessment of Observational Techniques   244
Advantages   244
Disadvantages   244

Observation in Human Service Practice   245

Main Points   246

Important Terms for Review   247

Exploring the Internet   247

For Further Reading   248

Exercises for Class Discussion   250

All methods of data collection involve some form of observation, but the term "observational technique" is used in this chapter to delineate a special type of data collection. **Observational techniques** refer to the collection of data through direct visual or auditory experience of behavior. With observational techniques, which include video or audio recordings of behavior, the researcher actually sees or hears the behavior or words that are the data for the research. Surveys, in contrast, involve people's *reports* to the researcher about what they said, did, or felt. With surveys and available data, the researcher does not directly observe what will be the focus of the research.

People often believe that direct observation provides a more accurate or honest picture of reality because we "see it ourselves" without anything to interfere with our perceptions. This belief, however, can be highly misleading, as Alice's experiences before her journey through the looking-glass illustrate. Alice introduced her black kitten to a place seen through the mirror above her fireplace, a place Alice called the "Looking-glass House":

> Now if you'll only attend, Kitty, and not talk so much, I'll tell you all my ideas about Looking-glass House. First, there's the room you can see through the glass—that's just the same as our drawing-room, only the things go the other way. I can see all of it when I get upon a chair—all but the bit just behind the fireplace. Oh! I do so wish I could see *that* bit! I want so much to know whether they've a fire in the winter: you never *can* tell, you know, unless our fire smokes, and then smoke comes up in that room too—but that may be only pretence, just to make it look as if they had a fire. Well then, the books are something like our books, only the words go the wrong way: I know *that,* because I've held up one of our books to the glass, and then they hold up one in the other room. [Carroll, 1946, pp. 8–10]

In her quest to know the Looking-glass House, Alice is inextricably trapped and limited by her perspective. She has tantalizing glimpses of that other world, but she can't see all of it no matter how hard she struggles. Distressingly, the clues she does observe—such as smoke seeming to come from a fire—are difficult to interpret. Do they mean what she thinks (or wants) them to mean? The Looking-glass House is forever partially shrouded in mystery and dissimulation.

Scientific research and practice in the human services also involve peering through a looking-glass—making observations of a world with our own, admittedly frail, perceptual apparatus. What is outside ourselves is as alien to us as the Looking-glass House is to Alice. We, too, are trapped by our perspective. We, too, cannot see all that we are convinced is "out there." Observation is difficult, it is tricky, and it can be faulty—but it is at the core of both scientific investigation and human service practice.

Accordingly, we need to take a lesson from Alice and approach observation in a careful and systematic fashion. Alice seems serenely unaware that it is *her perspective* that shapes the world she observes through the mirror. We need to recognize the force of our own perspectives and adopt observational techniques that minimize their distorting effect. This chapter discusses observational techniques in scientific research, beginning with the different types of observations that can be made. Following the presentation of designs for observation is a discussion of some important issues related to observation, including methods of recording observations, validity and reliability of observations, and the use of observational research on minority populations. The advantages and disadvantages of observational techniques are also assessed. Finally, we suggest some lessons that scientific observation can provide for those making observations in practice settings.

Designs for Observation

Observational studies can differ from one another along three dimensions. One dimension has to do with whether the data collected through the observations are quantitative or qualitative in nature. This distinction is discussed in Chapter 4 and will be explored in greater depth in this chapter. A second dimension deals with whether the observations are done in a naturalistic setting or in a laboratory or contrived setting. A *naturalistic setting* is a "real-life" situation in which people behave as they routinely would if they weren't the subjects of scientific observation. In fact, in some cases, people in naturalistic settings may not know that they are under observation. *Contrived settings* are ones that are created by the researcher and would not have occurred were it not for the research being conducted. The third dimension involves the extent to which the investigator participates in the activities of the people being observed. The two general possibilities are that of participant observer and that of nonparticipant observer. Various types of observational methods will be discussed that combine these dimensions in different ways.

Participant Observation

Participant observation is a method in which the researcher is a part of, and participates in, the activities of the people, group, or situation that is being studied (Burgess, 1984; Lofland and Lofland, 1984). Participant observation research is naturalistic and involves some participation by the investigator, although, as will be seen, the degree of such participation can vary. In some cases, the investigator may have belonged to the group prior to the start of the research and can use this position as a group member to collect data. For example, a social worker might be interested in staff adaptation to antidiscrimination legislation in hiring. If this person is on the agency personnel committee, such a position might serve as the context for participant observation. As new staff members are hired, the social worker could observe the reactions of the other staff in dealing with the new regulations. In

other cases, a researcher must first gain access to a group in order to be a participant observer. This was done by the anthropologist Sue Estroff in an effort to learn more about the daily lives and problems of former mental patients. She joined for 2 years in the lives of a group of deinstitutionalized mental patients, experiencing the drudgery and degradation of their daily routine (Estroff, 1978). She worked at low-paying jobs (such as slipping rings onto drapery rods) that were the lot of these ex-patients. She took the powerful antipsychotic drugs that were routinely administered to them and that had distinctive side effects such as hand tremors and jiggling legs. And she experienced the extreme depression and despair that result when one suddenly stops taking these potent drugs. From her position as participant in the subculture of these mental patients, she could observe the con games that characterized the relationships between patients and mental health professionals.

Through this type of participant observation, practitioners have access to a view of client groups that cannot be gained in an interview or therapy session. It is a unique view because it is seen from the perspective of the client, a perspective that is especially valuable to anyone who works with groups that are stigmatized or commonly misunderstood by both practitioners and laypeople. Like Alice, who could not clearly see the whole room in the Looking-glass House, human service workers can by no means clearly see the lives of their clients from their position as practitioners. In a sense, Estroff climbed *through* the "mirror" in much the same way little Alice did. Though many practitioners may not have the opportunity to engage in such observations personally, many such research efforts by behavioral scientists can be utilized to develop a better understanding of client groups. And human service professionals should seek opportunities to conduct this kind of research themselves in order to understand particular groups or subcultures. In fact, practitioners might consider periodically engaging in participant observation of their clients, if it is possible, in order to detect ways in which the practitioner perspective may limit understanding of client groups.

Qualitative Versus Quantitative Data

Chapter 4 discusses the distinction between qualitative and quantitative research. Although some quantitative data may be collected during participant observation, it is typically highly qualitative research, and its proponents argue that qualitative research offers access to a very valuable type of data: the subjective experiences of those under study (Guba and Lincoln, 1994). The importance of these subjective experiences is at the heart of a fundamental controversy in the social sciences about how to understand human social behavior. Although a complex controversy, it basically involves two potentially opposing positions in social science: the positivists versus the subjectivists (Smart, 1976; Benton, 1977; Wakefield, 1995). A brief introduction to this controversy should clarify how participant observation research differs from other types of research.

Positivism argues that the world exists independently of people's perceptions of it and that scientists can use objective techniques to discover what exists in the world (Durkheim, 1938; Halfpenny, 1982). Astronomers, for example, use telescopes to discover stars and galaxies, which exist regardless of whether we are aware of them. So, too, human beings can be studied in terms of behaviors that can be observed and recorded using some kind of objective technique. Recording people's gender, age, height, weight, or socioeconomic position are legitimate and objective measurement techniques—the equivalent of the physicist measuring the temperature, volume, or velocity of some liquid or solid. For the positivist, quantifying these measurements—assessing the *average* age of a group or looking at the percentage of a group that is male—is merely a precise way of describing and summarizing an objective reality. Such measurement provides a solid and objective foundation for understanding human social behavior. Limiting study to observable behaviors and using objective techniques, positivists argue, is most likely to produce systematic and repeatable research results that are open to refutation by other scientists.

Subjectivism (also called the interactionist or *verstehen* approach) argues that these "objective" measures miss a very important part of the human experience: the subjective and very personal *meanings* that people attach to themselves and what they do (Glaser and Strauss, 1967; Wilson, 1970). Max Weber, an early proponent of this view, argued that we need to look not only at what people do but also at what they think and feel about what is happening to them (Weber, 1957, orig. pub. 1925). This "meaning" or "feeling" or "interpretive" dimension cannot be adequately captured through objective, quantitative measurement techniques. Researchers need to gain what Weber called **verstehen**, or a subjective understanding. They need to view and experience the situation from the perspective of the people themselves. To use a colloquialism, the researchers need "to walk a mile in their shoes." They need to talk to the people at length and to immerse themselves in the lives of those people so they can experience the highs and lows, the joys and sorrows, the triumphs and the tragedies as seen from the perspective of the people being studied. Researchers need to see how the individuals experience and give meaning to what is happening to them. Qualitative research methods are an attempt to gain access to that personal, subjective experience; for subjectivists, quantitative research, by its very nature, misses this very important dimension of social reality. Positivists, for their part, do not necessarily deny the existence or importance of subjective experiences, but they do question whether the subjective interpretations of the *verstehen* method have any scientific validity.

Proponents of participant observation argue that it is the only method that enables the researcher to approximate *verstehen,* an understanding of the subjective experiences of people. Of course, actual access to such experience is impossible; thoughts and feelings, by their very nature, are private. Even when someone *tells* you how he or she feels, this person has objectified that subjective experience into *words* and thus changed it. Participant observers, however, can gain some insight into those subjective experiences by immersing themselves in the lives and daily experiences of the people they study. By experiencing the same culture, the same values, the same hopes and fears, researchers are in a better position to take on the point of view of these people. However, despite its focus on subjective experiences, participant observation is still empirical in the sense that it is grounded in observation, and those who use this method are also concerned about issues of reliability and validity. Researchers who use participant observation consider it no less systematic or scientific than the more positivistic research techniques.

Consider some examples. An investigator interested in the causes of poverty and unemployment might gain great insight by using participant observation to study such conditions. The anthropologist Elliot Liebow (1967) did precisely this. After spending considerable time with a group of African American men who hung around a street corner in Washington, D.C., Liebow wrote an account of their lives that is filled with compassion and understanding. He gained considerable comprehension of how the social conditions these men faced generated intense feelings of hopelessness that permeated all parts of their lives. He learned why these men worked little, if at all: The only jobs open to them were very menial and low-paying. He also came to understand how their past history of failure had left them lacking in the self-confidence necessary to address new challenges. In the 1980s, sociologist Terry Williams (1989) did participant observation research among teenage cocaine dealers in New York City. He spent 2 hours a day, 3 days a week, hanging out with these teens in the bars, discos, restaurants, parties, crack houses, and street corners where they spent their days. Through this exposure, he, like Liebow, was able to see why they couldn't get jobs—good entry-level jobs were disappearing—and why they dealt cocaine—the opportunity was there and they could make a lot of money. He also learned that these kids were shrewd businesspeople, worked very hard, and most of all sought the same kind of respect and reward that motivates people pursuing more conventional careers. By using participant observation, both Liebow and Williams were able to observe processes and grasp levels of meaning that other, more "objective" methods such as surveys or available statistical data would not have been able to uncover.

So once again, we see that the research question—in this case, the need for subjective understanding to explain something—influences the selection of a participant observation research design over other types of observation or over nonobservational techniques. Had the research question called for data of a more positivist nature, then a different design might have been needed. As shown later in this chapter, some observational techniques do lend themselves to more positivist, quantitative approaches.

There is another way in which the research question influences the choice of participant observation. This observational technique is often selected when the research question is exploratory in nature and theoretical development does not enable researchers to spell out relevant concepts or develop precise hypotheses. Participant observation permits the researcher to view human behavior as it occurs in the natural environment without the restrictions of preconceived notions or explanations. Through observation, the researcher can begin to formulate concepts, variables, and hypotheses that seem relevant to the topic and grounded in the actual behavior of people.

Observer Roles In many types of research, the relationship between the researcher and those participating in the research is fairly clear-cut. In surveys, for example, participants know who the researchers are and that they as respondents are providing data to the researchers. In observational research—and especially with participant observation—the researcher–participant relationship becomes more problematic in that it can take a number of different forms. Two critical issues arise: the extent to which the observer will change the setting that is being observed and the extent to which people should be informed that they are being used for research purposes. The way in which a researcher resolves these issues determines the nature of the observer–participant relationship for a given research project.

A participant observer is a part of the activities being studied and so is in a position to influence the direction of those activities. For example, the anthropologist Sue Estroff might have been inclined to organize the deinstitutionalized mental patients she studied into a lobbying group demanding better living conditions and improved treatment from mental health professionals. Yet, had she done this early in her participant observation, would it have interfered with her research goals? Would she have learned all the sources of despair and degradation that these people experienced? Would she have learned how such groups, without benefit of an intervening anthropologist, adapt to their plight? The resolution of this issue of the extent of intervention, of course, rests partly on the research question. If Estroff were interested in how such groups adapt without outside aid, then she should limit her influence on the group, even though humanitarian values might push her toward involvement. On the other hand, if she wanted to assess effective strategies for improving the lot of such groups, then intervention on her part would be called for by the research question. Human service providers, in particular, need to be sensitive to this issue because an important part of their role is intervention. Providers need to recognize that intervention may at times be counterproductive to research goals.

This problem of the degree of intervention is often referred to as a question of whether the researcher is, first and foremost, a *participant* or an *observer* (Gold, 1958). Which of these two aspects of the role should one emphasize? Let us look at each side of the issue. Those who would emphasize the importance of the *participation* of the observer argue that the investigator plays two roles—that of scientist *and* that of group member. In order to comprehend fully the activities of the group and the dynamics of the situation, the researcher must become fully involved in the group. Otherwise, group members may not confide in the researcher, or he or she may not become aware of the meanings that various actions and objects have for the group. In order to become fully involved, the researcher must act like any other group member—and this means intervening in those situations in which other group members might do so.

On the other side of the issue, those who emphasize *observation* over participation argue that the more fully one becomes a group member, the less

objective one becomes. The real danger is that researchers will become so immersed in the group that they take on completely the perspective of the group and can no longer view the situation from a scientific perspective (Shupe and Bromley, 1980). This is always a danger in participant observation. In fact, some researchers caution against the use of participant observation for this very reason. For example, one criminology professor joined a local police force in order to learn more about the police work that he talked about in his lectures. Over a period of time, he became so caught up in the world of the police that he could no longer view them objectively and critically, and any semblance of scientific investigation was lost. He identified with the police and viewed the world as a police officer rather than as a researcher (*see* Kirkham, 1976, and Manning, 1978, for a discussion of this case). Similarly, human service practitioners must guard against becoming so identified with their clients that they lose objectivity in evaluating situations. Imagine a counselor in a rape crisis center who sees many women who have experienced the terror and humiliation of sexual assault, only to be further humiliated by a clumsy or insensitive police staff. Improving the capacity of the criminal justice system to respond with sensitivity to victims would be an appropriate goal. However, the counselor's empathy with victims could so arouse her hostility that the worker might become incapable of working with police on a professional basis. Most participant observers attempt to strike a balance between total immersion and loss of objectivity on the one hand and total separation with its consequent loss of information on the other.

The second critical issue in the researcher–participant relationship is both practical and ethical: To what extent should the people studied be informed of the investigator's research purposes (Punch, 1986)? This is an especially troubling problem in participant observation because in some cases fully informing people would undermine the researcher's ability to gather accurate data. For example, a study of staff treatment of patients in a mental hospital was conducted by having researchers admitted to the hospital as patients without informing the staff of their research purposes

(Rosenhan, 1973). Undoubtedly, hospital staff would have behaved quite differently had they known they were under surveillance. Therefore, some researchers take the position that concealment is sometimes necessary in order to conduct scientific work and that researchers must judge whether the scientific gain justifies the deception of human beings and any potential injury—social or psychological—they might suffer. Others, however, hold adamantly to the position that any research on human beings must include "informed consent": The people involved should be fully informed concerning the purposes of the research, any possible dangers or consequences, and the credentials of the researcher. Anything less, they argue, would be unethical and immoral because it tricks people into cooperation and may lead to undesirable consequences of which they are not aware. This complex ethical dilemma is dealt with at greater length in Chapter 3.

In a classic piece on observational research, Raymond Gold (1958) identified three distinct observer roles that can emerge depending on how the issues of observer influence and informed consent are resolved: complete participant, participant-as-observer, and observer-as-participant. The major distinguishing feature of the *complete participant role* is that the observer's status as observer is not revealed to those who are being studied. The observer enters a group under the guise of being just another member and essentially plays that role while conducting the study. The researcher must be able to sustain this pretense for long periods because studies using the complete participant role are usually characterized by lengthy involvement with the group studied. The complete participant role has proved valuable in studying groups that otherwise might be closed to research if the observer's true identity were known. Drug users (Becker, 1953), homosexuals (Humphreys, 1970), drug dealers (Adler, 1985), and members of the Satanic Church (Moody, 1976) are among such groups that have been studied by using the complete participant role.

The *participant-as-observer role* differs from the complete participant role in that the researcher's status as observer is revealed to those who are being studied. In this role, the observer enters a group and participates in their routines but is known to be doing so for research purposes. As in the case of the complete participant role, the participant-as-observer will spend a considerable amount of time observing in the group being studied. The participant-as-observer role has often been used in community research. This is probably due to the large size of the groups involved and the need for direct access to information that the complete participant might find difficult or too time-consuming to obtain while maintaining a disguise. Whyte's (1955) classic study *Street Corner Society* is a fine example of the use of the participant-as-observer role. Research in Practice 9.1 illustrates the use of the participant-as-observer role in a human service context.

The *observer-as-participant role* is similar to the participant-as-observer role in that the observer's true status is known to those being studied but differs with regard to the length of time the observer spends with the group. As noted, the participant-as-observer role assumes a lengthy period of observation. The observer-as-participant role involves brief contact with the group being studied, possibly for as short as one day. This brief contact tends to preclude the deep, insightful results that characterize studies utilizing the two previous roles. The observer-as-participant role is likely to generate more shallow, superficial results. In fact, the brief contact that characterizes this role may lead the observer to misunderstand aspects of the group being studied. Because of these problems, the observer-as-participant role has been less popular for conducting serious social research.

Steps in Participant Observation Research

Any participant observation research encounters certain common problems. These problems are dealt with by organizing the investigation into a series of steps (Bailey, 1987). The first step, of course, is to establish the specific goals of the research and to decide that participant observation is the most appropriate research strategy. If you are trying to gain a comprehensive understanding of the values, perceptions, and other subjective elements of a particular group or subculture, then participant observation may well be the most appropriate mode of attack.

The second step is to decide which specific group to study. If you are interested in former mental patients living in residential care centers, with which groups of people will you be involved? One way this issue is commonly decided is simply by the accessibility of the group, but representativeness may also be considered.

The third step is very challenging: gaining entry into the group to be studied. In the complete participant role, this step may be less of a problem because the people do not know they are being studied. However, you must be sufficiently like those studied to gain access. In the other participant roles, however, you must find some way to convince the people to agree to accept your involvement as a researcher. Several methods increase the likelihood that people will cooperate (Johnson, 1975; Jorgensen, 1989). One way is to gain the cooperation of those with more status and power in the group and use your relationship with them to gain access to others. It would be best, for example, to approach the directors of a mental health center and enlist their aid before contacting caseworkers and ward staff. Another way to increase cooperation is to present your reasons for conducting the research to people in a way that seems plausible to them and makes sense in their frame of reference. Esoteric or abstract scientific goals are unlikely to be very appealing to an agency director or to a single parent struggling on welfare. You should emphasize that your major concern is understanding their thoughts and behaviors as legitimate, acceptable, and appropriate. Nothing will close doors faster than the hint that you intend to *evaluate* the group. The door of a welfare recipient may be opened if you tell him or her you are studying the difficulties confronting parents on welfare; it will surely be slammed if you say you want to separate the "good" welfare recipients from the "bad."

Cooperation is also enhanced if you have some means of legitimizing yourself as a researcher. This might be done through an affiliation with a university that supports the study or an agency that has an interest in the research. In a study of a sexually transmitted disease clinic, for example, Joseph Sheley (1976) gained entrance because he was involved with a larger community study of sexually transmitted disease. Such legitimation can backfire, of course, if the group you hope to study is suspicious of, or hostile toward, the organization with which you are affiliated. (Sheley, for example, although allowed into the clinic, found himself having a degree of "outsider" status because of his association with the community STD study.) Finally, it may be necessary to use informants to gain entry into some groups. An *informant* is an insider who can introduce you to others in the group, ease your acceptance into the group, and help you interpret how the group views the world. Especially with informal subcultures, the informant technique can be a valuable approach.

The fourth step in participant observation is to develop rapport and trust with the people being studied so that they will serve as useful and accurate sources of information. This can be time-consuming, trying, and traumatic. It is a problem with which the human service professional can readily identify. The community organizer attempting to gain the trust of migrant workers, the substance abuse worker dealing with a narcotics addict, and the child welfare worker running a group home for girls can all attest to the importance of establishing rapport. Although in many cases the human service worker can express a sincere desire to help as a means of establishing rapport, the researcher cannot always employ this approach because the research goals may not include the provision of such help. In the initial stages of the research, people are likely to be distant if not outright distrustful. You are likely to make errors and social gaffes that offend the people you have joined. More than one participant observation effort has had to be curtailed because the investigator inadvertently alienated the people being studied.

Many elements are involved in developing rapport or trust among one's informants (Johnson, 1975; Jorgensen, 1989). Rapport can emerge if the informants and group members view the investigator

Research in Practice 9.1

Program Evaluation: Participant Observation of a Token Economy Program Among Schizophrenics

Remember, these are locked wards. These are the worst patients. We chose the worst so we could prove our program works.
  —organizer of a token economy program

I think this system stinks. They can go shove the whole thing as far as I'm concerned.
  —patient in a token economy program
  [Biklen, 1976, pp. 53, 59]

These starkly contrasting views of a token economy program illustrate one dimension of the controversy that has swirled around such change efforts. Token economy is a form of behavior modification that has been trumpeted by some as a corrective for many social and personal ills and denounced by others as an instrument of coercion and repression. Token economy programs have been used as therapeutic efforts with many types of people, such as the developmentally disabled, the mentally ill, and criminal offenders.

A number of questions could be asked about these programs. Do they work? Is it ethical to use

such admittedly manipulative therapies with involuntary clients? Although these issues are being debated in the professional literature, another dimension of the problem often receives little attention: What do the recipients of behavior modification programs think of them? Do they share the optimistic views of the program organizers that token economies will usher in positive changes in behavior? Or do the patients echo, each in their own distinctive style, that program organizers should "shove the whole thing"?

This concern for the client's view of behavior modification was the catalyst for a research project designed and carried out by Douglas Biklen (1976). To gain this important, but too often neglected, client view, Biklen developed a research strategy based on unstructured participant observation. He spent 5 months observing a token economy program among schizophrenic women in a locked ward of a state mental hospital. Biklen adopted an observer role that fell somewhere between that of participant-as-observer and that of complete observer. He explained his presence to the patients by saying that he was there "to study mental hospital life and change in an institution"

as a basically nice person who will do them no harm. It matters little if the informants know of or agree with the research goals—only that they develop a positive attitude toward the investigator. Trust and rapport can also emerge if the investigator shows through behavior that he or she agrees with, or at least has some sympathy for, the perspective of the people being studied. If you join your field contacts in some of their routine activities, such as drinking beer or playing cards, they are likely to view you as one who accepts them and can be trusted. Here, of course, the researcher must balance the need for acceptance against personal

and professional standards of behavior. Finally, rapport can be enhanced if the relationship between investigator and group members is reciprocal; that is, both the observer and the group members have something that the other needs and wants. You might, for example, gain scientific data from your informants while they, in turn, hope to gain some publicity and attendant public concern from the publication of your results.

The fifth step in participant observation is to observe and record. This can only truly begin once you have established sufficient rapport to ensure that you are gathering useful data. We discuss

(Biklen, 1976, p. 54). However, he did not participate in the token economy program. He observed staff–patient interchanges that were a part of the program, and patients knew they were being observed. With such a stance, he hoped to avoid being identified with any one faction, such as the patients, the attendants, or the supervisory staff. This would place him in the most advantageous position to collect data regarding how both staff and patients perceived the program.

Participant observation was appropriate for Biklen's research because his study was exploratory in nature and specific hypotheses had not yet been developed. Biklen observed patient–staff encounters in 3-hour shifts, taking detailed field notes of his observations immediately after each session. He analyzed the field notes himself but guarded against unreasonable bias by subjecting his analysis and interpretation to the critical scrutiny of his colleagues—social scientists, educators, and psychologists. From this, he was able to develop hypotheses grounded in his data.

From his position as an outsider, Biklen observed elements of the token economy program that those organizing the program failed to perceive. For example, staff and client perceptions of the program were quite different. The staff placed great emphasis on what they called "activation" of patients, and helping became operationalized as "activating" the patients—getting them to move,

talk, play checkers, or *do* almost anything. In many cases, Biklen found, the patients didn't want to be "activated" and didn't perceive it as "helping" them. Their response to this program—which they perceived as being thrust unwanted into their lives—was one of anger, ironic humor, or withdrawal. In addition, the patients viewed the rewards offered by the staff—cigarettes and canteen privileges—as demeaning.

From his observations, Biklen raises a vexing issue: Do token economy programs—with their complex system of rewards, privileges, and denials meted out by the staff based on their judgment of the patient's conformity to certain standards—help the patient? Or do they merely intensify institutional control over patient behavior under the guise of "scientific" behavior change? Biklen's participant observation research makes us acutely aware that clients—all clients—have a legitimate perspective that needs to be considered:

> I sought to treat the patients not as "psychotics" but as people who, like other participants in the setting, had perspectives that were relevant for themselves. [Biklen, 1976, p. 54]

Participant observation research is one very valuable scientific tool for learning about that perspective.

---

recording observations later in this chapter, but first we need to look at nonparticipant forms of observation.

Unobtrusive Observation

Some research questions call for or require the investigator to refrain from participation in the group being investigated. The concern is that the intrusive impact of an outsider might change the behavior of group members in ways detrimental to the research question. In such cases, the relationship adopted

by the investigator would be what Gold labels the *complete observer role*—the observer has no direct contact with, or no substantial influence on, those being observed. One way of doing such nonparticipant observation is to use an observational technique that has been called **unobtrusive** (or **nonreactive**) **observation:** Those under study are not aware that they are being studied, and the investigator does not change their behavior by his or her presence (Webb et al., 1981; Sechrest and Belew, 1983). Unobtrusive observation can be done in naturalistic or contrived settings and could involve both quantitative or qualitative observations.

It can take a number of forms: hidden observation, disguised observation, and physical traces.

Hidden Observation   In some research projects, it is possible to observe behavior from a vantage point that is obscured from the view of those under observation. This might be done by observing people through a one-way mirror or by videotaping them with a hidden camera. For example, studies of aggressive behavior among children have utilized observations in naturalistic settings by videotaping children at play in school yards with the camera in a hidden location (Pepler and Craig, 1995). The camera can be set up in a classroom window, out of sight of the children, and modern cameras with zoom lenses make possible clear observation of children's behavior from long distances. As long as the children are not aware of the cameras and of the fact that they are being observed, the research is truly nonreactive in nature. This naturalistic, hidden observation is important in the study of aggression among children because children will behave more normally under these conditions; in a contrived setting or an interview, it would probably be impossible to make the same honest, natural observations that are possible when children are just being themselves among their peers. In fact, one group of researchers of such behavior noted that "the use of knives on our school playground tapes was so covert that it often took several passes through the audiovisual tapes to discern their presence" (Pepler and Craig, 1995, p. 550). Because the children are clearly attempting to hide the use of knives from observation by others, they would be unlikely to display such aggressive behavior to researchers in surveys or in a contrived setting. Naturalistic and hidden observations are key to making such discoveries.

A major problem with hidden observations is to ensure that the observations are, in fact, hidden and truly unobtrusive. The unobtrusive nature of the study of children's aggression, just mentioned, was compromised in two ways. First, the school principal and the teachers and other adults supervising the children at play were aware that observations were being made. All people have a tendency to react differently when they are being observed—they put their best foot forward or behave in a fashion that will be acceptable to the observer. The adults supervising these children may well have done the same thing—watching the children more closely or reacting more quickly to behaviors that hint of aggression. If these adults behaved differently with the children than they would have were the children not being observed, this would compromise the unobtrusive nature of the observations. A second compromise occurred because the researchers also wanted an audiotape of the children's conversations in order to fully understand the nature of their aggressive behavior. So, the children had a wireless microphone clipped to their clothing while they played in the school yard, thus making them aware that they were being observed. The researchers decided that both of these compromises were essential and that they had only minor effects on the validity of the observations made. The adults, for example, did not know exactly which children on the playground were being observed at a given time, and the children seemed, after a short period of being aware of the microphone, to ignore it and play naturally. Other research supports this idea that people often tend to forget they are being observed and to behave normally, especially if the observation occurs over a long period. This research on aggression among children does illustrate, however, the ways in which what appears at first to be hidden observation is not actually completely unobtrusive.

Disguised Observation   With some types of behavior, it is possible to observe people in a naturalistic setting, but without participating and without revealing that one is observing them. Any setting in which one can be present and not participate without calling attention to oneself is a potential scene for disguised observation. One setting, for example, that might lend itself to such disguised observation is a public establishment like a bar or a tavern. Exactly this kind of disguised observation was done by a group of investigators interested in alcohol-related aggressive behavior (Graham et al., 1980). They decided that information could best be gathered through an unobtrusive observation of the behavior of people as they consumed alcohol in various bars in Vancouver, British Columbia. Teams of observers spent from 40 to 56 hours per week making observations in drinking establishments. Each team consisted of a male–female pair. They would enter an establishment, locate a table with a good view of the saloon, and order a drink. They made every effort not to influence the people in the bar in any way. We would consider such research nonparticipant, rather than participant, because the investigators made efforts to have no contact with, or influence on, the behavior of the patrons. At times, this would be impossible—a patron would wander over to their table and engage them in a conversation. In those cases, they quickly terminated the observations and left the bar. In some other ways, one might question the unobtrusive character of their observation: The female observer was often the only white female in the bar (the others being Native Americans), the observers were sometimes a small island of sobriety in a sea of drunkenness, and there were often social class differences between the dress and behavior of the observers and the observed. Nonetheless, their impact on the behavior of the clientele was probably minimal, so we can consider this disguised, nonparticipant observation.

Physical Traces   The physical objects or evidence that result from people's activities that can be used as data to test hypotheses are known as **physical traces.** Commonly used in police investigations, physical traces might be fingerprints, tire tracks, or dirt stains. (It is in this realm that a scientific investigator is most likely to feel like a fledgling Sherlock Holmes.) Although such methods are less common in social research, an investigator with ingenuity and an unrestrained imagination can devise ways to utilize such observation. There are two types of physical traces. *Erosion measures* involve the degree to which some materials are worn, eroded, or used up. For example, nurses making home visits commonly observe the level of medicine in medicine bottles as an unobtrusive indicator of whether the patient is taking the prescribed amount.

Accretion measures are those involving materials that are deposited or accumulated because of human activity. For example, the archaeologist William Rathje (Rathje and Murphy, 1992) directed a project devoted to the study of modern household refuse as an accretion measure. Sometimes called "garbology," this research was designed to learn more about contemporary civilization by studying the things that we throw out in our garbage. Rathje provided his assistants with lab coats, surgical masks, gloves, and appropriate immunizations before sending them out to inspect people's garbage. The items in the refuse were sorted along a number of dimensions: whether an object was food, drugs, or something else; how much it weighed; cost; brand name; and the like. Such a study can serve a number of purposes. First, it can serve as a check on what a respondent tells an interviewer. If a person claims to consume a few cans of beer a day, inspection of refuse can validate or refute that claim. Second, it can measure people's responses to various social and economic changes. As food prices rise, one can measure the changing patterns of food consumption by people of various social classes.

Another, perhaps somewhat unusual, form of accretion analysis involves graffiti. At first dismissed as the play of those with too much time to kill and possessed of bad judgment, some forms of graffiti have been found to have considerable cultural significance. Ferrell (1995), after a lengthy 4-year study of "hip hop" graffiti writing, suggests that it represents an important form of youthful communication and expression. Graffiti writing, known as "tagging," for many youths is a form of protest against many of the unpleasant things they face in their urban lives. The most frequent targets are symbols of authority, such as public buildings or large businesses. The "tagging" crews are even looked at as surrogate families that significantly supplement the often fragmented and dysfunctional urban family. Studies have revealed that, although decried by many as vandalism, urban graffiti writing has become a part of urban youth subculture and is unlikely to yield to repressive policies. Accretion studies of things like graffiti that may seem insignificant or even repugnant can actually reveal much deeper meanings and can be useful in developing more effective public policies for dealing with such social phenomena.

Physical traces are not commonly used by themselves. However, in conjunction with other data collection efforts, they can add a valuable dimension to our knowledge of certain social phenomena. Through such nonreactive techniques, it is possible to discover some aspects of a problem that researchers are unlikely to find through more reactive measures.

Nonparticipant observation can be a valuable observational technique because it provides the investigator with access to behavior in social settings that has not been disturbed or changed as a result of scientific scrutiny. However, nonparticipant observation is highly behavioristic in that it is largely limited to the observation of visible behaviors. As such, it is not conducive to linking behavior with subjective or symbolic meanings important to people. Thus, nonparticipant observation is often used as an adjunct to research methods more capable of discovering these meanings.

Other Types of Observation

There are many forms of observation other than participant and unobtrusive. In fact, any time researchers look, listen, and record what they observe, they are engaging in observational research. For example, observation can be the primary mode of data collection in experimental settings where we would record the changes in behavior that result from our manipulation of an independent variable. (Experiments are discussed in detail in Chapter 10.) Observation also plays an important part in the activities of practitioners who are seeking some behavior change in clients. This can often take the form of single-subject designs, which are presented in Chapter 11.

Focus groups are another kind of research that often involve observational techniques. Although focus groups have many characteristics of surveys and thus are discussed at length in Chapter 7, the data from focus groups also often include direct observation of the participants' nonverbal behavior

as well as their verbal responses to questions. Focus group sessions are often videotaped or audiotaped, and field notes are prepared from these recordings. In some cases, these observational data from focus groups are more qualitative than quantitative in nature, so many of the issues discussed in this chapter relating to qualitative research would apply. As mentioned in Chapter 7, for example, some focus group data resemble the field notes of qualitative research, so many of the issues in observation discussed in the next section may be applicable to focus group research. A major advantage of focus groups over participant observation is that the former make it possible to observe a lot of social interaction on a specific topic in a limited amount of time (Morgan, 1994). Moderators have some control over this because they can direct discussion away from topics that are not fruitful whereas in participant observation the observer must let the scene unfold naturally. However, this is also a disadvantage of focus groups in that they are fundamentally *unnatural* settings.

One way in which observational settings differ from one another is in terms of the degree of structure imposed by the researchers on people's activities in the setting. In participant and unobtrusive observation, people are usually left to behave as they wish, with little interference from the researcher. Experimental observation, on the other hand, especially that done in contrived settings, is a more systematic observation in which researchers assign people very precise tasks to accomplish. Normally, the degree of structure imposed is greater in hypothesis-testing research and less in exploratory research. An exception to this is focus group research, which is often exploratory in nature but yet imposes at least a moderate degree of structure on the behavior of the participants. Whatever their specific form, all observational techniques raise certain issues that must be addressed by the researchers.

Issues in Observation

Because human perceptions are limited and frail—recall Alice's view of the Looking-glass House—observational research needs to be conducted in a way that reduces misperception and increases the accuracy of the data. We address problems of accuracy in terms of four issues: recording observations, sampling, the validity and reliability of observations, and the problem of reactivity.

Recording Observations

The manner in which observations are recorded depends in part on whether observations are primarily quantitative or qualitative in nature. Quantitative observation typically calls for more structured recording of data on *coding sheets,* whereas qualitative observation may use less-structured *field notes.*

Coding Sheets Observational research often involves a process of **coding,** or categorizing behaviors into a limited number of categories. To do this, one should specify as clearly as possible the behaviors to be observed or counted during data collection. When this can be done, the use of coding sheets is desirable. A *coding sheet* is simply a form designed to facilitate categorizing and counting of behaviors. For example, a typical coding sheet would have a listing of various behaviors with blanks following them in which the behaviors could be checked as they occur. If duration of a behavior is also important, additional blanks would be provided to record the timing of the behaviors.

The code sheet for a particular research project is likely to be a unique and highly specific document that reflects the special concerns of that project. Nevertheless, a number of coding schemes have sufficient generality that they can be useful in a number of different settings. For example, one coding scheme that has been applied to a diversity of research projects was developed by the sociologist Robert F. Bales (1952) to study the elements of social interaction in small, face-to-face groups. As can be seen in Figure 9.1, Bales's categories are very specific and behavioral: They refer to behaviors that the coder is to look for, such as "jokes," "laughs," "concurs," "withholds help," and the like. Bales's coding categories emerged from his operationalization of social processes and interactional strategies common to all groups. Bales argues that all behavior in groups can be classified as relating to either

task issues (instrumental or goal-oriented behavior) or social–emotional issues (behavior relating to the expression of feelings or the integration of motivations). Furthermore, all groups must contend with six separate problem areas in accomplishing these task and social-emotional goals (listed at the bottom of Figure 9.1). With this coding scheme, a profile of any group can be developed in relation to these issues and processes.

Table 9.1 presents a coding scheme, with similarities to that of Bales, that was used in a study of group work among institutionalized elderly. The goal of the research was to devise and evaluate intervention strategies that would increase people's participation in group activity. At each group meeting, two observers sat adjacent to the group where they could observe interaction without interfering with the group (a modified form of nonparticipant observation). Each observer had a stopwatch and a coding sheet (*see* Figure 9.2). Behaviors were recorded on the coding sheet at one-minute intervals for the group members and at one-half-minute intervals for the group worker who led each group. In this fashion, the researchers developed a running account of the verbal and nonverbal interaction between group members and group workers. The effect of various strategies by the group worker, such as directing questions at individuals or using tangible rewards for specific behaviors, could then be measured in terms of changes in interaction patterns. The parallels between Bales's and Linsk's categories should be clear: Linsk's categories of "questions," "statements," "positive comments," and "negative comments" are virtually identical to Bales's categories of "asks for orientation," "gives orientation," "shows solidarity," and "shows antagonism," respectively. This illustrates the utility of examining existing general coding schemes to determine whether they can be used directly or modified to serve one's purposes.

The development of an efficacious coding scheme requires considerable care. The coding categories should derive from the hypotheses being tested in the research. In the Linsk study, the researchers' concern was with the nature and quality of verbal and nonverbal interaction in a group, and the categories chosen reflect that focus. In addition,

Problem Areas: **Observation Categories:**

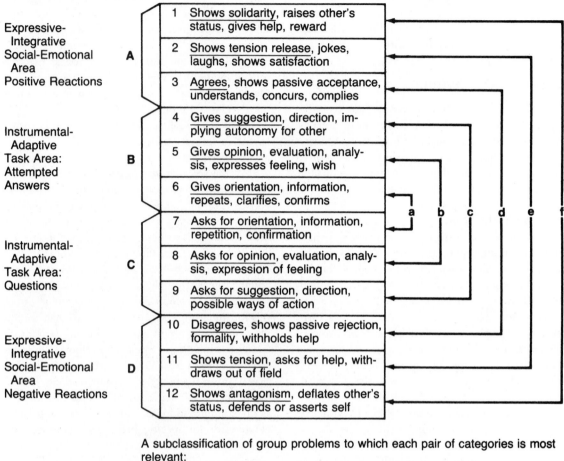

A subclassification of group problems to which each pair of categories is most relevant:

a Problems of orientation   d Problems of decision
b Problems of evaluation   e Problems of tension-management
c Problems of control   f Problems of integration

Figure 9.1   Categories for the Observation of Social Interaction

Source   From Robert F. Bales, "Some Uniformities of Behavior in Small Social Systems," in *Readings in Social Psychology,* edited by Guy E. Swanson, Theodore Newcomb, and Eugene L. Hartley. Copyright © 1952 by Henry Holt and Co.; © renewed 1980 by Holt, Rinehart and Winston. Reprinted by permission of the publisher.

coding categories should be highly specific and behavioral. The degree to which this can be achieved is obviously limited because overspecificity would become cumbersome and meaningless. For example, in Linsk's study, a category of "speaks" would be too general because it does not inform us of the type of verbal contribution the person makes. At the other extreme, a category such as "raises eyebrows" is so specific that we cannot determine the meaning of the behavior. It is essential to walk a fine line between being too specific and too general—providing a coding scheme that enables

Table 9.1 Behavioral Definitions and Symbols Used to Record Data

Behavior	Recording Symbols*	Definition
—*Social Group Worker Behaviors*—		
Questions	G, I	Verbal behavior that demands or suggests a response from one or more group members, indicated by words that suggest a question (i.e., why, how) or a direct request or demand for a response.
Statements	G, I	Verbal behavior that gives information and does not call for a response from group members and is not a direct consequence of a previous behavior of individual or group of residents. Includes reading to residents.
Positive Comments	G, I	Verbal behavior that followed the behavior of one or more group members and relates to this behavior to encourage similar responses. Suggests recognition, approval, or praise.
Negative Comments	G, I	Verbal behavior that followed the behavior of one or more group members and relates to this behavior to discourage similar responses. Suggests disapproval or displeasure.
Listening	✓	Silence on the part of the worker either while a group member verbalizes or while waiting for resident response in the absence of other worker behavior.
Demonstration/ Participation	✓	Demonstrating equipment or activity or participating in activity.
Attending to External Events	✓	Watching, listening to, or talking to a stimulus outside of the activity.
—*Group Member Behaviors*—		
Appropriate Verbal Behavior	◯	Verbal behavior related to current group task (subject under discussion, activity, or relating to activity stimuli, e.g., phonograph recording).
Verbal Behavior Related to Environment	◯	Verbal behavior related to another person present at activity or related to the room or other aspects of the environment, but not related to the current group task.
Inappropriate Verbal Behavior	⊘	Verbal behavior that does not relate to group task or other residents or staff present or the environment. Verbalizations not audible to the entire group or observers.
Appropriate Attention	△	Visual or apparent listening attention, indicated by head orientation or other observable response, that is directed toward social worker, a resident who is making or has just made an appropriate verbal response, or activity stimulus.
Appropriate Activity	☐	Manipulating equipment related to activity as worker has demonstrated or similar appropriate use, helping another resident to do so, nodding or head-shaking appropriately, raising hand for recognition.
Inappropriate Activity	╱	Repetitive actions, aggressive actions, manipulating materials not related to group task or activity stimuli, leaving activity, sleeping, talking to oneself, any attention directed away from worker, group task, activity stimuli, or a resident making a verbal response.

*Questions, statements, and comments were judged as to whether directed to an individual (I) or to the group (G).

Source Adapted from N. Linsk, M. W. Howe, and E. M. Pinkston, "Behavioral Group Work in a Home for the Aged." Copyright © 1975, National Association of Social Workers, Inc. Reprinted with permission from *Social Work,* Vol. 20, No. 6 (November 1975), p. 456, Fig.1; p. 457, Fig. 2.

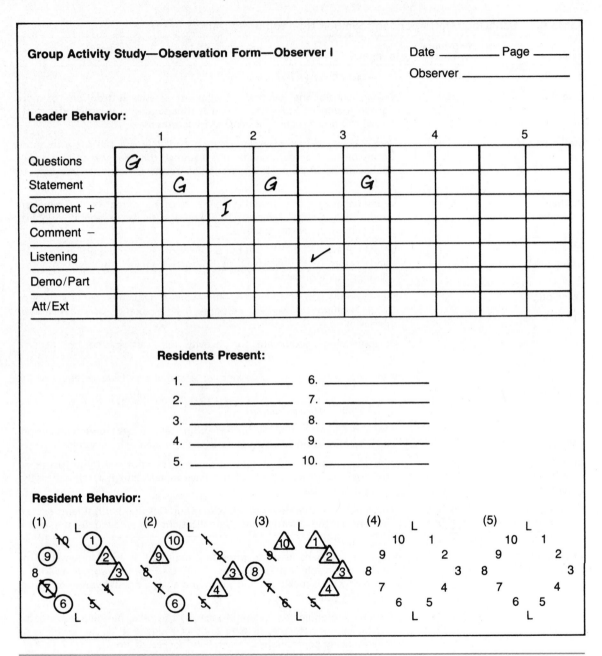

Figure 9.2   Sample Observation Form (Used to Record Data During 3-Minute Observation Periods at Group Meetings)

Source   From N. Linsk, M. W. Howe, and E. M. Pinkston, "Behavioral Goup Work in a Home for the Aged." Copyright © 1975 by National Association of Social Workers, Inc. Reprinted with permission from *Social Work,* Vol. 20, No. 6 (November 1975), Fig. 1, p. 456; Fig. 2, p. 457.

us to answer our research questions. It is important to recognize that, although coding behavior with such schemes may appear quantifiable and objective, a considerable degree of subjective interpretation is involved. The coder must decide, for example, whether a given response is positive or negative and shows solidarity or antagonism, and these judgments are necessarily subjective.

The use of coding schemes is not limited to situations in which a group is small, well organized, or engaging in highly structured behavior. If it is possible to specify concepts and hypotheses very precisely—in other words, if the research is clearly hypothesis testing rather than exploratory—then it may be possible to develop a precise coding scheme for data collection. In their disguised observation study of alcohol-related aggression, Kathryn Graham and colleagues (1980) were able to do this. Their basic hypothesis was that aggressive behavior among men when they drink is due to situational factors as much as to psychological predispositions toward violence. They hypothesized that aversive stimuli in bars (their independent variable) serve as cues that allow or encourage aggressive behavior (the dependent variable). The dependent variable was coded by using a dichotomous coding scheme: nonphysical aggression (swearing or other forms of abusive language) and physical aggression. Within the physical category, behavior was coded as physical threats or challenges to fight but no actual contact, aggressive but noninjurious physical contact (for example, grabbing and pushing), and actual physical violence (punching and kicking).

The independent variable—situational factors eliciting aggression—was, needless to say, more complex to code. First, the researchers spent some weeks in the field observing and developing precise definitions and coding schemes for the situational variables. Here are a few of the coding categories they developed:

location: 1 = downtown bar
2 = suburban bar
time of day: 1 = 9 A.M. to noon
2 = noon to 3 P.M.
3 = 3 P.M. to 6 P.M.
and so on

noise level: 1 = very quiet
2 = medium quiet
3 = medium loud
4 = loud
sexual bodily contact: 1 = none, very casual
2 = discreet necking
3 = heavy necking, touching
4 = flagrant fondling
friendliness to strangers: 1 = open, lots of conversation with strangers
2 = closed, people talk only to members of their own group

Each two-person observation team would spend from 2 to $2\frac{1}{2}$ hours in an establishment. Most recording of observations was done after leaving the establishment so that note taking would not attract attention.

This unobtrusive observation illustrates the manner in which a precise, quantifiable coding scheme can be used in field observation if the hypotheses to be tested are sufficiently developed. The investigators also found, however, that it was useful to collect qualitative data because, while they were in the field, more variables of importance began to emerge. The investigators decided that coding, although the major form of data collection, was not sufficient by itself. They found it useful to record descriptive accounts of aggressive incidents in order to ensure a complete record.

Coding schemes can become highly complex, involving many categories of behavior, timing of the behaviors, measures of intensity, and the like. However, more complex coding schemes can be used only in situations where it is possible to record accurately all that is necessary. Linsk's study of a single, small, task-oriented group enabled the use of a complicated coding scheme. In Graham's study, this would have been considerably more difficult, for the group (the clientele of a bar) was large and shifting in composition, much was going on, and actual recording had to be reserved until after the observation was concluded. This

Research in Practice 9.2
Assessment of Client Functioning: Home Observation of Marital Conflicts

The ability to negotiate conflict is crucial to a satisfying marital relationship. Because most marital therapists readily agree on this principle, the process of communication in marital disputes is considered a prime area of research for the advancement of intervention techniques. Therapists want to better understand not merely the explicit messages that marital partners send but also the process by which messages are sent and what implicit messages are received by the partner as well.

Direct observation of marital conflict would clearly be the ideal method for the study of such a topic because the complexities and subtle nuances of communication and interpersonal conflict cannot be captured by a questionnaire or interview. Obtaining access to real marital disputes, however, is fraught with logistical and ethical problems. Consequently, the closest that researchers have generally come to actual observation of conflict has been through simulated conflicts in laboratory settings and discussions of real-life conflicts in office settings.

However ideal the laboratory might be for control of extraneous variables, it is clearly an artificial setting in which to study real-life conflict processes. In actual conflicts in the home, couples may move about, leave one room and enter another, or withdraw from the conflict entirely. Objects such as a light left on or behaviors such as failing to close a door may stimulate conflict when a couple confronts them within the context of their own home. Most of these natural elements that might play a part in conflict processes are absent in the lab. In a laboratory study, couples might be asked to discuss a conflict for a set period of

time. This may be very foreign to the way many couples actually feud. Moreover, laboratory experiments often involve discussion of broad issues such as household management. At home, conflicts flare up around specific instances of management like, "Who left that pile of dirty dishes in the sink again?" As one illustration of the different results that can come from these research settings, previous research has concluded that studies of conflict in the laboratory tend to underestimate negative interaction patterns that are found in conflicts in the home (Gottman, 1979).

In order to study conflict under more realistic conditions, while retaining as much experimental control as possible, one group of researchers tried home observation of conflict (Margolin, Burman, and John, 1989). Their study evaluated intrapersonal and interpersonal factors associated with constructive versus destructive modes of handling marital conflict. They designed a study wherein the subjects permitted the researchers and a video camera to come into their own homes and observe them as they reenacted actual conflicts. The researchers recruited potential subjects by means of radio and newspaper announcements and through talks with community groups in the Los Angeles area. These efforts generated more than 500 inquiries, of which 73 actually completed the project.

The researchers were interested in comparing couples with differing conflict styles: couples who on occasion resort to physical aggression (PA); couples whose predominant pattern is verbal aggression (VA); couples who generally withdraw (WI); and couples who are nondistressed with low

research setting necessitated a simpler coding scheme. Furthermore, investigations using complex coding schemes that require intense concentration on the part of the observer often require a number of observers, each of whom records

for a short period and then is relieved by another observer. This reduces error due to observer fatigue or fluctuations in concentration. In some investigations, group behavior is recorded on videotape in order to reduce error and to allow researchers to

levels of conflict (ND). In order to determine which style each couple had, couples completed the Didactic Adjustment scale and the Conflict Tactics scale.

The in-home observation was the fifth session of a five-session project, with the four previous sessions taking place in a laboratory setting. For the in-home session, each spouse first worked independently with one of two researchers. The spouse was instructed to choose a typical serious conflict and to think about how the conflict begins, who does and says what, what room they are in, and how the conflict progresses and ends. The two researchers and both spouses then reconvened to reenact the selected conflicts. During these reenactments, the experimenter remained in the room to ask occasional clarifying questions or to keep the process moving but attempted to avoid influencing the substance of the conflict.

The resulting videotape record of the conflicts was evaluated using a coding system that evaluated behavioral, cognitive, and affective dimensions of marital interaction. The system contained 59 items derived from a review of the marital interaction literature and the experimenter's experience. Each of the items was rated on a six-point scale from (0) "not at all present" to (5) "highly representative." Each conflict was divided into three equal time segments, and three independent coders rated each spouse for each of the three segments. Coders were randomly assigned to each tape, and they did not know which group the couple had been assigned to. The 59 items were organized into seven scales that measured these dimensions of the spouses' behavior: Overt Hostility, Patronizing, Warmth, Problem Solve, Uninvolved, Despair, and Defensive. These behaviors were measured for each participant at the beginning, middle, and ending phases of the conflicts.

One of the main findings of the study was that PA couples exhibit more overtly hostile behaviors than do VA or WI couples. Furthermore, PA husbands, as compared to VA and WI husbands, tend to become more defensive and uninvolved toward the end of discussion. PA spouses were found to accelerate their use of patronizing behaviors and failed to show increased problem solving commensurate with other groups. The researchers noted that PA husbands differed from VA and WI husbands, but that PA wives did not appear different from their counterparts in other groups. PA husbands were described as appearing "to flail about in a sea of overt hostility present through the conversation, and after exhausting all other resources, finally withdraw and fall into despair" (Margolin, Burman, and John, 1989, p. 14).

The researchers suggest that further research be done in conjunction with the issue of violence against women. Given the patterns in their data, they hypothesize that violence may occur because PA husbands, having problem-solving deficiencies, rely on defensive and withdrawal strategies that are not very effective in the long run. Because these strategies do not lead to resolution of conflicts, PA husbands may then resort to physical aggression.

This study shows the versatility of observational methods. Although a quasi-laboratory study, the researchers used in-home observation to capture the realism of an important clinical topic. The study also illustrates the use of a fairly precise and highly quantified coding scheme to transform the videotape data into a quantifiable form. Thus, although observational research is often considered most appropriate for exploratory studies, it may also be the method of choice for studies such as the one described here, where variables were quite specific and where a fairly extensive theory base already existed.

view the group as often as needed to code behavior properly. In developing a coding scheme, in short, one must make sure that the scheme does not become more complex than is usable, given the resources at hand. Research in Practice 9.2 presents an observational study that used a number of coding schemes.

Coding schemes are not appropriate forms of recording observations in all observational research. In some cases, as with exploratory research, hypotheses cannot be developed with sufficient precision to make possible the operationalizing of concepts. The research is intended to explore and discover rather than explain and predict. In other cases, the hypotheses involve variables and relationships that require considerable interpretive effort on the part of the observer in the field and cannot easily be condensed to a few coding categories. In still other cases, the complexity and lack of structure in the group being observed render coding schemes useless. When these considerations lead to the conclusion that coding schemes are not appropriate, the investigator is likely to turn to field notes as a means of recording observations.

Field Notes   Detailed, descriptive accounts of the observations made during a given period are called **field notes.** Whereas the precise nature of field notes varies greatly from one study to another, all field notes should include five elements (Bogdan and Taylor, 1975; Lofland and Lofland, 1984):

1. A *running description* makes up the bulk of the field notes and is pretty much self-explanatory. It is simply the record of the day's observations. The primary concern of the running description is to record accurately the concrete events that are observed. The observer should avoid *analyzing* persons or events while in the field because there is not the time and it will interfere with observation of the ongoing scene. Instead, one should concentrate on faithfully recording what occurs.

2. Field notes also include *accounts of previous episodes that were forgotten or went unnoticed* but were remembered while the investigator was still in the field. When the field notes from any observation session are being prepared, it is likely that certain events may be forgotten and left out. During subsequent observations, events may transpire that bring the forgotten episodes back to mind. These events should be recorded when remembered, with the proper notation concerning when they originally occurred.

3. *Analytical ideas and inferences* refer to spur-of-the-moment ideas concerning such things as data analysis, important variables, speculation regarding causal sequences, and the like. "Flashes of insight" regarding any aspect of the study should be recorded when they occur. Reviewing these ideas after the completion of observations can be of great benefit to the final data analysis and writing of the report. Although most data analysis will be reserved until after the observation period is over, you would not want to forget whatever analytical ideas occurred to you while in the field.

4. *Personal impressions and feelings* should be noted, for the possibility for bias to color one's observations is always present. Recording personal impressions and feelings helps to minimize this bias by giving a sense of the perspective from which the observer is viewing various persons, places, or events. Does the observer just plain dislike a certain person in the setting who is being observed? If so, the observer should honestly record such a feeling when it first occurs. This can prove beneficial when reviewing accounts relating to this person to see if one's personal feelings may have influenced the description.

5. *Notes for further information* are notes observers write to and for themselves: plans for future observations, specific things or persons to look for, and the like. It is risky to rely on memory for anything important relating to the study.

Recording field notes is particularly problematic for participant observers whose status as observer is disguised. Because such observers must constantly guard against having their true identity revealed, note taking must be accomplished surreptitiously. In some settings, a bit of ingenuity on the part of the researcher can handle the problem quite nicely. For example, in her study of people's behavior in bars, Sheri Cavan (1966) solved the note-taking problem by making frequent trips to the rest room and recording her observations there. Given the well-recognized effect of alcoholic beverages on the human body, her trips probably raised little suspicion among the other bar patrons. The study mentioned earlier conducted by researchers who were admitted as patients to mental hospitals found another wrinkle on note taking in participant observation: They could take notes openly because the staff defined note taking as the meaningless activities of people who were "crazy" (Rosenhan, 1973).

In many participant observation settings, no amount of innovation will allow the researcher to record observations on the scene. In these situations, there is no alternative but to wait and record observations after one has left the observational setting. Relying on memory in this fashion is less than desirable because memory is quite fallible. The observer should record observations as soon as possible to minimize the likelihood of forgetting important episodes.

What to Record For someone who has never conducted participant observation research, collecting data through field notes can be a particularly frustrating and confusing affair. What to watch for? What to include in the field notes? These can be very difficult questions even for veteran observers. In addition, because participant observation research may be exploratory, one is often only partially aware of what might be relevant. It is possible, nevertheless, to organize one's thoughts around some general categories of things to be observed and recorded (Sellitz et al., 1976; Runcie, 1980):

1. *The setting:* Field notes should contain some description of the general physical and social setting being observed. Is it a bar, restaurant, or ward of a mental institution? Are there any physical objects or barriers that might play a role in the social interaction in the setting? Bogdan and Taylor (1975) suggest beginning each day's field notes with a drawing of the physical layout being observed. Such things as time of day, weather, or the presence of others who are not the focus of your observations might be useful information in some field research. In short, the field notes should serve to remind you—when you review them weeks, months, or years later—of the characteristics of the setting in which you observed behavior.

2. *The people:* Field notes should include a physical and social description of the main characters who are the focus of your observations. How many people? How are they dressed? What are their ages, genders, and socioeconomic characteristics (as well as you can observe from physical appearance)? Again, field notes should tell you, for each separate day of observation, who was present, who entered and left the setting during observation, and how the cast changed from one day to the next.

3. *Individual behavior:* The central observations in most studies are the behaviors of the people in the settings. How do people relate to one another? Who talks to whom, and in what fashion? What sequences of behavior occur? In addition, you may want to record the duration and the frequency of interaction among people. Are there repetitive cycles of behavior that occur? Is there a particular sequencing of behavior?

4. *Group behavior:* In some cases, the behavior of groups may be an important bit of information. How long does a group of people remain on the scene? How does one group relate to another? It might, for example, be useful to know what cliques have formed in a setting.

It should be clear that an enormous amount of information might be gathered in any setting. In addition, the more exploratory the research, the more information must be recorded because it is more difficult to be sure what is relevant. With experience in the field and the development of more narrowly focused hypotheses, it is often possible to reduce the amount of information collected.

Time Sampling

Many observational strategies involve the continual recording of observations throughout the length of the study. Participant observers record things as they happen, and more systematic observers mark coding schemes for as long as an interchange or social setting persists. However, in some situations continuous data collection is costly and unnecessary. In addition, as we discussed with other forms of sampling in Chapter 6, it is often not necessary to collect data from *all* elements of a population. In studies of child development, for example, it may not be necessary to record all that occurs during an hour, a day, or a week. Instead, we can gather valid data through **time sampling,** or making observations only during certain selected time periods (Irwin and Bushnell, 1980). For example, if one were doing an observational study of adolescents in a group home, the prime hours for observation would be those when the residents are most likely to be at the home, such as weekdays from 3:00 P.M. until lights out at 11:00 P.M. (40 hours per week) and Saturdays and Sundays from 7:00 A.M. until 11:00 P.M. (32 hours per week). The researcher could construct a sampling frame comprised of a weekly list of these 72 one-hour time segments and then select a random sample of these elements. To be sure that both weekdays and weekends are included, one might specify 8 hours during the week and 4 hours from the weekend. The resulting sample of 12 one-hour time segments would provide sufficient time coverage for observation while reducing biases that might occur if, say, all observations were made on weekdays after 8:00 P.M. when many youths would be tired at the end of the day.

When conducting time sampling, there are some guidelines to keep in mind (Suen and Ary, 1986). The length of each time-sampling interval and the distance between intervals depend on the nature of the behaviors being observed: They should occur with sufficient frequency that they are likely to be seen during the sampled time periods. Very infrequent behaviors might call for continual observations. The more frequently a behavior occurs, the smaller the number of intervals that will need to be sampled. Furthermore, the time interval should be long enough for the behavior to occur and for the observer to make whatever recordings are called for.

Many of the considerations in time sampling are like the issues in sampling subjects or respondents as discussed in Chapter 6. If the primary concern of the researcher is to be assured of observing *some* occurrences of the behavior under study, it is advisable to use the equivalent of a purposive sample. For example, in studying domestic violence, a researcher would want to observe instances of family quarreling. Doing observations at mealtime would be one way to increase the probability of

witnessing the desired events. On the other hand, if the researcher is concerned with accurately estimating the frequency of occurrence of a particular event or with studying the pattern of responses over a time period, it would be necessary to use the equivalent of a probability sample. For example, in observing nursing home residents for frequency of contacts with nonresidents, the week could be divided into hourly segments, and a random selection of hours could then be used as the basis for doing the observations.

Particularly when the observation process is highly complex and difficult to sustain for long periods of time, some form of time sampling can be of considerable help in improving the quality of data collected.

Validity and Reliability

Observational techniques, like other forms of data collection, need to be assessed in terms of how valid and reliable they are (Kirk and Miller, 1986). Observation rests on human sense organs and human perceptions—both of which are notoriously fallible. Just as Alice had difficulty perceiving the Looking-glass House, we have profound problems in perceiving the world around us. This is an especially difficult and insidious problem because we are so often totally unaware of the ways in which our senses and our perspective can lead us to misperceive situations. Especially with observational methods, people are inclined to resolutely say, "I was there. I saw it. I comprehend what was going on." Yet, as any trial lawyer will readily attest, eyewitnesses are often very unreliable spectators to events, and considerable experimental evidence indicates that firsthand accounts of events are often partially inaccurate (Buckhout, 1974). Given these problems, we need to consider the validity and reliability of observations carefully.

Little question exists that observational techniques have greater face validity as measures of behavior and events than do many techniques that rely on secondhand accounts. Surveys or questionnaires depend on someone else's perception and recollection, which can be shaped and clouded by many factors beyond the control of the researcher. Observational techniques, on the other hand, provide firsthand accounts of occurrences under conditions that are partially controlled by the investigator. Misperception may still occur, of course, but the researcher is in a position to recognize its impact and possibly control its magnitude. For these reasons, observation is considered to have greater face validity than many other data collection techniques.

As shown in Chapter 5, it is sometimes possible to measure the validity of an instrument through such means as correlating the results of the instrument with the results achieved by some other instrument known to measure the variable validly. When such direct measures of validity are not possible in observational research, it is helpful to evaluate the observational efforts in terms of factors that might work to *reduce* validity:

1. If the people being observed do not have *anonymity,* their behavior may not be a true reflection of how they behave normally. Especially when controversial, sensitive, or potentially embarrassing issues are investigated, validity will decline substantially if anonymity has not been ensured. For this reason, hidden or disguised observation and observation in which the researcher takes the complete participant role are more valid than other types of observation.
2. Our perceptions are drastically shaped by our *expectations or lack of them.* If we expect something to occur, we are much more likely to observe it—whether it actually occurs or not. If we expect welfare recipients to be lazy, then we will be acutely aware of all those behaviors among welfare recipients that seem to indicate laziness. Thus, validity of observations will be reduced to the extent that our expectations—whether recognized or not—mold our perceptions. On the other side of the coin, a lack of expectations may lead us to miss something of importance in a setting. This is especially a problem in participant observation research that is characterized by a lack of structure and organization.
3. Validity of observations is also influenced by *the condition of the observer.* Hunger, fatigue, stress, or personal problems can lead to very distorted perceptions and interpretations. Likewise, physical characteristics, such as the lighting in an establishment, may lead to invalid observations. (This is another good reason for keeping complete field notes—field conditions affecting validity can be assessed at a later point.) If a number of these conditions exist, it may be judicious to terminate observation and resume when conditions are more favorable.

Although many of the conditions influencing validity may be beyond the control of the investigator, it is important to assess their impact on the research honestly so that accurate appraisal of the results can be made.

Of course, a number of guides can be used to determine how confident we are of the validity of our results. First, some of the ways of assessing validity discussed in Chapter 5 can be adapted for use with observational techniques. For example, criterion validity might be assessed by comparing the results we achieve through observation with the results gained from other methods, such as surveys or experiments. If the various methodologies yield the same conclusions, then we have greater confidence that our observations have validity.

Second, the behavior of the people being observed may offer some hint as to how valid the observations are. If they engage in actions that are illegal or deviant or that might result in sanctions if publicly known, then you can assume that their behavior is an honest reflection of how they would act were you not present. In a study of police officers in a juvenile division, for example, Irving Piliavin and Scott Briar (1964, p. 207) made this argument:

> While these data do not lend themselves to quantitative assessments of reliability and validity, the candor shown by the officers in their interviews with the investigators and their use of officially frowned upon practices while under observation provide some assurance that their behavior accurately reflects the typical operations and attitudes of the law-enforcement personnel studied.

Likewise, in his study of a sexually transmitted disease clinic, Joseph Sheley (1976, p. 116) argued that the validity of his data was quite strong because "staff members dropped their professional masks and displayed quite unprofessional behavior and ideas in the company of the researcher." Under such conditions, you can assume that people are reacting to environmental stimuli that normally guide their behavior rather than shaping a performance for the benefit of the investigator.

Assessing the reliability of observational research may be quite easy and straightforward or impossible, depending on the type of observation employed. In the case of an individual researcher who is studying a single group or setting through participant observation, there is no practical way to assess reliability (Kirk and Miller, 1986). When observations are more structured, as when using a coding scheme, reliability can be readily assessed through tests of *intercoder reliability,* or the ability of observers to code behaviors consistently into the same categories of the coding scheme. Two or more observers code the same behavior, and the resulting codes are correlated to determine the degree of agreement between them. For example, in their study of barroom aggression, Graham and her colleagues (1980) did this by correlating the coding results from the two observers who visited each bar. They achieved reliabilities ranging from $r = .57$ to $r = .99$. Many experts suggest that structured observation should achieve an intercoder reliability of $r = .75$ or better (Bailey, 1987).

Reactivity

A major concern in any research is **reactivity,** or the degree to which the presence of the researcher influences what is being observed (Webb et al., 1981). To take an extreme example, suppose a researcher enters a group for the purpose of studying it through participant observation. Suppose, in addition, that the researcher takes a very active role in the group's proceedings by talking a great deal, offering suggestions, and the like. It should be clear that an observer behaving in this fashion will exert considerable influence on what occurs in the group, making the observer's presence highly reac-

tive. This affects the validity of the observations because you do not know whether you have measured the group's *natural* activities or their *reactions* to the observer. One is never sure if events very different from those observed may have taken place had the observation been conducted in a less reactive manner. Reactivity also relates to the generalizability of findings. If the observer's presence is reactive, it is difficult to generalize findings to similar groups which have not had an observer in attendance.

It is generally agreed that participant observation generates the best results when reactivity is kept to a minimum. This is a major argument in favor of the complete participant role, where the observer's true status is concealed (Johnson and Bolstad, 1973). It is logical to assume that a group will be less affected by observation if they are unaware of the observer's role-as-observer than if they are aware. Using the complete participant role will not, however, guarantee a lack of reactivity. The role must be played properly. The complete participant should play as passive a role in the group as possible without raising suspicion. Even when the beginning of an observational study is accomplished without undue reactivity, the researcher must be careful that reactivity does not increase during the course of the project. Such a situation occurred in a study of a group that had predicted the end of the world (Festinger, Riecken, and Schachter, 1956). On numerous occasions, situations arose that forced the observers to become active participants to the point where subsequent group activity was influenced by their actions.

Human service workers should be aware that reactivity is a problem that is confronted more frequently than just when they are conducting formalized observational research. Practitioners are routinely called on to make intervention decisions based on observational data. For example, a home visit may be called for in a case of suspected child neglect. The worker's presence during the home visit will undoubtedly cause a change in the interactional patterns of the family. The realization that their child-rearing practices are under scrutiny will likely place all family members on their best behavior during the visit. An appreciation for the reactivity of such a visit might help the practitioner avoid making an erroneous decision.

Observational Research on Minority Populations

In the previous chapter, we noted that the use of available data was good for studying sensitive topics because it minimizes the problem of reactivity. The same can be said for the use of some observational techniques, especially unobtrusive observation. Studies of the extent of racism in the United States, for example, have often relied on survey research, and the findings have shown a considerable decline in racism over the years, particularly in the late 1960s and 1970s (Crosby, Bromley, and Saxe, 1980). However, these surveys have been criticized on the grounds that they reflect not an actual decline in racist attitudes but rather a change in the social atmosphere, so that it is frowned on to *express* prejudice or racism overtly. To get around this problem of reactivity, some researchers have used unobtrusive observations to measure racism.

One approach has been to present people with the opportunity to assist someone who is obviously in need of help and then measure how much or what kind of help is proferred. These studies are often conducted in field settings with the subjects unaware that they are part of a research project. The help needed might be to pick up some groceries that have been dropped, to give spare change to a panhandler, or to contribute money to a charity. The race of the person needing help is varied in order to see whether African Americans receive less or more assistance than do whites (virtually all of these studies are of racism directed toward either African Americans or whites). Then, the extent and type of help offered is noted by the researcher unbeknownst to the subject. These studies suggest strongly that prejudicial attitudes are more common among Americans than the surveys would indicate and that Americans express those prejudices when there are few negative consequences to doing so.

Other unobtrusive studies of racism have used willingness to exhibit aggression as a measure of prejudice and discrimination. For example, subjects might be asked to give a person a series of electrical shocks as a part of an alleged experiment on learning. While no one actually receives any shocks, the subjects are convinced that they will. Then, comparisons can be made of whether more intense or longer shocks are given to African Americans than whites. These studies again find antiblack hostility to be pervasive but subtle.

An overall assessment concluded that "discriminatory behavior (among Americans) is more prevalent in the body of unobtrusive studies than we might expect on the basis of survey data" (Crosby, Bromley, and Saxe, 1980, p. 557). Americans today are more likely to say that they are not prejudiced but then behave in a discriminatory fashion. So it is only by combining survey and observational investigations that we can see this complexity.

The studies just discussed are general assessments of whether racism exists. In applied research, unobtrusive observation is sometimes used to see whether certain groups suffer discrimination in particular social and economic spheres. For example, discrimination in the rental and sale of dwelling units has been studied by sending white, African American, and Hispanic buyers to the same housing unit or realtor, without the renter or seller aware that they are a part of an observational study. They find that African American and Hispanic buyers are charged more for the rental and sale of homes, are more likely to be told an advertised housing unit is not available, and are more likely to be shown units in predominantly minority neighborhoods ("Study Finds Bias . . . ," 1991). The same thing has been done with people negotiating a purchase price for a new automobile. Automobile salespeople, in fact, make significantly lower final offers to white males than they do to white females or African Americans of either sex (Ayres, 1991). So minorities are treated differently, and to their detriment, in some significant social spheres. Undoubtedly, many realtors and salespeople would deny that they are racist or that they treat minorities differently. Unobtrusive observation enables us to get a more valid check on such behavior, although it can't tell us whether the cause of it is racist attitudes or something else.

Assessment of Observational Techniques

As this chapter has shown, observational techniques differ from one another in terms of how qualitative and naturalistic they are. Not surprisingly, the advantages and disadvantages of observational techniques also differ depending on whether they are qualitative versus quantitative and contrived versus naturalistic. The first two advantages described next would apply to all forms of observational research. The remainder of the advantages and disadvantages apply particularly to the more qualitative, naturalistic, or unstructured types of observational research.

Advantages

1. Unlike surveys, which are limited to dealing with verbal statements, observational research can focus on both verbal and nonverbal behavior. This is an advantage because *actual* behavior is being studied in addition to people's *statements* about how they behave. By dealing with behavior, observational research avoids a potential source of error: the gap between what people say they do and what they actually do. The ability of observational techniques to consider both verbal and nonverbal behavior puts the researcher in a better position to link the verbal statements with behavior.
2. Much observational research is longitudinal in nature and thus enables researchers to make statements concerning changes that occur over the time of the research. In addition, by following activities over time, observers will have less trouble establishing the correct causal sequence than would be the case with surveys. As noted in Chapter 2, establishing the causal order with survey data can at times be difficult.
3. The advantage most often claimed for observational research is that it provides deeper and more insightful data than those generated by most other methods. Especially with participant observation, researchers immerse themselves in

the daily activities of those studied to a greater degree than with other techniques. This places them in a position to gain information that would likely be missed with techniques such as a questionnaire or interview. This is especially so for the complete participant who, as an accepted member of the group, sees people behaving freely and naturally, unaware that they are being studied. The interviewer may generate socially acceptable responses and a carefully orchestrated presentation of self. The participant observer, however, is better able to go beyond these public fronts and penetrate the nether regions of human behavior.
4. Observational research is capable of studying groups and behavior that would be closed to other forms of research. Many studies cited in this chapter involve groups that, for various reasons, would not be open to research by other methods. They may have something to hide, or they may view intrusion by a stranger as threatening to their cohesion and values. The ability of the complete participant to conceal his or her identity and conduct research where it could otherwise not be conducted is a major advantage of this observational technique.
5. A frequently overlooked, but nevertheless significant, advantage of observational research is that the most qualified person is often directly involved in the collection of data because the senior researcher is often one of the observers (Denzin, 1989). This is very different from surveys, for example, in which the project director may rarely conduct interviews, leaving this to part-time interviewers hired for the job. This places the most knowledgeable person the farthest from the data collection effort.

Disadvantages

Most of the disadvantages of observational research relate to the more qualitative, naturalistic, and unstructured types. With less structure, the quality of the results of an observational study depends heavily on the individual skills of the researcher, and this leads to several criticisms.

1. A nagging concern with participant observation research has always been the possible effect of observer bias on the results. Such research does not have the structured tools of other methods that help ensure objectivity. If researchers are not careful, personal attitudes and values can distort research findings, rendering them virtually useless for scientific purposes.

2. Closely related to the issue of observer bias is the problem of the observer overidentifying with those who are studied (Shupe and Bromley, 1980). As the observer frequently becomes a part of a group for a substantial period of time, this possibility is quite real. Overidentification with subjects was first noted in anthropology, which contains much observational research, and was given the label "going native." Going native and allowing the research to deteriorate into a propaganda piece for the group studied can surely have as disastrous results for the utility of a study as would observer bias.

3. The lack of structure also makes exact replication—an important part of scientific research—virtually impossible. Observational studies are often such individualized projects that the possibility for exact replication is slight. Any observer in a natural setting will be forced to record what occurs selectively owing to sheer volume. There is little chance that a replication attempt would select precisely the same aspects of a given setting on which to focus.

4. The nature of the data gathered in some observational research makes them very difficult to quantify. We noted that some participant observers generate field notes that are basically rambling descriptions. Data in this form are quite difficult to code or categorize in summary form. This makes traditional hypothesis testing exceedingly problematic. As a result, many observational studies fail to get beyond a description of the setting observed.

5. Although unrelated to its lack of structure, the ethics of participant observation have been called into question by some critics, with the complete participant role generating the most controversy. Some social scientists see it as unethical to conceal one's identity for the purpose of conducting research. The strongest statement against concealed observation is that of Erikson (1967), who completely rejects all field studies that do not inform those being studied in advance. Whether disguised observation is ethical is still an open controversy in the social sciences. As noted in Chapter 3, disguised observation is considered a "questionable practice" that requires approval by an institutional review board. So long as the research is not trivial and the identities of participants are not revealed, disguised observation would likely be allowed.

6. As has been mentioned earlier, participant observation affords the researcher little control over the variables in the setting. A great deal may be occurring, and the researcher will not be in a position to control or moderate these influences. This often leads to situations in which the researcher is at a loss to select the important causal factors in a situation.

7. Because of the physical limitations on the observing capabilities of human beings, a participant observation study will almost certainly study a limited sample of people. Although one could, with a sufficient number of observers, study a large sample, this is rarely done. Observation is more commonly limited to a small group (such as a family or gang) or one setting (such as a bar or restaurant). The explanatory power that comes from a large sample size is, therefore, not available.

Observation in Human Service Practice

Observation is at the foundation of human service practice, and our analysis of scientific observation in this chapter has some important implications for observation in practice settings. Even though the goals of practice and research are somewhat different, some of the observational techniques developed by researchers can be carried over into practice. We will illustrate a few of the lessons to be learned.

1. It is critical for practitioners to realize that the type of observation engaged in affects the kind of information one can gather. Structured observation in a therapeutic setting offers practitioners considerable control over what occurs and comparability of information from one setting to the next. Yet, it is a somewhat artificial setting (from the client's perspective) and may not capture the dynamics of real-life situations as experienced by the client. For this, participant observation would be more valuable.

2. Reactivity is a serious concern in any observation—whether done by a researcher or a practitioner. Human service workers must be sensitive to the extent to which their presence affects, possibly profoundly, the behavior of others. Clients may put their best foot (or their worst foot!) forward when a caseworker is present. The effect may be subtle, and even the client may not be aware of the change. A concern about reactivity may dictate the use of observational techniques that reduce the extent of the problem. One may choose unobtrusive observation or the disguised observer role as a means of reducing the extent of reactivity.

3. Good observational techniques rest on sound methods of recording information. This means that the practitioner should spell out as clearly as possible beforehand the kinds of behaviors that will be observed. The more specificity, the better: "Aggression" is too general; one should plan to look for "hitting, kicking, or verbal insults." Thus, a precise and specific coding scheme is an important tool in both research and practice observation. This leaves fewer decisions to be made during observation when one is likely to be rushed and concerned about other matters.

4. Observation in research and practice have different purposes: The former focuses on hypothesis testing and knowledge accumulation while the latter is intended primarily as a tool for change or amelioration of undesirable conditions. However, as stressed in Chapter 1, practice observations, if done properly, can add to our body of scientific knowledge.

5. Both research and practice observations should be done systematically, which means that certain explicit and publicly agreed upon rules are followed so that others know precisely how the observations were made and could repeat them if desired. At times, departure from a previously established, systematic plan of observation may be called for in practice. As a practitioner–client relationship develops or circumstances change, the intuition of the practitioner may call for such departures in order to maintain progress toward the goals of practice. However, such departures are rarely justified in research and are practically always detrimental to the research process because observations made using different procedures are not comparable.

Main Points

- Observational techniques involve the collection of data through direct visual or auditory experience of behavior.
- *Verstehen* refers to observers' efforts to view and understand a situation from the perspective of the people involved.
- Positivism holds that human behavior should be studied only by objective means.
- A major decision for the participant observer is whether his or her status as observer will be revealed to those studied (participant-as-observer) or will be concealed (complete participant).
- A problem faced by observational researchers is reactivity: the extent to which the observer's presence influences what is observed.
- Unobtrusive measures, including hidden observation, disguised observation, and the analysis of physical traces, are designed to minimize reactivity.
- Coding schemes identify which behaviors are relevant to a study and how they will be recorded.
- Coding sheets contain the categories of the coding scheme and are designed to facilitate the recording process.
- Some participant observers record data as field notes, which are detailed, descriptive accounts of the observations made during a given period.

■ Time sampling is often used in observational research to reduce the volume of observations that have to be made.

■ Validity in observational research means that the observations correctly and accurately reflect reality.

■ Some observational techniques, especially unobtrusive observation, minimize reactivity and are thus good for studying sensitive topics such as racism and sexism.

■ Observational techniques are relevant to both research and practice settings.

Important Terms for Review

coding
field notes
nonreactive observation
observational techniques
participant observation
physical traces
positivism
reactivity
subjectivism
time sampling
unobtrusive observation
verstehen

Exploring the Internet

In seeking additional information on observation as a method of social research, it is a good idea to use such terms as "qualitative methods" and "participant observation" with Internet search engines such as Excite or Infoseek. Although qualitative methods and observation are not synonymous, qualitative researchers do rely heavily on observation as a research strategy, so many Web sites devoted to qualitative research will provide content on observation. One of the better launching points for an exploration of observational methods on the Internet is a site maintained by the School of Social and Systemic Studies at Nova South-

eastern University. One resource available through this site is *The Qualitative Report,* an online journal devoted to qualitative and critical inquiry. One component of this Web site is Qualitative Research Resources on the Internet. This page includes an exhaustive collection of links to qualitative research sites and materials available through the World Wide Web. Papers, dissertations, and syllabi are just some of the useful materials that can be found in the Resources section. To access Qualitative Research Resources on the Internet, point your World Wide Web browser to the following URL:http://www.nova.edu/ssss/QR/qualres.html.

Among the sites included in Qualitative Research Resources on the Internet is the WWW site for QUALIDATA at the University of Essex in England (http://www.essex.ac.uk/qualidata/index.htm). This site provides information relating to qualitative data analysis as well as providing a number of useful links to other social science research resources that include observational methods. In Exploring the Internet in Chapter 8, we listed a number of sources for available data, and from the sites listed there, one might assume that available data means statistical data. However, the Internet can also provide access to qualitative available data based on observation, and QUALIDATA is an excellent example of such a data resource. We suggest that you select the "Background" option at this site to learn more about the idea of making qualitative data available to the research community. Then you might browse through the catalog of archived data sets (QUALICAT) to appreciate the variety of data sets that are available.

For assistance with analysis of qualitative data obtained through observation, Computer Assisted Qualitative Data Systems (CAQDAS) is a worthwhile site to explore (http://www.soc.surrey.ac.uk/caqdas/). In addition to information on computer programs for analyzing data, the site includes an extensive bibliography on qualitative data analysis and links to other sites. Another Web site with an emphasis on qualitative observational research is maintained by the Centre for Applied Research in Education (CARE), a community of researchers

COMPUTERS IN RESEARCH
Collecting Observational Data by Computer

Precise monitoring of client behaviors is a prerequisite for many interventions derived from behavioral theory. Whether serving as a staff member in a residential facility for children, conducting group activities in a day treatment center for the mentally ill, or working with the developmentally disabled in a sheltered workshop, human service practitioners are frequently required to monitor the antecedents, consequences, and frequencies of the behaviors of clients. In the past, practitioners and behavioral researchers had to rely on paper-and-pencil methods to record observations, and these limit the amount and complexity of what can be recorded. Usually, the observer is restricted to using event recording, duration recording, or possibly a time-sampling procedure. But simply counting the frequency of events doesn't necessarily communicate the severity of a problem behavior when duration varies. On the other hand, it is very difficult to keep track of behavior duration if several behaviors are involved. Using manual recording, complex interactions between several behaviors may be impossible to capture because the demands on the recorder prohibit monitoring more than a few behaviors at a time.

Consider, for example, observing how a severely retarded child reacts to demands in a situa-

tion. The criterion or stimulus variable might be an instruction or a demand by a teacher. The response of interest might include the child's compliance, passivity, self-stimulation, aggression, or opposition. Questions to be answered with observational data might be: Does the child comply immediately or use some combination of the response options? What if we also want to know how the number of staff and other children in the room affect the child's behavior? The need to reliably measure such complex behavior chains as well as to keep track of multiple, simultaneous variables has led some human service researchers to develop an innovative computer system for data collection (Repp et al., 1989).

Their data collection system takes advantage of the advent of laptop and notebook computers. The researchers programmed the computer to record three types of entries: identifiers, behavioral data, and field notes. Identifiers include such variables as date, client name, observer name, and time and location. Collecting behavioral data begins by pressing the TAB key, which engages the computer's internal clock. With this feature, whenever a behavior of interest is recorded, the exact time of the observation is automatically recorded too. Self-adhesive labels to designate behaviors of interest

specializing in action research, naturalistic inquiry, evaluation, and the development of new methodologies to study sensitive issues. CARE is based in the School of Education and Professional Development, University of East Anglia in Norwich, United Kingdom, and may be accessed at http://www.uea.ac.uk/care/. The site includes descriptions of projects with which CARE is involved. You can review the descriptions for examples of how qualitative methods are being used in applied research projects in such fields as education and health care.

For Further Reading

Anderson, Elijah. *Streetwise: Race, Class, and Change in an Urban Community.* Chicago: University of Chicago Press, 1990. This is an excellent example of participant observation research in a community setting. In this case, changes in community life are described as the racial and social class composition of a neighborhood changes.

Berg, Bruce L. *Qualitative Research Methods for the Social Sciences,* 2nd ed. Boston: Allyn & Bacon, 1995. Berg provides more detail on the qualitative research methods discussed in this chapter, as well as some

are placed on the letter keys. Some keys are designated as "Event" keys; pressing them once records one event. Others are duration keys, and these are pressed once to indicate the beginning of a behavior and again to show termination. An attractive feature of this system is that the program accepts multiple entries. For example, if a client is rocking and screaming while the teacher is making a demand, each of the three keys (R-rocking, S-screaming, and D-demand) can be engaged concurrently. The data output displays the second at which each category began and ended.

Some data are mutually exclusive. The researchers give the example of the number of staff in the room, which can only be one value at a time such as zero, one, two, or three. A subset of keys is used to designate this variable; pressing any one in the subset automatically terminates the previous value. Thus, if three staff are present and one leaves, pressing the key for two automatically terminates the duration value for three staff. With training, not only can an observer monitor many more behaviors than is feasible with paper-and-pencil monitoring, but also the researcher obtains a much richer data set that can be used to answer questions about complex patterns of behavior.

These researchers employed the computerized data-gathering system in a study of the effects of moving a group of adults from institutions to group homes. The researchers studied behaviors of 19 clients and 9 staff members in these facilities. In addition to finding changes in the clients' engagement in their environments, the researchers were able to study how each staff person provided antecedents and consequences for client behavior. The researchers attribute their ability to monitor the large number of behaviors to the effectiveness of the computer system (Felce, deKock, and Repp, 1986).

Based on their experience with this computerized observation measurement system, the researchers conclude that the computer has two principal advantages. First, it delivers a tremendous savings of time in data gathering over traditional approaches such as time sampling. Second, the system provides a record of each event in sequence so that complex behavior patterns may be analyzed. They report that one can examine an environment of 20 to 30 variables and determine which antecedents, consequences, and setting events predict human behavior. Handling such complexity is the major advantage that they see, and one which should be of great value not only to researchers but to practitioners who are using behavior modification-based interventions. As we have seen with computer-assisted survey research (CASR) and computer-assisted telephone interviewing (CATI) (*see* Chapter 7), computerization not only enables researchers to collect the same data as with traditional methods, but it results in the capacity to investigate different and more complex relationships among variables as well.

others, such as ethnographies, that we have not included.

Denzin, Norman K., and Yvonna S. Lincoln, eds. *Handbook of Qualitative Research.* Thousand Oaks, Calif.: Sage, 1994. This book of readings provides a comprehensive overview of all aspects of qualitative research, including the historical development of the field. It is one of the most complete and authoritative statements about this form of research.

Fielding, Nigel G., and Raymond M. Lee. *Using Computers in Qualitative Research.* Newbury Park, Calif.: Sage, 1991. This book focuses on the ways in which computers can be used in qualitative data collection and analysis, including discussions of software available and how qualitative research might change to adapt to computer capabilities.

Liebow, Elliot. *Tell Them Who I Am.* New York: Free Press, 1993. This book is an observational research account in the genre of *Talley's Corner.* The author carefully documents the patterns and routines of homeless women, showing how they meet their needs and struggle to keep hope and humanity alive.

Marshall, Catherine, and Gretchen B. Rossman. *Designing Qualitative Research.* Newbury Park, Calif.: Sage, 1989. The authors of this book provide a good introduction to qualitative research methods in applied research and policy analysis. Although it emphasizes educational research, the book includes vignettes from other social science and human service areas.

Miles, Matthew B., and A. Michael Huberman. *Qualitative Data Analysis: An Expanded Sourcebook*, 2nd ed. Thousand Oaks, Calif.: Sage, 1994. This is a comprehensive guide to the analysis of data from qualitative observational research. It shows exactly how to do it.

Silverman, David. *Interpreting Qualitative Data*. Newbury Park, Calif.: Sage, 1993. This book discusses the theoretical issues involved in collecting and analyzing data from qualitative research as well as describing some of the particular data collection techniques.

Strauss, Anselm, and Juliet Corbin. *Basics of Qualitative Research: Grounded Theory Procedures and Techniques*. Newbury Park, Calif.: Sage, 1990. This is a good overview of how to do qualitative research.

Tesch, Renata. *Qualitative Research: Analysis Types and Software Tools*. New York: Falmer Press, 1990. This book discusses how to do analysis with qualitative data, documents, and some available data—basically, any data that are not in quantitative form. It also discusses computer software available for such research.

Whyte, William Foote. *Learning From the Field: A Guide From Experience*. Beverly Hills, Calif.: Sage, 1984. A delightful book by one of the premier field researchers in the social sciences. Whyte has used his 50 years of experience in the field to produce a practical and accessible volume on the gamut of issues related to field research.

Williams, Constance C. *Black Teenage Mothers: Pregnancy and Child Rearing From Their Perspective*. New York: Lexington Books, 1991. This book is a fine example of applying the ethnographic approach to the study of a human problem that is of great interest to human service practitioners. It is enlightening for its coverage of a social issue as well as being an example of a research approach.

Exercises for Class Discussion

9.1 A school counselor is asked by a teacher to assist her in controlling the behavior of four boys in her fifth grade class. The teacher complains that the boys "horse around" a great deal. They don't work on their assignments, throw paper wads, disrupt other children, get out of their seats, and make "smart remarks" instead of answering questions. The counselor suggests setting up a behavioral intervention but first wants to observe the class.

a. What problems will the counselor face in doing an observation?

b. One idea is to observe at random intervals throughout the week. Another is to observe for one full morning. What do you think would be the advantages and disadvantages of each approach? Can you think of a better method of time sampling for this situation?

c. Develop a coding sheet that the counselor could use to record the frequency of the problems mentioned by the teacher.

d. Besides the occurrence of these specific behaviors, what other things should the counselor attempt to observe?

e. What ethical issues would need to be addressed in conducting and reporting on this type of observation? For example, would it be necessary to have the students' permission? What about parents? What steps should be taken to assure confidentiality of the data that are collected as a result of the observation?

9.2 Select one of the following locations for an observational study, and spend approximately one hour there in actual observation: a veterinarian's waiting room, a beauty shop, a shoeshine stand, an adult bookstore, a fast-food restaurant, a bus stop, a hospital emergency room, or a garage sale. Answer each of the following questions:

a. For the location selected, what general categories of data will you look for?

b. How will you gain entry to the setting? Whose permission will you need, and how will you obtain it?

c. Would any particular time periods be preferable for making observations at the setting you have selected?

d. Which observational approach will you use—nonparticipant or one of the participant forms?

e. Conduct the observations and report your experiences to the class.

f. For the observational setting you have selected, would it be more appropriate to collect data in the form of field notes or to develop a coding scheme? Why?

9.3 For the observational settings discussed in Exercise 9.2, consider the issue of when a participant observer should intervene and bring about some changes in the setting. What kinds of things would have to occur to warrant such intervention even though intervening would be detrimental to research goals? Given the examples that you and others in the class have developed, can you deduce any principles that might help others make the decision about when intervention is justified?

CHAPTER 10

Experimental Research

The Logic of Experimentation   254
Causation and Control   254
Matching and Randomization   256
Internal Validity   258

Experimental Designs   264
Preexperimental Designs   264
True Experimental Designs   265
Quasi-Experimental Designs   270

External Validity   275
Reactive Effects of Testing   275
Unrepresentative Samples   275
Reactive Settings   276
Multiple-Treatment Interference   277
The Importance of Replication   278
Lack of Minority Participation and Analysis   278

Assessment of Experiments   279
Advantages   279
Disadvantages   280

Main Points   281

Important Terms for Review   282

Exploring the Internet   282

For Further Reading   282

Exercises for Class Discussion   283

When people think of "science" and "research," experiments are often the first things that come to mind. These terms conjure up images of laboratories and white coats and electronic gear that are often associated with experiments. This points to a considerable misunderstanding of the nature of experimentation. In fact, we all engage in casual experimenting in the course of our everyday lives. For example, when a mechanical device malfunctions, we probe and test its various components in an effort to discover the elements responsible for the malfunction. In essence, we are experimenting to find the component (or variable) that *caused* the device to malfunction. Human service practitioners also often engage in casual experimentation. For example, in working with clients with particular problems, human service workers often try new intervention strategies to see if they will prove beneficial to the client. If behavior modification or role rehearsal does not bring about the desired effect, then a cognitive learning strategy might be tried. While these are illustrations of casual rather than systematic experiments, they do point to the essence of **experimentation:** It is a controlled method of observation in which the value of one or more independent variables is changed in order to assess its causal effect on one or more dependent variables.

The term "experimentation" as used in research, then, concerns a logic of analysis rather than a particular location, such as a laboratory, in which observations are made. In fact, experiments can be conducted in many settings. **Laboratory experiments** are conducted in artificial settings constructed in such a way that selected elements of the natural environment are simulated and features of the investigation controlled. **Field experiments,** on the other hand, are conducted in natural settings as people go about their everyday affairs.

The logic of scientific experiments can be illustrated by taking a more careful look at two elements of the impromptu or casual experimenting that may occur in everyday human service practice. First, many casual experiments fail. That is, manipulating the variables involved does not produce the desired result. No matter which approach to a client is used, for example, improvement in functioning is not forthcoming. In part, failures in casual experiments stem from the fact that they are *casual* and thus not carefully planned. For example, the wrong variables may have been selected for manipulation so that no matter how they were changed, the desired result could not be obtained. In scientific experimentation, criteria exist to increase the likelihood of success by ensuring that the experiment is soundly planned and that crucial procedures are carried out. Not that following the formalized procedures will guarantee success — it will not. Failure — in the sense of not achieving desired results — is an unpleasant, but fully expected, outcome of experimenting. Actually, it may be best not to conceive of failure to achieve predicted results as failure. Not achieving predicted results — assuming the results are not due to poor research techniques — serves to rule out one possible explanation.

The second feature of casual experimenting is a tendency to jump to conclusions that later prove incorrect. An effort to improve the performance of a client, for example, may produce temporary changes that later disappear. What went wrong? It may be that the practitioner's change in intervention strategy was not the real source of the change in the client's behavior. Something else may have actually caused the temporary changes. For example, the client found a job or his or her mother-in-law recovered from surgery, and these led to temporary improvements in performance. Or it may be that *any change* from one intervention strategy to another will result in short-term improvements that quickly dissipate. The point is that many things influence people's behavior, and casual experimentation is not organized to sort out these influences. Scientific experimentation is designed to do this and thus reduce the likelihood of reaching false conclusions.

The focus of this chapter is experimental research, but the techniques discussed here can be applied to practice settings. Although the impromptu experimenting attributed to human service practice certainly has its place, a thorough grasp of the principles of experimentation can enhance the practitioner's knowledge-building and decision-making efforts. In this chapter, we first discuss the underlying logic of experimentation and the major terms associated with experimental research. Then we present major factors that can lead to incorrect inferences in experiments and discuss how these problems can be avoided by properly designing the experiment. Finally, we analyze the problem of generalizing experimental findings to other settings and review the advantages and disadvantages of experiments.

The Logic of Experimentation

Causation and Control

The strength of experiments as a research technique is that they are designed to enable us to make inferences about causality. The element that makes this possible is *control:* In experiments, the investigator has considerable control over determining who participates in a study, what happens to them, and under what conditions it happens. In order to appreciate the importance of this, let us look at some of the key terms in experimental research (Kirk, 1982).

At the core of experimental research is the fact that the investigator exposes the people in an experiment, commonly referred to as *experimental subjects,* to some condition or variable, called the *experimental stimulus.* The **experimental stimulus,** or experimental treatment, is an independent variable directly manipulated by the experimenter in order to assess its effect on behavior. Recall from Chapter 2 that independent variables are those variables in a study that are hypothesized to produce change in another variable. The variable affected by the independent variable is the dependent variable—so

called because its value is dependent on the value of the independent variable. An **experimental group** is a group of subjects who are exposed to the experimental stimulus. **Experimental condition** is the term used to describe the group of people who receive the experimental stimulus.

We can illustrate the logic underlying experimentation by means of a series of symbols. The following symbols are commonly used to describe experimental designs:

O = an observation or measurement of the dependent variable

X = exposure of people to the experimental stimulus or independent variable

R = random assignment to conditions

In addition, the symbols constituting a particular experimental design are presented in time sequence, with those to the left occurring earlier in the sequence than those farther to the right. With this in mind, we can describe a very elementary experiment in the following way:

$$O \; X \; O$$

In this experiment, the researcher measures the dependent variable (this is called a pretest), exposes the subjects to the independent variable, and then remeasures the dependent variable (the posttest) to see if there has been a change. One major yardstick for assessing whether the independent variable in an experiment has had an effect is a comparison of the pretest scores or measures with those of the posttest. (Note that this is a slightly different use of the term "pretest" from its use in Chapters 1 and 7. In those contexts, the purpose of the pretest was to assess the adequacy of a data collection instrument before actual data collection ensued. In this context, the pretest involves actual data collection, but before the introduction of the experimental stimulus.)

Suppose, for example, that we were interested in the ability of developmentally disabled children to remain attentive and perform well in classroom settings. We might hypothesize that behavior modification techniques, in the form of reinforcement with praise, would improve the children's performance. To test this hypothesis, we would first measure the children's performance so as to have a baseline against which to assess change. Then we would expose the children to rewards for performance, the independent variable. For a specified period, children would be given praise each time they showed certain specified improvements in performance. Finally, we would again measure their performance—the dependent variable—to see if it had changed since the first measurement.

This illustration shows one of the major ways that experiments offer researchers control over what happens: The researcher manipulates the experimental stimulus. In this illustration, the researcher is using praise as the reinforcer. The experimenter specifies how and under what conditions the reinforcement is delivered, including how much reinforcement is delivered for a given response. The researcher might use one standard level of reinforcement or use multiple levels of reinforcement to assess the impact of such variation. The key point here is that the "when" and "how much" of the experimental stimulus are *controlled* by the researcher.

The purpose of an experiment, again, is to determine what effects independent variables produce on dependent variables. Variation in the dependent variable produced by the independent variable is known as **experimental variability,** and is the focus of interest in experiments. However, variation in the dependent variable can occur for many reasons other than the impact of the independent variable. For example, measurement error may affect the dependent variable (*see* Chapter 5). Or the people in the experiment may have peculiar characteristics that influence the dependent variable separately from any effect of the experimental stimulus. It is also possible that chance factors can affect the dependent variable. Variation in the dependent variable from any source other than the experimental stimulus is known as **extraneous variability,** and makes inferences about change in the dependent variable difficult. Every experiment contains some extraneous variability because there will always be things other than the experimental stimulus that influence the dependent variable. Researchers need some way of discovering how much variation is experimental and how much extraneous; experiments can be designed to provide this information through the use of *control variables* and *control groups.* **Control variables** are variables whose value is held constant in all conditions of the experiment. By not allowing these variables to change from one condition to another, any effects they may produce in the dependent variable should be eliminated. In the study of developmentally disabled children, for example, we might have some reason to believe that, in addition to the presumed impact of the experimental stimulus, the environment in which learning occurs—factors such as the lighting and heating—could affect how well the children perform. To control this, we would conduct all the observations in the same setting with no changes in lighting or heating. With such controls, we have greater confidence that changes in the dependent variable are caused by changes in the independent variable and not by the variables that are controlled.

A **control group** is a group of research subjects who are provided the same experiences as those in the experimental condition with a single exception: The control group receives no exposure to the experimental stimulus. **Control condition** refers to the state of being in a group that receives no experimental stimuli. When we include the control group in the elementary experimental design just described, we end up with the following design:

Experimental group: $O \; X \; O$
Control group: $O \quad \; O$

The control group is very important in experiments because it provides the baseline from which the effects of the independent variable are measured. For example, in the study of developmentally disabled children, the experimental condition involves receiving reinforcement in terms of praise. However, it might be possible that the children's performance would increase even in the absence of praise, possibly because of the attention received by being a part of an experiment. To test for this, it would be desirable to have a control group that receives the same attention as the children in the experimental group but is not rewarded with praise. Because both experimental and control groups experience the same conditions with the exception of the independent variable, it can be more safely concluded that any differences in the posttest value of the dependent variable between the experimental and control groups is due to the effect of the independent variable. So another yardstick for assessing whether an independent variable has an effect—in addition to the pretest–posttest comparison—is the posttest–posttest comparison between experimental and control groups.

It is important that the ideas of a control variable and a control group be kept distinct because they serve quite different functions. The use of a control variable is an attempt to minimize the impact of a single, known source of extraneous variability on the dependent variable. The use of a control group, on the other hand, is an effort to assess the impact of extraneous variability from any source—including variables that are not known to the researcher—on the dependent variable.

Matching and Randomization

When comparisons are made between the experimental and control groups to determine the effect of the independent variable, it is of crucial importance that the two groups be composed of people who are as much alike as possible. If they are not, any comparison could be meaningless as far as the effects of the independent variable are concerned. For example, imagine that a teacher decides to experiment with a new teaching technique. As luck would have it, she has two classes on the same subject, one meeting in the morning and the other in the afternoon. She uses the new teaching technique in the afternoon—the experimental group—and her conventional teaching methods in the morning section—the control group. At the end of the term, she notes that the afternoon class did substantially better on tests than the morning class. Can she conclude that the new technique is more effective than her old methods? Not with any great certainty. The students in the two classes may have dif-

fered from one another in systematic ways, and it may have been these differences between students, rather than variation in teaching technique, that caused differences in performance. It may be, for example, that students involved in extracurricular activities take morning classes so that their afternoons are free for those activities. Furthermore, students active in extracurricular affairs may have less time to study or be less academically inclined. Thus, given the kind of students who tend to take morning classes, we would expect the afternoon class to perform better even if there had been no variation in teaching technique.

Two methods are used to avoid the problem encountered by the teacher and ensure that the experimental and control groups are equivalent: *matching* and *random assignment*. The first has a certain intuitive appeal, but on closer inspection, it proves to be the less desirable of the two. As the name implies, **matching** involves matching individuals in the experimental group with similar subjects for a control group. People are matched on the basis of variables that we presume might have an effect on the dependent variable separate from the effect of the independent variable. By matching, we make the experimental and control groups equivalent on these variables so that these variables could not account for any differences between the two groups on the dependent variable. For example, the teacher described earlier might use an IQ test as a matching tool. A high IQ student in the morning class would be matched with a high IQ student in the afternoon class. Any students without equivalent matches on IQ in the other class would simply not be used in the data analysis. But other variables in addition to IQ could affect the outcome. Race, sex, socioeconomic status, study habits, reading ability, math proficiency—the list goes on and on. Though matching on IQ would not be too great a problem, the difficulty of matching would increase geometrically with the addition of more variables. For example, the teacher might need to find a match for an African American female of middle-class background with good study habits and a ninth grade reading ability who is also in the 95th percentile in math proficiency.

This illustrates one of the problems with matching: So many variables might be used in matching that it is usually impractical to consider more than a few at a time. A second problem with matching is that the researcher needs to know in advance which factors might have an effect on the dependent variable so that these can be included in the matching process, but often such information is not available. On the positive side, matching is better than no attempt to control at all and may be the only type of control available. In our illustration, the teacher may very well have no control over which students get assigned to which class. Consequently, the best she could do is select subgroup members in one class who have counterparts in the other class on a few key variables.

The second approach to assuring equivalent groups is random assignment. As the name implies, **random assignment** uses chance to reduce the variation between experimental and control groups. This can be done in a number of ways. For example, each person in the experiment can be given a random number, then the numbers arranged in order and every other person on the list placed in the experimental condition. Or the names of all the people in the experiment can be listed alphabetically and given a number, then a computer used to randomly assign each number to either the experimental or the control group. (*See* Chapter 6 and Appendix B on the use of random numbers tables.) The point is to make sure that each person has an equal chance of being placed into either the experimental group or the control group. In the long run, this technique offers the greatest probability that experimental and control groups will have no systematic differences between them so that differences on the outcome measures can be confidently attributed to the effect of the independent variable. Chance rather than a priori knowledge of other variables is the foundation of random assignment.

The problem with relying on chance is that, even though in the long run and over many applications randomization generates equivalent groups, this approach can still yield nonequivalent groups on occasion. This is especially so when the study

sample is very small. Table 10.1 illustrates the extreme difference between groups that can occur by chance when using randomization. In this hypothetical data, eight subjects have been identified by sex and height. The subjects are ranked according to their true position on the dependent variable prior to the experiment with scores ranging from 2 to 18. The mean score for the entire group is 10. Thus, when divided into an experimental and a control group, the ideal situation (row labeled "Ideal groups") would be for each group to have the same mean score of 10, or at least very close to it, on the dependent variable. While probability theory tells us that, with random assignment, it is most likely that experimental and control group means will be close to the overall mean, it is possible to obtain groups with very different means because, by chance, any combination of subjects in the two groups is possible. Table 10.1 shows one possible arrangement of subjects into one group with a mean score of 5 and another with a mean score of 15 (labeled "Worst random").

To reduce the likelihood of such occurrences, researchers often use a combination of matching and randomization known as **blocking.** In blocking, the subjects are first matched on one or more key variables in order to form blocks. Members of each block are then randomly assigned to the experimental and control conditions. Blocking works by reducing the extreme range of groups that are possible. For blocking to be effective, it is necessary that the variable on which cases are blocked be associated with the dependent variable. Notice in Table 10.1 that males have low scores and females have high scores; so the variable, sex, and the dependent variable are clearly associated. There is no such association between height and the dependent variable. When blocking is done on the basis of sex, two males are randomly assigned to each group and two females are randomly assigned to each group. The most extreme difference between groups that is possible in our hypothetical illustration with sex as the blocking variable are group means of 8 and 12 (labeled "Worst block on sex"). This is a considerable improvement over the extremes of 5 and 15 that are possible with randomization alone. Notice,

Table 10.1 Randomization and Blocking Illustration

Subject	Sex	Height	True Dependent Variable Score
A	Male	Short	2
B	Male	Tall	4
C	Male	Tall	6
D	Male	Short	8
E	Female	Tall	12
F	Female	Short	14
G	Female	Short	16
H	Female	Tall	18
Total N = 8			Mean = 10

	Possible Groupings			
	Group 1	Group 1 mean	Group 2	Group 2 mean
Ideal groups	B C F G	10	A D E H	10
Worst random	A B C D	5	E F G H	15
Worst block on sex	A B E F	8	C D G H	12
Worst block on height	A B C D	5	E F G H	15

however, that when the groups are blocked on the basis of height (labeled "Worst block on height"), there is no improvement; the worst possible group difference is still 5 and 15, as it was under randomization. This demonstrates that blocking on an appropriate variable can help reduce differences between groups. Choosing a variable for blocking that is unrelated to the dependent variable won't make matters any worse than random assignment, but it also won't improve the chances of achieving equivalent groups. Whether or not it is worth it to use blocking basically comes down to the anticipated improvement in group equivalency versus the cost and complexity of carrying out the blocking procedure. Research in Practice 10.1 describes a field experiment in which randomization and blocking were combined with other procedures to ensure equivalence between experimental and control groups.

Internal Validity

The central issue in experimentation is its utility in enabling us to make statements about causal relationships between phenomena. This is the reason for such things as control variables, control groups, randomization, and matching. In what has come to be considered the definitive work on experiments and experimental designs, Donald Campbell and Julian Stanley (1963) discuss the importance of *internal validity* in experiments (*see also* Cook and Campbell, 1979). Recall from Chapter 5 that the *validity* of a measure refers to whether it accurately measures what it is intended to measure. Likewise, **internal validity** in experiments refers to whether the independent variable actually produces the effect it appears to have had on the dependent variable; it is concerned with ruling out extraneous sources of variability to the point where we have confidence that changes in the dependent variable were caused by the independent variable. In the preceding discussion, we presented the basic logic involved in designing experiments that have internal validity. However, the problem is much more complex than we have so far stated because internal validity can be threatened in many ways. We now turn to the seven most serious threats to internal validity, as identified by Campbell and Stanley.

History   The threat of history concerns events that occur during the course of an experiment, other than the experimental stimulus, that could affect the dependent variable. History is more of a problem for field experiments than for those conducted in the confines of a laboratory because field experiments typically last longer, allowing more time for events that could affect the outcome to occur. For example, many commentators have made the observation that the reduction in the nation's highway speed limit to 55 miles per hour in the early 1970s appeared to produce a reduction in deaths in traffic accidents. This conclusion may not be warranted, however, for contemporaneous with the reduction of the speed limit there occurred rapidly rising fuel prices and a reduced fuel supply. These two events produced a sharp cutback in the number of miles people drove. It should be evident that the effects of these historical events make it very difficult to ascertain what effect the reduction of the speed limit actually had on accident rates.

Maturation   Maturation refers to changes occurring within experimental subjects that are due to the passage of time. Such things as growing older, hungrier, wiser, more experienced, or more tired are examples of maturation changes. If any of these changes are related to the dependent variable, their effects could confuse the effect of the independent variable. For example, many believe that people pass through a natural series of stages when grieving over the loss of a loved one: First, there is shock, then intense grief and sense of loss, followed by recovery (Kamerman, 1988). In other words, time brings its own change, or maturation, to the grieving individual. If we wanted to assess the ef-

fectiveness of some therapeutic intervention in helping people cope with the death of a loved one, any improvements people show over time might be due to maturation, or the natural progression of the grief process, rather than to the therapeutic intervention.

Testing   The threat of testing may occur any time subjects are exposed to a measurement device more than once. Because many experiments use paper-and-pencil measures and "before" and "after" measurements, testing effects are often of concern. For example, people taking achievement or intelligence tests for a second time tend to score better than they did the first time (Nachmias and Nachmias, 1992). This improvement occurs even when alternative forms of the test are used. Similar changes occur on personality tests. It should be quite clear that these built-in shifts in paper-and-pencil measures could lead to changes in the dependent variable that are due to testing rather than to the impact of the independent variable.

Instrumentation   The threat of instrumentation refers to the fact that the way in which variables are measured may change in systematic ways during the course of an experiment, resulting in the measurement of observations being done differently at the end from the way they were in the beginning. In observing and recording verbal behavior, for example, observers may become more adept at recording and do so more quickly. This means that they could record *more* behaviors at the end of an experiment than at the beginning. If the observers do learn and become more skillful, then changes in the dependent variable may be due to instrumentation effects rather than to the impact of the independent variable.

Statistical Regression   The threat of statistical regression can arise any time subjects are placed in experimental or control groups on the basis of extremely high or low scores on a measure in comparison to the average score for the whole group. When remeasured, those extreme groups will tend, on the whole, to score less extremely. In other

Research in Practice **10.1**
Program Evaluation: Meeting the Challenges to Experimentation in a Drug Prevention Program

Societal concern over the harmful effects of to-bacco, alcohol, and other drugs has led to a prolif-eration of school-based substance abuse prevention programs. Evaluations of these programs have pro-duced mixed results, which frustrates human ser-vice professionals eager to address these serious so-cial problems. The evaluations have suffered from a number of weaknesses that reduce their capacity to provide direction for program development. One weakness has been samples that include too few schools to make reasonable generalizations; other common weaknesses are that studies do not in-clude enough students or do not adequately ad-dress ethnic and racial diversity. Lack of random assignment, faulty implementation of the interven-tion, questions about accuracy of reported drug use, and inadequate statistical controls have been cited as other flaws.

These problems, however, are not endemic to drug prevention research, as one research team de-cisively demonstrated in their evaluation of a pro-gram called Project ALERT (Ellickson and Bell, 1992). Their study not only illustrates that true ex-perimental designs are feasible in drug prevention research, but also shows the clear benefits that can be derived from a well-planned and executed de-sign. What really makes this project noteworthy are the mechanism used for ensuring equivalence be-tween experimental and control groups and the care taken to make sure that the treatment was im-plemented correctly. These are two elements of field experiments that often detract from the valid-ity of the experimental design.

To begin, the designers of the program learned from the negative findings of projects whose sole intervention was to provide information about drugs and teach students general communication skills. Instead, they designed an intervention in which information about the negative conse-quences of drug use was presented as only one of several motivators for resisting drugs. In addition, the program emphasized skills the designers felt were specifically linked to situations in which

young people might feel pressured to use drugs. The program was based on a social influence model of prevention. According to this model, the key factors that keep young people from using drugs are influence by family, friends, and others, plus the young person's own beliefs about drugs. One aim of the program was to puncture myths about drugs and to help young people understand how drug use can affect daily lives and social rela-tionships. A second aim was to teach skills to aid in resisting internal and external pressures to use drugs. This was accomplished through skill demon-strations by instructors, role-playing of solutions by the students, and reinforcement of successful per-formance. In addition to finding out if the pro-gram content was effective or not, the researchers were interested in whether the program could be delivered more effectively by adults or other teenagers. Consequently, the study used three groups: a control group with no treatment, a treat-ment group with instruction delivered by an adult educator, and a treatment group using an educator assisted by teenage peers from neighboring schools.

One concern in designing the study was to ensure that the program would be tested in differ-ent environments. Many previous studies had fo-cused on white, middle-class, suburban communi-ties. To avoid this, the researchers began by listing all California and Oregon school districts and then distinguishing them by several dimensions, such as geographic location, racial/ethnic composition, so-cioeconomic level, and school size. Potential dis-tricts were first contacted by phone, then by per-sonal visit. As some districts joined in, the researchers concentrated on obtaining other dis-tricts that would complement them in terms of demographic features. The process netted eight school districts including 19 California schools and 11 Oregon schools.

Although the process generated a sample of schools that met the researchers' requirements in terms of diversity, the next challenge was to assign the schools to treatment and control conditions. It was not feasible to randomly assign individual students to study conditions because the nature of the intervention required that it be delivered to a whole school at one time. Consequently, whole schools were assigned to treatment and control groups; thus, the study sample consisted of all 30 schools. For reasons covered in our discussion of randomization and blocking, simple random assignment could produce nonequivalent experimental and control groups, especially with a sample as small as 30 cases. To reduce the likelihood of this, the researchers buttressed randomized assignment with *blocking,* but with a special twist that they labeled *restricted assignment.*

School district was used as the blocking factor. The researchers reasoned that schools within the same district could be expected to have similar underlying substance abuse rates. Socioeconomic status, norms about drug use, and school policy about substance use are also likely to be similar, if not the same, across schools in the same district. With such a small sample, then, it is possible by chance that most or all of the schools in one district could end up, even with random assignment, in the same experimental condition. To prevent this, schools from each district were randomly spread over the experimental conditions. If a district contained three schools, one was randomly assigned to each study condition. In the case of four schools, each condition was assigned one school and the remaining school was randomly assigned to one of the study conditions. For districts with five schools, one condition received one school and the other conditions got two schools each. Blocking in this fashion helped assure that schools from the same district were spread more evenly among the three conditions of adult-only curriculum, teenager-leader curriculum, and control condition.

Although blocking could be expected to be of some help, the researchers also knew from their demographic analysis that substantial differences did exist within some districts. Because there were only 30 schools from eight districts to be distributed over three experimental conditions, the researchers were concerned that randomization, even with blocking, might result in nonequivalent groups. Their solution to this problem was to make

use of publicly available data on each school and the results of an 11-item questionnaire that eighth-graders had previously completed at potential Project ALERT schools. These sources provided valuable information about not only demographic variables, such as parental education and mobility between schools, but also cigarette and marijuana use as well.

Under the design of the research, pairs of school districts entered the project at about the same time. So, instead of assigning schools from each district to experimental conditions independently, the researchers created blocking units by pairing schools from one district with schools from the other district and then randomly assigning these pairs of schools to treatments. The secret to this procedure was to create the best possible pairings. Figure 10.1 identifies school districts by letters and individual schools by numbers. (Schools A1 and A2, for example, are different schools, but both are in district A.) As the figure illustrates, there are six possible ways that three schools from one district (A1, A2, and A3) could be paired with three from a second (B1, B2, and B3).

The researchers evaluated each of the six sets of pairs to see which set had the best balance on the available variables such as race, socioeconomic status, and reported drug use. The best set was the one in which the three pairs were most equivalent on these variables. This set was then used as the basis for blocking. One pair of schools in the set was randomly assigned to the adult-educator condition, the second to the peer-instructor condition, and the third to the control group. The researchers called this *restricted assignment:* Randomization and blocking were used, but the outcomes of that process were restricted by eliminating those possible combinations of schools that were most likely to differ on important variables.

Obviously, the collection of preliminary data and assignment to conditions by blocking with restricted assignment was a painstaking process, but one that paid off in having three groups of schools that were very well balanced on almost all variables thought to possibly produce differences in the outcome variable. This increased the researchers' confidence that the outcomes were produced by

continued on next page

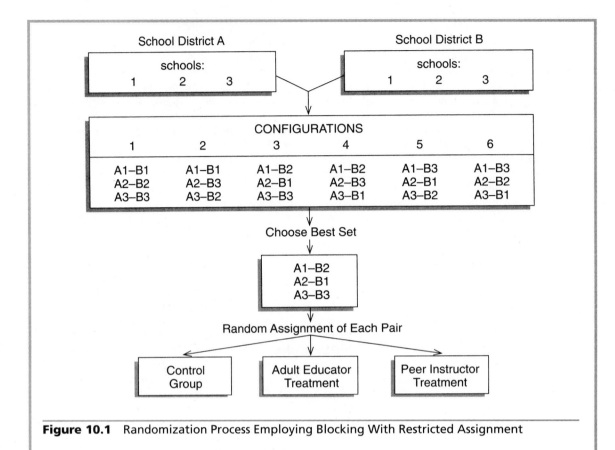

Figure 10.1   Randomization Process Employing Blocking With Restricted Assignment

experimental variability rather than nonequivalent groups. In addition to being as certain as possible that the groups were well balanced, the researchers took steps to assure that the treatment model would be implemented precisely as planned. If Project ALERT failed, they wanted to be confident that failure was due to the intervention model itself and not because a good idea was poorly executed. Several steps were taken to guard against faulty implementation. First, training of de-

words, they will *regress toward the overall group average.* For example, suppose the bottom 10 percent of scorers on a standard achievement test are singled out to participate in a special remedial course. On completing the course, they are measured with the achievement test again and show improvement. Could you conclude that the remedial course was responsible for the higher scores? You would certainly be hesitant to make this inference because of the effects of testing and maturation we have already discussed. In addition, however, there would also be a regression effect. Some of those people

scoring in the bottom 10 percent undoubtedly did so for reasons other than their actual level of ability—because they didn't get enough sleep the night before, were ill, or were upset over a quarrel. (How many times have you scored lower on an exam than you normally do because of factors like these?) If these people take the exam a second time, the conditions mentioned will have changed, and they will likely perform better—even without the special remedial course. Recognize that many, possibly most, people at the lowest 10 percent *are* performing at their normal level. However, in any

livery personnel strongly emphasized adhering to the model. Second, the researchers monitored almost half of the 2,300 classroom sessions scheduled during the program. At the end of a lesson, an independent monitor rated the session on completeness and fidelity to program content and the model's teaching process, and evaluated the session overall.

Obtaining accurate measures of such sensitive behaviors as drug usage is another concern in any field experiment. Because students may not tell the truth if asked about their substance use, the researchers included saliva samples as part of the data collection strategy, explaining to students that marijuana and tobacco use could be detected in this manner. During data collection, the researchers used a variety of techniques known to improve reporting on surveys. Aware of the controversial nature of the study, the researchers also obtained a certificate of confidentiality from the Department of Health and Human Services (*see* Chapter 3). Finally, students were given the option of withdrawing from participation at any time during the study.

The results of the experiment showed that the program effectively prevented or reduced both cigarette and marijuana use during the junior high years and had modest effects on adolescent drinking. For marijuana, the program generally had positive effects across the different levels of risk for future use. For cigarettes, the program's impact depended on prior use: Youths who had only experimented with cigarettes showed the greatest positive effect; but for students whose experience

with cigarettes had gone beyond experimentation, subsequent smoking rates were higher than for controls. The program also reduced alcohol use, but the impact eroded within 12 months of the end of the program. As for differences in type of instruction, there was no significant difference between adult-only and peer-assisted instruction.

In reflecting on the research experience, the researchers identified several lessons they learned:

- Communities and organizations will abide by experimental conditions, including randomization, if they understand the importance and feel that the inconvenience of doing so has been dealt with.
- Field experiments using large and limited units of assignment such as school districts need to go beyond simple random assignment to assure balanced groups.
- Careful efforts to encourage truthful and accurate reporting can deliver reliable drug use reports.
- When large organizations such as schools must be used as the unit of assignment, a large-scale study may be a necessity for meeting the research objectives. There may be no alternative to a large-scale study when issues such as diversity and generalizability are at stake.

Studies such as Project ALERT require large investments of money, time, and effort, but the promise of quality information for policy decision making underscores the value of such projects for the human services.

such group based on a single test administration, a certain number of people will probably be scoring lower than their normal level. If the whole group repeats the exam—even without any intervening experimental manipulation—they can be expected to perform better and thus the average score of the group will improve.

Selection   Selection is a threat to internal validity when the kinds of people selected for one experimental condition differ from the people selected for other conditions. The threat of selection derives

from experimental and control groups being improperly constituted. Recall the importance of random assignment or matching to equalize these groups. As noted, improper composition of these groups can make findings based on comparisons between them meaningless.

Experimental Attrition   The attrition threat occurs when there is a differential dropout of subjects from the experimental and control groups. Especially in experiments that extend over long time periods, some people will fail to complete the experiment. People will die, move away, become incapacitated, or simply quit. If there is a notable difference in attrition rates between the experimental and control groups, the groups may not be equivalent at the end of the experiment although they were at the beginning. An example of the attrition threat can be found in a study of the effects of sex composition on the patterns of interaction in consciousness-raising counseling groups (Carlock and Martin, 1977). One group was all women while the other was composed of both men and women. The women were randomly assigned to one or the other of the groups. Originally the all-female group contained 9 members, and the male–female group had 16 members. Before the experiment was completed, however, two female members of the male–female group dropped out. When the interactional patterns in the groups were compared, substantial differences were found. The authors concluded that these differences were due to the differing sex compositions of the groups, but, as they note, their findings are weakened because of the dropouts from the male–female group. With such small groups to begin with, the loss of two members from one group could have substantially affected the results.

With this lengthy list of threats to the internal validity of experiments, can one ever have confidence that changes in the dependent variable are due to the impact of the independent variable and not to some extraneous variability? In fact, such confidence can be established—and threats to internal validity controlled—through the use of a good experimental design, and it is to this topic that we now direct our attention.

Experimental Designs

There are three categories of experimental designs. **Preexperimental designs** lack both the random assignment to conditions and the control groups that are such a central part of good experimental designs. Although they are still sometimes useful, they illustrate some inherent weaknesses in terms

of establishing internal validity. The better designs are called *true experimental designs* and *quasi-experimental designs*. **True experimental designs** are more complex ones that use randomization and other techniques to control the threats to internal validity. **Quasi-experimental designs** are special designs for use in the approximation of experimental control in nonexperimental settings.

Preexperimental Designs

On the surface, Design P.1 might appear to be an adequate design. The subjects are pretested, exposed to the experimental condition, and then posttested. It would seem that any differences between the pretest measures and posttest measures would be due to the experimental stimulus.

P.1 The One-Group Pretest–Posttest Design

Experimental Group: $O \ X \ O$

However, there are serious weaknesses in this design as it stands. With the exceptions of selection and attrition, which are irrelevant owing to the lack of a control group, Design P.1 is subject to the other five threats to internal validity. If a historical event related to the dependent variable intervenes between the pretest and the posttest, its effects could be confused with those of the independent variable. Maturation changes in the subjects could also produce differences between pretest and posttest scores. If paper-and-pencil measures are used, a shift of scores from pretest to posttest could occur owing to testing effects. Regardless of the measurement process used, instrumentation changes could produce variation in the pretest and posttest scores. Finally, if the subjects were selected because they possessed some extreme characteristic, differences between pretest and posttest scores could be due to regression toward the mean. In all these cases, variation on the dependent variable produced by one or more of the validity threats could easily be mistaken for variation due to the independent variable.

The other preexperimental design—the Static Group Comparison—involves comparing one group that experiences the experimental stimulus with another group that does not.

P.2 The Static Group Comparison

Experimental group: $\_\ \underline{X\ O}\ \_$
Control group: O

In considering this design, it is important to recognize that the comparison group that appears to be a control group is not, in the true sense, a control group. The major validity threat to this design is selection. Note that no random assignment is indicated that would make the comparison groups comparable. In Design P.2, the group compared with the experimental group is normally an intact group picked up only for the purpose of comparison. There is no assurance of comparability between it and the experimental group. For example, we might wish to test the impact of a local assistance program by comparing a city in which the program exists with one that does not have the program. Any conclusions we might reach about the effects of the program might be inaccurate because of other differences between the two cities.

Despite their weaknesses, preexperimental designs are used when resources do not permit the development of true experimental designs. Human service practitioners especially are likely to be faced with this dilemma. It should be evident, however, that conclusions based on such designs are to be regarded with the utmost caution and the results viewed as suggestive at best. These designs should be avoided if at all possible. If they are used, efforts should be made to test the validity of those findings further by using one of the true experimental designs.

True Experimental Designs

Probably the most common true experimental design is the Pretest–Posttest Control Group Design with random assignment, which is identical to the design on page 255 except for randomization. This design is used so often that it is frequently referred to by its popular name: the *classic* experimental de-

sign. In all of the true experimental designs, the proper test of hypotheses is the comparison of posttests between experimental and control groups.

T.1 The Pretest–Posttest Control Group Design with Randomization—the "classic" experimental design

Experimental group: $R\ O\ X\ O$
Control group: $R\ O\ \ \ \ O$

This design utilizes a true control group, including random assignment to equalize the comparison groups, which eliminates all the threats to internal validity except certain patterns of attrition. Because of this, we can have considerable confidence that any differences between experimental and control groups on the dependent variable are due to the effect of the independent variable.

Let us take a closer look at how the classic design avoids the various threats. History is removed as a rival explanation of differences between the groups on the posttest because both groups experience the same events except for the experimental stimulus. Because the same amount of time passes for both groups, maturation effects can be assumed to be equal and, therefore, do not account for posttest differences. Similarly, as both groups are pretested, any testing influences on the posttest should be the same for the two groups. Instrumentation effects are also readily controlled with this design because any unreliability in the measurement process that could cause a shift in scores from pretest to posttest should be the same for both comparison groups.

In situations where regression could occur, the classic experimental design can control it through random assignment of subjects with extreme characteristics. This ensures that whatever regression does take place can be assumed to be the same for both groups. Regression toward the mean should not, therefore, account for any differences between the groups on the posttest. Randomization also controls the validity threat of selection by making sure that the comparison groups are equivalent. Furthermore, the pretest results can be used as a check on precisely how similar the two groups actually are. Because the two groups are very similar, attrition rates would be expected to be about the same for each group. In a lengthy experiment with a large sample, we would fully expect about the same number of subjects in each group to move away, die, or become incapacitated during the experiment. These can be assumed to be, more or less, random events. Attrition due to these reasons, therefore, is unlikely to create a validity problem. Attrition due to voluntary quitting is another matter. It is quite possible that the experimental stimulus may affect the rate of attrition. That is, subjects might find something about the experimental condition either more or less likable than the subjects find the control condition, so the dropout rate could differ. If this occurs, it raises the possibility that the groups are no longer equivalent at the time of the posttest. Unfortunately, there is no really effective way of dealing with this problem. About all one can do is to watch for its occurrence and interpret the results cautiously if attrition bias appears to be a problem.

A second true experimental design—the Solomon Four-Group Design—is more sophisticated than Design T.1 in that four different comparison groups are used.

T.2 The Solomon Four-Group Design

Experimental group 1:	R	O	X	O
Control group 1:	R	O		O
Experimental group 2:	R		X	O
Control group 2:	R			O

As should be evident, the first two groups of the Solomon design constitute Design T.1, indicating that it is capable of controlling the same threats to internal validity as did that design. The major advantage of the Solomon design is that it can tell us whether changes in the dependent variable are due to some *interaction effect* between the pretest and the exposure to the experimental stimulus. Experimental group 2 is exposed to the experimental stimulus without being pretested. If the posttest of experimental group 1 differs from the posttest of experimental group 2, it may be due to an interaction effect of receiving both the pretest and experimental stimulus—something we would not find out with

the classic design. Suppose, for example, that we wanted to assess the effect on prejudice toward racial minorities (the dependent variable) of receiving positive information about a racial group (the independent variable). We pretest groups by asking them questions regarding their prejudice toward particular groups. Then we expose them to the experimental stimulus: newspaper articles reporting on civic deeds and rescue efforts of members of those racial groups. If we find lower levels of prejudice in experimental group 1 than in control group 1, it might be due to the independent variable. But it could also be that filling out a pretest questionnaire on prejudice sensitized people in the first group to these issues and they reacted *more strongly* to the experimental stimulus than they would have without such pretesting. If this is so, then experimental group 2 should show less change than experimental group 1. If the independent variable has an effect separate from its interaction with the pretest, then experimental group 2 should show more change than control group 1. If control group 1 and experimental group 2 show no change but experimental group 1 does show a change, then change is produced only by the interaction of pretesting and treatment.

It should be apparent that the Solomon design enables us to make a more complex assessment of the causes of changes in the dependent variable. In addition, the combined effects of maturation and history can be controlled (as with Design T.1) as well as measured. By comparing the posttest of control group 2 with the pretests of experimental group 1 and control group 1, these effects can be assessed. However, our concern with history and maturation effects is usually only in *controlling* their effects, not *measuring* them.

Despite the superiority of the Solomon design, it is often bypassed for Design T.1 because the Solomon design requires twice as many groups. This effectively doubles the time and cost of conducting the experiment. Not surprisingly, many researchers decide that the advantages are not worth the added cost and complexity. If a researcher desires the strongest design, however, Design T.2 is the one to choose.

There are times when pretesting is either impractical or undesirable. For example, pretesting might sensitize subjects to the independent variable. In these cases, it is still possible to use a true experimental design, the Posttest-Only Control Group Design.

T.3 The Posttest-Only Control Group Design

Experimental group: R X O
Control group: R O

Despite the absence of pretests, Design T.3 is an adequate true experimental design that controls validity threats as well as do the designs with pretests. It uses random assignment to conditions, which distinguishes it from the preexperimental Design P.2. The only potential validity question raised in conjunction with this design is selection. The absence of pretests means that random assignment is the only assurance that the comparison groups are equivalent. Campbell and Stanley (1963), however, argue convincingly that pretests are not essential and that randomization reliably produces equivalent groups. Furthermore, they argue that the lack of popularity of Design T.3 stems more from the tradition of pretesting in experimentation than from any major contribution to validity produced by its use.

The preceding experimental designs are adequate for testing hypotheses when the independent variable is either present (experimental group) or absent (control group). Yet, many hypotheses involve independent variables that vary in terms of *degree* or *amount* of something that is present. For example, *how much* treatment of a client (intensity level) is needed to produce some desired behavioral change? In a study of abusive parents, the independent variable was exposure to positive parenting sessions (Burch and Mohr, 1980). Rather than just assess the effect of the presence or absence of such sessions, the researchers exposed some groups to *more* sessions than others. In cases such as this, an extension of Design T.1 with multiple experimental groups and one control group is used.

T.4 The Multiple Experimental Group With One Control Group Design

Experimental group 1: R O X_1 O
Experimental group 2: R O X_2 O
Experimental group 3: R O X_3 O
Control group: R O O

The symbols X_1, X_2, and X_3 refer to differing amounts or intensities of a single independent variable or treatment. Comparing the posttests of the experimental groups enables us to determine the impact of the differing amounts of the independent variable.

The experimental designs considered thus far can assess the impact of only a single independent variable at a time on the dependent variable. We know, however, that variables can *interact* with one another, and the combined effects of two or more variables may be quite different from the effects of each variable operating separately. For example, one experimental study investigated the impact of both social class and race on people's stereotypes of women (Landrine, 1985). People in the study were asked to describe society's stereotype of four different women: a middle-class black, a middle-class white, a lower-class black, and a lower-class white. They found that social class and sex did affect stereotyping: Lower-class people received more negative stereotyping than did middle-class people, and African Americans were viewed less favorably than whites. They did not find an interaction effect, however. In other words, various class/race combinations did not produce more changes in stereotyping than the effects of class and race separately. To assess the effect of such interactions, experimenters have to expose the subjects to more than one independent variable. A convenient experimental design for accomplishing this is the Factorial Design. Design T.5 illustrates the simplest factorial design in which two independent variables (X_1 and X_2) are involved, each with only two values (present or absent).

T.5 The Factorial Design

Experimental group 1: R X_1 X_2 O
Experimental group 2: R X_1 O
Experimental group 3: R X_2 O
Control group: R O

Research in Practice 10.2
Program Evaluation: Field Experiments on the Police Handling of Domestic Violence Cases

The police telephone operator answered the call from a weeping woman: "Police."

VOICE: I want a . . . a battered woman.
OPERATOR: What, ma'am?
VOICE: I am a battered woman.
OPERATOR: Do you want the police to come, ma'am?
VOICE: (sob) Yes.
OPERATOR: Is he in the house now?
VOICE: Yes—he's in the house now and I'm scared. [Sherman, 1992, p. 80]

This interchange between a victim of wife battering and the police was recorded in the course of a landmark experiment on law enforcement intervention in domestic violence conducted in Minneapolis. At first glance, this dialogue appears to stand as eloquent testimony to ethical and logistical barriers that prohibit using true experiments in the real world of human service. No matter how valuable the potential research findings, it would be unthinkable to tell a victim, "Sorry, you're in the control group, we can't help you." And how could the researcher get the police officer on the scene to administer treatment A and not treatment B or C on a truly random basis?

On the other hand, the urgency of human need demands that researchers find the best ways of responding to such critical social problems. The most powerful rationale for using experiments is that they deliver a more convincing case for causal relationships between variables than do other research methods. The main reason for this is the

control that researchers have over the variables—independent, dependent, and extraneous—in experimental research. If an intervention does prevent future assaults, a randomized experiment is the best way to find that out. Lawrence Sherman presents a fascinating account of the Minneapolis study and five replications in Omaha, Charlotte (North Carolina), Milwaukee, Metro-Dade (Miami), and Colorado Springs. His presentation documents how researchers can overcome the barriers to experimentation in field settings and the lessons learned from the experience (Sherman, 1992). We will highlight three of these studies on responding to domestic assault and focus on how they dealt with three potential barriers to experimentation—the ethics of withholding treatment, randomization, and assuring that treatments are actually delivered as assigned.

The catalyst for this series of studies was an investigation by criminologist Lawrence Sherman and sociologist Richard Berk (1984). The researchers randomly assigned 314 misdemeanor domestic assault cases to three types of police intervention: advising the couple (including informal mediation), separating the couple by ordering the offender to leave the house for 8 hours, and arresting the offender so that he stayed in jail overnight. The independent variable was the mode of police intervention, and the dependent variable was whether or not the perpetrator was involved in another domestic violence incident in the 6 months following police intervention.

Factorial designs involve enough groups so that all possible combinations of the independent variables can be investigated. Assessment of interaction is accomplished by the comparison of experimental group 1, which is exposed to both independent variables, with experimental groups 2 and 3. We can see whether the combined effects of the independent variables differ from their separate effects.

Factorial designs can be expanded beyond the simple example used here. More than two variables can be investigated, and each variable can have more than two values. However, as the complexity of factorial designs increases, the number of groups required rapidly increases and can become unmanageable. For example, with three independent variables, each with three values, we

For ethical and practical reasons, the study was restricted to misdemeanor assaults, milder cases lacking severe injury, or a life-threatening situation. With such misdemeanor offenses, police *could* make an arrest, or they could advise or separate, but no one of these responses was *required*. Under normal conditions, police would use their own judgment as to which intervention is called for. When participating in the Sherman-Berk study, police officers responding to a call first determined if the case fit the study criteria and then applied one of the three intervention techniques if it did. The ethical concerns raised by withholding treatment and random assignment to treatments were thus addressed by responding to all calls, by providing one of three standard treatments to each case, and by restricting the study to only misdemeanor cases.

Random assignment to experimental conditions was achieved by requiring each police officer to use a pad consisting of color-coded forms corresponding to the three different treatments: arrest, separation, and mediation. The forms were randomly ordered in the pad, and the officers were instructed to select their intervention according to whatever color form came up when they intervened in a case that met the study guidelines. In this study, then, the officers doing the intervening were responsible for making sure that the randomization was done properly. In order for the study to work as planned, officers had to follow the instructions faithfully. In addition, the forms were sequentially numbered so that the researchers could monitor how well the officers followed the assigned interventions. The researchers tried riding patrol with some of the officers to check on this, but this proved impractical because of the sporadic occurrence of assault complaints. Another approach was to have officers complete a brief form after each

call describing what happened. In spite of these efforts, the study was criticized on the grounds that the treatments might not have been delivered as assigned.

Sherman and Berk concluded that arrest was the most effective of the three options for dealing with a spouse abuser: Those arrested were significantly less likely to be involved in a repeat episode of domestic violence in the following 6 months. Encouraged by these findings, many communities developed more aggressive arrest policies toward domestic assault. However, researchers and policymakers cautioned against placing too much faith in the results of this one study. One criticism was that the study had a small sample size. In addition, a disproportionate number of cases had been submitted by a few officers. This may be because these officers patrolled a more violent section of town and, because of experience, were particularly effective at making an arrest an effective deterrent. The other officers, who did not turn in many cases, may have been more effective at mediation or separation. If this was the case, then the study was really about variations in the skills of police officers rather than variations in the effectiveness of different treatments. This points to the importance of assessing *internal validity:* Is it variation in the independent variable that produces changes in the dependent variable, or is something else producing these changes?

Yet another criticism of Sherman and Berk's study is that there were inadequate controls over which treatments were actually delivered. There was also the possibility that surveillance effects from the multiple follow-up interviews distorted the impact of the treatment. Finally, if the sample was biased for any of the foregoing reasons, the

continued on next page

would need a 3 × 3 × 3 factorial design, or 27 different groups. However, field experiments designed to assess the impact of social programs sometimes involve such complex designs.

We have covered the major types of true experimental designs in this section. However, circumstances often require researchers to use a variant of

one of these designs. Research in Practice 10.2 illustrates such a variation that, nonetheless, retains randomization. The designs presented here also form the basis for many other more complex designs capable of handling such problems in experimenting as multiple independent variables and order effects.

results may not be generalizable to other settings (Hirschel, Hutchison, and Dean, 1992).

A follow-up study in Omaha differed from the Minneapolis project in several key respects (Dunford, Huizinga, and Elliott, 1989). First, in addition to evaluating the three treatments of arrest, mediation, or separation, the research included a unique facet. If the assailant was not present when officers arrived, but the case otherwise met study criteria, the suspect was randomly assigned to either receive or not receive a warrant for the offender's arrest.

In order to improve generalizability, the researchers wanted to be sure the project covered all areas of the community, including sections populated by minorities. A competing goal was to maintain control by using those officers most likely to encounter assault cases rather than training and monitoring the entire police force. A review of the 911 dispatch log revealed that about 60 percent of domestic assault calls occurred on the "C" shift (4:00 P.M. to midnight). Focusing the project only on this shift kept the project more manageable. As in Minneapolis, the Omaha study was restricted to cases of probable cause of misdemeanor-level assault.

A criticism of the Minneapolis study had been the reliance on police officers to carry out randomization. The Omaha project addressed this criticism by having random assignment to treatment performed by the Information Unit of the Omaha police force. Upon establishing control at the scene, responding officers determined if the case met project eligibility requirements such as being a misdemeanor offense. After information such as time, date, and victim and suspect characteristics had been reported to the Information Unit, the *operator* assigned an intervention based on a computer-generated randomization procedure. In this way, randomization was done in a central location, and data about the case and the assigned treatment were immediately stored in the computer file.

For results to be valid, it was crucial that officers actually deliver the assigned treatment. This problem was controlled by three forms of monitoring. First, officers reported dispositions on a Domestic Violence Report form and forwarded it to the project. Second, victims were asked to describe what treatment was delivered. Finally, official records of police, prosecuting attorneys, and courts were compared with the other forms of monitoring data. Analysis of these various case-monitoring systems indicated that 92 percent of the treatments were delivered as assigned.

Still another replication of the original Minneapolis study, this time in Charlotte, North Carolina, also had unique features (Hirschel et al., 1992). It included only cases involving female victims and male offenders where both parties were at least 18 years old. The study covered the entire patrol division in round-the-clock, citywide sampling. The interventions also differed somewhat from the other studies. In addition to arrest, the police could issue a citation requiring a court appearance by both victim and offender, or they could advise and separate (a combination of the mediation and separation treatments of the other studies). An additional explicit criterion addressed the concern of victim and officer safety: Cases were excluded if the victim insisted on arrest, if the assailant threatened or assaulted the police, or if officers believed that the offender posed an immi-

Quasi-Experimental Designs

There are many times when it is impossible, for practical or other reasons, to meet the conditions necessary for the development of true experimental designs. The most common problems in this regard are an inability to assign people randomly to conditions and the difficulty of creating a true control group with which to compare the experimental groups. Although this can be a problem in experiments in any context, it is especially acute in field experiments and in practice settings. Rather than rule out experimentation in such settings, however, one may be able to use a *quasi-experimental design*. These designs allow the researcher to approach the level of control of true experimental designs in situations where the requirements of the latter cannot be met. Quasi-experimental designs afford considerable control, but they fall short of the true experimental designs and should, therefore, be used only

nent danger to the victim. After restoring order at the scene, all victims were provided information on community resources, including the Victim Assistance Program and the Battered Women's Shelter.

In a manner similar to the Omaha project, Charlotte researchers used the police department's computer-assisted dispatch system to automatically generate random assignment of the three treatments, thus eliminating potential human manipulation or error. So we see that the replication studies not only provided more data to answer the research question, but served to refine the research techniques to reduce error.

Choosing the best way to operationalize key variables is an important lesson from these studies. One approach was to measure whether or not the assailant committed another offense. Another conceptualization was "time to failure," defined as the number of months before an additional offense. Both approaches were used. A related issue was whether to rely on official arrest records or interview reports of victims. If repeat incidents of domestic assault are measured by *re-arrest* of the perpetrator, then repeat incidents appear to be rather small; however, if the occurrence of repeat events is measured by reports of the victims to interviewers, then repeat incidents appear to be common. Measured in the latter way, an important conclusion of these studies was to underscore the alarmingly high level of repeat incidents. This is another example of the issue of validity discussed in Chapter 5: How accurately does a measurement tool measure some theoretical concept? Which is the best measure of repeat domestic assault: arrest records or victim reports?

The original Minneapolis study, based on 314 cases, concluded that arrest significantly reduced future assaults, and the policy implication appeared clear-cut: Implement an aggressive pro-arrest policy to reduce wife assault. Based on a total sample of thousands in six cities in the various replications, the general conclusion now is that the issue is far from clear-cut. Sherman (1992, p. 247) offers these summary conclusions:

- Arrest increases domestic violence among people who have nothing to lose, especially the unemployed.
- Arrest deters domestic violence in cities with higher proportions of white and Hispanic suspects.
- Arrest deters domestic violence in the short run, but escalates violence later in cities with higher proportions of unemployed African American suspects.
- A small but chronic portion of all violent couples produce the majority of domestic violence incidents.
- Offenders who flee before police arrive are substantially deterred by warrants for their arrest, at least in Omaha.

The research underscores the point that social problems and societal responses are complex and unlikely to yield singular solutions. Based on these findings, policymakers should not assume that mandatory arrest practices will reduce a community's family violence. There is still much to learn about both the nature of the problem and its solutions, and communities need to continue to monitor and refine their approaches.

when conditions do not allow the use of a true experimental design (Achen, 1986). As we will see in Chapter 11, quasi-experimental designs also form the basis of single-subject designs used in clinical practice.

One of the simplest and most useful of the quasi-experimental designs is the Time Series Design. This design involves a series of repeated measures, followed by the introduction of the experimental condition, and then another series of measures.

Q.1 The Time Series Design

Experimental group:
$$O_1 \, O_2 \, O_3 \, O_4 \, X \, O_5 \, O_6 \, O_7 \, O_8$$

The number of pretest and posttest measurements can vary, but it would be unwise to use fewer than three of each. Time series designs can be analyzed by graphing the repeated measures and inspecting the pattern produced. We can conclude whether

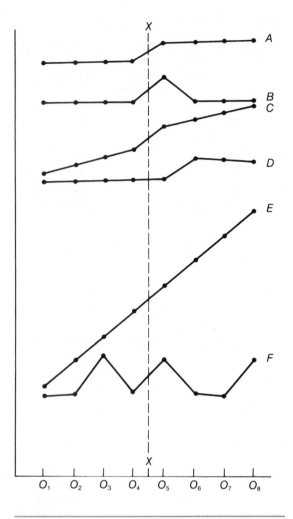

Figure 10.2   Hypothetical Examples of Time Series Data

Source   Adapted from Donald T. Campbell and Julian C. Stanley, *Experimental and Quasi-Experimental Designs for Research.* Copyright © 1963 Houghton Mifflin Company. Used with permission.

the independent variable produced an effect by observing when, over the whole series of observations, changes in the dependent variable occur. Figure 10.2 illustrates some possible outcomes of a time series experiment. Of major interest is what

occurs between O_4 and O_5 because these are the measures that immediately precede and follow the experimental stimulus. The other measures are important, however, because they provide a basis for assessing the change that occurs between O_4 and O_5. As Figure 10.2 shows, some outcomes suggest that the stimulus has had an effect whereas others do not. In cases *A, B,* and *C,* stimulus *X* appears to produce an effect. In each case, the differences between measures O_4 and O_5 are greater than the differences between any other adjacent measures. Cases *E* and *F* illustrate outcomes where we can infer that changes result from something other than the stimulus because the differences between measures O_4 and O_5 are not substantially different from those between some other adjacent measures. The results of a time series design are not always clearcut, as illustrated by case *D.* The sharp change between measures O_5 and O_6 could be a delayed effect of *X,* or it could be due to something else. More careful analysis would be required to come to a firm conclusion in that case.

In field studies involving a time series analysis, the experimental stimulus is often not something that the researcher manipulates; rather, it is something that occurs independently of the research. Thus, any natural event presumed to cause changes in people's behavior could serve as an experimental stimulus. In a study of the mass media and violence, for example, the experimental stimulus was the heavyweight championship prize fights that occurred between 1973 and 1978 (Phillips, 1983). The dependent variable was the daily counts of all homicides in the United States provided by the National Center for Health Statistics, so an assessment could be made of the daily homicide rates after championship prize fights. They found a sharp increase in homicides after such fights, peaking on the third day after each fight. Apparently, in some Americans, viewing heavyweight prize fights stimulates aggressive behavior that turns fatal in a few cases.

The time series design fares quite well when evaluated on its ability to control threats to internal validity. With the exception of history, the other threats are controlled by the presence of the series of premeasures. Maturation, testing, instrumentation, regression, and attrition produce gradual changes that would be operating between all measures. As such, they could not account for any sharp change occurring between O_4 and O_5. Because this design does not use a control group, the issue of selection is not a factor. Thus, history is the only potential threat to internal validity. It is always possible that some extraneous event could intervene between measures O_4 and O_5 and produce a change that could be confused with an effect of X. In many cases, there may not be an event that plausibly could produce the noted effect, and we could be quite sure it was due to X. Nevertheless, the inability of the time series design to control the threat of history is considered a weakness.

The time series design requires that we be able to measure the same group repeatedly over an extended period. Because this requires considerable cooperation from the subjects, there may be times when the time series design cannot be used. A design that avoids this problem and yet maintains the other characteristics of the time series is the Different Group Time Series Design. Rather than make repeated measures on one group, this design substitutes several randomly selected groups, each of which is measured only once but at different times.

Q.2 The Different Group Time Series Design

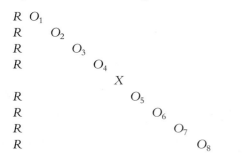

Design Q.2 produces the same type of data as the regular time series and can be analyzed using the same graphing procedure. In terms of internal validity, Design Q.2 controls the same threats as the time series. Random sampling is relied on to equate the several comparison groups. Design Q.2 also has the same weakness as the time series design: Historical events can intervene between O_4 and O_5, possibly confusing the results.

Because of the many random samples required by this design, it is limited to situations where the cost of those samples is inexpensive. For example, if it is possible to draw the samples and collect data by telephone, this design is ideal. This is essentially the approach used by commercial pollsters when they repeatedly measure public opinion by conducting monthly telephone surveys of different random samples. Although the pollsters do not conduct experiments, their repeated measures allow the assessment of the impact of events on public opinion. The event in question becomes the X in the design, and levels of opinion are compared before and after it occurred. For example, the 1991 war against Iraq known as Desert Storm caused the popularity of President Bush to soar. His popularity later declined substantially, but because of the many before and after measurements there is little doubt that it was the war that temporarily increased the president's popularity.

As noted, both the preceding designs suffer from the validity threat of history. By the addition of a control group to that time series design, this last remaining threat is controlled. Design Q.3 illustrates this and is known as the Multiple Time Series Design.

Q.3 The Multiple Time Series Design

Experimental group:
$$O_1 \ O_2 \ O_3 \ O_4 \ X \ O_5 \ O_6 \ O_7 \ O_8$$
Control group:
$$O_1 \ O_2 \ O_3 \ O_4 \quad O_5 \ O_6 \ O_7 \ O_8$$

Design Q.3 controls all the threats to internal validity, including history. Events other than X should affect both groups equally, so history is not a rival explanation for differences between the groups after the experimental group has been exposed to X. A design that uses a control group without random assignment might be thought suspect on the threat of selection. This is less of a problem than with pre-experimental designs, however, because the series of before measures affords ample opportunity to see how similar the comparison groups are.

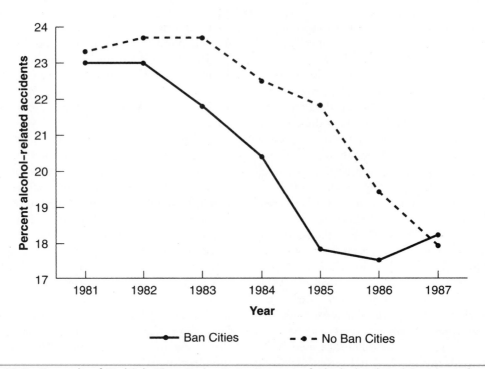

Figure 10.3 Example of Multiple Time Series Data: Percent of Alcohol-Related Accidents for "Ban" and "No Ban" Cities in California, 1981–1987

Source Carol W. Kohfeld and Leslie A. Leip, "Bans on Concurrent Sale of Beer and Gas: A California Case Study," *Sociological Practice Review,* Vol. 2 (April 1991), p. 109. Reprinted with permission of the American Sociological Association and the authors.

Data from Design Q.3 are plotted and analyzed in the same way as with the two preceding designs. This time, however, there are two lines on the graph, one for the experimental group and one for the control group. The patterns of the two groups are compared to see what effect X produced. As a demonstration of the utility of quasi-experimental designs, Carol Kohfeld and Leslie Leip (1991) looked at the impact of a policy in California that restricted the sale of beer and wine in stores that also sell gasoline. The idea was that people would be less likely to drink and drive if they could not purchase gasoline and alcohol at the same place. They measured the effectiveness of the policy in terms of the percentage of all alcohol-related automobile accidents. They collected data on 77 cities from 1981 to 1987, 37 of which had instituted the ban on concurrent sales of alcohol and gasoline by 1986. As Figure 10.3 illustrates, the percentage of

alcohol-related accidents did decline over the period, especially between 1983 and 1986, from a high of about 24 percent to a low of about 18 percent. This would suggest that the ban had an effect. But was the decline due to the ban? Comparing cities with the ban to a control group of cities without such a ban over the same period, it appears that the ban had little effect since the "no ban" cities had a comparable decline. The best that could be said is that the cities with the ban experienced the decline slightly sooner than the "no ban" cities.

Quasi-experimental designs have considerable potential for human service research, much of which involves repeated contact with the same clients. Records of clients' situations and progress are routinely kept, which means that the repeated measures required by the time series designs might not be difficult to obtain. Various treatments or programs used with the clients would constitute the experimental condition. Plotting the data as suggested for time series analysis would reveal whatever impact those procedures produced. Some of these topics and the intricacies of such designs are discussed in more detail in Chapter 11.

External Validity

In experiments, researchers make something happen that would not have occurred naturally. In laboratory experiments, for example, they construct a social setting that, they believe, simulates what occurs in the everyday world. In addition to being artificial, this setting is typically more simple than what occurs naturally because researchers try to limit the number of social or psychological forces operating in order to observe more clearly the influence of the independent variables on the dependent variable. Even field experiments, which are considerably more natural than those in the laboratory, involve a manipulation of an independent variable by the researcher—a change in the scene that would not have occurred without the researcher's intervention.

This "unnaturalness" raises a validity problem different from internal validity discussed earlier in the chapter. **External validity** concerns the extent to which causal inferences made in an experiment can be generalized to other times, settings, or groups of people (Cook and Campbell, 1979). The basic issue is whether an experiment is so simple, contrived, or in some other way different from the everyday world that what we learn from the experiment does not apply to the natural world. This problem is a part of the problem of generalizing findings from samples to populations discussed in Chapter 6. With experiments, however, some special problems arise that are not found with sampling in other types of research methods. Indeed, resolving the problem of external validity can be difficult and is less straightforward than is the case with internal validity. Campbell and Stanley (1963, p. 17) succinctly state the problem:

> Whereas the problems of internal validity are solvable within the limits of the logic of probability statistics, the problems of external va-

lidity are not logically solvable in any neat, conclusive way. Generalization always turns out to involve extrapolation into a realm not represented in one's sample.

We will review four major threats to external validity and ways in which these threats can be reduced.

Reactive Effects of Testing

In any design using pretesting, the possibility exists that experiencing the pretest can alter subjects' reactions to the independent variable. For example, items on a paper-and-pencil pretest measure might make subjects more or less responsive to the independent variable than they would have been without exposure to those items. The problem this raises for generalizability should not be difficult to understand. The populations to which we wish to generalize findings are composed of people who have not been pretested. Therefore, if the subjects are affected by the pretest, findings may not accurately generalize to the unpretested population.

Whether reactive effects of testing are a threat to generalizability depends on the variables involved in the experiment and the nature of the measurement process used. Paper-and-pencil measures may be quite reactive; unobtrusive observation is likely not to be reactive. When one is planning an experiment, it is therefore important to consider whether reactive effects of testing are likely to be a problem. If they are, then it would be desirable to choose a research design that does not call for pretesting, such as Design T.3, or one that includes groups that are not pretested, such as the Solomon design. With the latter design, it is possible to measure the extent of any pretesting effects.

Unrepresentative Samples

As emphasized in Chapter 6, the representativeness of the people studied in any form of research is crucial to the issue of generalizability. Unfortunately, it is often difficult to experiment on truly representative samples of any known population. Often, experimental subjects are volunteers, people who are enticed in some way to participate, or people who happen to be available to the researcher. The implications of this for generalizing experimental findings are quite serious. For example, one review of a large number of studies concluded that people who volunteer for experiments differ systematically from the general population in the following ways: The volunteers are better educated, come from a higher social class, have higher intelligence, have a greater need for social approval, and are more sociable (Rosenthal and Rosnow, 1975). Clearly, these differences could be related to any number of the variables likely to be used in human service research. Generalizing findings from such volunteer subjects could be quite hazardous.

Although the use of coerced subjects may reduce the differences between experimental subjects and the general population from which they are drawn, it has problems of its own as far as generalization is concerned. Coerced subjects are likely to have little interest in the experiment and may be resentful about the coercion used (Cox and Sipprelle, 1971). This effect has been found even where the nature of the coercion was quite mild, such as gaining extra credit in a college class for agreeing to participate in an experiment. It is reasonable to assume that these effects would be amplified where the level of coercion was greater, such as court-ordered participation in a treatment program under threat of incarceration. In fact, a study of a drug treatment program involving court-ordered clients found this anticipated pattern (Peyrot, 1985). The coerced clients were resentful, uncooperative, and unwilling to commit to the therapeutic objectives of the program.

The threat to external validity created by unrepresentative samples is of great importance to human service workers because most efforts to evaluate the effectiveness of treatment approaches are conducted on volunteers or coerced subjects. Volunteers may make programs look good because they are interested in the treatment and motivated to change in the direction promoted by the treatment. It should come as no surprise that apparently effective treatment approaches on volunteers often fail when applied to nonvolunteer groups. Alternatively, because of their lack of interest and resentment, coerced subjects tend to make treatments appear ineffective when they might be effective on persons who are not coerced.

Reactive Settings

In addition to the reactivity produced by testing, the experimental setting itself may lead people to behave in ways that are different from their behavior in the everyday world. One reason for this is that experimental settings contain *demand characteristics:* subtle, unprogrammed cues that communicate to subjects something about how they should behave. For example, people in experiments tend to be highly cooperative and responsive to the experimenter. In fact, the psychologist Martin Orne (1962) deliberately tried to create boring and repetitive tasks for subjects so that they would rebel and refuse to do them. One task was to perform a series of additions of random numbers. Each page required 200 additions, and each person was given 2,000 pages. After giving instructions, the experimenter told them to continue working until he returned; $5\frac{1}{2}$ hours later the subjects were still working, and it was Orne who gave up and ended the experiment! On the basis of this and other research, it has become evident that experimental settings exercise a powerful influence on subjects that can damage the generalizability of experimental findings. This has been labeled as the problem of the *good subject*—that is, the subject in an experiment who will do whatever the investigator asks, even to the point of confirming the experimenter's hypotheses if they are communicated to the subject (Wuebben, Straits, and Schulman, 1974).

Subjects' reactions are not the only way in which experimental settings can be reactive. Experimenters themselves can introduce distortion into the results that reduce generalizability. Experimenters, of course, usually have expectations concerning the results of the experiment, wanting it to come out one way or another. These *experimenter's expectations* can be communicated to subjects in such a subtle fashion that neither experimenter nor subjects are aware the communication has taken place (Rosenthal, 1967). A classic illustration of how subtle this can be is recounted by Graham (1977) and involves a horse, not humans. The horse was called Clever Hans because of his seeming ability to solve fairly complex arithmetic problems. Hans and his trainer toured Europe in the early 1900s, amazing audiences and becoming quite famous. Hans would stand on stage pounding out the answers to problems with his hoofs. Amazingly, Hans was hardly ever wrong. Hans would perform his feats as well even when his trainer was not present. Could Hans really do arithmetic? After very careful observation, it was discovered that Hans was picking up the subtle cues given off by those who asked him questions. As Hans approached the correct number of hoofbeats, questioners would move or shift just enough to cue the horse that it was time to stop.

The same phenomenon has been thoroughly investigated in the physician–patient relationship (Kline, 1988). When giving a patient a treatment known to be effective, a physician exudes confidence, and the patient picks up on this and expects to get better. The patient's hopeful mood then increases the likelihood that the patient will actually improve. However, when a physician is giving a patient a placebo—an inert substance the physician doesn't expect to work—his or her manner communicates doubt; the patient senses, without being aware of it, what the physician's expectations are and then helps create that reality. People in experiments do the same thing. Subjects react to subtle cues unconsciously given off by an experimenter that tell them to behave in a way the researcher would like them to.

Reactive experimental settings can threaten external validity because changes in the dependent variable might be due to demand characteristics or experimenter expectancies rather than to the independent variable. One procedure for reducing the problem of reactivity in experimental settings is to conduct the experiment in such a way that subjects are *blind*—that is, unaware of the experimental hypotheses—so that this knowledge will not influence their behavior. In fact, subjects are commonly given a false rationale for what they are to do in order to reduce the reactions of subjects that might

interfere with the generalizability of the findings. As an ethical matter, subjects should be informed of the experiment's true purpose during the post-experimental debriefing session.

The surest way of controlling reactivity due to the experimenter is to run what is called a *double-blind* experiment. In a **double-blind experiment,** neither the subjects nor the experimenter knows which people are in the experimental and which are in the control condition. This makes it impossible for the experimenter to communicate to subjects how they ought to behave because, for any given subject, the experimenter would not know which responses would confirm the experimental hypotheses. Though it is simple in theory, maintaining a double-blind procedure in practice can be difficult. Another layer of personnel must be added to accomplish the assignment of subjects, issue sealed instructions to the experimenter, and keep track of the results. Furthermore, all information relating to these activities must be kept from those actually running the experimental groups. It is easy for this structure to break down so that the double-blind feature is lost. However, for true protection against such reactivity, double-blind experiments need to be used. Unfortunately, there are times when the nature of the treatment interferes with the use of the double-blind approach. Because of the different activities involved, it may be obvious which condition is experimental and which is control. Clearly, this would prevent the use of a double-blind experiment.

Multiple-Treatment Interference

In an experiment in which there is more than one independent variable, it may be the particular combination and ordering of experimental treatments that produce change in the dependent variable. If this same combination and this same ordering do not occur outside the experimental setting, the findings from the experiment cannot be generalized. Suppose, for example, that an experiment calls for subjects to experience four independent variables in succession. Furthermore, suppose that the last variable in the series appears to produce an interesting effect. Could the effect of that fourth variable be safely generalized on the basis of the experimental findings? The answer is no. The subjects in the experiment would have experienced three other independent variables first. Experiencing those other variables first might have affected the way they reacted to the last one. If people outside of the experimental setting do not experience all the variables in sequence, generalization concerning the fourth variable is risky. The problem of multiple-treatment interference is similar to reactive effects of testing in that the subjects in the experiment experience something that the people in the population at large do not.

The threat of multiple-treatment interference can be effectively eliminated through the use of complex designs in which the independent variables are experienced by the different experimental groups in every possible sequence. If a given variable produces a consistent effect regardless of the ordering of the variables, then multiple-treatment interference is not a threat to the generalizability of the findings. An alternative is to isolate the variable of interest in a multiple-treatment experiment and conduct a follow-up experiment with that variable as the only treatment. If it produces an effect similar to that found when it was a part of a series of treatments, multiple-treatment interference can be ruled out.

In designing experiments, especially those to be conducted in laboratory settings, problems of external validity need to be considered. Properly designed experiments can offer researchers substantial confidence in generalizing from an experimental sample to other settings or groups. However, efforts to enhance external validity may affect our ability to achieve internal validity, which brings us to the importance of replication for external validity.

The Importance of Replication

Although both internal and external validity are important to experimental research, there is a tension between the two. On the one hand, internal validity is enhanced through greater control. Consequently, the researcher seeking internal validity is attracted to the laboratory experiment and to precise testing. Yet, we have just seen that the reactive effect of testing is a threat to external validity. Seeking control, the researcher may use a homogeneous sample to avoid the confounding effects of other variables. In the effort to achieve internal validity, one might, for example, use a sample of white, male 18-year-olds. Although the effects of race, sex, and age are now controlled, the external validity threat of unrepresentative samples is increased. We have suggested the use of complex designs to reduce the threat to external validity of multiple-treatment interference. However, complex designs are more difficult to implement in a way that retains the integrity of the research design. Thus, there appears to be a dilemma between seeking internal validity on the one hand and external validity on the other.

The basic solution to this problem is not to seek a solution to both internal validity and external validity in a single study. As Thomas Cook and Donald Campbell (1979, p. 78) put it with regard to experiments: "In the last analysis, external validity . . . is a matter of replication." Confidence in generalizing from experimental findings increases as the same hypotheses are tested and supported in a variety of settings with a variety of designs. Often this takes the form of initial testing in the laboratory under ideal conditions to see if the hypothesis is supported at all. Then the same hypothesis can be tested under the less-than-ideal conditions of the field. Through replication, the dual objectives of internal and external validity can be achieved.

Lack of Minority Participation and Analysis

Depending on the setting in which an experiment is conducted, women and minorities may well find themselves underrepresented in laboratory or field experiments. This is a problem that can affect external validity as well as internal validity. Researchers often choose as subjects for experiments people who are easily accessible to them. In basic research in psychology and sociology, for example, students in introductory psychology or sociology classes are often selected as research subjects. The sex ratio of college students is fairly even: 47 percent male and 53 percent female. However, African Americans constitute only about 9 percent of all college students while they account for 13 percent of our total population (U.S. Bureau of the Census, 1991). This means that experiments using a representative sample of college students will tend to underrepresent African Americans, Hispanics, and some other minorities. And this underrepresentation is more severe at some colleges than at others: Some major research universities even today have only 1 percent or 2 percent black enrollment. So whenever experimental subjects are selected from a setting, care must be taken to ensure representation of minorities in a sample if the minorities are to be included in the generalizations made from the data. Otherwise, mention should be made that no special procedures were used in the sampling to enhance minority involvement.

A related problem is what one sociologist calls *gender insensitivity:* "ignoring gender as an important social variable" (Eichler, 1988, p. 66). In experiments, this can happen when no mention is made of the sex ratio of the subjects in the experiment or data are not analyzed separately for each sex. Eichler reports one issue of a psychology journal in which the only article to mention the sex of the subjects was one that used rhesus monkeys; none of those using human subjects did so. This was true despite the fact that practically all those articles focused on variables (such as perception, verbal ability, and learning) on which people's gender might well have an influence.

A final problem relating to minority participation in experiments is the failure to consider the gender or minority status of all participants in the experiment. In addition to the researcher and the subject, this might include interviewers, confederates of the experimenter, and any others who interact with the subject during data collection. We know, for example, that people of the same gender interact differently from people of the opposite gender. Thus, a male interviewer will respond differently when asking questions of a female subject from when interviewing a male subject. In the former case, he might be more friendly, attentive, or

engaging without even realizing it, and this could influence the subject's response to questions.

These threats to external validity can be reduced by reporting the sex or minority status of the various people involved in experiments and analyzing the data with sex or minority status as an experimental or control variable. There are, of course, reasons to have a homogeneous sample in an experiment: It can reduce extraneous variation when trying to establish a causal relationship between independent and dependent variables. However, if the results are to be generalized to all racial and ethnic groups and both sexes, then experiments need to be replicated using subjects from these groups.

Assessment of Experiments

By now you should more fully appreciate the extent to which experimentation can be used in human service research. In addition, you should recognize how the logic of experimentation can be translated into valuable guidelines that can enhance human service intervention. We close the chapter with a brief summary of the advantages and disadvantages of experiments.

Advantages

Inference of Causality   The major advantage of experimental research is that it places us in the most advantageous position from which to infer causal relationships between variables. Recall from Chapter 2 that causality can never be directly observed. Rather, we infer that one thing caused another by observing changes in the two things under the appropriate conditions. A well-designed and controlled experiment puts us in the strongest position to make that causal inference because it enables us to control the effect of other variables, which raises our confidence that it is the independent variable that is bringing about changes in the dependent variable. Experiments also permit us to establish the time sequence necessary for inferring causality. We can measure the dependent variable to see if it has changed *since* the experimental manipulation. With other research methods, such as the survey, it is often not possible to directly observe whether the changes in one variable preceded or followed changes in another variable.

Control   Experimenters are not limited by the variables and events that happen to be naturally occurring in a particular situation. Rather, they can decide what variables will be studied, what values those variables will take, and what combination of variables will be included. In other words, they can create precisely what their hypotheses suggest are important. This is in sharp contrast to other research methods, such as the use of available data (*see* Chapter 8) or observational techniques (*see* Chapter 9), in which hypotheses need to be reshaped to fit the existing data or observations.

The Study of Change   Many experimental designs are longitudinal, which means that they are conducted over a period of time, and measurements are taken at more than one time. This makes it possible to study changes over time. Many other research methods, such as surveys, tend to be cross-sectional—they are like "snapshots" taken at a given point in time. In cross-sectional studies, we can *ask* people how things have changed over time, but we cannot *directly observe* that change.

Costs   In some cases, experiments—especially those conducted in laboratory settings—can be considerably cheaper than other research methods. Because of the element of control, the sample size can be smaller and this saves money. The costly travel expenses and interviewer salaries found in some surveys are eliminated. Some field experiments, however, can be expensive because they may require interviewing—possibly more than once—to assess changes in dependent variables.

Disadvantages

Inflexibility   Experimental designs generally require that the treatment, or independent variable, be well developed and that the same treatment be applied to all cases in the experimental group. If the nature of the independent variable changes as the experiment progresses, this is extraneous variation that makes it difficult to say what changed the dependent variable. Because of this inflexibility, experimental designs are not suitable in the early stages of research when treatments may not be well developed. This requirement for consistently measuring the independent variable is especially true of large-scale, longitudinal experiments, which are best suited for clearly designed treatments (Rossi and Freeman, 1993).

Randomization Requirement   Human service organizations may be unwilling to accept random assignment to treatment and control conditions in spite of the value of this technique for controlling extraneous effects. This is especially so when the design calls for a control group to receive no treatment at all. Organizations may have ethical concerns about randomization, or they may want to be sure that they "get something" for participating in a study and so be reluctant to serve as the control condition. In addition, with field experiments, there are times when it is impossible to find or create a control group that is truly comparable to the experimental groups and thus the true experimental designs are ruled out. In spite of the fact that randomization was achieved, both Research in Practice illustrations in this chapter emphasize the considerable difficulty in carrying out randomization.

Artificiality   The laboratory setting in which some experiments are conducted is an artificial environment created by the investigator, which raises questions of external validity. We often do not know what the relationship is between this artificial setting and the real world in which people live out their daily lives. We cannot be sure that people would behave in the same fashion on the street or in the classroom as they do in the laboratory. Even field experiments of human service interventions are vulnerable to this criticism to an extent, especially when they create conditions that would never exist naturally. For example, the recipients of social services who are the subjects of research may be treated better by the research team than they would be in their everyday contacts with human service agencies. Under the watchful eye of a research team, much greater care may be taken in the form of monitoring and supervision to assure that the treatment delivered is true to the theoretical model than is taken when the same intervention is delivered as a routine part of an agency's service.

Experimenter Effects We have just pointed out the artificiality of experimental settings in comparison to the real world. Yet, there is another side to this coin: The experimental setting itself is a real world—a social occasion in which social norms, roles, and values exist and shape people's behavior (Wuebben et al., 1974). Social processes arising within the experimental setting—and not a part of the experimental variables—may shape the research outcome. Thus, changes in the dependent variable may be due to the demand characteristics of experiments, such as repeated measurement, or to the impact of experimenter expectations—factors that obviously do not influence people in the everyday world.

Generalizability The logistics involved in managing an experiment often necessitate that experimenters use small samples. Furthermore, the goal of holding measurement error to a minimum often compels researchers to make these samples as homogeneous as possible. Despite the advantages of random sampling, the experimenter must frequently settle for availability samples in order to obtain subjects who will participate in the study. The net result is that experiments are often conducted on small, homogeneous availability samples, and it may be difficult to know to whom such results can be generalized. It is often assumed that representative sampling is not as essential in experiments as in other types of research because of the randomization and control procedures used. Although these help, one still must be cautious regarding the population to which generalizations are made.

Timeliness of Results Although experiments may produce the strongest evidence of causation, they are often time-consuming to conduct. The urgency of policy decisions may preclude using experimentation simply because it takes too long to generate funding for the project, design the research, and carry it out. If results do not come in quickly enough, they may not be considered in the debate over a rapidly developing policy (Rossi and Freeman, 1993).

Main Points

- Experiments are a controlled method of observation in which the value of one or more independent variables is changed in order to assess the causal effect on one or more dependent variables.
- Owing to the great control afforded by experiments, they are the surest method of discovering causal relationships among variables.
- Major elements of control in experiments include control variables, control groups, matching, and randomization.
- Internal validity refers to whether the independent variable does in fact produce the effect it appears to produce on the dependent variable.
- Numerous conditions may threaten the internal validity of experiments, but all of them can be controlled by using true experimental designs.
- Quasi-experimental designs are useful for bringing much of the control of an experiment to nonexperimental situations.
- External validity concerns the degree to which experimental results can be generalized beyond the experimental setting.
- Threats to external validity are generally not controllable through design, being more difficult and less straightforward to control.
- Double-blind experiments, in which neither the subjects nor the experimenters know which groups are in the experimental or control condition, are used to control both experimental demand characteristics and experimenter bias.

■ To avoid race, ethnicity, or gender insensitivity, the minority composition of experimental groups should be reported, consideration should be given to analyzing the data by controlling for minority impact, and the minority status of all experimental participants should be considered.

■ An understanding of experimental procedures can contribute to practice effectiveness as well as research endeavors.

Important Terms for Review

blocking
control condition
control group
control variables
double-blind experiment
experimental condition
experimental group
experimental stimulus
experimental variability
experimentation
external validity
extraneous variability
field experiments
internal validity
laboratory experiments
matching
preexperimental designs
quasi-experimental designs
random assignments
true experimental designs

Exploring the Internet

If you've been taking advantage of Internet resources that apply to the previous chapters, then you've no doubt discovered the value of using key chapter terms with various Internet search engines. For example, using such terms as "random assignment" or "randomized control group" with the AltaVista search engine will help you locate a number of Web sites that relate to experimental design in

social science. One site we located by using the search engine was The Hypertension Nework (http://www.bloodpressure.com/index html.) The site is primarily devoted to health-related information and research on high blood pressure, so its relevance to experimental design is not immediately apparent. However, it includes a link to a page on clinical trials. Here you'll find a discussion of experimental design and how it is being applied to the study of hypertension.

The American Psychological Association maintains a Web site devoted to research experiments that are being conducted on the Net entitled Psychological Research on the Net. Its URL is http://psych.hanover.edu/APS/exponnet.html. By contacting this site, you will find links to experiments on the Internet that are related to psychological issues. They are organized by general topic area with the topic areas listed alphabetically. We recommend that you explore some of these sites and participate in some of the projects that appeal to you. Keep in mind that not all the projects included here are true experimental designs complete with control groups, but many of the projects do employ features of experimental design.

For Further Reading

Adair, J. *The Human Subject: The Social Psychology of the Psychological Experiment.* Boston: Little, Brown, 1973. A good analysis of the many kinds of reactivity and experimenter expectancies that can be found in experimental settings.

Fairweather, George W., and William S. Davidson. *An Introduction to Community Experimentation: Theory, Methods, and Practice.* New York: McGraw-Hill, 1986. An interesting book ideally suited to those involved in community action programs. It outlines the reasons for experimentation and supplies the designs to evaluate the effectiveness of various intervention programs.

Gabor, Peter A., and Richard M. Grinnell, Jr. *Evaluation and Quality Improvement in the Human Services.* Boston: Allyn & Bacon, 1994. Although this book covers many other research issues, it is especially good at showing the importance of experimental designs in program evaluations. It describes the use of many different kinds of designs used in human service settings.

Gottman, John M. *Time-Series Analysis: A Comprehensive Introduction for Social Scientists.* New York: Cambridge University Press, 1981. Comprehensive is certainly the operative word in describing this book as it details the mathematical analysis of time series designs. The author also argues persuasively against the common "eyeballing" approach to time-series analysis.

Kirk, R. E. *Experimental Design: Procedures for the Behavioral Sciences,* 2nd ed. Belmont, Calif.: Brooks/Cole, 1982. This is a thorough overview of how to design experiments, both simple ones and complicated ones. It goes well beyond the review in this chapter.

Pechman, Joseph, and P. Michael Timpane, eds. *Work Incentives and Income Guarantees: The New Jersey Income Tax Experiment.* Washington, D.C.: The Brookings Institution, 1975. An excellent discussion of methodological and political problems in conducting an applied experiment in a controversial field setting.

Ray, William, and Richard Ravizza. *Methods Toward a Science of Behavior and Experience.* Belmont, Calif.: Wadsworth, 1993. This book covers many research topics, but it also devotes considerable attention to experimentation, especially describing the logic behind and the value of experimental designs.

Exercises for Class Discussion

A senior citizens service organization is concerned about the large number of purse snatchings and other attacks on elderly people in the community and decides to apply for a Department of Justice grant intended to assist local communities in fighting crime. A requirement for receiving such a grant is that an evaluation be done to assess the effectiveness of any program established.

The idea of the staff of the center is, first, to hire local teenagers to work out of the center as escorts to those people who request the service. Second, they plan to use the teenagers as a crime watch in those areas where attacks have been fairly frequent. Initially, the center will not be able to serve everyone, and the crime watch staff will only be able to cover some of the neighborhoods.

The senior center staff believes that this program will serve two objectives. First, it will reduce the threat of crime to the elderly. Second, if young people are put into positions where they can work with and help the elderly, it will increase feelings of understanding between the generations.

You have been asked to help the center develop a research design whose purpose is to assess how well the program attains its objectives.

10.1 What would be the independent and dependent variables for such a project? Give some examples of possible indicators for these variables. Given the various types of experimental designs available—preexperimental, quasi-experimental, and true experimental—which two would be the most appropriate to the research question and the most feasible?

10.2 One decision that needs to be made is whether to use the presence or absence of the program as the independent variable or to test different combinations of the independent variables. List some possible combinations of intervention efforts that could be used in a factorial design.

10.3 A major issue in experimental research is how to assign participants to experimental and control conditions.

a. Consider just the escort service. How could participants be assigned to treatment and control conditions? Would random assignment be ethical? Indicate why or why not.

b. Now consider the crime watch component, which serves anyone who happens to be in the patrolled area. Assume the center serves about a 50-block area of the city. Suggest some ways of developing experimental and control conditions.

c. Are there any control variables that might be usefully considered in this study? How would these control variables assist you in making causal inferences?

10.4 How would you collect data to evaluate the effectiveness of the program in meeting its goals of reducing crime and increasing intergenerational understanding? Consider the alternatives of personal interviews, mailed questionnaires, observations, and existing data.

Now there's trouble in River City. It seems a local, very influential politician has gotten wind of the project. His mother lives in the impact area, and under no circumstances will he support an evaluation where his mother may wind up as a control subject who will not be provided services. Without his support, there will be no grant.

10.5 How could you design a quasi-experimental study that would not involve designating certain people or areas as experimental and control? What deficiencies would this design have in comparison to a true experiment?

10.6 What are the major threats to internal and external validity in this research project? How have the designs considered in the preceding exercises helped to reduce these threats?

CHAPTER 11

Single-Subject Designs

The Clinical-Research Model   286

The Clinical-Research Process   288
Identify Problems   288
Establish Goals   288
Select a Single-Subject Design   289
Establish and Measure the Baseline   289
Introduce Treatment   294
Assess Treatment Effects   295

Types of Single-Subject Designs   297
Single-Treatment Designs   299
Specialized Designs   303

Generalizability of Single-Subject Designs   309

Assessment of the Clinical-Research Model   310
Advantages   310
Disadvantages   311

Main Points   311

Important Terms for Review   313

Exploring the Internet   314

For Further Reading   316

Exercises for Class Discussion   316

Much human service work occurs in clinical settings in which practitioners attempt to improve the functioning of individual clients. This one-to-one relationship may at first appear far removed from research settings involving the experimental groups, independent variables, and matching described in the preceding chapter. Although research findings are clearly useful in such practice settings, can the practitioner–client encounter itself be considered a part of that research process? Increasingly, the practitioner–client relationship is becoming an arena for social research. Not only is this individual client interaction being recognized as able to serve the purposes of scientific research and knowledge accumulation, but practitioners are also calling on procedures commonly used in research to help enhance their intervention efforts (Fischer, 1981).

We saw in Chapter 1 that there is a growing tendency for human service professionals to view their role as that of clinician-researchers. The purpose of this chapter is to present a fundamental tool of this role and a central mechanism through which valid research can be conducted in clinical settings: the *single-subject design*. **Single-subject designs** are quasi-experimental research designs that involve assessing change in a dependent variable on a single research subject. Actually, the term "single-subject" is somewhat of a misnomer because the focus of the research may be a couple, family, group, organization, or other human aggregate as well as an individual person. In the literature, the general study design is variously referred to as single-case, case-study, same-subject, repeated measures, intensive, clinical-experimental, applied behavior analysis, time series, ideographic, N = 1, and single-system as well as single-subject (Krishef, 1991). We continue to use the single-subject designation because it is the most widely accepted term. However, it must be emphasized that the subject may be something other than a person. For example, two of our students recently conducted a single-subject design study on improving group cohe-

siveness in a social skills group for chronic mentally ill adults. In this case, the group was the subject and cohesion was the dependent variable. Other students evaluated a medication program in a community mental health system. They measured the proportion of clients who received their weekly dosage of medication on time. Here the service delivery program was the subject and the proportion of patients treated as scheduled was the dependent variable. However, the most common application is to focus on a behavior of an individual client. The feature that unites these various projects under one design is the fact that the dependent variable is repeatedly measured during a baseline phase and during one or more intervention phases when the independent variable is manipulated. Experimental effects are inferred by comparisons of the subject's responses across baseline and intervention phases. We begin by discussing how and why a *clinical-research model* has emerged in the human services. Then we analyze the clinical-research process, showing how research can be merged with clinical practice. Building on the discussion of experimental designs in Chapter 10, we then present the various kinds of single-subject designs available to clinician-researchers. Finally, we analyze the advantages and disadvantages of single-subject designs.

The Clinical-Research Model

A fundamental driving force behind the development of single-subject designs is the human service practitioner's professional concern about knowing how a client is responding to intervention. This basic desire to know has been intensified by the pressure for more accountability in the human services. Funding sources and review organizations demand documentation that services have been delivered according to standards, and they want to see evidence that clients have in fact improved. Unfortunately, traditional research designs have significant limitations for meeting these needs of the practice community (Alter and Evens, 1990; Gingerich, 1990; Orcutt, 1990; Russell, 1990; Barlow and Hersen, 1984). For example, one major source of new knowledge for many practitioners prior to single-subject designs was group experiments. However, group experiments are often inappropriate or impossible to conduct in clinical settings. It may be too time-consuming and costly to assemble clients with similar problems and randomly assign some to treatment and others to control groups. A second problem with group experiments in terms of practice implications is that the results are often an average of the whole group's response, obscuring individual reactions. It is, of course, precisely the effects on individuals that are of most interest to clinicians. For example, knowing that a given treatment was effective on 70 percent of an experimental group may be interesting, but it helps relatively little in predicting the reaction of a particular client seated in a practitioner's office.

Another problem in some traditional group experimentation is the failure of the research design to capture the process by which change was induced. Thus, traditional research has sometimes been referred to as "black box" research because subjects receive some treatment and are then compared with other subjects who did not receive the treatment. With only a pretest and posttest measure, experimenters may not have information on the process of how change occurred but only on whether or not it occurred. It is as if the subjects passed through a mysterious black box and came out either improved or not improved. A fourth complaint about traditional group experiments has been that the complicated nature of the statistical analysis associated with data interpretation necessitates that quantitative methodologists, not regular practitioners, carry out the research. This reliance on direction from outside of practice may have contributed to studies' being viewed as not relevant to practice.

Finally, the use of control groups, from whom treatment is withheld, has been a source of ethical concern to human service professionals. Thus, although group experiments are appropriate for some purposes, the deficiencies inherent in the method have led both practitioners and researchers to seek an alternative approach for evaluating individual change and refining intervention techniques. Single-subject designs, as we shall see, effectively avoid the unattractive features of group experiments.

A second source of clinical knowledge prior to single-subject designs was case histories. A case history, of course, is a report from a clinician about a client who has undergone treatment. Although many of these reports are intriguing, they often do not provide a sound basis for the accumulation of knowledge. First of all, they exhibit to only a limited degree the characteristics that distinguish science from other sources of knowledge (*see* Chapter 2). For example, vague treatments are often reported to have produced vague improvements. Because of this, other practitioners would have grave difficulty replicating the procedures if they wished. And the ability to replicate is, of course, a fundamental characteristic of the scientific method, especially when one is working with a single case at a time. In addition, case histories are often prepared only on successes, so information about failures, which may be of equal importance, is not communicated to other practitioners. Another problem with case histories is a failure to report valid and reliable data to support conclusions. In the absence of hard data, exaggerated claims of success become commonplace (Barlow and Hersen, 1984). Finally, these studies, with no controls, fail to consider the possible impact of extraneous variables on the client.

So it was against this backdrop of unsatisfactory research techniques for clinical settings that the *clinical-research model* emerged. The **clinical-research or empirical-practice model** became an effort to merge research and practice, and it includes much more than single-subject designs. It involves a stance toward practice that is defined by the following characteristics (Siegel, 1984):

1. Maximum use is made of research findings for understanding human service practice issues.

2. Data is collected systematically in order to monitor the intervention.
3. Interventions are evaluated empirically to determine their degree of effectiveness.
4. Problems, interventions, and outcomes are specified in terms that are concrete, observable, and measurable.
5. Research ways of thinking and research methods are employed in defining clients' problems, in formulating questions for practice, in collecting assessment data, in evaluating effectiveness of interventions, and in using evidence.
6. Research and practice are viewed as parts of the same problem-solving process.
7. Research is accepted as a tool to be used in practice.

The systematic evaluation of practice through the use of single-subject designs is a core component of this model of practice. It is through the mechanism of single-subject designs that research and practice merge into one enterprise. It should be noted, however, that this approach does not reject traditional large-group research. Such research is necessary for testing total programs and for confirming the generalizability of intervention effectiveness. With this note of clarification, we now turn to examining the stages in the clinical-research process and how single-subject designs are incorporated into practice.

The Clinical-Research Process

At the outset, we wish to make it clear that the clinical-research model is not a radically new approach to intervention. In fact, there are many parallels between this model and traditional practice. Much of what the model calls for, many practitioners are likely to do anyway. The model does, however, inject greater specificity, objectivity, and empiricism into the clinical process. By following the model, clinician-researchers are in a position to know precisely what treatment was applied and how much effect was produced and to have supporting data for proof. The model links research

and practice by putting the practitioner in the enviable position of not only bringing about change but also having valid evidence as to why the change occurred. What follows in this section is an outline of the clinical-research process divided into six stages, which are summarized in Figure 11.1.

Identify Problems

Like all practice approaches, the clinical-research model begins with an assessment of the client's problem. Typically, the problem will involve some aspect of the client's functioning: behaviors, perceptions, attitudes, or feelings. During the initial stage, the practitioner strives to obtain as clear and specific an understanding of the problem as possible, using assessment strategies such as interviewing or paper-and-pencil assessment tools commonly used by practitioners.

Establish Goals

After the problem is identified, the next step is to determine what goals are to be achieved through treatment. At this point, the first real difference between the clinical-research model and traditional practice is encountered. The model requires, first,

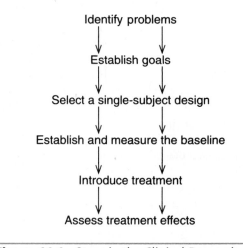

Figure 11.1   Steps in the Clinical-Research Process

that goals be more specific and precisely defined than is often done in conventional practice, and, second, that they be measurable in some way (Kazdin, 1985). Although these requirements of specificity and measurability are more rigorous under the clinical-research model than in traditional practice, they are best seen as an extension of normal practice procedures rather than as something strangely different. As to the requirement of measurability of outcomes, some practitioners would argue that some beneficial outcomes of intervention are so subtle that they are unmeasurable. Countering this attitude in the field of social work, two researchers contend: "When the outcome is not measurable, social workers are probably engaging in self-delusion" (Newman and Turem, 1974, p. 16). The self-delusion is believing that a real but unmeasurable change has occurred when actually it has not. Rather than try to settle this debate, we make the important point that the clinical-research model places strong emphasis on measurable outcomes.

One common problem encountered in establishing goals is that they are often long term, making it impractical for the clinician-researcher to monitor progress all the way to achievement of the final goal. In these cases, it may be necessary to identify proximate, intermediate goals whose achievement is evidence of progress toward the final goal. For example, the final goal for an underachiever might be improved academic performance—a long-term goal. Proximate goals that would evidence progress might include improved note taking, longer study hours, and more regular class attendance. Achievement of these proximate goals would be expected to be related to achievement of the final goal. Which measurable, intermediate goals can serve as valid indicators of long-term goals depends, of course, on a theoretical understanding of the long-term changes sought through intervention.

Select a Single-Subject Design

Once a problem and a corresponding goal for intervention have been identified, the next phase of the clinical-research process is to select an appropriate single-subject design. Whereas the general principle of single-subject research consists of comparing a series of preintervention measurements with a series of postintervention measurements, there are many variations on this basic scheme. Later in the chapter we present several common designs and discuss their strengths and limitations. At this point, however, we simply want to alert you to the fact that there are many design options from which to choose and also to point out that, early in the process, the practitioner should be thinking about the design choices that will best suit the goals and constraints of a particular clinical case. For example, if the practitioner's primary objective is to provide treatment and simply monitor the client's progress, then a simple design will be adequate. In other cases, there may be a general behavior deficit where the proposed intervention involves working on increasing the desired behavior in different realms of the client's life such as at home, in school, and in visiting with friends. There are designs that take advantage of such an intervention strategy both to monitor client behavior and maximize validity for research goals.

The point is that single-subject designs are very flexible and adaptive to many practice situations. To take advantage of this flexibility requires that the practitioner have a clear notion of the problem to be addressed, an understanding of how the proposed intervention is supposed to effect changes, and an awareness of single-subject design strengths and limitations. Once a particular design has been chosen, the practitioner can address the next step in the clinical-research process, establishing and measuring a baseline.

Establish and Measure the Baseline

Single-subject designs are based on the quasi-experimental time-series designs discussed in Chapter 10, although modified to make them more appropriate for use with a single subject. As such, single-subject designs call for repeated measures of the client's condition so that trends and changes can be noted. Typically, what is measured is the frequency, intensity, or duration of some behavior of the client, such as how many cigarettes are smoked, the severity of pain, or how long a depression lasts. Thus, the fourth step in the clinical-research process is to establish a **baseline,** or a series of measurements of the client's condition prior to treatment; the baseline is used as a basis from which to compare the client's condition after treatment is implemented. By comparing measurements after treatment with those of the baseline period, the clinician can trace the effect the treatment is having. Typically, three measurements are needed, as an absolute minimum, to establish a baseline (Barlow and Hersen, 1973). More measurements are better, especially if the client's condition is unstable. It is important to note that all single-subject designs rule out the simple procedure of using only two measurements—one pretest and one posttest—because this results in a preexperimental design (*see* Design P.1 in Chapter 10) that is extremely weak on internal validity.

Figure 11.2 illustrates how baseline measurement can serve as a basis for assessing treatment effects. The hypothetical data show a high level of undesirable client behavior prior to treatment. After treatment is instigated, this drops sharply. Results are not always as dramatic as these, so making interpretations can be more difficult. We deal with the issue of assessing treatment effects in more detail later.

Two major issues to be settled in establishing the baseline are what to measure and how to measure it. Typically, the clinical problem itself will suggest the appropriate trait to measure. In general, what we seek to change through treatment is what needs to be measured. For example, a child whose problem is disruptive behavior in school could be monitored as to the frequency of disruptions he or she causes each day. On the other hand, treatment philosophy might suggest monitoring frequency of *appropriate* behavior as a means of not only measuring behavior but also setting the stage for change.

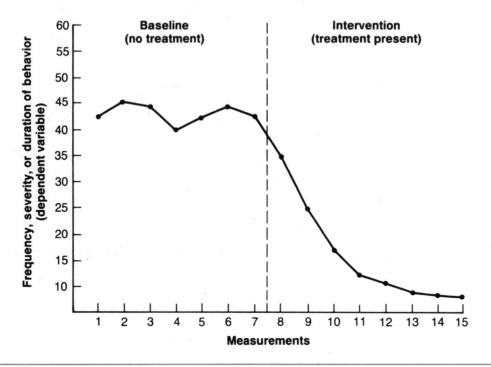

Figure 11.2 Hypothetical Baseline Followed by Successful Treatment

As emphasized in Chapter 5, measurement and operational definitions should be deduced from theoretical concepts, whether those concepts emerge from research or practice theories.

Client problems that do not have specific behavioral outcomes or manifestations are more difficult to measure (Bloom, Fischer, and Orme, 1995). Depression, for example, can be displayed in many different behavioral forms, and in such cases it is preferable to use several measures. Also, where there is such an indirect link between a concept and behavioral manifestations, the use of multiple indicators helps to reduce the effects of error in those measures. In the case of depression, we might establish a separate baseline for a behavioral indicator (say, percent of day spent alone), a paper-and-pencil measure of depression, and a self-report from the client about his or her subjective assessment. If the treatment produced positive gains on all measures, we would have greater evidence of the treatment's effectiveness than if we relied on only one indicator.

Having decided on what aspects of the client's condition to measure, we confront the question of *how* to measure them. Basically, the clinician-researcher has four choices: observation, existing records, paper-and-pencil measures, and client self-reports. Of these, observation is of most general utility and is the most valid and reliable (Jayaratne and Levy, 1979; Weiss and Frohman, 1985). Unfortunately, as noted earlier, many client problems are not directly observable, so there is a limit to the applicability of observation. When it is used, however, there are three important considerations. (These issues regarding observation are discussed in greater detail in Chapter 9.) First, the observations should be unobtrusive. If they are not, the client may behave differently owing to the presence of the observers. This could result in faulty baseline data, which could obscure treatment effects. Second, multiple observers should be used where possible in order to assess the extent of observer reliability. In some cases, videotapes might be substituted for multiple observers, but in natural settings their use is likely to be difficult. Third, if possible, observers should not be aware of when treatment is begun.

If they are, their expectations for improvement might affect the objectivity of their observations. For example, borderline behaviors that were counted as disruptive during the baseline phase might be ignored during the treatment phase. This shift would tend to overstate the apparent effectiveness of the treatment to reduce disruptive behavior.

A second measurement approach is to use existing records. Some client problems relate to matters on which data are routinely gathered by people other than the clinician or client. For example, existing records, such as grades and school attendance, are often used in assessing a child's school performance. Where existing records are appropriate, they are often a good choice. They are unobtrusive because they are collected whether the client is under treatment or not. Furthermore, because they are collected by persons other than the clinician-researcher, time and cost factors are likely to be favorable. There are several problems associated with using existing records for research purposes, however, and these can be reviewed in Chapter 8.

A third common measurement approach is paper-and-pencil measures, which are often used when the client's problem does not lend itself to direct observation. If the decision is made to use a paper-and-pencil measure, it is advisable to use an existing one, if available, rather than devise a new one. In addition to the practical benefits of avoiding the time and trouble of developing a new measure, existing measures usually have established levels of validity and reliability. Furthermore, their use contributes to the accumulation of knowledge because the standardized measuring devices make for greater comparability across studies. Fortunately, a large number of measures are available, covering a wide array of client problems. (The following are only some of the compilations of such measures: Bonjean et al., 1967; Lake et al., 1973; Chun, Cobb, and French, 1975; Groth-Marnat, 1984; Mitchell, 1985; Magura and Moses, 1986; Corcoran and Fischer, 1987; Fredman and Sherman, 1987; Miller, 1991; and Robinson, Shaver, and Wrightsman, 1991.) Research in Practice 11.1 discusses such measures in detail.

Research in Practice 11.1
Assessment of Client Functioning: Rapid Assessment Instruments

Although single-subject designs hold much promise for improving the precision with which practitioners evaluate the outcomes of intervention with individual clients, a stumbling block to reliable and valid applications from the time this design was first advocated has been the lack of sound measurement tools. While a practitioner could rely on direct observation or available records, many existing standardized measures were not suitable for the repeated measurements required by the single-subject design. This situation is no longer the case, thanks to the development of a variety of measurement tools known collectively as *rapid assessment instruments,* or RAIs.

RAIs are distinguished from other measures by several main features. They are short, easy to administer, and easy to complete. RAIs are written in clear, easy-to-understand language with uncomplicated directions so that disruption of the intervention process is kept to a minimum. Scoring can normally be done in a few minutes without the need for special equipment. They have been applied in family service agencies (Toseland and Reid, 1985) and in agencies serving children and youth (Edlesen, 1985). Levitt and Reid (1981) identify sources for RAIs covering anxiety, depression, assertiveness, social interaction, and marital problems. Probably the best current reference for the practitioner seeking measurement instruments to aid in single-subject evaluation in practice is *Measures for Clinical Practice: A Sourcebook,* compiled by Corcoran and Fischer.

One can gain an appreciation for the effort and creativity required to develop sound measure-

ment tools for single-subject designs from the ongoing work of Walter Hudson and his colleagues, who set out to design a measurement package that would be appropriate for single-subject work, easy to administer and score, and relevant to the clinical problems likely to be encountered in practice (Hudson, 1982). In the early 1970s, they began work on this project, culminating in the *Clinical*

Table 11.1   Hudson's Index of Self-Esteem (ISE)

This questionnaire is designed to measure how you see yourself. It is not a test, so there are no right or wrong answers. Please answer each item as carefully and accurately as you can by placing a number by each one as follows:

1 = Rarely or none of the time
2 = A little of the time
3 = Some of the time
4 = A good part of the time
5 = Most or all of the time

_____ 1. I feel that people would not like me if they really knew me well.
_____ 2. I feel that others get along much better than I do.
_____ 3. I feel that I am a beautiful person.
_____ 4. When I am with other people I feel they are glad I am with them.
_____ 5. I feel that people really like to talk with me.

Source   From W. W. Hudson, *The Clinical Measurement Package* (Homewood, Ill.: Dorsey Press, 1982). Scales may be obtained from WALMYR Publishing Company, P.O. Box 6229, Tallahassee, FL 32314-6229.

Paper-and-pencil measures have some characteristics that make them less than ideal for use in single-subject designs, however. First, they are obtrusive, because clients obviously know they are being measured, and this can create many problems. For example, completing a questionnaire concern-

ing family relationships might make parents aware that they have been paying less attention to their children than they should, and they could change their behavior because of this awareness. Recall from Chapter 10 that this is the "testing" threat to internal validity in experiments. (Although such

Measurement Package (CMP). This manual includes nine 25-item paper-and-pencil scales for the assessment of (1) depression, (2) self-esteem, (3) marital discord, (4) sexual discord, (5) parent–child relationships as seen by the parent, (6) mother–child relationships as seen by the child, (7) father–child relationships as seen by the child, (8) intrafamilial stress, and (9) peer relationships. (Table 11.1 contains the first five items of the self-esteem scale.)

With regard to research, the CMP illustrates several key points. First, good data collection techniques are essential for both research and practice. Recall from Chapter 2 that theory provides hypotheses for research and interventions for practice and that the outcomes of research and interventions contribute to theory development (*see* Figure 2.1). Without good data collection strategies and sound measurement procedures, utilization of single-subject designs is doomed to failure. Efforts to overcome these problems culminated in the development of this scale package, and creation of the scales involved repeated application of the scales in various research projects to determine reliability and validity. Second, the package illustrates the kind of achievements necessary to link practice and research more closely in the human services. The scales are relevant to the clinical problems practitioners face, they are easy to administer, they are relatively innocuous in work with clients, and they yield reasonably clear interpretations. Third, the manual illustrates some of the differences in applying such scales for practice as compared with research. For example, one difference, Hudson argues, is in the type of design chosen. For practice purposes, a simple design with a single baseline and a single treatment can be extremely powerful for documenting client improvement and for making clinical decisions. As we point out in this chapter, however, such a simple design is weak for research

purposes. Another difference between practice and research, Hudson argues, is in reliability: Practitioners require higher reliability in a measurement tool than do researchers. The reason for this is that researchers, even in single-subject work, may be able to combine cases and use statistical analysis to determine significance of effect, thus easing the distortions of a somewhat unreliable measure. The clinician, on the other hand, is concerned with helping one client, not in simply knowing what in the long run would be the probability of a certain effect on a group of people. According to Hudson, the estimates for reliability of the CMP scales are all over .90, suggesting that they should be well suited to the needs of both practice and research.

The CMP manual illustrates another issue in research, namely, that the construction of good instruments is a painstaking, time-consuming process that goes far beyond simply making up a list of questions (*see* Chapters 5 and 13). We mention in this chapter problems with data based on self-reports. The CMP manual overcomes many of these problems through careful tests for reliability and validity. Because of this, the package of nine instruments illustrates that careful assessment of client functioning and single-subject design are well within the reach of human service providers in a wide variety of practice settings. Hudson developed the Computer-Assisted Social Services (CASS), a computer software package for maintaining client records and evaluating client progress (Nurius and Hudson, 1993). In addition to the scales described in the CMP, the CASS contains many new scales, some of which are often evaluated for reliability and validity. Some of the new scales measure (1) personal stress, (2) anxiety, (3) alcohol abuse, (4) sexual attitude, (5) homophobia, (6) partner abuse: nonphysical, (7) partner abuse: physical, and (8) peer relations.

change may be desirable, the problem from a research standpoint is that it is not possible to determine if the treatment or the measurement process caused the change.) The second problem with paper-and-pencil measures is that of *demand characteristics,* also discussed in Chapter 10. Clients may de-

liberately change responses in the direction indicating improvement. This effect can occur because of a desire to fulfill the expectations of the clinician for improvement in the client. Furthermore, because of frequent exposure to the measure, the client will become familiar with it, raising the specter of multiple-testing effects (*see* Chapter 10). Finally, some paper-and-pencil measures are projective tests, such as the Rorschach Inkblot Test, the Thematic Apperception Test, sentence completion tests, and figure drawings. These tests all rely heavily on the examiner's interpretation of client responses. After reviewing the evidence, Barlow and Hersen (1984) strongly advise against the use of these types of measures because they do not have sufficient validity and reliability to provide a sound basis for single-subject experiments.

The last measurement alternative is to use self-reports of clients who monitor their own behavior or feelings. Although clients' perceptions of their condition are important, there are many problems associated with overreliance on self-reports.

First, there is evidence that self-reports do not correlate well with objective indicators. For example, studies of assertiveness among female college students have made use of people's own reports of how assertive they are and of trained observers' assessments of how assertively these people actually behave. Generally, researchers find that the self-reports do not correlate with the observers' assessments (Frisch and Higgins, 1986).

Second, self-monitoring is reactive because it sensitizes the client to some aspect of his or her behavior (Barlow et al., 1992). Research has shown that the mere process of monitoring can change one's behavior. In one study, for example, objective baselines were gathered on how many cigarettes were consumed by a group of smokers (McFall, 1970). Half the subjects were then asked to monitor and record the extent of their smoking. The other half were to keep track of the times when they didn't smoke. Both groups showed a change from their baseline levels but in the opposite direction. Those monitoring their smoking smoked *more,* and those monitoring their nonsmoking smoked less! Similar self-monitoring effects have been noted concerning study habits among college students (Johnson and White, 1971). This phenomenon has been put to use in a variety of treatment programs, which include self-monitoring as the intervention that brings about behavior change. This effect, however, is hardly desirable when the goal is

to assess the effects of treatments other than self-monitoring. Because of the multitude of problems associated with self-report data, they should be used with caution, preferably as an adjunct to other measures that are less subject to false reports.

From our discussion of measurement options available to clinician-researchers, it is evident that some are better than others. The most objective, valid, and reliable measure available in a given research context should be selected. As noted, direct observation is usually best if the client's problem lends itself to such observation. Otherwise, a more indirect measure will be necessary, although these have the limitations we have outlined. However, by using multiple measures, the weaknesses of the indirect measures can be reduced and the quality of the single-subject experiment improved (Gottman, 1985).

Introduce Treatment

Once the baseline is established, the next stage in the clinical-research process is to begin treatment. When the treatment is applied, it is important that only a *single,* coherent treatment be applied during any treatment phase (Barlow and Hersen, 1984). The reason for this derives from the fact that each application of the clinical-research model is essentially an experiment, with the treatment being the independent variable in that experiment. If more than one treatment is used and the client exhibits behavior change in comparison to the baseline, we would not know *which* treatment produced the change and would have learned nothing that might be valuable with similar clients in the future. In order to assess the effects of the independent variable, we must be able to specify precisely what the treatment consisted of and also be consistent in its application during the treatment phase.

The demand for a single, specific treatment is one aspect of the clinical-research model that has led to a cold reception in some human service circles, particularly among nonbehaviorists (Nelsen, 1981). Nonbehavioral treatments often lack the specificity that allows practitioners to trace a particular treatment over the period of the treatment phase. In addition, nonbehavioral treatments can be very complex and may even mix a number of treatment modes, making it difficult to identify the precise factors that presumably resulted in change. However, this is less a criticism of the clinical-research model than a challenge to those using nonbehavioral treatments: "[nonbehaviorists] must work hard at choosing interventions that may be effective and at defining their interventions precisely, preferably by addressing both what they do and how they do it" (Nelsen, 1981, p. 35).

Resistance to the discipline imposed by the clinical-research model appears to be greatest among those who are least familiar with it. After some initial frustration with the specificity and single treatment required by the model, practitioners learning to apply the model come to accept it (Johnson, 1981). They come to appreciate that the model increases rationality in the selection of treatments, forces an explicit consideration of the assumptions on which treatment is based, and requires the use of specific practice skills rather than a reliance solely on their own intuition or ingenuity. Greatest satisfaction, however, comes from the fact that the model provides solid evidence regarding whether the client benefited from treatment. While it is rewarding to feel that one has been of assistance, it is even more rewarding to have some objective evidence to support those feelings.

During the treatment phase, the measurement of the client's condition, started during the baseline phase, is continued. This, of course, is done to track what changes (if any) the treatment is producing in the client's condition. It is crucial that the conditions under which measurements are made during the treatment phase remain consistent with those under which the baseline measurements were obtained (Jayaratne and Levy, 1979). Any change in such things as observers, settings, examiners, or instructions could confound apparent treatment effects. Remember that a single-subject design is an experiment, and only one variable—the treatment—should be allowed to change from one phase to another.

Assess Treatment Effects

When is a treatment judged effective? This seemingly simple question, which is addressed in the last stage of the clinical-research process, has a surprisingly complex answer. Assessing effectiveness depends, first of all, on the pattern produced during the baseline measurements: The ease and clarity with which baseline measures can be compared with treatment measures depends in part on the *stability* of the baseline measures. Figure 11.3 illustrates four possible baseline patterns: (1) a stable baseline, (2) a rising trend (client worsening), (3) a descending trend (client improving), and (4) an

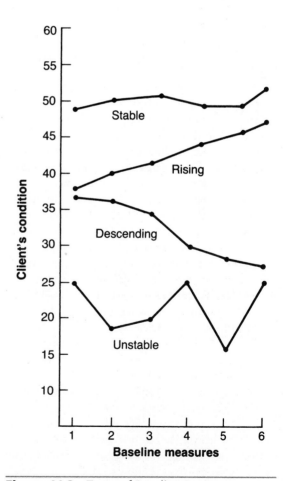

Figure 11.3 Types of Baseline Patterns

unstable baseline. (In this discussion of baseline stability, we will assume that lower measurement scores represent improvement, as in the case of reducing the incidence of some problem behavior. If the goal of treatment is to increase some aspect of client functioning, as it often is, improvement would be indicated by higher measurement scores.) A stable baseline is the ideal since posttreatment comparisons will then readily reveal treatment effects. If the treatment is helpful, there should be a pronounced downward move in measurement levels. A treatment producing negative effects would yield an upward move in measurement levels. Ineffective treatment would be revealed by little change from the baseline levels. The value of a stable baseline is that it allows all three possible treatment outcomes to be readily noted.

Unfortunately, client conditions are often not stable. Their condition may worsen, improve, or be highly variable. Assessing treatment effects with baselines of these types is more difficult and often puts limits on what can be inferred. A baseline with a rising trend (client worsening) is not too problematic because an effective treatment will produce a reversal of the baseline trend. Such a change provides strong evidence that the treatment was effective. With ineffective or harmful treatments, however, it is difficult to tell if this is just a continuation of the baseline trend (ineffective treatment) or if the continued deterioration is due to some harmful treatment. A baseline with a decreasing trend, showing client improvement, has the opposite effect. If the treatment proves harmful, the trend will reverse, and the negative effect will be readily apparent. But if the client continues to improve during treatment, it is unclear whether the treatment produced that improvement (effective treatment) or whether it was just a continuation of the baseline trend (ineffective treatment).

The most troublesome baseline is one that is unstable. With the client's condition changing from one measurement to another, it becomes very difficult to identify changes due to treatment. There are, however, a couple of strategies for dealing with an unstable baseline (Barlow and Hersen, 1984). One is to extend the period of baseline measure-

ments with the hope that a stable pattern will emerge. There is no guarantee, of course, that it will. In addition, there may be practical as well as ethical constraints on how long treatment can be postponed while awaiting baseline stability. A second strategy is the application of statistical techniques that can reveal trends and differences between pre- and posttreatment too subtle to be noted by visual inspection (Gottman, 1981; Achen, 1986). These statistics are of limited effectiveness, however, if the pattern is very unstable.

The use of statistics in assessing treatment effects also raises a problem beyond that of baseline stability, namely, how much change is necessary before one can say that a treatment is effective. From a research perspective, any change from pretest measures to posttest measures is evidence that the treatment was effective in the sense of bringing about change in the dependent variable. However, in clinical settings, *change* can take the form of improvement or deterioration in a client's status. Practitioners are seeking improvement, of course, so treatment effectiveness in single-subject designs is normally defined as an improvement in performance after treatment. Yet, assessing whether improvement has occurred can be complex because effectiveness can be based on three different criteria: therapeutic, experimental, or statistical.

A treatment is *therapeutically effective* when it leads clients to achieve fully the goals set for them to accomplish. The disruptive student is no longer disruptive, the underachiever is now achieving, or the teenage mother can care for her infant independently. When treatment produces these kinds of improvements in a client's condition, its effectiveness is obvious. Visual inspection of the measurements taken during the treatment phase will clearly reveal the improvement wrought when compared with the baseline measurements.

A treatment is *experimentally effective* when it produces a pronounced improvement in the client's condition although ultimate goals have not been reached. For example, a claustrophobic may have come to the point where he or she can use an elevator alone but remains unable to use a crowded one. As with therapeutic effectiveness, the change in the client's condition from baseline to treatment phase is sufficiently dramatic that visual inspection is normally adequate to reveal it. Figure 11.4 displays two data plots from single-subject designs conducted by one of the text authors in a school classroom. In the first case, the teacher monitored disruptive classroom behavior. The second case represents a child in kindergarten who had difficulty adjusting to school. The problem was monitored by counting the number of requests she made during school to go home. These cases illustrate two criteria for establishing experimental effectiveness (Kazdin, 1982). The first case has nonoverlapping data. All the measurements taken during the treatment phase are higher or lower (whichever direction represents improvement) than those taken during the baseline phase. Stated another way, performance during treatment does not overlap with that of the baseline period. This is a fairly severe guideline and one that, if met, is a strong demonstration of experimental effectiveness. The criterion achieved by the second case is somewhat less rigorous: All the measurements taken during the treatment phase are higher or lower than the *average* level of the baseline. This guideline would be preferred over the first if the baseline were not especially stable. It is important to emphasize that these are only guidelines, not rigid rules. It is quite possible that a given single-subject experiment could evidence clear experimental effectiveness and achieve neither of these guidelines. Following them, however, does make visual inspection more systematic and less a matter of judgment on the part of the clinician-researcher.

Statistical effectiveness is achieved when the treatment produces statistically significant improvement in the client's condition. In other words, the difference between baseline and treatment levels is too great to be due to chance variation. (The concept of statistical significance is discussed in detail in Chapter 15.) Because statistics are sufficiently sensitive to detect smaller changes than can visual inspection, statistical effectiveness sometimes requires the least improvement in the client. This raises the issue of the difference between statistical significance and therapeutic or experimental significance.

A treatment judged effective because it produced a statistically significant improvement in the client might be judged a near failure according to the other criteria. For example, reducing an alcoholic's consumption from 20 ounces of whiskey a day to 15 might be a statistically significant reduction, but we would hardly call the treatment a rousing success. Because statistical significance may be only remotely related to treatment success, statistical analysis is usually limited to cases with an unstable baseline, which makes visual analysis difficult. When statistical analysis is used, single-subject data require the use of special statistical techniques because many commonly used statistics assume that each measurement is independent of the others. Because all the measurements in a single-subject experiment are from the same person, statistical tests based on the assumption of independence would be inappropriate. Fortunately, statistics specifically designed for analyzing single-subject data are available (*see* Barlow and Hersen, 1984; Jayaratne and Levy, 1979; Kazdin, 1982; Marascuilo and Busk, 1988; Gottman, 1981; Achen, 1986). Furthermore, several of these techniques are fairly easy to apply without using a computer or other equipment to do the analysis.

So we see that the question of treatment effectiveness depends in part on the particular criterion of effectiveness applied. With the varying criteria, it is important to be aware of the differences and to be precise when discussing what is meant by effectiveness. Furthermore, it is important to recognize that the effect of a treatment may be relatively permanent, or the effect may decrease after treatment is withdrawn. To test for this, the posttreatment measurements become, in effect, a new baseline. Deviation from this baseline as time passes suggests that there is a limit to how long the treatment is effective.

Types of Single-Subject Designs

Although numerous types of single-subject designs exist, all involve repeated measurements during baseline and treatment phases and a comparison

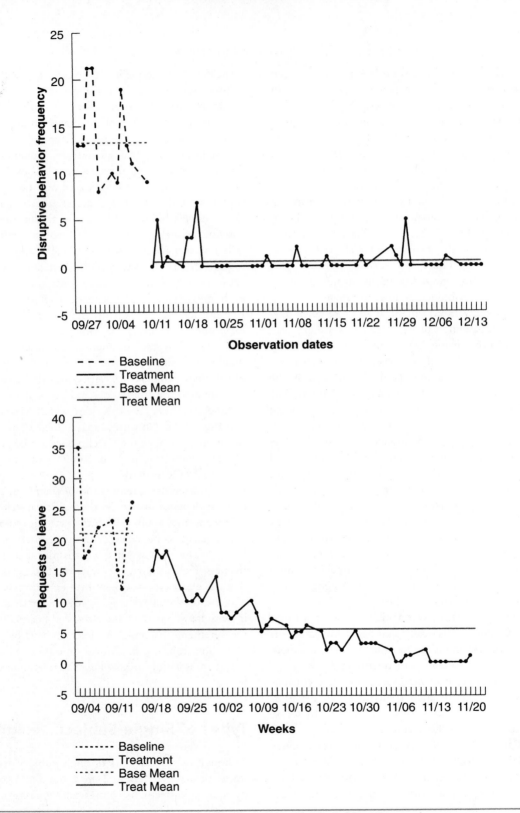

Figure 11.4 Establishing Experimental Effectiveness in Single-Subject Research

across phases as evidence of treatment effects. The designs differ in the number of phases involved, the number of treatments applied, and the number of baselines employed. Perhaps the most important differences are in the internal validity of the designs. Some are more capable of providing evidence for the effect of a treatment when such an effect actually exists. Ideally, of course, clinician-researchers should select the most valid design that fits their particular case (*see* the discussions of validity in Chapters 5 and 10).

Single-Treatment Designs

The Basic *AB* Design   It has become customary to present single-subject designs by using the first letters of the alphabet to symbolize various phases of the design. The letter *A* signifies a phase in which the client is not receiving treatment. This would be the baseline period in all designs, but it could also refer to a period when treatment is withdrawn in some of the more complex designs. The letter *B* indicates a treatment phase during which some specific intervention is in progress. Subsequent letters of the alphabet, *C, D,* and so on, are used as needed to symbolize the application of treatments different from *B*.

The *AB* design is the simplest of the single-subject designs and forms the basis for the others. The *AB design* consists of one baseline phase followed by one treatment phase. Treatment effectiveness is determined by comparing the client's condition during treatment with that of the baseline. The basic *AB* design is less than ideal because its validity is threatened by *history:* Events other than the intervention could be responsible for the change in the client. Despite the limitations of the *AB* design, it provides better evidence of treatment effects than nonexperimental case histories. It also has the advantage of being applicable to most clinical situations, especially in cases where more rigorous designs might be precluded.

Reversal Designs   The *AB* design can be strengthened substantially by moving to a *reversal design,* so called because, after one treatment phase,

the treatment is withdrawn for a period of time. There are basically two versions of the reversal design: *ABA* and *ABAB*. The two versions differ only in that the *ABA* design ends in a no treatment phase whereas, in the *ABAB* design, the treatment is reintroduced a second time (*see* Figure 11.5).

The value of the reversal designs stems from their ability to demonstrate more conclusively that the treatment and not some extraneous factor is producing change in the client's condition. If the client's condition deteriorates when the treatment is withdrawn, we have evidence that the treatment is the controlling factor. Even more evidence is provided with the *ABAB* design if the reintroduction of the treatment coincides with renewed improvement of the client. Although it is possible for a set of extraneous factors to produce the first client improvement, it is less likely that the same set of factors would recur at precisely the right time to produce improvement on reintroduction of the treatment. As Figure 11.5 illustrates, especially with the *ABAB* design, we would have great confidence in the efficacy of a treatment that produced similar real-life results.

Despite their strengths on internal validity, practical considerations often restrict the use of reversal designs. First, treatments that produce permanent changes in clients—which is often the goal of intervention—are not reversible. For example, if the treatment involves clients' learning something, it is obvious that they cannot "unlearn" it at the command of the clinician-researcher. In such cases, reversal designs are simply not applicable. Second, it might be unwise or unethical to attempt returning clients to their pretreatment state. An obvious example would be a case where the suicidal tendencies of a client were alleviated. It is up to the clinician-researcher to decide on a case-by-case basis whether a reversal design can be ethically justified.

Multiple-Baseline Designs   The *multiple-baseline design* involves establishing baselines for more than one aspect of the client's condition. Multiple baselines can be established for different behaviors, for one behavior in different settings, or for different clients who suffer from a similar problem. For

The *ABA* Design

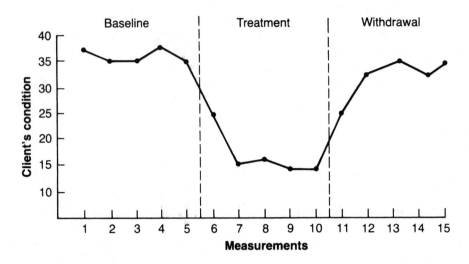

The *ABAB* Design

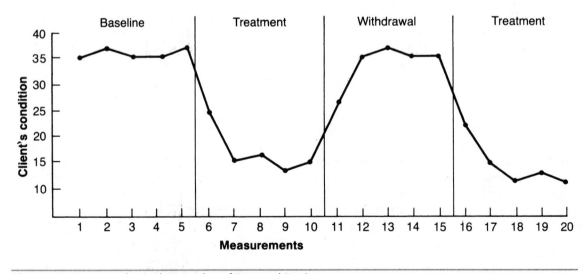

Figure 11.5 Hypothetical Examples of Reversal Designs

example, a practitioner working with several alcoholics could establish separate baselines for each, thus applying the multiple-baseline design across individuals. Although it is recommended that a minimum of three baselines be utilized, clinician-researchers should not be deterred from using only

two if conditions do not permit more. The more baselines that are used, however, the stronger in terms of internal validity the design becomes (Barlow and Hersen, 1984; Jayaratne and Levy, 1979).

The multiple-baseline design is essentially a stacked set of *AB* designs, with the same treatment being introduced sequentially into each of the baseline conditions:

First client: A_1B
Second client: A_1A_2B
Third client: $A_1A_2A_3B$

In the illustration, the initial baseline measurement (A_1) is made on each client, and then the treatment is introduced to the first client only. A second baseline measurement is taken from the remaining two clients, and then treatment is introduced to the second client. A third baseline measurement is taken from the third client, who then receives treatment. Figure 11.6 illustrates the multiple-baseline design with a successful outcome. In each of the three conditions, the introduction of the treatment is followed by improvement. The multiple-baseline design is fairly strong on internal validity.

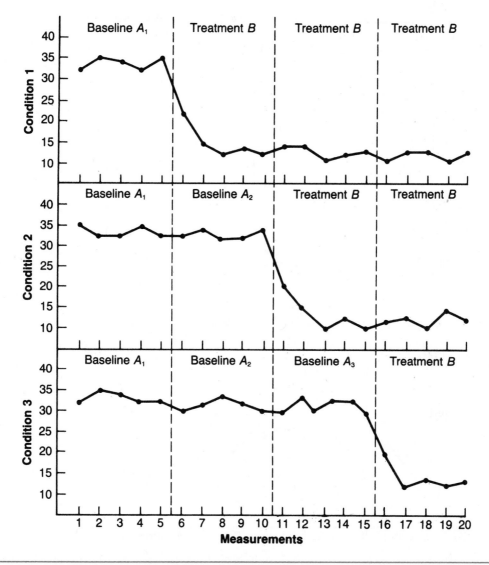

Figure 11.6   Hypothetical Example of Multiple-Baseline Design

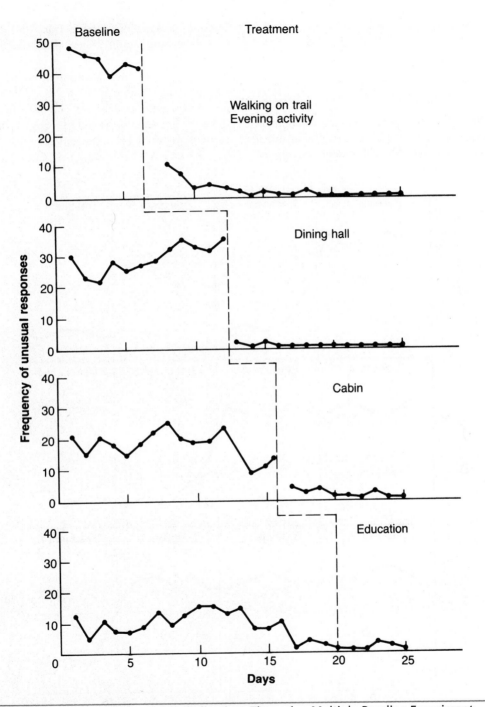

Figure 11.7   Reduction of Unusual Verbalizations Through a Multiple-Baseline Experiment

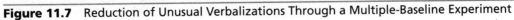

The efficacy of the treatment is assessed across three or more behaviors, settings, or individuals. Furthermore, the sequential introduction of treatments makes it highly unlikely that extraneous factors can account for apparent treatment effects across the several baseline conditions. The multiple-baseline design is thus generally superior to the *AB* design, but the *AB* design with replication also overcomes some of the threats to internal validity, such as history (Harris and Jenson, 1985). The multiple-baseline design is not as strong on internal validity as are the reversal designs; but where reversal designs are inappropriate, the multiple-baseline design is a good alternative.

The application of the multiple-baseline design is sufficiently complex to warrant a detailed example, illustrating the design as applied across settings (Allen, 1973). The client was an 8-year-old boy with an unusual fascination with penguins. He would fantasize about them for up to 8 hours a day and had an imaginary menagerie populated with the creatures, each with its own name. The child talked about his imaginary pets with great frequency. These verbalizations made him an object of scorn and ridicule among other children and interfered with his interpersonal relations with adults. The experiment was conducted while the boy was attending summer camp. For the first 6 days, camp counselors made baseline observations of the frequency of penguin statements in four settings around the camp: evening-activity, dining-hall, cabin, and education settings. On the 7th day, treatment—consisting of ignoring the penguin statements and showing attention when he interacted more appropriately—was instituted during evening activity. At successive intervals, the treatment was extended to cover another setting until it was operative in all four (*see* Figure 11.7).

Every time treatment was introduced in a setting, there was a decline in the unwanted responses in that setting, some quite dramatic. Only in the education setting was the effect modest. This setting, however, had the lowest baseline rate to begin with, and it is probable that treatment effects from the other settings carried over to education, where treatment was introduced last. Overall, the pattern

across baselines provides very strong evidence that it was the treatment that brought about behavior change.

Multiple-baseline designs can provide strong evidence for the validity of single-subject outcomes, as Research in Practice 11.2 illustrates. They do have weaknesses, however. The seepage of treatment effects from one setting to another, as in the "penguin case," illustrates a major limitation of the multiple-baseline design. The behaviors, settings, or individuals traced by the several baselines must be relatively independent, or the treatment effects in one condition can produce changes in other, as yet untreated, conditions. For example, it would be unwise to attempt a multiple-baseline design with members of the same family. Because of their routine interaction, treatment applied to one family member could affect the others. If the baseline conditions are highly interrelated, the treatment will show effects after the initial introduction not only in the condition where it is applied, but in one or more of the other conditions as well. If interrelatedness is sufficiently severe, the power of the multiple-baseline design can be destroyed, rendering it little more than an *AB* design with multiple indicators.

One final note concerning the multiple-baseline design is its ability to reveal *contravariation*: positive changes in one area, but negative changes in another (Jayaratne and Levy, 1979). For example, a multiple-drug abuser might respond to treatment by reducing intake of one substance but increasing intake of another. If we traced only one drug, perhaps the most dangerous, the contravariation would remain undetected. A multiple-baseline design covering all the abuser's drugs would readily reveal such an occurrence.

Specialized Designs

The designs just discussed comprise the simplest and most generally useful single-subject designs and have in common the use of only a single treatment (although applied more than once in the *ABAB* design). However, some situations call for variations of these simpler designs to

Research in Practice 11.2
Practice Effectiveness: A Multiple-Baseline Evaluation of Treating Panic Disorder

"It just happened . . . I was walking and all of a sudden my heart started to beat fast and I started to sweat . . . I didn't know what was going on . . . I just felt weird . . . that something bad was happening to me but I didn't know what." [Quoted in Ollendick, 1995, p. 217]

These are the words of a 14-year-old adolescent describing her first panic attack, a condition characterized by discrete periods of intense fear or discomfort in which certain somatic and cognitive symptoms develop abruptly. One can imagine the concern that such experiences would raise for a person, wondering what caused it, when it might happen again, as well as embarrassment produced by behaving in a bizarre manner. Although the problem of panic disorder (PD) and panic disorder with agoraphobia (PDAG—anxiety about being in places from which escape is difficult or where help is unavailable in case of a panic attack) have been widely studied and successfully treated in adults, one researcher discovered that little work had been done on these conditions with adolescents (Ollendick, 1995). Research by Barlow et al. (1989) and Ost, Westling, and Helstrom (1993) had documented the effectiveness, with adults, of behavioral-theory–based interventions, such as applied relaxation, exposure in vivo, and cognitive methods for treating panic disorder. In addition, the researcher's review of the literature found that the same methods had also been used successfully in treatment of separation anxiety and overanxious disorder in youth. So, the researcher set out to evaluate the effectiveness of such cognitive behavioral treatments with panic disorders in adolescents.

We have stated that single-subject designs may be superior to group experiments for documenting the progress of individual clients and for capturing the process by which change is induced. On the other hand, simply comparing a client's base-line scores to treatment scores, as is the case in an *AB* design, is less than ideal in terms of demonstrating causality because of the threat to validity posed by history. The multiple-baseline design is one strategy that reduces the threat of history while still providing a detailed record of individual process through treatment. This feature made the multiple-baseline the design of choice for the research project on the treatment of panic disorder in adolescents (Ollendick, 1995). The particular research design was a multiple-baseline across subjects. Four adolescents who were being seen at an outpatient clinic specializing in anxiety disorders of children and adolescents participated in the study. The subjects were evaluated on several screening instruments and each met full criteria for panic disorder with agoraphobia. They reported that "they sometimes felt really scared, for no reason at all, that out of the blue they felt really scared and that they didn't know why," and that there were places that they didn't want to go because they were afraid they "would get scared all of a sudden and couldn't get help or get away." It was hypothesized that the cognitive behavioral treatments found effective among adults in treating such conditions would also prove effective with adolescents.

Several measures were used to assess the effectiveness of treatment. One indicator was the frequency of panic attacks. The adolescents were asked to monitor the date, time duration, location, circumstance, and symptoms experienced using a Panic Attack Record (PAR) based on a recording format that the researcher located in the literature (Rapee, Craske, and Barlow, 1990). This provided a weekly measure of the frequency of panic attacks. Another indicator was self-efficacy in coping with three potential agoraphobic situations that were included in one of the screening tests used during assessment. Subjects were asked to rate from 1 to 5 how sure they were that they could cope with situations (1 = not at all sure, 5 = definitely sure).

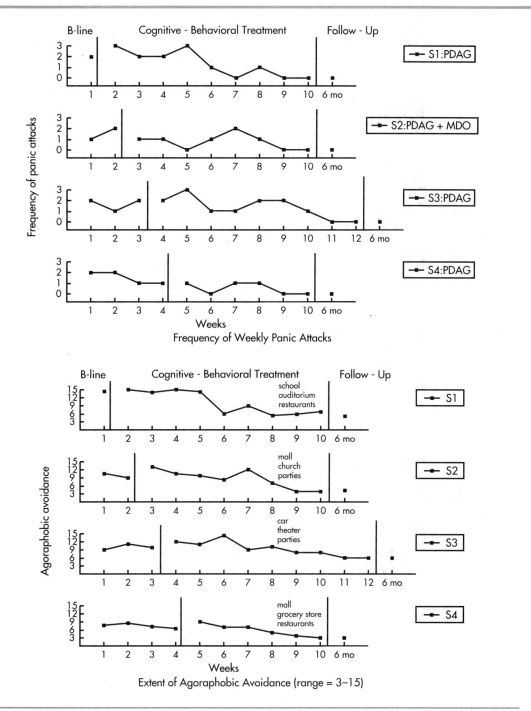

Figure 11.8 Outcomes Assessment Using a Multiple-Baseline Design

Source Adapted from Thomas H. Ollendick, "Cognitive Behavioral Treatment of Panic Disorder With Agoraphobia in Adolescents: A Multiple-Baseline Design Analysis," *Behavior Therapy,* Vol. 26 (1995), pp. 517–531.

continued on next page

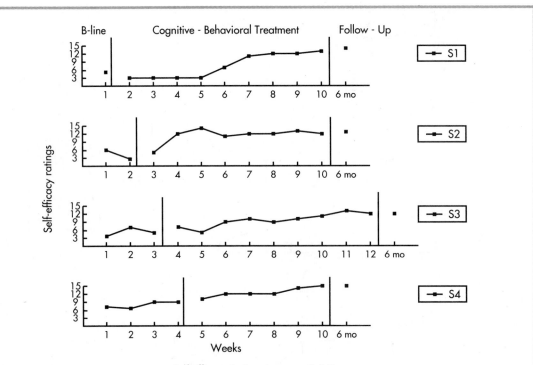

Self-Efficacy Ratings (range = 3–15)

The subjects considered three circumstances: simply being in the agoraphobic situation, first noticing some symptoms, and experiencing more intense symptoms. The adolescents were also asked to rate the extent to which they had actually avoided agoraphobic situations such as going to school, being in an auditorium, or going to restaurants. The self-efficacy and avoidance measures were also modeled on measures found in the existing literature (Clum, 1990).

Baseline measures were obtained for 1 week for S1 (subject 1), for 2 weeks for S2, 3 weeks for

handle special problems. So many complex and specialized designs exist that we can touch on only a few.

Multiple-Treatment Designs   In some settings, it may be necessary to apply several treatments before an effective one is found. By an extension of the reversal designs, *multiple treatments* can be accommodated. A fairly simple extension is the *ABACA* design. It should be apparent that the *ABA* segment comprises a basic reversal design. To

that is added a second treatment phase with treatment *C* instead of *B* and another return-to-baseline phase. This design can be extended to include as many treatments as a given case requires. One important limitation of this design is that it is not possible to determine which is most effective if both treatments show some effect (Barlow and Hersen, 1984). The culprit is history, as extraneous variables occurring during the *B* phase cannot be assumed to be the same as those occurring during the *C* phase.

S3, and 4 weeks for S4 (*see* Figure 11.8). Following baseline, a treatment regime was begun that included providing information on the nature of panic attacks and training in progressive muscle relaxation and proper breathing techniques. The adolescents were taught to use positive self-statements and cognitive coping strategies. Later sessions involved in vivo exposure to the situations that had aroused panic symptoms. The actual length of treatment varied from one subject to another, based on the termination criterion of 2 consecutive weeks with an absence of attacks. Brief maintenance sessions were held 2 weeks and 1 month following treatment. A systematic follow-up occurred 6 months posttreatment.

The data plots for frequency of attacks, agoraphobic avoidance, and self-efficacy provided positive evidence that the treatment was effective in eliminating panic attacks. In addition, standardized self-report measures were used at pretreatment, posttreatment, and follow-up, and these measures also showed improvement.

The project illustrates several points about the research–human service practice relationship. First of all, in searching for a potential intervention strategy, Ollendick relied on the empirical literature to identify promising intervention methods. He also used this literature to devise measurement strategies that would be consistent with previous research and more likely to be reliable and valid. In selecting a research design, it was important to have a design that would not interfere with treatment and that would permit documentation of the progress of each case. For these purposes, a single-subject design was ideal. However, the researcher also wanted to demonstrate that the intervention was the cause of change. Although an *AB* single-subject design is weak in terms of demonstrating the cause of change, the researcher was able to improve confidence in the effectiveness of the treatment by using the multiple-baseline design. He also improved confidence in the outcome by using multiple measures of the problem (frequency of attacks, agoraphobic avoidance, and self-efficacy) and by selecting measurement strategies that had already been reported in the literature. Furthermore, he used standardized tests prior to treatment, after treatment, and at 6-month follow-up. Such a pretest–posttest design is also weak in and of itself, but using it in combination with the multiple-baseline strategy gives more confidence in the outcome of the project as a whole. It would be relatively easy to expand this project into a larger-scale pretest–posttest project simply by replicating the intervention with more clients. It should also be noted that in this project, the problem of "seepage" that we discussed as a potential weakness of multiple baselines was not an issue because all the clients were independent from one another. Through use of the single-system design, the researcher was able to both individualize the treatment to meet the needs of each client and use four subjects in a multiple-baseline design, resulting in greater confidence that the intervention caused the change.

Special designs can also be used when treatments are not applied individually, but in combination. In these cases, it is desirable to assess the relative effects of the components of the treatment package. The *A-B-A-B-BC-B-BC* design, a complex extension of the reversal designs, allows this to be accomplished. The first half, *ABAB*, is one of the basic reversal designs. This part provides a strong demonstration of component *B*'s effects. The *BC-B-BC* segment indicates the effects of *C* beyond those of *B* alone. This design can, of course, be extended farther to indicate additional treatments. Because both of these design extensions are based on reversal designs, they cannot be used with treatments that are irreversible or that are unethical to reverse.

Changing-Criterion Designs Another specialized design that has considerable utility is called the *changing-criterion design* (Barlow and Hersen, 1984). With this design, the goal or criterion of success changes over time as the client is led to

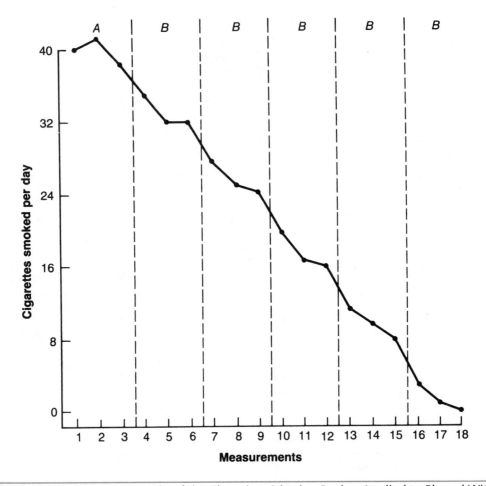

Figure 11.9 Hypothetical Example of the Changing-Criterion Design Applied to Phased Withdrawal of Smoking

attainment of the final treatment goal in stages by achieving a series of subgoals. For example, a smoker could be brought to the final goal of abstinence through phased withdrawal. Figure 11.9 illustrates what a successful application of treatment with a changing-criterion design might look like with such a case. Following the baseline measurement of cigarettes smoked per day, treatment is instituted. For example, let us assume the treatment consists of reinforcement. During the first treatment phase, the client is reinforced for achieving the first subgoal, say, a reduction of eight cigarettes per day. In the second treatment phase, reinforce-

ment is received for achieving a reduction of an additional eight cigarettes—the second subgoal. The third treatment phase would require another reduction to receive the reinforcement. The process is continued until the client has progressed through the subgoals and achieved the final goal of no longer smoking.

The changing-criterion design is related to the multiple-baseline design. In the multiple-baseline design, intervention is independently implemented in relatively distinct areas of the subject's environment. In the changing-criterion design, each time a subgoal is achieved and a new, more stringent subgoal is established, the preceding level essentially becomes a new baseline from which further improvement is measured. Like the multiple-baseline design, the changing-criterion design provides greater evidence of treatment effectiveness than the simple *AB* design. Each time the treatment leads to the achievement of another subgoal, further evidence of its effectiveness is obtained. The only major limitation associated with the changing-criterion design is that it cannot be applied to all client problems. Unless the problem can be meaningfully broken up into subgoals, the changing-criterion design is not applicable.

Generalizability of Single-Subject Designs

In order to build a knowledge base for clinical practice, researchers must have findings that are generalizable to a wide variety of situations and cases. It should come as little surprise that *one* successful single-subject experiment has very little generalizability beyond that particular case. Despite success and hard evidence to prove that the treatment produced it, there is no assurance that the same treatment would be effective on other clients, in different settings, or when used by another practitioner. This lack of generalizability, however, does not detract from the value of single-subject experiments because generalizability can be achieved through replication. It requires many replications before a knowledge base is developed concerning which clients can be helped by a given treatment, which settings it will work in, and what the clinician must do to apply it successfully. As you may gather, this is a process of slow accretion. Each replication provides a little more knowledge concerning the extent of generalizability of treatment effectiveness.

It is valuable in this context to make a distinction between *direct* and *systematic* replication. **Direct replication** involves the repeated application of the same treatment by the same clinician to clients suffering from the same basic problem. In direct replication, only the individual clients vary,

with all other conditions remaining constant. Direct replication serves two important functions (Barlow and Hersen, 1984). First, it increases confidence in the reliability of findings. For example, a clinician with a series of successes in treating claustrophobics would have far greater confidence in the effectiveness of the treatment than was present after success with the first case. Second, direct replication builds generalizability across clients. We discover that the initial success was not a fluke, as the treatment repeatedly proves effective with additional clients. Direct replication is the beginning of establishing the generalizability of a treatment. It cannot, however, answer questions concerning generalizability across settings, practitioners, or other client problems.

Systematic replication is an attempt to extend the treatment to different settings, practitioners, or client disorders by varying one of these conditions or any combination of them. It is normally conducted after there is evidence from direct replication that the treatment may work. For example, the clinician mentioned earlier with the successful history of intervention with claustrophobics might begin systematic replication by applying the treatment to agoraphobics. If this is successful, it would indicate that the treatment was generalizable to a different client disorder from that with which success was originally obtained. Additional replications that vary settings and clinicians would, of course, be required to establish generalizability across these conditions.

An example of a successful systematic replication where all three conditions—change agent, setting, and client disorder—were varied is provided by the earlier example of the 8-year-old boy with the penguin fixation (Allen, 1973). Recall that treatment consisted of having counselors ignore the penguin remarks and show attention when the boy interacted more normally. Prior to this case, James Gardner (1967) reported success with the same treatment applied to a client suffering from a different disorder, in a different setting, and using different change agents. The client was a 10-year-old girl suffering from seizures. When examinations failed to locate a physical cause, the interaction patterns within the girl's family were observed. It was discovered that she and her sister were fiercely competitive for attention from their parents. Furthermore, it was observed that the seizures never failed to attract attention. Treatment consisted of the same type of reinforcement later used with the 8-year-old boy—ignoring the seizures and showing attention during normal behavior. Following intervention, the rate of seizures markedly decreased. Further proof of treatment effectiveness was obtained by applying an *ABAB* reversal design. The parents returned to paying attention to the seizures, and the rate increased. When treatment was reinstated, the girl's seizure rate dropped to zero. Permanent cessation of seizures was apparently achieved—a follow-up a year later revealed that no additional seizures had occurred.

When, as in this case, the same treatment evidences effectiveness in a replication with so many differences from a previous situation, it suggests that the treatment may have broad generalizability. Many more successful replications, of course, would be needed before the parameters of effectiveness for this or any other treatment would be firmly established.

When single-subject experiments and their replication are conducted, two practices are crucial. First, substantial information about client characteristics and backgrounds should be collected. This information can serve as *control variables* in assessing the complex effects that treatment can have on dependent variables. The necessity for this arises from the fact that replications often show that treatment is not consistently effective or ineffective. The background information may be useful in sorting out the reasons for these mixed results. A simple example would be a treatment that was effective with men but either ineffective or less effective with women. A second essential practice is that treatments be kept uniform from case to case so that the results of replications are truly comparable. In addition, reports must be clear and include all information relevant for future replication efforts. At the outset, we noted that one source of dissatisfaction with traditional case histories is the ten-

dency of reports to be too vague to allow for replication. The full potential of single-subject experiments will not be realized if reports include inadequate information for sound replication.

Assessment of the Clinical-Research Model

Advantages

Promotes Better Service for Clients   The requisites of the clinical-research model—careful assessment of treatment goals, use of specific treatments, and continuous monitoring of client progress—tend to promote more effective treatment for clients and encourage the use of scientifically tested intervention strategies (Nelsen, 1981; Johnson, 1981). The model encourages the use of specific practice skills applied in a systematic and rational fashion rather than a reliance on personal idiosyncracy, intuition, or vague and shifting treatment efforts. Furthermore, the model promotes a consideration of the assumptions underlying various treatment approaches, such as why a given treatment should produce positive results with a particular case. The net result is an increased likelihood that a successful intervention will be selected and that the client will be helped.

Promotes Research Activity   The merger of practice and research in the clinical-research model allows practitioners, who might otherwise not conduct research, to do so. For quite obvious and practical reasons, the opportunities for most human service practitioners to be involved in traditional group research are limited. The clinical-research model makes each client a possible subject for a single-subject experiment. In addition, single-subject research is more practical for the typical clinician because it is research on a small scale, involving minimal cost and avoiding the complexities of group research. Furthermore, involvement in single-subject research can enhance the status of the practitioner because publication of results is often possible. On a broader scale, increased research ac-

tivity can promote the image of the human services as scientifically based professions.

Results Are of Both Immediate and Future Value
Following the clinical-research model provides hard evidence of a client's progress, which is of immediate value to the practitioner. Tracking progress aids in the selection and application of treatments that prove effective. After successful treatment, the data provide a clear demonstration that the client has been helped. In an age of increasing accountability, vague feelings of having helped clients or even client testimonials are no longer adequate. In order to prove that intervention does work, critics will increasingly demand scientifically based evidence, and single-subject experiments hold the promise of providing that evidence (Russell, 1990).

Disadvantages

Impracticality
Under current practice conditions, the application of the clinical-research model may often be impractical (Barth, 1981). Some of the most rigorous of the single-subject designs, such as the reversal designs, are especially difficult to apply because irreversible treatments and ethical considerations may preclude their use. Furthermore, some designs contain many phase segments that may require too much time to complete. Beyond these problems is the fact that some client disorders call for immediate attention, precluding baseline measurements so crucial to single-subject designs.

Limited Generalizability of Results
As noted, results from one single-subject experiment have virtually no generalizability beyond that particular case, and they provide less powerful tests of therapeutic effects than do traditional group experiments (Barlow and Hersen 1984; Jayaratne, 1977). Generalizability is obtained only through successful replication across clients, settings, disorders, and practitioners. This is a slow process, meaning that

the potential of single-subject research to increase the knowledge base of the profession will not be realized quickly.

Main Points

- Single-subject designs are quasi-experimental designs used to trace changes induced by treatments to individual clients in a clinical setting.
- Interest in single-subject designs developed out of dissatisfaction with group experiments and case histories as sources of knowledge useful in clinical settings.
- The clinical-research model utilizing single-subject designs is not a radical departure from traditional clinical practice, but rather an effort to increase the specificity and objectivity of practice and to enhance opportunities for replication and knowledge accumulation.
- Although there are many specific single-subject designs from which to choose, all involve a series of pretreatment measures (the baseline) and a series of posttreatment measures that are then compared with the baseline.
- Measurements typically consist of observations, available records, paper-and-pencil measures, or self-reports, with observations usually being the most desirable and self-reports the least desirable.
- Effectiveness may be judged against three different standards—therapeutic, experimental, or statistical—with therapeutic effectiveness demanding the greatest client improvement and statistical effectiveness the least.
- The simple *AB* design is highly flexible, but is not strong on internal validity.
- Reversal designs, such as *ABA* or *ABAB,* are strong on internal validity, but are often impractical to apply.
- Multiple-baseline designs are quite strong on internal validity and are reasonably flexible, making them a good choice when a reversal design cannot be used.
- In addition to these basic designs, there are many specialized designs that can accommodate

COMPUTERS IN RESEARCH
Computer-Aided Single-Subject Data Analysis

In the discussion of analyzing the data on single-subject designs, the point was made that visual analysis is often preferred for single-subject data but that statistical analysis can be used. Whichever one chooses, the computer can be a big help in the analysis. One can simply adapt existing software, tailor it to the demands of single-subject design analysis, or select special packages designed specifically for evaluating clinical data.

Many software packages are available for personal computers that will quickly provide line graphs, histograms, pie charts, and other visual displays for single-subject data. One of the most popular is the spreadsheet. With it the researcher can graph data and perform statistical calculations. The computer spreadsheet derives its name from the common accounting system of organizing financial data on special grids of columns and rows known as spreadsheets. In the computerized version, the display format of the screen is organized into columns and rows of cells, with letters designating the columns and numbers the rows, as in Figure 11.10.

Thus, the first row consists of cells A1, B1, C1, and so on, and the first column consists of cells A1, A2, A3, and so on. Users can enter words or other nonnumeric characters into cells, in which case the spreadsheet treats the cell content as a *label*. In the illustration, "Observation," "Baseline," "Treatment," "Base Mn," and "Treat Mn" are examples of labels. Users can also enter numerical data, such as the observation numbers in cells A2..A17; these are referred to as *values*. A third type of entry, and one which makes spreadsheets really useful, is the *formula*. Although you cannot see it in Figure 11.10, cell B18 actually contains

the formula @avg(B2..B17). In this software, the @ sign is used to designate formula functions. This formula averages the values in cells B2 through B17 and displays the result, 11.125, in cell B18. Spreadsheets can accomplish almost any calculation one might want by specifying the proper formula.

Although accounting applications were the impetus for spreadsheets, many other uses have been discovered for this ubiquitous program, including social science research. Here we illustrate how the program can be used for simple single-subject research. The data in this illustration are for a hypothetical case where the evaluator has monitored the number of tantrums that a child has on each of 16 days. After an 8-day baseline, time-outs are used each time the child has tantrums. Comparing baseline to treatment enables us to determine whether the time-outs produce fewer tantrums.

We can use a spreadsheet program to quickly perform a visual analysis of the results. The key to the analysis is laying out the data correctly in the appropriate columns and rows. We use five columns. In column A, we list the time order for each observation, both baseline and treatment (1 through 16). In column B, we list the baseline data for the first eight tantrum counts. In column C we list the intervention phase tantrum counts. Note that the tantrum count for each observation is entered in the row corresponding to its time-order number. Cells B18 and C18 have formulas to compute the mean of the respective columns, @avg(B2..B17) and @avg(C2..C17). The baseline average, 11.1, is then entered into cells D2..D9, and the mean of the treatment observations is entered in E10..E17; this

such things as changing treatments, combined treatments, or phased achievement of the treatment goal.
■ Positive results from one single-subject experiment are not generalizable, but generalizabil-

ity can be built up over time through replication.
■ Computer software is available that can simplify and speed both the visual analysis and the statistical analysis of data from single-subject research.

	A	B	C	D	E	F	G	H
1	Observation	Baseline	Treatment	Base Mn	Treat Mn			
2	1	10		11.1				
3	2	14		11.1				
4	3	11		11.1				
5	4	9		11.1				
6	5	12		11.1				
7	6	11		11.1				
8	7	13		11.1				
9	8	9		11.1				
10	9		7		4.6			
11	10		5		4.6			
12	11		6		4.6			
13	12		3		4.6			
14	13		5		4.6			
15	14		4		4.6			
16	15		4		4.6			
17	16		3		4.6			
18		11.125	4.625					
19								
20								

Figure 11.10 Illustration From Spreadsheet Computer Software

is done so that a line representing the mean observations can be printed on the resulting graph to use as a comparison.

The data can be analyzed visually by preparing a graph using the data laid out in the configuration of Figure 11.10. The values in cells A2..A17 are used for the X (or horizontal) axis of the graph, or the day on which an observation is made. The Y

(or vertical) axis represents the number of tantrums. Four series of data points are printed on the graph:

Series 1: data from cells B2 through B17
            (tantrums during baseline)

continued on next page

Important Terms for Review

baseline
clinical-research model

direct replication
empirical-practice model
single-subject designs
systematic replication

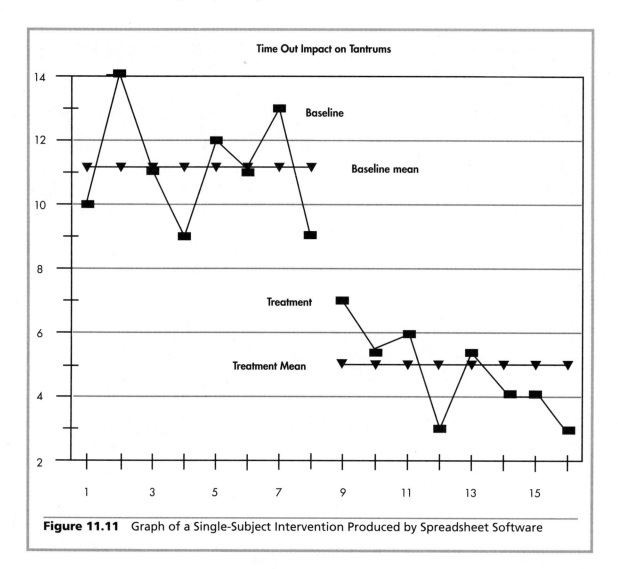

Figure 11.11   Graph of a Single-Subject Intervention Produced by Spreadsheet Software

Exploring the Internet

Single-subject design is a relatively narrow, specialized topic, so locating resources on the Internet will prove more challenging than seeking material on more general research topics. Using such terms as "single case experiments" with standard search engines may locate some useful sites, but the search

process can be frustrating. As an alternative to using general search engines, you can turn to some more specialized tools for assistance. Single-subject designs have long been used in the field of psychology, so a promising starting point is the American Psychological Association home page at http://www.apa.org/. One of the resources available here is PsychCrawler, a search engine that fo-

Series 2: data from cells C2 through C17
  (tantrums after treatment)
Series 3: data from cells D2 through D17
  (baseline mean)
Series 4: data from cells E2 through E17
  (treatment mean)

The resulting graph is displayed in Figure 11.11. Any single-subject data can be plotted by simply adapting this pattern of data entry to the data obtained from the study. One common visual analysis standard with a stable baseline is whether or not all treatment observations are better than the baseline mean. The frequency of temper tantrums for every treatment observation in Figure 11.11 is clearly lower than the baseline mean; so, by this standard, there is a significant difference. A second, more stringent standard, is if all treatment observations are better than the best baseline observation. Here again, the standard is met; we can thus conclude that tantrum behavior has been reduced by the intervention.

Unfortunately, the most common data analysis software packages, such as SPSS, SAS, and Minitab, do not include single-system design data analysis options. One program currently available for this is the Single-Case Randomization Tests or SCRT, distributed by ProGAMMA. This package is used to design single-case experiments and to perform graphical and statistical analyses on data collected within such a design. A very promising option for human service practitioners is the program SPPC

developed by Walter Hudson. The Windows 95 version of this program is being designed to include features to graph time-series data and to do several statistical procedures that are commonly used with single-subject designs (Bloom et al., 1995).

Another computer option for the practitioner wanting to incorporate single-subject designs into practice is Computer-Assisted Social Services (CASS) from Walter Hudson, the scales of which were described in Research in Practice 11.1. This system is much more than a collection of scales; it is a software package that incorporates the capacity to do single-subject analysis with the scales provided or any others that the user may wish to include with the package. CASS will provide graphs for visual analysis. The system is designed in such a way that clients can complete the computerized scales on a regular basis and see a printout of their progress. Because many clients can complete the scales on their own, interruptions and interference with treatment are kept to a minimum while still providing good data for monitoring client progress.

As more human service settings install personal computers and as software such as SPPC and CASS becomes available, the incorporation of single-subject design as a routine part of practice becomes increasingly feasible. The specialized SPPC and CASS programs not only permit single-subject evaluation but also open the door to using the computer as an integral part of human service delivery and evaluation.

cuses on psychology-related topics. By using single-subject research terms with this more specialized search engine, you are more likely to locate useful Internet sites.

An interesting way of exploring how single-subject designs have been applied to various human service practice evaluation studies is to use the search engine provided for the *Journal of Applied*

Behavior Analysis. The URL address for this site is http://www.envmed.rochester.edu/wwwrap/behavior/jaba/jabaindx.htm. The search engine provides a menu of suggested search terms, but you can include your own as well. Using the term "multiple baseline" will return a listing of previously published journal articles related to multiple-baseline designs. You can then select articles of interest to you and review an abstract of each article. If you have a practice situation in mind for evaluation, perusing these abstracts can provide guidance for planning and conducting a single-subject design.

For Further Reading

Behavior Therapy and *Research on Social Work Practice*. These journals publish numerous articles on single-subject design research. Some articles report the results of such research while others analyze methodological issues relating to single-subject designs.

Bloom, M., ed. *Single-System Designs in the Social Services: Issues and Options for the 1990s*. New York: Haworth, 1993. A compilation of thought-provoking articles by leading human service professionals on the application of single-system designs to practice.

Bloom, M., J. Fischer, and J. Orme. *Evaluating Practice: Guidelines for the Accountable Professional*. Boston: Allyn & Bacon, 1995. A thorough textbook on all aspects of single-system design for social work and other human services.

Gabor, Peter A., and Richard M. Grinnell, Jr. *Evaluation and Quality Improvement in the Human Services*. Boston: Allyn & Bacon, 1994. Although this book covers many other research issues, it includes significant material on using single-subject research in evaluating human service programs. It also describes some case studies.

Haynes, S. N. *Principles of Behavioral Assessment*. New York: Gardner, 1978. A thorough coverage of a variety of issues important to single-subject designs, including the design of measurement instruments.

Kazdin, A. E. *Single-Case Research Designs*. New York: Oxford University Press, 1982. A concise overview of single-subject research with illustrative applications in several areas of human service practice.

Tripodi, T. *A Primer on Single-Subject Design for Clinical Social Workers*. Washington, D.C.: NASW Press, 1994. A good basic text on how to do single-subject evaluations of practice, including measurement, statistical analysis procedures, and a number of appendices on practical measurement scales.

Videka-Sherman, Lynn, and William J. Reid, eds. *Advances in Clinical Social Work Research*. Silver Spring, Md: NASW Press, 1990. This edited volume contains articles from top scholars in the field in which they discuss and sometimes debate numerous issues confronting clinical social work research.

Exercises for Class Discussion

11.1 A foster parent complains to the foster care worker that the 14-year-old child placed in her home chronically oversleeps in the morning and is late for school. She wakes him every morning about 7 A.M., leaving him 2 hours to get ready for school and be there on time.

a. Establish the problems that the foster care worker might tackle with this youngster and the goals to be accomplished. As you do this, keep in mind the importance of specificity and measurability.

b. Identify some alternative ways of measuring a baseline for assessing change in this case.

c. What would be the advantages and disadvantages of having the foster parent versus the foster son do the data collecting? Can you identify any outside sources of data?

11.2 Select a behavior from one of the following, devise a means of measuring it, and collect baseline data for a week, using yourself or someone else as the client. Report your results to the class.

a. Cigarette smoking

b. Speeding while driving

c. Snacking

d. Feeling depressed

e. Praising your child

f. Completing homework

11.3 A counselor in a spouse abuse shelter has been working with women in the shelter on assertiveness in dealing with men. She would like to do a single-subject design with a woman client to evaluate the effectiveness of the assertiveness training. She intends to have the staff collect data on the client's level of assertiveness in a variety of situations, using a coded observation form.

What would be the advantages and disadvantages of the following designs for this research?

a. *AB*

b. *ABA*

c. *ABAB*

What steps would need to be taken to conduct this study in an ethical manner? Are there any special problems that are unique to each design type (*AB, ABA,* or *ABAB*)? Are there more complex designs that you might want to use in this situation?

11.4 An intensive foster care worker is responsible for six adolescent clients in separate foster homes. She has been receiving complaints from most of the foster parents that the kids do not pick up their clothes or do other chores around the house such as washing dishes, mowing lawns, or cleaning walks. She decides to implement a reinforcement program by enabling the foster children to earn points toward special activities such as a trip to a large amusement park. One such activity would be scheduled each week.

a. Describe how this worker might design a multiple-baseline study across clients.

b. Describe how the worker might design a multiple-baseline study across behaviors.

c. How might she devise a changing-criterion design?

CHAPTER 12

Evaluation Research

What Is Evaluation Research? 319
  Why Evaluate? 319
  Evaluation Research and Basic Research 320
  Types of Evaluation Research 321

Formative Evaluation Research 322

Summative Evaluation Research 323
  Evaluability Assessment 324
  Specification of Variables 325
  Measuring Variables 327
  The Evaluation of Minorities in Evaluation Research 328
  Designs for Evaluation Research 328
  Cost-Benefit Analysis 332
  Cost-Effective Analysis 336

Barriers to the Use of Evaluation Research 337

Main Points 341

Important Terms for Review 341

Exploring the Internet 341

For Further Reading 342

Exercises for Class Discussion 343

A major theme of this book is the benefits accorded to the human service field by linking human service practice with scientific research to form a single endeavor seeking common goals. In various places, we have labeled this *scientific practice* (*see* Chapter 1) or the *clinical-research model* (*see* Chapter 11). In this chapter, we encounter a new element of this linkage in the form of *evaluation research,* which really points to a reason for conducting research rather than a new research methodology. **Evaluation research** refers to the use of scientific research methods to plan intervention programs, to monitor the implementation of new programs and the operation of existing ones, and to determine how effectively programs or clinical practices achieve their goals.

Although evaluation research has been around for many years, it has risen to considerable prominence over the past two decades as the amount of public and private funds channeled into social programs has grown. As funding has increased, those providing the funds have sought valid and reliable evidence regarding whether programs achieve their goals, how efficiently they do so, and whether they produce any unintended consequences. Evaluation research is a mechanism for gathering evidence about these issues, and it has become an integral part of most social programs today.

In this chapter, we provide an overview of the field of evaluation research. First, we discuss in more detail what evaluation research is, distinguishing it from basic research. Then we discuss the two major forms of evaluation research, formative and summative. This is followed by a review of how evaluation research is conducted, including an assessment of the various research designs commonly used. Cost-benefit analysis and cost-effective analysis are also explained as they relate to evaluation research. We conclude with a discussion of the problems that often arise when it comes time to utilize the outcomes of evaluation research.

What Is Evaluation Research?

Evaluation research is a means of supplying valid and reliable evidence regarding the operation of social programs or clinical practices—how they are planned, how well they operate, and how effectively they achieve their goals. For example, a medical care facility may need to know if there is a community need for a day care program for the elderly. Corrections officials may wish to know the size at which a probation officer's caseload becomes too large to provide effective services to those on probation. Or hospital administrators may need to assess the impact on patient care of a 15 percent reduction in the nursing staff. In these situations and others like them, evaluation research uses many of the research techniques discussed in other chapters to provide evidence about the workings of programs and practices in the human services. A typical evaluation effort might involve some combination of interviews, questionnaires, observation, available data, and an experimental design. In fact, we have already discussed evaluation research in many places in this book without calling it by name. In Chapter 11, for example, many of the single-subject design studies described can be considered evaluation research of the effectiveness of clinical interventions.

Why Evaluate?

Evaluation research is conducted for three major reasons (Rossi and Freeman, 1993). First, it can be conducted for *administrative purposes,* such as to fulfill an evaluation requirement demanded by a funding source, to improve service to clients, or to increase efficiency of program delivery. Evaluations done for administrative reasons tend to focus on assessing the daily operations of a program rather than its overall impact, and the goal is typically to find the most efficient means of running a program or agency. A second reason for conducting evaluation research is *impact assessment:* A program is assessed to see what effects, if any, it is producing. Typically, the goals of the program are identified, and the program is measured in terms of how well it achieves those goals. The results of the impact assessment are then used to make policy decisions regarding whether to expand, change, or curtail a program. Third, evaluation research may be conducted to *test hypotheses* or *evaluate practice approaches.* These often amount to the same thing, because practice strategies are typically based on hypotheses derived from social and psychological theories. Such evaluation not only provides information about a particular practice intervention but also adds to the fund of social-scientific knowledge, which may be useful in the design of new intervention strategies.

Evaluation Research and Basic Research

Evaluation research is a form of applied research (*see* Chapter 1), and as such it involves a special application of the general research techniques used in basic research. Because of this, there are similarities between the two. But there are also some important differences (Weiss, 1972; DeMartini, 1982). First, the results of evaluation research have immediate practical use in assessing operating programs. Basic research, on the other hand, is oriented toward more general information gathering and hypothesis testing.

Second, in contrast to evaluation research, where the needs of the decision makers sponsoring the study are paramount in shaping the form and content of the research, the basic researcher has more control over which issues are to be investigated (Rossi and Freeman, 1993). In some evaluations, there may be some latitude for the evaluator to expand beyond the issues of direct interest to the decision makers, but control over the content of the research is shared with them. This may become a source of conflict between researchers and sponsors of the evaluation.

A third difference is that evaluation, by its very nature, has a judgmental quality about it that is of-ten not a part of basic research. The evaluation may deem a program as a "success" or "failure" on the basis of how well it achieved its purposes, and this judgmental quality can be a source of tension between an evaluator and the sponsors of the evaluation. Understandably, the sponsors are concerned that a negative evaluation could have dire consequences for the existence of the program and for their own livelihoods and careers.

The fourth difference between basic and evaluation research relates to the issues given priority in the research process. In basic research, quite naturally, the requisites for producing a scientifically sound study are given strong weight. Evaluation research, on the other hand, takes place in a context in which an ongoing program is in operation, and the demands of the program may conflict with the demands for sound scientific practices. When this happens, the program administrators may give higher priority to the program than to the evaluation. The scientific demands of an evaluation, for example, might call for the random assignment of nurses from a home health-care agency to each new client of the agency. The agency administrator, on the other hand, may prefer to assign nurses on the basis of his or her assessment of their competencies and "fit" with the client, and the agency head will likely be able to override the requests of the evaluators, forcing the latter to modify their scientific procedures. These conflicts can be aggravated by differences in approach sometimes found between practitioners and researchers (Weiss, 1972). Practitioners tend to emphasize the importance of providing services to people and the role of empathy and concern in the intervention process. Researchers, on the other hand, may give more weight to the understanding provided by rigorous scientific analysis and objectivity. Although these differences should not be overdrawn—for researchers do have empathy and practitioners do recognize the value of scientific analysis—there can be a difference in emphasis between practitioners and researchers, and it can be a source of tension. In fact, one of the beneficial outcomes of developing linkages between practice and research is that it encourages people to develop ways of combining the two approaches so that advantages accrue to both.

A final difference between basic and evaluation research relates to making the results of the research public. One of the canons of science is that research results be made public for others to see and criticize in order to reduce the likelihood that errors or personal bias might find their way into scientific research (*see* Chapter 2). In the past, wide dissemination of evaluation results was uncommon. A review of the journals *Social Work* and *Social Casework* between 1958 and 1972 found not one article describing a carefully conducted evaluation. The few references to evaluation were more in the nature of "afterthoughts" (Segal, 1972). It was not until 1976 that a journal specifically devoted to evaluation reports, *Evaluation Quarterly,* came into existence. Today about a dozen journals are devoted to this topic, and a number of professional organizations serve as outlets for the dissemination of the results of evaluation research. However, all too frequently, sponsors of an evaluation are supplied with a few copies of the report, which are promptly filed away to gather dust on shelves and clutter already overcrowded offices. This has the effect of thwarting the accumulation of information so necessary for progress. Even if evaluation results show no effect, those findings are valuable in preventing ineffective programs from proliferating.

Despite the differences between evaluation research and basic research, there are important similarities. First, both may choose from the entire array of data-gathering techniques those that best fit their needs. In fact, as noted, evaluation projects often involve a synthesis of data gathered in a variety of ways. Second, both forms of research can focus on determining cause-and-effect relationships. In basic research, researchers seek cause-and-effect relationships between variables of their own choosing, whereas in evaluation research the investigation is focused on variables that are a part of the program being assessed.

It should be apparent that the differences between evaluation and basic research are of a practical nature, deriving mainly from the context in which evaluation research is conducted. Although these differences are important—and the potential conflicts alluded to quite real—the actual process of inquiry is very much the same in both types of research. In fact, evaluation research illustrates the dynamic and flexible quality of basic social research methods in that the core methods and techniques can be expanded and changed to confront new problems and issues. Evaluation research is a novel and challenging application of methods that have been used in many other contexts. As such, the distinction between basic and evaluation research is really one of degree rather than kind.

Types of Evaluation Research

The term "evaluation research" is somewhat misleading in that there is not a separate set of research techniques that are distinctly applied for a single purpose. Rather, the term applies to a diverse collection of strategies that can be used for a broad range of evaluative purposes. One way in which evaluation research methods may be classified is in terms of the unit of analysis. For example, the single-subject designs covered in Chapter 11 may be considered evaluation methods where the unit of analysis is a single individual. Because of the unique features involved in doing such individual studies, we have chosen to devote a separate chapter to them. This chapter considers those evaluations that focus on programs or organizations as the unit of analysis.

Another useful way of conceptualizing the diversity of evaluation research is in terms of the goals of the study. Evaluation research can achieve two basic goals. **Formative evaluation research** focuses on providing information to guide the planning, development, and implementation of a specific program. It is primarily concerned with ensuring a smooth-running, well-integrated program rather than with the ultimate worth or impact of the program. **Summative evaluation research** is concerned with the program's effects. Here the purpose centers on assessing the effectiveness and efficiency of programs and the extent to which the outcomes of the project are generalizable to other settings and populations. Formative evaluation research has traditionally received less attention in the evaluation literature than has summative. However, the two forms are closely linked and may be likened to a foundation and a building. The formative component of evaluation may not be especially glamorous or attract much attention, but, unless it is carefully prepared and well done, the summative type of study will be very difficult to carry out and obtain high-quality results. We will discuss each type of evaluation research separately.

Formative Evaluation Research

Formative research involves applying research to the types of questions that arise in the planning, implementation, and operation of programs. For initiating a program, certain basic information is essential. First, it is necessary to gather data on the target population and their characteristics. The nature of the problems they have, the number of potential program users, their location in the community, and other demographic information would also be essential to planning a good program. Second, it is important to be aware of existing services that the program under development might duplicate or on which it may rely for referrals or auxiliary services. Third, the program planners need to be knowledgeable about the specific intervention strategies that might be applied to the problems. Fourth, the program operators must be able to specify the skills that staff must have to deliver the program. Fifth, it must be determined if it is feasible to offer and monitor the program as it has been conceptualized.

To provide answers to these questions, formative research might take the form of a **needs assessment:** collecting data to determine how many people in a community will need particular services and to assess what level of services or personnel already exist to fill a need (McKillip, 1987). In doing needs assessments, researchers commonly uti-

lize a sampling strategy and then survey members of the target population. Thus, survey research methods form the backbone of such needs assessments. However, one could also rely on direct observation or utilize existing data to gain a profile of the population and identify needs. Essentially, any techniques used for descriptive research may be employed to answer this question. Knowledge of existing and related services might be gained through interviewing potential clients and representatives of existing agencies. Knowledge of possible intervention strategies and program components often comes from conducting a thorough literature search, a fundamental step in any research project. Appendix A in this book, on the use of the library, is directly applicable to such a task.

Formative evaluations also sometimes utilize *focus groups,* the group interview technique discussed at length in Chapter 7. Focus groups are especially useful when the formative evaluation is exploratory in nature or when planners need to learn about the very personal and subjective meanings and experiences of people. Focus groups can be a useful strategy for drawing such information from people.

Formative evaluation research can also take the form of a *pretest* or *trial run,* in which all the procedures to be used in a program are tested before the full program is implemented. An example of this can be found in a program to provide financial aid to newly released offenders (Rossi, Berk, and Lenihan, 1980). The researchers began with a very modest project involving 6 released inmates who received six weekly payments of $60 and 20 controls who received no payment. Relying on a review of the literature and existing statistics on the problems of released offenders, this modest project helped prepare for a large-scale program in several ways. It helped determine that it was logistically possible to make the payments and to interview and keep track of ex-inmates in the community. Had this pilot project shown that these operational elements could not be accomplished effectively, then it would have been foolish to continue with a larger project even though one might be convinced of the overall effectiveness of the program.

Because the questions addressed in formative research are often modest in scope, the research is frequently conducted by the staff of the agency administering the program. However, such research may also be done on a national scale in conjunction with large programs. Programs such as AFDC, food stamps, and vocational rehabilitation involve large sums of money, and initiation of such programs involves estimating the number of potential recipients, which can vary considerably depending on what definition of poverty is applied. Before initiating such programs, formative research based on needs assessment is essential. Many programs fail because there are really no potential users of the program or the design of the program precludes clients from using it. A fascinating account of one such program is *Implementation: Or How Great Expectations in Washington Are Dashed in Oakland* (Pressman and Wildavsky, 1973). The authors describe the pitfalls encountered in an effort to develop a major antipoverty job creation program. After initial fanfare and allocation of several million dollars, only a few jobs were created. Although formative evaluation cannot ensure success, it can help reduce instances of unnecessary intervention and increase the potential for success among those programs that are initiated.

Besides serving as a tool for the planning of an intervention program, formative research may also be used to monitor the implementation of new programs and the ongoing operation of existing ones. Experience with evaluations for program effectiveness has shown that a major factor in program failure is often the fact that the program as planned was never really implemented (Berman and Pauly, 1975). Several basic issues in program monitoring are counterparts to program planning. First, is the target population in fact being served? Second, are the services that are supposed to be delivered actually being delivered? Third, is the quality of the service adequate? As a means of supplying answers to the first question, it is common to use a census of program users and compare their characteristics with the characteristics of the population for whom services were intended. Any discrepancy suggests that some members of the target population are not receiving services intended for them. Service delivery may be assessed in a variety of ways, including questionnaires and direct observation. As in single-subject designs, time samples may be used to determine if behaviors associated with service delivery are occurring as planned. Quality control techniques not unlike those used in industry are employed to monitor the delivery of services in many settings. Major financial assistance services such as AFDC are routinely monitored by state departments of social services. Typically, this process involves selecting a random sample of recipients and examining the most recent action on their files to determine if the action resulted in a correct payment, an overpayment, or an underpayment. States are expected to keep their error rate within certain specific limits. Other settings may use follow-up questionnaires to service users to determine if expected services were delivered.

Finally, agencies commonly use a time-reporting system to make sure that staff are spending the expected amount of time on specified aspects of the program. Figure 12.1 illustrates one type of time-reporting system. Such studies do not address the question of whether or not the program is actually doing any good. Rather, they address the narrower issue of the extent to which the services actually being delivered are true to the intended plan.

Summative Evaluation Research

Summative evaluation research involves assessing the impact of a program, although good summative evaluations usually investigate other matters concerning the program's operation. The results of summative evaluations are intended to be used for policy-making decisions—whether to continue, expand, or cancel a program, and whether to generalize the findings of this project to other settings and populations. Summative evaluations are typically large-scale projects involving considerable time, personnel, and resources. For this reason, as well as to avoid the biasing effect of personal

Case Name _____

Case No. _____

Worker _____   Page _____

_____

Date	Type	Time	

Code:
    1—Telephone Contact   8—Foster Parent Training
    2—In-office Visit   9—Court Visit
    3—School Visit   10—Visit to Family of Origin
    4—Foster Home Visit   11—Case Staffing & Supervision
    5—Referring Worker Visit   12—Other Collateral
    6—Paperwork   13—Client
    7—Driving Time

Time Interval—
1–15 Min.

Figure 12.1   Example of a Time-Reporting Form

interest, summative evaluations are often conducted by outside consultants rather than by agency staff.

Although the steps in the research process are much the same for all types of research, including evaluation research, some special planning is called for to take into consideration the unique problems of evaluation research.

Evaluability Assessment

During the planning of evaluation research, an **evaluability assessment** is often conducted to enable investigators to decide whether a program has the necessary preconditions to be evaluated. An evaluability assessment involves four steps (Rutman,

1984; Smith, 1989). First, the purpose of the evaluation—from the standpoint of the eventual users of the results—is determined. This identifies which aspects of the program are to be assessed for impact. To be evaluated, a program needs clearly specified goals. Having clear goals is necessary because they are the major criteria of a program's success. Goals are the dependent variables that the input variables are supposed to affect. Unfortunately, the goals of many programs are either vague or so global (improving family functioning, for example) that they are unusable for evaluation purposes. As we will see, it may be necessary for an evaluator to become actively involved, together with the staff, in developing a set of clear goals before a program is evaluable.

The second step in an evaluability assessment is to study and gather information about the program. What are the inputs, the expected results or goals, and the linkage between the two? This linkage is essentially the theory on which the program is based. It involves answering the question: Why, given these program inputs, should certain outcomes be expected? This theoretical linkage may be explicitly recognized as the basis of the program, or it might be implicit but derivable from the program's operation. The purpose of identifying this rationale is that it is important in understanding the success or failure of the program. For example, some programs may identify certain outcomes as goals but not direct any effort toward realizing them. (Quite obviously, if evaluated against these goals, the program would likely turn out to be a failure.) If we do not specify the linkage, the reason for failure may be unclear, and, in the case of a success, we would be at a loss to explain why. Knowledge of the linkage would reveal the source of the problem as the failure to direct input resources toward those particular goals. During this step, it is important to monitor the program *as implemented* because gaps sometimes develop between the stated program and the program as operated.

Third, information gathered during the second stage is used to develop a flow model of the program. This model traces program inputs, clients, and interventions as they affect the expected results,

specifying any assumed causal linkages along the way. Modeling of programs is extremely useful in evaluation research because it provides a clear picture of the structure and operation of the program. It can also help explain a program's successes or failures. For example, as a part of an evaluation of a group counseling program in a correctional system, a careful model of the program was developed (Kassebaum, Ward, and Wilner, 1971). When the results of the evaluation showed that inmates in the counseling program did not have lower recidivism rates than other inmates, the evaluators were hardly surprised. Their model revealed that counselors were poorly trained and unmotivated, counseling sessions tended to be unfocused "bull" sessions, inmate participation was motivated largely by a desire to impress the parole board, and the inmates did not view the sessions as likely to be helpful to them. Against this backdrop, the failure of counseling to reduce recidivism is understandable. The flow model of the program helped identify these elements.

The final stage of the evaluability assessment is to review the program model to identify those aspects of the program that are sufficiently unambiguous in terms of inputs, goals, and linkages that evaluation of them appears feasible. The result of the assessment may be that the whole program can be evaluated, none of the program can be evaluated, or, most commonly, only certain parts of the program are amenable to evaluation.

Specification of Variables

As in any research, an important part of evaluation research is the specification of variables and how they will be measured. In some evaluations, the variables of interest take the form of independent and dependent variables. The inputs to a social program, for example, might constitute the independent variables. In some cases, the independent variable takes the form of a dichotomous variable: participation or nonparticipation in a program. In other cases, the independent variable might be the degree or duration of participation in a program, such as the frequency of contact with a counselor, the level of financial aid received, or the length of time a service is provided. Commonly, the dependent variables in evaluation research are the goals of a program: precisely what it is supposed to accomplish. Some evaluation research, of course, especially the formative type, would not involve independent and dependent variables. Whatever form the variables take, a central issue in evaluation research is that the variables be clearly and properly specified, and numerous problems can arise along these lines. This is especially true when measuring the goals of a program, and we will illustrate some of the measurement problems in evaluation research in this realm.

A frequent problem is that the goals, as articulated by program administrators, do not easily lend themselves to evaluation. They may be vague, overly broad, or so long term that evaluation is not feasible. For example, a goal of Head Start preschool education is to develop capable and functioning adults who can rise out of poverty. Although the success of Head Start in achieving this goal may be its ultimate test, it would be necessary to wait 20 to 30 years before evaluating the program. Although this may be a laudable and essential part of the program, funding agencies are understandably reluctant to expend funds for that length of time with no evaluation. Thus, such programs normally include what are called *proximate* goals, or goals that can be realized in the short run and that are related to the achievement of the long-term goals (Weiss, 1972). In the case of Head Start, academic achievement would be a reasonable proximate goal because performance in school is associated with social and occupational success in adulthood.

There are programs, of course, in which it is possible and desirable to assess the long-term impact. For example, there was a 30-year follow-up of the Cambridge-Sommerville Youth Study, a 5-year experiment in delinquency prevention begun in Boston in 1939 (McCord, 1978). This field experiment focused on 506 young boys, half receiving counseling and other assistance while the remainder served as a control group. The experimental condition consisted of counseling sessions every 2 weeks, tutoring, medical and psychiatric assistance, summer camps, and organized youth activities. Thirty years later, 95 percent of the participants in the experiment were located. Many of the comparisons showed no differences between the two groups. But what differences were found suggested that the experimental variables had the *opposite* effect from what was expected! The experimental group committed more crimes as adults, had higher rates of alcoholism, poorer mental and physical health, and less occupational success. The only positive result for the program appeared to be the participants' own subjective evaluations. Two thirds of the experimental group indicated that they thought the program had been helpful to them even though their objective situation was worse than that of people in the control group. The program may have produced harmful effects because it raised participants' expectations to an unrealistically high level. When those expectations were not realized, participants suffered frustration and added stress, which resulted in a greater tendency toward criminality and alcoholism as well as the deleterious effects on their mental and physical health (McCord, 1978). Despite the need for early program evaluations, long-term evaluation, accomplished so well in this study, is still essential in assessing many programs.

When goals are vague or overly broad, they must be clarified or reduced in scope so that they are amenable to evaluation. In this regard, it is helpful if program administrators consult with evaluators in developing the goals for a program. During discussions with program administrators, it is important that evaluators not simply accept as all-inclusive the goals articulated by the administrators. In fact, one of the major reasons for finding that a program does not have the intended result is that program goals are too limited (Chen and Rossi, 1980). Too often, administrators state program goals from the standpoint of what they desire, resulting in goals that are unattainable given program inputs. When evaluated against these goals, the program naturally appears to be a failure. Evaluators should "cast a wide net" in seeking program effects, including not only those suggested by administrators but also others logically expected given the nature of the program. The model developed during the evaluability assessment and the theoretical basis of the program are productive places to look for possible program effects to be included in the evaluation. This approach promises to provide a better chance of finding nonzero program effects and supplying information on what the program does as well as what it does not do.

Measuring Variables

The goals specified for an evaluation program tend to be abstract statements of desired outcomes. Before an actual evaluation can proceed, measurable criteria or operational definitions specifying exactly what observations will be made to determine goal achievement must be developed. Evaluators thus distinguish between *goals,* which are the desired end states for a program, and *objectives,* which are the measurable criteria for success. For example, a program goal of a substance abuse prevention program might be to reduce experimentation with alcohol and cigarettes among junior high students. An objective of the program might be that 85 percent of program participants be able to correctly list at least five health hazards associated with alcohol use. Some goals can be readily measured because they have clearly quantifiable outcomes. For example, the academic effects of compensatory education programs can be readily measured by standard achievement tests. Such effects of Head Start as improved self-esteem, better adjustment to the classroom environment, or enhanced parent–child relationships will likely require more inventiveness on the part of the evaluator to measure.

When measures for program effects are being considered, there may be alternative indicators of the same program effect. For example, in measuring the effects of a family planning program, we might use as a measure (1) the proportion of participants adopting contraceptive practices, (2) the average desired number of children, (3) the average number of children actually born, or (4) the attitudes toward large families (Rossi and Freeman, 1993). All these indicators are logically related to the effects of a family planning program. Multiple indicators—

though sometimes prohibited by budget—are more useful than single ones. Multiple indicators are more sensitive and, therefore, more likely to show an effect if the program produced one (Weiss, 1972, p. 36). If multiple indicators are impractical, a decision must be made as to which of the alternatives is best. In the case of the four alternatives for the family planning program, the clearest indicator of program success would be a low birth rate among participants. This indicator, however, might be impractical for some purposes because we would have to wait many years before the evaluation could be completed. The two indicators dealing with attitudes would not be the best choices because attitudes can change, and sometimes only a weak relationship exists between attitudes and behavior. Indeed, attitudinal measures should be avoided whenever a behavioral alternative is available. Of the four possible measures, then, the proportion of participants who adopt contraception is probably the best single indicator of the effectiveness of the family planning program. It would not be perfect, because contraceptives must be used conscientiously for them to be effective, but for a short-run measure it would be adequate.

As recommended on a number of occasions (for example, in Chapter 11), it is preferable to use existing measures where possible. This avoids the work involved in creating new measures, pretesting them, and establishing their validity and reliability. Furthermore, existing measures contribute to the accumulation of knowledge because they make evaluations of different programs more comparable. The preference for existing measures extends only to the point where good existing measures for the variables of interest can be found. If existing measures are only tangentially related to what one seeks to measure, then it is far better to develop new measures. Good measurement is so crucial to meaningful evaluation that shortcuts that compromise quality should not be tolerated.

Assuming that some new measures must be created, it is important to keep in mind the dual criteria for assessing them: validity and reliability. Measures used in evaluation research must meet the same standards of validity and reliability as those used in basic research, and the methods for assessing those characteristics considered in Chapter 5 apply here.

The Evaluation of Minorities in Evaluation Research

One area in which evaluation research has played an important role is in assessing the operation and impact of policies and programs affecting minorities. When the women's movement hit full stride in the 1970s, women began rapidly to enter what had generally been considered exclusively male occupations. Before long, studies were being done assessing the relative performances of men and women working the same jobs. As more and more of this research was amassed, serious questions began to be raised concerning the quality and fairness of these evaluations, particularly toward the women in traditionally male occupations.

Take the case of evaluating male and female police officers. Merry Morash and Jack Greene (1986) reviewed the nine major evaluations of women police officers that had been conducted up to that time. Not surprisingly, given the varying methodologies of the several studies, results were inconsistent. With one exception, however, the studies concluded that female police officers were neither better nor worse than their male counterparts, but that they were different. That is, women were better than the male officers at some policing activities, but they were not as good as the male officers at others. If these differences are real, such information could be quite valuable in allocating police personnel to maximize the strengths and minimize the weaknesses of both male and female officers. But what if the differences are merely artifacts of faulty study design? Because assignments in police departments have implications for career advancement, we had better be sure that the findings of such evaluations are indeed valid before we proceed to use them as a basis for allocating personnel—or for any other reason.

Morash and Greene's review of the nine studies is not encouraging on the validity issue, but it does point out issues that future researchers should address. Among the problems they found were a tendency to emphasize conformity to male stereotypes (such as marksmanship or the frequency of arrests), a failure to evaluate performance on a representative sample of police tasks, an overemphasis on the violent and dangerous aspects of police work, a failure to consider the differences between men's and women's experiences in the workplace (there is greater camaraderie among male officers, for example), a failure to evaluate variations in performance among male officers as well as variation between the sexes, and unclear or unspecified definitions of what constituted good police work. Quite a litany of criticisms!

The authors also found that performance evaluations may be subject to deliberate political manipulation. A study conducted in Philadelphia concluded that women performed at least as well as did the men. In a second study, certain behaviors that had been positively evaluated in the first study were now negatively evaluated. This time the results came out against the female officers.

Morash and Greene's analysis clearly indicates that conducting performance evaluations of men and women in job settings can be very difficult and fraught with possibilities for invalid conclusions. The fact that such evaluations will continue to be done and their results acted upon means that those who conduct evaluations must be cognizant of the potential pitfalls that await and be ready to guard against biased results through the use of sound study designs and a firm resistance to any efforts at political manipulation.

Designs for Evaluation Research

Summative evaluation research is often concerned with cause-and-effect relationships. For example, the program being evaluated is presumed to bring about some changes in such factors as client behavior. A research design developed for such an evaluation needs to be based on an awareness of this cause-and-effect dimension. In Chapter 10, we noted that true experimental designs involving randomization are the better choice for establishing cause-and-effect relationships because they best control the validity threats that can lead to false causal inferences. The ideal approach to determining the effects of a program, therefore, is the randomized experiment. Any of the true experimental designs discussed in Chapter 10 is appropriate for evaluation purposes.

Randomized Experimental Designs   As you recall, the requirements of a true experiment are two randomized equivalent groups, one that experiences the experimental condition and one that does not and serves as a control group. In summative evaluation research, the experimental condition requires some level of participation in the program under consideration. The crucial feature of the true experiment is that members of the comparison groups are randomly assigned. This is the surest and most reliable way of producing equivalent groups.

Virtually all randomized experiments in evaluation are field experiments, taking place in the setting where the actual program is administered. Because of this, evaluators may encounter a number of impediments to conducting a randomized experiment. The first impediment centers around the control group and the randomization procedure used to obtain it. It is necessary, in order to have a control group, to deny some members of the target population access to the program under evaluation, and that denial must be on a random basis. Evaluators may encounter substantial resistance to such denials. For example, the enabling legislation of some programs mandates that all persons who meet the eligibility requirements have a legal right to participate in the program. If such is the case, random denial of service is ruled out.

In other programs, resistance to random denial of services may spring from program administrators and staff. Practitioners are accustomed to providing services on the basis of need and may be disinclined to use a table of random numbers instead. It seems cold, insensitive, even immoral, to withhold available services from people who need them, especially if intuition leads us to believe that the provision of services would have beneficial effects. In advocating a randomized experiment, evaluators

sometimes find themselves in a "no win" situation. If they discover that the program produces harmful effects, they are blamed for subjecting the experimental group to the harmful program. If the program produces positive results, they are blamed for withholding this valuable service from the control group. Imagine the ethical implications of a randomized experiment for evaluating something like a suicide prevention program where life-and-death issues are at stake.

Along these lines, it is important to keep in mind that our intuition regarding the impact of programs is often faulty. In fact, the literature on evaluation research strongly suggests that practitioners' assumptions of positive program effects are often wrong. Leonard Gibbs (1991) documents this point with a diverse list of well-intentioned intervention efforts from the annals of medicine and human service—efforts that appeared to be reasonable in their time but proved to be ineffective. Included are bloodletting, use of mercuric chloride as a drug, oxygen therapy for premature infants, neuroleptic medication for tardive dyskinesia, a juvenile awareness program known as "Scared Straight," encounter groups, and a program of aggressive relocation of the aged. In the last illustration, a study on providing a full range of human services to the mentally impaired elderly reported that the death rate for clients receiving the intensive services was 25 percent in contrast to only 18 percent for the controls. Although not statistically significant, the results should make one pause before assuming that good intentions assure a positive outcome. One review of numerous efforts to evaluate social casework concluded: "Not only has professional casework failed to demonstrate it is effective, but lack of effectiveness appears to be the rule rather than the exception across several categories of clients, problems, situations, and types of casework" (Fischer, 1973, p. 14). Because services that intuition suggests are effective often turn out not to be so, the arguments against withholding services in a randomized experimental design are severely weakened, and, as demonstrated in Research in Practice 10.2, studies involving true control groups are clearly feasible.

A second impediment to conducting randomized experiments in evaluation research is that they may be more time-consuming and expensive than other designs. Experimental evaluations of programs are typically longitudinal: Sufficient time must pass for programs to have an effect. With many social programs, such as compensatory education or job training, the minimum length of the experiment might be at least a year. Furthermore, a listing of the target population, required for randomization, may be difficult or expensive to obtain. These practical considerations mean that randomized experiments are limited to those cases where the money and time are available for an elaborate, rigorous evaluation. Before succumbing to pressure to settle for a weaker design, however, the lesson of the Salk polio vaccine trials should be considered. Two experimental methods were used. One was a nonrandomized trial wherein 1 million volunteer second-graders were given the vaccine while unvaccinated first- and third-graders served as the control group. The other study was an experiment involving 800,000 volunteers who were randomly assigned to receive either the vaccine or a placebo without doctors, parents, or the children knowing which group they were in. Although the first study involved a larger sample and may have seemed easier to conduct without the complicated randomization process, its design proved inadequate for estimating the effect of the vaccine. It seems that polio was more prevalent in the middle class because better hygiene prevented building up the natural immunity that lower-class children developed. Second-graders who volunteered tended to be middle class and thus different from second-graders who did not volunteer and also different from the first and third grade controls. In citing this case in his argument for randomized experiments, Lawrence Sherman (1992, p. 59) concludes, "Only the randomized, fully controlled Salk vaccine experiment provided the clear estimate of the vaccine's benefits which was needed to adopt a national policy of vaccination."

Randomized experiments are clearly the best designs from which to assess causality, and many statistical procedures are based on the assumption of equivalent experimental and control groups. Reports in journals such as *Evaluation Quarterly* document the widespread use of these designs today. With some inventiveness on the part of evaluators, much of the resistance to randomized experiments can be overcome. Indeed, there is a growing consensus about the desirability of randomized experiments and an expanding literature documenting their use. This should work to reduce the barriers to future randomized experiments in evaluation (Rossi and Freeman, 1993).

One common situation in particular contributes to the possibility of a randomized experiment. When the target population is larger than the program's capacity to serve it—in short, when demand for services exceeds supply—services must be denied to some people. Because many programs are initially instituted on a small scale, this excess demand often occurs. Because some members of the target population will not be served anyway, the determination of who will be served might as well be random unless there is some other clear-cut and defensible criterion that could be used, such as severity of need. In fact, a reasonable argument can be made that random allocation of services is the fairest method when resources are inadequate to serve all and no other criteria seem applicable.

If an evaluator is successful in obtaining approval for a randomized experiment, the random assignment process must be carefully monitored to ensure that it is properly implemented. Lack of such monitoring can destroy the experimental design. For example, an employment and training program, with which one of the authors of this book once consulted, had agreed to a randomized study. However, when a large group of eager youths appeared at the agency on the first day, the staff was overwhelmed and simply threw the program open to all of them, thus totally destroying the randomization procedure. When such events go undiscovered, the comparison groups will not be equalized and the eventual results may be misleading. A two-step procedure is desirable in which client information is gathered by personnel different from those who do the random assignment. In this way, those doing the assignment would do so without knowledge of client identities or characteristics. Insulating the assignment process in this way reduces the opportunity for deviations from randomness to creep in and eases the monitoring task (Cook, Cook, and Mark, 1977).

The Alternatives to Randomized Experiments

The barriers to randomized experiments may be sufficiently formidable that an alternative design must be utilized. It is important to remember that anything other than a randomized experiment will produce results in which confidence is reduced because such alternative designs are weaker on internal validity (*see* Chapter 10). Properly conducted, however, these designs can allow evaluation with a reasonable degree of certitude (Achen, 1986).

One alternative to the randomized experiment is to use a quasi-experimental design. When a program is meant to affect behavior about which data are routinely collected, a time-series design may be appropriate. One research group, for example, used a time-series design to evaluate the impact of a Massachusetts gun control law that mandated a 1-year minimum prison sentence for anyone convicted of carrying a firearm without a permit (Deutch and Alt, 1977). The law went into effect in April 1975. The researchers traced the monthly occurrences of homicide, assault with a gun, and armed robbery in Boston from 1966 to 1975, which provided a baseline of gun-related offenses for about 9 years prior to the introduction of the gun control law. Their analysis revealed that in the first 7 months the law was in effect, statistically significant decreases in both armed robbery and assault with a gun occurred. No change was registered for homicide, however. Despite their frequent utility for evaluation, it is important to remember that the chief weakness of time-series designs is the validity threat of history. Unless it is possible to use a control group, as in the multiple time-series design, it is always possible that some extraneous variable can intervene and confound the results.

A second alternative to randomized experiments is *matching*. If randomization is not feasible, it may be possible to match persons in the experimental group with persons having similar characteristics in a control group. Recall, however, that matching can be unreliable because relatively few variables can be used for matching, which leaves uncontrolled variables that might confound the results.

An example of an evaluation in which a form of matching was used was a study of the effects of a housing allowance program implemented by the Department of Housing and Urban Development (HUD) in 1970 (Jackson and Mohr, 1986). Because of the nature of the program, people could not be assigned to experimental and control groups. Instead, for the experimental group, a random sample of clients enrolled in the program was used. For a control group, a sample was selected from the Annual Housing Survey administered by HUD. The HUD survey contained data similar to that collected from the experimental group. The matching involved selecting clients from the Annual Housing Survey who were eligible for, but not enrolled in, the housing allowance program. This provided a comparison group to assess the impact of enrollment in the housing allowance program on such things as changes in housing quality and the extent of the rent burden.

A third alternative to the randomized experiment, really another form of matching, is the use of *cohort groups*. Cohorts are groups of people who move through an organization or a treatment program at about the same time. For example, the following are cohorts: students in the same grade in a school, people receiving public assistance at the same time from a particular agency, and people in a drug rehabilitation program at the same time. Cohorts are valuable alternatives to randomized experiments because we may be able to assume that each cohort in an organization or program is similar to the cohort preceding it in terms of the characteristics that might affect a treatment outcome. In other words, each group should be alike in age, sex, socioeconomic status, and other characteristics that may be important. However, there can also be very significant differences, and cohorts should always be assessed to detect any possible systematic variation between one cohort and another.

An elaborate cohort study evaluating curriculum revision and televised instruction was conducted in El Salvador from 1969 to 1973 (Mayo,

Hornick, and McAnany, 1976). Seventh grade classes in 1969, 1970, and 1971 made up three separate cohorts of students. Within the cohorts, some classes received a new curriculum, some received the new curriculum with televised instruction, and some received the old curriculum. The cohorts from 1969 and 1970 were followed for 3 years, and the one from 1971 was followed for 2 years. Comparisons among the groups produced mixed results. The new curriculum was consistently superior to the old one, and televised instruction was superior during the first year it was experienced. However, the superiority of televised instruction wore off as the students became accustomed to it.

The major weakness of cohorts is, again, the threat to validity from history. Because the measurements are taken at widely spaced times, extraneous variables may intercede and possibly affect the results. The El Salvador example is instructive on this point. It would be unlikely that a similar cohort study could have been reliably conducted 10 years later as the country became unstable owing to guerrilla warfare. Comparing a cohort from a period of peace with one from a period of near civil war would have obvious problems.

A fourth alternative to the randomized experiment is called the *regression discontinuity design:* People are selected to receive a treatment based on their score on a test, their eligibility for a program, or some other criterion. The study of recidivism in California discussed in Research in Practice 12.1 was a regression discontinuity design in which prison inmates were eligible for the experimental group if they had worked sufficient hours in prison to be eligible for unemployment benefits when released. Inmates who had worked fewer hours were put in the control group. This design is often implemented for evaluation research field experiments, and it can be very useful. However, regression discontinuity designs suffer from some of the threats to internal validity, particularly selection and, in some cases, statistical regression. (Incidentally, the summative evaluation described in Research in Practice 12.1 was an outgrowth of the formative evaluation project, described earlier in this chapter, about the provision of financial aid to newly released prisoners.)

The last major alternative to randomized experiments is the use of *statistical controls,* which are procedures that allow the effects of one or more variables to be removed or held constant so that the effects of other variables can be observed. These procedures allow comparisons to be made between groups that differ from one another on some characteristics thought to be important. The effects of the variables on which the groups differ are removed through statistical manipulation so that they cannot obscure the results. Statistical controls, however, even in their most elaborate application, can only approximate the level of control achievable in randomized experiments. Like matching, only variables known to the researcher to be potentially important can be statistically controlled, so there is always the possibility of important extraneous variables left uncontrolled. Furthermore, statistical controls tend to underadjust for differences between groups because of the error component in the measurement of the control variables (Weiss, 1972; Berk and Rossi, 1990). The error allows at least some of the effects of the control variables to remain even after the statistical controls have been applied. Because of these limitations, statistical control alone may not be appropriate. However, it is well suited as an adjunct to the physical control obtained through design. For example, in a matched design we might find out, after the fact, that an important variable was left unmatched. Assuming the necessary data were collected, we could make up for this error by applying statistical control to that variable.

The use of both design control and statistical control is probably the best overall approach for evaluation, because statistical control can even be useful in randomized experiments (Rossi and Freeman, 1993).

Cost-Benefit Analysis

One particular type of evaluation research—one that has become the darling of some policymakers and the bane of others—is cost-benefit analysis. Because it involves some unique issues and premises, it warrants special attention. In an era of increasing accountability for social programs, this controversial approach to program evaluation is probably here to stay. If it is going to be used, it is important that it be used properly, with its limitations well understood.

On the surface, **cost-benefit analysis** appears seductively simple. All we need do is add up the costs of a program, subtract them from the dollar value of the benefits, and we have the result: either a net gain (benefits exceed costs) or a net loss (costs exceed benefits). Such an approach is very appealing to many policymakers because it seems to clarify complex issues and programs through quantification. They would logically support and perhaps expand programs showing a net gain and curtail those producing a net loss. If only it were that simple. As we shall see, quantifying benefits and costs can be extremely difficult and often involves a number of unproved assumptions and estimates.

Cost-benefit analysis can be applied to a program during its planning stages (called *ex ante* analysis) or after it has been in operation (*ex post* analysis) (Rossi and Freeman, 1993). The major difference between the two is that an ex ante analysis requires the use of more estimates and assumptions because no hard data exist on either costs or benefits. In an ex post study, there are records of actual cost outlays, and benefits can be empirically determined through normal evaluation research procedures. The use of estimates in ex ante analyses means that results are far more tentative. This also accounts for why ex ante analyses conducted by different parties sometimes come to widely divergent conclusions: They use different estimates and assumptions. Sorting out whose estimates are most valid has produced some lively debates among policymakers. Ex post analyses require fewer estimates and are, therefore, more reliable.

Estimating Costs   The easiest part of cost-benefit analysis — although by no means simple — is determining the **direct costs** of a program. There is either a record of actual expenditures (in ex post analysis) or a proposed budget for the program (in ex ante analysis). A budget proposal, however, is based on certain assumptions that may not be accurate. For example, the budget for a supplemental unemployment compensation program must assume a certain unemployment rate. If the actual rate changes, the cost of the program could skyrocket or fall dramatically.

Considerably more difficult to estimate than the direct costs of programs are what economists call *opportunity costs*. **Opportunity costs** are the value of forgone opportunities. Suppose, for example, that you are fortunate enough to win a $1,000 prize in a contest. You can invest the money and receive a monetary return or spend it on anything you like. Suppose you decide to spend it on a stereo. The direct cost of the stereo is the $1,000 you spent on it, but there are opportunity costs. The opportunity costs are what you forgo by buying the stereo. You lose the return that you could have received by investing it or the value of other items you might have purchased, such as new clothes or the down payment on an automobile.

A similar situation applies to the funding of social programs. Agencies have limited resources. If they decide to fund a given program, the cost of the program includes the opportunity costs of not funding alternative programs. Normally, the estimated value of benefits of competing programs is used as the basis for computing the opportunity costs of the program being analyzed. Computing the benefits that are lost by not initiating a program can be very complex, which makes it difficult to calculate the opportunity costs of the funded program. Such estimates need to be done, however, to provide an accurate picture of the total costs of a program.

Estimating and Monetizing Benefits   The really difficult and often unreliable part of cost-benefit analysis comes in determining program benefits and *monetizing,* or attaching a dollar value to, them. This may be a fairly straightforward process or a mystical one, depending on the program. In general, if a program's benefits are related to some economic activity, they are easier to monetize. For example, the value of subsidized day care can be easily monetized. The market price of private day care plus the added income of the parent who otherwise could not work would constitute the major dollar benefits from the program. But what about program benefits less related to

Research in Practice 12.1
Program Evaluation: The Effectiveness of Financial Assistance in Reducing Recidivism

Even the most reformed and well-intentioned former prisoner faces a host of obstacles in his or her efforts to begin a new life outside prison. Family members are often not supportive or too poor to help, or the ex-inmate has no relatives or friends outside prison on whom to rely. The newly released prisoner suddenly becomes responsible for innumerable decisions: where to live, buy clothes, obtain meals, find work, and how to make friends and keep out of trouble. These problems are frequently compounded by an uncertain financial status: no job prospects, a bus ticket to one's hometown, and $25 to $200 gate money.

Policymakers concerned about the welfare of former prisoners and hoping to reduce recidivism have considered programs that provide financial assistance to former prisoners to help them make the transition to civilian life. The thrust of such programs is typically to provide a payment, like unemployment insurance, to provide financial support while the ex-inmate gets settled and finds a job. Because many crimes are economically motivated, it seems reasonable to hypothesize that such financial assistance would reduce the likelihood that a newly released inmate would turn to such crimes.

To test this hypothesis, the Baltimore Living Insurance for Ex-prisoners (or Baltimore LIFE) Project was developed (Lenihan, 1977; Rossi et al., 1980). This field experiment was an intermediary

stage between a small pilot project involving only six people and a much larger program involving several thousand inmates in Texas and Georgia. In the Baltimore LIFE Project, high-risk inmates scheduled for release by the Maryland Department of Corrections were randomly divided into four groups, three experimental groups and one control group. One experimental group received financial assistance of $60 per week for 13 weeks after release and was offered job placement services. A second received the financial assistance but no job placement services. The third experimental group received only the job services, whereas the control group received neither financial assistance nor job services. The intent of this phase of research was to determine if the two independent variables—financial assistance and job placement services—would have any positive effect on recidivism. For 2 years, the ex-prisoners were observed and their experience in employment and criminal activity was noted. When the analysis was done, a number of factors were considered, such as race, age at first arrest, number of prior arrests, education, marital status, parole status, and work experience.

The Baltimore LIFE Project illustrates several key features of careful program evaluation. First, the project was preceded by a much smaller exploratory study that enabled the project staff

economic activity? How can a dollar value be placed on such program benefits as improved mental health, improved self-esteem, reduced domestic violence, or other noneconomic outcomes? Cost-benefit analysis attempts, through complex procedures, to place a dollar value on practically anything. Doing so, however, requires many assumptions and value judgments that are likely to be controversial. Because of this, cost-benefit analysis is of the greatest utility when the relationship

between program benefits and a certain dollar value is fairly clear.

Another complicating factor in cost-benefit analysis is that benefits and costs do not accrue at the same time. Costs are incurred immediately upon the program's implementation, whereas benefits may accrue at some later date, possibly far in the future. In some programs, such as education or job training, at least part of the benefits may be very long term, indeed. This temporal gap is a

to test and refine some of their procedures. Second, the evaluation utilized a variety of research techniques. In addition to the basic experimental design, the research relied on structured interviews and case studies of several participants to provide insight into the problems, reactions, and frustrations of these men as they attempted to cope with life in the community. Third, a cost-benefit analysis was conducted to ascertain if the program was worthwhile. Finally, great care was taken in selecting participants, in explaining the program to the participants, and in dispensing the financial aid and job counseling according to the design.

The results of the study indicated that the men who received financial aid had an 8 percent lower rate of arrest for charges of theft. Arrests for other types of crime were not significantly different. Also, those not receiving financial aid were arrested earlier, were more likely to be convicted, and were more likely to be returned to prison. Job placement services had no apparent impact on recidivism or occupational success.

Based on the modestly optimistic findings of this research, a much larger program, which involved dispensing financial aid through the existing Employment Security Offices in the states of Texas and Georgia, was implemented. In that project, the overall findings were not positive. The researchers concluded that the disappearance of positive outcomes may have resulted from the way the larger program was administered, thereby emphasizing the need for careful program implementa-

tion as well as research. Thus, evaluation research focuses not only on the outcome of programs but also on how they can be best implemented.

The LIFE experiment also served as a model for a legislatively mandated program in California (Berk et al., 1985). It was designed much like the LIFE program, except the inmates actually applied for unemployment benefits once released from prison and were eligible if they had worked sufficient hours per week in prison. Because of this, however, the random assignment of inmates to experimental and control groups for evaluation purposes was not done, and thus the best research design for assessing program impacts—the randomized experiment—was not used. Instead, investigators used a regression discontinuity design, in which the experimental group consisted of those inmates who had worked enough to be eligible for unemployment benefits and the control group contained those who had not. This did not affect the operation of the program, but it did make the evaluation of it more difficult and less certain. Nonetheless, a conservative evaluation of its effects concluded that the program saved California $2,000 for each inmate involved. In other words, the costs of the program were far outweighed by the money saved because some inmates in the program did not commit further crimes and the state saved the cost of incarcerating them. Despite this, the program was ended, partly because of ideological hostility to the idea of giving support to inmates and partly because California was facing a budget crisis.

problem because the value of both costs and benefits changes with time. We are well aware, for example, that a given number of dollars today does not have the same purchasing power it did 10 years ago. To make meaningful comparisons over time, we must adjust costs and benefits so that comparisons are made in constant dollars. This involves the calculation of what is called the *discount rate*. The discount rate is the amount that future costs and benefits are reduced to make them comparable to

the current value of money. Actual determination of the discount rate involves some highly complex accounting procedures. There are also several competing approaches to its calculation (Rossi and Freeman, 1993). As many saddened investors will attest, predicting the future value of money is a risky business. Furthermore, the discount rate used has a marked effect on the outcome of the analysis. For all these reasons, it is commonplace to run several analyses with differing discount rates to see how the program fares under different sets of assumptions.

Whose Costs, Whose Benefits?   An important consideration in cost-benefit analysis is that costs and benefits are calculated from particular perspectives. Three different perspectives may be used: program participants, the funding source, or society as a whole. A comprehensive cost-benefit analysis would include all three.

Let us take the example of subsidized day care and consider its costs and benefits from the three perspectives. For the parents who use day care service so they can work at paying jobs, the costs are the loss of other public assistance they would receive if they stayed home or did not work. Their benefits would be the income received by working, together with less tangible benefits such as enhanced social status, job satisfaction, and freedom from child care responsibilities. In general, from the standpoint of participants, benefits usually outweigh costs because program costs are paid by others. However, there may be many intangible costs for participants, such as inconvenience, negative labeling, and concern over adequacy of care received by children. Consequently, participants may view the "price" as not worth it.

From the perspective of the funding source — in this case we will assume it is the federal government — the costs and benefits are quite different. The costs would be the direct costs of running the day care service, together with the opportunity costs of not using the money for something else. The benefits would be the reduced costs of other public assistance programs and an increase in tax revenues on the incomes of working parents.

The societal perspective is the broadest and frequently the most difficult to calculate. (Furthermore, if the funding source is the government, we should not assume that the government's perspective coincides with the societal perspective. The government represents those groups that happen to control a particular government agency.) The costs to society of the day care service would be the increased taxes or federal borrowing necessary to fund the program plus the opportunity costs involved. Costs would also include lost jobs to private child care providers and lost income of workers displaced by the parents who now compete for their jobs. Benefits would be increased productivity of parents who are now freer to make economic, social, and cultural contributions to society (although we need to remember that performing as a parent or homemaker is also an essential contribution in our society). Other less direct benefits might accrue if working and the additional income it provides have positive effects on family relationships, the children's well-being, future aspirations, and the like. If day care happened to produce negative effects in these or other areas, such effects would be considered additional social costs.

An important contribution of the societal perspective is that it leads to a consideration of the distribution of costs and benefits across society. Most social programs involve some redistribution of wealth. In other words, program costs are typically not borne by the same segments of society that receive the benefits. Farm subsidy programs redistribute wealth from urban areas to rural areas, whereas Social Security transfers wealth from the young to the old, to cite only two of many possible examples. Whether these transfers are in the best interests of society is ultimately a political decision. A comprehensive cost-benefit analysis will make that a more informed decision. Some of the complexities and attributes of a cost-benefit analysis are illustrated in Research in Practice 12.2.

Cost-Effective Analysis

Because it is difficult to monetize benefits, interest has developed in an alternative approach that does not require that benefits be ascribed a dollar value. **Cost-effective analysis** compares program costs measured in dollars with program effects measured in whatever units are appropriate, such as achievement test scores, skill performance level, coping abilities, or whatever effect the program is supposed to produce. Such analysis is most useful for choosing among competing programs rather than evaluating a single program. For example, a cost-effective appraisal of a compensatory education program might reveal that total per-pupil costs of $300 raised reading performance by one point on a standard achievement test. This can then be compared with other programs in terms of the cost to raise reading performance by one point. A cost-effective comparison of remedial programs for disadvantaged children conducted by the General Accounting Office (GAO) found programs with wide-ranging cost effectiveness (Socolar, 1981). The average per-pupil cost of all such programs was $778. Interestingly, the GAO found that six especially effective programs cost only $180 per student. Such cost-effective analyses of many competing programs make it possible to select the most efficient approach. Interpreting a single cost-effective analysis, however, is less clear-cut than a cost-benefit analysis because the costs and benefits are not expressed in the same units. For this reason, cost-effective analysis is not an interchangeable substitute for cost-benefit analysis. They answer very different questions.

Although cost-benefit analysis is a valuable tool in assessing programs, it is important that it not be oversimplified or overemphasized. Results must be carefully interpreted in light of the data used to produce them. The complex components that go into a cost-benefit analysis need to be considered when interpreting the results. Like all forms of analysis, cost-benefit is only as good as the data, the estimates, and the assumptions on which it is based. All these components should be explicitly discussed in the report, and the users should be encouraged to evaluate the soundness of them. The real risk associated with cost-benefit analysis comes when bottom-line results are accepted blindly and become the overriding factor in decision making. At its current level of development, cost-benefit analysis can be very useful, but it must be cautiously interpreted as only one of many factors in the decision-making process concerning social programs.

Barriers to the Use of Evaluation Research

At the beginning of this chapter, we described the purposes of evaluation research as improving service to clients, aiding in the policymaking process, and testing social science theories and practice approaches. In all these areas, the assumption is made that the research results will be used to produce some change in the status quo. In actuality, this is often not the case, since there are many barriers to the use of the results of evaluation research.

One barrier is the fault of evaluators. Owing to poor design or execution, the evaluation may not produce clear-cut results. It is obviously difficult to overcome resistance to change unless the reasons for change are strong and the direction that change should take is clear. All too often, the basic conclusion of an evaluation is this: "The program as currently operated is not achieving its intended goals." What is one to do with such a conclusion? There is no indication of why the program is failing nor are there any suggestions for improving it. To avoid such results as this, we suggested earlier that evaluation be broadly conceived so that findings indicate not only what the program does not do, but also what it does do and why. Such detailed findings are of far greater utility for pointing the way for the future and for producing positive program changes (Bedell et al., 1985).

A second barrier to the use of evaluation research results is poor communication on the part of evaluators (Miller, 1987). Researchers are used to communicating with other researchers who share a common technical language and background. When communicating with one another, researchers assume those commonalities and write their reports accordingly. If this is done in an evaluation report, the results may be quite unclear to practitioners, program administrators, and policymakers who are supposed to use those results. Evaluation reports should be written so that they are understandable to the audience who will use them, and evaluators should work through the report with sponsors, explaining it thoroughly and answering all questions. Those sponsoring an evaluation or using the results should demand such accountability from evaluation researchers.

A third barrier to the use of evaluation research is the failure of evaluation researchers to press for the adoption of their research findings. Such an advocacy role is foreign to many researchers who feel that their job terminates once the data have been analyzed. However, implementation of modifications

Research in Practice 12.2
Program Evaluation: Cost-Benefit Analysis of a Personnel Program

A major goal of personnel programs is to improve the earning capacity of the people receiving training. One such program was the Supported Work Program (SWP), designed to provide work experience for several groups of people with long-standing employability problems (Kemper, Long, and Thornton, 1981). The target population included AFDC recipients, high school dropouts, former drug users, and ex-inmates. The program provided temporary employment (up to 18 months) and utilized various approaches to improve functioning, such as peer support and graduated stress, in which job demands are increased gradually as the participant becomes more accustomed to the job. The SWP was a large-scale project involving sites at 15 locations across the country. Understandably, a question often asked of such programs is this: Are the expenditures for the program worth the results? To answer this question, a cost-benefit evaluation was conducted. A sample of eligible applicants was randomly assigned to either a treatment group receiving the supports just mentioned or a control group not receiving them. Both participants and controls were interviewed at 9-month intervals for a period of 36 months.

Although an employment program may seem more straightforward than other types of intervention in terms of computing costs and benefits in dollars, Table 12.1, which shows expected benefits and costs, clearly illustrates that it can be a challenging task. Benefits and costs are considered from three alternative perspectives: the participants, the funding source (taxpayers), and society as a whole. An important element of conducting cost-benefit analyses, as Table 12.1 illustrates, is specifying the range of possible costs and benefits of a program and then clearly indicating which ones will be used in the assessment and how they will be estimated. Some benefits and costs can be readily translated into dollar values. It is relatively easy, for example, to monetize the earnings of program recipients who find employment and the taxes they would pay on their earnings. It is considerably more complex, however, to place a dollar amount on the reduced cost of operating the criminal justice system when program recipients avoid committing crimes or on the improved health status of people who are working and eating well. Finally, some benefits are probably impossible to monetize, such as the reduction in fear and psychological tension that results from a lower crime rate.

The results of the Supported Work Program were mixed. From the perspective of society as a whole, the long-term benefits exceeded costs by over $8,000 per recipient. For former drug addicts, the net benefit was $4,000 per participant. For high school dropouts, the cost exceeded the benefits by about $1,500 per participant. For ex-inmates, on the other hand, the researchers were unable to specify a clear net cost or benefit. In drawing their conclusions, the researchers caution that the estimates are partially based on extrapolating future benefits, that some of the benefits in participant earnings may have been at the expense of other workers who were displaced, and that many benefits are not inherently evaluable in financial terms.

Table 12.1 Expected Effects of Benefit–Cost Analysis Components, by Accounting Perspective

	Accounting Perspective		
	Society	**Participants**	**Funding Source (nonparticipants)**
Benefits and Costs			
I. Produced by Participants			
Value of in-program output	+	0	+
Increased postprogram output	+	+	0
Preference for work over welfare	+	+	+
II. Increased Tax Payments	0	−	+
III. Reduced Dependence on Transfer Programs			
Reduced transfer payments	0	−	+
Reduced administrative costs	+	0	+
IV. Reduced Criminal Activity			
Reduced property damage and personal injury	+	0	+
Reduced stolen property	+	−	+
Reduced justice system costs	+	0	+
Reduced psychological costs	+	+	+
V. Reduced Drug and Alcohol Use			
Reduced treatment costs	+	0	+
Psychological benefits	+	+	+
VI. Reduced Use of Alternative Education, Training, and Employment Services			
Reduced education and employment costs	+	0	+
Reduced training allowances	0	−	+
VII. Other Benefits			
Improved participant health status	+	+	+
Income redistribution	+	+	+
VIII. Program Operating Cost			
Overhead cost	−	0	−
Project cost	−	0	−
IX. Central Administrative Cost	−	0	−
X. Participant Labor Cost			
In-program earnings plus fringes	0	+	−
Forgone earnings plus fringes	−	−	0
Forgone nonmarket activities	−	−	0
XI. Increased Work-Related Cost			
Child care	−	−	−
Other	−	−	0

Note A plus (+) indicates an expected benefit from a given perspective, whereas a minus (−) indicates a cost, with a zero (0) indicating neither a cost nor a benefit.

Source Adapted from P. Kemper, D. Long, and C. Thornton, *The Supported Work Evaluation: Final Benefit-Cost Analysis* (Princeton: Mathematica Policy Research, Inc., 1981), p. 12. Used with permission.

to a program is often complex, and program staff are faced with competing interests. Without active participation by the researcher, adoption of recommendations may very well not take place.

A fourth barrier is the resistance to change that can be found in many quarters. People become accustomed to established procedures and may be disinclined to change. There are vested interests that are difficult to overcome. One of the most arrogant rejections of research was President Richard Nixon's reaction to the findings of the President's Commission on Pornography. Nixon appointed the commission to study the societal impact of pornography, fully expecting negative effects to be found, thus justifying a crackdown. When the commission reported no negative effects of viewing pornography and possibly even some salutary ones, Nixon simply dismissed the report as wrong.

Such blatant dismissals are rare. More common is what happened to a study of group counseling in a correctional system (Kassebaum et al., 1971). This was a very well conducted study that not only found few positive effects of counseling, but also provided many suggestions as to why these effects did not occur. The reaction to the report by the Department of Corrections was swift, but not what would be predicted given its contents. The counseling program was not dropped but was expanded to every prison in the system, and the expanded program was not modified to take into account suggestions in the report (Ward and Kassebaum, 1972). The evaluators speculated in a rather discouraged tone that the main effect of their report would be to limit future outside evaluations of prison programs.

One change suggested to improve research utilization is increased dissemination of results (Weiss, 1972). Earlier we expressed concern over the fact that evaluation reports are often not widely circulated. Broader dissemination may bring a report to the attention of someone willing to use the results.

Evaluation research reports are published in a number of ways. Sometimes they are published in social science or human service research journals, such as *Evaluation Review, Journal of Applied Behav-*

ioral Science, or *Journal of Applied Sociology.* In the past 10 years, more outlets for the publication of evaluation research have developed. Evaluation research reports are also published in government documents and reports, especially when the study concerns a government program; these can be accessed like other government documents (*see* Appendix A). Some evaluation reports are not published, however, and this can make them more difficult, but not impossible, to find. Even though unpublished, the results may be presented at meetings of applied research organizations, such as the Society for Applied Sociology, the NTL Institute for Applied Behavioral Science, and the National Association of Social Workers. In some cases, unpublished research reports can be obtained from the researchers themselves or from the organizations or agencies for whom the research was done. Unpublished reports can be difficult to locate because they are not included in indexes or abstracts that can be found in the library. This explains why researchers participate in a communication network with others doing research in the same area: These personal contacts are a way to learn what others are doing and obtain unpublished research reports. Another change that has been shown to increase the use of the results of evaluations is to involve the potential users in the evaluation research itself. Users can help design the research or serve as interviewers. When they do, there is better communication between evaluators and users, the users perceive the evaluation as more relevant and credible, and they are more committed to the evaluation (Dawson and D'Amico, 1985; Greene, 1988).

What is really needed to improve research utilization is for policymakers and program administrators to develop an increased willingness to put evaluation results to use. In fact, resistance to research utilization appears to be declining, and there may be a growing awareness that common sense and conventional wisdom are inadequate bases for designing and operating effective social programs (Rossi and Freeman, 1993). Years of experience with ineffective programs have made this conclusion quite evident. Such changing perspectives are encouraging for the future of evaluation research and its increased utilization.

Main Points

▪ Evaluation research is the use of scientific research methods to plan intervention programs, to monitor the implementation of new programs and the operation of existing ones, and to determine how effectively programs or clinical practices achieve their goals.

▪ Formative evaluation focuses on the planning, development, and implementation of intervention programs.

▪ Summative evaluation assesses the effectiveness and efficiency of programs and the extent to which program effects may be generalized to other settings and populations.

▪ Prior to beginning evaluation, an evaluability assessment is conducted to gain knowledge about the program as operated and to identify those aspects of it that can be evaluated.

▪ Proximate goals are evaluable short-run goals logically related to the achievement of long-term goals that are impractical to evaluate.

▪ Despite frequent difficulties associated with their use, randomized experiments constitute the strongest, most desirable designs for assessing program impact.

▪ Cost-benefit analysis, through the use of complex assumptions and estimates, compares the costs of a program with the dollar value of its benefits.

▪ Cost-benefit analysis and cost-effective analysis are not interchangeable. Cost-benefit analysis is useful for evaluating a single program, whereas cost-effective analysis is useful for choosing the most efficient program from among competing approaches.

▪ It is important that bottom-line results from either cost-benefit or cost-effective analyses not be accepted blindly, but that the data, estimates, and assumptions on which the results are based be carefully considered.

Important Terms for Review

cost-benefit analysis
cost-effective analysis
direct costs
evaluability assessment
evaluation research
formative evaluation research
needs assessment
opportunity costs
summative evaluation research

Exploring the Internet

One way to broaden your understanding of program evaluation research is to review examples of completed evaluation studies. The Internet is an excellent source for locating illustrative projects in any human service field. If the field of substance abuse interests you, then we suggest that you contact the National Clearinghouse for Alcohol and Drug Information (NCADI) PREVLINE database at http://www.health.org/dbases.htm. NCADI offers substance abuse information via searchable databases. You can access each database by clicking on the button for each database at this URL and then using the search engine made available by each database. You can research these databases for bibliographic abstracts pertaining to such subjects as alcohol, tobacco, marijuana, cocaine, and other drugs.

The Justice Information Center, operated by the National Criminal Justice Reference Service and located at http://www.ncjrs.org/homepage.htm, provides access not only to bibliographic references but to the full text versions of a wide range of evaluation projects in criminal justice. By selecting "Research and Evaluation" from among the menu options, you can review the studies and learn about the actual methodology used to evaluate the projects. One of the pages associated with this site is devoted to evaluation grants (http://www.ncjrs.org/fedgrant.htm). Here you can review grant application instructions. We pointed out that evaluation research differs from basic research in the role of the decision makers in program evaluation. We suggest that you review the specifications for one of the program evaluation projects with an eye toward how the sponsoring organization's needs affect the design of the research project.

An excellent source of program evaluation-related resources in the field of education is the ERIC Clearinghouse on Assessment and Evaluation (http://ericae2.educ.cua.edu/). In addition to directing you to various evaluation studies, the site provides links to assessment tools and professional organizations involved in evaluation. One such site worth mentioning in its own right is the American Evaluation Association. The home page of the American Evaluation Association is located at http://www.eval.org/. The AEA is an international professional association of evaluators devoted to the application and exploration of program evaluation, personnel evaluation, technology, and many other forms of evaluation. This organization maintains a current listing of Internet sites of interest to program evaluators, so whether you are interested in health, education, or any other human service area, this site will help you to locate additional resources.

For Further Reading

Alkin, Marvin C. *A Guide for Evaluation Decision Makers.* Beverly Hills, Calif.: Sage, 1985. This book is intended for administrators who commission evaluation research or who are responsible for seeing that evaluations are performed properly. It is a useful guide for developing meaningful evaluations.

Blalock, Ann Bonar, ed. *Evaluating Social Programs at the State and Local Level: The JTPA Evaluation Design Project.* Kalamazoo, Mich.: W. E. Upjohn Institute, 1990. This book provides an excellent overview of how to conduct program evaluations by analyzing specific evaluations of employment and training programs. It is a useful case-study approach.

Boruch, Robert. *Randomized Experiments for Planning and Evaluation.* Thousand Oaks, Calif.: Sage, 1996. This author stresses the point made in this chapter that good program evaluations should be based on randomized experimental designs. The book is packed with many useful examples of how to do this, often in situations where it might seem impossible.

Carley, Michael. *Social Measurement and Social Indicators: Issues of Policy and Theory.* Boston: Allen & Unwin, 1983. This book presents an in-depth look at various social indicators that may be monitored to assess aspects of social change. These indicators may be useful in measuring the impact of social programs for evaluation purposes.

Glaser, Daniel, with Edna Erez. *Evaluation Research and Decision Guidance: For Correctional, Addiction-Treatment, Mental Health, and Other People Changing Agencies.* New Brunswick, N.J.: Transaction Books, 1988. The authors provide a thorough review of how to assess the effectiveness of organizations or agencies whose goal is to change people in some fashion—make them drug free, law-abiding, mentally healthy, or educated. Studying the effectiveness of these organizations is different and more difficult than doing so in organizations that produce things, like cars or pizzas.

Guba, Egon G., and Yvonna S. Lincoln. *Fourth Generation Evaluation.* Newbury Park, Calif.: Sage, 1989. This book focuses mostly on program evaluation in educational settings. It challenges conventional ways of thinking in that it takes an "interpretive" approach, viewing all knowledge as a social construction. Even scientific knowledge is seen as socially constructed, as only one version of reality.

Krause, Daniel R. *Effective Program Evaluation: An Introduction.* Chicago: Nelson-Hall, 1995. A very readable textbook that covers all the basics of conducting a program evaluation, this book also includes some selected readings that help facilitate the research process.

Nas, Tevfik F. *Cost-Benefit Analysis: Theory and Application.* Thousand Oaks, Calif.: Sage, 1996. The author shows, in much more detail than could be included in this chapter, how to conduct good cost-benefit analyses. The book covers all the relevant issues.

Patton, Michael Quinn. *Utilization-Focused Evaluation,* 3rd ed. Thousand Oaks, Calif.: Sage, 1996. This book considers both theoretical and practical issues in conducting program evaluations. It also uses a case-study approach and stresses the perspective that good program evaluations must be designed to be useful to program managers and policymakers.

Shadish, William R., Jr., Thomas D. Cook, and Laura C. Leviton. *Foundations of Program Evaluation.* Newbury

Park, Calif.: Sage, 1993. This volume looks at the origins of program evaluation and at the accumulated experiences of veteran program evaluators to provide an insightful discussion of the development of the field and of key issues that are relevant today.

Stake, Robert E. *Quieting Reform: Social Science and Social Action in an Urban Youth Program.* Urbana, Ill.: University of Illinois Press, 1986. This is an excellent case study of a program for disadvantaged youth—the evaluation of it and the politics that surrounds the whole process. It examines the many pressures on evaluation researchers, the many interests that get involved in such a process, and the varying definitions of what constitutes success.

Weiss, Heather B., and Francine H. Jacobs, eds. *Evaluating Family Programs.* New York: Aldine de Gruyter, 1988. This book provides an interesting summary of the kinds of research evaluations that have relevance for the family as a social institution. Many programs are evaluated and numerous methodological issues are discussed. This is a very good resource.

Exercises for Class Discussion

It is a commonly known fact that many elderly people have strong emotional attachments to their pets. However, the necessity of moving into a nursing home or medical care facility generally entails severing the relationship that the older person has developed with a dog or cat. Recently, experts in gerontology have been "discovering" the important role that animals can play in making residents feel at home in residential facilities. Consequently, some facilities have begun experimenting with pet therapy, a program in which volunteers bring pets to the nursing home on a regular basis so that interested residents may pet and play with the animals. The idea of having dogs and cats running around in a nursing home may seem contrary to the medical goals of a sterile, clean environment but has proved to be quite popular with the patients.

Assume you are a human service worker with a nursing home, and you have been approached by some residents or staff about starting such a program. You are aware that there may be some local foundation money available to support the project,

and some local organizations such as the Humane Society, the area kennel club, and a cat fanciers group could probably be induced to provide both the animals and the volunteers to help with the project. You also know that to get the money for the program, you will have to convince the administration that the program is worth the trouble and also show the foundation that you have a well-designed program that is effective in meeting its goals.

12.1 In order to make a formal proposal for funding, you must first do some formative evaluation research to determine if the program is needed and, if so, feasible. What are some research questions you think would be important to ask in this regard?

12.2 What kinds of data would be necessary, and how might you collect them?

12.3 State some specific goals that such a program might be expected to achieve.

Assume you have done some formative evaluation work, and the facility administrator has given the go-ahead to apply for a grant for the project. However, the board was somewhat skeptical about the idea, so the compromise that resulted specifies the program be tried for 6 months, at the end of which time a thorough evaluation must be done to determine the effects of the program and the relative costs and benefits.

12.4 What are some possible effects that the program might have? Remember to look for both positive and negative impacts. How would you suggest measuring these potential effects?

12.5 In terms of doing a cost-benefit analysis, make a list of both costs and benefits. For each list, do as follows: Make a column for three different accounting perspectives—society, the nursing home residents, and the funding source. For each cost and each benefit you identify, place a plus (+) sign in the column if that party stands to benefit, a zero (0) if the impact is neutral, or a minus (−) if that party stands to have a net cost. (*See* the table in Research in Practice 12.2 for an example.)

12.6 Given the kinds of benefits that might result from such a program, which ones lend themselves to cost accounting? Which ones are not readily translatable into dollars? All things considered, do you think a cost-benefit analysis is appropriate for this project?

12.7 The program as planned will be available to any resident in the facility who wants to participate. Thus, it will not be possible to assign residents randomly to receive or not receive the program. Given this condition, what are some alternate ways of providing experimental control for the project? What potential validity problems do your suggestions pose?

CHAPTER 13
Scaling

Advantages of Scaling   346

Developing Scales   347
  Sources of Scale Items   348
  Characteristics of Scale Items   348

Scaling Formats   350
  Likert Scales   350
  Thurstone Scales   353
  Semantic Differential Scales   356
  Guttman Scales   358
  Multidimensional Scales   362

Scaling in the Human Services   363

Main Points   366

Important Terms for Review   366

Exploring the Internet   366

For Further Reading   367

Exercises for Class Discussion   368

Measurement in research is discussed at some length in Chapter 5, which explains that some measurement is fairly straightforward and involves the use of only a single *item,* or indicator of a variable. We can, for example, measure a person's age with one question that asks how old the person is. Likewise, such variables as marital status or number of children in a family would normally be measured with a single item. These variables refer to phenomena in the world that are fairly unambiguous and for which a single indicator provides a valid and reliable measure. Many other variables, however, are much more difficult and complex to measure. In some cases, there may be more than one indicator of a variable. In other cases, the variable may involve a number of dimensions that calls for multiple indicators. In still other cases, we may be concerned with the *degree* to which a variable is present. In these cases, a single-item measuring instrument would probably be inadequate, and we would use a **scale,** a number of items that are combined to form a composite score on a variable. To measure people's attitudes toward having children, for example, we could ask how much they agree with a series of questions, which are the items that make up the scale. Their composite score on the scale would indicate their overall attitude toward having children.

This chapter provides an introduction to how scales are constructed. We begin by discussing the benefits of scales as opposed to single-item measures, and then we present some basic considerations involved in selecting scale items. Following this, we assess the various scaling techniques and the reasons for choosing a particular format. Finally, we consider some of the special scaling needs likely to be confronted by human service practitioners.

Advantages of Scaling

Scales have four major advantages over single-item measures.

Improved Validity When measuring abstract or complex variables, a multiple-item measure is generally more valid than a single-item measure. Consider the variable "self-esteem." The Rosenberg Self-Esteem Scale, developed to measure self-esteem, contains 10 statements (*see* Table 13.1). It does so because no single question or statement could possibly measure something as complex, multifaceted, and constantly changing as a person's self-esteem. What single question could we ask you that might encompass all the feelings that you have about yourself? Clearly, self-esteem involves many aspects of a person's life situation—family, occupation, financial and social status, to name a few. Multiple-item scales provide more valid measures of such complex phenomena.

Improved Reliability In general, as shown in Chapter 5, the more items contained in a measure, the more reliable it will be. This is so because the statements comprising a scale are actually just a sample of the entire universe of statements that could have been used. A single-item measure is a sample of one, and it is less likely to be *representative* of the universe of statements than more than one item would be. Multiple-item scales are larger samples from this universe and are, therefore, more likely to be representative. Being more representative, they are more reliable than single-item measures.

Increased Level of Measurement Single-item measures are likely to produce data that are nominal or, at the very best, partially ordered. The term "partially ordered data" refers to data with a few ordered categories but with many cases "tied" for each category. Although superior to nominal, these data are less desirable than fully ordered data in which every, or nearly every, case has its own rank (*see* Chapter 14). Multiple-item scales are capable of producing fully ordered and possibly interval-level data. A higher level of measurement means

Table 13.1 Rosenberg Self-Esteem Scale

	1 Strongly Agree	2 Agree	3 Disagree	4 Strongly Disagree
(1) On the whole, I am satisfied with myself.	SA[4]	A[3]	D[2]	SD[1]
(2) At times I think I am no good at all.	SA[1]	A[2]	D[3]	SD[4]
(3) I feel that I have a number of good qualities.	SA[4]	A[3]	D[2]	SD[1]
(4) I am able to do things as well as most other people.	SA[4]	A[3]	D[2]	SD[1]
(5) I feel I do not have much to be proud of.	SA[1]	A[2]	D[3]	SD[4]
(6) I certainly feel useless at times.	SA[1]	A[2]	D[3]	SD[4]
(7) I feel that I'm a person of worth, at least on an equal plane with others.	SA[4]	A[3]	D[2]	SD[1]
(8) I wish I could have more respect for myself.	SA[1]	A[2]	D[3]	SD[4]
(9) All in all, I am inclined to feel that I am a failure.	SA[1]	A[2]	D[3]	SD[4]
(10) I take a positive attitude toward myself.	SA[4]	A[3]	D[2]	SD[1]

Source Morris Rosenberg, *Conceiving the Self*, rev. ed. (Malabar, Fla.: Krieger Publishing Company, 1986).

better measurement in terms of precision and increased flexibility in data analysis.

Increased Efficiency in Data Handling Because the items in a scale are all related (in that they all measure the same variable), responses to these items can be summarized into a single number or score for each respondent. This achieves the quantification goal of measurement and means that all the separate responses to each of the items do not have to be analyzed individually. Each score summarizes a great deal of information about each respondent and facilitates analysis of the data.

So when the concept to be measured is complex, multiple-item scales offer substantial advantages for the researcher—advantages that often outweigh the difficulty of their construction.

Developing Scales

Once it is decided to use scales as a measuring device, an appropriate scale needs to be found or developed. In most cases, scales consist of questions to which people respond or statements to which they

indicate their level of agreement. In Chapter 7, we present guidelines for wording questions in questionnaires or interviews, and those same general rules apply to the development or selection of scale items. You should review those guidelines now, considering them in the context of scale construction. In many cases, it is possible to use a complete scale developed by someone else if it is a valid and reliable measure of the variables under investigation. Or a scale can be made up of statements or even of whole sections that are taken from previously developed scales. A major advantage of using existing items or scales is that their validity and reliability have usually already been established. A few of the many compilations of measurement scales are listed in the For Further Reading section of this chapter. In addition, scales are reported in the many research journals in the behavioral sciences.

If no existing scale will do the job, then a new scale should be developed (De Vellis, 1991). A certain logic is common to the development of scales, which generally involves the following steps:

1. Developing or locating many potential scale items, far more than will appear in the final scale.

2. Eliminating items that are redundant, ambiguous, or for some other reason inappropriate for the scale.
3. Pretesting the remaining items for validity, reliability, or other measurement checks to be described shortly.
4. Eliminating items that do not pass the tests of step 3.
5. Repeating steps 3 and 4 as often as necessary to reduce the scale to the number of items required.

Sources of Scale Items

One of the most accessible sources of scale items is a researcher's own imagination. Once a concept has been developed and refined, the researcher has a pretty good idea of what is to be measured. The researcher can then generate a range of statements that seem to satisfy the criteria to be discussed. At this early stage in scale construction, one need not be too concerned with honing and polishing the statements to perfection because much pretesting remains before any statement is ever seen by an actual respondent.

A second source of scale items is people, sometimes called "judges," who are considered to be especially knowledgeable in a particular area. If one is seeking items for a delinquency scale, for instance, it would seem reasonable to discuss the issue with juvenile probation officers and others having daily contact with delinquents. Two social psychologists used this approach to find items for a scale to measure people's tendency to manipulate others for their own personal gain (Christie and Geis, 1970). They turned to the writings of Niccolò Machiavelli, a sixteenth-century adviser to the prince of Florence in Italy. In his classic book *The Prince,* Machiavelli propounded essentially a con artist's view of the world and politics: People, according to Machiavelli, are to be manipulated for one's own benefit, in a cool and unemotional fashion. Lying, cheating, and underhandedness are justified if they advance one's own personal position. In the writings of this Florentine of four centuries ago, these

social psychologists found such statements as: "It is safer to be feared than to be loved" and "Humility not only is of no service but is actually harmful." They constructed a scale made up of Machiavelli's statements, somewhat revised, and asked people whether they agreed with each statement. The scale is now known as the Machiavellianism Scale and has been used widely in scientific research. One is tempted to wonder whether Signore Machiavelli, were he able to peer through the mists of time, would consider this scale a sufficiently cunning and beguiling use of his prose. In any event, this illustrates a particularly creative use of "judges" in the development of scales.

A third source of scale items is the people who are the focus of the research project. Claudia Coulton (1979), for example, was interested in person–environment fit among consumers of hospital social services. In developing her scale, she obtained a large number of verbatim statements from hospital patients and then began to form these into a scale. In like manner, if one were interested in attitudes among teenagers toward unwanted pregnancies, an excellent beginning would be to discuss the topic with teenagers and gather from them as many statements as possible regarding the issue. When items are garnered from people in this fashion, only rarely would statements be usable without editing. Many statements would ultimately be rejected, and most would have to be considerably rewritten. Such people, however, are likely to provide a range of statements that have meaning from the perspective of the group under investigation.

Characteristics of Scale Items

Once a large number of scale items have been found, the best ones have to be selected for the final scale. Good scale items have the following characteristics.

Validity A primary concern in item selection is the validity of the statements (*see* Chapter 5 on validity). Each statement considered for inclusion should be assessed for content validity. For example, if we were creating a self-report delinquency scale, each statement would be assessed as to how it related to measuring delinquent activity. Statements concerning a person's participation in various delinquent acts would be reasonable as valid measures of how delinquent that person is. On the other hand, an item relating to how well the respondent gets along with his or her siblings would probably not be a valid indicator of delinquency.

Range of Variation

Variables that are measured with multiple-item scales are normally considered to consist of a number of possible values or positions that a person could take. If we wanted to measure people's attitudes toward growing old, for example, people's positions on that variable could be extremely positive, extremely negative, or anywhere in between. In selecting items for measurement scales, we should ensure that the items cover the actual range of possible variation on the variable being measured. Failure to do so will result in a poor scale. When selecting items on the basis of variability, the researcher needs to exercise care to avoid defining the range either too narrowly or too broadly. Failure to include a sufficiently wide range of items will result in respondents' "piling up" at one or both ends of the scale's range. If many respondents tie with either the lowest or highest possible score, the range in the scale is inadequate. This "piling up" effect reduces the precision of the measurement because we are unable to differentiate among the respondents with tied scores.

Going to extremes with items to define the range is not desirable either. If we include items that are too extreme, they will apply to few, if any, respondents. In the case of a delinquency scale, for example, an item pertaining to engaging in cannibalism would be such an extreme item as to warrant exclusion. The act is so rare in our culture that it is unlikely that any juvenile has done it, and it thus contributes nothing of benefit to the scale. The goal is to select items with enough range of variation to cover the actual range of alternatives that people are likely to choose, without including items that are so extreme that they do not apply to anyone.

Unidimensionality

In the construction of a multiple-item scale, the goal is to measure one specific variable, and we do not want the results confounded by items on the scale that actually measure a different, although possibly related, variable. The items of a **unidimensional scale** measure only one variable. If a scale actually measures more than one variable, then it is called multidimensional. In creating our delinquency scale, we might be tempted to include an item about school performance on the grounds that delinquents seem to perform poorly in school. Although an empirical relationship may exist between delinquency and school performance, they are separate variables and should be treated and measured as such.

In assessing the unidimensionality of scales, one must distinguish between *different variables* and *different aspects of the same variable*. A single variable may have more than one aspect, and we need to be careful to recognize these so that they can be measured appropriately. Delinquency, for example, contains at least two aspects: severity and frequency. In terms of severity, it seems reasonable to distinguish between an adolescent who committed petty theft and one who committed aggravated assault. In terms of frequency, an adolescent who regularly commits petty theft might be properly considered as delinquent, or even more delinquent, than one with a single case of assault.

The different aspects of a variable need to be distinguished and analyzed carefully because one may correlate with an independent or dependent variable, whereas another does not. This again suggests the complexity of some variables. In a study of person−environment fit, for example, Claudia Coulton (1979) distinguished between the many aspects that might be parts of this variable. "Person−environment fit" refers to the extent to which an individual's needs can be satisfied and aspirations fulfilled in the context of the demands and opportunities available in a particular environment. Coulton distinguished between "fit" in relation to one's economic activities, "fit" in terms of the amount and relevance of information available to a person, "fit" in terms of one's family relations, and the like. In this case, the "person−environment fit" scale is unidimensional in that it measures one underlying variable, but it also contains a number of distinct aspects that are a part of that variable.

To gain systematic evidence of the unidimensionality of a scale, the researcher can intercorrelate each item in the scale with every other scale item. This is often done during a pretest. If some items do not correlate with the others, it is possible that they do not measure the same variable or that they are separate aspects of the variable that vary independently of one another. If we suspect that these items measure a different variable, then they should be eliminated from the scale. If we find a few items that have nearly perfect correlations, we only need to use one of them in the scale. Two items to which people respond identically are simply redundant, and using both adds nothing to the measurement abilities of the scale. Occasionally, however, highly correlated items should be included to detect response inconsistency or random answering. That exception notwithstanding, the final scale will be composed of statements that correlate fairly highly, but not perfectly, with one another.

A knowledge of the characteristics and sources of scale items provides an important and necessary foundation for the development of scales. By themselves, however, these offer only a general guide to scale development. The more complex intricacies to developing scales can best be grasped by looking at specific types of scales and illustrations of how they have been developed. Moreover, some types of scales have unique requirements that are not adequately covered by our previous discussion. We turn, then, to a discussion of the most important types of scales used in human service research.

Scaling Formats

Scaling can utilize a number of formats, and each format calls for some unique elements in its design.

Likert Scales

One of the most popular approaches to scaling is that developed by Rensis Likert (1932). A **Likert scale** consists of a series of statements, each followed by four or five response alternatives. An illustration of a Likert scale is presented in Table 13.1. Five is the most common number of alternatives because it offers respondents a sufficient range of choices without requiring unnecessarily minute distinctions in attitudes. However, more or fewer than five alternatives are sometimes used. Notice in Table 13.1 the numbers ranging from 1 to 4 in brackets next to each response alternative. These numbers are included on the scale here for purposes of illustration only; they would not be printed on a scale for actual use because their presence might influence respondents' answers. The numbers are used when scoring the scale. The numbers associated with each response are totaled to provide the overall score for each respondent. In this case—a 10-item scale—individual scores can range from a low of 10 (if alternative 1 were chosen every time) to a high of 40 (if alternative 4 were chosen every time). Note that, as discussed in Chapter 5, each item in a Likert scale is an ordinal measure, ranging from a low of "strongly disagree" to a high of "strongly agree." Because the total score of a Likert scale is the sum of individual, ordinal items, many researchers contend that a Likert scale is therefore ordinal in nature. Technically, one should refrain from using statistics such as the mean and standard deviation with ordinal-level data. However, especially with well-established Likert scales, it is common to see published studies in which scores are treated as if they were interval level. Whether this application of interval procedures is appropriate is a debated topic among researchers and cannot be resolved here.

The Likert scale is one example of scales known as **summated rating scales.** These are scales in which a person's score is determined by summing the number of questions answered in a particular way. We could, for example, ask respondents to agree or disagree with statements and then give them a 1 for each statement they agree with and a 0 for each disagreement. Their scale score is then the sum of their responses. Summated rating scales can take a number of different forms, although the Likert format is the most common.

Constructing a Likert scale, as with all scales, requires considerable time and effort. One begins by developing a series of statements relating to the variable being measured. The general criteria for statements outlined previously should be carefully considered during this stage. No matter how diligent we are in following those guidelines, however, some of the statements will turn out to be inadequate for a variety of reasons. Because we anticipate having to drop some unacceptable items, substantially more statements than desired in the final scale should initially be written. A common rule of thumb is to start with three times the number of statements desired for the final scale.

Likert scales are designed to avoid certain kinds of response patterns that affect the validity of the scale. You will notice in the items in Table 13.1 that choosing "strongly agree" on items 1, 3, 4, 7, and 10 would be an expression of high self-esteem; choosing "strongly agree" on items 2, 5, 6, 8, and 9, on the other hand, would be an expression of low self-esteem. If "strongly agree" were an expression of high self-esteem for all items, some respondents would have to choose the same alternative on every item in order to express their opinion. This is not desirable because it can cause *response pattern anxiety:* Some people become anxious if they have to repeat the same response all the time and change their responses to avoid doing so. If this occurs, then their reactions to statements do not reflect their actual attitudes but rather their reaction to a certain response pattern, and the validity of the scale is reduced. (As students, you have probably had this experience when taking a multiple-choice exam. If several consecutive questions all have the same answer, you become concerned and may doubt answers that you are fairly sure of just because the pattern of responses differs from the more random pattern you expect.) If both positive and negative statements are provided in a scale, all respondents should find some statements with which they agree and others with which they disagree so that response pattern anxiety is avoided.

Having the same response alternative be an expression of the same opinion or feeling on all items can produce another problem with scales: *response set.* Some people tend to be either "yea-sayers"

or "nay-sayers," tending either to agree or disagree with statements regardless of their content. If the self-esteem scale were constructed so that "strongly agree" always indicated high self-esteem, then people who tend to agree with statements would score higher on self-esteem than they actually should because they tend to agree with statements irrespective of content. This again would throw into question the validity of the scale. Mixing the response pattern of items is taken into account in scoring Likert scales. The alternatives that indicate an expression of the same opinion or feeling are given the same numerical score. In our example, for instance, all high-esteem alternatives (whether they be "strongly agree" or "strongly disagree") are given a score of 4. Then each person's responses to all items can be summed for a total scale score.

In deciding which items will ultimately be used in a Likert scale, a final criterion is whether the scale items *discriminate* among people. That is, we want people's responses to an item to range over the four or five alternatives rather than bunch up on one or two choices. Imagine a scale with an item that reads: "Persons convicted of shoplifting should have their hands amputated." If such an item were submitted to a group of college students, it is likely that most would respond with "strongly disagree" and maybe a few "disagrees." It is highly unlikely that any would agree. Of what use is this item to us? We cannot *compare* people—assess who is more likely to agree or disagree—because they all disagree. We cannot correlate responses to this item with the social or psychological characteristics of the students because there is little or no variation in responses to the item.

We want, then, to eliminate nondiscriminating items from consideration for our scale. *Nondiscriminating items* are those that are responded to in a similar fashion by both people who score high and people who score low on the overall scale. Nondiscriminating items in a scale can be detected on the basis of results from a pretest in which people respond to all the preliminary items of the scale. One way of identifying nondiscriminating items is by computing a **discriminatory power score** (or DP score) for each item. The DP score essentially tells us the degree to which each item differentiates between respondents with high scores and respondents with low scores on the overall scale. Although this approach is now used less in actual practice because of the availability of other, more complex, procedures that depend on computer support, it is a straightforward technique that illustrates well the principles of item selection.

The first step in obtaining DP scores is to calculate the total scores of each respondent and rank the scores from highest to lowest. We then identify the upper and lower quartiles of the distribution of total scores. The *upper quartile* (Q_3) is the cutoff point in a distribution above which the highest 25 percent of the scores are located, and the *lower quartile* (Q_1) is the cutoff point below which the lowest 25 percent of the scores are located. With the quartiles based on *total* scores identified, we compare the pattern of responses to *each* scale item for respondents whose scores fall above the upper quartile with the pattern for respondents whose scores fall below the lower quartile. Table 13.2 illustrates the computation of DP scores for one item in a scale to which 40 people responded. Ten respondents are above the upper quartile, and 10 are below the lower quartile. It can be seen that the high scorers tended to agree with this item because most had scores of 4 or 5. Low scorers tended to disagree because they are totally concentrated in the 1 and 2 score range. The next step is to compute a weighted total on this item for the two groups. This is done by multiplying each score by the number of respondents with that score. For example, for those above the upper quartile, the weighted total is: $(1 \times 0) + (2 \times 1) + (3 \times 2) + (4 \times 4) + (5 \times 3) = 0 + 2 + 6 + 16 + 15 =$

39. Next, the weighted mean (average) is computed by dividing the weighted total by the number of cases in the quartile. For the upper quartile, we have $39 \div 10 = 3.9$. The DP score for this item is then obtained by subtracting the mean of those below the lower quartile from the mean of those above the upper quartile. In this example, we have $3.9 - 1.8 = 2.1$ DP. This process is repeated for every item in the preliminary scale so that each item has a calculated DP score. It should be clear that figuring DP scores for all preliminary items would be extremely tedious if done by hand. Fortunately, computers can be readily programmed to accomplish this task.

Once we have DP scores for all the preliminary items, final selection can begin. The best items are those with the *highest* DP scores because this shows that people in the upper and lower quartiles responded to the items very differently. As a rule of thumb, as many items as possible should have DP scores of 1.00 or greater, and few, if any, should drop below 0.50. Applying this rule to the item in Table 13.2, we would conclude that it is a very good item and would include it in the final scale.

Occasionally, one will encounter DP scores with negative signs. Under no circumstances should an item with a negative DP score be included because this means that high scorers on the overall scale scored lower on this item than did the low scorers. If the size of the negative DP score is small, it is probably an ambiguous statement that is being variously interpreted by respondents. If the negative DP score is large, however, it is possible that the item was accidentally misscored; that is, a negative item was scored as if it were positive or vice versa.

Table 13.2   Calculation of Discriminatory Power Score for One Item in a Scale

Quartile	N	Response Value					Weighted Total	Weighted Mean	DP Score
		1	2	3	4	5			
Upper	10	0	1	2	4	3	39	3.90	
Lower	10	2	8	0	0	0	18	1.80	2.10
								2.10	

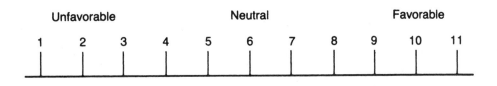

Figure 13.1   Equal-Appearing Intervals as Used in Thurstone Scale Construction

Many computer software packages have procedures for item analysis that rely on other principles but accomplish largely the same task. For example, the popular package SPSS includes the procedure RELIABILITY, which performs an item analysis on the components of additive scales by computing commonly used coefficients of reliability. The procedure computes a correlation matrix that shows how each item correlates with every other item. It also provides the reliability coefficient Cronbach's alpha (*see* Chapter 5) for the proposed scale, with each item deleted. Using the output of this procedure, the researcher can exclude from the scale those items that detract from or contribute little to the overall reliability of the instrument.

The Likert scale is one of the most popular multiple-item scales because of the many advantages it possesses. First, it offers respondents a range of choices rather than the limited "yes–no" alternatives used in some other scales. This makes Likert scales valuable if our theoretical assessment of a variable is that it ranges along a continuum rather than being either present or absent. Second, data produced by Likert-type scales are considered to be ordinal level, which enables us to use more powerful statistical procedures than with nominal-level data. Third, Likert scales are fairly straightforward to construct.

Although its advantages make the Likert scale one of the most widely used attitude scales, it has the same disadvantages as many other scales. In particular, one must be careful in interpreting a single score based on a Likert scale because it is a summary of so much information (separate responses to a number of items). Whenever we summarize data we lose some information. (Your grade in this course is a summary measure of your performance,

and in calculating it your instructor loses information regarding those high—or low—scores you received on individual exams.) The summary score might hide information about patterns of variation in responses or about possible multidimensionality of the scale.

Research in Practice 13.1 discusses the development of a Likert scale to be used for research in human service practice settings.

Thurstone Scales

Another approach to scaling was developed by L. L. Thurstone and E. J. Chave (1929). **Thurstone scales** are constructed so that they use *equal-appearing intervals*—that is, it is assumed that the distance between any two adjacent points on the scale is the same. This provides us with data of interval-level quality and enables us to use all the powerful statistical procedures that require interval-level data. (You may want to review levels of measurement in Chapter 5 to ensure that you understand the importance of this characteristic of Thurstone scales.)

Construction of a Thurstone scale begins in much the same way as for Likert scales, with the selection of many statements that relate to the variable being measured. Once a sufficient number of statements is at hand, the next step is to provide a value between 1 and 11 for each statement. As illustrated in Figure 13.1, Thurstone scales utilize an 11-point scale ranging from 1, the most unfavorable statement regarding an object, event, or issue, to 11, the most favorable. Point 6 on the scale is called "neutral" and is used for statements that are neither favorable nor unfavorable. For example, the statement "teenage girls who get pregnant are

Research in Practice 13.1
Program Evaluation: Developing a Scale to Measure Client Satisfaction

In our efforts to evaluate the human services, one important group whose opinion is often neglected is that of the clients themselves, in spite of the fact that the jargon of the human services is filled with such phrases as "start where the client is" and "promote client self-determination" and labels such as "client-centered" therapy. This lack of a client focus in evaluation has been attributed in part to the fact that services are delivered through public settings where agencies are not dependent on the client for financial support. It has also been suggested that the user of social services is viewed as a patient in need of treatment rather than as a consumer who is making use of professional services in pursuit of his or her own personal goals (Rein, 1970). A consequence of this oversight has been a lack of measurement tools to assess what clients think of the services they receive.

Recognition that client evaluation of services should be an integral part of program evaluation efforts served as the challenge to a team of researchers who set out to develop a Likert scale that would serve as a valid and reliable indicator of client satisfaction (Reid and Gundlach, 1983). The process they followed in developing their scale illustrates many of the points made in our discussion of scale construction.

The first step in the process involved collecting possible scale items that would reflect social service consumer attitudes. The researchers relied on two main sources for scale items. First, one of the authors had extensive experience in practice and consultation with service users, so this personal expertise served as a source of items. Second, the authors consulted the provocative book *The Client Speaks,* which was based on interviews with family service agency users in London (Timms and Mayer, 1971).

Items were developed to measure three attributes of a service:

immoral" would be considered very unfavorable toward teenage pregnancies.

The task of rating each statement as to how favorable or unfavorable it is with regard to the measured variable is assigned to a group of people known as "judges." With each of the preliminary statements printed on a separate card, the judges rate the items by placing them in piles corresponding to points on the 11-point scale. The judges place in each pile statements that they assess to be roughly equivalent in terms of their favorableness.

Once the scale values are computed for all the preliminary items, the next step is to determine which items are the least ambiguous and, therefore, best for inclusion in the final scale. If the judges differed widely in their ratings on an item, it is likely something is unclear about the statement itself that leads to varying interpretations. Therefore, the degree of agreement among judges about the rating of an item is used as one indicator of ambiguity.

Scales should include the items with the most agreement among judges, and there should be a roughly equal number of items for each of the 11 scale values ranging from unfavorable to favorable, moving upward in half-point increments. This would mean that a minimum of 21 items is required, although some argue that if reliability of .90 or better is desired, as many as 50 statements may be needed (Seiler and Hough, 1970). Regardless of the number actually used, the last step in Thurstone scale construction is to order the items randomly for presentation to respondents.

Table 13.3 presents the first 13 statements contained in the original 45-item Thurstone scale developed by Thurstone and Chave, with the scale

1. Relevance—did a service correspond to the client's perception of his or her problem and needs?
2. Impact—did the service reduce the problem?
3. Gratification—did the service enhance self-esteem and contribute to a sense of power and integrity?

The items were included in a study of social service use involving 166 families in a midsize Michigan community. The respondents were heads of households served by the Head Start program. The authors describe this sample as a high-service user group. During the 3 months prior to the study, 78 percent had received AFDC, 75 percent had received Medicaid, and 56 percent had received food stamps. The sample had also used a variety of other public services.

To analyze the scale items, the authors turned to the SPSS statistical package and used its procedures for item analysis. They used Cronbach's alpha to determine which items to eliminate. A full explanation of the process is beyond the scope of this book; however, it basically involves comparing the reliability coefficient of the scale when an item is included with the reliability coefficient obtained when an item is dropped from the scale. If the reliability is greater without a given item included, it is dropped from the scale. Items that contribute very little to the overall reliability may also be dropped to make the scale as concise and convenient to complete as possible.

On completion of the scale construction process, the authors reported that the total scale had a reliability of .955. Reliability for the Relevance subscale was .848, Impact was .821, and Gratification was .857.

Additional analysis was conducted to determine relationships between the subscales and background characteristics of the service users, such as race, sex, and marital status. Comparisons were also made between respondents based on the particular service they viewed as most important. The authors concluded that a measurement tool for client satisfaction was feasible and recommended that the scale could be used by agencies seeking to assess the effect of differing services on client attitudes.

value of each item indicated in parentheses. This particular scale is designed so that items with high scale values are "unfavorable" toward the church, and items with low scale values are "favorable." The scale values would not, of course, be included on a working version of the scale and are presented here for purposes of illustration. Note that respondents are required only to check the statements with which they agree, making the Thurstone format particularly easy for respondents.

Scoring a Thurstone scale is different from the simple summation procedure used with Likert scales. Because the respondents will agree to differing numbers of statements with different values, the simple sum of the item values is worthless. Rather, a respondent's score is either the mean or median of the scale values of the items that the person agrees with. For example, if a person agreed with statements 2, 4, 8, and 12 in Table 13.3, that person's Thurstone scale score would be 3.13. Another person choosing 1, 7, 10, and 13 would have a score of 8.18. This scoring procedure distributes respondents along the original 11-point scale.

Thurstone and Likert scaling techniques are essentially interchangeable methods of measuring attitudes. A major advantage of the Thurstone technique is that it provides interval-level data. However, if the interval-data properties are not needed, the Likert technique is probably preferable owing to its higher reliability with fewer items and its reputed greater ease of construction. A second advantage of Thurstone scales is that people can respond to the items more quickly than with a Likert scale because they need only indicate whether they agree with an item and need not ponder how much they agree or disagree. However, because

Table 13.3   Attitude Toward Church Scale

Check (√) every statement below that expresses your sentiment toward the church. Interpret the statements in accordance with your own experience with churches.

(8.3)*   1. I think the teaching of the church is altogether too superficial to have much social significance.

(1.7)   2. I feel the church services give me inspiration and help me to live up to my best during the following week.

(2.6)   3. I think the church keeps business and politics up to a higher standard than they would otherwise tend to maintain.

(2.3)   4. I find the services of the church both restful and inspiring.

(4.0)   5. When I go to church, I enjoy a fine ritual service with good music.

(4.5)   6. I believe in what the church teaches but with mental reservations.

(5.7)   7. I do not receive any benefit from attending church services, but I think it helps some people.

(5.4)   8. I believe in religion, but I seldom go to church.

(4.7)   9. I am careless about religion and church relationships, but I would not like to see my attitude become general.

(10.5)   10. I regard the church as a static, crystallized institution, and as such it is unwholesome and detrimental to society and the individual.

(1.5)   11. I believe church membership is almost essential to living life at its best.

(3.1)   12. I do not understand the dogmas or creeds of the church, but I find that the church helps me to be more honest and creditable.

(8.2)   13. The paternal and benevolent attitude of the church is quite distasteful to me.

*Scale value

Source   L. L. Thurstone and E. J. Chave, *The Measurement of Attitude* (Chicago: University of Chicago Press, 1929). Used with permission of the University of Chicago Press.

reliability calls for Thurstone scales to be longer, this advantage may be minimal. In fact, this can become a disadvantage if the longer scale leads people to be overly quick or careless in responding to statements. Another major disadvantage of Thurstone scales is that they are costly and difficult to construct. However, modern data-processing techniques have substantially reduced the construction time of Thurstone scales (Seiler and Hough, 1970).

Semantic Differential Scales

Another scaling format, which has proved quite popular, is the semantic differential (SD) developed by Osgood, Suci, and Tannenbaum (1957). The **semantic differential** format presents the respon-

dent with a stimulus, such as a person or event, that is to be rated on a scale between a series of polar opposite adjectives. Normally, the scale has 7 points, but scales can have fewer or more points if theoretical or methodological considerations call for it. Table 13.4 illustrates an SD designed to measure people's attitudes toward the elderly. In this study, college students were shown pictures of people of varying ages and then asked to describe the characteristics of each person by placing an X on the line between each adjective pair that best represented their assessment of the person. So, on the first line, placing an X over the 6 means that you view the person as quite active, while placing an X over the 1 is an assessment of very passive. In this example, all the "positive" adjectives are on the left

Table 13.4 Semantic Differential Scale Assessing Attitudes Toward the Elderly

	Scale							
	7	6	5	4	3	2	1	
Active	——	——	——	——	——	——	——	Passive
Competent	——	——	——	——	——	——	——	Incompetent
High IQ	——	——	——	——	——	——	——	Low IQ
Powerful	——	——	——	——	——	——	——	Weak
Healthy	——	——	——	——	——	——	——	Sickly
Secure	——	——	——	——	——	——	——	Insecure
Creative	——	——	——	——	——	——	——	Uncreative
Fast	——	——	——	——	——	——	——	Slow
Attractive	——	——	——	——	——	——	——	Ugly
Pleasant	——	——	——	——	——	——	——	Unpleasant
Reliable	——	——	——	——	——	——	——	Unreliable
Energetic	——	——	——	——	——	——	——	Lazy
Calm	——	——	——	——	——	——	——	Irritable
Flexible	——	——	——	——	——	——	——	Rigid
Educated	——	——	——	——	——	——	——	Uneducated
Generous	——	——	——	——	——	——	——	Selfish
Wealthy	——	——	——	——	——	——	——	Poor
Good memory	——	——	——	——	——	——	——	Poor memory
Involved	——	——	——	——	——	——	——	Socially isolated

Source William C. Levin, "Age Stereotyping: College Student Evaluations," *Research on Aging*, Vol. 10 (March 1988), pp. 134–148. Reprinted with permission of Sage Publications, Inc.

and the "negative" adjectives are on the right. Sometimes the positive responses to some adjectives are put on the right in order to discourage uninterested respondents from placing all their responses in the same column. If we found respondents who had done so, we would probably discard their data because they obviously had not marked the scale seriously. (Incidentally, this study found considerable age stereotyping still persisting among college students: The elderly were consistently evaluated more negatively than younger people on most of these adjectives.)

Based on their research with the SD, Osgood and colleagues have suggested that, depending on the sets of adjectives used, three different dimen-

sions of a concept are commonly measured. These dimensions are evaluation, potency, and activity. Semantic differentials can be designed to measure any one or all three of these dimensions. The measure illustrated in Table 13.4 contains adjectives relating to all those dimensions.

One major problem in constructing an SD is the selection of relevant adjectives for rating a given concept. For example, the adjective pair "alive–dead" would not be very relevant for an SD rating self-concept. If one is unsure about the relevance of a set of adjectives, it is possible to supply the adjectives to a group of subjects and have them rank-order them according to their relevance to the concept to be rated. One would then use the pairs of adjectives ranked highest by the subjects (Mitsos, 1961).

A second problem with SDs is determining which of those three dimensions a given pair of adjectives is measuring. Generally, intuition is not reliable for making this determination (Heise, 1970). Accurate identification of the dimension measured by a given adjective pair can be accomplished through the use of a rather complex statistical procedure called *factor analysis,* which correlates each variable with every other variable. Its use in SD construction is to indicate which of the three dimensions correlates most highly with a given set of adjectives and hence which dimension is being tapped by those adjectives. Unfortunately, it is often impractical to do a factor analysis every time we wish to construct an SD because of the very large sample size needed for reliable results. A number of researchers, however, have factor-analyzed many adjectives and determined their SD dimension. When one is constructing an SD, it is wise to consult one or more of these sources: DiVista, 1966; Osgood, May, and Miron, 1975; Osgood et al., 1957; Wright, 1958.

Many SDs are set up like the one in Table 13.4 with only the ends of the scale labeled with the adjectives. Some scales, however, employ adverbs such as "extremely," "quite," and "slightly" at appropriate points between the adjectives. One study found that the use of adverbs improved the quality of responses to SD scales (Wells and Smith, 1960). In light of these findings, it appears advisable to include adverbs when constructing SDs.

Scoring an SD can be done in a variety of ways depending on the researcher's needs. One way is to treat the response to each adjective pair separately. This procedure is not common, however, because usually we want a summary score for each respondent. For this to be accomplished, responses on the adjective pairs that constitute each dimension can be summed to provide an overall score on each of the dimensions measured—another variant of the summated ratings scale.

Semantic differentials have several advantages in comparison with both Likert and Thurstone formats. Unlike the other scaling techniques that re-

quire 20 or more items for adequate reliability, SDs require only four to eight adjective pairs for each dimension to reach reliabilities of .80 or better. Approximately 10 adjective pairs are often used to ensure adequate validity. This brevity means that many concepts can be rated by respondents in a reasonable amount of time. In addition, because an SD is fairly easy to respond to, people can be expected to make at least 25 judgments in 15 minutes (Heise, 1970; Miller, 1991). Another advantage is that SDs are much easier and less time-consuming to construct than either Likert or Thurstone scales. Adjective pairs are easier to develop than are unambiguous and unbiased statements about an issue. In addition, adjective pairs from prior studies are more readily adaptable to other studies because of the general and nonspecific nature of the adjectives. This is particularly important if a measuring scale is needed quickly. If, for example, we wanted people's reactions to some unanticipated event, time would be of the essence. We would have to get their reactions while the event was still fresh in their minds. Only an SD-type scale could be readied in time.

About the only disadvantage of an SD is that, like Likert scales, SDs generate data considered to be ordinal. If interval data are desired, a Thurstone scale would be preferable.

Guttman Scales

At the outset of this chapter, we noted that efforts are made to create scales that are unidimensional—that is, they measure a single variable or a single aspect of a variable. With a **Guttman scale,** the procedures used in construction help ensure that the resulting scale will truly be unidimensional (Guttman, 1944).

Researchers using Guttman scaling achieve unidimensionality by developing the items in such a way that, in a perfect Guttman scale, there is only one pattern of response that will yield any given score on the scale. For example, if an individual's score is 5, we would expect that he or she had agreed with the first five items on the scale. This can be contrasted with other scaling techniques that allow obtaining the same score by agreeing or disagreeing with any number of items and having completely different response patterns. Guttman scaling is able to do this because the items in the scale have an inherently progressive order, usually relating to the intensity of the variable being measured. In the parlance of Guttman scaling, the least intense items are referred to as "easy" because more people are likely to agree with them, and the most intense items are considered "hard" because fewer are expected to agree with them. If a person agrees with a certain item, we would expect him or her also to agree with all the less intense items; conversely, if a person disagrees with a particular item, we would also expect that person to disagree with all the more intense items.

Table 13.5 contains a Guttman scale designed to measure the effects of volunteering on people's career development. The items are arranged with the "easiest" first and the "hardest" last. Often, only two response categories, either "agree" and "disagree" or "yes" and "no," are provided. Some Guttman scales, however, make use of the Likert-type response categories, as does the scale in Table 13.5. Because these categories are collapsed to a dichotomy at a later point in working with the scale, little is gained by their inclusion other than allowing the respondents greater freedom of expression.

The fact that the items in a Guttman scale are progressive and cumulative leads to the basic means of assessing whether a set of items constitutes a Guttman scale. This criterion is called *reproducibility*, or the ability of the total score of all respondents to reproduce the pattern of the responses to the scale items of each individual. For example, all persons with scores of 2 will have agreed with the two "easiest" items and disagreed with the rest, persons with scores of 3 will have agreed with the three "easiest" items and disagreed with the rest, and so on. In a perfect Guttman scale, each respondent's score will reproduce one of these patterns, as is illustrated in Table 13.5. There is always one more perfect response pattern in a Guttman scale than there are items in the scale; therefore, the five-item scale in Table 13.5 would have six possible response patterns. In actual practice, perfect Guttman scales are virtually nonexistent. Usually, some respondents

will deviate from the expected pattern. Nevertheless, Guttman scales with very high levels of reproducibility have been developed.

Constructing a Guttman scale is difficult and to an extent risky because we will not know whether the scale we have devised will have sufficient reproducibility to qualify as a Guttman scale until after we have applied it to a sample of respondents. As with the other scaling techniques, a basic first step is creating and selecting items for inclusion in the scale. In Guttman scaling, this task is further complicated by the need for the items eventually selected to have the characteristic of progression. The procedure for selecting items for a Guttman scale is known as the *scale discrimination technique* (Edwards and Kilpatrick, 1948). As was done with both Likert and Thurstone scaling techniques, we begin by writing a large number of statements relating to the variable to be measured. These statements are rated by a group of judges along the 11-point Thurstone equal-appearing interval scale. Scale values and interquartile ranges (upper quartile minus lower quartile, or $Q_3 - Q_1$) of the judges' ratings are obtained for each item. The half of the items with the lowest interquartile ranges are kept, with the remainder being discarded. The items on which judges were in the greatest agreement are given a Likert-type response format and presented to a pretest group. The pretest results are used to calculate discriminatory power (DP) scores as described under Likert scaling. Items for inclusion in the final Guttman scale are selected so that they cover the full Thurstone scale range and have the highest DP scores. Despite the effort involved in this approach, all it accomplishes is to increase the likelihood that the selected items will have sufficient reproducibility to constitute a Guttman scale; it does not guarantee reproducibility.

The only way to determine if we have succeeded in developing a true Guttman scale is to administer it to another pretest group and see if it has adequate reproducibility (Dotson and Summers, 1970). Table 13.6 illustrates the most common way of assessing reproducibility of items. For the sake of simplicity, the illustrated scale contains only four items and data from only 20 subjects. As can be

Table 13.5   A Guttman Scale Measuring the Effect of Volunteering on Career Development

To what extent have the skills you have developed volunteering for the Red Cross helped you to:

1. develop new interests?
   helped not at all _____   helped at least a little to a great deal _____

2. accept other volunteer jobs?
   helped not at all _____   helped at least a little to a great deal _____

3. make career decisions?
   helped not at all _____   helped at least a little to a great deal _____

4. secure a paid job?
   helped not at all _____   helped at least a little to a great deal _____

5. return to school?
   helped not at all _____   helped at least a little to a great deal _____

Note   The response alternatives in the study were "helped not at all," "helped not much," "helped very much," and "helped a great deal"; they were collapsed into the above two categories for the Guttman analysis.

Coefficient of reproducibility: .9253

	Guttman Scale Patterns						% Saying Volunteering Helped at Least a Little
	0	1	2	3	4	5	
Develop new interests	no	yes	yes	yes	yes	yes	49%
Accept other volunteer jobs	no	no	yes	yes	yes	yes	32
Make career decisions	no	no	no	yes	yes	yes	21
Secure a paid job	no	no	no	no	yes	yes	19
Return to school	no	no	no	no	no	yes	11

Source   Adapted from Michael J. Zakour, "Measuring Career-Development Volunteerism: Guttman Scale Analysis Using Red Cross Volunteers," *Journal of Social Service Review,* Vol. 19, nos. 3/4 (1994), p. 112.

seen from the table, subjects are arrayed according to their total score for the four statements, from highest (4) to lowest (0). Subjects' responses to each statement are indicated by an X under either 1 or 0 corresponding to an agree or disagree response, respectively. The statements are arranged from left to right from "hardest" (most disagreements) to "easiest" (most agreements). The lines drawn across each of the statement columns are called *cutting points* and indicate where the pattern of responses tends to shift from agree to disagree. The position of the cutting points must be determined carefully because they form the basis from which error responses are counted. Any "1" (agree) response below the cutting points and any "0" (disagree) response above the cutting points constitute error responses. Cutting points are drawn at positions that minimize the number of error responses. Inspection of the cutting points in Table 13.6 will reveal that locating them in any other position will not reduce the number of error responses.

With the cutting points established, tabulating error responses is straightforward. In the example under statement 1 are three "1" responses below the cutting point with no "0" responses above it. Note that in the row marked "error," these responses are tabulated as 3 and 0, respectively. The same counting procedure was followed for the other statements. As Table 13.6 illustrates, the error responses for individual statements are summed to indicate the total number of error responses. It should be clear that tabulating error responses for a longer scale by hand would be exceedingly tedious. However, computer software, such as the SAS

Table 13.6 Example of Error Computation for a Guttman Scale

	Statements								
	1		**2**		**3**		**4**		
Subjects	**1**	**0**	**1**	**0**	**1**	**0**	**1**	**0**	Scores
1	X		X		X		X		4
2	X			X	X		X		3
3	X			X	X		X		3
4		X	X		X		X		3
5		X	X		X		X		3
6		X	X		X		X		3
7		X	X		X		X		3
8		X	X		X		X		3
9		X		X	X		X		2
10	X			X		X	X		2
11		X		X	X		X		2
12		X		X	X		X		2
13	X			X		X	X		2
14		X	X			X	X		2
15	X			X		X		X	1
16		X		X		X	X		1
17		X		X	X			X	1
18		X	X			X		X	1
19		X		X		X	X		1
20		X		X		X		X	0
Frequency	6	14	8	12	12	8	16	4	
Error	3	0	2	2	1	1	2	0	e = 11

package, can assess the reproducibility of even a long scale quite rapidly (*SAS User's Guide,* 1979).

The total number of errors is used in the following simple formula to calculate the coefficient of reproducibility (R_c):

$$R_c = 1 - \frac{\text{number of errors}}{\text{no. of items} \times \text{no. of subjects}}$$

Inserting the values from Table 13.6 we have:

$$R_c = 1 - \frac{11}{(4)(20)} = 1 - .14 = .86$$

Guttman (1950) suggested that a coefficient of reproducibility of .90 is the minimum acceptable for a scale to qualify as a Guttman scale. According to this criterion, our example does not qualify. However, scales with reproducibility coefficients of somewhat less than .90 have given satisfactory results. In general, the more items in a Guttman scale, the more difficult it is to achieve a high level of reproducibility. For a very short scale, such as the one in Table 13.5, .90 would certainly be the minimum acceptable, and its reported coefficient of reproducibility is .92. With a longer scale, the minimum reproducibility level can be adjusted downward slightly.

Suppose that we developed a scale of 11 items, submitted it to a pretest group, determined the reproducibility coefficient, and found it too low. The game is not over because of this initial failure. It is perfectly legitimate to rearrange the order of the items or drop items in an effort to achieve the necessary reproducibility. We might, for example, drop three or four of the items containing the most error responses, leaving us with a seven- or eight-item scale with adequate reproducibility to qualify as a Guttman scale. In addition, situations arise in which the coefficient of reproducibility can be misleading, and A. L. Edwards (1957) suggests additional analysis may be necessary to assess the reproducibility of a scale.

It is important to note that a given Guttman scale may be group specific. This means that if we achieve adequate reproducibility with a given set of items with one sample of respondents, nothing guarantees that the same items will scale when applied to another sample. Only after-the-fact analysis of each sample will reveal if the Guttman scale properties hold for subsequent applications of a scale.

The data generated by Guttman scaling is ordinal level. Given the relatively few items characteristic of these scales and the common "agree–disagree" format used, there are few possible scores for respondents to achieve. This means that large numbers of respondents will have tied scores on the scale, so many statisticians believe it is better to consider these numbers as ranks (ordinal) rather than interval- or ratio-level data (see Chapter 5). Guttman scales are unique, however, for the characteristics of unidimensionality and reproducibility. If these attributes are desired, they are apt to more than outweigh the presence of all the tied scores.

Given the extreme complexity of creating Guttman scales, most human service workers will seldom have occasion to develop one. There are, however, a substantial number of such scales in existence, making an understanding of their operating characteristics worthwhile. This is especially true because of the need to check the reproducibility level of a scale each time it is applied to a new sample.

Multidimensional Scales

As you may have noticed, all the scaling techniques presented so far were developed a number of years ago. More recent activity in scaling techniques has centered on what is called the **multidimensional scale,** which is a scale measuring variables that are composed of more than a single dimension. These scaling techniques are too complex for full presentation here, but we can discuss the basic logic that underlies them.

Recall that one purpose of the preceding scaling techniques is to locate respondents' scores along some continuum. Accomplishing this, we are able to determine that various groups or people exhibit more or less of the variable measured. With these unidimensional techniques, the straight line of a single scale is sufficient to indicate the location of all people on a given variable. When we come to variables of more than one dimension, however, this single line is no longer adequate. We must think of locating responses somewhere in either two-, three-, or *N*-dimensional space. A common analogy is made between multidimensional scaling and cartography, or mapmaking. Just as the cartographer locates various places along the dimensions of latitude and longitude, multidimensional scaling locates people along the various dimensions of a variable. For example, if we conceive of people's motivation as composed of the two dimensions of "discomfort" and "hope," then Figure 13.2 illustrates how multidimensional scaling might serve to locate these people with regard to these dimensions (Kogan, 1975). It might be possible, for example, to use multidimensional scaling of client motivation to predict chances of success with clients undergoing various forms of treatment.

Multidimensional scaling can, of course, deal with variables composed of many more than two dimensions. As more dimensions are added, however, presentation and interpretation become increasingly complex. Persons interested in a detailed presentation of multidimensional techniques are

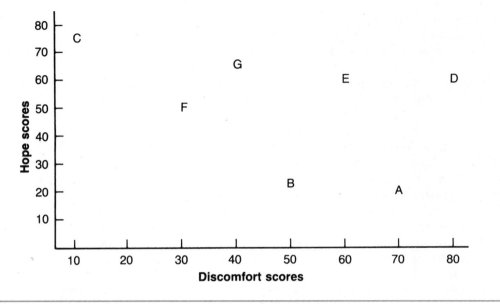

Figure 13.2 Hypothetical Two-Dimensional Space of Client Motivation

advised to consult Schiffman, Reynolds, and Young (1981). Be forewarned that multidimensional scaling utilizes some fairly sophisticated statistical techniques that you may need to review before you develop a thorough understanding of it.

Scales are most commonly used in research problems in which the unit of analysis is the individual (*see* Chapter 4), and this emphasis is reflected in the preceding discussion. However, scales can be used with other units of analysis, such as the characteristics of organizations.

Scaling in the Human Services

In the past few decades, the use of scaling techniques has become quite widespread in the human services, both for clinical and for research purposes. In some cases, practitioners are called on to develop a scale themselves to measure a variable that is of interest for some clinical or research reason. More commonly, however, practitioners find it desirable to use a scale that has been developed by someone

else. Many scales, for example, are useful tools in assessing the functioning of clients or organizations. Recall the rapid assessment instruments (RAIs) and Walter Hudson's *Clinical Measurement Package* discussed in Research in Practice 11.1. In other cases, practitioners find themselves involved in survey or evaluation research in which scales are used as data collection techniques. At the very least, human service providers utilize research related to intervention strategies that can be incorporated into practice, and increasingly this research involves the use of scales. For any of these uses, knowing how to develop, evaluate, and use scales is essential because their misuse can have devastating consequences.

The major danger in the uninformed use of scales is that a poorly constructed measuring device will provide false or misleading information about the world. And false data are in some ways worse than no data at all because people *believe* they have gained some understanding when, in fact, they have not. Social policy or practice techniques based on such erroneous data may actually exacerbate problems rather than alleviate them. For these reasons, one needs to be exceedingly cautious about using scales that have been developed without the extensive pretesting and analysis outlined in this chapter. Many people are under the very mistaken impression that one can gather usable data from statements that have been constructed with no pretesting or analysis. It is tempting to believe that a couple of intelligent people can sit down and write unbiased, valid, and reliable statements to measure variables. This is a dangerously erroneous belief. Great care is always called for in constructing scales. These concerns regarding scale construction illustrate the profound responsibility of social researchers to take all steps necessary to ensure that their findings are valid. Scientific results can have a powerful influence on the way we deal with other people, including clients, and such results must therefore be approached cautiously and rigorously. Any investigator—including a human service practitioner—who casually develops scales without rigorous safeguards and distributes results based on those scales is, many would argue, engaging in unethical behavior.

This point is aptly illustrated by a study that reported on the validity of several measures of aggression in children (Seibert and Ramanaiah, 1978). The authors comment that there has been a proliferation of aggression measures involving self-report data, teacher ratings, peer ratings, and projective techniques. However, there had been very little research to test the validity of these measures. Because lack of demonstrated validity both limits the usefulness of these scales and also makes it difficult to compare results from studies using different scales, the researchers set out to investigate the validity of three of the more commonly used aggression measures and three measures of impulsivity. For both impulsivity and aggression, teacher ratings, peer ratings, and self-report data constituted the three measures. The researchers found strong empirical support for the validity of peer ratings and teacher ratings, but only marginal support for self-report measures.

The researchers suggest that a strong tendency of children to respond in a socially desirable way may be the cause of the low validity of the self-report methods. In other words, children may respond to items not in terms of their true feelings, but rather in terms of what they believe the researchers or other adults would find socially acceptable. They also comment that the fact that the teacher and children had known each other for 8 months contributed to the validity of the peer and teacher rating scales, presumably because experience enabled them to learn which behavioral manifestations represented aggression or impulsivity in particular individuals. This example illustrates not only the importance of testing the validity of a scale but also the importance of considering the characteristics of the subjects in the research. Suppose you were doing a research study on aggression in children and the research design included the use of one of the scales discussed here. According to this research, the best results would be achieved by using a peer or teacher rating scale near the end of the school year rather than at the beginning. Furthermore, you would probably be best off not using self-report measures.

In short, human service providers need to be in a position to assess whether research is methodologically sound. In the case of scale construction, this requires considering how rigorous the investigator was in developing items, whether pretesting was conducted, and whether validity and reliability were tested. If you encounter a discriminatory power, or DP, score, you need to be able to evaluate it in deciding whether to accept the research results as scientifically sound. In some cases, after reviewing a piece of research, you may decide that, although the results are tantalizing, the study lacks the methodological rigor necessary to convince you to incorporate those results into your practice. Just as the U.S. Food and Drug Administration is very cautious about approving new drugs for medical use, you should also be prudent about adopting research results for practice purposes—especially results based on a single study or studies that do not meet strict scientific standards. Research in Practice 13.2 illustrates a case in which issues of validity and reliability of scales, along with the time and cost necessary to administer them, were taken into account in deciding which scales to incorporate into practice.

Research in Practice 13.2
Client Functioning: Measurement for What? Benefits of Sequential Assessment

Although there is no one-to-one correlation, it is generally true that the most reliable and valid measurement procedures are also the most expensive to develop and use. Therefore, human service agencies sometimes find themselves confronting the question of whether the added cost of using a more valid and reliable scale is worth it.

One agency dealt with this issue in the assessment of alcohol-related problems of new clients in a treatment organization. Client problems were screened in three levels: brief screening, basic assessment, and specialized assessment (Skinner, 1981).

The first consisted of a structured interview, conducted by a professional, for intake purposes. It included only a few questions about alcohol usage in addition to demographic items, work history, family background, legal status, and so on. The second level, basic assessment, consisted of a scale to measure involvement with alcohol called the Michigan Alcohol Screening Test (MAST). This scale contained 25 items on various problems associated with problem drinking, including the social, legal, medical, and interpersonal consequences of alcohol abuse for the individual. This scale has been tested for reliability and exceeds the conventional rule of .80. The third level of measurement, specialized assessment, consisted of the Alcohol Use Inventory (AUI). This is a multiscale inventory of 147 questions and is designed to measure styles of alcohol use, unfavorable consequences of use, and perceived benefits of drinking. Within the instrument are 22 separate scales. This instrument also has been found to meet acceptable levels of reliability and validity. The overall research question was whether the longer, more valid, and reliable scale was worth the added cost of administering it.

The researcher administered the three forms of measurement to a sample of 327 individuals who had problems with alcohol in order to assess the relative benefits and liabilities of each approach. In addition, several other instruments were used to assess further the validity of the three procedures. These included the Lifetime Drinking History, which is a detailed, structured interview procedure that yields quantitative indexes of drinking patterns. Other measures included several scales to test for understanding of scale items and measures of the tendency to present oneself in a favorable light.

The study found that asking individuals a few simple questions during the intake process was effective in obtaining useful data about alcohol usage. However, although the intake interview permitted detection of a potential problem, the MAST procedure produced reliable information on the severity and nature of the alcohol problem. More important, this additional information was gained at only a slight increase in time and money required for the assessment process. In contrast, the AUI procedure required considerably more time in order to complete the 147-item, multiscale instrument and also considerable time and skill to score and interpret the results. For the added cost, it provided detailed information about styles of use, patterns of symptoms, and perceived benefits of use.

The researcher concluded that human service professionals who are in a position to detect alcohol-related problems would definitely benefit from including a procedure such as MAST in their client screening routine. The added reliability and validity over and above what can be obtained in a brief screening are obtained for very little additional cost. On the other hand, the added precision and fine distinctions that are possible through use of the AUI cannot be justified for referring agencies. The AUI is better suited for specialized treatment facilities that can set up efficient procedures for scoring and analysis and that can make use of the added information in treatment planning for alcoholics. Therefore, the selection of measurement tools and the decision to incorporate scales into practice should be based on the demonstrated capacity of the measurement tools weighed against the added costs in terms of time, money, and skill required for their use.

Main Points

■ Multiple-item scales are particularly valuable for measuring complex variables because they enhance validity and reliability, can increase the level of measurement, and improve the efficiency of data handling.

■ The five basic steps common to most scaling techniques are: develop many preliminary items, eliminate obviously bad items, pretest the remaining items, eliminate bad items on the basis of pretest results, and select items for the final scale.

■ Likert scaling is a very popular scale format involving a series of statements to which respondents select from five alternatives ranging from strongly disagree to strongly agree.

■ An important consideration in selecting items for inclusion in a Likert scale is their discriminatory power: the ability of each item to differentiate between high and low scorers on the overall measurement scale.

■ Thurstone scaling uses judges to assign a value from 1 to 11 to each item in the scale, which results in a scale capable of producing interval-level data.

■ Items for inclusion in a Thurstone scale have scale scores that cover the full 1 to 11 range and were most agreed on by the judges.

■ The semantic differential scaling format presents respondents with a concept to be rated and a series of opposite adjective pairs separated by a seven-point scale that is used to evaluate the concept.

■ Semantic differentials are a convenient scaling format as they are considerably easier to construct than the alternatives.

■ Guttman scales have the unique characteristic of reproducibility, meaning that a given total score reflects one and only one pattern of responses to the items in the scale.

■ Multidimensional scaling uses two or more dimensions or components of a complex variable to locate people with regard to the various components of the variable.

■ The use of scales or the results of research based on measurement scales should be approached cautiously with careful consideration given to whether adequate development has gone into the scale, particularly in terms of assessing its validity and reliability.

Important Terms for Review

discriminatory power score
Guttman scale
Likert scale
multidimensional scale
scale
semantic differential
summated rating scales
Thurstone scale
unidimensional scale

Exploring the Internet

Information about a potential scale for a research project, and sometimes even copies of the scale itself, can be obtained through the Internet. In conjunction with discussions related to measurement and scales in previous chapters, we have mentioned Computer-Assisted Social Services (CASS) and the *Clinical Measurement Package* developed by Walter Hudson. The URL for the home page of Walmyr Publishing Company, the company that publishes these materials, is http://www.syspac.com/~walmyr/. From this site, you can download samples of the scales to view with an Acrobat file viewer program. Easy-to-follow instructions are provided for downloading both the sample scales and the Acrobat program. There is also information on ordering scales for professional and educational purposes as well as information about other products.

Another Internet source for locating assessment scales for human service purposes is Mental Health Net. This site's URL is http://www.health.org/dbases.html. This site includes many links to resources on assessment, including news groups and journals on the Web related to assessment. For scales related to children's mental health problems, an excellent source is the Technical Assistance Center (TAC) for the Evaluation of Children's Mental Health Systems. The Internet site for TAC's list of outcome measurement scales can be found at http://tac.pie.org/TM/3618.

Another promising Internet site that is still under construction at this writing is that of the Center for Mental Health Services Research, affiliated with the George Warren Brown School of Social Work at Washington University, at the following URL: http://www.gwbssw.wustl.edu/~cmhsr/?16,16. They are in the process of developing a measurement instrument collection page at http://www.gwbssw.wustl.edu/~cmhsr/measure.html#idiographic. The site lists a large number of scales that are appropriate for many human service needs.

Another way of using the Internet to learn more about scaling is to use such key terms as "guttman" or "likert" with a specialized search engine, such as the one provided in conjunction with the General Social Survey Internet site at http://www.icpsr.umich.edu/gss/home.html. The search engine returns bibliographic citations and also full-text reports related to the General Social Survey. Many different scales have been used in the General Social Survey, making this site an excellent source of research articles about scaling issues.

The National Clearinghouse for Alcohol and Drug Information also provides a search engine in conjunction with its databases. The Internet site location is http://www.health.org/dbases.html. Simply select the database that you wish to search and then enter your search terms in the designated windows. We suggest that you try such terms as "Likert," "Guttman," "semantic differential," or "multidimensional scale." In addition to the bibliographic citation, the database provides abstracts to help you decide whether to pursue the article. This source will not only help you find specific scales, but also help you locate articles discussing validity, reliability, and actual use of the scale.

While exploring each of these sites, or others related to scaling, pay attention to whether and in what ways the sites include information about the methods of assessing scales discussed in this chapter: validity, reliability, reproducibility, discriminatory power, and so on.

For Further Reading

Bech, Per. *Rating Scales for Psychopathology, Health Status and Quality of Life: A Compendium on Documentation in Accordance with the DSM-III-R and WHO Systems.* New York: Springer-Verlag, 1992. Oriented particularly toward researchers and clinicians in the mental health field, the book provides details on a range of instruments suitable for measuring client problems and conditions and intervention outcomes.

Bloom, Martin, Joel Fischer, and John Orme. *Evaluating Practice: Guidelines for the Accountable Professional.* Boston: Allyn & Bacon, 1995. Primarily a text devoted to single-subject design evaluation, one full chapter is devoted to standardized scales, including many illustrations of complete scales.

De Vellis, Robert F. *Scale Development: Theories and Applications.* Newbury Park, Calif.: Sage, 1991. This is an understandable guide to all the various stages in developing good scales. It includes discussions of how to generate items, how long scales should be, and other useful topics.

Fischer, Joel, and Kevin Corcoran. *Measures for Clinical Practice: A Sourcebook,* 2nd ed. New York: Free Press, 1994. A two-volume set that includes actual scales as well as reliability and validity data. Volume I covers instruments for couples, families, and children; volume II is devoted to instruments for adults.

Magura, Stephen, and Beth Silverman Moses. *Outcome Measures for Child Welfare Services: Theory and Applications.* Washington, D.C.: Child Welfare League of America, Inc., 1986. Another compendium of scales that can be used in both research and practice.

McDowell, Ian, and Claire Newell. *Measuring Health: A Guide to Rating Scales and Questionnaires,* 2nd ed. New York: Oxford University Press, 1996. This volume discusses the theoretical and technical aspects of constructing and evaluating scales relating to such health issues as social health, psychological well-being, and depression. It presents and evaluates many actual scales.

Miller, Delbert C. *Handbook of Research Design and Social Measurement,* 5th ed. New York: Longman, 1991. The latest edition of a classic in the field of measurement. Miller's book provides an overview of the various types of scale construction along with many examples of proven scales.

Mueller, Daniel J. *Measuring Social Attitudes: A Handbook for Researchers and Practitioners.* New York: Teachers College Press, 1986. A step-by-step guide to developing any of the major scaling formats (Likert,

Thurstone, semantic differential, etc.). It also contains many useful examples of existing scales.

Ollendick, Thomas H., and Michael Hersen, eds. *Handbook of Child and Adolescent Assessment*. General Psychology Series, vol. 167. Boston: Allyn & Bacon, 1992. A multiauthor handbook exploring the principles and procedures of child and adolescent assessment. Emphasizes the theme that measurement should be guided by a body of principles that will lead to a set of developmentally sensitive and empirically validated procedures. The volume is organized into three parts: fundamental issues, specific assessment strategies, and the assessment of specific populations.

Schutte, Nicola S., and John M. Malouff. *Sourcebook of Adult Assessment Strategies (Applied Clinical Psychology)*. New York: Plenum, 1995. A text for practitioners, researchers, and instructors in the mental health field, presenting over 70 scales on a wide range of adult mental disorders, reviews of their psychometric properties, and user instructions. The scales include self-report, observer-based, and clinician-rating measures.

The following are some other compilations of scales that can be useful in human service research:

Fredman, Norman, and Robert Sherman. *Handbook of Measurements for Marriage and Family Therapy*. New York: Brunner/Mazel, 1987.

Robinson, J. P., P. R. Shaver, and L. S. Wrightsman, eds. *Measures of Personality and Social Psychological Attitudes*. San Diego: Academic Press, 1991.

Straus, M. A. *Family Measurement Techniques*. Minneapolis: University of Minnesota Press, 1969.

Exercises for Class Discussion

One point we have made in this chapter on scaling is that the human service professional may not have occasion to construct new scales. However, in many situations you could use scales that have already been developed and that are reported in the literature.

13.1 For one of the following topics, find one or more scales that are included in the professional literature:

Depression	Life satisfaction
Alcoholism	Stress
Child abuse	Marital satisfaction or adjustment

We suggest using *Psychological Abstracts, Sociological Abstracts,* and *Social Work Research and Abstracts* as aids in your research. See also Appendix A (on the use of the library) in this volume.

13.2 For each scale you locate, indicate what kind of scale it is, for example, Likert, Guttman, or semantic differential. Is reliability and validity information available on the scale? If you wanted to use a scale on this topic, what would be the problems with, and advantages of, using the one you found?

One source of scales for human service practice is the Clinical Measurement Package by Walter Hudson. As a class project, have members complete and score the Generalized Contentment Scale. (A trial set of the scales may be obtained from the Dorsey Press, 1820 Ridge Road, Homewood, IL 60430.)

13.3 What value does such a scale have over and above data that might be gathered in interviews?

13.4 These scales are intended for repeated use with single-subject designs. How do you envision clients might respond to such a scale, especially with repeated applications?

CHAPTER 14

Data Analysis I: Data Preparation and Presentation

Preparation for Data Analysis   370
  Coding Schemes   371
  Preparing and Using a Codebook   375

Data Entry   376
  Raw Data Entry   376
  Data Cleaning   378
  Creating New Variables   379

Data Distributions   379
  Types of Data Distributions   380
  Constructing Frequency Distributions   380

Graphical Display of Data Distributions   385
  Bar Graphs   385
  Histograms and Frequency Polygons   387
  Pie Charts   387

Contingency Tables   388
  Bivariate Relationships   388
  Multivariate Analysis   390

Main Points   397

Important Terms for Review   397

Exploring the Internet   398

For Further Reading   398

Exercises for Class Discussion   399

All research involves some form of **data analysis,** which refers to deriving some meaning from the observations that have been made during the research project. Data analysis can take many forms. In some cases, it is qualitative, such as a summary description of an investigator's field notes from a participant observation study. Our focus in this chapter, however, is with quantitative data analysis, in which observations are put into numerical form and manipulated in some way based on their arithmetic properties. The analysis of quantitative data typically involves the use of **statistics,** which are procedures for assembling, classifying, tabulating, and summarizing numerical data so that some meaning or information is obtained.

This chapter begins our coverage of common data analysis methods, which is continued in Chapter 15. Primarily designed for those who have not taken a course in statistics, these chapters may also serve as a refresher for those who have. Actually, to learn how to do statistical analysis would require at least a full course devoted solely to that topic. However, our goals are more basic: to acquaint you with the issues of preparing a data set for analysis, to help you select the most appropriate statistics to accomplish a particular task, and to provide guidance in the interpretation of statistical results. This will prepare you to better understand various statistics when you encounter them in research reports and the popular media and also to assess whether the statistics are being used properly. This chapter explores some of the fundamentals of preparing and managing data. This often overlooked portion of the research process falls between the generation of observations by the research design on the one hand and the production of statistical results on the other. Although it may not seem as challenging or intellectually demanding as developing the design or analyzing the data, it is a critical step that can well determine the success of the overall project. After discussing how observations are put in a form that makes it possible to perform statistical proce-

dures on them, we then examine initial steps in describing and displaying the data and in exploring relationships between variables through the use of tables and graphs. In Chapter 15, we present a discussion of statistical procedures for detecting and estimating relationships between variables.

Preparation for Data Analysis

In this chapter, we generally assume that the data have already been collected and that our task is now to enter the data into a computer file and begin the data analysis. Recall from Chapter 1 that data analysis is part of the overall research process and that many questions regarding data analysis should be resolved before any data are actually collected. As emphasized in Chapters 2, 4, and 5, theoretical and conceptual considerations are important in determining the nature of the data to be collected, and the nature of the data determines the kinds of statistics that can be applied. Furthermore, as we discussed in Chapter 7 in relation to survey data collection, procedures such as computer assisted telephone interviewing (CATI) essentially merge the steps of data collection, data coding, and data set creation into one process because responses of participants are entered directly into a computer file data set. So, even though the actual data analysis occurs toward the end of a research project, many of the issues discussed in this chapter will have been settled, or at least envisioned, *before* any data are actually collected.

Imagine that you have completed a survey of sample size 400. The completed questionnaires are neatly stacked on your desk. Presumably, the questionnaires contain much information and contain the data for assessing the hypotheses you set out to test with the survey. But, as long as the data are on the questionnaires, or in any other raw form for that matter, they are useless. In such a state, the data are in a highly inconvenient form from the standpoint of deriving some usable meaning from them. Indeed, even if we tediously read through the 400 questionnaires, we would have little idea of the overall contents. The data were collected in an organized way that made sense in terms of the collection process, but this format is inconvenient for drawing conclusions. The collected data must be reorganized before we can go on and apply the necessary statistics for their analysis.

Coding Schemes

In the current context, *coding* refers to the process by which a researcher transforms raw data into a machine-readable format suitable for data analysis, and this requires that each observation be translated into a numerical value or set of letters. The numbers or letters assigned to an observation of a variable are called a *code*. The raw data set may have resulted from an observational study, a survey, an experiment, or an analysis of existing data, and it can be in one of several forms, including completed written questionnaires, survey interview schedules, observation notes, or agency records. In the following discussion, we will use survey data to illustrate the coding process, but the basic principles apply to other research methods as well. Coding data requires adapting the data as collected to the constraints of the program used for statistical analysis. On the one hand, the researcher must consider the data source, such as a completed questionnaire, and determine how the data can be translated into a coded form. On the other hand, the researcher must also be cognizant of the capabilities and restrictions of the computer program that will be used to analyze the data. Although we present these perspectives somewhat independently, in practice the researcher must give simultaneous attention to both. The plan by which the researcher organizes responses to a variable or an item, together with how the variable is defined for computerization, constitutes the **coding scheme** for a variable.

The initial purpose of the coding scheme is to provide the rules and directions for converting the observations into code. Referring to our illustra-tion of the 400 completed questionnaires stacked on your desk, the first task is to convert the responses into numbers and letters for computer entry.

As explained in Chapters 8 and 9, coding refers to categorizing a variable into a limited number of categories. Sometimes this coding is built into the way a question is asked and answered (*see* Chapter 7). This is the case with the following question format:

Which of the following best describes where you live? (Circle the number of your choice.)

1. Large city.
2. Suburb of a large city.
3. City of 50,000 or less.
4. Rural but nonfarm.
5. Rural farm.

In this case, the circled number would be the code for how a particular respondent answered a question. This example also illustrates one reason why coding and data analysis issues need to be considered before data collection is initiated. The number of options in the question predetermines the maximum number of response categories that can be used later in looking at possible relationships between "residential area" and other variables. Because we did not provide an option for "City of 50,000 to 300,000," we could not use this as a category in our data analysis.

With some variables, the actual value of the response is a number and can be used to code the data. Family size, income, and number of arrests are variables of this type. However, when the data take the form of responses to open-ended survey questions, field notes, or other nonnumerical entities, for quantitative analysis, the data must be translated into numbers. This process is essential for most data analysis because the substitution of numbers for observations greatly reduces the volume of data that must be stored and facilitates its analysis, especially by computer. (As we noted in Chapter 9, qualitative analysis often does not involve the substitution of numbers for the actual observations.) Many computer programs permit you to use words or letters to stand for categories, but these are generally more cumbersome and only infrequently used. (Recall from Chapter 5, however, that assigning a number to coding categories does not necessarily mean that we can perform the various mathematical functions, such as addition and subtraction, on them. Whether we can do this depends on the level of measurement.)

When coding categories are being established, two general rules should be followed. First, the coding categories should be *mutually exclusive;* that is, a given observation is coded into one and only one category for each variable. The universal practice of categorizing people by sex as either male or female exemplifies mutually exclusive categories. Second, the coding categories should be *exhaustive,* which means that a coding category exists for every possible observation that was made. For example, it might be tempting not to bother to code the "no opinion" response with Likert-type questions on the grounds that you will probably not include those responses in the data analysis. You might very well decide not to analyze those responses in the end, but the coding stage is not the time to make such decisions. If you fail to code a response and later decide to include it in the analysis, it would be necessary to develop a new coding scheme and reenter the data into the computer. A good rule of thumb when coding is to do it in such a way that *all* information is coded. Coding is usually a difficult task, and the coder can become careless and fatigued. But it is critical that the job be done well. Searching out errors after the fact is often time-consuming and expensive. Unless caught and rectified, coding errors can ruin the most carefully collected data set by causing distortions in relationships and resulting in meaningless or misleading results.

Today, virtually all quantitative, and much qualitative, data analysis is done using computers. This means that not only must the coding scheme specify logically meaningful catagories as we have discussed thus far, but the coding system must also provide specifications that the computer program requires in order to use the data once they are entered into a computer file. These specifications include attributes for each variable that permit the computer program to display the data on the monitor, to use the data in calculations, and to write the data to various files for storage and retrieval. In its most basic form, a computerized data set can be conceptualized as a rectangular table of cells where the columns represent variables and the rows designate individual cases. Figure 14.1 illustrates a portion of a simulated data set showing how it would appear on a typical computer program data entry screen. The first column consists of respondent last names; the remaining columns designate first names, birth dates, prior arrests, date of offense, relationship to victim, and annual income. Notice that the top of each column displays the variable name (lname, fname, and so on). The variable names and other variable attributes, together with information about the position of the variable in the data set, are also vital elements of the coding scheme for computerized data. At a minimum, a computer coding scheme identifies a variable name and a variable format.

For variable names, computer program data entry screens typically use a default designation, such as C1, C2, C3 (in the case of Minitab) or var001, var002, var003 (in SPSS) to identify variables. Spreadsheet programs, such as Lotus, Excel, and Quattro, label them a, b, c, . . . aa, ab, and so on. Obviously, such designations convey little information about the meaning of a particular variable. With even a few variables, relying on such designations quickly becomes confusing, so the researcher needs to provide more recognizable variable names. Variable names should be short, in order to minimize entering long lists of variable names when conducting statistical analysis. In addition, some statistical programs, such as SPSS, limit names to a maximum of eight characters. Although short, a variable name should be an indicator of the content of that variable. A common practice is to use a mnemonic device when naming variables. Thus "lname" and "fname" clue the reader that the variable names stand for last name and first name, respectively. Variable names may also be selected to help group variables together. For example, a data

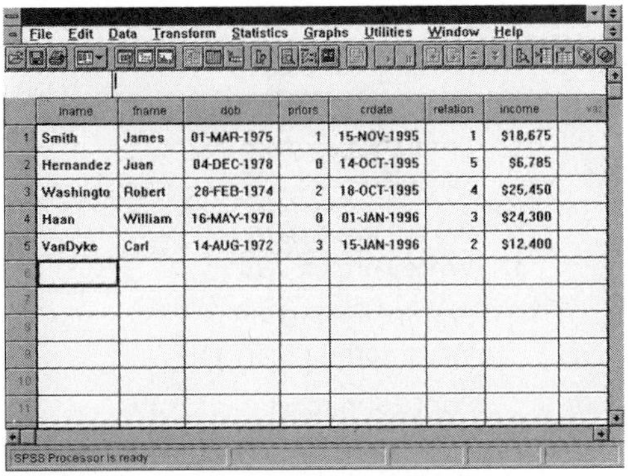

Figure 14.1 Data Entry Screen Commonly Used in Windows Versions of Statistical Software

format determines how many characters a coded entry may have, whether it is nonnumeric or some form of numeric variable, and where identifiers such as decimals, commas, or dollar signs should be placed. Figure 14.1 displays several types of variables; some consist of letters, others include letters and numbers, and some are only numbers. Data analysis programs vary in terms of the kinds of variables that they accept, but the two major types are numeric and alphanumeric. **Numeric variables** are sometimes called "values," because they have the property of a quantitative value. **Alphanumeric variables,** on the other hand, consist simply of type characters; they are sometimes also referred to as "string" variables or labels. An alphanumeric variable has no quantitative meaning and cannot be used in mathematical computations. Thus, the variable "lname" is clearly an alphanumeric variable because its field (column) consists of text, such as "Smith" and "Hernandez." However, what makes a variable alphanumeric is determined by how the variable is defined in the coding scheme and not simply by what characters are displayed on the computer monitor. For example, we could enter Social Security numbers in a data set and designate these as alphanumeric values. Even though the entire column consists of numerical characters, such as 375426174, a statistical program such as SPSS would not compute the mean, standard deviation, or other statistics on this variable because it is designated as an alphanumeric or string variable. Data analysis programs commonly accept almost any keyboard character in a variable that has been designated to be alphanumeric. Although one can enter numerical characters in an alphanumeric variable, statistical packages such as SPSS and Minitab only accept numerical symbols in a variable designated numeric.

In addition to simply designating a variable as either string or numeric, many programs also permit the specification of subtypes of numeric variables. Typical options include: integer, decimal, currency, and date or time. Although the format code is not visible on the screen, it is stored with the data file and tells the program how much space to

set on domestic violence may include similar variables on both the suspect and the victim, such as date of birth, age, and alcohol use. Beginning each variable related to victims with the letter "v" and each suspect-related variable with an "s" helps the researcher to quickly distinguish to which party a given variable refers. Another benefit of this approach is that data analysis programs commonly display variable lists alphabetically. Beginning all victim-related variables with "v" causes them to be grouped together whenever the computer displays a variable list. This reduces the need to scroll through a long list of variables when selecting variables for inclusion in a data analysis procedure. When a variable is measured by combining people's responses to a number of separate items, it is often useful to use a number as part of the name to identify the variable's position in the set. Variables representing individual items of a 10-item self-esteem scale, for example, might be designated as se1, se2, se3, and so on through se10. Such a designation can reduce the amount of work in combining the items into a single score. Thus, a total score on self-esteem can be generated by a computer command like "Sum se1 to se10" instead of requiring a separate listing of all 10 individual items.

In addition to the variable name, a coding scheme specifies the *variable format*. The variable

Table 14.1 Domestic Violence Study Codebook

Item	Variable Name	Variable Label	Variable Formats	Position
1. List offender last name	LNAME	last name	Print Format: A12 Write Format: A12	1
2. List offender first name	FNAME	first name	Print Format: A10 Write Format: A10	2
3. Enter date of birth	DOB	date of birth	Print Format: DATE11 Write Format DATE11	3
4. How many prior arrests for domestic violence?	PRIORS	number of prior arrests	Print Format: F8 Write Format: F8 Missing values: $-1,9$	4
5. What was the date of offense?	CRDATE	crime date	Print Format: DATE11 Write Format: DATE11	5
6. What was offender's relationship with victim?	RELATION	relation to victim	Print Format: F8 Write Format: F8 Value Label 1 married 2 cohabitating 3 separated 4 divorced 5 dating 6 other	6
7. What was offender's adjusted gross income reported to IRS for 1995?	INCOME	1995 income	Print Format: DOLLAR8 Write Format: DOLLAR8 Missing values: $-1, 99$	7

reserve for a given variable in the data set and how to display it. These format codes are included in the variable information as "Print Format" and "Write Format" provided in the codebook, as shown in Table 14.1. In the case of the variable LNAME, these are specified as "A12." The "A" designates the variable as alphanumeric and the "12" indicates the maximum number of characters that the computer will permit for printing the variable when it is displayed or when the program writes the variable to a file. Similarly, the date-of-birth variable is identified as DATE11, indicating that the variable is a date with 11 characters in it. The numeric variable PRIORS is designated as "F8," indicating that it is a numeric variable with no decimal places. If it were a decimal variable with two decimal places, it would be "F8.2." Currency variables are displayed

with two decimal places, a dollar sign, and commas separating thousands. So, the variable INCOME has a format of DOLLAR8, indicating that it is a currency variable that can be as large as "99,999,999.99." In Table 14.1, the variables DOB and CRDATE are defined as date variables. Even though the displayed entries consist of both letters and numbers, the actual entry for a date is stored in the computer file as a single (and very large!) number representing the number of seconds from some point in time that the program specifies as zero. SPSS stores dates as the number of seconds from midnight, October 14, 1582 (SPSS, 1994). The date, 8–November–1957, is actually stored as $1.2E+10$. Although this may seem bizarre, this convention permits the data analysis program to do computations with dates. If we want to determine how old each suspect was at the time of the offense, we can enter a computer command that will subtract DOB from CRDATE and display the result in years. Although different computer programs use their own conventions of designating variable types, the important point is that how the variable is defined before data entry determines its type, rather than being determined by how the variable looks on a computer monitor or printout. The researcher must plan how variables will need to be used in the analysis and define them accordingly.

Additional elements may be added to a coding scheme to enhance its usefulness. Besides a variable name, which is very brief, the researcher may specify a variable label, which is an extended description of a variable that the data analysis program will print in addition to the variable name whenever output is generated for that variable. Thus, in a table using the variable CRDATE, the designation "crime date" can be printed to make the table more understandable. Similarly, the coding scheme may include "value labels," which designate in words what a given value represents. For example, in Table 14.1, numbers are used to designate the following relationship possibilities between offender and victim: 1 = married, 2 = cohabitating, 3 = separated, 4 = divorced, 5 = dating, and 6 = other. Because this is a nominal variable and thus without an inherent quantitative meaning to the numbers, the value labels are printed on outputs to help make it clear what quality each number represents.

Finally, the coding scheme should also show how to interpret special codes, such as *missing values*. Missing values arise when there is no response recorded for a particular item. Depending on why the item is a nonresponse, the researcher may either leave the variable blank in the computer data set or enter a value that signifies why the item was missing. For example, an item might be coded "−1" if the respondent refused to answer the question or "99" if the item does not apply to a particular respondent. This could be an important distinction for some types of analysis, so the coding scheme must specify how these various entries should be handled in computations. For example, if "99" is a missing value code for a variable of respondent age, the computer program must treat this respondent's age as missing and not as 99 years old when computing statistics such as the mean or standard deviation on the variable.

Preparing and Using a Codebook

The coding scheme results in a specification of the variable name, variable format, the range of permissible response codes, location of the variable in the data set, and optional features, such as variable labels, value labels, and missing value codes. Researchers commonly develop a *codebook* for the data set, which is an inventory of all the individual items in the data collection instrument together with the coding schemes (*see* Table 14.1). We stated that the initial use of the coding scheme is to guide the process of converting responses into codes. But the need for a codebook does not end once the data are entered into a computer file. The codebook provides lasting documentation on how the data set is constructed. Anytime there is a question about how a variable is constructed or how it can be used in analysis, the researcher can turn to the codebook for help. Not only does the researcher who collected the data need the codebook, but without such documentation, it would be impossible to conduct a replication study on a previously collected data set or to explore new hypotheses with existing data. Finally, the codebook is invaluable for data file management. A data set may consist of hundreds of variables, so to make analysis more efficient, researchers commonly create subfiles containing only the variables needed for a particular analysis. The codebook plays an essential role in selecting the variables and creating new files.

The preliminary codebook is normally prepared before data are entered into the computer and is used as a guide for data entry. However, the codebook is not a static document. As will be described in more detail shortly, researchers often recode original variables and compute new ones. It is critical that these manipulations of the original data also be documented in the codebook so that any researcher can determine how these new variables were derived, what they mean, and where they are located in the data set.

Data Entry

The goal of the data entry process is to produce a complete data set, free from errors, that the data analysis software program can access and process. Although sometimes seen as a laborious, repetitive task devoid of intellectual skill requirements, data entry is a critical part of the research process, and the researcher needs to take steps to ensure that it proceeds with accuracy and efficiency. Significant strides have been made in recent years to both minimize data entry error and to increase the speed of transforming raw data into a data set that is ready for analysis.

Raw Data Entry

When the raw data must be extracted from existing documents such as court records, or from printed questionnaires or survey schedules, the data must be manually entered into the computer. Several options exist for this process. Sometimes the questionnaire data are coded onto pages known as "transfer sheets," consisting of numbered rows and columns that look much like the computer screen in Figure 14.1. In other cases, questionnaires have space along the border for writing the code, referred to as "edge coding." Whether one uses a transfer sheet, edge coding, or simply the raw questionnaires themselves, a common way to enter a data set is to use the data entry facility of the statistical package that will eventually be used to analyze the data. Modern statistical packages for the personal computer, such as SPSS and Minitab, include full-featured data entry facilities as part of the package. Conventions and individual features vary from program to program, but the basic process is similar.

The data entry screen is laid out in columns and rows, as shown in Figure 14.1. Each column represents one variable (field), and each row represents one case (record). Assuming that the variable names, labels, and other specifications have already been entered during the preparation of the codebook, the value for each variable is simply typed into the respective cell in the row corresponding to the individual case. Errors can be corrected by moving the cursor with mouse or arrow keys to the cell in question and reentering the correct code. If the coding scheme's data definition for the computer has not already been entered into the computer file, this step can be completed as data are entered into each variable.

Although data entry directly into a statistical package is relatively easy and convenient, there are additional options that may be more attractive. On the one hand, you may not have immediate access to the data analysis package itself. Another possibility is that the data are being collected for purposes other than your research for use with a program such as a spreadsheet or a database that human service agencies commonly use to collect and store data for management purposes. Spreadsheet programs were originally developed for financial data, but are now widely used for many other purposes, and human service agencies commonly use them to enter and store data. Such spreadsheets as Lotus, Excel, and Quattro have made popular the row-by-column cell display now used by statistical packages that we discussed earlier. Major statistical packages can read data files generated by popular spreadsheet programs. So, even though you may not have the latest version of SPSS or Minitab installed on your own personal computer, you can basically prepare a data set on your spreadsheet program, save it on disk, and load it into the statistical package and begin analysis. In addition to the wide availability of spreadsheet programs, another reason for using them is their powerful capacity to compute complex variables through the use of formulas. It may be easier to compute a variable on the spreadsheet and import it into a statistical package than to rely on the statistical package's capacity to compute new variables.

Database programs such as Access and Paradox are also popular options for data entry. Actually, modern spreadsheets and database program features tend to overlap, although databases are designed primarily for the storage, retrieval, and manipulation of data files while a spreadsheet's strong suit is quantitative calculation. A major reason for turning to a database for data entry is the control that such a program affords over the data entry process. An appealing database feature is the ability to specify a default value or an acceptable range of values for a variable. Thus, if males are coded "1" and females are coded "2" and the vast majority of respondents are males, the database can be set up to enter a default value of "1." The computer will automatically enter that value as data are entered for each case unless a "2" is manually inserted. Alternatively, an acceptable range, such as "1–5," may be defined for a variable. If the data entry person types a "6," the computer will not accept it, thus reducing the potential for error. Setting up a database program this way prevents entry of out-of-range values.

A second reason for choosing a database program for data entry is the form design feature that these programs offer. For example, the researcher can prepare a data entry form that looks very similar to the questionnaire. The form may also provide coding instructions to the data entry person for complex items. Instead of staring at an endless sea of rows and columns, the data entry person views a form with blanks in which data may be entered. The actual data are stored in a standard file structure, but the form helps guide the data entry process. The form can even be programmed to follow the skip pattern of the questionnaire (see Chapter 7), eliminating the need to make decisions about where to enter the next response. In addition, data entry can be greatly simplified by the use of "pull down menus" and "buttons." These features are ideal for closed-ended questions. Pull down menus display a small window and an arrow on the data entry form. The user simply clicks on the menu bar and the program displays all the possible acceptable choices for that item. The user then selects the respondent's choice from the list with the mouse pointer or arrow key, and the program

enters that value in the database. For simple items, such as those with a Yes–No response choice, a button is used. The computer screen displays a button next to each response choice. The user simply clicks the mouse pointer on the desired choice and the response is coded into the data set. Such features greatly speed up the data entry process and reduce the possibility of error.

A final option worth considering for data entry is a specialized data entry program, such as QDATA, which we discuss in the Exploring the Internet section of this chapter. QDATA is a modest program compared to a full-featured database or spreadsheet, but it is very effective for the specific task of data entry. It will define a data set, including specifying variable labels, value labels, and range of values. Once the data are entered, the file can be saved in a statistical package format or in ASCII, which is a generic format many programs accept.

Instead of making data entry a distinct step in the research process, it may be combined with data collection. One way of doing this, as described earlier, is to use a data entry form prepared with a database as the actual questionnaire. Either the interviewer or the respondent views the items on the computer monitor and enters the responses. For studies consisting primarily of closed-ended question items, which readily lend themselves to employing buttons and pull down menus, recording the responses directly into the computer data set can reduce error and increase the speed of data entry.

Another innovation in data entry is the use of optical scanning technology. A data collection instrument is designed using a special program. Respondents may either mark a circle corresponding to their choice or, in more sophisticated programs, write a response. The questionnaire is then read by a scanning machine or faxed into the computer and the coded values are entered directly into the database for analysis. Whether one uses a specialized data entry such as this or relies on manual entry into the data analysis program depends on several factors. The specialized equipment is cost effective for large projects where a staff of data entry personnel would otherwise need to be employed. On the other hand, designing, setting up, and testing an automated data entry program would be prohibitively expensive for a small data set. Researchers today have many options to chose from, and the most important issue is to select the process that will yield an accurate, usable data set.

Data Cleaning

No matter how much care one takes during the data entry process, errors can be expected. Errors include such things as skipping variables for certain cases, entering the wrong value, entering the value in the wrong column, or entering an alphanumeric character in a numeric variable column. If uncorrected, some errors might cause the analysis program to abort a statistical procedure, or at least they may seriously distort the findings of the analysis. So, before analysis begins, it is highly recommended that the researcher examine the data set carefully and make corrections. Although no system is foolproof, researchers have developed a variety of techniques for locating errors.

If the data set is small, you may be able to detect some errors simply by scanning the data with the data editor screen. Scrolling through the rows and columns of data on the screen can turn up some obvious errors, such as blank cells, unusually large numbers, or stray alphanumeric characters. However, it is best to rely on a more systematic approach. One simple technique with a statistical package, spreadsheet, or database is to use a *sort* procedure. Sorting rearranges the order of all cases in the data set on the basis of the values of the variable selected as the sort key. Alphanumeric variables are sorted alphabetically, and numerical variables are sorted in numerical order. Scanning the sorted data on the monitor, one can detect misspellings and missing or out-of-range values. For example, if the variable used in the sort procedure is a scale item where expected values are integers from 1 to 5, blank entries and entries of "0" would be at the top of the list, decimals such as 1.5 would show up between "1" and "2," and values of 6 or more would be at the end of the list. This can be a cumbersome process with large data sets, but if there are

only 50 or so variables, sorting the data works well. With a statistical package such as SPSS, another option is to use a "Frequencies" procedure on all variables. This generates a list of every value that actually occurs in the data set for each variable in ascending order and the number of cases for each respective value. This aids in detecting variables with out-of-range values or values that should not be present. Of course, knowing that there are some cases somewhere with the wrong entries for a variable and finding those cases are very different things, especially when there may be a thousand or more cases in the data set. Having identified a variable with one or more suspect cases, the researcher can use a conditional selection process. The exact command differs from program to program, but basically you enter a command to select those cases for which the value for the variable in question meets a certain condition. For example, if no one in the data set should have an age greater than 18, you execute a command to select all cases where AGE > 18. You then include a second command to list the case numbers or the last and first names of all cases meeting that condition. Armed with this information, you can scroll through the data set to the identified cases and correct them. You may edit the entry by replacing it with the correct value, enter a missing value code if the correct value is not available, or, in really serious cases, eliminate the whole case entirely.

The techniques covered thus far will help find data entries that are too large or too small, but sometimes the data are within the acceptable range, but simply wrong for that case. Some of these errors can be detected by looking for logical inconsistencies. For example, if the value in a month variable is April, June, September, or November, then the value in a day variable associated with that month should not be greater than 30. If the variable entry for the number of adults in the household is 2, and the number of children is 4, then the entry for total household size should be 6. Depending on the software program, it is possible to build queries that detect cases where such inconsistencies are present. The program QDATA has a built-in facility for doing such logical consistency checks. Large-scale, professional surveys have the benefit of specialized software to help detect errors as well as having supervisory personnel review data entry to detect problems, but most human service practitioners are unlikely to have access to such services. However, rigorous application of the procedures discussed here can help locate many errors even without benefit of specialized programs. Finally, error detection underscores the importance of numbering the questionnaires or other raw data sources and keeping the raw data in a safe, accessible location so that you can compare the original data to the computer file when needed.

Creating New Variables

The data have all been entered and checked for error, but one task remains before proceeding to data analysis. The variables as recorded may not be in the final form for the desired analysis procedures, and, if so, the researcher will need to modify the variables or generate new ones that can be used. Such data manipulation may sound unusual, but, as you will see, it is a legitimate and a necessary part of the research process. Here is one example of how and why this is done. Recall from Chapter 13 that some scale items are stated in positive terms and other items stated in negative terms to avoid problems such as response set. With a 10-item Likert scale for depression, for instance, with choices ranging from 1 to 5, half of the items would be stated such that a positive response (such as "strongly agree" or "1") would indicate low depression. The other half of the items would be stated such that a negative response ("strongly disagree" or "5") would indicate low depression. To conduct statistical analysis on them, some items need to be reverse scored so that a score of 1 on all items signifies a low value on the concept being measured and a 5 signifies a high value. This can be accomplished by use of a *recode* procedure in statistical programs. A recode statement specifies the existing values in a given variable and what the new values should be. In our example, for the five negative items, we would change the values as follows:

Old Item Value		Revised Item Value
1	⟶	5
2	⟶	4
3	⟶	3
4	⟶	2
5	⟶	1

Having recoded the negative items, we now have 10 consistent items where low values indicate a lack of depression and high values, a presence of depression. However, what we really need is a total scale score on depression. This can be obtained by using a *compute* procedure in the data analysis program. A compute procedure creates a new variable by performing mathematical computations using one or more existing variables. Depending on the conventions of the particular software, we would enter a command like this:

Let DEPSCORE = sum(DEP1 to DEP10)

A new variable called DEPSCORE, which is the total scale score, is computed by summing all 10 individual items that make up the depression scale (DEP1 through DEP10). The new variable is added to the data file. As with the existing variables, the researcher can attach a variable label and value labels to such newly created variables. Whenever the researcher modifies the data set, whether by recoding or computing new variables, the steps used in the data manipulation must be recorded and added to the codebook. Fortunately, this is easy to do because statistical programs typically record all executed data transformations in a special file. In SPSS it is called an output file; in Minitab it is designated as a history file. Documenting the transformations this way assures that any researcher using the data file will be able to confirm how new variables were generated. As we shall see, recoding and computing new variables is an essential step in the process of unlocking the findings contained in the data set.

Data Distributions

Once the data have been stored as a computer file, systematically inspected for error, cleaned, and possibly revised through recoding and variable creation, we are ready to begin actual data analysis. Data analysis is the process of seeking out patterns within individual variables, and, more important, seeking out patterns in relationships between variables. The term *univariate analysis* refers to the process of describing individual variables. Even though our ultimate goal in a research project is usually to determine how two or more variables are related, the process of describing the data by specifying the characteristics of individual variables is critical to a research project. Learning how individual variables are distributed can help determine which variables to use in studying relationships and which data analysis procedures we should use.

Types of Data Distributions

One of the first steps usually taken with a data set is to look at the range of values for each variable. To accomplish this, a *frequency distribution* is constructed. In Table 14.2, the variable is the grade for a college class, with the traditional five categories. The frequency column shows the number of class members who received each grade. Of particular interest is the *shape* of a frequency distribution. A distribution's shape derives from the pattern the frequencies produce among the various categories of the variable. A number of labels are used to describe the shapes of distributions. First, distributions may be symmetrical or asymmetrical (*see* Figure 14.2). *Symmetrical distributions* are balanced, with one half of the distribution being a mirror image of the other half. In reality, most distributions only approach perfect symmetry. *Asymmetrical distributions* have cases bunched toward one end of the scale, with a long "tail" caused by a

small number of extreme cases trailing off in the other direction. Asymmetrical distributions are said to be *skewed,* with positively skewed distributions having long tails extending in the direction of the higher values and negatively skewed distributions having tails going in the direction of lower values. (Note that the concepts of positive and negative skewness apply only to distributions of data of ordinal level or higher. Because the categories of nominal data have no inherent order, the shape of a distribution of nominal data is purely an arbitrary matter of how one chooses to arrange the categories.) Determining the amount of skewness is an important preliminary step for later analysis. Certain inferential statistics, for example, are based on the assumption that the variables are normally distributed. One of the basic properties of a normal distribution is that of being symmetrical. Therefore, our analysis at this stage may be critical for helping to decide later which inferential procedures are appropriate.

Constructing Frequency Distributions

Simple Frequency Distributions   When data are collected, they are in the form of a *raw data distribution,* which means that the distribution contains all the different values that were observed on a variable. Table 14.3 displays a raw data distribution of the ages of a sample of 71 residents in a veterans' facility. A first step in data analysis might be to construct a *simple frequency distribution,* in which each value of a variable is listed only once along with the number of cases that have that value. Table 14.3 includes a simple frequency distribution of the ages of the people in the veterans' facility. The "X" column refers to the values or categories of the variable, while the "*f*" column indicates the frequency, or number of cases that have each value.

Simple frequency distributions can be constructed on variables at any level of measurement. In Table 14.3 notice how much easier it is to gain some sense of the age distribution of the residents from the simple frequency distribution in comparison to the raw data distribution. However, sometimes simple frequency distributions are too cumbersome. In Table 14.3, there are still a lot of

Table 14.2   Hypothetical Grade Distribution for a Social Science Research Class

Grade	Frequency
A	4
B	7
C	10
D	5
F	3
	$N = 29$

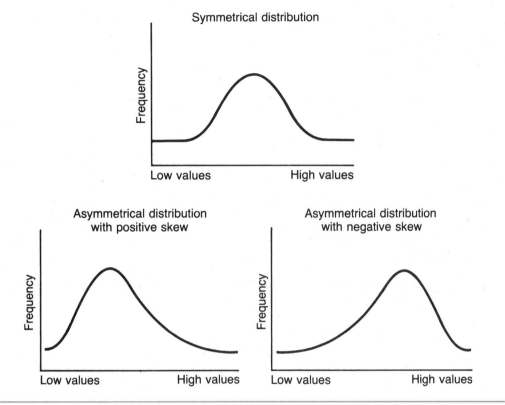

Figure 14.2 Symmetrical and Asymmetrical Distributions

categories to look at, and many categories have no case or only a few cases. In these situations, it is often preferable to collapse a distribution further by creating a grouped frequency distribution.

Grouped Frequency Distributions At its core, data analysis is basically a search for patterns in data. However, sometimes searching for patterns in raw data is akin to the old adage of not being able to see the forest for the trees. Even if we order the observations by using a simple frequency distribution, the large number of observations, the small variations between some observations, and large gaps between others combine to hide the pattern inherent in the data. *Grouping* is the process of combining a large number of individual variable categories into a smaller number of larger categories. It permits us to step back from the data and see the big picture by ignoring minor variations between cases and focusing attention on larger patterns. One reason for grouping is to summarize the data into a manageable number of categories; a table or graph may be unreadable if it has too many categories. Another purpose would be to eliminate categories that have no or very few cases in them. In addition to making it easier to see patterns in the data, grouping is often necessary for certain data analysis procedures. For example, a statistical computation may require that there be enough cases so that each cell in a table could theoretically have at least five cases in it. Grouping may help meet this requirement because reducing the number of categories increases the number of cases falling into the newer and larger categories.

The manner in which grouping is done depends in large part on the level of measurement of

Table 14.3   Two Types of Data Distributions of Patients' Ages

A. Raw Data Distribution

98	82	78	70	68	60
96	81	76	70	68	60
95	80	76	70	68	59
92	80	75	70	68	59
91	79	74	70	68	59
89	79	73	70	67	58
87	79	72	70	66	56
85	79	72	70	66	54
85	79	71	70	66	52
84	79	71	69	64	51
82	79	71	69	63	50
82	79	71	69	63	

Total $N = 71$

B. Simple Frequency Distribution

X	f	X	f	X	f
98	1	76	2	59	3
96	1	75	1	58	1
95	1	74	1	56	1
92	1	73	1	54	1
91	1	72	2	52	1
89	1	71	4	51	1
87	1	70	9	50	1
85	2	69	3		
84	1	68	5		
82	3	67	1		
81	1	66	3		
80	2	64	1		
79	8	63	2		
78	1	60	2		

the data. Table 14.4 shows the hypothetical results of a small survey that includes the variable "religious affiliation." This frequency distribution clearly is in need of grouping: Some categories have no cases at all, others have few cases, and there is a large number of categories in the coding scheme. When grouping nominal data such as these, one must rely on logic and common sense to group categories together that fit in some way with each other. For example, it is logical to group all the Protestant denominations into a new category called "Protestant," because they all share some core beliefs and practices. On the other hand, those categories with few or no frequencies could reasonably be grouped into a category called "other," simply because there is an insufficient number of cases in any one of them. The difference in reasoning behind forming each group is important to note, because it may be significant for later analysis. For example, if we are evaluating how religious affiliation relates to attitudes toward volunteering for community service, "Catholic," "Jewish," and "Protestant" are meaningful categories, whereas "other" is a hodgepodge of cases that we really can't describe in terms of common theology. For analysis purposes, we may want to classify these latter cases as "missing" and exclude them from analysis.

Table 14.4 Illustration of Grouping a Nominal Variable

| | Original Code Scheme | | | | Recoding Scheme | |
| | *RELIGION* religious affiliation | | | | *RELIG2* religious affiliation groups | |
Value	Label	Frequency		Value	Label	Frequency
1	Roman Catholic	10		1	Roman Catholic	10
2	Methodist	3		2	Protestant	20
3	Presbyterian	2		3	Jewish	10
4	Lutheran	5		4	Other	5
5	Baptist	4				
6	Unitarian	3				
7	Episcopalian	3				
8	Jewish	10				
9	Moslem	1				
10	Eastern Orthodox	0				
11	Hindu	1				
12	Buddhist	1				
13	Shintoist	0				
14	Atheist	2				
15	Other	0				

Total *N* = 45

Grouping ordinal data can be a very straightforward process of merging adjacent categories. For example, if it were decided that the nine social class categories in Table 14.5 were too many, it would be easy to collapse them down to the conventional three as shown in the table. In this illustration, going from nine to three categories makes logical

Table 14.5 Grouping Ordinal Data

Social Class	f	Social Class	f
upper-upper	8		
middle-upper	14	upper	57
lower-upper	35		
upper-middle	56		
middle-middle	92	middle	212
lower-middle	64		
upper-lower	44		
middle-lower	32	lower	87
lower-lower	11		
Total (*N*) = 356		Total (*N*) = 356	

sense because the nine small categories are gradations of the three larger groupings. However, this is not always the case. A survey may include an item that asks for years of education but not have a variable for highest degree attained. The desired variable could be approximated by grouping the existing variable. Although years of education could conceivably be construed of as a ratio level variable, if it is applied as an indicator of preparation for employment, then it might better be treated as ordinal. In terms of getting a job, having a high school diploma, an associate degree, or a bachelor's degree may be the critical determinants. People who dropped out without completing the twelfth grade are all dropouts, whether they completed 9, 10, or 11 years. People who have 13–15 years of education probably have some college, but not a bachelor's degree. Rather than using equal multiples as in the social class example, a researcher might approximate employment preparation by grouping years of education into the following categories: 1 = <9 years (no high school), 2 = 9–11 years (some high school), 3 = 12 years (high school grad), 4 = 13–15 years (some college), 5 = 16+ (college grad). The scheme would not be perfect because not everyone with 12 years of schooling graduated, but it would approximate the desired variable. As this example illustrates, the fact that the original categories are ordered is a starting point for grouping a variable, but the researcher must still rely on logic and knowledge of the application to which the grouped variable will be put to decide on the boundaries of the intervals.

Grouping interval level data is a fairly direct process. Unlike ordinal data, the distance between units of interval level data are by definition equal, so one general principle is to use equal width intervals when grouping data. Nevertheless, common sense and knowledge of the use to which the grouped data will be put are essential to planning the group intervals. Intervals of $10 might make perfect sense if grouping data on weekly earnings of high school students, but completely inappropriate if the data concern annual income of single-parent households. All raw frequency distributions of interval data have units of 1, such as length of jail sentence in days, earnings in dollars, or live births per year. In grouping, one merely increases the number of units in each new interval from 1 to 3, 10, 1,000 or whatever amount makes logical sense given the data and provides the desired number of intervals for describing the data and doing data analysis. The size of the grouped intervals is called the *interval width*. Consider the distribution of un-grouped ages for residents in a veterans' residential facility in Table 14.3. These scores are clearly in need of grouping as they are so spread out that any pattern is difficult to see.

We will illustrate grouping interval data by grouping the scores in Table 14.3 into 10 new intervals. On the one hand, we want enough intervals so that we don't obscure significant variation in the data; on the other hand, we want to reduce the clutter of too many categories. Once the decision on the number of intervals is made, one must determine the number of measurement units that will go into each new interval; in other words, we need to determine the interval width. In our particular example, with a range of 48 years in the age variable and the number of grouped intervals set at 10, it is quite obvious that the interval width should be 5.

In other situations, however, the interval width may not be so easy to determine, so there is a formula that one can apply to find the interval width:

$$Interval\ Width = \frac{(H_s - L_s)}{N_i}$$

where:

H_s = Highest score
L_s = Lowest score
N_i = Number of desired intervals

If we applied this equation to the data in Table 14.3, we would have:

$$Interval\ Width = \frac{(98 - 50)}{10} = \frac{48}{10} = 4.8$$

In many cases, the result of this formula is a decimal of some sort that one merely adjusts up or down to the nearest convenient interval width. In our case, we would adjust upward for an interval width of 5. The resulting frequency distribution is displayed in Table 14.6.

When selecting interval widths, it is suggested that the width be an odd number, such as 3, 5, or 7. This should be done because intervals with an odd-numbered width have a whole number for their *midpoints*. For example, an interval sized 5, 50−54 has a midpoint of 52, but an interval sized 4, 46−49 has a midpoint of 47.5. When working with grouped interval data, the midpoints have a number of uses (such as category labels in Table 14.6), and it is far more convenient to work with midpoints that do not have decimals. Compare the grouped data in Table 14.6 with the ungrouped and simple frequency distributions in Table 14.3. Do you notice anything in the grouped distribution that you did not see when you first looked at those distributions, especially the ungrouped distribution? The grouped distribution clearly shows the characteristic accumulation of people in the middle of a distribution with the frequencies tapering off toward both tails of the distribution. Such a distribution is commonly referred to as a "normal curve" and is an important characteristic of data distributions that is used in choosing some statistics in Chapter 15.

Table 14.6   Patient Age Data Grouped by Intervals of 5 Years

Interval Width	Value	Frequency	Percent	Valid Percent	Cum Percent
50–54	52	4	5.6	5.6	5.6
55–59	57	5	7.0	7.0	12.7
60–64	62	5	7.0	7.0	19.7
65–69	67	12	16.9	16.9	36.6
70–74	72	17	23.9	23.9	60.6
75–79	77	12	16.9	16.9	77.5
80–84	82	7	9.9	9.9	87.3
85–89	87	4	5.6	5.6	93.0
90–94	92	2	2.8	2.8	95.8
95–99	97	3	4.2	4.2	100.0
	Total	71	100.0	100.0	

Valid cases   71   Missing cases   0

Graphical Display of Data Distributions

In addition to describing variables by means of a frequency distribution, another common procedure is to use a graph. The visual impact of a graph can help identify and summarize patterns in data that might not be detected as readily by perusing frequency distribution tables. Although long recognized as valuable for communicating information about data, constructing graphs has been an expensive and labor-intensive process until recently. However, modern data analysis packages have greatly changed that. Not only is a diverse array of full-color graph options available as a special set of tools, but some packages include graphs as an extra feature of basic analysis procedures, such as frequency analysis. For example, by simply checking a box in the SPSS Frequencies Menu, the program provides a histogram with each frequency distribution table. The easy access to graphical presentation of data, however, is a two-edged sword. Used correctly, graphs are a powerful tool for communicating information about data; used incorrectly, they can confuse and even mislead viewers on t he meaning of a distribution. One situation in which graphs are popular occurs when the results

of a frequency distribution must be presented to an audience that is unfamiliar with reading such tables.

We present a few of the more common ways of graphing individual variables. Basically, these graphs are visual representations of a frequency distribution. Earlier, we discussed ways of grouping data for presentation in a frequency distribution table. Many of the same issues apply to graphing data. For example, a graph is more effective if there are a manageable number of categories. If several categories have a very low frequency, they will be hard to see on a graph. An effective graph, then, begins with organizing the data appropriately as one would for a frequency distribution table.

Bar Graphs

One of the most commonly used types of graphs is the **bar graph.** A distinguishing feature of the bar graph is the space between the bars. These spaces illustrate that the categories of the variable being represented are separate, or *discrete*. In Chapter 5 we pointed out that only certain categories are theoretically possible in a discrete variable such as race, religious affiliation, and household size. Nominal and ordinal variables are by definition discrete

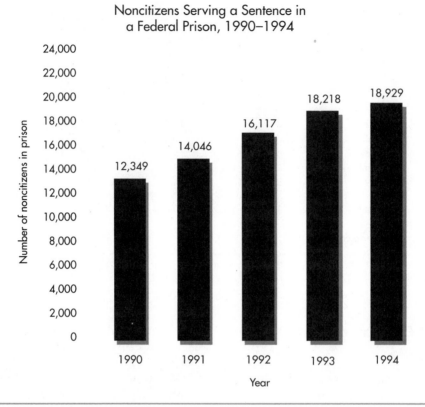

Figure 14.3   Example of a Bar Graph
Source   Based on Bureau of Justice Statistics, *Noncitizens in the Federal Criminal Justice System 1984–1994* (Washington, D.C.: U.S. Department of Justice, 1996), p. 9.

variables, so bar graphs are especially useful for these levels of data. Figure 14.3 illustrates a typical bar graph, with the height of the bars representing the frequencies in each category of the variable. As can be seen from the figure, a bar graph makes it easy to note any trends, such as the upward one in Figure 14.3.

When constructing a bar graph (and most other types of graphs, for that matter), care should be taken when establishing the dimensions of the graph. The vertical axis, which represents the frequencies, and the horizontal axis, which represents the categories of the variable, should be about equal with reasonably equal spacing of the categories on both axes. Again, Figure 14.3 illustrates this. This concern for roughly equal dimensions is

important because it is possible to accidentally or purposely construct a graph that gives a false impression. For example, by expanding the dimensions of the vertical axis, a graph can be constructed that makes small differences among categories appear large, at least to the casual observer. On the other hand, expanding the horizontal dimension has the opposite effect. A graph can be constructed that appears to minimize differences among the categories. Purposeful manipulation of graph dimensions in an attempt to deceive viewers is considered unethical. It should be noted, however, that misleading graphs are produced all the time, so always carefully inspect any graph you are reading to be sure that you are not being misled by its initial appearance.

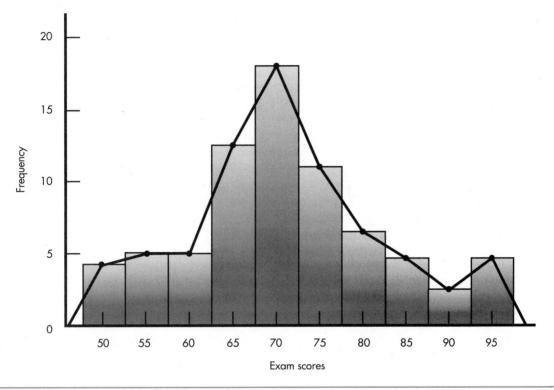

Figure 14.4   Histogram and Frequency Polygon of Hypothetical Exam Scores

Histograms and Frequency Polygons

Although some variables, such as household size or a frequency count of a behavior, are discrete variables, at the interval or ratio level of measurement, variables are conceived of as being *continuous,* meaning that, unlike the discrete variables, there are no gaps or spaces between the categories. Thus, age is a continuous variable. This continuous nature of interval and ratio data should be reflected in graphs used to present them. One wishing to graph interval or ratio data has a choice of two popular methods. The first is called a **histogram** and bears a considerable resemblance to the preceding bar graph. Once again, as can be seen in Figure 14.4, bars of various lengths are used to represent the magnitude of the frequencies from a frequency distribution. The only difference between a bar graph and a histogram is that the bars in a histogram touch, signifying the continuous nature of the data.

Figure 14.4 also illustrates the alternative technique of graphing interval or ratio data, the **frequency polygon.** A frequency polygon is simply a line graph that connects the midpoints of each category of the variable. The choice of either a histogram or frequency polygon is purely a matter of personal preference as they are interchangeable.

Pie Charts

Pie charts are another type of commonly used graph that are particularly good for showing how some whole amount is divided. As such, pie charts are often used to illustrate how budgets are distributed for varying functions. If you ever have occasion to prepare a grant proposal, it will most likely contain one or more pie charts indicating how you intend to spend the money. Figure 14.5 is a pie chart based on projected revenue to the federal government for the 1997 fiscal year.

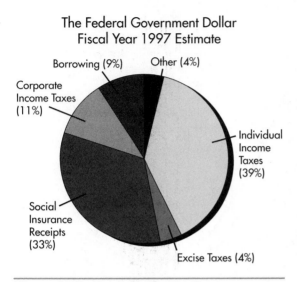

The Federal Government Dollar
Fiscal Year 1997 Estimate

Borrowing (9%) Other (4%)
Corporate Income Taxes (11%)
Social Insurance Receipts (33%)
Excise Taxes (4%)
Individual Income Taxes (39%)

Figure 14.5   Example of a Pie Chart
Source   *Budget Supplement Fiscal Year 1997* (Washington, D.C.: U.S. Government Printing Office, 1996), p. 2.

The pie chart, quite obviously, gets its name from its resemblance to the slices of a pie. The size of each "slice" gives a visual depiction of the percentage of the whole that each category represents. Preparing a pie chart via a computer program now involves simply choosing a variable and the pie chart option from the graphing menu. However, the process that the graphing program uses involves determining how many of the 360 degrees of an entire circle are to be allocated to each of the categories. For example, Figure 14.5 indicates that 11 percent of revenues are expected to come from corporate income taxes. To determine how large a slice to allocate to corporate income taxes, the data analysis software multiplies 360 by 11 percent, obtaining a value of 39.6 degrees. So, the slice devoted to corporate income taxes is drawn such that it occupies 39.6 degrees of the 360 degrees of the circle.

Research in Practice 14.1 provides an example of how the preparation and presentation of univariate data described thus far in this chapter can have utility in human service program planning.

Contingency Tables

Thus far we have discussed ways of describing the distribution of cases on a single variable and ways of presenting single variable data in the form of frequency distributions and graphs. Now we turn our attention to ways of describing and exploring how two or more variables are distributed together. That is, given the values in a data set on one variable, how are values distributed on one or more other variables? Classifying or organizing the data on one variable according to values on a second variable is the basis for contingency table analysis.

Bivariate Relationships

The statistics we have considered so far are used to describe the distribution of a single variable and are, therefore, called **univariate statistics.** Most data analysis in research involves dealing with two or more variables simultaneously. Statistical procedures used to describe the relationship between two variables are called **bivariate statistics,** whereas **multivariate statistics** deal with three or more variables. When two or more variables are analyzed with descriptive statistics, the major feature of interest is the relationship between the variables, especially the extent to which they covary, or vary together. If two variables are related, a change in one of the variables is associated with a change in the other.

Contingency and Percentage Tables   A convenient way of investigating bivariate relationships is to cross-tabulate the data in the form of a table. A *contingency table* contains raw frequencies, whereas in a *percentage table* the frequencies have been converted to percentages. Both types of tables are useful for studying relationships. We discuss these tables for only two variables. However, you should be aware that contingency table analysis can be applied to three or more variables.

Table 14.7 illustrates the general form of a contingency table. We utilize two conventions to standardize the construction of contingency tables. First, when there is an independent variable and a

Table 14.7   Contingency Table

		Independent Variable			
		Low	Medium	High	Totals
	High	21	47	12	80
Dependent	**Medium**	38	41	20	99
Variable	**Low**	79	14	28	121
	Totals	138	102	60	N = 300

dependent variable, the vertical *columns* are used to represent categories of the independent variable, with the horizontal *rows* representing categories of the dependent variable. Second, when ordinal level or higher data are cross-tabulated, the categories should be ordered as illustrated in Table 14.7, with columns running from lowest on the left to highest on the right and rows from lowest at the bottom to highest at the top. Be advised that these conventions are not universally applied, and you may encounter tables constructed differently. Following the conventions, however, contributes to consistency and ease of interpretation. Furthermore, the computational routines for some statistics assume that tables are constructed according to this convention and must be modified to produce correct results with tables structured differently.

Several labels are used to refer to the various parts of tables. The squares of the table are called *cells,* with the frequencies within the cells labeled *cell frequencies.* Values in the "totals" column or row are called *marginals.* Tables are often identified according to the number of rows and columns they contain. A table with two rows and two columns becomes a 2 × 2 (read "2 by 2") table. A table such as Table 14.7 is a 3 × 3 table. In addition, because the number of rows is always designated first, a 2 × 3 table is *not* the same as a 3 × 2.

Contingency tables are generally used as a starting point for creating percentage tables or as the basis for applying many statistics. By themselves, contingency tables are difficult to interpret if the number of cases vary in each column and row. Converting a contingency table to a percentage table makes interpretation far easier, and this can be

done by dividing each cell frequency by the appropriate marginal total and multiplying the result by 100. The column marginals would be used if we were interested in seeing how the dependent variable is distributed across categories of the independent variable. Table 14.8 illustrates contingency Table 14.7 converted to a percentage table. Percentages in the first column were obtained by dividing the cell frequencies 21, 38, and 79 by the column marginal 138, with the result multiplied by 100. Below each column, the percentages are totaled and indicated as equaling 100 percent. This informs the reader that the column marginals were used to compute the percentages. The numbers in parentheses are the column marginals from the original contingency table. They supply valuable information regarding the number of cases on which the percentages are based and should always be presented with a percentage table.

Reading percentage tables is a straightforward process similar to constructing them. Whereas we computed the percentages down the columns, we read percentage tables by comparing percentages along the rows. Of particular interest is the *percentage difference* (% d) between any two categories within a given row. For example, Table 14.9 presents hypothetical data on the relative effectiveness of two different treatments for depression. The difference between the two cells in the top row is 6.8%, meaning that more of those receiving treatment B improved than those receiving treatment A. The % d suggests that treatment B was somewhat more effective on this sample of clients. Note that with a 2 × 2 table such as Table 14.9, the same

Table 14.8   Percentage Table

		Independent Variable		
		Low	Medium	High
	High	15.2%	46.1%	20.0%
Dependent	**Medium**	27.5%	40.2%	33.3%
Variable	**Low**	57.3%	13.7%	46.7%
	Totals	100%	100%	100%
		(138)	(102)	(60)

Table 14.9   Relative Effectiveness of Two Treatments for Depression

	Treatment A	Treatment B	
Improved	35.3%	42.1%	
No improvement	64.7%	57.9%	
	100%	100%	%d = 6.8%
	(34)	(34)	

% d will result by subtracting within the bottom row, so a single % d summarizes the complete 2×2 table. As the number of rows and columns in a table increases, the number of % d's that can be calculated increases rapidly.

The magnitude of % d's is a crude indicator of the strength of relationships. It should not be surprising that small differences of 1 or 2 percent indicate very weak and possibly meaningless relationships. On the other hand, % d's of 15 percent or more usually indicate substantial relationships. Unfortunately, no hard and fast rules concerning evaluating the magnitude of % d's can be offered because of the complicating factor of sample size. For example, if we are dealing with employment data for the entire nation, a difference of 1 percent or less could represent a million more workers with or without jobs. With very large samples, smaller % d's are more important. Alternatively, with small samples, % d's must be large before they indicate a substantial relationship.

Multivariate Analysis

As noted in Chapter 2, analyzing an independent and a dependent variable and finding a bivariate relationship between them does not prove that the independent variable actually *causes* variation in the dependent variable. To infer causality, the possible effects of extraneous variables must be investigated. Although research projects may focus primary attention on two variables, they will typically consider others to assess the full complexity of social phenomena. A set of procedures for conducting this kind of multivariate analysis is called either *table*

elaboration or *contingency control*. Contingency control involves examining a relationship between an independent and a dependent variable while holding a third variable constant. Three variable tables are constructed such that the relationship between the independent and dependent variable can be examined within each category of that third variable. The general format of contingency control is illustrated in Figure 14.6. Although contingency control can be applied to variables with any number of categories, for the sake of simplicity and space we use dichotomous variables throughout this presentation.

The subtables Z_1 and Z_2 are referred to as *partial tables* and the relationships within them as *partial relationships*. A partial relationship is a relationship between an independent and a dependent

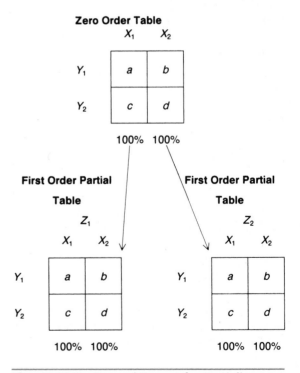

Figure 14.6   General Format for Partialing Tables:
X = categories of the independent variable
Y = categories of the dependent variable
Z = categories of the test variable

variable within one category of the test (or control) variable.

The original table that is divided into partials is called the *zero order table,* and the relationship contained within it is known as a *zero order relationship.* The "zero" in these labels indicates that no test variables are being controlled. As we introduce test variables, partial tables are referred to by the number of test variables being controlled at one time. If we are controlling one test variable in our partial tables, they are referred to as *first order partials,* clearly indicating that the number of variables controlled is one. If more variables than one are simultaneously controlled, the tables are called second order partials, third order partials, and so on. Although possible, it is rare to go beyond the first order with contingency control. One reason is that as we add more test variables, the number of partial tables that are generated increases rapidly, and interpreting all of these tables may be extremely difficult. The other reason table elaboration is rarely taken beyond the first order is that the sample gets divided quickly, to the point that individual cell frequencies may become too small and reduce our confidence in the results. We literally run out of cases. This effect can be seen in Figure 14.6, where in the zero order case the sample is divided among the four cells of that table; but when we move to the partials, the same number of cases is spread among eight cells, thus reducing the magnitude of the cell frequencies. For analyzing multivariate relationships beyond the first order, techniques other than table elaboration normally are used.

When a test variable is introduced and partial tables created, the tables will reveal that one of four possible results has occurred. First, there may be *no effect.* This result is indicated when the relationship in the partial tables is approximately the same in terms of strength as it was in the zero order table. In this case, we have tested a variable that is unrelated to either the independent or the dependent variable; therefore, it could not affect the relationship between those variables. In all cases, the direction and the strength of the relationships among the three variables determine the result that occurs when partialing. Figure 14.12 illustrates the no-

effect condition by indicating no linkage between the test variable and either the independent or the dependent variable.

A second possibility when doing table elaboration is that the strength of the relationship found in the zero order table may be substantially reduced or even disappear entirely in the partials. This result may be difficult to interpret because there are two possibilities and we need more information (which may or may not be available) to choose between the two. One possibility is that in terms of temporal order, the test variable intervenes between the independent and the dependent variable (Figure 14.12). When such an intervening variable is controlled, the relationship between the independent variable and the dependent variable is effectively blocked, so the partial tables show little relationship.

The other possibility is that the zero order relationship is either all or partly *spurious.* In this case, the test variable is temporally located before either the independent or dependent variable and is related directly to both (Figure 14.12). When the effects of the test variable are controlled, the apparent relationship between the independent variable and the dependent variable is reduced because the operation of the test variable was to inflate the actual relationship between the other two variables in the zero order table. In a case of complete spuriousness, the independent and dependent variables appear to be related in a zero order table only because of the influence of the test variable. With this influence blocked in the partials, the zero order relationship disappears. Be sure to note the importance of being able to establish the appropriate temporal location of the test variable relative to the other two variables. If that cannot be done, as might occur with survey data, we cannot be sure whether the partials are indicating the presence of an intervening variable or that of a spurious relationship. As noted in Chapter 2, determining temporal order is crucial in sorting out causal relationships among variables.

Another possibility can occur when controlling on a third variable. The partial tables may show an even stronger relationship between the independent and dependent variables than was indicated by

Research in Practice 14.1
Needs Assessment: Does Deer Hunting Really Prevent Domestic Violence?

One of the most significant ways that social science research methods and human service practice can be linked together is by using research data to make better informed human service planning decisions. To illustrate this point, we've selected one of our own projects, the Marquette County Coordinated Response to Domestic Violence Program. Through a cooperative effort between community agencies, spearheaded by the Women's Center and the Marquette County Prosecuting Attorney, the project is seeking ways of responding more effectively to cases of domestic violence. A brief description of this project will illustrate how the skills of data preparation and presentation are often used in human service settings.

A portion of this effort involves designing a data collection system to identify domestic violence cases and to track their progress through the various organizations involved in responding to the problem. Just setting up the data collection system proved to be a complex undertaking. There were several possible sources of data, such as 911 calls to Central Dispatch; hot-line calls to the Women's Center; legal system reports from police, the prosecutor, district court, and probation; as well as reports from hospitals and mental health and substance abuse programs. These records include police report information as well as case disposition data. Such records are not particularly "user friendly" to an outsider; the jargon seems strange, and the reports are not laid out with the needs of a data collector in mind. Furthermore, there were so many possible variables that decisions had to be made as to what to use and what to ignore. Fortunately, the primary project staff member was an attorney by profession. Using a database program, he developed a data entry form, including coding directions, that permitted a student intern to enter data from all cases, beginning with 1995, the year before program initiation. These data were intended to serve as a baseline for program planning. Approximately 180 completed case files for of-

fenses occurring in 1995 were entered into the initial data set.

Although the database was a good start, many of the variables were not in a form that lent itself to ready data analysis by a statistical package such as SPSS. For example, information on the severity of injury to the victim had been entered as descriptive labels, such as "Pushed and Shoved—No lasting pain" or "Weapon Involved—Wounded by Weapon." As a result, such variables were recoded into an ordinal scale, ranging from no physical contact through serious injury requiring medical attention. The database program is also being revised, so that in the future, the data set will already contain a numerical code and not require recoding.

When data analysis is being used to inform human service practice, an important part of the process is to identify variables that can be of practical use. In this case, one such variable turned out to be the victim's ZIP Code. The simple frequency distribution in Table 14.10 shows the distribution of 1995 domestic violence cases in Marquette County, Michigan, for ZIP Codes of the larger communities. The county is the largest in the state in area, but in terms of population, communities are small. Marquette has only about 27,000 inhabitants. Under these circumstances, ZIP Codes are convenient because they include surrounding suburban areas while still representing distinct communities for program planning. In this case, the

Table 14.10   Program Evaluation Data Showing Domestic Violence Cases by ZIP Code

VZIP   *victim zip code*

Value Label	Value	Frequency	Percent
Gwinn	49841	15	8.3
Ishpeming	49849	50	27.6
Marquette	49855	69	38.1
Neguanee	49866	24	13.3

data show that Ishpeming, which is about one half the size of Marquette, has a disproportionately large number of domestic violence calls. Marquette is the county seat and has many more human service resources, including a major hospital, a university, and the Women's Center. Analyzing cases by geographic distribution is hardly a ground-breaking data analysis procedure, but this simple analysis played a major role in the decision to allocate a new full-time staff member to Ishpeming, which was felt to be underserved.

Other basic descriptive data are also useful for program planning. An often discussed issue in the field of domestic violence is the role of alcohol. The pie chart in Figure 14.7 shows the distribution of alcohol involvement by both the suspect and victim. Such information can help agencies plan services based on actual data rather than on conjecture. The pie chart in Figure 14.8 depicts the distribution of severity of injury in the domestic violence cases that came to the attention of the police. Knowing not only how many cases were referred, but also the severity of assaults can be useful in planning services. Such graphical presentations are also an effective way to share statistical data with audiences who have little knowledge of statistics.

Of course, not all data can be translated into program policy decisions. One variable we exam-

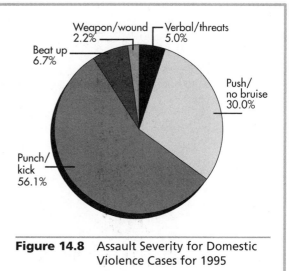

Figure 14.8 Assault Severity for Domestic Violence Cases for 1995

ined was the distribution of domestic violence cases by month. Figure 14.9 seems to suggest that domestic violence cases were comparatively few in number during November and relatively high during April. What could be the explanation? Several local people who looked at the graphs had an immediate explanation. It's deer season in November and tax time in April. On the face of it, it seems plausible. There are over 700,000 licensed deer hunters in Michigan. In the Upper Peninsula region, deer season may be more important than Christmas. Schools close for the opener, fluorescent orange clothing is everywhere, and men head off to deer camp in droves. If a large proportion of men are not around their partners, there's less opportunity for domestic violence. The tax time in April doesn't appear to have quite the same impact, but the April rate is high. However, before the NRA begins touting big game hunting as domestic violence prevention or the IRS gets bad press for being the cause of domestic violence, there are some more likely (and less entertaining) explanations. Probably the most likely explanation is simply random variation in the data. Furthermore, months are not equal intervals. Not only do some have more days than others, but some have more *weekends,* and one thing that is clear is that most

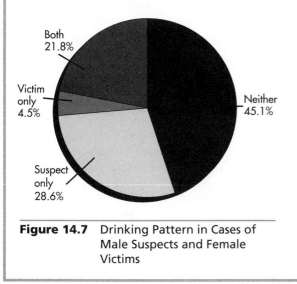

Figure 14.7 Drinking Pattern in Cases of Male Suspects and Female Victims

continued on next page

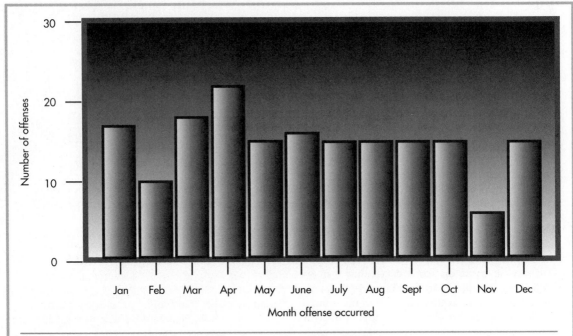

Figure 14.9   Domestic Violence Offenses per Month for 1995

violence happens between Friday evening and Sunday morning (see the bar chart in Figure 14.10). The pattern (or lack thereof) in the data is more apparent by graphing the data by week instead of month (see Figure 14.11). April 15 falls in week 15 and deer season opens on November 15 in week 46. The number of cases around tax time is large, but many other weeks show the same or more numbers of cases. No cases of domestic violence were reported during the week of opening day, but there were three other weeks with no cases, and several weeks with only one or two cases. Conclusions about the impact on domestic violence of both the tax deadline and deer season are less clear when we categorize data by week rather than month.

This situation illustrates some important points. First, there is more random variability to data than we often think. We must be cautious about reaching "ad hoc" conclusions just because they seem plausible or interesting. Second, how data are organized or grouped in frequency distributions and graphs can reveal meaningful patterns, but can also lead to confusion if the categories are flawed. Finally, the evaluator must keep in mind the purpose of the evaluation. In this instance, identifying in what communities domestic violence occurs is an important, useful contribution because it has direct implications for how services should be allocated. On the other hand, finding a few more cases of domestic violence around tax time or a few less around deer season would not be of much use for needs assessment or program planning. Such relationships might be of sociological interest, but the purpose of the study determines which variables are important.

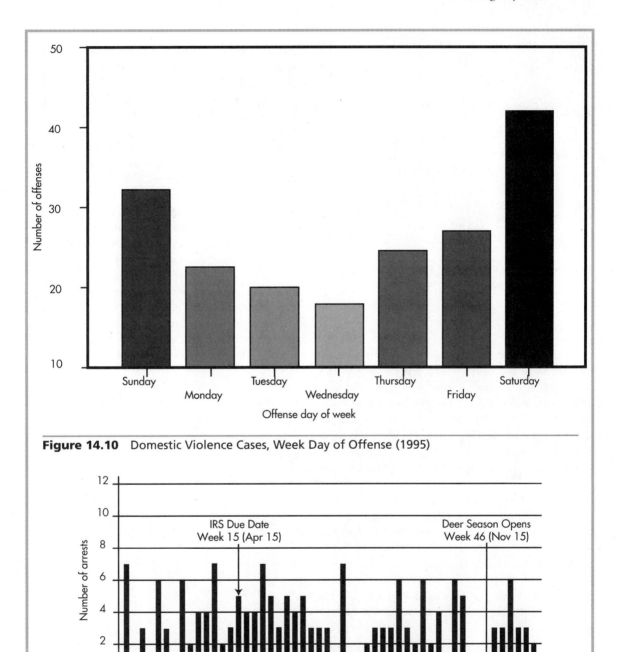

Figure 14.10   Domestic Violence Cases, Week Day of Offense (1995)

Figure 14.11   Domestic Violence Arrests by Week of the Year (1995)

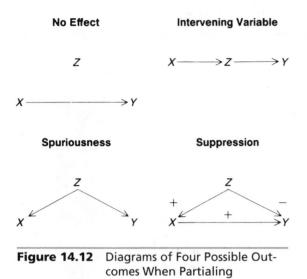

Figure 14.12   Diagrams of Four Possible Outcomes When Partialing

the zero order table. This outcome occurs because the action of the uncontrolled test variable in the zero order table is to suppress the relationship between the independent and the dependent variables. In fact, variables that produce this result are called *suppressor variables,* and the result itself is known as *suppression.* Figure 14.12 illustrates one way suppression can occur. Note that positive relationships are indicated between the independent and dependent variables and between the independent variable and the test variable. A negative relationship exists between the test variable and the dependent variable. It should be evident that the test variable and the independent variable are exerting forces on the dependent variable that are, at least in part, offsetting. That is, as values of the independent variable increase, they influence the dependent variable to increase, but as the test variable increases, it is influencing the dependent variable to decrease, thus masking part of the relationship between the independent and the dependent variables. When the influence of the test variable is controlled, this masking effect is removed and the relationship between the independent variable and the dependent variable is now revealed to be stronger than in the zero order table.

The last, but often most intriguing, of outcomes is that of *interaction.* Interaction refers to a relationship between an independent and a dependent variable that is inconsistent. That is, the relationship between the variables differs depending on the condition of the test variable. For example, one partial table might show a no-effect result while another might show a "spurious" result. This result means that the relationships among the three variables are more complex than in the previous outcomes. When interaction is present, we can no longer speak of a simple, singular relationship between the independent variable and the dependent variable with the effects of the test variable controlled. Because the condition of the test variable affects the relationship, we must specify the condition of the test variable before discussing the independent–dependent relationship. In the preceding example, we would have to indicate that in condition 1 of the test variable, the relationship found between the independent variable and the depen-

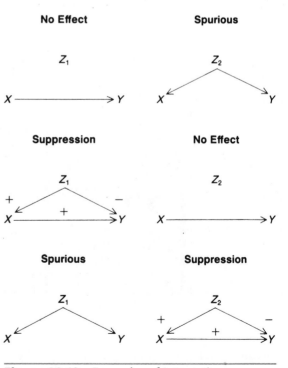

Figure 14.13   Examples of Interaction

dent variable at the zero order stayed roughly the same and controlling on the test variable had "no effect." In condition 2, however, controlling on the test variable caused the zero order relationship to disappear, indicating that it was "spurious" or possibly the test variable operates as an intervening variable. Be sure to note that this combination of "no effect" and "spurious" is only one possible combination of the various outcomes that may indicate interaction. Any combination that produces inconsistent results across the partial tables could be interaction. Figure 14.13 illustrates some of these combinations. Interaction results are not at all uncommon in social research. One common test variable—gender—routinely produces interaction effects because men and women react to numerous independent variables differently.

Main Points

■ Data analysis refers to deriving some meaning from the observations that have been made as a part of a research project; quantitative data analysis involves putting observations into numerical form and manipulating them based on their arithmetical properties.

■ Most data analysis is currently performed by computer, with data entered into a computer file from a computer terminal.

■ Data analysis begins by developing a coding scheme and a codebook, which is a set of mutually exclusive and exhaustive numerical codes into which the raw data are categorized.

■ After data have been entered into a computer file, they must be carefully checked for coding or input errors.

■ New or revised variables may be created through recoding existing variables or by computing new variables based on existing variables.

■ Frequency distributions may be effectively communicated by using bar graphs, histograms, frequency polygons, and pie charts.

■ Frequency distributions reveal the pattern the frequencies produce among the various categories of the variable and may be symmetrical or asymmetrical.

■ Contingency tables and percentage tables are particularly useful for analyzing bivariate and multivariate relationships with categorical or partially ordered data.

Important Terms for Review

alphanumeric variable
bar graph
bivariate statistic
coding scheme
data analysis
frequency polygon
histogram
multivariate statistic
numeric variable
pie chart
statistics
univariate statistic

Exploring the Internet

The emphasis in most of the Exploring the Internet sections in this text has been on locating information that will help expand your knowledge of research. But the Internet can not only provide interesting illustrations of research methods, it can also provide you with tools for actually doing research. The step of data entry is an example of this. An important goal of the data entry step is to obtain a data set that is complete, free from errors, and ready for analysis. Although one can enter data directly into a statistical software program, such as SPSS, Minitab, or SAS, it is not always convenient to do so, nor are there always safeguards against entering wrong values. A solution is a freeware (so called because there is no charge for obtaining it) program called QDATA that is available over the Internet. QDATA is an easy-to-use program specifically for designing data sets, entering the data, and cleaning the data. One can begin by defining variables to be included in the data set, including variable names, extended labels, whether the variable is text or numeric, the range of acceptable values, and labels for the values. Once the variables are defined, you can enter your data set. After the data are entered, the program guides you through several data cleaning steps. By downloading the program and its manual, you can either use the program with actual data that you collect or simply experiment by making up a hypothetical data set to gain a sense of the process involved.

Graphical aids to data analysis and presentation have exploded with the advent of the personal computer, and the Internet has an abundance of resources available to enrich your understanding of graphical data analysis and to provide tools to aid you in generating graphs of your data. One of the most inclusive sites on the Internet related to graphical use of data is Michael Friendly's site, Statistics and Statistical Graphics, which can be accessed at URL http://www.math.yorku.ca/SCS/StatResource.html. This page provides a topic-based collection of available resources for statistics, statistical graphics, and computation related to research, data analysis, and teaching; it now contains over 350 links. An interesting feature of this Internet site is a page devoted to illustrating some of the best and worst examples of using graphs to depict data. Examining these graphical depictions of data will show you the value of using graphs and some of the pitfalls to avoid as well. The Gallery of Data Visualization can be accessed at http://www.math.yorku.ca/SCS/Gallery/.

We can provide only a cursory introduction to graphs in the text, but entire courses are devoted to the subject. An excellent example of using the Internet for instruction and for learning more about graphical data analysis is an Internet course offered by Jeff Banfield. A perusal of his site will provide leads to texts and other Internet resources as well as show you a variety of graphing procedures. The URL for this site is http://math.montana.edu/~umsfjban/STAT438/Stat438.html#Graphics.

For Further Reading

Bowen, R. W. *Graph It! How to Make, Read, and Interpret Graphs.* Englewood Cliffs, N.J.: Prentice-Hall, 1992. This short book provides more detail on creating

graphs than we could include in this chapter, and it covers some graphing techniques that we did not cover. It is profusely illustrated, easy to read, and an invaluable guide.

Computers in Human Services. New York: Haworth, Quarterly. A journal that began publication in 1984, focusing on the potential of computer technology to help us deal with mental health, developmental disabilities, and other human problems. It provides a timely contribution to this area.

Craft, John L. *Statistics and Data Analysis for Social Workers,* 2nd ed. Itasca, Ill.: Peacock, 1990. This brief introduction to statistical analysis provides many good illustrations of the kinds of statistical analysis that involve human service workers.

Evans, James D. *Straightforward Statistics for the Behavioral Sciences.* Pacific Grove, Calif.: Brooks/Cole, 1996. This is a standard but well-written introductory textbook in statistics. It covers all the topics discussed in this and the next chapter, going into more detail and including additional topics.

Fox, William. *Social Statistics Using Microcase.* Chicago: Nelson-Hall, 1992. Written in a light and accessible style, this book teaches statistics through the use of the increasingly popular and easy-to-use Microcase software, a copy of which is included with each book.

Healey, Joseph F. *Statistics: A Tool for Social Research,* 4th ed. Belmont, Calif.: Wadsworth, 1996. This is another standard but well-written introductory textbook in statistics. Along with the Evans book, it can help you understand all the material in this and the next chapter.

Henry, Gary T. *Graphing Data: Techniques for Display and Analysis.* Newbury Park, Calif.: Sage, 1994. Presents techniques for making data from the social sciences accessible to nontechnical audiences. Discusses insights from visual perception research relating to graphing data, and explores graphs for data summarization, display of multiple units, tabular displays, alternatives to tables, two-variable scatterplots, and creating effective legends and titles on displays.

Jones, Gerald E. *How to Lie With Charts.* Alameda, Calif.: Sybex, 1995. An ideal guide for all who want to understand how presenters can use charts to deceive an audience. Readers will learn how to make their presentations more effective.

Kachigan, S. *Multivariate Statistical Analysis,* New York: Radius Press, 1982. Another advanced textbook covering a variety of more sophisticated statistics, with primary emphasis on multivariate techniques.

SPSS. *SPSS 6.1 for Windows Brief Guide.* Chicago: SPSS Inc., 1995. This is a brief introduction to using the Windows version of the statistical package SPSS that is mentioned a number of times in this chapter. Windows software is so easy to use that this short introduction to SPSS will actually equip the student to begin using other Windows statistical software.

Wallgren, Anders, Britt Wallgren, Rolf Persson, and Ulf Jorner. *Graphing Statistics and Data: Creating Better Charts.* Walnut Creek, Calif.: Altamira Press, 1996. Suggests how to create graphs and charts that make viewers aware of the qualities of data. Introduces the elements of charts, such as axes, scales, and patterns; describes steps to make charts clearer, using real data for examples; and walks through the entire process from data to finished chart.

Zeisel, Hans. *Say It With Figures,* 6th ed. New York: Harper & Row, 1984. A classic analysis of how to present data with statistics. It is very useful for policy-makers who wish to improve their understanding of the statistics presented to them.

Exercises for Class Discussion

Assume that you have just completed the data collection on a needs assessment on the need for a volunteer visitation program for the elderly in your community. You have a random sample of 500 questionnaires completed by people 55 and older that must now be analyzed. The program will cost about $45,000 a year to pay for the coordinator's salary and administrative and advertising costs. Variables included in the survey are sex, age, annual income, proximity to family members, a scale score on perception of neighbors' capacity to help, and a scale indicating desirability of a visitation program. Finally, the question was asked: "If this program were implemented, would you use it?" The question could be answered yes or no.

14.1 Describe the general process you would follow in analyzing the data by listing the main steps to be completed.

14.2 Develop a hypothetical coding scheme for the following variables: age, sex, income, and desirability scale score (assume the scale scores can range from 0 to 30).

14.3 In terms of bivariate relationships, using the final question as the dependent variable, indicate which indicators would be appropriate for each of the independent variables. What if the dependent variable is the scale score?

CHAPTER 15

Data Analysis II: Descriptive and Inferential Statistics

Considerations in Choosing Statistics   401
Level of Measurement   401
Goals of the Data Analysis   403
Number of Variables   403
Properties of the Data   403
Audience   404

Descriptive Statistics   405
Measures of Central Tendency   405
Measures of Dispersion   406
Measures of Association   407
The Normal Distribution   411

Inferential Statistics   413
Probability Theory   413
Sampling Distributions   414
Statistical Hypothesis Testing   415
Statistical Procedures   417

Main Points   422

Important Terms for Review   424

Exploring the Internet   424

For Further Reading   424

Exercises for Class Discussion   425

This chapter is a continuation of the introduction to data analysis that begins in Chapter 14. You will recall from Chapter 14 that data analysis is the process of deriving some meaning from the observations that have been made during the research process. Thus far, the focus has been on describing data using relatively simple procedures, such as frequency distributions, data plots, and contingency tables. Although these means of summarizing and displaying data are useful, in order to describe data precisely and to examine relationships between variables, researchers rely on more sophisticated statistics. Statistics have become common to the lexicon of modern living. We often hear people casually referring to something being "above the norm," "below average," or "correlated" with something else. Tune in to the evening news and you might assume that death from cancer is imminent because research has shown a "statistically significant correlation" between your favorite food and the dreaded disease. Or you might hear a report stating that the relationship between underage drinking and traffic-related injuries to adolescents is "statistically significant." Because statistics are ubiquitous in our modern world, people may use statistical terms, such as "correlation" or "statistical significance," without fully comprehending what they mean. It is imperative to have a basic understanding of statistical concepts in order to be an informed consumer of both the popular media and the professional literature in the social sciences and human services.

However, it is very likely that, as a human service professional, you will also need to compile data, analyze it, and present the findings as part of a needs assessment, funding proposal, or documentation of program outcome. This requires knowing not only how to interpret a statistic, but also which statistics to use and how to compute them. We believe that it is especially important to emphasize choosing the correct statistic. Computer technology has made statistical computation relatively easy,

but the proper selection of statistical procedures and interpretation of statistical results cannot be done by the computer—it requires an intellect informed about statistical analysis. We begin this chapter with some guides to help you identify which statistical procedures might be appropriate in a given situation. Next we introduce common statistics for describing the characteristics of the actual data that have been collected. Finally, we examine inferential statistics, which are used to draw conclusions about populations from samples drawn from those populations.

This chapter is not intended as a thorough coverage of statistical procedures; to provide such coverage would require a book devoted solely to the subject. However, the chapter does provide a basic introduction to the fundamentals of doing statistical analysis in order to draw conclusions from the data and to understand their broader implications.

Considerations in Choosing Statistics

Once the data are coded and in a computer file, the researcher is ready to begin the data analysis that will unlock the information that the data contain. One of the major errors that can occur in data analysis is selecting a statistic that is inappropriate for the kind of data gathered in a research project. Although many factors need to be taken into account in choosing statistics appropriately, five major considerations are especially important.

Level of Measurement

One consideration is the level of measurement of the data collected. Chapter 5 addresses the four levels of measurement: nominal, ordinal, interval, and ratio. Each level of measurement involves different rules of permissible mathematical operations that can be performed on the numbers produced while measuring variables at that level. As you will recall, the nominal level involves merely classifying observations into categories; the categories have no order, and the numbers associated with a category only serve as a label for the category—the numbers have no mathematical value and performing any arithmetic operations on them is inappropriate. On the other hand, a ratio level of measurement has a true zero point, making all mathematical operations permissible.

Each statistical procedure involves mathematical operations that are appropriate at one of the levels of measurement. For example, a nominal statistic assumes that the data have only mutually exclusive and exhaustive categories and none of the mathematical properties of the other levels of measurement; likewise, a ratio statistic assumes that the data have a true zero point and requires mathematical operations appropriate to that. The basic rule is that variables that are measured at a given level can be analyzed with a statistic that is designed for that level of measurement or with a statistic that is designed for a lower level of measurement. As Table 15.1 illustrates, nominal, ordinal, interval, or ratio data can be treated as nominal and used with a statistical procedure designed for nominal data. For example, a frequency distribution, as described in Chapter 14, can be used with a nominal level variable, such as religious affiliation; however, a frequency distribution can also be used to classify data at higher levels of measurement, such as levels of agreement to Likert scale items (ordinal level) or annual income in dollars (ratio level). Because it can handle data at all levels of measurement, a frequency distribution is a good statistical procedure with which to begin data analysis.

However, even though data measured at higher levels can be analyzed with lower level statistics, there is a trade-off in terms of the kind of information and relationships that can be discovered about the data based on the statistics. With annual income, for example, it is much more informative to be able to say that the people in the upper 10 percent of the income distribution earn eight times more money than people in the bottom 50 percent than to simply report the number or percent of people who are in a particular income category. Therefore, it is generally preferred to use the highest level of statistic that is appropriate for a particular variable. In addition, it is definitely inappropriate to use a statistic designed for a higher level of measurement than the level of measurement of the data being analyzed.

Thus far, we have been discussing the role of levels of measurement in selecting a statistic on the basis of individual variables. However, many research questions involve examining relationships between two or more variables simultaneously, and these may involve different levels of measurement. For example, we might study whether substance abusers abstain or use drugs (nominal) after attending one of several treatment programs (nominal), while also taking into account religious affiliation (nominal), age (interval), and severity of addiction (ordinal). One reason why there are so many different statistical procedures is that they address

Table 15.1   Relationship Between Statistics and Level of Measurement

Level Statistic Is Designed For	Type of Data With Which Statistic Can Be Used			
	Nominal	*Ordinal*	*Interval*	*Ratio*
Ratio	No	No	No	Yes
Interval	No	No	Yes	Yes
Ordinal	No	Yes	Yes	Yes
Nominal	Yes	Yes	Yes	Yes

different possible combinations of levels of measurement among variables. For any data analysis problem, then, the researcher must be able to classify each variable in terms of its level of measurement.

Goals of the Data Analysis

The second consideration in assessing the appropriateness of statistics is to determine what goals the statistic is to accomplish. Each statistical technique performs a particular function, revealing certain information about the data. A clear conception of the analytical goals of the data analysis is a prerequisite for selecting the best statistics for achieving those goals. Statistical techniques have one of two goals: *description* or *inference*. **Descriptive statistics** are procedures that assist in organizing, summarizing, and interpreting data. The data might be from a sample or they might be from a whole population (*see* Chapter 6); in either case, descriptive statistics organize and summarize the body of data. **Inferential statistics** are procedures that allow us to make generalizations from sample data to the populations from which the samples were drawn. Recall from Chapter 6 that the ultimate reason for making observations on samples is to draw conclusions regarding the populations from which those samples were drawn. We make observations on a sample of clients in an agency because it is too expensive, time-consuming, or impractical to observe all the clients; yet we want to draw conclusions about all the clients. Inferential statistics are based on probability theory, and they basically tell us the probability of being wrong if we extend the results found in a sample to the population from which the sample was taken.

Statistics must be chosen that are appropriate to the goals of the data analysis. In some cases, both descriptive and inferential statistics are used because the analysis is intended to accomplish both goals. However, if a population were small enough that the data were collected from every element in the population, then inferential statistics would not be necessary and would be inappropriate. In addition, inferential statistics should not be used if the goals of the analysis are descriptive, and descriptive statistics should not be used if the goal is inference.

Number of Variables

A third consideration in choosing an appropriate statistic is the number of variables to be analyzed. **Univariate statistics** are those that analyze only one variable; **bivariate statistics** analyze two variables; **multivariate statistics** analyze three or more variables. An example of a univariate statistical problem would be an investigation of the average income paid to correctional officers in a particular correctional facility. The only variable in the problem is "amount of income"; the correctional facility is not a variable but a constant—it has only one value or category. This problem could be changed into a bivariate problem by introducing a second variable: How does gender affect the average income paid to the correctional officers in the facility? Now the problem has two variables: gender and amount of income. A multivariate problem could be hypothesized by adding additional variables: How do gender, race, and seniority influence levels of income in the facility?

Each statistic is designed to be used on either a univariate, bivariate, or multivariate problem. However, a point of clarification is warranted: Some univariate statistics are also calculated as a *part* of some bivariate or multivariate statistics. For example, among the statistics to be discussed in this chapter, the mean is a univariate statistic, but it is also calculated as a part of some bivariate statistics (such as Student's t) and some multivariate statistics (such as MANOVA). In these cases, however, the univariate statistic is only one step in the more complex and lengthy calculation of the bivariate and multivariate statistics.

Properties of the Data

To be properly used, some statistics require that the data to be analyzed have certain mathematical or other properties. Actually, an example of this was already discussed as levels of measurement, which involves the mathematical properties required for particular statistical tests. This is discussed separately because it is of paramount importance and relates to every statistical procedure. There are, however, other assumptions about the properties of the data that need to be considered.

One important assumption of many statistical procedures is that the observations on the dependent variable are independent of one another. For example, if we are evaluating the effectiveness of a counseling program for men who batter their partners, we might randomly assign 20 men to receive the treatment and 20 to be in the control group. Upon completion of the program, each subject participates in a videotaped simulation exercise where an observer rates his use of controlling tactics with his partner. First, the 20 control tapes are graded and then the 20 treatment tapes are graded. The grading process is a complex task, and the observer becomes more skilled in grading as he or she gains practice and counts more controlling behaviors as a consequence. In this situation, subjects scored later are likely to have higher scores than those rated first, so the scores are correlated with (are "dependent" on) rating order. This condition is referred to as *serial dependence* because the scores are dependent on their position in the series of measurements. Serial dependence is often hard to detect but can be a serious problem because one may reach erroneous conclusions when comparing the average rating for the treatment group with the average rating of the control group. (Without going into detail, it can be noted that statistical procedures exist that can detect such a correlation with serial position and estimate how much of the difference between groups is due to it.)

In other situations, it is more obvious that observations are not independent; in fact, some research problems call for designs that include related observations. This is particularly the case when one wishes to study change over time. For example, one might classify homeless shelters by funding source in 1986 and again by funding source in 1996 in order to determine if there is a trend. A similar situation occurs when the same group of people are given a pretest and a posttest, or possibly several tests over the course of an interven-

tion. Other research problems that don't satisfy the assumption of independence are the single subject designs discussed in Chapter 11. In these three examples, because the same organizations or individuals are being observed at different points in time, the observations are not independent, and one would use a statistic that adjusts for this fact.

Another important assumption for some statistics, which is discussed in the next section, concerns the shape of the distribution of observations on a variable. Some statistics require that this distribution be normal or symmetrical. If the distribution is not normal, the statistic calculated on the data may be misleading.

As a part of the process of selecting an appropriate statistic, researchers review these various assumptions about the nature of the data they are analyzing and assess the risk of using a statistic that requires assumptions that are not met, or not fully met, by the data. The more the data violate these assumptions, the greater the risk of producing a misleading result.

Audience

If all the preceding considerations are weighed and more than one statistic could be appropriately used, then consideration is given to the audience for whom the data analysis is intended. If that audience has limited statistical expertise, then a relatively simple statistic that can be understood by the audience would be preferred over a more complex statistic that might confuse. Among the simpler statistics would be the visual forms of presenting data discussed in Chapter 14 and the univariate statistics described in the next section. Some bivariate statistics, and especially the multivariate statistics, may well be beyond the comprehension of audiences without at least an elementary introduction to statistics.

With these considerations in mind, the chapter now turns to the descriptive statistics that are most commonly used in the social sciences and human services.

Descriptive Statistics

Imagine that you are selected to spend a year studying abroad. You say good-bye to your friends and family and board a plane for Europe, Asia, or other far-off locale. In the course of your stay there, you would likely be asked by your hosts to describe what Americans are like. For example, you might be asked to describe American college students. One way to respond would be to talk about what is typical or common among American college students. American college students are middle-class kids who like to attend sporting events such as football, basketball, and hockey. They head south during spring break to party; they eat junk food; they pay for school by relying on their parents and taking out loans. They love to use e-mail and the Internet to communicate, and they watch a lot of TV. That's not a complete description, however, and hardly a fair one. Many students don't attend athletic events at all, nor do they get to sport a tan after spring break. Some don't get any financial aid, and, although a majority of freshmen may be 18, we personally know some who are 50! So in trying to describe what American college students are like, you really need to talk about the diversity among students, not just what is most common. Beyond describing similarities and differences, you might also get into discussing characteristics of particular groups. You might say, for example, that women at your school are more likely to major in social work and men are more likely to major in criminal justice. As you engage in this process of describing what students are like, you would be using, albeit in a casual way, the basic principles of descriptive statistics. Descriptive statistics provide quantitative indicators of what is common or typical about a variable, how much diversity or difference there is in the variable, and how values on one variable are associated with values on one or more other variables.

Measures of Central Tendency

Although valuable for revealing patterns within the data and the shape of the distribution, frequency distributions, discussed in Chapter 14, can be cumbersome. In fact, with variables that can take on many values such as age or income, a frequency distribution can become so massive that it is difficult to detect patterns in it. **Measures of central tendency,** more commonly known as *averages,* summarize distributions by identifying the "typical" or "average" value. They are one of the most commonly used statistics. The three most widely used measures of central tendency are the *mode, median,* and *mean,* each designed for use with a particular level of measurement and having unique qualities.

The *mode* is the category in a frequency distribution that contains the largest number of cases. The mode for the grade distribution in Table 14.2 is C because more people received that grade than any other. Although the mode can be determined for data of any level of measurement (such as the grade distribution, which is ordinal), it is usually used with data of the nominal level, for two reasons. First, the mode is the least stable of the three measures, that is, its value can be changed substantially by rather minor additions, deletions, or changes in the values making up the distribution. With the other measures of central tendency, adding more cases produces less dramatic shifts in their values. Second, if two or more categories are tied with the largest number of cases, we could have two, three, or more modes, none of which would necessarily be very "typical" of the distribution. The presence of several modes also undermines its utility as a summary statistic to describe the average case.

With ordinal data, the *median* is the appropriate measure of central tendency. The median is the point in a distribution below which 50 percent of the observations occur. For example, a distribution of six scores—10, 14, 15, 17, 18, 25—results in a median of 16. Note that when the distribution contains an even number of values, an observed score may not fall on the median. The median is then the value halfway between the two central scores. If we add another score greater than 16 to the preceding distribution so that it contains 7 cases, the median is 17, an observed score. Because the median does not take into account the actual value of the scores, only the number of observations, whether the score we add is 17, 100, or 1,000 makes no difference—the median is still 17. This makes the median very stable because the presence of extremely high or low scores in a distribution has little effect on the value of the median.

The *mean*, the measure of central tendency most people think of when they hear the word "average," is calculated by summing all the values in a distribution and dividing by the number of cases. The mean, however, is only suitable for interval or ratio level data, where there is equal spacing along a scale and various mathematical functions can be performed (*see* Chapter 5). (There is one exception to this: dichotomous nominal or ordinal level variables that have only two values. Many interval level statistics, such as the mean, can be meaningfully computed on such variables. This is called dummy variable analysis and is beyond what we wish to introduce in this chapter.) Because the mean takes into account the actual value of all scores in a distribution, it is less stable than the median. The presence of a few extreme scores will "pull" the mean in that direction. Because of this, the median is often the preferred average when summarizing skewed distributions, even with interval level data, as it more accurately reflects the central value. For example, although the mean could be used to summarize income data, the U.S. Bureau of the Census typically reports median income because the presence of the relatively few wealthy people tends to pull the mean to such a high level that it overstates the average family income. Because it is less affected by extreme scores, the median is also often preferred in clinical practice research, where treatment and control groups are usually small and violate the assumptions required for statistics based on the mean.

Selecting the most appropriate measure of central tendency for a given set of data is not difficult. Level of measurement and skewness are the primary considerations. With relatively symmetrical distributions, the only factor is level of measurement.

Measures of Dispersion

Like measures of central tendency, measures of dispersion are used to describe and summarize distributions. Whereas central tendency indicators describe the middle or average of the distribution, **measures of dispersion** indicate how dispersed or spread out the values are in a distribution. Measures of dispersion add valuable information about distributions. On the basis of central tendency measures alone, we might assume that two distributions with similar averages are basically alike. Such an assumption would be erroneous, however, if the spread of the distributions were different. As illustrated in Figure 15.1, distribution *A* is more dispersed, with values deviating widely from the central value. The values in distribution *B* are more tightly clustered near the average. For avoiding possible erroneous assumptions about the spread of distributions, it is desirable to report a measure of dispersion along with a measure of central tendency.

Three commonly used measures of dispersion are the *range, semi-interquartile range,* and the *standard deviation*. The *range* is the simplest of these, referring merely to the difference between the highest and lowest scores in the distribution. As such, the range indicates the total spread of a distribution. Knowing the end points of a distribution, however, tells us nothing about how the remainder of the values

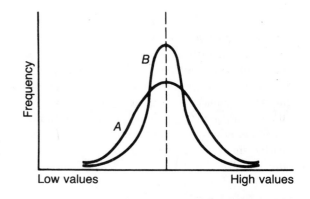

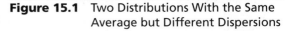

Figure 15.1   Two Distributions With the Same Average but Different Dispersions

are dispersed within the distribution. Furthermore, because the range is based on only two values, it is unstable. Adding or deleting extreme scores causes the range to vary widely, whereas the bulk of the distribution may change little. Moreover, despite its simplicity, the range is suitable only for interval data. The operation of subtraction used to obtain the range assumes that the values of the scores in a distribution have meaning, and that is true only for interval and ratio level data. Because of these limitations, the range is usually used as an adjunct to other measures of dispersion and not reported alone.

The *semi-interquartile range* (sometimes called the quartile deviation) is conventionally symbolized by the letter Q. The semi-interquartile range is obtained by first dividing a frequency distribution into fourths, or *quartiles.* The first quartile is the score below which 25 percent of the scores occur, and the third quartile is the score below which 75 percent of the scores occur. Q is calculated by subtracting the first quartile from the third quartile and dividing by 2. The semi-interquartile range is closely related to the median and is the measure of dispersion usually reported with it. In fact, the median is actually the second quartile, the point below which 50 percent of the scores occur. The semi-interquartile range is equal to half the difference between the third quartile and the first quartile. The larger the value of the semi-interquartile range, the more dispersed the scores are from the median.

The *standard deviation,* symbolized by the letter *s,* indicates the average (or mean) spread of the scores from the mean and is, therefore, the measure of dispersion usually reported along with the mean. The larger the value of the standard deviation, the more dispersed the scores are from the mean. Actual calculation of the standard deviation is relatively complex and beyond the scope of this chapter. In addition to its use as a descriptive statistic, the standard deviation has important applications in inferential statistics.

One final note on measures of dispersion. Although their overall purpose is to assist in the description of distributions, a single dispersion value from a single distribution is not particularly revealing. The major utility of dispersion indicators is in comparing several distributions because they enable us to tell at a glance which has more or less spread.

Measures of Association

Measures of association describe the nature of relationships between variables, particularly the *strength* of the relationship or how closely variables are related. The strongest relationship is a *perfect* one in which a given change in one variable is always associated with a given change in the other variable. Perfect relationships are rarely found in human service research. A less than perfect relationship indicates only a tendency for the variables to vary together. With ordinal or higher-level data, relationships between variables can also be positive, negative, or curvilinear. Recall that a positive relationship is one in which the change in value of the variables is in the same direction; that is, both increase or both decrease. And recall that a negative relationship is one in which one variable increases while the other decreases. Finally, recall that a curvilinear relationship is one in which the direction of change in one variable is not consistent with changes in the other. For example, in a U-shaped curvilinear relationship, both low and high values of the independent variable may be associated with high values of the dependent variable. In this case, a negative relationship exists between the two variables for low values on the independent variable and a positive relationship with high values on the independent variable. Most measures of association indicate a perfect positive relationship by 1.00 and a perfect negative one by −1.00. The closer the value of the measure is to −1.00 or 1.00, the stronger the relationship. The closer the value is to zero, the weaker the relationship.

The overriding determinant in selecting a measure of association is the level of measurement of the data at hand, so we will consider measures of association according to the level of measurement for which each was designed.

Nominal Data   Some data are dichotomous in form. That is, the variables have only two values, such as yes or no, male or female. A useful measure of association for two dichotomous variables is the *phi* (pronounced *phee*) coefficient (ϕ). The data are cast into a 2 × 2 table as illustrated by Table 15.2. Phi indicates the strength of the relationship between variables by yielding a value between −1.00 and 1.00. Although phi may yield negative values, the negative sign is simply ignored because it has no meaning in the case of nominal data.

Phi is considered a good measure of association for three reasons. First, it is quite easy to compute. Second, it is mathematically related to measures of association suitable for other levels of measurement, which makes comparing the strength of different relationships possible. Measures of association that are not mathematically related have different operating characteristics and produce values that are not comparable, precluding meaningful comparisons. Third, phi is a member of a group of measures of association that can be given what is called a **proportional reduction in error (PRE)** interpretation. The PRE interpretation means that the measure shows how much the independent variable helps to reduce error in predicting values of the dependent variable. To interpret phi in this way, it is first necessary to square it (ϕ^2). For example, $\phi = .39$ is squared to become $\phi^2 = .15$. This latter value is treated as a percentage and is interpreted to mean that the independent variable reduced the error in predicting values of the dependent variable by 15 percent. All PRE statistics are interpreted in this way.

Because phi is suitable only for two dichotomous variables, a different measure of association

Table 15.3   Nominal Data Suitable for Lambda

| | | Independent Variable (X) | | |
		X_1	X_2	X_3
Dependent	Y_1	200	60	40
Variable	Y_2	50	90	10
(Y)	Y_3	10	10	50

$\lambda = .20$

must be used for nominal data with more categories. The most generally useful measure for data of this type is lambda (λ). As with phi, the data are cast into tabular form, as illustrated in Table 15.3.

Lambda is a bit different from most measures of association in that its value can range only from 0 to 1.00. Lambda is never negative, but this is not a disadvantage because the negative sign is meaningless with nominal data anyway. Lambda is always positive because it is a direct reading PRE statistic. That is, lambda indicates the proportional reduction in error as calculated and need not be squared as phi does. This is an important point to remember as the values lambda produces usually look rather small. The reason is not that lambda understates relationships, but that the lambda values are "presquared," which makes them appear small.

Although phi and lambda are the most common nominal measures of association, several others are available. For two dichotomous variables, an alternative to phi is Yule's Q. However, Q cannot be given the PRE interpretation and tends to make relationships appear stronger than they actually are. For nominal data with more categories, Goodman and Kruskal's tau (τ) is often used. Tau is sometimes preferred to lambda because the former uses data from all cells in the table while the latter only includes in its computation data from some of the cells. However, tau does not always vary from 0 to 1.00, especially when the dependent variable has more categories than the independent variable.

Ordinal Data   There are many commonly used measures of association for ordinal data. A major consideration in selecting one to use has to do with

Table 15.2   Nominal Data Suitable for Phi

| | | Independent Variable (X) | |
		X_1	X_2
Dependent Variable (Y)	Y_1	15	35
	Y_2	40	18

$\phi = .39$

whether or not the data are *fully ordered*. In situations where every or nearly every case has its own unique rank and there are no or few ties, the data are said to be fully ordered. Table 15.4 illustrates fully ordered data. The most popular measure of association for fully ordered data is Spearman's rho (r_s). Rho, like phi, is mathematically related to other measures and thus facilitates comparisons of relationships. It also has the desirable characteristic of varying between -1.00 and 1.00. Note that now, with ordinal data, the negative sign has meaning and indicates a negative relationship. Rho also may be squared (r_s^2) and given the PRE interpretation.

When there are only a few ordered categories and many cases to place into them, the data will contain many ties, far too many for Spearman's rho to be usable. Data of this type are called *partially ordered* and are handled in tabular form, as illustrated in Table 15.5. Several alternative measures of association are available for data of this type. Gamma (γ), Somer's *D*, and Kendall's tau (τ) are all suitable and vary between -1.00 and 1.00. There are, however, some subtle differences among them that make one or another most appropriate in a given situation.

Gamma is the easiest of the three to compute, but unfortunately it does not take into account any of the tied scores and tends to overstate the strength of the relationship. Indeed, on the basis of a positive gamma alone, we cannot safely assume that as *X* increases, *Y* also increases, which is a nor-

Table 15.4 Ordinal Data Suitable for Spearman's Rho

Independent Variable	Dependent Variable
Ranks	*Ranks*
10	9
8	10
1	1
3	5
2	2
9	6
4	7
6	3
5	4
7	8

$r_s = .77$

Table 15.5 Ordinal Data Suitable for Gamma, Somer's *D*, or Kendall's Tau

		Independent Variable (X)		
		Low	Medium	High
Dependent	High	8	10	12
Variable	Medium	10	14	8
(Y)	Low	18	11	4

$\gamma = .38$
$D_{yx} = .27$
$\tau = .27$

mal assumption of a positive relationship. Because of its failure to consider ties, all a positive gamma allows us to conclude is that as *X* increases, *Y* does not decrease, which, of course, is a much weaker conclusion.

Somer's *D* is used when we are only interested in our ability to predict a dependent variable from an independent variable. When predicting *Y* from *X*, Somer's *D* takes into account ties on the dependent variable. This has the effect of reducing the value of *D* in comparison with gamma when the two are computed on the same data. Somer's *D*, however, gives a more accurate indication of how much the independent variable reduces error in predicting the dependent variable.

Finally, Kendall's tau takes into account all the tied scores. It indicates the degree to which the independent variable reduces error in predicting the dependent variable *and* how much the latter reduces error in predicting the former. Because it considers the relationship both ways, tau is particularly appropriate when we do not have a clearly identifiable independent and dependent variable and merely wish to determine if two variables are related. By including all the ties, a positive tau allows us to conclude correctly that as *X* increases, *Y* also increases. As this is the type of statement we expect to make on the basis of a positive result, Kendall's tau is more generally useful than gamma.

Interval Data The most used measure of association for interval data is the *correlation coefficient* or *Pearson's r*. The correlation coefficient is

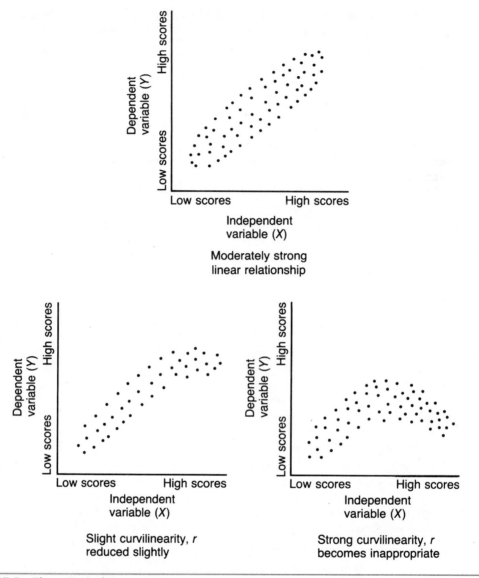

Figure 15.2   Three Typical Scattergrams

mathematically related to both phi and Spearman's rho, making comparisons among them possible. As with the other two, Pearson's r varies between -1.00 and 1.00 and may be squared (r^2) and given the PRE interpretation. When squared, this value is called the *coefficient of determination*.

The correlation coefficient has a unique characteristic that is important to remember when ap-

plying or interpreting it. Pearson's r indicates the degree to which the relationship between two interval level variables can be described by a straight line when plotted on a scattergram as in Figure 15.2. The formula for r mathematically determines the best fitting line and then considers the amount the scores deviate from perfect linearity. This feature of Pearson's r means that, if the relationship between the two variables is somewhat *curvilinear*, r will understate the actual strength of the relationship. Therefore, it is advisable to plot, or have the computer plot, a *scattergram*. A scattergram is a table with the scores of both variables plotted on it. The scattergram provides a visual indication of the relationship between the two variables and is useful for uncovering curvilinearity that might adversely affect the correlation coefficient. Figure 15.2 illustrates three typical scattergrams. In those instances in which curvilinearity is discovered, a measure of association other than Pearson's r should be selected. Curvilinear measures of association do exist, but they are beyond the scope of our discussion. They may be found in more sophisticated textbooks about statistics.

Before we leave measures of association, one important matter requires emphasis. Association or correlation does not imply causality! Just because one variable is labeled independent and another dependent and a relationship is found between them does not prove that changes in one variable caused changes in the other. As we emphasized in Chapter 2, correlation is only one step toward inferring causality. In addition, it is necessary to affirm the appropriate temporal sequence and rule out rival causal variables.

The Normal Distribution

Chapter 14 discusses frequency distributions as descriptive statistical procedures that transform a raw data distribution into a form that is more meaningful. There is another way to transform raw data to derive additional meaning from it, and this transformation will also serve as our transition from descriptive to inferential statistics. A transformation is a set of arithmetical operations that are executed on a variable to obtain a new variable. One common transformation is known as *standardizing*. Raw scores are transformed into *standard scores,* also known as *z-scores.* Symbolically, a standardized score, z, is given by:

$$z = \frac{x - \bar{x}}{s}$$

Standard scores are obtained by following these two steps:

a. Subtract the mean, $\bar{x}$, from each raw score, x.
b. Divide the $x - \bar{x}$ difference by the standard deviation, s, of the distribution.

If all the raw scores in a distribution are transformed to z-scores, a new distribution is obtained that will always have $\bar{x} = 0$ and $s = 1$. This is called a *standard normal distribution,* and, as it turns out, this distribution has some quite convenient properties.

One way to think about the z-transformation is that it expresses raw scores in a distribution in terms of standard deviation units rather than the original unit of measurement. A z-score of 1.5 indicates a score point that is 1.5 standard deviations greater than the mean, whereas a z-score of −1.5 indicates a score point 1.5 standard deviations below the mean. In other words, a standard score, z, is a number indicating the distance that a raw score deviates from the mean as measured in standard deviation units. Furthermore, the sign of a z-score indicates whether the score point is above (+) or below (−) the mean of the distribution.

On first encounter, it may seem strange to express raw scores in terms of standard deviation units, but doing so allows one to make comparisons between distributions that otherwise would be difficult to make because their original units of measurement differ. Standardizing equalizes the units so that a meaningful comparison can be made. For example, the comparison of a person's raw scores on two different IQ tests would not be legitimate unless the IQ tests have a common unit of measurement and operate on the same scale. Therefore, mental testers commonly employ the z-transformation as a way of making different IQ tests comparable.

Consider the data in Table 15.6. In both tests, someone received a score of 99, but are both of those scores really equal? In terms of raw scores they certainly appear to be, but in relative terms — that is, compared to the other scores in the distribution — the 99 on Test 2 is far more remarkable and a z-score transformation will reveal this. On Test 1, with a relatively high mean and small

Table 15.6 Two Sets of Hypothetical Test Scores

	Test 1		Test 2	
	99		99	
	98		45	
$\bar{x} = 94.6$	96		44	$\bar{x} = 49.6$
	95		44	
$s = 3$	95		43	$s = 20$
	93		41	
	91		41	
	90		40	

standard deviation, the 99 transforms to a z-score of 1.46, which means it is 1.46 standard deviations above the mean of 94.6. The 99 on Test 2, with a low mean and high standard deviation, transforms to a z-score of 2.47, which means it is 2.47 standard deviations above the mean of 49.6. The comparison of z-scores shows that the two scores of 99 are, in fact, far from equal compared to the other scores in their respective distributions. Allowing for these types of comparisons to be made is one important use of z-scores.

Another important use of z-scores has to do with what is called the normal distribution. The normal distribution is a continuous, bell-shaped distribution, as shown in Figure 15.3. The **normal distribution** is a symmetrical, unimodal distribution in which the mode, median, and mean are identical. Actually, there is not a single normal dis-

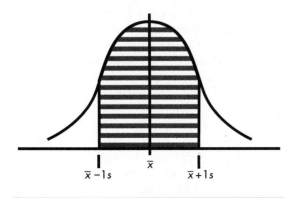

Figure 15.3 Area Under a Normal Distribution at Plus One and Minus One Standard Deviations

tribution, but many. Normal distributions may have different means and different standard deviations, for example. What makes them all normal is that they all are symmetrical and unimodal, and have the three measures of central tendency at the same point. In addition, all normal distributions have the same proportion of cases between the same two ordinates. This statement means that between, say, $+1$ and -1 standard deviations from the mean for any normal distribution, the proportion of the total cases bounded by those points will be the same for all those normal distributions.

In Figure 15.3, the shaded area is the proportion of the total area under the curve bounded by points that are 1 standard deviation on either side of the mean. For any normal distribution, no matter what the mean and standard deviation happen to be, the area bounded by $\bar{x} - s$ and $\bar{x} + s$ is always equal to 68.26 percent of the total area under the curve, whereas 95.46 percent of the total area is between $\bar{x} - 2s$ and $\bar{x} + 2s$. In place of $\bar{x} - s$ and $\bar{x} + s$, one may substitute any two points one wishes and carve out a proportion of the total area that will be the same for all normal distributions. Figure 15.4 shows selected points and the proportions of the total area that fall between them for any and all normal distributions.

This points to another use of z-transformations: They are used to assess the relative position of a score in a distribution of scores. For example, suppose you took a national merit exam and received a score of 580. How well did you do compared to the others who took it? If you know that the scores on this exam are normally distributed, and you know the mean score and standard deviation, then you can calculate your position relative to the others who took the exam. Suppose the mean was 490 and the standard deviation was 72. You could then use the z formula to transform your exam score of 580 into a z-score (standard deviation unit) of 1.25. Tables are available (although not in this book) to look up what proportion of cases fall above or below any point in a normal distribution. From those tables, it can be determined that 89.44 percent of all cases in a normal distribution fall below 1.25 standard deviations

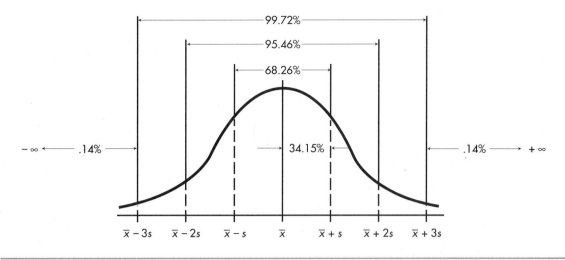

Figure 15.4 Proportions of the Area Under the Normal Curve Between Selected Points

above the mean. So you did better than over 89 percent of all the people who took that examination! Transforming your test score into a *z*-score enables you to make a very precise statement about your place in the distribution relative to others in the distribution.

The standard normal distribution is useful for comparing distributions with different means and standard deviations, and it helps us make precise statements about relative position in a distribution. A third important use of this distribution is that it serves as the foundation for inferential statistics, which will now be the focus of attention.

Inferential Statistics

As noted in Chapter 6, most social research is conducted on relatively small samples drawn from much larger populations, and all the statistical procedures discussed so far are designed to assist in describing, summarizing, and interpreting data from samples. Findings from sample data, however, would be of little scientific value if they could not be generalized beyond the members of the sample to the larger population from which the samples were drawn. For example, it would do other practitioners little good to learn that a researcher had suc-

cessfully raised the school performance of 50 underachievers unless they could reasonably expect the new approach to work on children who were not in the researcher's sample. In other words, for the new technique to be worthwhile, it must be generalizable to members of the population of underachievers.

Probability Theory

How do we know when research findings are generalizable? Generalization is always an uncertain business, but inferential statistics can reduce the uncertainty to the point where reasonably safe generalizations can be made and the probability of a given amount of error estimated. Inferential statistics are based on probability theory, the same probability theory that works to make probability samples representative. Because of this, inferential statistics can be meaningfully applied only to data based on probability samples or experiments in which random assignment has been implemented.

Probability theory allows the mathematical calculation of the likelihood or probability that random events or outcomes will occur. For example, if 10,000 raffle tickets are issued and the winning ticket is chosen in such a way that each ticket has an equal chance of being selected, then each person who purchases one ticket has 1 in 10,000 chances of winning. However, if you buy 10 tickets, then you have 10 in 10,000 or 1 in 1,000 chances of winning. You have increased the probability of your winning even though the mechanism for selecting the winner is unchanged. This does not mean, of course, that you *will* win. Less likely events do occur, although with less frequency than more likely ones, and a person who purchased one ticket could certainly win the raffle. In other words, probability theory tells us the *likelihood* of something's occurring; it does not tell us what *will* occur. For this reason, inferential statistics can tell us whether the odds are on our side that a particular generalization is accurate, but they do not make it a sure bet.

As noted in Chapter 6, probability samples are supposed to represent the populations from which they were drawn, but we expect differences between a sample and its population owing to chance alone. Because these differences are due to the random process used in the selection of samples, their probability can be readily calculated. For example, suppose a researcher draws a probability sample of 50 delinquent boys and applies a special intervention designed to reduce future delinquency involvement. At the end of one year the success rate of the sample is 75 percent, whereas for the population of untreated delinquents the rate is 60 percent. Can we conclude that the experimental intervention was a success? At the level of the sample alone, it is clear that the treated boys had a better rate, but the differences could be due, all or in part, to sampling error. Even with random sampling, the researcher could have obtained a sample of boys who were on average better risks than those in the general population of delinquent boys. The question that inferential statistics answers is whether the difference between the sample results and the population results is too great to be due to chance alone. In the example, running the appropriate inferential statistic would tell us what the chances are of obtaining, through random error, a 15 percent difference between a population and a probability sample drawn from that population. If such a difference were highly probable, we would conclude

that the seeming effect of the experimental treatment was due to chance differences between sample and population. On the other hand, if the result indicated that there was only a small likelihood that a 15 percent differential was due to chance, we would conclude that the treatment did produce a generalizable effect.

Sampling Distributions

Our ability to determine the likelihood that a sample difference is due to chance derives from the properties of the normal distribution, which is discussed earlier in this chapter, and what are called *sampling distributions*. A **sampling distribution** is a distribution of sample statistics. For instance, in the example in the preceding section, a sample of 50 delinquents was selected and had a success rate of 75 percent. We could have selected more samples than this one. We could have selected 10 samples of 50 boys each and computed a success rate on each sample. The success rate found in each sample would probably be slightly different because each sample consists of a different set of 50 boys. For the 10 samples, we might have found the following success rates: 72 percent, 71 percent, 73 percent, 69 percent, 66 percent, 70 percent, 73 percent, 69 percent, 71 percent, 67 percent. These 10 sample results are called a sampling distribution. If we knew the success rate among all delinquent boys in the population that these samples were taken from, this would be referred to as the *population parameter.* Some of the samples will show the same success rate as in the population; other samples will show a success rate higher than the success rate in the population, whereas other samples will show a lower success rate. In other words, the sample success rates will be distributed around the actual success rate in the population from which the samples are taken. Or, a sampling distribution involves sample statistics that are distributed around a population parameter.

This sampling distribution has certain properties that are very important in inferential statistics. In particular, the **central limit theorem** from mathematics tells us that, when a large number of large random samples are selected from a population, the resulting distribution of sample statistics has two key properties: First, the sampling distribution will approximate a normal distribution, and second, the population parameter will be equal to the mean of the sampling distribution. In the example in the preceding paragraph, this means that the distribution of all sample success rates will be normal, and the success rate in the population will be equal to the average of all those sample success rates. This means that we can determine the probability that a sample result will fall between any two points in the sampling distribution, just as we did with z-scores and the normal distribution. It also means that we can determine the probability that a sample result will fall far away from the population parameter. Recall from the earlier discussion that approximately 68 percent of all cases in a normal distribution fall within 1 standard deviation above and below the mean of the distribution, and approximately 95 percent of cases fall within 2 standard deviations. Likewise, in a distribution of samples, 95 percent of the sample results will fall within 2 standard deviations of the mean of the sampling distribution, which is also the population parameter. Only 5 percent of samples will fall more than 2 standard deviations away from the population parameter. Going back to our previous example, we can choose one of two alternatives: (1) the treatment didn't work, and we have selected a sample of boys that, by chance, is very different from the boys in the population (i.e., sampling error), or (2) the treatment worked, and this is what makes the treatment boys very different from the nontreated boys in the population. However, if the success rate in the population is 60 percent and the sample success rate of 75 percent is more than 2 standard deviations away from 60 percent, then the z-transformation will tell us that 75 percent is way out in one of the tails of the normal distribution and obtaining such a sample by chance would be highly unusual. Therefore, we would be on safer grounds, just in terms of probabilities, to conclude that the 75 percent is probably not due to sampling error, but rather is showing that the treatment had an effect on this group of boys.

Although many different kinds of inferential statistics are used, they all follow the basic logic involving sampling distributions and normal distributions just described. The formal process by which researchers decide whether the results of data analysis could be due to chance or are better explained by relationships between variables is called statistical hypothesis testing.

Statistical Hypothesis Testing

When utilizing inferential statistics, we are engaging in a special form of hypothesis testing in which two hypotheses that are precisely opposite of each other are developed. The outcome of a statistical test is then used to determine which hypothesis is most likely correct. The first hypothesis, called the **null hypothesis,** states that no relationship exists between two variables in the population or that there is no difference between a sample statistic and a population parameter. "There is *no* relationship between variable X and variable Y in the population" or "There is *no* difference between the success rate of the sample and the success rate of the population" would be two examples of possible null hypotheses. Alternatives to null hypotheses are called **research hypotheses.** Suitable research hypotheses to go with the two preceding null hypotheses would be: "There *is* a relationship between variable X and variable Y at the level of the population" and "There *is* a difference between the sample success rate and the population success rate." In each application of a statistical test, we assess the research hypothesis by determining whether the opposite null hypothesis is probable or improbable.

It is not uncommon, upon first exposure to statistical hypothesis testing, to question the utility of null hypotheses. If we believe the research hypothesis is true, why not just test that hypothesis? The need for null hypotheses stems from the fact that it is not possible with inferential statistics to prove research hypotheses directly. However, by determining that it is very likely that the null hypotheses are false, we indirectly provide evidence that their opposite, the research hypotheses, are probably true.

To illustrate this point, we will use an example where there is a clear criterion to use in testing a hypothesis. Imagine attempting to determine whether a die is unbiased. If it is, each side should appear approximately an equal number of times—about one sixth of the times the die is thrown. If the die is biased, one or more outcomes will occur a disproportionate number of times—one or more numbers occurring substantially more than one sixth of the time. Suppose the die is tossed 12 times, with each outcome occurring twice, or one sixth of the time. Would this prove the die unbiased? The answer is no. The bias, if it exists, might be too slight to appear after only 12 trials. What if the die is tossed 144 times and still each outcome occurs one sixth of the time? Such a result would still not make it certain that the die is unbiased, for a slight bias might be revealed by even more trials. Indeed, no number of trials would provide absolute assurance that the die is unbiased. However, a large number of trials with no evidence of bias would make the hypothesis of a biased die so unlikely that it is reasonable to reject it. By finding no evidence of support for one hypothesis, we indirectly obtain support for its alternative. In all applications of statistical hypothesis testing, if the evidence fails to support the null hypothesis, then the opposing research hypothesis is accepted as probably true.

Although their computational routines vary, all inferential statistical tests use the properties of sampling distributions and normal curves to yield a result indicating the probability that the null hypothesis is true. In choosing between the competing hypotheses, we ask: How unlikely must it be for the null hypothesis to be true before we are willing to reject it as false and accept the research hypothesis? This is determined by the **alpha level,** or the probability at which the null hypothesis will be rejected (*see* Table 15.7). Researchers have some discretion in setting alpha levels but must guard against the two types of inferential errors that can be made. **Type I** or **alpha error** is the probability of rejecting a null hypothesis that is actually true. The alpha level selected determines the amount of alpha error we are willing to tolerate, so the re-

searcher directly controls Type I error by setting alpha. Alpha levels are usually written as "$p < .20$" and read as "a probability of less than 20 percent." Alpha levels can be understood in the following way. Suppose the null hypothesis is that "no relationship exists between variable X and variable Y in the population." We draw a sample from that population to test the hypothesis and indeed find a relationship in the sample data. An alpha level of .20 means that we would find a relationship as large as we did in 20 percent of the samples we draw even though the null hypothesis is actually true and there is no relationship between the variables in the population. We are now faced with a difficult dilemma: Is the null hypothesis true and our sample an unusual one, or is the null hypothesis false? Inferential statistics can't answer that question for us. It can tell us that, in the long run and by testing many hypotheses, we would be correct 80 percent of the time by rejecting null hypotheses when differences of a given size have an alpha level of .20.

Setting an alpha level as low as .20 makes it easy to reject the null hypothesis, but we are also assured of rejecting true null hypotheses quite frequently. To avoid so much Type I error, we might establish a very stringent alpha, such as .001, meaning that we would reject the null hypothesis only if its odds of being true were less than 1 in 1,000. If the null hypothesis can be rejected at such an alpha level, we would be quite confident that it was false and that we were not committing a Type I error.

But setting extremely rigorous alpha levels raises the probability of making the other possible inferential error. **Type II** or **beta error** is the probability of failing to reject null hypotheses that are actually false. Alpha levels such as .001 make it so difficult to reject null hypotheses that many false ones, which should be rejected, are not. Thus, in selecting suitable alpha levels, we face a dilemma. Guarding against one type of error increases the chances of making the other type. Fortunately, conventions regarding appropriate alpha levels have developed. In general, social researchers operate with alpha levels of .05, .01, or .001. Although these lev-

TABLE 15.7   Illustration of Type I and Type II Errors

	Condition in Population	
Decision	Null Hypothesis Is True	Null Hypothesis Is False
Reject null hypothesis	Type I (alpha) error prob. = alpha	Correct decision (power of test) prob. = 1 − beta
Fail to reject null hypothesis	Correct decision prob. = 1 − alpha	Type II (beta) error prob. = beta

els are the most common ones you will see in research reports, nothing is sacred about them. The researcher must consider the purpose of the research and the alternative risks in selecting a given level. For example, medical research into the safety and effectiveness of new drugs or treatments typically operates with very stringent alpha levels because life and death are at stake. If the null hypothesis in a research project is "Drug X is not safe," then we would want to reject it only if we were very sure that it is false. If it is wrongly rejected, people would be exposed to an unsafe product. On the other hand, a practitioner with a null hypothesis of "Reminder phone calls do not reduce the number of no-shows for clinic appointments" might select an alpha level as low as .10. If the procedure shows any chance of working, the clinic may want to try it. In this case, the consequences of rejecting a true null hypothesis would not be very severe. Some additional issues related to hypothesis testing and alpha and beta errors are discussed in Research in Practice 15.1.

A common way of expressing that the null hypothesis was rejected is to indicate that a given result is "statistically significant" at some specified alpha level. Unfortunately, the use of the word "significant" can cause some confusion. In popular usage, "significant" means important or notable. Its meaning in statistics, however, does not have the same connotation. Whether a set of research findings is important or notable depends far more on the topic, theory, sample, and quality of measurement than it does on statistically rejecting null hypotheses. Research on trivial matters or research that

is procedurally flawed cannot produce important results no matter how many "statistically significant" findings it might contain. Be sure to remember that the meaning of "significant" in statistics is simply that a null hypothesis has been successfully rejected.

Statistical Procedures

Some of the basic considerations for selecting inferential statistical procedures are much like those for selecting descriptive statistics. One important consideration is the nature of the dependent variable. For nominal dependent variables, the commonly used procedures such as chi-square are discussed later. Many additional procedures, such as log-linear analysis, go beyond the scope of this book but are rapidly gaining prominence in the research literature. With ordinal dependent variables, many procedures are, in addition to being applicable to ordered data, compatible with small clinical samples. Furthermore, many procedures that are technically appropriate for interval level data are also used with ordinal variables because they are "robust," or not readily affected by violation of their theoretical assumptions. Finally, many procedures have been developed to handle interval level data, such as Student's *t*, ANOVA (analysis of variance), and regression, which we discuss later.

Beyond the level of measurement in the dependent variable, another consideration is the character of the independent variable. Some procedures are designed for single independent variables with only

Research in Practice 15.1

Program Evaluation: Designed for Failure: Statistical Power in Human Service Research

Although much attention is given to the issue of statistical significance or alpha levels in evaluation research, a related and equally important issue, statistical power, is often overlooked (Kraemer and Thiemann, 1987). *Statistical power* refers to the probability of *correctly* rejecting a null hypothesis in a research study (*see* Table 15.7). Another way of looking at statistical power is to conceptualize a study designed with low power as being a study with a high probability of failure because it cannot detect an intervention that works. For example, if family intervention does actually reduce the extent of problems in families, does the statistical test we apply to a sample of families tell us this? This is a very real problem as evidenced by examinations of published human service research that indicate that almost half of the studies reviewed could not detect even a medium-sized effect (Orme and Combs-Orme, 1986). A consequence of this shortcoming is that policy decisions may be made to curtail or not implement potentially useful innovations. Another important consideration is that a research effort is wasted if it is unable to detect a program effect when it is present.

In the typical human service program evaluation, the investigator formulates a null hypothesis, such as "There is no difference between the treatment group and the control group," expecting to reject it at the specified level of statistical significance or alpha level. The sample data are analyzed and the null hypothesis is then rejected if the difference between the experimental group and the control group is sufficiently large to be considered

an improbable event at the preselected alpha level, such as .05, .01, or .001. An unfortunate error of interpretation is to assume that failure to reject the null hypothesis is equivalent to "proving" that the treatment had no effect. A more correct assessment is that the data generated from this study, *as designed,* failed to detect a difference between the treatment and the control conditions. Unless care is taken in the design of the study, it could well be that the study could not detect an effect, even if it were present.

One reason why inadequate attention has been paid to the issue of statistical power in the past has been that estimating statistical power was a difficult undertaking. Fortunately, this is no longer the case. One major advance was the publication of texts on the subject that included tables making determination of power relatively straightforward (Cohen, 1988). More recently, the task has been simplified even further by the introduction of computer software such as Design Power, previously discussed in Chapter 6 in relation to sampling. Statistical power is determined quantitatively as:

$$1 - beta$$

or

$$1 - (\text{the probability of a Type II error})$$

The beta level is complex to calculate and beyond the scope of this book. For a particular research problem, beta can be looked up in a reference work such as Cohen (1988) or calculated by

two levels. Other procedures handle two or more independent variables simultaneously as well as estimating combined effects.

Finally, another issue concerns how the data were generated. Some procedures such as ANOVA are intended for data generated by an experiment

in which you are comparing one or more control groups with one or more treatment groups. Other procedures, such as regression analysis, are well suited for analyzing large samples, such as surveys, in order to estimate effects. Still other procedures, such as MANOVA (multivariate analysis of vari-

appropriate computer software. Once this is done, the adequacy of beta can be assessed by the following rule of thumb: The minimum acceptable ratio of Type II errors to Type I errors should be about four to one. Thus, if alpha is set at .05, beta should be $4 \times .05$, or .20. Because power equals $1 - $ beta, power equals $1 - .20$, or .80. (This means we have an 80 percent chance to correctly reject the null hypothesis.) Similarly, if alpha is .01, power should be a minimum of .96, and if alpha is .001, power should be a minimum of .996. However, the four-to-one rule is only a general guideline. Which power level is acceptable in a particular research project should be determined by the nature of the research project and its implications.

Reviews of published research studies in the human services and other fields have consistently reported that the actual power of a large proportion of studies is well below these standards of .80, .96, and .996 (Orme and Tolman, 1986). What can be done to improve the power of a research project? Although the concept of power is complex, it has three major determinants: sample size, alpha level, and effect size. By manipulating them, one can improve statistical power.

The larger the sample, the greater the statistical power of a research project. Therefore, a simple solution to increasing power may be to increase the sample size. Another potential solution is to reduce the alpha level or probability of a Type I error. Because Type I and Type II errors are related, it may be preferable to use a lower alpha level such as .1 instead of .05 as a way of increasing power.

Although these two strategies may be an important part of a solution, the best approach may be to take steps to increase the effect size of the independent variable in the study sample. Other things being equal, the larger the effect of the independent variable relative to other factors, the more likely the null hypothesis will be rejected. One way to increase effect size is to select samples that minimize error and assure that a high proportion of the difference between treatment and control groups is due to the independent variable (see Chapters 6 and 10 on error). Another solution lies in taking steps to eliminate as much extraneous variation as possible. Thorough training of service providers, careful rehearsal of procedures, and attention to program detail can all serve to eliminate variation due to factors other than the program effect. We don't often think of social interventions in terms of "dosage," but the evaluation researcher should also make sure that the participants receive a sufficient dose of the independent variable to make a difference. If the program is financial aid, it might be better to give a small sample large amounts of aid instead of giving a little aid to many. If the program is counseling, the program should provide an intensive counseling experience. Using the most valid and reliable measurement tools can help detect a difference that exists between groups.

The issue of statistical power in research underscores the necessity of planning projects thoroughly from the initial stage of problem formulation. By the time data analysis is conducted, it is probably too late to take steps to achieve adequate power. The solutions lie in the design formulation, the sampling procedure, and the conduct of the study. Only by envisioning the data analysis requirements from the beginning of the project can studies achieve their goal of determining the effect of an intervention effort.

ance and covariance), are suitable for both statistical control of nonexperimental variables and analysis of experiment-generated variables at the same time. Many of these procedures are highly complex and beyond the scope of this text. However, our point is that specific factors favor the use of some statistical procedures over others. It is important to select the appropriate procedures. Through other courses, you may learn to utilize and select the procedures yourself, or, as a human service professional, you may rely on outside consultants to assist you with this aspect of your research.

In experimentation, one often makes comparisons between a control group and a treatment group. If these two groups are comparable in all respects except for the treatment received, a commonly used statistic is Student's t. This statistic compares the mean of one group against the mean of the other. Recall from the chapter on sampling that the groups may have different means by chance alone. Large differences, however, suggest a treatment effect. But what is a large difference? The answer depends on the scale of the variable being measured and on the size of the samples. The t test results in a statistical value that is referred to a table for samples of different sizes. The table indicates the probability of obtaining a value that is as large or larger by chance. If the table value is less probable than the alpha level, one rejects the null hypothesis and concludes that the difference is significant. Tables indicating the value of t and of other inferential statistics necessary for rejecting null hypotheses at various alpha levels may be found in any introductory statistics textbook. If you are using a computer package such as SPSS, the significance value is provided for you.

In many experimental situations, the research involves more than only two groups. The researcher may also want to measure the difference between groups. For example, if four treatment groups each receive different amounts of tutorial help, we might be interested in the effect each level of help has on the number of problems the members of the different groups can solve. For this situation, involving an experimental design and an interval level dependent variable (number of problems solved), a commonly applied statistical procedure is analysis of variance (ANOVA). ANOVA compares the variability in the scores of members within each group (within group variance) with variability between treatment groups. We would not expect all members of a treatment group to do equally well. In fact, even if one level of treatment works better than another, some members of a lower group might do better than some members receiving a better tutorial program. ANOVA permits the researcher to estimate how much of the variance in performance between groups is due to the treatment.

Another commonly used statistical procedure is multiple regression analysis. Multiple regression is used for a variety of purposes, but a typical application involves estimating the effect of multiple independent variables. For example, we might be interested in determining if a person's income is influenced by gender, race, and age—plus, *how much* each of these variables affects income. As discussed earlier, correlation will indicate whether two variables are associated, but regression permits one to estimate how much change in the dependent variable is produced by a given change in an independent variable. Multiple regression is especially useful in that it can handle a large number of independent variables simultaneously, thus permitting researchers to estimate the effects of one variable while controlling for others. We know, for example, that income is correlated with race, education, age, and occupation, among many other variables. If we collect these data from a number of respondents, regression permits us to estimate the contribution of each independent variable to income. Multiple regression produces coefficients that indicate the direction and amount of change in the dependent variable to be expected from a unit change in the independent variables. Thus, if the dependent variable is dollars of income, a regression coefficient of $+580$ for the variable "years of education" indicates that one more year of education is "worth" an additional \$580 in income, assuming the other independent variables are held constant. In our illustration, regression would produce an equation as follows:

$$Y' \text{ (income)} = a + b_1 \text{ (race)} + b_2 \text{ (education)} + b_3 \text{ (age)} + b_4 \text{ (gender)}$$

where a = value of Y before other factors' effects are considered, b_1 is an estimate of the effect of race on income, b_2 is the estimated effect of education, b_3 is the estimated effect of age, and b_4 is the estimated effect of gender.

A widely used inferential statistic suitable for nominal data is chi-square (χ^2), which is applied to data in tabular form. The several versions of chi-square allow its application to data of different types. All these versions, however, operate by com-

TABLE 15.8 Hypothetical Data Relating Race and Religion

Religion	Race			
	White	**Black**	**Other**	
Protestant	actual: 50 expected: 123	actual: 120 expected: 61.5	actual: 35 expected: 20.5	205
Catholic	actual: 150 expected: 108	actual: 20 expected: 54	actual: 10 expected: 18	180
Jewish	actual: 100 expected: 69	actual: 10 expected: 34.5	actual: 5 expected: 11.5	115
	300	150	50	*N* = 500

paring the number of cases actually found in the cross-classification of two or more variables with what would be expected by chance. For example, Table 15.8 shows a sample of 500 community residents cross-classified by religion and race. Chi-square compares the actual values in a table such as this with what would be expected if the variables were unrelated. Table 15.8 also contains these expected values, which can be determined from the marginals in the table. For example, because whites make up 60 percent of the whole sample, we would expect 60 percent of the Jews, or 69 out of 115, to be white if the variables of religion and race were unrelated. Due to random variation, one would expect that the actual values will not be exactly the same as the theoretically expected values even when there is no relationship. However, the more the actual cell frequencies in a sample diverge from the expected frequencies, the more likely it is that an association exists between the two variables at the level of the population.

Small values of chi-square indicate little or no association, whereas large values indicate that an as-

sociation is likely. With chi-square, the value of the statistic is influenced by sample size and by the number of categories on each variable. Computer data analysis packages automatically take this into account in reporting significance level; however, when doing hand calculations, one must refer the statistical value to a special table that states the probability of obtaining a χ^2 of that magnitude by chance, given the sample size and number of variable categories. Chi-square does not indicate the strength of the association but whether one exists at the level of the population.

In this chapter, we have presented a basic introduction to the statistical analysis of data. For the consumer of research, this introduction provides some basic guidelines for interpreting statistical analyses that you will encounter in reading research. Those who will conduct research and engage in statistical analysis themselves will need to go beyond the materials presented in this chapter. For such people, we have suggested a few valuable books to consult in the For Further Reading section.

COMPUTERS IN RESEARCH
Statistical Software

Although computing statistics by hand or by pocket calculator is possible, most data analysis today is done with a computer. In the past, and sometimes even today, statistical analysis was done on mainframe computers. Four of the more popular statistical packages for mainframe computers are SPSS, SAS, BMDP, and MINITAB. With the advance in computer technology, however, microcomputers are replacing mainframes for many of these tasks. This has placed computerized statistical capability at the disposal of virtually anyone who wishes to use it. At the same time, the bewildering array of software has made program selection a complicated choice.

Because researchers now use the computer for so many different tasks, we can no longer evaluate statistical software solely on the basis of the number of statistical procedures it can run—we must also consider the other applications of the software. Fortunately, several excellent sources are available for assistance in selecting statistical software. Many popular periodicals about computers, such as *Byte* and *InfoWorld,* publish articles evaluating software (*see,* for example, Carpenter, Deloria, and Morganstein, 1984; Fridlund, 1986; Lehman, 1987). These and other magazines are widely available in bookstores and at newsstands. In addition, many professional journals also contain articles on statistical software. One of the better sources for social

research applications is *Social Science Computer Review.* Because of rapid innovation in software, it is best to consult current issues for up-to-date developments.

Although this wide availability of computer software makes statistical analysis easier, it also may tempt some into using statistical procedures inappropriately: just because they are listed on the menu, look familiar, sound exotic, or produce impressive looking output. One need only specify the procedure and identify the data to be used, and the computer does the rest. However, even though the procedure may be "successful" in the sense that output is generated, the analysis may not be the most appropriate—it may even be wrong and cause a misleading conclusion. So how does one determine the best data analysis procedure or the most appropriate statistic to use? There is no substitute for a solid grasp of the objectives of the research and an understanding of the assumptions underlying statistical procedures on the part of the researcher. However, several computer programs can help the researcher identify key issues and systematically put that knowledge to use.

One example is the program *Statistical Navigator Professional* (Malcolm, 1992). This program does not analyze data; rather, it generates a report that presents options for data analysis from more than 200 statistical procedures and a description of how

Main Points

- The major considerations in choosing statistics properly are the level of measurement of the variables, the goals of the research, the number of variables involved, the properties of the data, and the audience.
- Descriptive statistics are procedures that assist in organizing, summarizing, and interpreting sample data.

- Measures of central tendency, or averages, summarize distributions by locating the central value of frequency distributions.
- Measures of dispersion indicate how dispersed or spread out the values are in a distribution, with most indicators revealing the average spread of the scores around the central value.
- Measures of association indicate the strength of relationships, and, with ordinal or higher-level

well each option fits the stated objectives and assumptions of the research. The program is an example of a so-called expert system in that the program contains information for decision making that the user accesses by answering questions presented by the computer. The software leads the user through an interview by presenting questions on the screen. The answer to one set of questions determines the next set of questions to appear. Based on the user's responses, the computer selects appropriate data analysis procedures. It should be emphasized that the program does not select the statistic for the user; rather, it guides the user through the steps necessary to choose a proper statistic.

The steps of the computerized process are revealing in that they parallel how a careful researcher should go about selecting a statistical procedure. A "consultation" begins with the specification of the objectives of the analysis. One way of doing this is to choose the appropriate description from several lists of research objective categories. For example, you could indicate whether the objective is descriptive (that is, to provide summary statistics) or inferential (to draw a conclusion about a population). Another option is to enter a phrase describing the research and have the program attempt to identify the desired category. After determining a general category, the program then asks questions regarding the researcher's assumptions about the data, such as whether the data distribution is normal and whether observations are independent. Finally, the

program asks which statistical analyses would customarily be used in this area of research and compares these with the choices made.

The program prepares a report that includes as many as four statistical procedures, rated by how well they match the assumptions and objectives of the researcher as well as the expectations of the intended audience. The report also includes a comprehensive description of each selected test, complete with references and a list of statistical software packages that include the test. In addition to conducting a "consultation," the program has a "browse" feature that enables the user to review the program's material on definitions and information about statistical procedures. This feature enables the user to learn more about statistical procedures or to recall specifics about procedures without need of an outside reference source.

Using a computer program such as *Statistical Navigator Professional* does not ensure that a researcher will always select the appropriate statistic. Nor can one expect it to replace a knowledge of research methods and data analysis. But using the program requires the researcher to consider assumptions about the data and requirements for analysis as well as the objectives of the study. Thus, the program does not eliminate the researcher's responsibility to evaluate and select the best data analysis option. Instead, it systematizes the selection process, makes a large amount of technical information immediately accessible, and encourages the researcher to consider design options that might otherwise be overlooked.

data, they also indicate the direction of relationships.

■ Data are sometimes transformed into z-scores or standard normal distributions. These distributions enable us to compare distributions with one another, assess the relative position of cases in a distribution, and conduct inferential statistics. The properties of the normal distribution are very important in this regard.

■ Inferential statistics are procedures that allow generalizations to be made from sample data to populations from which the samples were drawn. Inferential statistics derive from the properties of the normal distribution, sampling distributions, and the central limit theorem.

■ In inferential statistics, a research hypothesis is paired with an opposite null hypothesis and the results of a statistical test are used to decide which is most likely correct.

■ Particular inferential statistics are linked to level of measurement. Among the inferential statistics are Student's *t*, analysis of variance, regression, and chi-square.

Important Terms for Review

alpha error
alpha level
beta error
bivariate statistics
central limit theorem
descriptive statistics
inferential statistics
measures of association
measures of central tendency
measures of dispersion
multivariate statistics
normal distribution
null hypothesis
proportional reduction in error (PRE)
research hypothesis
sampling distribution
Type I and Type II errors
univariate statistics

Exploring the Internet

One of the exciting features of the Internet is that it permits you to quickly access and use resources from anywhere in the world. A great example of this is a Web site in Australia called SurfStat. It's worth going "down under" if more information on data analysis is what you seek. The URL for Surf Stat is http://frey.newcastle.edu.au/Stats/surfstat/surfstat.html. Actually, this site is much more than simply a site devoted to statistical methods. It contains some excellent illustrations of many research issues, including the concepts of spurious relationships, sampling, and statistical inference. This site also includes links to many other sites devoted to statistics.

Other Web sites can help you to actually carry out data analysis tasks. For example, we have discussed the issue of statistical power in Research in Practice 15.1. There are Internet sites that permit you to enter parameters about your data set and to receive statistical power calculations as output. One such site is Power Calculator, provided at the following URL: http://www.stat.ucla.edu/~jbond/HTMLPOWER/. This Internet site permits you to determine power statistics for several different kinds of data analysis problems. Another site, which is easier to use but limited to only a few types of statistical problems, calculates the power of a design for a given sample size. It can also be used to determine the size sample you need, depending on the statistical power requirements that you specify. This Internet site is called Inference for Means: Comparing Two Independent Samples; it can be accessed at http://www.health.ucalgary.ca/~rollin/stats/ssize/n2.html.

Finally, we have mentioned several different data analysis software programs in the course of this chapter. You can learn more about data analysis software by contacting software firms at their Internet addresses. One way to locate such sites is to simply enter the name of the software, for example, "SPSS," in a search engine. Many social science research–related sites also include links to these sites. For example, the Internet site for ERIC (located at http://ericae2.educ.cua.edu/) has a link entitled "statistics." Simply select it and the site provides links to SPSS, SAS, and several other software sites.

For Further Reading

Aron, Arthur, and Elaine N. Aron. *Statistics for the Behavioral and Social Sciences.* Upper Saddle River, N.J.: Prentice-Hall, 1997. This very readable introduction to statistics explains the issues clearly and minimizes the use of formulas.

Cuzzort, R. P., and James S. Vrettos. *Elementary Forms of Statistical Reasoning.* New York: St. Martin's, 1996. This fairly brief textbook introduces statistical analysis to the student. It focuses more on the logic of statistics and how to reason through problems rather than on computational issues.

Evans, James D. *Straightforward Statistics for the Behavioral Sciences.* Pacific Grove, Calif.: Brooks/Cole, 1996. This is a standard but well-written introductory textbook in statistics. It covers all the topics discussed in this and the preceding chapter, going into more detail and including additional topics.

Gravetter, Frederick J., and Larry B. Wallnau. *Statistics for the Behavioral Sciences,* 4th ed. Minneapolis: West, 1996. This text provides a fairly comprehensive introduction to both descriptive and inferential statistics. It can serve as an important resource and reference work as you learn statistics.

Healey, Joseph F. *Statistics: A Tool for Social Research,* 4th ed. Belmont, Calif.: Wadsworth, 1996. This is another standard but well-written introductory textbook in statistics. Along with the Evans book, it can help you understand all the material in this and the preceding chapter.

SPSS. *SPSS 6.1 for Windows Brief Guide.* Chicago: SPSS Inc., 1995. This is a brief introduction to using the Windows version of the statistical package SPSS that is mentioned a number of times in this chapter. Windows software is so easy to use that this short intro-duction to SPSS will actually equip the student to begin using other Windows statistical software.

Exercises for Class Discussion

A community mental health agency operates a program called Assertive Community Treatment for chronic mentally ill persons. The goal of the program is to enable the mentally ill to live in their own community with as few restrictions as possible and to prevent rehospitalization, which is extremely expensive. In addition to providing and monitoring medications, the program provides a drop-in center, therapy groups, arts and crafts, a 24-hour emergency service, and regular contact with a case management team. The agency converted its record keeping to computer databases several years ago, but has not used the data in any systematic way to evaluate program effectiveness. The agency asks your help in deciding which of several hundred

Variable Name	Description	Permissible Range of Values
HOSPDAYS	Number of days hospitalized during fiscal year	Integer values from 0 to 366
HYESNO1 to HYESNO12	Was patient hospitalized at all during a given month? (HYESNO1 = January, HYESNO2 = February)	0 = No, 1 = Yes
CMANHR1 to CMANHR12, CMANHRAL	Case manager hours devoted to the case each month (CMANHR1 = January, CMANHR2 = February, CMANHRAL = sum for year)	Any value from 0 to 200
GAS1 to GAS12	Goal attainment rating score; completed by case manager on each client each month on client progress toward treatment goals	1 = low, 2 = medium, 3 = high
RESSTAT	Residential status: living alone, with roommate, in group home, or with family member	1 = alone, 2 = roommate, 3 = group home, 4 = family, 5 = other
MEDUSE1 to MEDUSE12	Case manager estimate about patient compliance with medication regime	1 = poor, 2 = good, 3 = excellent
CRISIS1 to CRISIS12	Did the patient have an emergency contact with center during month?	0 = No, 1 = Yes

variables they should use, and what statistical procedures would be appropriate. The table below presents a selection of some of the variables available, together with coding information.

1. Classify each of the variables in this data set as nominal, ordinal, interval, or ratio. Compare your classification with other students and discuss any cases that are difficult to classify.
2. You run a frequency distribution procedure on all the variables. There are 120 total cases. You notice that HOSPDAYS range from 0 to 57. However, 117 of the cases had 15 days or less hospitalization while the remaining 4 cases are 35, 48, and 57, respectively. Which measures of central tendency and dispersion would you use with this variable and why?
3. Which measure(s) of association would be appropriate for examining each of the following relationships?

HOSPDAYS — CMANHRAL
HYESNO1 — MEDUSE
MEDUSE — GAS1
CRISIS1 — HYESNO1
HYESNO1 — CMANHR1
CRISIS1 — GAS1
GAS1 — GAS2

4. Similar programs are used throughout the state with approximately 15,000 patients. Assume that the same data are available from the other programs and that a random sample of 600 patients is selected. Identify three research questions that you could ask from this data. For each question, state the research and null hypotheses and indicate the alpha level to use for Type I error.

CHAPTER 16

Writing for Research: Grant Proposals and Report Writing

The Grant-Funding Process   428
  Federal Government Funding Sources   428
  State Government Grants   429
  Private Funding Sources   430
  Learning About Funding Opportunities   434

Grant Proposal Planning   435
  Proposal Development as a Process   435
  Identifying the Topic   437
  Needs Assessment   438
  Specifying the Organization's Mission   438
  Developing a Program   439
  Targeting a Funding Source   440
  Contacting and Visiting Funding Sources   441

Writing the Grant Proposal   443
  Appearance and Writing Style   443
  Components of the Proposal   444
  Submitting the Proposal   447

Writing a Research Report   447
  Consideration of the Audience   448
  Organization of the Report   449
  The Process of Writing   451

Main Points   452

Important Terms for Review   453

Exploring the Internet   453

For Further Reading   453

Exercises for Class Discussion   454

This chapter focuses on two very important elements of applied research that are often neglected in introductory research methods texts: the role of grants in research and the importance of good writing. The term **grant** refers to the provision of money or other resources to be used for either research or service delivery purposes. Grants are an important funding source for both social research and the provision of human services. In fact, the amount of grant monies awarded each year is truly staggering. For example, at the federal level, the National Science Foundation (NSF), a major provider of grants for research, distributed more than 2.75 billion dollars in 1992. The National Institutes of Health, which provides grants for both research and action programs, served up more than 10 billion dollars in 1992 (*Chronicle of Higher Education,* 1992). Private foundations gave out grants worth more than 8 billion dollars in 1995, the last year for which data are available (*The Foundation Directory,* 1996). Indeed, vast sums are dispersed through the system of grants. Given the large role grants play in funding research and some activities of nonprofit human service organizations, it is highly likely that you will be directly involved in a grant-funded project as a professional human service worker.

Despite the pervasiveness of grants, a person might properly feel shell-shocked if given the task of preparing a grant proposal without previous experience. Grant writing is sometimes perceived as a mystical process with strange jargon and convoluted procedures in which only seasoned professionals with an inside track are successful in receiving funds. The neophyte would understandably have many questions. What do I do first? Whom do I contact? What do they want to know? Although the prospect of one's first grant proposal can be daunting, preparing a fundable proposal involves many of the principles of sound practice and research that are part of professional education. If approached systematically, writing grant proposals can be an interesting challenge rather than something to be feared.

In the space available, we can neither explore all aspects of grantsmanship nor go into much detail. We focus on obtaining grants for agency functions, including both service delivery and research purposes. In fact, grants for service delivery typically include a call for needs assessment data and an evaluation of the service delivery; therefore, many grants combine practice and research activities. Depending on the demands of the funding source, minor differences may arise between preparing a proposal for a research project, service delivery, or a combination of the two. Those serious about seeking grants should consult one or more of the listings in For Further Reading. We conclude this chapter with a more general discussion of the writing process—to assist in writing grant proposals as well as research reports.

The Grant-Funding Process

Sources of grant money fall into three general categories: government agencies, private foundations, and corporations (Smith and McLean, 1988; Bauer, 1995). Of these, government agencies are by far the largest source of grant monies. They are also about the only sources of large grants of more than a few thousand dollars. Even in the case of smaller grants, it often pays to start first with government sources because many of the private foundations refuse funding automatically unless you can prove that efforts to obtain government funding have failed. Among government agencies, branches of the federal government are the largest source for grant money, so we discuss these first.

Federal Government Funding Sources

Project or Categorical Grants *Project* or *categorical grants* (the terms are synonymous) are narrowly focused on some specific need or problem as defined by some agency of the federal government.

Grant seekers design approaches, within specified guidelines provided by the government agency, to meet the need or ameliorate the problem specified by the government agency. The agencies make their requests for programs or research opportunities known through what is called a Request For Proposals (RFP), which is a formal request for people or agencies to submit proposals on how they would conduct some research or establish and run some program. Agencies or researchers then submit proposals in a competition to obtain the grant money. Grants are then awarded to those submitting the best proposals within the guidelines established by the granting agency.

Formula Grants   *Formula grants* are part of large-scale, nationwide federal programs and serve as mechanisms for allocating the funds for the programs. For example, at a time of high unemployment, the federal government commonly sponsors various "job-creating" activities through formula grants. Because unemployment is experienced in varying levels of severity in various places in the country, the money would be allocated by a "formula" (hence their name) that provides most of the funds to those areas hardest hit by the problem and prorates the remainder of the funds to other areas as needed. Normally, formula grants are channeled through state and local governments until they reach the agency level. This allows each state and locality to tailor its approach to the problems of its particular situation. For example, unemployment in one locale may be concentrated among displaced factory workers, while in another among minority teenagers. The most effective approach in the first locale may be retraining programs, but the second locale may benefit more from having its teenagers taught basic job skills such as showing up regularly and on time for work. So, unlike the categorical grants, formula grants allow the applicant more freedom in designing the research project or program as long as it serves the general goals of the grant monies.

Block Grants   *Block grants* are similar to formula grants in that they are a transfer of funds from the federal government to the states, which then do the final allocating to state agencies and on through to nonprofit service providers. Block grants are different in that they cover much broader areas, such as maternal and child health or elementary and secondary education, and are ongoing year after year. In fact, there are only nine categories of block grants, but they represent the largest transfer of funds from the federal government to the states.

Federal Contracts   Though not strictly grants, federal government contracts can be an important source of funds. With contracts, it is the government that decides precisely what it wants and how it wants it done. Very little flexibility is left to the researcher or service provider. The government is looking for agencies that can perform the desired tasks at the lowest price. Sources of information about contracts and the rules under which they are awarded are different from grants. Also, the number and variety of contracts is vast, so that considerable research may be needed to get involved with the contract side of the federal government. However, despite the obstacles, nonprofit agencies are moving into contracts as a new way to fund research and services. To describe how to begin dealing with contracts requires a whole book; our purpose in mentioning contracts is to alert you to a resource that is not currently being fully exploited by agencies.

State Government Grants

Although states have always dispersed some of their own tax revenue through the granting process, the rise of federal block grants and the occasional formula grant have greatly expanded the dispersal of funds at the state level. Because each state disperses these monies differently, we cannot make any blanket statements about how to bid successfully for these funds. Regarding block grants, something consistent across all states is a federally mandated series of open meetings to discuss how the grant money should be used. Although showing up and speaking at these meetings will not ensure that you

Table 16.1   50 Largest Foundations by Total Giving

Name	Total Giving	Assets	Fiscal Date
1. The Ford Foundation	$285,226,002	$6,600,562,000	09/30/94
2. W. K. Kellogg Foundation	222,691,781	6,034,576,655	08/31/95
3. The Pew Charitable Trusts	157,169,536	3,298,723,548	12/31/94
4. The Robert Wood Johnson Foundation	135,861,955	3,754,153,612	12/31/94
5. John D. and Catherine T. MacArthur Foundation	116,279,275	2,914,554,520	12/31/94
6. The Annenberg Foundation	112,996,033	1,387,238,383	06/30/95
7. The Andrew W. Mellon Foundation	105,627,655	2,191,323,000	12/31/94
8. Lilly Endowment, Inc.	99,354,052	3,093,752,921	12/31/94
9. The Rockefeller Foundation	93,260,988	2,364,552,922	12/31/93
10. Robert W. Woodruff Foundation, Inc.	63,217,640	1,732,729,896	12/31/94
11. The David and Lucile Packard Foundation	62,745,546	1,544,060,433	12/31/94
12. The Kresge Foundation	60,083,081	1,470,803,425	12/31/94
13. DeWitt Wallace-Reader's Digest Fund, Inc.	58,925,583	996,413,188	12/31/94
14. Soros Humanitarian Foundation	54,166,275	67,653,205	11/30/93
15. The McKnight Foundation	53,800,000	1,100,000,000	12/31/94
16. The Annie E. Casey Foundation	52,919,831	1,057,683,986	12/31/94
17. Charles Stewart Mott Foundation	51,505,688	1,203,825,430	12/31/94
18. The Harry and Jeanette Weinberg Foundation, Inc.	51,000,000	990,900,000	02/28/95
19. The New York Community Trust	50,965,342	964,123,681	12/31/94
20. The Duke Endowment	48,002,147	1,260,115,470	12/31/94
21. Carnegie Corporation of New York	45,723,708	1,126,710,522	09/30/94
22. The Starr Foundation	45,061,546	1,053,640,633	12/31/94
23. Arthur S. DeMoss Foundation	44,645,433	321,830,798	12/31/94
24. Lila Wallace-Reader's Digest Fund, Inc.	43,539,839	756,689,830	12/31/94
25. Alfred P. Sloan Foundation	40,986,123	789,637,993	12/31/94
26. Lucille P. Markey Charitable Trust	36,813,070	138,597,600	06/30/94

will get a grant, it will help to assure that some money is allocated for the area of your greatest concern. Another way to increase your chances of getting state grant monies is to keep in contact with the state departments and agencies that oversee and fund research and services related to the human services, such as the department of corrections, the department of mental health, and the department of social services. These state agencies may also publish RFPs as a way of soliciting grant proposals.

Private Funding Sources

Foundations   A *foundation* is a nonprofit, legally incorporated entity organized for the purpose of dispersing funds to projects that meet the guide-

lines of its charter. The number of private foundations is staggering, upwards of 35,000 (Krathwohl, 1988; Bauer, 1995). However, you probably won't need to search through all of these to find one to support your project. First, not all foundations are created equal. The largest 20 percent of foundations control 97 percent of foundation assets, so this narrows the number of likely prospects considerably. Second, most foundations award only small grants. Only about 500 foundations typically give grants in excess of $5,000 each. Submitting a proposal, no matter how noble the purpose or how well prepared the paperwork, that calls for a grant of, say, $20,000 to a foundation that has never awarded more than $5,000 in any one grant is probably a waste of time. The person looking for a small grant must begin looking at some of the other character-

Table 16.1 *Continued*

Name	Total Giving	Assets	Fiscal Date
27. The William Penn Foundation	35,996,782	636,000,000	12/31/94
28. John S. and James L. Knight Foundation	34,406,412	742,507,878	12/31/94
29. Open Society Institute	33,778,501	6,349,939	12/31/93
30. Houston Endowment, Inc.	32,416,988	834,433,658	12/31/94
31. AT&T Foundation	32,155,414	128,300,496	12/31/93
32. The Freedom Forum International, Inc.	32,077,001	728,610,392	05/31/94
33. The Cleveland Foundation	30,723,125	733,950,639	12/31/94
34. The Corella & Bertram Bonner Foundation, Inc.	30,140,704	55,123,448	06/30/94
35. The Lincy Foundation	30,114,645	76,233,137	09/30/94
36. The Brown Foundation, Inc.	29,244,114	645,837,056	06/30/95
37. Robert R. McCormick Tribune Foundation	29,060,610	685,950,254	12/31/94
38. The San Francisco Foundation	28,762,376	325,268,333	06/30/95
39. Marin Community Foundation	28,241,000	563,199,000	06/30/94
40. The James Irvine Foundation	28,055,673	664,190,220	12/31/94
41. The Ahmanson Foundation	27,379,600	546,412,884	10/31/94
42. The Chicago Community Trust	26,957,224	406,536,600	09/30/94
43. Howard Heinz Endowment	26,887,433	557,781,996	12/31/94
44. The Whitaker Foundation	26,184,884	364,115,016	12/31/94
45. W. M. Keck Foundation	25,974,000	843,941,117	12/31/94
46. US WEST Foundation	25,830,483	16,029,000	12/31/94
47. Joseph B. Whitehead Foundation	25,639,000	587,644,539	12/31/94
48. The William and Flora Hewlett Foundation	25,612,008	985,735,924	12/31/94
49. Weingart Foundation	25,470,597	489,789,727	06/30/94
50. The Lynde and Harry Bradley Foundation, Inc.	25,306,728	393,142,629	12/31/94

Source Reprinted with permission from *The Foundation Directory,* 18th ed., © 1996 by the Foundation Center, 79 Fifth Ave., New York, NY 10003.

istics of foundations in order to sort through the possibilities and find those few most likely to fund the proposal. In general, however, private funding sources are good places to seek grants for agency activities or applied research because they prefer to fund action programs that produce immediate results rather than research projects that, at best, have some long-term payoff. Also, the complexity of proposal preparation and submission is much less than that encountered with federal agencies. Table 16.1 presents a list of the 50 largest foundations by total giving.

Types of Foundations There are five distinct types of foundations. *Community foundations* exist to serve their immediate local area. Therefore, if a project is modest in scale and serves some local need, a

community foundation may be a good choice. *General purpose foundations* are often large, such as the Ford Foundation, and operate nationwide. If a project is large in scope, with the potential of having an impact broader than the local community, these large foundations may be ideal. They particularly like innovative demonstration projects that may show the way for other communities to solve various problems. *Special purpose foundations* carve out a particular area of interest and award grants only to projects that deal directly with that area of specialization. Successful funding from these sources requires some research into which foundations fund what kinds of projects. Fortunately, large foundations typically publish annual reports, much as corporations do, outlining recently funded projects (Krathwohl, 1988). From these lists, one can

over 450,000 children in fiscal years 1988 and 1989.

REGULATIONS, GUIDELINES, AND LITERATURE: Chapter XIII of Title 45 Code of Federal Regulations, including 45 CFR parts 1301, 1302, 1303, 1304, 1305. These are available on request at no charge.

INFORMATION CONTACTS:

Regional or Local Office: Regional Program Director, Children, Youth and Families (see Appendix IV of the Catalog for list of addresses of Regional Offices).

Headquarters Office: Administration for Children, Youth and Families/Head Start, Office of Human Development Services, Department of Health and Human Services, P.O. Box 1182, Washington, DC 20013. Telephone: (202) 755-7782.

RELATED PROGRAMS: 10,550, Food Distribution.

EXAMPLES OF FUNDED PROJECTS: (1) Full-Year and Full-Day Head Start Programs: (2) Full-Year and Part-Day Head Start Programs; and (3) Parent and Child Center Programs.

CRITERIA FOR SELECTING PROPOSALS: (1) The degree to which the proposed project will meet the Head Start Program Performance Standards or other program objectives as specified in a program announcement; (2) reasonableness of cost; (3) qualification of staff; and (4) other criteria, which are detailed in every program announcement.

13.608 ADMINISTRATION FOR CHILDREN, YOUTH AND FAMILIES—CHILD WELFARE RESEARCH AND DEMONSTRATION

FEDERAL AGENCY: OFFICE OF HUMAN DEVELOPMENT SERVICES, DEPARTMENT OF HEALTH AND HUMAN SERVICES

AUTHORIZATION: Social Security Act, as amended; Title IV, Part B, Section 426, Public Law 86-778; Public Law 96-248, 42 U.S.C. 626.

OBJECTIVES: To provide financial support for research and demonstration projects in the area of child and family development and welfare.

TYPES OF ASSISTANCE: Project Grants.

USES AND USE RESTRICTIONS: Grants are for: (1) special research and demonstration projects in the field of child welfare which are of regional or national significance; (2) special projects for the demonstration of new methods which show promise of substantial contribution to the advancement of child welfare; and (3) projects for the demonstration of the use of research in the field of child welfare. Contracts are for the conduct of research, evaluation, or demonstration projects.

ELIGIBILITY REQUIREMENTS:

Applicant Eligibility: Grants: State and local governments or other non-profit institutions of higher learning, and other nonprofit agencies or organizations engaged in research or child welfare activities. Contracts: any public or private organizations.

Beneficiary Eligibility: Children and families.

Credentials/Documentation: Nonprofit organizations which have not previously received OHDs program support and must submit proof of nonprofit status. Applicable costs and administrative procedures will be determined in accordance with Parts 74 and 92 of Title 45 of the Code of Federal Regulations, which implement the requirements of applicable OMB Circulars No. A-87, No. A-21, and No. A-122.

APPLICATION AND AWARD PROCESS:

Preapplication Coordination: Limited consultation available at Headquarters Office. The standard application forms, as furnished by DHHS and required by OMB Circular No. A-102, must be used for this program. This program is excluded from coverage under E.O. 12372.

Application Procedure: Application form, including budget request and narrative description of project proposal to be submitted to the headquarters Office. This program is subject to the provisions of OMB Circular No. A-110 and No. A-102.

Award Procedure: Review by at least three nonfederal professionals.

and Families.

Deadlines: Determined annually for new projects. Application for continuation grants must be received 90 days prior to the start of the new budget period.

Range of Approval/Disapproval Time: From 90 to 180 days.

Appeals: None.

Renewals: Renewals and extensions available through formal submission of progress reports and continuation application.

ASSISTANCE CONSIDERATIONS:

Formula and Matching Requirements: There is no statutory formula. Grantees are required to provide at least 5 percent of total direct costs. Amount of matching required is specified in all announcements of availability of grants. This may be either cash or in kind, fairly evaluated.

Length and Time Phasing of Assistance: Grant may be for 1 to 3 years; average duration is 17 months.

POST ASSISTANCE REQUIREMENTS:

Reports: Financial and progress report quarterly; final report and final expenditure report at completion of study.

Audits: In accordance with the provisions of OMB Circular No. A-128, "Audits of State and Local Governments," State and local governments that receive financial assistance of $100,000 or more within the State's fiscal year shall have an audit made for that year. State and local governments that receive between $25,000 and $100,000 within the State's fiscal year shall have an audit made in accordance with Circular No. A-128, or in accordance with Federal laws and regulations governing the programs in which they participate. All other grantees are required to have institutional audits every 2 years in accordance with 45 CFR 74.62.

Records: All financial records are to be maintained 3 year after termination of study, or until audit is completed, whichever occurs first.

FINANCIAL INFORMATION:

Account Identification: 75-1636-0-1-506.

Obligations: (Grants and Contracts) FY 87 $7,786,000; FY 88 est $8,457,000; and FY 89 est $13,244,000. (NOTE: The funds in this program are also available for program contracts. The amounts which can be used for such contracts cannot be predetermined.)

Range and Average of Financial Assistance: $10,000 to $250,000; $100,000.

PROGRAM ACCOMPLISHMENTS: (1) Supported efforts to design models to improve service system response to the needs of emancipated or nearly-emancipated youth; (2) developed coordinated approaches between child welfare, developmental disabilities, and mental retardation agencies to maximize available resources at service at the State and local level; (3) provided public social service agencies, State and local juvenile and family court judges with guidelines or criteria for determining what constitutes "reasonable efforts" to avoid out-of-home placement for children, including an analysis of the factors contributing to the failure of Family Based Child Welfare Services; (4) assisted States in implementing effective Child Welfare licensing policies and procedures; (5) implemented or improved the delivery of preplacement preventive services, particularly through the provision of these services by non-profit organizations; (6) developed effective techniques for the intervention and provision of emergency services to depressed and suicidal youth; (7) disseminated and documented the use of information concerning positive characteristics that produce strong families and responsible family guidance in matters such as health, education, career preparation, and the social and emotional growth of children and youth.

REGULATIONS, GUIDELINES, AND LITERATURE: No regulations specific to this program. Annual Priority Statements, applications and submission deadline information are available at no charge.

INFORMATION CONTACTS:

Regional or Local Office: Not applicable. All requests should be directed to Headquarters Office.

Headquarters Office: Chief Discretionary Program Branch, Administration for Children, Youth and Families, Office of Human Devel-

---

Figure 16.1 Illustration from the *Catalog of Federal Domestic Assistance*

opment Services, OS, P.O. Box 1182, Washington, DC 20013. Telephone: (202) 755-7420.

RELATED PROGRAMS: 13.623, Administration for Children, Youth and Families—Runaway and Homeless Youth; 13.652, Administration for Children, Youth and Families—Adoption Opportunities; 13.670, Administration for Children, Youth and Families—Child Abuse and Neglect Discretionary Activities; 13.766, Health Care Financing Research, Demonstrations and Evaluations.

EXAMPLES OF FUNDED PROJECTS: (1) Achieving Economic Self-Sufficiency; (2) A Unique Partnership to Promote a New Method of Funding Child Care; (3) Defining Reasonable Efforts; (4) Illinois Child Welfare Licensing Initiative; (5) Comprehensive Child Care Benefits Package; (6) A Knowledge Transfer Project for Strengthening Families; and (7) Demonstration of the Utilization of the Minority Volunteer Network for Child Welfare.

CRITERIA FOR SELECTING PROPOSALS: An assessment is made of the degree to which a proposal promises to meet the specific program objectives defined in the program announcement, considering reasonableness of cost, qualifications of staff and adequacy of methodology.

13.612 NATIVE AMERICAN PROGRAMS— FINANCIAL ASSISTANCE GRANTS

FEDERAL AGENCY: OFFICE OF HUMAN DEVELOPMENT SERVICES, DEPARTMENT OF HEALTH AND HUMAN SERVICES

AUTHORIZATION: Native American Programs Act of 1974, Section 803, Public Law 93-644, 42 U.S.C. 2991 et seq., as amended.

OBJECTIVE: To provide financial assistance to public and private nonprofit organizations including Indian Tribes, urban Indian centers, Native Alaskan villages, Native Hawaiian organizations, rural off-reservation groups, and other Native American organizations for the development and implementation of social and economic development strategies that promote self-sufficiency. These projects are expected to result in improved social and economic conditions of Native Americans within their communities and to increase the effectiveness of Indian Tribes and Native American organizations in meeting their economic and social goals.

TYPES OF ASSISTANCE: Project Grants (Contracts).

USES AND USE RESTRICTIONS: Grants may be used for such purposes as, but not limited to: (1) Governance Projects, to promote self-governance of programs formerly operated by Federal employees; (2) Economic Development Projects, to promote business starts for Indian-owned businesses in manufacturing, trade, retail, and agriculture; improve Indian housing management; and to develop a Tribal health care system; and, (3) Social Development Projects to assume local control of planning and delivering social services in Native American communities. In addition, funding is now available for a revolving loan fund for Native Hawaiian organizations.

ELIGIBILITY REQUIREMENTS:

Applicant Eligibility: Public and private nonprofit agencies, including but not limited to, governing bodies of Indian tribes on Federal and State reservations, Alaskan Native villages and regional corporations established by the Alaska Native Claims Settlement Act, and such public and nonprofit private agencies serving Hawaiian Natives, and Indian organizations in urban or rural nonreservation areas.

Beneficiary Eligibility: American Indians, Native Alaskans, and Native Hawaiians.

Credentials/Documentation: Nonprofit organizations which have not previously received OHDS program support must submit proof of nonprofit status. Applicable costs and administrative procedures will be determined in accordance with Parts 74 and 92 of the Code of Federal Regulations, which implement the requirements of applicable OMB Circulars Nos. A-87, A-21, and A-122.

APPLICATION AND AWARD PROCESS:

Preapplication Coordination: The provisions of OMB Circular No.

A-102 apply to grantees which are State and local governments. The standard application forms, as furnished by DHHS and required by OMB Circular No. A-102, must be used for this program. This program is excluded from coverage under E.O. 12372.

Application Procedure: Information regarding the availability of grant funds will be published from time to time in the Federal Register as Program Announcements, which will provide details on program objectives for which applications are being solicited and other application requirements. The Administration for Native Americans will provide each applicant agency with the appropriate forms for the application for Federal Assistance and instructions for applying for grants from OHDS programs. Applications should be submitted to OHDS Grants Management Branch, Department of Health and Human Services, Room 345-F, 200 Independence Avenue, SW., Washington, DC 20201. This program is subject to the provisions of OMB Circulars No. A-110 and No. A-102.

Award Procedure: All funds are awarded directly to the grantees.

Deadlines: Program Announcement 13612-881, Competitive Financial Assistance for Projects to promote Social and Economic self-sufficiency for Native Americans has a closing date for receipt of applications on May 20, 1988.

Range of Approval/Disapproval Time: Applicants will receive notice of approval/disapproval approximately 90 days after receipt of application.

Appeals: Appeals procedures are published in 45 CFR 1336.52.

Renewals: Not applicable.

ASSISTANCE CONSIDERATIONS:

Formula and Matching Requirements: This program has no statutory formula for distribution of funds. A matching share of 20 percent is required unless waived in accordance with criteria which are also published in 45 CFR 1336.50. This program has maintenance of effort requirements; and waiver requirements are contained in 1336.50. See funding agency for further details.

Length and Time Phasing of Assistance: Grantees may apply for competitive continuation support within a project period of 1 to 3 years.

POST ASSISTANCE REQUIREMENTS:

Reports: Quarterly Financial Status Reports, Report of Federal Cash Transactions, and Project Progress Reports are required.

Audits: In accordance with the provisions of OMB Circular No. A-128, "Audits of State and Local Governments," State and local governments that receive financial assistance of $100,000 or more within the State's fiscal year shall have an audit made for that year. State and local governments that receive between $25,000 and $100,000 within the State's fiscal year shall have an audit made in accordance with Circular No. A-128, or in accordance with Federal laws and regulations governing the programs in which they participate. All other grantees are required to have institutional audits every 2 years in accordance with 45 CFR 74.62.

Records: Financial records, supporting documents and all other related records pertinent to ANA grants must be maintained for a period of 3 years. If an audit is not completed by the end of the 3-year period, or if audit findings have not been resolved, records shall be retained until resolution of the audit findings.

FINANCIAL INFORMATION:

Account Identifications: 75-1636-0-1-506.

Obligations: (Grants) FY 87 $27,300,000; FY 88 est $28,257,000; and FY 89 est $27,979,000. (NOTE: The funds in this program are also available for program contracts. The amounts which can be used for such contracts cannot be predetermined.

Range and Average of Financial Assistance: (Tribal Grants) $20,000 to $860,000; $125,000 (Urban Grants) $30,000 to $210,000; $100,000.

PROGRAM ACCOMPLISHMENTS: The program currently serves approximately 968,000 out of an estimated 1.6 million Native Americans. Financial assistance is provided for Native American community projects, research evaluation, technical assistance and

Figure 16.1 *Continued*

tell the sorts of issues and projects that various foundations are interested in and willing to support.

Family foundations are the most difficult to categorize because there are so many—more than 30,000 according to Bauer (1995)—and they are so different. Some are large and have the resources to award fairly substantial grants, whereas others have a cap on grant size of a few thousand dollars. Some are quite general in the projects they fund, whereas others have very narrow interests. For example, some may fund only projects that benefit a particular religious or ethnic group while others fund only projects that address a particular problem, such as alcoholism or child abuse.

Corporate foundations are used by some corporations as the conduit for corporate philanthropy. Other corporations engage in philanthropy but do not use the foundation mechanism. In either case, nonprofit agencies are common recipients of corporate giving. To maximize your chances of sharing some of this corporate wealth, you must understand a few things about corporate giving. As investor-owned, profit-making enterprises, corporations are giving away the stockholders' money. As such, the directors who make the philanthropic decisions are cautious to fund only those activities that can be justified to the stockholders. This tends to mean that the corporation or its employees must stand to benefit in some way from funded projects. For example, a nonprofit child care facility used by many corporate employees might receive a corporate grant or other corporate support. Also, because of this need to benefit, corporate giving is concentrated largely in areas where the corporations have their offices, headquarters, or manufacturing facilities.

Learning About Funding Opportunities

Given all the separate agencies and organizations that disperse grants, how do you find specific funding opportunities? Publications and computer databases are available that can help. The *Catalog of Federal Domestic Assistance (CFDA),* for example, describes all federal government programs. Figure 16.1 provides an illustration from the catalog of a

program run by the Department of Health and Human Services. As you can see, the catalog supplies information valuable to the grant seeker. It explains the objectives of the program, the steps in the application process, examples of funded projects, and criteria for selecting proposals. To make the search of the catalog quick and effective, an online computerized system called the Federal Assistance Program Retrieval System (FAPRS) has been developed. The FAPRS allows you to use certain key words to match your proposed project with federal agencies that would be the most likely funding source. This system is similar to some you may have used to conduct library searches. For information on how to obtain an FAPRS search, write to the Office of Management and Budget, Budget Review Division, Federal Program Information Branch, Washington, DC 20503. Another electronic version of the CFDA is called *GrantSearch CFDA,* available from Capitol Publications.

Grant seekers can use their personal computers to search for funding opportunities through the use of the *Grants Database* prepared by Oryx Press. This is also available in CD-ROM or online (contact Oryx Press or Knight Ridder Information Services). Oryx Press also has a printed version available titled *Directory of Research Grants.* It is the most comprehensive source of current information on grants offered by government, corporate, and private funding sources. In addition to its convenience, the database has the advantage of being updated monthly, unlike conventional publications that may become dated. Any agency that depends on grants as a routine source of funding should investigate subscribing to the *Grants Database.*

Another useful publication is the *Federal Register.* This daily, magazine-size volume reports on the activities of the federal government. Although it includes a lot of information of little use to the grant seeker, new programs are announced first in it; so it is a good resource for the ever-changing opportunities in obtaining federal funding. Guidelines for obtaining funding under the new programs are also first provided in the *Federal Register.* Eventually, this information gets into the CFDA, but because that is only published annually, many months could pass before a new program gets listed in the latest edition. The *Federal Register* is also available through several computer search services, and there is a CD-ROM version called Compact Disc Federal Register.

Many funding agencies publish periodic newsletters or bulletins describing their latest activities and programs. It is easy to get on these mailing lists. They often contain RFPs; searching the RFPs, you may find an opportunity for your organization.

A special guide to corporate foundations, *Corporate Foundations Profiles,* is offered by the Foundation Center. This useful volume presents detailed descriptions of the largest 250 corporate foundations and less detailed information on 470 more. This directory, among other things, allows you to determine which corporations have operations in your area and might therefore be likely prospects for funding.

Also published by the Foundation Center is *The Foundation Directory.* It contains a list of foundations of all types, organized by the state in which they are incorporated. While at first this may seem strange, remember that except for the very large nationwide organizations, foundations tend to limit their funding geographically. As illustrated in Figure 16.2, the directory supplies a considerable amount of information about each foundation—information that is useful in the sorting-out process. For example, the financial information gives some idea of the size of grants that a foundation typically makes. It also provides information on "purpose and activities," "types of support," and "limitations" to further screen potential funders. Also, procedures for making applications are described and memberships of boards of directors are provided. For those in the business of seeking grants, *The Foundation Directory* is an essential tool. Another publication from the Foundation Center, *Foundation Fundamentals: A Guide for Grant Seekers* (Margolin, 1991), is particularly useful for the beginner. It outlines the services of the center along with information on locating foundations, preparing proposals, and submitting proposals to private foundations.

The Annual Register of Grant Support: A Directory of Funding Sources, like *The Foundation Directory,* is an excellent source of information on grant sources. Of particular interest to human service professionals is that funding sources are organized according to funding purposes. One category is "Special Populations," which includes subcategories for African Americans, Native Americans, Spanish-speaking people, and women. Additional listings for children and youth, community development, crime prevention, and public health and social welfare are covered under "Urban and Regional Affairs" (*Annual Register of Grant Support,* 1996).

The Foundation Center also provides a computerized search service called COMSEARCH. Several different types of searches can be made. For example, foundations can be selected by type of topic area that they fund, geographical region they focus on, or the dollar amount of grants typically made. These searches quickly and easily narrow the range of foundations to the most likely prospects.

For more information on locating funding opportunities, see Krathwohl (1988), Smith and McLean (1988), or Bauer (1995).

Grant Proposal Planning

The grant-funding process involves two players: the funding sources, who sift through proposals seeking worthy projects in which to invest, and the agencies with project ideas that deserve funding. Getting the two together is the heart of the granting enterprise. Having described the funding sources, we now turn to the second process, namely, the development of a fundable proposal (Miner, 1996).

Proposal Development as a Process

Let us explode one myth about obtaining grants: Successful proposals are not started and finished in short order. Rather, they are developed in detail and carefully honed over time. The preparation of grant proposals should be considered an ongoing, continuing function within an agency, rather than a sporadic event. The reasons for this will become clear as we proceed through the grant preparation

Entry number — 1228
The Philip L. Graham Fund ▼
Street address — c/o The Washington Post Co.
1150 Fifteenth St., N.W.
Person to whom inquiries should be addressed — Washington 20071 (202) 334-6640
Contact: Mary M. Bellor, Pres.

Establishment data — Trust established in 1963 in DC.

Year-end date of accounting period

Assets at market value (M) or ledger value (L)

Total expenditures figure

Amount and number of grants paid

Separate information on amount and number of employee matching gifts, grants to individuals, or loans

Donor(s): Katharine Graham, Frederick S. Beebe, ‡ The Washington Post Co., Newsweek, Inc., Post-Newsweek Stations.
Foundation type: Independent
Financial data (yr. ended 12/31/94): Assets, $55,803,245 (M); expenditures, $2,916,512; qualifying distributions, $2,886,262, including $2,826,485 for 145 grants (high: $300,000; low: $1,000; average: $5,000–$25,000).

Areas of foundation giving — Purpose and activities: Support for raising standards of excellence in journalism. Grants also for arts and culture, education, social welfare with an emphasis on youth agencies, and civic and community affairs.
Fields of interest: Journalism & publishing; arts/cultural programs; early childhood education; education; human services; youth, services; community development.

Types of grants and other types of support — Types of support: Capital campaigns; building/renovation; equipment; endowment funds; program development; seed money; matching funds.

Specific limitations on foundation giving by geographic area, subject focus, or types of support — Limitations: Giving primarily in the metropolitan Washington, DC, area. No support for national or international organizations, or for religious organizations for religious purposes. No grants to individuals, or for medical services, research, annual campaigns, operating expenses, conferences, publications, tickets, films, or courtesy advertising; no loans.
Publications: Application guidelines, program policy statement, grants list.

Printed material available from the foundation

Application information — Application information: Application form not required.
Initial approach: Letter, telephone, or proposal
Copies of proposal: 1
Deadline(s): Feb. 1, May 1, Aug. 1, and Nov. 1
Board meeting date(s): Spring, summer, fall, and winter
Final notification: 6 months
Officers and Trustees:* Mary M. Bellor, Pres.; Martin Cohen,* Treas.; Donald E. Graham, Katharine Graham, Theodore M. Lutz, Vincent E. Reed, John W. Sweeterman.

Officers and trustees or other governing bodies

Staff — Number of staff: 1 part-time professional.
EIN: 526051781

Selected grants — Selected grants: The following grants were reported in 1993.
$60,000 to Federal City Council, DC. 2 grants: $35,000 (For DC COPE (Committee on Public Education)), $25,000 (To develop staffing and management plan for DC Public Schools).
$25,000 to Youth for Tomorrow, Bristow, VA. For residential school for teenage boys.
$20,000 to Allen Community Outreach Center, DC. For social services to poor.
$20,000 to Archbishop Carroll High School, DC. For computer lab for school programs.
$15,000 to Ellington Fund, DC. For Duke Ellington School for the Arts.
$10,000 to Arizona State University, Walter Cronkite School of Journalism and Telecommunication, Tempe, AZ. For equipment for broadcast department.
$10,000 to Dance Exchange, DC. For community outreach programs.
$10,000 to Family Friends of the National Capital Area, DC. For respite care for medically fragile children.
$10,000 to Youth Leadership Metropolitan Washington, Springfield, VA. For youth leadership training.

IRS Identification Number

Figure 16.2 Explanation of Sample Entry From *The Foundation Directory*

Source Reprinted with permission from *The Foundation Directory,* 18th ed., copyright © 1996 by the Foundation Center, 79 Fifth Ave., New York, NY 10003.

process, but all too often grants are begun in haste and rushed to partial completion to meet some fast-approaching deadline. The result, too often, is rejection.

When conceptualized as a process instead of a single event, grant development has many principles in common with the research process introduced in Chapter 1. When the grant is for the purpose of conducting a research project, the connection with the research process is obvious, but a sound understanding of research principles is also directly applicable to grants for service delivery. In seeking funds, the prospective grantee must identify a problem, hone this into a well-defined and manageable topic, develop objectives for the project, search the literature to devise a method of intervention, and plan an evaluation strategy. Furthermore, just as one research study leads to new questions for study, lessons learned in one grant-funded project lead to new ideas for further projects.

In this section, we describe a number of key elements of the grant-funding process. They are not a series of sequential steps but rather a number of separate and interconnected elements that can be accomplished in different orders at different times. Some are ongoing activities of agencies while others are specific things that must be done at a particular point. Together, they culminate in and make possible the actual writing of the grant proposal, which we discuss in the next section. As a way of promoting the concept of the generation of grant proposals as an ongoing part of agency activities, the use of a *proposal development workbook* (PDW) is recommended (Bauer, 1995). This looseleaf binder becomes the mortar that holds the building blocks of a proposal together. As the proposal develops from a vague idea to a full-blown project— complete with demonstration of need, evidence of community support, funding source possibilities, and much more—the PDW is used to organize all the things that go into a successful proposal. As the various components of the proposal are obtained or completed, they are placed conveniently in the PDW. Agency staff should be encouraged to be watchful for items to contribute.

For example, favorable news stories about the proposed project are effective demonstrations of community support that help to influence funding decision makers. Some of the materials in the PDW for one project might also be useful for a later project.

Identifying the Topic

Before we can begin filling our PDW, of course, we need an idea that can be developed into a fundable proposal. Problems that need to be solved exist in abundance, and many sources of research problems are discussed in Chapter 4. What tend to be in short supply, however, are innovative ways of attacking them. One approach is to organize brainstorming sessions (Bauer, 1995). Members of the staff are divided into small groups and told to develop as many possible solutions or approaches to the selected problem as they can. All of these proposed solutions are recorded for further consideration. The goal is to generate ideas, not come to a consensus as to which solution is "best." In fact, it is desirable to maintain alternative approaches to the problem. One or another may be more palatable politically to a particular funding source, and the chances of obtaining a grant can be significantly enhanced by choosing a solution favored by a funding source.

Once ideas are produced in the brainstorming sessions, they need to be evaluated. Thanks to group dynamics, wildly impractical or just plain stupid ideas usually never make it out of the group. Realistically, however, some of the ideas will be better than others. We want to sort the best few to save for building into a proposal. One important part of this evaluation is to work out cost-benefit or cost-effectiveness analyses (*see* Chapter 12). The cost-benefit analyses reveal whether the suggested solutions are economically viable. With any luck, one or more of the considered approaches will show benefits outweighing costs. The cost-benefit analyses of the chosen approach will also be important later as they become one of the arguments for funding the proposal. Cost-effectiveness analyses, of course, allow selecting the approaches that produce the greatest effect for the least cost. Being able to argue that the project for which you are seeking funding was the most cost effective of the several considered can only be looked on favorably by the decision makers at the funding source.

Needs Assessment

One of the most important components of a successful grant application is establishing the existence of some problem or need that requires amelioration. All funding sources must operate within their annual budgets, so the competition for available funds is fierce. If you can make the case that the problem or need you wish to address is most pressing, you will have greatly increased your chances of being funded. There are a variety of ways of making a case for your proposal, and those successful include information from more than one source. The core of the evidence supporting the existence of need will likely come from a *needs assessment survey.* With a properly drawn sample, it is possible to make quite accurate estimates concerning the extent of some need within a given population. Additional supporting evidence can come from *key informants,* or people who are particularly close to and knowledgeable about the problem at issue. *Community forums* can be held to gather testimony about the problem. Examples of individuals suffering from the problem can be used as *case studies,* which illustrate the problem in more human terms than abstract statistics. Finally, data from *public records* may be used as additional evidence of need. Bauer (1995) makes the useful analogy between the grant seeker and a lawyer preparing a case for trial. Each wishes to prepare as persuasive a case as possible to influence a set of decision makers (jury or review panel) to reach the desired conclusion. In the case of obtaining grants, documenting need is a crucial part of making your case. Just as it is not enough for a defendant to be innocent of the crime to be found not guilty by a jury, it is not enough for a need to exist in order to convince a funding source to fund a proposal that deals with it. In both situations, evidence must be gathered and the case presented to the decision makers with great care in order to generate a favorable verdict.

In some cases, it may be possible to obtain a grant to conduct needs assessment research. Recall that needs assessment is one of the focal areas considered in this text. Especially with problems we know little about, funding agencies might be willing to fund a survey to obtain more information. In other cases, a funding agency may require that a needs assessment survey be included as part of a larger funding proposal which may include a service delivery program that affects the problem. In any event, needs assessment often plays an important part in the grant-funding process.

Specifying the Organization's Mission

Not only must you document the need for services or research, you must also convince the funding source that your organization is the proper site for a program to address that problem. This entails demonstrating to the funding source that the problem described in the needs assessment is within your organization's domain or mission. Many organizations such as universities have formal mission statements that appear in official publications. However, such statements are often global in nature and may not be adequate for your purpose. At a minimum, the mission statement should include how and why the organization was started and its primary goals. Generally, funding sources look more favorably on organizations with a history and a track record of accomplishment related to the project to be funded. A new organization might have to work hard to prove its viability. The mission statement should also address current activities of the agency because organizations change with the changing needs of society—an organization that originated for one purpose may be doing very different things today. Finally, the mission statement should include future plans. Funding sources like organizations that appear to be serious and well managed. One way of demonstrating this is by showing that your group plans its future moves carefully.

Another way to convince a funding source that your agency is best suited for a particular project is to focus on the "uniqueness" of your agency. The goal here is to set your agency apart from others that might be similar. There is a tendency to think that one agency is not that much different from others that provide similar services. But with some thought (and perhaps another brainstorming session) you should be able to come up with some things about your agency that make it special in some way. Perhaps it is your geographical location, such as a particularly remote area or proximity to a large minority population. Possibly, something is unusual about your clientele or staff. Or maybe your problem-solving approach is different and uniquely successful. With a little careful consideration, you should be able to develop ways to portray your agency as uniquely qualified to address the need you have documented.

Developing a Program

The most crucial component of any proposal is the research or service project itself. Having established a need, it is necessary to translate that need into specific outcomes for the project and to develop a plan by which those objectives can be achieved. In the case of a research grant, such as a proposal to evaluate the effectiveness of a client advocacy program in a state department of mental health, the task is fundamentally one of preparing a detailed blueprint of the stages of the research process presented in the first chapter. Hypotheses must be developed and a method of testing these hypotheses devised. Issues of subject selection, study design, and data collection and analysis must be taken into account. A service delivery grant requires specification of exactly what will be done to address the need. Direct connections between the goals of the project and the program content must be explicated. Even though service delivery may be the primary emphasis of the proposal, most grants require an evaluation component; so a strategy for monitoring the program and securing data for evaluation purposes must be included.

An important consideration is the time-sequencing of the project. Before subjects can be interviewed, interviewers must be trained and instruments need to be selected or developed. How long will each of these steps take? Must certain staff be hired before the activities can take place? Accounting for all these details requires developing a work plan. The work plan shows the flow of procedures from beginning to end of the project and identifies how the various activities fit into a coordinated plan. Although a simple time schedule with beginning and ending dates for various phases may suffice for some projects, the use of graphics, such as a flow chart, is often convincing—and may be preferred. Such charts can clearly portray the relationships among elements of the project, when each element begins and ends, and which elements overlap. Planning the steps of the project and determining the amount of time for each requires a great deal of effort, but it is effort well spent. For one, it forces the agency to analyze how the various parts of the program fit and function together. It also serves to uncover difficulties before the proposal is written and approved, avoiding, for example, the discovery midway through the project that some significant and expensive component was overlooked. Finally, when the time comes to develop the budget and ask for dollars, the plan serves as justification for the resources.

A number of tools have been developed to aid in developing the work plan. Two of the most common tools are PERT (Program Evaluation Review Technique) and CPM (Critical Path Method). In using these techniques, a collection of tasks is specified that, when completed, results in a final outcome, which in this case is the completed project. Circles, rectangles, and arrows are used to graphically illustrate the progression of events. The technical details of PERT and CPM are beyond the scope of this text. Computer programs are also available that employ these program-planning principles. For IBM and compatibles there are *SuperProject* from SORCIM/IUS and *Microsoft Project for Windows* from Micro Software. Apple has a similar program for its Macintosh line called *MacProject*. A major advantage of these programs is that you can readily see the budgetary impact of changing situations by manipulating the variables that affect the budget (that is, play "What if"). For example, you could readily determine how much an extra full- or part-time employee would cost over the life of the program by inputting a single different number. Likewise, all other costs can be easily evaluated and a final budget prepared far more accurately than without this useful technology.

Targeting a Funding Source

By this point, you will have amassed the raw material of a proposal, including a clear idea of the problem, data on the need, the preferred program alternative, and cost estimates for the components of that alternative. Before one can organize the final proposal, though, consideration must be given to potential funding sources. As a first step, the most appropriate organizations should be identified from among the myriad government agencies and private foundations. However, sending numerous duplicate proposals to whichever funding sources appear most receptive probably won't work. Proposals must be tuned specifically for each funding source because each has different rules and needs. This requires research into the various funding sources—their rules of submission, project areas they have funded in the past, and their particular political viewpoints. Once you have a list of possible funding agencies, you begin to narrow the list. One consideration is whether your organization has any advocates who are associated with the funding agency or can make contact with the agency.

By *advocates,* we are referring to individuals who can not only speak on your behalf to funding sources but also offer guidance and advice throughout the funding process. Previously, we described the grant seeker preparing a proposal as analogous to a lawyer preparing a case for trial. That analogy applies once again in the area of using advocates to help make your case for the grant. The lawyer uses witnesses to help convince a jury. Advocates are the grant seeker's witnesses, and they supply testimony favorable to your proposal to funding sources. Like the attorney, grant seekers need to envision how advocates might be viewed and select those who can make the most favorable impression because advocates can play a key role in the final outcome.

The best advocates are people who are favorably disposed toward your agency and the proposed project and who have some influence on the funding source. In this respect, securing grant funding is a political process, requiring strategies similar to those used by practitioners in community practice. The range of people who could help influence a funding source is vast and difficult to discuss in general terms, but some possibilities include people with membership on both your agency's and a funding source's governing boards, members of your staff (don't forget spouses) with special contacts at funding sources, politicians at all levels who support your efforts, and agency volunteers who may have useful contacts.

Once your advocates are identified, along with the funding sources they can help with, it is time to put them to use. Advocates can be helpful in a variety of ways. At the initial stage, they can help put you in contact with representatives of the funding sources in order to establish a working relationship. They can set up appointments for you with funding sources, they may even accompany you while visiting a funding source, and they may know someone at the funding source who can help ensure that your proposal receives a fair and complete review. When you actually write the proposal, advocates can provide letters of support. All these efforts are intended to increase the likelihood that a proposal will receive attention. Funding agencies have limited resources, and they receive many more proposals than they can possibly fund. No matter how numerous or powerful, no collection of advocates substitutes for a worthy project and a well-prepared proposal. In all of this we are assuming that those two conditions are met. Advocates are important because a meritorious proposal is in competition with others also deserving. It is when decision makers are forced to choose from among numerous worthy proposals that advocates come into play.

```
                              Date:


Name
Title
Address

Dear _____:

    Our organization is interested in carrying out a project
under your program title _____. The project will
deal with meeting the needs in the area of _____.

    Please add me to your mailing list to receive the necessary
application forms, program guidelines and any existing
priorities statements or information that you feel would be
helpful to me. Please include a list of last year's grant
recipients under this program.

    If my project is ineligible under your current guidelines or
there are no funds available, could you please refer me to a
more appropriate agency?

    I have enclosed a self-addressed stamped envelope for your
convenience in returning the list of successful grantees. Thank
you for your cooperation and assistance in this matter.

                         Sincerely,



                         Name
                         Title
                         Phone Number
```

Figure 16.3   Elements to Be Included in a Letter to a Federal Agency to Obtain Information About Grants

Contacting and Visiting Funding Sources

Having identified a particular agency or foundation as a likely funding source, contact them quickly. Doing so can substantially increase the chances of funding (Krathwohl, 1988; Margolin, 1991). If effective advocates are available, they could make the first contact. Otherwise, contact first by letter. Figure 16.3 contains some of the elements that such a letter might include. A letter based on these elements would inform the agency of your intent, and it will obtain for you some much needed forms and other information. Assuming that the agency's initial response is not negative, such as "no funds available," it is then time to arrange for a personal visit. Call the agency and request an appointment. Before the meeting, though, you have some homework to do.

Note that one element in Figure 16.3 requests a list of last year's grant recipients. Before visiting the agency, you should contact one or more of these successful organizations. The range of useful information they can supply is vast. They have experience with the agency, and there is no substitute for that in learning the ins and outs of successful grantsmanship with that particular agency. Each agency develops its own particular style of operating as well as a perspective on problems and ways to solve them. You must learn about these bureaucratic idiosyncrasies from the past grant recipients so that you can tailor your proposal to best fit what the agency is looking for.

With your homework now complete, it is time to make the actual visit to the agency. This visit is to accomplish three general purposes. First, it will confirm or reject the selection of this agency as a likely funding source. With large federal agencies that offer funding under numerous special programs, information gained during your visit assures that you are applying to the agency most appropriate for your project (Krathwohl, 1988; Margolin, 1991). For example, a research proposal would likely be rejected if submitted to a program designed to fund action-oriented projects even though it might have been funded under some other program controlled by the same agency. Depending on their reaction, you should leave the agency with a pretty good sense of the chances of receiving funding from them. Second, the visit supplies you with additional information on how best to tailor the proposal to the agency's special needs, thus increasing the chances for funding (Table 16.2 suggests some things that can be learned during a visit to an agency). Krathwohl (1988) suggests that agency personnel may be enthusiastically helpful for some proposals because funding successful projects reflects positively on the agency and its employees. He urges seeking out and obtaining as

Table 16.2 Things to Learn on a Visit to a Granting Agency

- Does the funding agency have a real commitment to funding in the area of the proposed project as evidenced by previous grants funded?
- Does the amount of funds requested in the proposed grant fit within the granting agency's typical range of funding?
- What proportion of agency grants go to new projects as opposed to the continuation of currently running projects? Will this proportion change in the coming year?
- Does a new grant from an agency like mine have a chance for funding, especially when competing against those requesting a continuation of funding?
- To see what has worked in the past, can we review grant proposals that have received funding from this agency in the past?
- What are the most common reasons for rejecting a grant proposal submitted to this agency?
- What is the most common mistake that people make when submitting a grant request to this agency?
- Can we submit a draft of our grant proposal to this agency and receive feedback before submitting the final proposal?
- Are there any "packaging" guidelines that must be followed or the proposal will not be seriously considered (e.g., length, number of copies, binding, format, etc.)?
- What are the deadlines for submitting a grant proposal?

much assistance as agency staff are willing to provide. Third, the visit provides a personal touch for your proposal when it is submitted. Instead of representing a faceless organization, the proposal will be from people who are known personally and who made an impressive presentation of a serious need and their plans to fill it.

At some point during your visit, you will have the opportunity to discuss your plans with one or more agency executives. This, quite obviously, is a very important part of the visit and should be prepared for carefully. The most important part of this presentation is the demonstration of need, so present all the evidence you can marshal. Even if the agency has reservations about either your organization or your plans to satisfy the need, if you have convinced them of genuine need, they are more likely to work with you to modify your plans rather than give you an outright rejection. Be sure to use whatever video aids are appropriate because a visual impact can be effective and helps to demonstrate thorough preparation.

Writing the Grant Proposal

Having identified a topic, collected supporting documentation that confirms the need for action or research, formulated a method for addressing the problem, and targeted a funding source, you have completed the groundwork. Actually writing the proposal, with the information gleaned from these earlier steps, should be a relatively straightforward endeavor—but one that requires a great deal of care. In a number of places in this book, we emphasize that a very important part of both research and practice is to communicate to others what you plan to do and what you have accomplished. Such communication can occur at a number of different points in the research process, of which we will emphasize two in this chapter: preparing a grant proposal and writing a research report. If you cannot prepare a comprehensible and convincing grant proposal, you will not gain the financial support needed to complete a research project. If you cannot write a clear and thorough research report, your research findings—no matter how important—will not be translated into policies and practices by practitioners. We do not pretend that we can make you an accomplished writer by reading this chapter, but we hope to offer some useful suggestions and point you in the direction of useful resources.

Appearance and Writing Style

The old adage that you cannot judge a book by its cover may be true, but people routinely make such superficial judgments anyway. Because of this, both outward appearance and style of presentation in a grant proposal are crucial to success. Because demand for grant monies is great, funding agencies may look for any excuse to reject proposals in order to reduce the number that have to be given full review. Failure to follow any guideline may be seized on as a reason not to consider your proposal further. So, to begin with, follow the guidelines to the letter, even if they appear senseless to you. In particular, be careful about length restrictions. Submitting an overly long proposal, no matter how worthy, may result in rejection.

Reviewers have a limited amount of time to review many proposals, so you want to make your proposal attractive and capable of being "skimmed" easily. Using uncomplicated sentences and short paragraphs works toward this end. Underlining key phrases or the use of "bullets" (solid dots used to set off a series of points in a text) for highlighting purposes helps, too. Using different type styles, boldface headings, and variable margins and spacing further contribute to overall appearance and readability. Don't forget to include charts and graphs. They enhance visual impact and can convey much information in a far more abbreviated form than text. For example, a graph depicting the increasing incidence of some problem is far more effective at making the point than a simple reference to that fact in the text. The graph is also less likely to be unintentionally passed over by busy reviewers.

Not too long ago, great effort and a professional printer were required to produce a proposal with these desirable features. The advent of word processing and computerized desktop publishing systems, however, has placed the ability to produce high-quality documents in reach of most agencies. Such systems are strongly recommended for producing your grant proposals. You can bet that at least some of the grant applicants you will be competing against will produce a slick and attractive grant request on a computer. If your agency does not have this kind of technical support available, it may be worth contracting with another organization that can assist you in preparing a polished document. Although unlikely that you could secure funding strictly to purchase such equipment, you may be able to incorporate acquisition of desktop publishing equipment into a future grant request.

Beyond appearance, the style of the text is important. A dull, lifeless proposal, regardless of merit, will have less chance of being funded than one that exudes interest and excitement. Use action words and express emotions wherever appropriate. You want to interest the reviewers in the problem and your innovative approach to it. If you can reach the reviewers at an emotional level, it may positively influence your chances of being funded. Citing dialogue is one effective approach: Presenting possible future clients describing their problems in their *own words* is likely to be better received than some third-party description. As a general rule, try to maintain a fairly "light," readable style.

As in all writing, a sense of one's audience is crucial to preparing a successful grant proposal. Of particular importance is the fact that review panels, for both federal agencies and private foundations, may contain at least some nonspecialists (Krathwohl, 1988). This means that you must be careful to communicate your intentions in language that will be clear to someone who is not a professional in your field. More specifically, jargon should be avoided or, if unavoidable, explained. Beyond that, no assumptions can be made regarding such things as prior knowledge of the problem, its importance, previous approaches, measurement devices, or analytical techniques. Everything must be explained in detail and in terms the typical layperson can understand. Doing so and at the same time not boring the specialists requires a difficult balancing act in your writing.

The writing of the proposal requires such extreme care because the proposal represents you and your agency to the funding source. It will be seen as an indicator of the quality of your personnel and of their work. A great idea presented in a sloppy proposal will not get the funding it deserves. If you develop a worthy idea, it deserves to be properly presented so that funding can be obtained to implement it. The ultimate goal, after all, is not just to get grant money but to finance programs that accomplish some good.

Once a draft of the proposal is completed and before it is submitted, it is a good idea to have several members of your agency who were not directly involved in its production proofread it. This step is important because people unfamiliar with the proposal will approach it more as a reviewer will, with no prior knowledge of its content. The proposal will have to stand on its own just as it will during review by the funding source. In addition to looking for the usual typographical and grammatical errors, the proofreaders should be assessing the total package for content and presentation. Is all the needed information included? Is the problem adequately documented by the needs assessment? Does the proposed project logically address the problem identified in the needs assessment? Is the budget adequately detailed to justify the requested funds? These and many other questions regarding the content of the proposal should be addressed at this final proofreading stage.

All these suggestions regarding the appearance, style, and presentation of a proposal should not distract from the central importance of the proposed project itself. No amount of fancy wrappings will make up for an ill-conceived idea. The importance of these matters is to separate your deserving proposals from all the other deserving proposals to the point that yours gets funded.

Components of the Proposal

A typical proposal to a government agency or major foundation will contain most or all of the components shown in Table 16.3, probably in the order listed. The precise components depend on the

Table 16.3 Typical Proposal Contents and Sequence

1. Cover letter	6. Methods
2. Title page	7. Evaluation
3. Summary	8. Future funding
4. Problem/Need	9. Dissemination
5. Objectives	10. Budget
11. Attachments	

Table 16.4 Title Page Specifications

1. Title of project
2. Program being applied to
3. Grant program contact person
4. Name, position, and institutional affiliation of principal investigator
5. Name of other sources, if any, to which you have applied for funding for this project
6. Proposed start-up date and anticipated completion date

requirements of the specific agency or organization and on whether the proposal is to fund research, service delivery, or both. Notice that the order in Table 16.3 is quite different from the grant development sequence that we have presented. This is because the proposal is organized according to the needs of the reader and not necessarily according to the order in which one prepares the parts.

The Cover Letter   The cover letter is probably the last item to be completed, but because it is the first thing read by those who will evaluate your proposal, it is crucial. One very important function of the cover letter is to remind agency personnel of who you are and that you bothered to visit the agency and take into account their suggestions when designing the proposal. The idea is to show that you have done everything right (according to the agency's views) so that, now, your proposal deserves careful consideration.

Title Page   The title page is often a standard form supplied by the granting organization. Table 16.4 illustrates the common elements of a title page. A good title is one that describes the project and communicates the anticipated results. Thus, the title "Reducing Homicide in Family Disputes" is preferable to "Applying Mental Health Crisis Intervention Techniques to Family Violence" because the first title indicates what the project plans to achieve with the funds while the second merely

describes a service. Beyond serving as a label for your proposal, the title page is used to route your application to the various officials who must process it. The page should clearly identify the applicant's name and address as well as the specific program being applied for and the granting organization contact person.

Summary   Most granting agencies request a brief summary of the proposal so that agency administrators can quickly assess who should receive a copy. This should be no more than a paragraph and should briefly mention all elements of the proposal: research problem or service to be delivered, methods used, and anticipated results.

The Problem or Needs Statement   This is where you really begin to make your case. What should go here has already been discussed in the previous section while analyzing the needs assessment and mission of the organization. What must be done in the proposal is put clearly and coherently into prose describing what the problem is and why your agency can help solve it.

Objectives   Here you state very clearly and precisely what it is your proposal will achieve—exactly what research will be done or what service will be delivered. These objectives need to be very concrete and achievable. No funding agency will be impressed if your objective is to discover the "real truth" about spouse abuse. A more concrete objective would be to learn about the role of economic independence in the ability of women to avoid abuse. List all the objectives with no more than a sentence or two devoted to each. They should be presented in the order of their potential importance and contribution, with the most important listed first. In a research proposal, this section should contain theoretical considerations and the development of hypotheses.

Methods   The proposal should include a complete description of how you plan to conduct research or provide a service. In a research proposal, this section should contain all the mechanics of carrying out the research: sample size, sampling technique, research design, and statistical procedures to be used in analyzing the data.

Evaluation   Federal funding sources place particular emphasis on evaluation. It is politically (as well as practically) important to gather evidence that shows that the funded activities are achieving the objectives claimed for them. Therefore, virtually all proposals must contain adequate methods for assessing whether and how well your program is achieving its goals. In the case of a service delivery grant, this typically involves conducting research to assess whether the program resulted in the improvements or changes that were intended. A review of Chapter 12 along with some of the suggested readings should be helpful in preparing this part of the proposal.

Future Funding   A grant, by its very nature, is a onetime dispersal of funds. Human service organizations, on the other hand, typically support ongoing programs that require continuous funding. The disjunction between the onetime grant and the ongoing needs of the program should be addressed in the proposal. When the grant money ends, what then? The agency will want to see that you have thought through this problem and laid plans to deal with it. Plans for local funding, other grants, fundraisers, telethons, whatever, should be included. Agencies like to see lasting and successful programs develop out of their "seed" money. Inclusion of money in the budget for future fund-raising efforts is perfectly appropriate.

Dissemination   Dissemination refers to spreading the word about your research, service delivery program, the grant, the funding source, and, hopefully, your successes. Inclusion of comments regarding dissemination of results is looked on as an indicator of confidence. Agencies like positive publicity about the "good" that they do and tend to look favorably on opportunities to obtain it. This is a small thing and alone it will not get you a grant, but successful grantsmanship is ultimately a result of doing

a lot of little things right and better than the competition.

Budget   A carefully detailed budget is an important part of any grant proposal because granting agencies are punctilious in their accounting demands of grant recipients. Essentially, every dollar you request must be accounted for. The methods section of your proposal, where you spell out precisely what the program will do, provides the guide for developing the budget. All costs that will be incurred must be identified and included. Novice grant seekers often underestimate costs or leave out expenses. Because the developers of the project are usually researchers or practitioners and not financial officers, it is important to seek consultation in determining costs. Your organization may have standard formulas for fixing fringe benefit costs, travel, and overhead and may require bidding procedures for purchasing equipment. Be realistic. Promising the moon on a shoestring budget will not endear your proposal to an agency. It will merely be seen as the amateurish effort it is. If costs are reasonable and well justified, it may be possible to negotiate reductions if the total amount is too high.

Attachments   The attachments section provides important supporting evidence for claims made elsewhere in the proposal. Bauer (1995) suggests the following as appropriate for inclusion in the attachments section: needs assessment and other supporting research, résumés of key personnel, minutes of advisory committee meetings, names of board members, auditor's financial statement, letters of support from advocates, a copy of your tax-exempt status from the Internal Revenue Service, any pictures or diagrams, and copies of any organization publications.

Documentation of community support is also very important. Some funding sources demand a demonstration that the community is behind a project, but it should be provided even for those who do not require it. Evidence of community support generally comes from two sources: advisory board minutes and newspaper articles. Many agencies of the type we are discussing here have advisory boards that oversee their operations. These boards, composed primarily of other professional service providers, former consumers of the agency's services, and people whose expertise lies in the area of fund-raising, hold regular meetings to discuss the activities of the agencies they oversee. Minutes from meetings when the project for which you are seeking funding was discussed can be used as evidence of community support. Newspaper articles reflecting positively on the project form the other major source of evidence of community support. You can actively seek publicity for the agency and the project you are trying to get funded.

Submitting the Proposal

Public funding sources have quite rigid guidelines, not to mention firm deadlines, that govern the submission process. You, of course, will have obtained these along with all the other information from the funding agency. Because deadlines are involved, the proposal should be submitted either in person or by registered mail. In either case, it is a good idea to telephone the funding source a bit later to verify that they received the proposal.

With many of the private foundations, generalizing about submission procedures is difficult because each foundation has its own peculiar way of doing things. This places an added burden on the grant seeker. In some cases, private foundations do not require the lengthy and detailed proposals that we have described. They do not have the resources in the form of reviewers to evaluate such complex documents. Instead, they rely on what is called the *letter proposal*. As the name suggests, the letter proposal outlines the need, your plans to meet that need, and your grant request all in a fairly brief letter of no more than a few pages in length. Even something as important as the budget is abbreviated. Usually, the estimated total cost is all that is required. Rather than the voluminous detail characteristic of a federal proposal, each important issue in the letter proposal must fit into a paragraph. Brevity and clarity are the watchwords of a letter proposal.

Because you have done your homework, chances are good that the grant will be approved. But what if it is not? Understandable disappointment aside, rejection is an opportunity to learn. Contact the funding source and inquire about what was wrong (and right) about your proposal. Learn from them how to do a better job the next time. And remember, the only grant seekers never turned down are those who never submit a proposal. It is the nature of the game.

Grantsmanship is an exciting and increasingly essential element of human service research and practice. We hope that this chapter has made the prospect of preparing a grant proposal less daunting. Remember, however, that we have been able to present only a limited amount of material on obtaining grants. We strongly recommend that you read carefully a complete book devoted to grantsmanship, such as one of those listed in For Further Reading at the end of this chapter.

Writing a Research Report

One of the strengths of the scientific method is the public character of scientific results. Publicizing scientific findings accomplishes several important functions. First, unless research findings are made public, they accomplish little social good. How can others learn from the findings of research if those findings are withheld? Clearly, publication of research findings is necessary in order to apply those findings in developing programs and policies.

Second, publication allows the process of replication to ferret out errors, frauds, and falsehoods that inevitably creep into the products of human endeavor. The self-correcting nature of science that has contributed so much to its success depends on the wide dissemination of research results.

Third, publication of research findings makes attempted suppression of those findings more difficult. Recall that in Chapter 12 we noted that historically this had been a problem for evaluation research reports. A few copies were supplied to a sponsor who then had complete control over what was (or was not) done with the results. Broader publicity concerning research findings makes it more likely that they will come to the attention of someone who will use them.

Finally, the publication of research findings, like any written publication, is an effort at persuasion. It is an attempt to influence the readers to accept your ideas or conclusions. Chapter 3 discusses the idea of advocacy in research and shows that human service researchers are especially likely to advocate some particular use of their research findings. To be effective, advocates must communicate positions to others, and one major mode of communication is through the written word. An interesting, well-written, and smooth presentation is more likely to be persuasive.

Given the central role communication of research results plays in the entire scientific enterprise, the proper preparation of the research report is vital. In this section, we assume that you have learned appropriate English grammar and usage. The complexity of the English language being what it is, we strongly recommend that you consult one or more of the style manuals listed in For Further Reading. No matter how well you think you write, your writing will benefit from regular usage of a style manual.

Consideration of the Audience

An important consideration before beginning any writing assignment is the intended audience. For the writing to be most effective, it must be tailored to its specific audience. Although possible to identify several distinct audiences for research reports, the most significant distinction is between a *professional* audience and a *lay* audience. Of course, within these two broad categories are several more specific audiences that may require special consideration. Not all professionals are created equal. Even in the social sciences and human services, those pursuing research careers develop a different expertise and professional jargon than those following a more practice-oriented career. Likewise, those concentrating on clinical practice gain different expertise from those in administration or community practice. They may all be "professionals" within the

same discipline, but they do not share the same knowledge. It is important to keep these distinctions in mind when writing reports.

When a report is aimed at an audience of other professionals, certain assumptions can be made, such as familiarity with basic concepts of the discipline and knowledge of common statistical terms. Although these assumptions make writing for other professionals easier, such an audience is likely to be more critical of such things as following a proper format, elements of style, and substantive content.

If the intended audience is the lay public, or others less familiar with research and the human services, the preceding assumptions cannot be made. In that case, minimize the use of professional jargon, which is likely to be meaningless or possibly misleading to such an audience. Occasionally, jargon cannot be avoided. Social science disciplines do not make up jargon for its own sake but rather to enhance precision or to describe phenomena that our everyday language does not have words for. When used, professional jargon should be carefully explained to the lay reader. Presentation of data to a lay audience must also be simplified. They probably won't know what a probability coefficient is and may even have difficulty grasping the importance of a percentage table. Use the visual impact of graphs and charts to help get your message across. Also, explain fully what each statistic used accomplishes, and what the result means. Professionals who do not work routinely with statistics and data analysis may also need some of this sort of assistance. If you believe in the importance of your research and want it to be useful, careful attention to one's audience will further that goal immensely.

Because different journals are read by different audiences, requirements of professional periodicals vary from one publication to another. If a research report is being prepared for possible publication, care must be taken to follow the specifications of the particular journal to which the manuscript will be submitted. A helpful resource toward this end is *An Author's Guide to Social Work Journals* (Mendelsohn, 1992). Published by the National Association of Social Workers, the guide includes more than 130 social work, social welfare, and human service journals. Readers will find information on the journal's review process, editorial focus, format, and suggested style guide. In addition, the guide indicates where each journal is abstracted and indexed.

Organization of the Report

Despite the variation depending on the audience, research reports usually include most or all of the following elements.

Title The title is an important part of a report and the first thing a reader sees. The major function of the title is to give prospective readers an idea of what the study is about so they can decide whether they are interested in reading further. Therefore, a good title informs the reader about the major independent and dependent variables and, possibly, the major findings. A second reason to develop a good title is that the computerized library searches discussed in Appendix A use key words in titles as one means of selecting articles. Therefore, a report with a misleading or poor title may be lost from these searches. The following examples are from a recent issue of a social work journal:

> Socialization and the Belief Systems of Traditional-Age and Nontraditional-Age Social Work Students
> The Korean Protestant Church: The Role in Service Delivery for Korean Immigrants
> The Effect of Short-Term Family Therapy on the Social Functioning of the Chronic Schizophrenic and His Family

Note that each of these titles provides sufficient information for a reader to decide whether to pursue the article further and for a computer retrieval system to identify key words.

Abstract Most scientific journals and reports contain an abstract, which is a terse summary of the study that allows the reader to learn enough to decide whether to read the whole thing. (Some examples of this type of abstract are presented in Chapter 4.) Abstracts are also often collected and published in reference volumes, some of which are

discussed in Appendix A. In these collections, the abstracts allow the reader to decide whether to locate the complete articles. Because of their importance and brevity (125–175 words), abstracts must be carefully written. The first sentence should be a clear statement of the problem that was investigated by the study. The research methodology and sampling techniques are then indicated. A brief summary of findings and conclusions completes the abstract. Figure 16.4 shows an abstract with its component parts identified.

Introduction and Problem Statement The first part of the body of the report states the research problem and its importance. This should include a literature review of the history of the problem in previous research and theory. This material indicates how the current study flows from that which has gone before. Presentation of the theoretical material sets the stage for presenting the hypotheses that were tested in the study. Of necessity this section must be kept relatively brief. For example, the literature review typically consists of numerous citations of previous work on the topic area, with only the most relevant aspects of each study commented on. This emphasis on brevity should not be overdone, however. Clarity of presentation in this section is a must because without it, the remainder of the report loses its meaning.

Methods The methods section describes the sample that was studied and the research techniques employed. It also shows how concepts are operationalized and what measurement devices, such as scales, were used. This section is very important because it provides the basis on which the validity and generalizability of conclusions will be judged. It is also the basis for any future replication efforts. As such, this section must be written with sufficient detail so that it can perform both of these functions. Readers must be able to tell precisely what was done in the study and who participated.

Results This section is a straightforward presentation of the findings of the study, devoid of any editorializing or comment as to the meaning of the

507. ARNTZ, A. & VAN DEN HOUT, M.
Psychological treatments of panic disorder without agoraphobia: cognitive therapy versus applied relaxation.
Behavior Research and Therapy, 34(2): 113–21, Feb. 1996.
Dept. of Medical Psychology, Univ. of Limburg, PO Box 616, NL-6200 MD Maastricht, The Netherlands

1 { This study compared two psychological treatments of panic disorder and tested whether cognitive therapy (CT) was superior to applied relaxation (AR); and whether treatment was superior to waiting.

2 } Thirty-six outpatients of the community mental health center with the *DSM-III-R* diagnosis of panic disorder with no or mild agoraphobia were randomly assigned to CT or AR. Eighteen similar patients who were referred after the treatment conditions were complete constituted a waiting-list group.

3 { Treatment consisted of 12 weekly sessions. Patients self-monitored panic attacks during the whole treatment period, and the following four weeks, and during one week at a half-year follow-up. Questionnaires were filled out before and after treatment, and at four-week and half-year follow-ups. After the first follow-up additional treatment was provided if clinically indicated. One patient dropped out of AR and was replaced.

4 } Treatment was superior to waiting in reducing panic and questionnaire scores. CT was clearly superior to AR in reducing panic frequency, and somewhat less strongly superior to AR in reducing the questionnaire scores. Depending on the assessment point, 77.8–83.3 percent of the CT patients was panic-free after treatment, compared to 50 percent of the AR and 27.7 percent of the waiting-list patients. In conclusion, cognitive therapy for panic is especially effective in reducing the incidence of panic attacks. (Journal abstract, edited.)

Figure 16.4   Example of an Abstract, With Its Component Parts Identified: 1. Statement of problem, 2. Sample selection, 3. Method of study, 4. Results

results. That comes later. Typically, the presentation of results involves the use of tables, graphs, and statistics. The one exception to this is the results from a participant observation study, which is likely to have little quantitative data. As noted previously, you should consider your audience and fashion your presentation so that the data can be readily understood.

Discussion   In this section, conclusions are drawn regarding the implications of the data presented in the results section. Each tested hypothesis should be related to relevant data and a conclusion stated about the degree of support, or nonsupport, the data provide for it. Beyond that, any broader implications of the findings for either research, practice, or social policy should be noted. Any limitations or weaknesses of any of the results should be honestly noted as well. Often, research results raise new questions as they answer others. It is common practice, therefore, to identify those opportunities for future research.

References   A list of all works cited in the report is presented, usually as the last element of the report. A variety of formats can be used, but the one known as the *Harvard method* is the most common in the social sciences, and in a somewhat modified form it is the format used in this book. As sources are cited in the body of the text, the author's last name and date of publication are placed in parentheses at the end of the sentence. The references are then listed in alphabetical order by author's last name, with the publication date prominently displayed on the line below. Any common journal such as the *American Sociological Review, Social Problems,* or the *American Journal of Sociology* may be consulted for examples of this format.

An alternative format is called the *serial method,* in which the citations are indicated numerically in the body of the text. The references are then presented in the reference section in the same order as cited. This method is an older style than the Harvard method and is generally less used by researchers because it is more complicated to prepare and not justified except for long research reports with extensive references. Others, however, prefer it because there is less intrusion in the text. The journals *Social Work* and *Social Work Research* use this format.

Preparing a list of references or a bibliography for a grant or research report is generally a difficult and not very pleasant task. All the names of the authors must be spelled correctly, the page numbers and dates must be correct, and the punctuation is not like that used anywhere else. New computer software, however, can take some of the drudgery out of preparing bibliographies. Bibliography-formatting software will create a file of references with all the required information for each reference (still a lot of work). Once the file is complete, the program will reformat the information into a variety of popular bibliography styles. So long as the information in the file is correct, the bibliography will be correct, down to the last punctuation mark. In addition, some programs will interface with word processor programs and "search" documents for citations and make up a correct bibliography from the file of references. It will also flag any citations that are not in the file and any references in the file that are not cited. Trust us, when revising a long document (such as a book or grant proposal), this feature can save a lot of work and reduce errors. When shopping for bibliography-formatting software, one should investigate the capabilities of each package carefully. The more than 40 such programs on the market range in price from less than $100 to more than $600. They also range in capabilities from rather simple (formatting a bibliography into only one of the several bibliography formats) to those with all the features mentioned earlier. Bibliographic software does not do all of the busywork for you, but it can reduce the drudgery considerably and greatly enhance the accuracy of the finished product.

The Process of Writing

It is not possible, of course, to cover in a brief chapter all the elements involved in writing. This is done in writing courses and through practice at writing. However, a few points are of special importance.

First, writing is a process rather than a product. You never finish writing, although you may finish a paper or a report because it has to be submitted by a deadline. However, this doesn't mean that you couldn't write and revise further. Writing aims at the expression and communication of clear thought. It is difficult to write because, in some respects, language is a poor mechanism for communicating the subjective reality of our thoughts. If you tell someone about the car that almost hit you on the way to school this morning, words like "car" and "hit" seem straightforward and comprehensible. But do those words encompass the reality that you experienced? It was a bright red car, and it was speeding, and the driver seemed not to notice you, and . . . . How much detail do you provide to communicate your experience? You tell the person you were frightened by the close call, and then realizing he or she might not understand the wrenching terror that shot through you, you repeat that you were "really" frightened, using qualifiers, emphasis, and inflection to make your point. The words may seem inadequate to communicate your experience, but this is precisely the challenge that any writer confronts: using words to describe a very complex and confusing reality. Researchers face the challenge of using words to describe a very complex theoretical and methodological reality to various audiences.

A second point, which really flows from the first, is that rewriting and revision are an inherent part of the writing process. Very few writers are capable of making their first draft the final draft. Most writers, especially professional writers, must rewrite their material several times before it can be considered clear, comprehensible, and smooth. (The term "smooth" in this context simply means the writing contains very few errors or awkward constructions that distract the reader from the content.) One of the keys to revision is to be able to read your prose through the eyes of the intended audience. Would they understand a particular word, phrase, or sentence? Can they follow the sequential organization in the report? Do they grasp the transitions that move the reader from one sentence to another, from one paragraph to another? What is perfectly clear from the writer's perspective may be muddled and unclear from the reader's. The writer's talent is to perceive his or her writing from that other perspective.

Rewriting is an essential, if sometimes tedious, task, and it is also creative. As with other creative efforts, the energy and attention needed to create is greater at some times than at others. This means that the best writing is usually not produced in one sitting. Most writers find it useful to approach revision after they have been away from a paper for some time. This enables them to approach it with fresh insight and attention. For this reason, things that are written at the last minute, with a deadline rapidly approaching, may not be the best.

The task of writing and rewriting, of course, is made easier by modern computers and word-processing software. As writers who have spanned both the pre–word-processing and word-processing eras, we can attest that the latter is far preferable to the former. However, word processors do not write. The writer must still tap words onto the

screen. Writing still takes creativity, perception, persistence, and hard work.

Main Points

- Grants have become a very important source of funding for both social research and human services. If they are to successfully gain funding, grant proposals must be written well.
- Sources of grant money fall into three categories: government agencies, private foundations, and corporations, with government being the largest source.
- Government funds come in a number of different forms: project (categorical) grants, formula grants, block grants, federal contracts, and state government grants.
- Although many foundations fund grants, most fund only small projects and some fund research on only limited subject areas. Corporations tend to fund grants that can be justified to the stockholders, such as for services or improvements from which the corporation or its employees will benefit.
- Many funding sources can be located through online computerized search services.
- The preparation of grant proposals should be considered an ongoing, continuing function of a human service agency. The steps in the grant development process are analogous to the steps in the research process.
- The first step in grant development is to identify a fundable topic; this can be assisted by conducting a needs assessment.
- Once the project has been identified, you need to target a funding source that will be interested in your project; this might call for visits to potential funding sources to assess their interest.
- To be successful, grant proposals must be written well, and this requires paying attention to the appearance and to the writing style. Proposals must be neat, interesting to read, and addressed to the audience that will read them.
- A grant proposal should contain all the components necessary to provide a funding source with adequate information to assess it.

■ Research reports should also be well written be-cause the communication and publication of scientific results accomplish important functions for science.

■ A research report should be written at the level of the audience for whom it is intended. These might be researchers conversant with the jargon of research and statistics, practitioners unfamiliar with such jargon, or the lay public.

■ Most research reports include the following elements: a title, an abstract, an introduction and statement of the problem, a description of methods and results, a discussion of the implications of the findings, and a list of references.

Important Terms for Review

grant

Exploring the Internet

Although the Internet is proving to be a boon to students and researchers for locating research infor-mation, it has produced some new problems in terms of how to properly cite sources that one finds on the Internet. One aid that you can use to handle Internet citation problems is "MLA-Style Citations of Electronic Sources," by Janice R. Walker. You can locate this source at http://www.cas.usf.edu/english/walker/mla.html. Not only does this site provide information about how to correctly cite Internet sources, but it provides many links to other Internet sites that can provide addi-tional guidance on the topic.

In this chapter we devoted considerable atten-tion to the grant-funding process and writing the grant proposal. You can greatly enrich your knowl-edge of the grant-writing process by using the In-ternet to locate sites devoted to this topic. Simply entering such terms as "research grants" or "grant funding" in one of the search engines, such as Ly-cos or Infoseek, will generate a large number of potential sites to explore. You might also combine the term "grants" with a key word for a subject of interest to you, such as crime, aging, or education. Some of the major governmental human service sites have extensive material on grants, including abstracts of funded projects and RFPs that you can examine to better understand the issues of writing successful proposals. For example, the Justice Infor-mation Center (http://www.ncjrs.org/) has exten-sive information available on grants from the Na-tional Institute of Justice, the Office of Juvenile Justice and Delinquency Prevention, the Office for Victims of Crime, the Bureau of Justice Assistance, and other grant opportunities from the Depart-ment of Justice.

The General Services Administration's home page (http://www.gsa.gov/default.htm) is a good launching point for exploring federal government funding opportunities. From here, you can access the Federal Domestic Assistance Catalog (or go to it directly at http://www.gsa.gov/fdac/default.html). The Federal Domestic Assistance Catalog (FDAC) is a government-wide compendium of federal pro-grams, projects, services, and activities that provide assistance or benefits to the public. It contains fi-nancial and nonfinancial assistance programs ad-ministered by departments and agencies of the fed-eral government. The Internet site has a search engine where you can query the catalog. By enter-ing terms for a human service issue, you can quickly locate information about related grant op-portunities.

A good way to get a better sense of how to write grant reports is to read some completed stud-ies. One source you might try is the National Clearinghouse on Alcohol and Drug Information (http://www.health.org/dbases.htm). You can easily search their databases and review abstracts of com-pleted projects. The references indicate where and how to obtain complete reports.

For Further Reading

American Psychological Association's Guide to Research Sup-port, 3rd ed. Hyattsville, Md.: American Psychological Association. A complete guide for social scientists looking for support for their research. It includes in-formation on funding sources—including names, addresses, and telephone numbers—application procedures, and submission deadlines.

Austin, Ruth. *The Grants Register, 1997.* New York: St. Martin's, 1996. This volume is mainly focused on graduate or professional students who are looking for grants to assist them in research and travel that are a part of their educational experience, but it does include some granting organizations that support research by human service agencies.

Becker, Howard S. *Writing for Social Scientists: How to Start and Finish Your Thesis, Book, or Article.* Chicago: University of Chicago Press, 1986. A prolific researcher and writer, Howard Becker shares what he has learned with others. This book goes beyond the basics of style and grammar and offers practical suggestions for such things as overcoming writer's block, how to rewrite and revise, and how to develop a lucid style of prose.

Belcher, Jane C., and Julia M. Jacobsen. *From Idea to Funded Project: Grant Proposals That Work,* 4th ed. Phoenix: Oryx, 1992. This is an excellent guide to the preparation of effective grant proposals. It provides much sound advice and helpful hints to those about to embark on the process.

Chicago Manual of Style, 14th ed. Chicago: University of Chicago Press, 1993. Prepared by the editorial staff of the University of Chicago Press, the *Chicago Manual* has long been considered the definitive writing reference work. If you take your writing seriously, you should have a copy.

Cuba, Lee. *A Short Guide to Writing About Social Science,* 3rd ed. New York: Longman, 1997. This book is a good review of the things you need to know about writing research papers and preparing presentations on topics in the social sciences.

Hall, Donald, and Sven Birkerts. *Writing Well,* 7th ed. New York: HarperCollins, 1991. Hall, the author of dozens of books, brings his experience and expertise to a book that can help anyone improve his or her writing. Unlike many such books that present the rules in a rather stiff and direct fashion, Hall makes learning to write well interesting.

Hult, Christine A. *Researching and Writing in the Social Sciences.* Boston: Allyn & Bacon, 1996. This is an excellent guide to the writing process that focuses on the social sciences. It covers topics from using the library to planning your time to the actual writing process itself.

Jones, Francine, ed. *Corporate Foundation Profiles,* 7th ed. New York: The Foundation Center, 1992. This volume lists the many corporate foundations that provide grant money for a variety of endeavors. It is very useful because it indexes corporate foundations by the subject matter they fund, the geographic region in which they prefer to give funds, and the type of support they offer (e.g., seed money, research, continuing support, and so on).

Murphy, C. Edward, ed. *National Data Book of Foundations: A Comprehensive Guide to Grantmaking Foundations,* 16th ed. New York: The Foundation Center, 1992. This is one of the most comprehensive listings of active grantmaking foundations.

Ries, Joanne B., and Carl G. Leukefeld. *Applying for Research Funding: Getting Started and Getting Funded.* Thousand Oaks, Calif.: Sage, 1995. This book is an excellent overview of the steps in preparing a successful grant application for research in the human services.

Schumacher, Dorin. *Get Funded! A Practical Guide for Scholars Seeking Support From Business.* Newbury Park, Calif.: Sage, 1992. This is an especially helpful guide for seeking funding from businesses; it points out the differences between the corporate, academic, and human service mentalities and how to incorporate this knowledge into the preparation of grants.

Shertzer, Margaret. *The Elements of Grammar.* New York: Macmillan, 1986. This little book covers all aspects of correct English usage. It draws upon hundreds of examples from the greatest contemporary authors.

Exercises for Class Discussion

16.1 Portage Bay is a resort-oriented, medium-sized city of about 40,000 persons. Recently, the city council has been receiving numerous complaints from downtown merchants about vagrants and homeless people taking over the parks and public areas along the waterfront mall. A large mental institution is located near the city, and deinstitutionalized patients are accused of driving tourists away and hurting sales. Representatives of several organizations such as the Community Mental Health Center and Community Action Agency counter that the mentally ill are also residents and are being unfairly blamed for the problem. The advocates for the patients contend that the services are inadequate to meet the needs of the homeless in the community. A task force is formed to study the problem and develop a plan to resolve the conflict with the merchants while meeting the community's desire to be compassionate and meet the needs of the homeless. It becomes immediately clear that outside funding will be necessary to do a comprehensive study and to implement a plan of action.

a. Make a list of materials to which the task force might turn to locate funding sources. Do you think government grants or foundation grants would be more appropriate?

b. By using the *Catalog of Federal Domestic Assistance* and the *Monthly Catalog of Government Documents,* identify a list of several potential grant sources related to the problem faced by the city of Portage Bay.

16.2 Request sample grant application forms from organizations in your state that fund human service research projects. Your college or university probably has an office of research and development that can provide the guidelines, or you might contact such agencies as the state departments of mental health, social services, or corrections.

a. Compare the grant applications in terms of the kind and detail of information that each requires.

b. For each application, determine the problems for which the granting organization will dispense funding. What special priorities, if any, does the granting organization specify? Who is eligible to apply for the grant?

16.3 Select a human-service-related research article from a recent professional publication and review it from the standpoint of the criteria presented in the discussion of writing a research report.

a. To what audience does the article appear to be addressed (e.g., professional social workers, researchers, or the general public)?

b. Is the title effective?

c. Is there an abstract? If so, does it communicate the necessary information?

d. Examine the organization of the study to determine if it contains the basic components described in the text. How are the problem statement, methods description, results, and discussion handled by the author(s)?

APPENDIX A

A Guide to the Library

Organization of the Library   457
Library Departments   457
Computers in Research: The Library   458
Accessing Library Materials   459

Books   459
The Classification System   459
The Public Catalog   461

Periodicals   462
Journals Important to the Human Services   463

Abstracts and Indexes   464

Reference Books for the Human Services   467

Government Documents   467
The *Monthly Catalog*   467
Subject Bibliographies and State Government Documents   470

Sources of Data in the Library   470
Government Sources   470
Nongovernment Sources   471

Information Literacy and Critical Thinking Skills   471

Exploring the Internet   472

For Further Reading   472

A library is both a repository of information and a gateway for accessing information stored at other sites. Libraries own some of the information products they make available to customers, and libraries assist customers in locating and accessing information resources at other libraries or other locations. Some human service research projects can be completed in the library if the necessary information or data can be found there. More commonly, the library and its services are used as means of reviewing existing literature to see what has been done on a particular topic, gaining help in developing a research design, locating existing scales, and the like. However, because of the proliferation of materials accessed through libraries these days, finding what you want can be a daunting task for those unfamiliar with the organization of the library. To make effective use of the library you must, first, define precisely what it is you need to know; second, determine the best strategy for locating that information; and third, evaluate the information that you do find. This appendix focuses primarily on the second step by providing a basic introduction to the organization of the library and the services provided there. In addition, we point to some specific resources in the library that would be useful to practitioners in the human services.

Organization of the Library

There are two key elements in the organization of a library that you need to understand to use the library effectively. First, the library contains certain *departments* that perform special functions in the search for information. Second, the library contains a number of important mechanisms for *accessing* information.

Library Departments

One of the most valuable departments in the library for students seeking materials is the *reference department*. In most libraries, the reference department contains the basic tools for searching for information: encyclopedias, indexes, abstracts, dictionaries, handbooks, yearbooks, government documents that summarize statistical data, and an array of other such resources. Familiarity with this department is critical for efficient use of the library. In addition to the materials in the reference department, reference librarians are another valuable asset to the researcher. Highly trained and knowledgeable about how to locate materials, librarians have as one of their major duties helping library patrons. By working closely with a reference librarian, you will not only locate a specific item, but you can also learn the techniques of thorough and efficient searching for materials. Although you should probably try to locate materials yourself first, do not hesitate to consult the reference librarian if you have difficulties. One rule of thumb is to spend 30 minutes searching on your own before seeking help (Lolley, 1974).

Unless you have access to a very large library, such as the New York Public Library or the Library of Congress, you will undoubtedly find that some books or resource materials you need are not available in your library. To overcome this problem, you need to make use of the *interlibrary loan department*. Most libraries participate in a local or regional interlibrary loan program that permits them to borrow books and other materials from other libraries. Libraries first attempt to secure materials from libraries within their own region; if this is not possible, they will use computers to locate materials in libraries around the nation or, in some cases, the world. All participating libraries benefit because they can provide a greater range of materials and services to patrons than their own budgets allow. Books are usually sent by mail from one library to another, with the borrower sometimes asked to pay postage and insurance (usually not a large fee because the books are mailed at a very inexpensive "book rate"). In addition, lending libraries sometimes require that books they lend be used only in the borrowing library, in which case the borrowing library will not allow the books to be taken out. Many libraries, as a part of their interlibrary loan service, also participate in a periodical reprint service through which you can request a duplicated copy of an article from a periodical.

All libraries provide some *copying services* that enable you to photocopy certain library materials for a nominal fee. Most libraries also have machines that will make copies from microfilm or microfiche because much valuable library material, including old journals and newspapers, is put on microforms to save library space. Effective use of the library's copying services is important because it gives you a permanent copy of those materials that cannot be removed from the library. In using these services, however, you should be familiar with the federal copyright laws to ensure that you do not violate them. Normally, reproducing one copy for your private use is permissible.

The *documents division* of the library houses government publications, magazines, pamphlets, and sometimes collections of special books. Many government documents are now issued on microfiche and in electronic formats. In a small library, the documents division might be integrated with the reference department.

The *stacks* are the part of the library where most books and periodicals are stored. At large universities, there is usually more than one library, so all the books and journals will not necessarily be in the same building. Some libraries permit anyone to roam the stacks, whereas others are more restrictive, distributing "stack passes" to a limited number of people such as university faculty, graduate students, or other serious researchers. You should gain as much access to the stacks as possible because browsing in the stacks is a valuable adjunct to the other ways of finding appropriate resource materials. In the stacks, you can review the table of contents and the index of a book, which provide more information about how useful it will be to you than does the brief description of the book found in the public catalog. In addition, because books on similar topics are normally placed near one another

in the stacks, you can browse for books that might be useful once you find the right area in the stacks. Furthermore, if a book is misshelved slightly, you may accidentally find it if the library staff sent to retrieve it were unable to do so.

Computers in Research: The Library

The usefulness of computers in the research process extends into the library. To cope with the proliferation of materials, libraries over the past few decades have made extensive use of computerization to make library searches faster and more effective. For example, most libraries now have a computerized online public access catalog (OPAC) of all the books, periodicals, and other materials in the library. In some cases, the OPAC includes the holdings of all libraries in a region. Library patrons can search for materials by author, title, subject, or by the use of keywords. We describe this in the next section. In addition, many abstracts, indexes, and government documents described later in this appendix are now available on compact disc, commonly referred to as CD-ROM (compact disc read-only memory), and readily accessible by microcomputers.

A variety of computerized information-retrieval systems exist that can provide a list of citations to books, articles, and government publications on particular topics. In most cases, the user provides a list of keywords that relate to the topic of interest. The computer then searches through abstracts, indexes, and other materials in its files for citations that are filed under those keywords or contain a keyword or words in the title of the book or article.

Keyword searches work like this: If one were interested in child abuse, then keywords such as "child abuse," "discipline," "cruelty to children," "battered children," and "parent–child relationship" could be entered into the computer. It is also possible to narrow the search by cross-referencing a number of keywords. For example, we could request only materials listed under *all* the following keywords: "battered children—Native American—male—aged 1 to 4—Michigan." It is also possible to limit the search to works published between specified dates, sponsored by certain organizations, or qualified by any number of other criteria, depending on the search service and the database searched. Obviously, the more encompassing terms ("parent–child relationship") will result in the retrieval of a longer list of articles than will narrower terms ("battered children") or terms that are cross-referenced. This is something to take into consideration if there is a charge for this search service based in part on the number of references provided. Also, the longer list will include many sources not directly relevant to your concerns and could waste your valuable time. The librarians operating the computer search service can give you advice on whether a computer search is appropriate to your topic (sometimes a manual search is better) and also suggestions on useful keywords to maximize your search. Many search services provide a dictionary of terms used in the database. One such database, for example, is ERIC, or Educational Resources Information Center. If your library has this database, then it will also have a volume titled *Thesaurus of ERIC Descriptors* that contains all the subject terms used in the ERIC database.

Computers have also made it feasible to provide another service that gives patrons greater access to materials: table-of-contents and document-delivery services. *Table-of-contents services* make available the tables of contents of thousands of periodicals, providing author and title as well as other information relevant to accessing the articles. This means that a user can review the contents of many journals rapidly, even journals not owned by the particular library being used. *Document-delivery services,* often a part of table-of-contents services, actually deliver copies of articles to patrons. Even if the library being used doesn't own the journal, the article will be mailed or faxed to the patron from a library that does own it. These services have made it possible for libraries to provide materials for patrons even when the library does not physically possess the materials. The electronic and computer era has shifted libraries' focus away from ownership of materials and toward providing access to materials.

Many of these computerized library services are operated by the patrons themselves, although

some require assistance from library personnel. Some of these services are free or provided at low cost, but some of the services can be expensive. Some of the document-delivery services, for example, can get rather costly. Check with library personnel to determine precisely what services are available to you and what costs you might incur by using them.

Accessing Library Materials

Having a library available with ample materials and services is of little use unless you know how to *access* the materials you want. Patrons unfamiliar with the library can easily feel overwhelmed because there seem to be so many crannies, both physical and electronic, in which relevant resources can hide. There are, however, four basic strategies for locating materials. Following these strategies can unlock the secrets of the library. First, you must know how to use the OPAC, or *online public access catalog.* Second, you can use a variety of *abstracts* and *indexes.* Third, although many government documents can be found through the OPAC, the *Monthly Catalog of U.S. Government Publications* is a valuable additional resource in searching for government publications. Fourth, the *Internet* and the *World Wide Web* have become increasingly important in the search for information, and their use is explored in Appendix D and in the Exploring the Internet sections in this appendix and in each chapter. Thus, to do a thorough search that locates the most up-to-date sources, you must be familiar with all four strategies for accessing information.

Books
The Classification System

Small, local libraries might contain a few thousand books. Small to medium-sized universities have libraries with hundreds of thousands of volumes. Large university and public libraries contain millions of books. Despite the tremendous variations in size of libraries, the systems to classify books in them are so flexible that the system used in the smallest library can also be used in the largest, and, despite the tremendous size of some libraries, a person can easily retrieve a book if he or she knows how the book is classified. Most classification systems arrange books according to *subject matter.* First, books are classified into very general categories, such as history, science, or social sciences. Then, within each general category, they are further arranged into more precise subcategories. The category of social sciences, for example, is further divided into economics, sociology, and so on. In this fashion, the subject matter of a book is further narrowed until it fits into a fairly specific category. Then each book is given a unique *call number,* which contains all the necessary information from the classification system to identify that particular book.

There are primarily two classification systems used in the United States: the *Library of Congress system* and the *Dewey decimal system.* The Library of Congress system uses a combination of letters and numbers to classify books (*see* Table A.1). The first letter in the call number is one of 21 letters of the alphabet used to classify books into the most general categories. The letter *H,* for example, indicates the general category of the social sciences. The second letter (if there is a second letter) further narrows the subject matter within the social sciences. The letter *Q,* for example, indicates that the book falls in the more specific social science subject matter of "Family, Marriage, Women," whereas *V* refers to the subject of "Social Pathology." The letters of the call number are followed by a number that further narrows the subject matter. Within the classification *HV,* for example, numbers between 701 and 1420 refer to works on the topic of "protection, assistance, and relief of children," whereas the numbers from 5001 to 5840 refer to books on "alcoholism." This number is followed by a letter that is the first letter of the last name of the author of the book. This is followed by a number that further identifies the author. These sets of letters and numbers of the call number provide an identification that is unique to this book: No other book has ex-

Table A.1 Library of Congress Classification System

A	General Works
B	Philosophy and Religion
C	History (General—Civilization, Genealogy)
D	History—Old World
E	American History and General U.S. History
F	American History (Local) and Latin America
G	Geography, Anthropology, Folklore, Sports, and Other
H	Social Sciences

	HA	Statistics
	HB–HD	Economics
	HF	Commerce
	HG–HJ	Finance
	HM	Sociology
	HQ	Family, Marriage, Women
	HV	Social Pathology

J	Political Science
K	Law
L	Education
M	Music
N	Fine Arts
P	Language and Literature
Q	Science
R	Medicine
S	Agriculture, Forestry, Animal Culture, Fish Culture, Hunting
T	Technology
U	Military Science
V	Naval Science
Z	Bibliography and Library Science

Example: HV
      875
      F6

actly the same call number. Books are placed on the shelves in the order of their call numbers. All the *H*'s are placed together, and within the *H*'s all the *HM*'s go together. Within the *HM*'s, books are arranged according to the other letters and numbers.

The Dewey decimal system arranges books into 10 general categories based on a three-digit number on the top row of the call number (*see* Table A.2). Numbers in the 300 range comprise the social science category. The second and third digits of this top row further narrow the classification

Table A.2   Dewey Decimal Classification
System

Broad subject areas or classes:

000   Generalities
100   Philosophy and Related Disciplines
200   Religion
300   The Social Sciences
400   Language
500   Pure Sciences
600   Technology (Applied Sciences)
700   The Arts
800   Literature and Rhetoric
900   General Geography and History, and the like

*Each class can be subdivided into smaller classes or
subclasses:*

300   The Social Sciences
310   Statistical Method and Statistics
320   Political Science
330   Economics
340   Law
350   Public Administration
360   Welfare and Association
370   Education
380   Commerce
390   Customs and Folklore

Example: 362.7
         N34

within the social sciences. For example, the 360s deal with "welfare and association."

The three-digit number is followed by a decimal point and numbers that indicate narrower classifications. In the second row of the Dewey call number is a letter, which is again the first letter of the last name of the author of the book, followed by a number that further identifies the author. This may be followed by a lowercase letter that is the first letter in the first word of the title of the book (excluding "a," "an," and "the"). The Dewey system also provides each book with its own unique call number.

The Public Catalog

With knowledge of the classification system in use at your library, you can locate any book. To do so,

you need to find the *public catalog,* which is a listing of all the holdings in the library. In many libraries today, the public catalog is an online computerized catalog of holdings. In some cases, these computer files can tell you not only whether a library owns a particular item but also its status: whether it is checked out, at the bindery, lost, and so on. Some libraries are involved in regional networks with other libraries, and their computerized public catalogs will list which libraries in the network own a particular book or other holding. Thus, if a book is not available at your library, you can see where it can be found.

In some libraries, the public catalog still takes the form of a *card catalog,* where each holding is listed on a separate card; in the computerized version of the public catalog, each library holding has a separate entry or record that can be called up onto the computer screen. To locate a book or other item in the library, find the card or record of the book, make note of the location (e.g., reference, documents, or stacks) and the call number, and find it on the library shelves. (Remember that books with similar call numbers will be about similar topics, so it is a good practice to browse through books in the immediate vicinity of the one whose call number you have located.) Figure A.1 presents a computer record for a book, with the various elements of the record identified. The record shows the author and title of the book, the subject headings under which it can be found in the public catalog, the library in which the book is located, and so on. To find a record in the public catalog, look it up under the author's name, the title of the work, the subject heading under which it is listed, or, in the computerized version, by keywords that appear in the record. Author and title searches are fairly straightforward, but searching by subject can be a little more problematic because library patrons sometimes have difficulties finding useful subject headings for their topic. To assist in this task, a volume titled *Library of Congress Subject Headings* can be used. It lists headings acceptable for use in a public catalog, cross-referencing a number of different topics. This volume is usually located

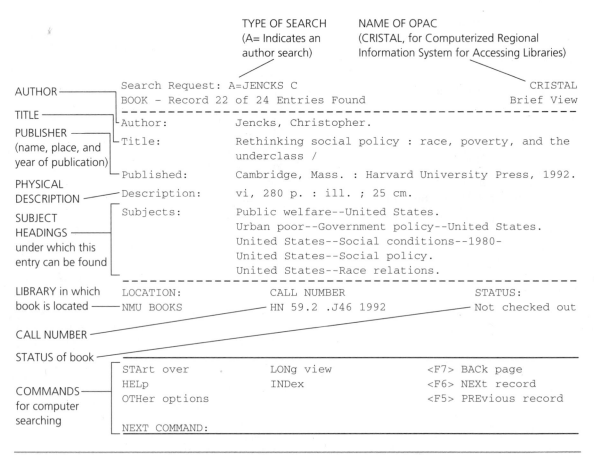

TYPE OF SEARCH
(A= Indicates an
author search)

NAME OF OPAC
(CRISTAL, for Computerized Regional
Information System for Accessing Libraries)

AUTHOR ——

TITLE ——

PUBLISHER ——
(name, place, and
year of publication)

PHYSICAL
DESCRIPTION ——

SUBJECT
HEADINGS ——
under which this
entry can be found

LIBRARY in which
book is located ——

CALL NUMBER ——

STATUS of book ——

COMMANDS ——
for computer
searching

```
Search Request: A=JENCKS C                                    CRISTAL
BOOK - Record 22 of 24 Entries Found                        Brief View
---------------------------------------------------------------------
Author:          Jencks, Christopher.

Title:           Rethinking social policy : race, poverty, and the
                 underclass /

Published:       Cambridge, Mass. : Harvard University Press, 1992.

Description:     vi, 280 p. : ill. ; 25 cm.

Subjects:        Public welfare--United States.
                 Urban poor--Government policy--United States.
                 United States--Social conditions--1980-
                 United States--Social policy.
                 United States--Race relations.
---------------------------------------------------------------------
LOCATION:            CALL NUMBER                   STATUS:
NMU BOOKS            HN 59.2 .J46 1992             Not checked out

STArt over        .    LONg view             <F7> BACk page
HELp                   INDex                 <F6> NEXt record
OTHer options                                <F5> PREvious record

NEXT COMMAND:
```

Figure A.1   An Example of a Record From an Online Public Access Catalog

somewhere near the public catalog itself. We described keyword searching earlier in the Computers in Research section. It is done the same way with the computerized public catalog. If you use the public catalog to locate books, you will have to determine from the title of the book and the brief description of the contents contained in the record whether a book will be useful to you. When you do this, it is better to err on the side of jotting down too many call numbers rather than too few.

Once the organizational key to the library is unlocked, it is easy to locate the information stored in books. There are, however, other repositories of information in the library, one of the most important of which is periodicals.

Periodicals

One of the most valuable and heavily used resources of the library, in addition to books, is *periodicals.* Periodicals are published periodically, such as weekly or monthly (hence, the name "periodicals"), and they often contain articles by a number of different authors on a variety of topics. Periodicals come in two basic types, although some are a blend of both. *Magazines* are directed at the general public, are written in a light and popular style, and are often commercial ventures. *Journals* are professional periodicals that publish articles primarily intended for members of a particular profession. The *American Sociological Review,* the *Journal of Social Ser-*

vice Research, and the *Journal of the American Medical Association* are examples. We will focus primarily on journals, but both magazines and journals can be very helpful in researching a problem because, first, periodicals tend to be more current than books, especially in reporting research findings. This is so, in part, because the production process for books is longer than that for periodicals. In addition, in many scientific fields, including the human services, much research is reported first in journals. In fact, many books contain primarily summaries or assessments of research that has already appeared in journals. Second, the articles in periodicals are brief and specific, enabling you to gather more information about a particular topic in a shorter period of time.

Periodicals, like books, can be given a call number, although not all libraries classify their periodicals according to call number. When periodicals are given a call number, they can be housed in the library in two ways: along with the books in the library by call number or separately from books by call number. When this procedure is used, you will need to look in the public catalog or other location to find the call number of the periodical you wish. The advantage of classifying periodicals by call number is that periodicals on a similar topic will be near one another. Some libraries, however, do not use the periodical call number, arranging periodicals separately from books in alphabetical order by the title of the journal (excluding the first "the" or "a" in the title). Once you locate where the periodicals are stored in your library, any particular periodical can then easily be found because no two periodicals have the same title or call number. Each issue of a journal is further identified by a volume number, the year of its publication, and an issue number indicating its place in the sequence of issues making up a particular volume. Some journals also identify their issues with the month or season (for example, Summer) in which it was published. To locate an issue of a journal, then, you need the following information: the call number or name of the journal, year of issue, volume number, and issue number (or month or season of publication).

There are usually three locations for periodicals in the library. First, most libraries store the *current* periodicals, or most recent issues, in a separate place where users can browse through them. Typically, the most recent one or two years are kept there. Second, *bound* periodicals contain several issues that have been bound together in one hardcover volume for extended storage. Each bound volume normally contains one year's worth of issues. Most of a library's periodical holdings are in this form. Third, old volumes are often put on *microfilm* or some other space-saving device for long-term storage. These are usually kept in large cabinets located near the machines that magnify them for viewing. A problem can arise when accessing periodicals that, though minor, is irksome to both patrons and librarians. The problem is that the separate issues that make up a volume of a journal must be bound together. This is done by sending the volume to a bindery, which means that the issues in that volume are temporarily unavailable to library patrons. The period is usually brief, but the periodicals are also usually recent ones because the binding is done within the first few years of publication. Students need to be aware that this problem can occur; it is one reason to begin library research early because some recent journals you are looking for may be available now but sent to the bindery a month from now.

Journals Important to the Human Services

Literally hundreds of journals in the library contain materials of use to human service researchers and practitioners. Although no one can be expected to read all these journals, awareness and occasional perusal of them can uncover much valuable source material. One way to spend free time is to browse through some of these journals in the current periodicals section of the library. Numerous journals are published primarily for human service professionals. Among the more important of these are:

Administration in Social Work
British Journal of Social Work

Child Welfare
Clinical Social Work Journal
Current Contents—Social and Behavioral Sciences
Exceptional Children
Families in Society
Federal Probation
Health & Social Work
International Journal of the Addictions
International Journal of Aging and Human Development
International Social Work
Journal of Social Work Education
Journal of Social Service Research
Journal of Sociology and Social Welfare
Public Welfare
School Social Work Journal
Smith College Studies in Social Work
Social Security Bulletin
Social Service Review
Social Work
Social Work Abstracts
Social Work in Education
Social Work in Health Care
Social Work Research
Social Work With Groups

Because the human service professions use knowledge developed by many of the behavioral sciences, many journals not published directly for human service providers can be of great value. Among the more useful of these are:

Administration and Policy in Mental Health
American Journal of Orthopsychiatry
American Journal of Public Health
American Journal of Sociology
American Sociological Review
Archives of General Psychiatry
Behavior Therapy
Child Development
Child Psychiatry and Human Development
Clinical Sociology Review
Community Mental Health Journal
Crime and Delinquency
Criminology
Gerontologist
International Journal of Group Psychotherapy
Journal of Abnormal Psychology
Journal of Applied Behavioral Science

Journal of Applied Sociology
Journal of Clinical Psychology
Journal of Consulting and Clinical Psychology
Journal of Counseling Psychology
Journal of Criminal Law and Criminology
Journal of Drug Issues
Journal of General Psychology
Journals of Gerontology (Series A and B)
Journal of Health and Social Behavior
Journal of Marital and Family Therapy
Journal of Marriage and the Family
Journal of Personality and Social Psychology
Journal of Research in Crime and Delinquency
Journal of Studies on Alcohol
Merrill-Palmer Quarterly
Psychological Bulletin
The Public Interest
Social Forces
Social Policy
Social Problems
Social Psychology Quarterly
Sociological Quarterly

Given this diversity of periodicals, how does one find those articles that relate to a particular topic? Two types of reference publications, called *abstracts* and *indexes,* are the major keys to accessing the information contained in periodicals.

Abstracts and Indexes

Some periodicals provide an *abstracting* service for library patrons. An *abstract* is a brief description, usually no more than a paragraph, of the contents of a book or article. A good abstract provides a complete summary of the work, including the thesis of the author, a description of any data collected, the conclusions drawn, and limitations of the study. Abstracts help you locate relevant research and decide whether it is sufficiently useful to warrant reading the entire work. Abstracting services provide a list of the journals whose articles are abstracted, usually in the first few pages of the volume of abstracts. Likewise, some journals list in each issue the abstracting and indexing services in which they are included.

Author Index

Milgrom, P., 795
Miller, A., 903
Miller, J., 625
Milling, L., 808
Mills, L., 893
Minton, C., 726
Minty, B., 479
Mitchell, C., 834
Mizrahi, T., 486
Molidor, C.E., 702, 753
Monaco, G.W., 611
Montel, K.H., 553
Mongomery, A., 903
Montiroli, P.M., 640
Morell, C., 651
Morgan, J., 798
Morris, F., 552
Morrison, B.J., 665
Morrissey, M., 828
Morrow-Howell, N., 536, 786
Mosher-Ashley, P.M., 666
Mueser, K.T., 806
Mullen, P.E., 727
Mulroy, E.A., 869
Munsch, J., 728
Murdock, B., 732
Murphy, K.R., 819
Murphy, M., 748
Murray, R.P., 652

N

Nardi, P.M., 480
Neck, C.P., 591

Abstract

— 753. MOLIDOR, C.E. —
Female gang members: a profile of aggression and victimization.
Social Work, 41(3): 251–57, May 1996.
School of Social Work, Univ. of Texas at Arlington, PO Box 19129, Arlington 76019–0129

Most research on gang membership has concentrated on the male population. When female gang membership is examined, it is usually in reference to the young women as sex objects or to their secondary roles in the gang. Minimal work has been done to examine the etiology of female gang membership. This article presents themes of female gang membership that emerged from in-depth structured interviews with 15 young women in a residential treatment facility. Demographic material, family structure, initiation rites, and criminal behaviors are examined. In addition, specific implications for social work practice and research are explored. (Journal abstract.)

Subject Index

and natural support systems, 883
people in midlife caring for parents as, 738
psychiatrically impaired, adult foster care for, 666
social work with, as ethnic minority, 659
stress among, as Holocaust survivors, 667
study of, in social work curriculum, 462
Aggression
association of rejection to, 677, 725
among female gang members, 753
Aging
role of, in co-residence of parents and adult children, 712
Agoraphobia
psychological treatments of panic disorder without, 507
Aid to Families With Dependent Children (AFDC)
and non-payment of child support by non-custodial parents, 686
participation of never-married and divorced mothers in, 718
AIDS
and anal sex among heterosexuals, 774
feminization of, 781
gay men with, and family of origin, 890
knowledge of, among junior high school students, 770
prevention of, in Turkey, 771
and promiscuity among gay men, 874
respite care for families with, 794
suicide among persons with, 780, 784
training of telephone intake workers on prevention of, 454

Figure A.2 Use of an Abstract
Source   Copyright © 1996, National Association of Social Workers, Inc. Reprinted with permission from *Social Work Abstracts,* Vol. 32, No. 2 (June 1996).

Using an abstract is relatively simple. Suppose you are interested in problems surrounding aggression and violence among gang members. First, you need to find a topic heading in the subject index of the abstract that will point you toward relevant articles (see Figure A.2). Obviously, "assaults" or "gangs" would be such topic headings and should be consulted. Because these headings are very specific, however, they might not be used by an abstracting service. More general topic headings would be "aggression" or "violence." After locating a specific heading, glance over the subtopics listed under it for one directly related to your interests. When you find the relevant subheading, there will be one or more numbers following it, each referring to a separate abstract. The abstracts are listed in the volume in numerical order. Abstracting services also provide an author index should you be searching for works by a particular author.

In addition to the summary description, the abstract provides the complete reference so that you can locate the work. In our illustration, the information presented in the reference, in the order it is presented, is this: author's name, title of article, name of journal, volume of journal, issue in volume, pages of that article in the journal, year journal was published, and an address where the author can be contacted. If an abstract suggests that an article will be useful to you, the complete reference should be written down.

The following are some of the major abstracting services useful for topics in the human services:

Abstracts in Gerontology: Current Literature on Aging
Child Development Abstracts and Bibliography
Criminal Justice Abstracts (formerly *Crime and Delinquency Abstracts*)
Dissertation Abstracts International
Exceptional Child Education Resources (*ECER,* formerly *Exceptional Child Education Abstracts*)
Human Resources Abstracts (formerly *Poverty and Human Resources Abstracts*)
Psychological Abstracts
Social Work Abstracts
Sociological Abstracts
Wilson Social Science Abstract
Women Studies Abstracts

Some abstracts and indexes are available on CD-ROM. *Sociological Abstracts'* CD-ROM version, for example, is called *Sociofile,* while *Psychological Abstracts'* is called *PsychLit.* Although these are some of the more important abstracts relevant to the human services, there are others. You should consult your reference librarian and become familiar with all the abstracts in your library relevant to the human services. If you make a list of them, you will

have a quick reference for any research you need to do while in college or on the job.

In addition to abstracting services, there are other publications that provide indexing services. An *index* is an alphabetical arrangement of materials based on some element of the materials, usually the author's last name, the title of the work, or the subject matter. (This text, for example, has separate name and subject indexes at the end.) Indexing publications usually provide an author index, which lists all the articles published by a particular author, and a subject index listing all articles on a given subject. An index will also present a list of the journals it indexes. Indexes have both advantages and disadvantages in comparison with abstracts. One advantage is that, because they take less time to prepare, they tend to be more current. Some abstracts are not published until more than a year after the articles covered have appeared. One disadvantage of indexes is that the user must rely on the title of the article to determine whether it is sufficiently relevant to spend the time seeking out the actual work itself. Anyone who has used indexes will attest to the many wild-goose chases where a seemingly useful article turned out to be irrelevant to a particular topic. Likewise, there are undoubtedly useful articles that are ignored because their titles do not seem sufficiently relevant.

Numerous indexes can be of value to human service professionals. A list follows.

Criminal Justice Periodical Index
Cumulative Index to Nursing and Allied Health Literature (*CINAHL*)
New York Times Index
Nursing and Allied Health Index
PAIS International
Readers' Guide to Periodical Literature
Social Sciences Citation Index
Social Sciences Index
United States Government Periodicals Index
Women's Studies Index

As with abstracts, you should make a list of all the indexes in your library relevant to the human service field.

Reference Books for the Human Services

One group of highly useful books that are, unfortunately, often overlooked are general reference books. Included in this rather broad category are encyclopedias, directories, and bibliographies. Although such works will not substitute for a thorough library search, they can save you time, as well as efficiently answer many routine questions. The following is only a partial listing of common reference works:

An Author's Guide to Social Work Journals
Encyclopedia of Adolescence
Encyclopedia of Aging
Encyclopedia of Alcoholism
Encyclopedia of Associations
Encyclopedia of Drug Abuse
Encyclopedia of Social Work
Encyclopedia of Sociology
National Directory of State Agencies
Public Welfare Directory
Social Service Organizations and Agencies Directory
Social Work Almanac
State Executive Directory Annual

Government Documents

The United States government is one of the largest publishing houses in the world, pouring forth mountains of books, bulletins, circulars, reports, and the like. Practitioners and researchers in the human service field will find government documents especially important because much of the research done in this area is sponsored by the government. Demonstration projects, program evaluations, and needs assessments, for example, are commonly funded by the government, and the resulting research reports are published by the government. Government documents also include information on model programs, funding sources, and bibliographies of topics of interest to human service professionals.

The *Monthly Catalog*

Locating government publications of use to you may at first seem a bewildering endeavor. With the aid of a few basic tools, however, the task can be done quickly, thoroughly, and with relatively little pain. The first thing to learn is whether your library is a *depository library,* a designation made by the superintendent of documents at the U.S. Government Printing Office. A *regional depository* library, of which there can be up to two in any state, receives everything published by the printing office. *Selective depositories* receive only some government publications, a listing of which can be found in *List of Classes of U.S. Government Publications Available for Selection by Depository Libraries.* Nondepository libraries will have some government documents, depending on which they choose to purchase.

The next thing you need to determine is which government documents are relevant to your particular topic of interest. Many libraries today list government documents along with other books in the online public access catalog. They can be located through name, title, subject, or keyword searches. Another major source for information on government documents is the *Monthly Catalog of U.S. Government Publications,* which has been published since 1895 and is now available on CD-ROM and accessible by computers. This publication includes a listing of most government publications along with the information necessary to locate them in the library or to purchase them from the office of the superintendent of documents.

Every government document submitted to the office of the superintendent of documents is given a *Monthly Catalog* entry number (*see* Figure A.3), and documents are listed in the *Monthly Catalog* in order of this number. This number has two components. The first two digits indicate the year the document was published (1988 in the illustration). The second group of digits locates the record in the *Monthly Catalog.* This second number is derived from sequencing the publications alphanumerically according to the classification number of the superintendent of documents, or SUDOCS number. The

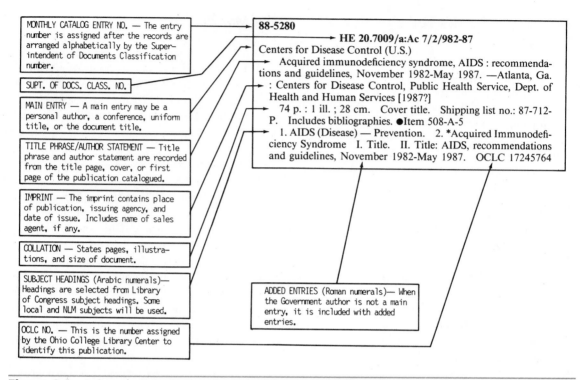

Figure A.3 A Sample Entry in the *Monthly Catalog of U.S. Government Publications*

SUDOCS number is like the call number in the public catalog for locating books because the government documents are filed in the library according to this number. However, although the Dewey decimal and Library of Congress classification systems classify entries according to subject matter, the SUDOCS system classifies materials according to the agency issuing the materials. In Figure A.3, for example, the *HE* in the SUDOCS number means that this document was issued by the Department of Health and Human Services. Thus, the *Monthly Catalog* entry number helps you locate the document in the *Monthly Catalog,* and the SUDOCS number enables you to locate where the document is shelved in the library.

Simply looking through the *Monthly Catalog* is an inefficient way of finding publications on the exact topic you want. Several aids can make your search both quicker and more thorough. These are the subject index, the author index, the title index,

and the title keyword index (*see* Figure A.4). Thus, if you actually know the author or title of a publication, you can simply look these up in the appropriate index. The index will give the *Monthly Catalog* entry number (and, since 1987, the SUDOCS number). If you know neither the exact title nor the author, the subject index will provide a listing of documents according to subject matter and again will provide the title and *Monthly Catalog* entry number (and, since 1987, the SUDOCS number). If you know a keyword associated with the title, the title keyword index will similarly direct you to the *Monthly Catalog* number. Armed with this number, you simply go to the correct volume of the *Monthly Catalog* according to the entry number. The *Monthly Catalog* provides a variety of details about the publications (*see* Figure A.3). Generally, in addition to the SUDOCS number that allows you to locate the document, the entry will give the author, title, publication information, price, and

Author Index

Center of Military History.

The Annapolis Convention., 88-3726

Armies, corps, divisions, and separate brigades /, 88-4957

The Army historian: a publication of the United States Army Center of Military History., 88-664

The Army Medical Department, 1818-1865 /, 88-3731

Army museum newsletter., 88-663

David Brearly., 88-3727

Dissertation year fellowships /, 88-7892

The German campaigns in the Balkans (spring, 1941)., 88-1990

German tank maintenance in World War II., 88-7894

Jonathan Dayton., 88-3728

The medics' war /, 88-1987

Moscow to Stalingrad : decision in the east /, 88-6529

The profession of arms : the 1962 Lees Knowles lectures given at Trinity College, Cambridge /, 88-1988

The staff ride /, 88-1989

Thomas Fitzsimons, 88-3729

U.S. Army mobilization and logistics in the Korean War : a research approach /, 88-7893

Warfare in the far north, 88-7895

William Jackson., 88-3730

Centers for Disease Control (U.S.)

Acquired immunodeficiency syndrome, AIDS : recommendations and guidelines, November 1982-May 1987. (88-5280)

The agents of non-A, non-B viral hepatitis /, 88-2364

AIDS in Africa : an epidemiologic paradigm /, 88-2361

Title Index

Acid rain. (I 19.114:R 13), 88-5751

Acoustic emission/flaw relationship for in-service monitoring of nuclear pressure vessels : progress report / Hutton, P. H. (Y 3.N 88:25/4300/v.4, no.1), 88-6126

Acoustic emission monitoring of fracture development / Anderson, Sterling J. (I 28.23:9077), 88-8443

Acoustic-televiewer and acoustic-waveform logs used to characterize deeply buried basalt flows, Hanford Site, Benton County, Washington [microform] / Paillet, F. L. (I 19.76:85-419), 88-9555

Acquiescence rulings United States. Social Security Administration. (HE 3.44:(date)), 88-844

Acquired Immune Deficiency Syndrome (AIDS) and the Veterans' Administration : hearing before the Subcommittee on Hospitals and Health Care of the Committee on Veterans' Affairs, House of Representatives, One hundredth Congress, first session, June 17, 1987, United States. Congress. House. Committee on Veterans' Affairs. Subcommittee on Hospitals and Health Care. (Y 4.V 64/3:100-19), 88-6304

Acquired immunodeficiency syndrome (AIDS) : fifteenth update, July 1987 through September 1987. 845 citations / Abrams, Estelle J. (HE 20.3614/2:87-13), 88-5261.

Acquired immunodeficiency syndrome AIDS : recommendations and guidelines, November 1982-May 1987. Centers for Disease Control (U.S.) (HE 20.7009/a:Ac 7/2/982-87),(88-5280)

Acquired immunodeficiency syndrome (AIDS) : sixteenth update, October 1987 through December 1987, 1028 citations,

Keyword Index

January — June 1988

** to families with dependent children (AFDC) pro 88-2233

** to students, Financial 88-2219

**AIDS /, Foreign policy implications of 88-9914

** /, Progress on the treatment of 88-5246

** : facts about the disease : how to protect yo 88-4098

** : need for immediate OSHA regulations to pro 88-3409

** : Opportunities for international scientific 88-10204

** : recommendations and guidelines, November 19 (88-5280)

** & hepatitis B., Worker exposure to 88-9857

** and teenagers : 88-8795

** and the education of our children : a guide f 88-3754

** and the education of our children : a guide f 88-7933

** and the law enforcement officer / 88-9805

** and the Veterans' Administration : 88-10232

** crisis as related to the federal budget: 88-7526

** drug development program at NCI. 88-8121

** for health services research /, Selected bibl 88-9485

** for policymakers /, An Annotated bibliography 88-6630

** in Africa : an epidemiologic paradigm / 88-2361

** knowledge and attitudes for September 1987: 88-6869

** knowledge and attitudes : provisional data fr 88-6868

** patients /, New drug therapy developed for pn 88-6852

** prevention program operations, Guidelines fo 88-2367

** published in the Morbidity and Mortality Week 88-4101

** research : 88-4776

** research and medical care within the Veterans 88-4794

** research and medical care within the Veterans 88-8971

** research program /, NCI's 88-5245

** to navigation bulletin 88-1451

** vaccine /, Research on development of an 88-5244

** a public health challenge : state issues, po 88-5227

**), CDC reports on acquired immunodeficiency s 88-2344

**), fifteenth update, July 1987 through Septem 88-5261

**). Informe del jefe del Servicio de Salud Pub 88-6826

** Public Health Service guidelines for counse 88-5283

** : sixteenth update, October 1987 through Dec 88-9474

** Straight facts about 88-2265

**.. Tips on avoiding 88-6861

**) : twelfth update, October 1986 through Decem 88-2298

**.. Viruses in cancer and 88-8125

Subject Index

Agriculture — United States.

Country-of-origin labeling on imported perishable agricultural commodities : hearing before the Subcommittee on Domestic Marketing, Consumer Relations, and Nutrition of the Committee on Agriculture, House of Representatives, One hundredth Congress, first session, on H.R. 692, H.R. 1176, and H.R. 1246, March 30, 1987. United States. Congress. House. Committee on Agriculture. Subcommittee on Domestic Marketing, Consumer Relations, and Nutrition. (Y 4.Ag 8/1:100-14), 88-6150

Agriculture — United States — Periodicals.

Semiannual report to Congress. United States. Dept. of Agriculture. Office of the Inspector General. (A 1.1/3:987), 88-4801

AIDS (Disease) — Bibliography.

Acquired immunodeficiency syndrome (AIDS) : fifteenth update, July 1987 through September 1987. 845 citations / Abrams, Estelle J. (HE 20.3614/2:87-13) 88-5261

AIDS (Disease) — Prevention.

Acquired immunodeficiency syndrome, AIDS : recommendations and guidelines, November 1982-May 1987. Centers for Disease Control (U.S.) (HE 20.7009/a:Ac 7/2/982-87)(88-5280)

Human T-lymphotropic virus type III/lymphadenopathy-associated virus : agent summary statement (HE 20.7009/a:H 88/6), 88-5282

Public Health Service guidelines for counseling and antibody testing to prevent HIV infection and AIDS. (HE 20.7009/a:H 88/7), 88-5283

Recommendations for prevention of HIV transmission in health-care settings. (HE 20.7009/a:H 88/8), 88-5284

Summary : recommendations for preventing transmission of infection with human T-lymphotropic virus type III/lymphadenopathy-associated virus in the workplace. (HE 20.7009/a:H 88/2), 88-5281

Figure A.4 Four Indexes Useful in Locating Documents in the *Monthly Catalog of U.S. Government Publications*

subject headings. This is useful for determining whether that particular document is of further interest to you.

To summarize, then, the steps followed in using the *Monthly Catalog* to find government documents are these: First, consult an appropriate index and obtain *Monthly Catalog* entry numbers and SUDOCS numbers; second, consult the *Monthly Catalog* for more information about the document, a complete reference, and the classification number of the superintendent of documents; and third, locate the document itself.

In addition to the *Monthly Catalog of U.S. Government Publications,* the following agencies publish separate catalogs of their own publications: the Bureau of the Census, the Commerce and Labor departments, and the Civil Rights Commission.

Subject Bibliographies and State Government Documents

The government also provides useful bibliographies of government documents on a wide range of topics. If one or more of these topics coincides with your interest, the subject bibliographies can provide access to many publications in your topic area. These bibliographies are indexed in the same way as the *Monthly Catalog.* For example, social welfare is subject no. 30. Turning to bibliography no. 30, one finds a listing of publications on the general topic of social welfare. The entries provide title, author, the SUDOCS number, and the stock number for ordering. There are also subject bibliographies on aging (no. 39) and childhood and adolescence (no. 35).

Documents published by state governments are often stored in libraries and are listed in the online public access catalog (OPAC). If your library does not receive the state publications, you can probably order them for a small fee.

Sources of Data in the Library

In Chapter 8, we discussed research using available data—data collected by someone else but available to others for analysis. The library is a repository rich in such available data. Some of it can serve as a useful beginning for a research project, and in some cases it can also be used for hypothesis testing and evaluation of programs. In either event, you should be familiar with the major sources of such data in your library.

Government Sources

The United States government is a major source of data available in libraries. Many of the government documents discussed previously report research findings, describe programs, or analyze social policy. These are not, strictly speaking, sources of raw data to be analyzed but rather interpretations, assessments, or summaries of data. Other government publications, however, present raw data on health, crime, poverty, and many other topics relevant to the human service professions, often without any accompanying interpretation or assessment. We will discuss such publications as are produced by two government agencies, the Bureau of the Census and the Department of Labor.

The U.S. Bureau of the Census publishes a vast array of statistical data of use to behavioral scientists and human service workers:

Bulletin of Criminal Justice Statistics. This publication, from the Department of Justice, contains valuable data on prisons, prison populations, and the criminal justice system in general.

Census of Population. The nationwide census is conducted once every decade and provides data on employment, income, race, occupation, poverty, and much more.

County and City Data Book. This is a supplement to the *Statistical Abstract,* reporting data on a local or regional basis. This book is only published every 5 years.

Current Population Reports. These are a series of annual publications that report on many of the same issues that the census does but are based on a probability sample of the population. There are series on income, household and family characteristics, marital status, living arrangements, and geographic mobility. These are useful publications for keeping current on changing social trends and problems.

Historical Statistics of the U.S.: Colonial Times to 1970. This volume provides historical data to supplement the *Statistical Abstract,* which often includes data from only the past decade or less.

Statistical Abstract of the U.S. This is an annual summary of statistical information about the United States. It contains data on population, birth and death rates, marriage and divorce rates, crime, health, education, and social services. This is probably the single most useful statistical summary.

The Bureau of Labor Statistics of the Department of Labor publishes many volumes relating to the labor force, employment, and earnings in the United States:

Employment and Earnings and Monthly Report on the Labor Force. Published monthly.

Employment and Earnings, States and Areas. An annual summary of state and regional trends.

Employment and Earnings Statistics for the United States. An annual summary.

Monthly Labor Review. A journal that presents both statistical and analytical articles relating to work and the labor force.

The Women's Bureau of the Department of Labor also publishes a number of periodicals focusing specifically on women workers, their earnings, their educational attainment, and legislation that affects them.

Several of these government sources of data are now available on CD-ROM and some over the Internet. The Census Bureau, for example, makes some data available over the Internet, and a program called GPO Access also links into online data sources. Information about Internet access to data is found in some of the Exploring the Internet sections in this book; in addition, you should check with the reference librarian at your library about CD-ROM and online sources of government data.

Nongovernment Sources

Amassing vast amounts of data as the government does each year is, of course, beyond the resources of most nongovernment organizations, such as businesses or nonprofit agencies. Many of them, however, do collect limited amounts of data that can be useful to researchers, and libraries can sometimes assist in gaining access to these data.

In some cases, libraries purchase *codebooks* that indicate the data available in a particular data set. Especially if some other arm of the university, such as the computer center or one of the behavioral science departments, has purchased the data set, the library may purchase such codebooks. However, libraries sometimes purchase the data sets themselves and make them available to faculty and students for research purposes. This has become especially true in recent years because data are increasingly available on CD-ROM, a technology libraries already use, as we have seen, for things like bibliographic searching and abstract searching. For example, the Sociometrics Corporation produces a number of data sets relevant to the social sciences and makes them available on CD-ROM or tapes for mainframe computers. The company has data sets relevant to adolescent sexuality and health; AIDS knowledge, attitudes, and behavior; women's health; and others. These data sets and others like them are often purchased by libraries or academic departments in universities and made available to students. Faculty and students can retrieve the data from the CD-ROM and import this information to a mainframe computer or microcomputer and analyze it with whatever statistical software is available in those environments (*see* Chapter 14). You should learn what data sets are available in your library.

Information Literacy and Critical Thinking Skills

A library is a veritable cornucopia of information, and we have tried to provide you with basic information on how to access that information. However, the best way to learn about your library is to *use* it. Roam around the stacks, browse through the public catalog, delve into government documents, explore the Internet. We have emphasized the ways in which you can systematically access information in the library. However, you can also find much useful material in random and casual rovings through the library. Above all, consult with the reference librarians, who are there primarily to assist you. These professionals are trained to help students and faculty devise programs and strategies for finding, analyzing, synthesizing, and evaluating information. Such information literacy is increasingly essential in the modern world, whether such information is found in a book, on a CD-ROM, or online. Information literacy is an important part of critical thinking, or the ability to judge the authenticity, accuracy, and worth of information.

This guide to the library has emphasized its utility to human service practitioners. However, a library is not meant solely to help you write a term paper or complete a research project. A library is a repository of cultural knowledge. It houses research reports on alcoholics along with the epic myths of Homer and the ancient and sacred literature of Hinduism, the Vedas. Literature, philosophy, and theology accompany engineering and celestial mechanics. And you can read the daily newspaper there! The point is that a library is, in a sense, the storehouse of a culture, and we hope that you use it to its fullest extent throughout your life as a source of enrichment and fulfillment. The search programs and strategies devised with the help of reference librarians in your college years can be used after college to help you find and analyze information about social issues or personal problems and to help you keep current in your chosen field of endeavor.

Exploring the Internet

All libraries today serve as gateways to the Internet, although one can access the Internet in other ways. The Internet has become an essential adjunct to the library in the search for information. For example, some of the table-of-contents and document-delivery services mentioned in this chapter can be accessed through the Internet, either through a library or your own personal computer. One such service is the UnCover system, whose Web site is http://www.carl.org/uncover. At this site, you can arrange to view the tables of contents of many thousands of periodicals and to have copies of arti-

cles mailed or faxed to you. This Web site will also tell you what the costs are for these various services.

There are also Web sites that enable you to review the holdings of libraries other than your own. This is especially useful if the library you have access to is small, with limited holdings. By exploring these other libraries, you can find resources, especially books and journals, that may not be in a smaller library. The Web site for the Library of Congress, for example, is at http://lcweb.loc.gov/homepage/lchp.html. Another Web site that provides access to many libraries is http://library.usask.ca/hywebcat/. Maintained by the University of Saskatchewan, this Web site will link you to the OPACs of many libraries around the world. You can search by geographical area or by the type of library desired. Under the latter, there are many options, such as medical, religious, or public libraries as well as the libraries of colleges and universities. This Web site also has links to many publishing companies.

Another way to gain library access is to use a search engine. We used Webcrawler in searching for "library access." This produced menus that enabled us to locate many libraries in the United States and abroad, as well as many specialized libraries in areas such as art and law.

The Sociometrics Corporation has a World Wide Web site located at http://www.socio.com. You can explore that location to get more information about the data sets the company has available, what variables they contain, and how much they cost—even the response options to questions that were asked in surveys. This can give you an idea about what kind of data sets might be available in your university.

For Further Reading

Bolner, Myrtle S. *Library Research Skills Handbook*, 2nd ed. Dubuque, Iowa: Kendall-Hunt, 1995. This book provides a comprehensive overview of how to do research in the library.

Cuba, Lee. *A Short Guide to Writing About Social Science*, 3rd ed. New York: Longman, 1997. This book is mostly about writing term papers and research reports, but it also includes a significant amount of material on using the library and the Internet.

Gates, Jean K. *Guide to the Use of Libraries and Information Sources,* 7th ed. New York: McGraw-Hill, 1993. This book is designed as a text for basic courses in library resources, so it can be an excellent introduction to the library that extends the topics in this chapter considerably.

Hahn, Harley. *The Internet Yellow Pages.* Berkeley, Calif.: Osborne McGraw-Hill, 1996. As the name implies, this book is an excellent resource for finding materials on the Internet.

McLaren, Bruce J. *Understanding and Using the Internet.* Minneapolis/St. Paul: West, 1996. This book is an excellent introduction to the Internet, providing all the information you need to utilize that online source of information.

Reed, Jeffrey G., and Pam M. Baxter. *Library Use: A Handbook for Psychology,* 2nd ed, Washington, D.C.: American Psychological Association, 1992. Focused as it is on psychology, this book is nonetheless a valuable guide to the library for someone preparing to conduct a social research project. Among other things, it covers using abstracting services, doing computer searches, and locating various scales and measurement devices.

The Sociology Writing Group. *A Guide To Writing Sociology Papers,* 3rd ed. New York: St. Martin's, 1994. This book provides useful guidance in terms of doing library research in the social sciences, organizing time and materials, and preparing and writing analyses based on both quantitative and qualitative data.

Generating Random Numbers

Random numbers are used for many purposes in social research. They are often used, for example, in constructing a probability sample in which elements are selected from a population and placed in the sample on a random basis. In some cases, this is done with a table of random numbers. Tables of random numbers can be found in many places, such as textbooks on statistics. A few volumes contain nothing but random numbers. Table B.1 in this appendix is a brief table of random numbers. In Chapter 6, while discussing simple random samples, we describe in detail how to use such a table.

Computer spreadsheets, such as Microsoft Excel, Lotus 1-2-3, or Borland Quattro Pro, make generating random numbers easy. Although the specific command varies from program to program, the basic approach is the same. The following command, used in Quattro Pro, serves as an illustration for generating a random number from 0 to 1,000:

$$@INT(@RAND \star 1001)$$

"@RAND" generates a decimal random number between 0 and 1. This random decimal is multiplied by 1,001, resulting in a number that ranges from a low of less than 1.0000 to a high of less than 1,001.0000. The "@INT" command drops the decimal portion and displays the integer portion.

Hence, the resulting random number ranges from 0 to 1,000. For example, if the random decimal were 0.0002, the result would be:

$$@INT(0.0002 \star 1001) = @INT(0.2002) = 0$$

If the random decimal were 0.9999, the result would be:

$$@INT(.9999 \star 1001) = @INT(1000.8999) = 1000$$

The range of random numbers may be changed by simply substituting a different value for 1,001. To generate a list of random numbers, the formula is copied into as many cells as needed using the "Cell Copy" command. An advantage of using a spreadsheet is that the random numbers can easily be ordered from lowest to highest. This feature is convenient for such tasks as selecting a random sample of case records. To reorder the numbers, the cell formulas are first converted to values using the "Values" selection from the "Edit" menu. Next, the "Sort" option is selected from the "Database" menu. The result is a list of random numbers in rank order.

Finally, random numbers may also be generated by standard statistical packages, such as SPSS and MINITAB. As with the spreadsheet, SPSS and MINITAB have a sorting procedure available that can be used to order the random numbers.

Table B.1   List of Random Numbers

894	920	220	614	090	805	668	331	745	136	071	056	205
493	974	737	304	049	109	097	660	275	036	819	132	807
768	450	669	873	510	712	613	059	924	377	090	315	507
482	379	669	549	746	814	424	217	883	969	246	777	454
621	422	255	762	718	431	883	645	341	148	212	527	557
488	005	671	472	511	746	446	425	889	766	248	860	956
472	782	194	854	272	001	465	118	514	892	258	367	599
554	576	110	002	045	940	724	975	533	401	603	047	221
333	797	019	563	344	349	210	261	204	225	739	730	872
653	346	789	798	616	377	724	625	760	845	430	239	647
018	792	713	967	411	189	654	392	789	308	733	343	168
446	165	992	185	650	158	738	758	284	900	822	217	809
733	098	756	628	982	258	875	694	463	772	162	788	537
324	338	369	374	975	389	657	310	552	951	242	626	135
800	408	564	050	120	844	656	122	270	638	712	442	293
994	349	174	326	424	016	645	595	383	578	393	114	426
776	410	150	051	532	844	219	710	207	763	085	314	858
835	234	461	844	543	475	105	274	191	122	549	991	696
408	051	655	449	318	302	574	581	586	466	123	866	301
356	581	735	113	285	188	235	863	096	585	783	817	030
336	130	491	288	437	351	650	325	673	807	311	844	363
935	737	202	656	201	553	387	933	546	203	930	201	322
975	455	421	422	173	767	163	860	167	939	304	318	227
484	564	624	002	801	589	140	125	059	875	848	345	944
848	669	356	665	029	902	247	804	133	374	407	316	773
836	906	596	608	598	956	481	982	742	757	635	746	967
425	895	530	807	924	685	325	894	571	925	705	559	532
122	251	638	926	678	852	779	707	320	649	809	203	333
034	451	574	656	354	387	913	663	375	079	743	503	635
145	849	295	003	709	118	762	068	784	616	147	959	292
428	232	529	095	487	039	387	957	546	864	107	120	661
755	154	664	651	508	033	915	809	328	137	452	291	539
826	104	222	160	209	051	502	331	146	686	883	400	246
776	604	739	131	166	298	637	123	561	890	701	131	288
407	824	285	927	235	029	020	693	109	638	896	498	486
618	200	842	317	347	457	092	399	155	282	524	001	843
471	229	629	918	141	025	058	833	729	715	300	293	346
820	378	250	979	367	537	907	692	685	185	282	276	351
466	615	866	805	239	138	372	292	787	350	852	026	586
694	817	184	101	428	277	646	584	674	582	545	348	245
378	839	626	595	447	107	403	426	421	177	414	308	652
126	857	405	000	284	823	588	927	228	559	376	230	786
728	088	417	036	171	603	988	692	995	285	056	823	211
719	148	527	527	334	371	726	435	651	414	908	170	684

Source   This table of random numbers was generated by the Computer Center at Northern Michigan University with the assistance of John Limback.

APPENDIX C
Professional Codes of Ethics

American Sociological Association 478
National Association of Social Workers 480

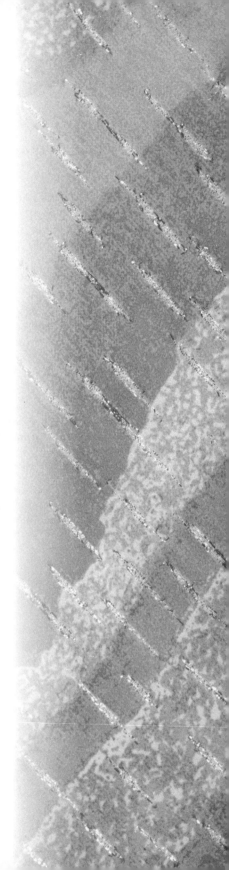

American Sociological Association

I. The Practice of Sociology

A. *Objectivity and Integrity*

Sociologists should strive to maintain objectivity and integrity in the conduct of sociological research and practice.

1. Sociologists should adhere to the highest possible technical standards in their research, teaching and practice.

2. Since individual sociologists vary in their research modes, skills, and experience, sociologists should always set forth *ex ante* the limits of their knowledge and the disciplinary and personal limitations that condition the validity of findings which affect whether or not a research project can be successfully completed.

3. In practice or other situations in which sociologists are requested to render a professional judgment, they should accurately and fairly represent their areas and degrees of expertise.

4. In presenting their work, sociologists are obligated to report their findings fully and should not misrepresent the findings of their research. When work is presented, they are obligated to report their findings fully and without omission of significant data. To the best of their ability, sociologists should also disclose details of their theories, methods, and research designs that might bear upon interpretations of research findings.

5. Sociologists must report fully all sources of financial support in their publications and must note any special relations to any sponsor.

6. Sociologists should not make any guarantees to respondents, individuals, groups or organizations—unless there is full intention and ability to honor such commitments. All such guarantees, once made, must be honored.

7. Consistent with the spirit of full disclosure of method and analysis, sociologists, after they have completed their own analyses, should cooperate in efforts to make raw data and pertinent documentation collected and prepared at public expense available to other social scientists, at reasonable costs, except in cases where confidentiality, the client's rights to proprietary information and privacy, or the claims of a fieldworker to the privacy of personal notes necessarily would be violated. The timeliness of this cooperation is especially critical.

8. Sociologists should provide adequate information and citations concerning scales and other measures used in their research.

9. Sociologists must not accept grants, contracts, or research assignments that appear likely to require violation of the principles enunciated in this Code, and should dissociate themselves from research when they discover a violation and are unable to achieve its correction.

10. When financial support for a project has been accepted, sociologists must make every reasonable effort to complete the proposed work on schedule, including reports to the funding source.

11. When several sociologists, including students, are involved in joint projects, there should be mutually accepted ex-

plicit agreements at the outset with respect to division of work, compensation, access to data, rights of authorship, and other rights and responsibilities. Such agreements may need to be modified as the project evolves and such modifications must be agreed upon jointly.

12. Sociologists should take particular care to state all significant qualifications on the findings and interpretations of their research.

13. Sociologists have the obligation to disseminate research findings, except those likely to cause harm to clients, collaborators, and participants, or those which are proprietary under a formal or informal agreement.

14. In their roles as practitioners, researchers, teachers, and administrators, sociologists have an important social responsibility because their recommendations, decisions, and actions may alter the lives of others. They should be aware of the situations and pressures that might lead to the misuse of their influence and authority. In these various roles, sociologists should also recognize that professional problems and conflicts may interfere with professional effectiveness. Sociologists should take steps to insure that these conflicts do not produce deleterious results for clients, research participants, colleagues, students, and employees.

B. *Disclosure and Respect for the Rights of Research Populations*

Disparities in wealth, power, and social status between the sociologist and respondents and clients may reflect and create problems of equity in research collaboration. Conflict of interest for the sociologist may occur in research and practice. Also to follow the precepts of the scientific method—such as those requiring full disclosure—may entail

adverse consequences or personal risks for individuals and groups. Finally, irresponsible actions by a single researcher or research team can eliminate or reduce future access to a category of respondents by the entire profession and its allied fields.

1. Sociologists should not misuse their positions as professional social scientists for fraudulent purposes or as a pretext for gathering intelligence for any organization or government. Sociologists should not mislead respondents involved in a research project as to the purpose for which that research is being conducted.

2. Subjects of research are entitled to rights of biographical anonymity.

3. Information about subjects obtained from records that are opened to public scrutiny cannot be protected by guarantees of privacy or confidentiality.

4. The process of conducting sociological research must not expose respondents to substantial risk of personal harm. Informed consent must be obtained when the risks of research are greater than the risks of everyday life. Where modest risk or harm is anticipated, informed consent must be obtained.

5. Sociologists should take culturally appropriate steps to secure informed consent and to avoid invasions of privacy. Special actions may be necessary where the individuals studied are illiterate, have very low social status, or are unfamiliar with social research.

6. To the extent possible in a given study sociologists should anticipate potential threats to confidentiality. Such means as the removal of identifiers, the use of randomized responses, and other statistical solutions to problems of privacy should be used where appropriate.

7. Confidential information provided by research participants must be treated as such by sociologists, even when this

information enjoys no legal protection or privilege and legal force is applied. The obligation to respect confidentiality also applies to members of research organizations (interviewers, coders, clerical staff, etc.) who have access to the information. It is the responsibility of administrators and chief investigators to instruct staff members on this point and to make every effort to insure that access to confidential information is restricted.

8. While generally adhering to the norm of acknowledging the contributions of all collaborators, sociologists should be sensitive to harm that may arise from disclosure and respect a collaborator's wish or need for anonymity. Full disclosure may be made later if circumstances permit.

9. Study design and information gathering techniques should conform to regulations protecting the rights of human subjects, irrespective of source of funding, as outlined by the American Association of University Professors (AAUP) in "Regulations Governing Research on Human Subjects: Academic Freedom and the Institutional Review Board," *Academe,* December 1981: 358–370.

10. Sociologists should comply with appropriate federal and institutional requirements pertaining to the conduct of research. These requirements might include but are not necessarily limited to failure to obtain proper review and approval for research that involves human subjects and failure to follow recommendations made by responsible committees concerning research subjects, materials, and procedures.

Source   American Sociological Association. *Code of Ethics.* Washington, D. C., 1989. Reprinted by permission of the American Sociological Association.

National Association of Social Workers

1. Social Workers' Ethical Responsibilities to Clients

1.01 Commitment to Clients

Social workers' primary responsibility is to promote the welfare of clients. In general, clients' interests are primary. However, social workers' responsibility to the larger society or specific legal obligations may on limited occasions supersede the loyalty owed clients and clients should be so advised. (Examples include when a social worker is required by law to report that a client has abused a child or has threatened to harm self or others.)

1.02 Self-Determination

Social workers respect and promote the right of clients to self-determination and assist clients in their efforts to identify and clarify their goals. Social workers may limit clients' right to self-determination when, in their professional judgment, clients' actions or potential actions pose a serious, foreseeable, and imminent risk to themselves or others.

1.03 Informed Consent

(a) Social workers should obtain clients' informed consent for services delivered to them. Social workers should use clear and understandable language to inform clients of the purpose of the service, risks related to the service, relevant costs, reasonable alternatives, clients' right to refuse or withdraw consent, and the time frame covered by the consent. Social workers should provide clients with an opportunity to ask questions.

(b) In instances where clients are not literate or have difficulty understanding the primary language used in the practice setting, social workers should take steps to ensure clients' comprehension. This may include providing clients with a detailed verbal explanation or arranging for an interpreter and/or translator.

(c) In instances where clients lack the capacity to provide informed consent, social workers should protect clients' interests by seeking permission from an appropriate third party, and inform clients consistent with their level of understanding. Social workers should take reasonable steps to enhance such clients' ability to give informed consent.

(d) In instances where clients are receiving services involuntarily, social workers should provide information about the nature and extent of services, and of the extent of clients' right to refuse service.

(e) Social workers should provide services only in the context of a negotiated professional relationship based on informed consent. Social workers who provide services via electronic mediums (such as computers, telephone, radio, and television) should inform recipients of the limitations and risks associated with such services.

(f) Social workers should obtain clients' informed consent before audiotaping or videotaping clients, or permitting third party observation of clients.

4. Social Workers' Ethical Responsibilities as Professionals

4.01 Competence

(a) Social workers should accept responsibility or employment only on the basis of existing competence or the intention to acquire the necessary competence.

(b) Social workers should strive to become and remain proficient in professional practice and the performance of professional functions. Social workers should critically examine, and keep current with, emerging knowledge relevant to social work. Social workers should routinely review emerging professional literature and participate in continuing education relevant to social work practice and social work ethics.

(c) Social workers should base practice on recognized knowledge, including empirically based knowledge, relevant to social work and social work ethics.

5. Social Workers' Ethical Responsibilities to the Social Work Profession

5.01 Integrity of the Profession

(a) Social workers should work toward the maintenance and promotion of high standards of practice.

(b) Social workers should uphold and advance the values, ethics, knowledge, and mission of the profession. Social workers should protect, enhance, and improve the integrity of the profession through appropriate study and research, active discussion, and responsible criticism of the profession.

(c) Social workers should contribute time and professional expertise to activities that promote respect for the value, integrity, and competence of the social work profession. These activities may include teaching, research, consultations, service, legislative testimony, presentations in the community, and participation in their professional organizations.

(d) Social workers should contribute to the knowledge base of social work and share with colleagues their knowledge related to practice, research, and ethics. Social workers should seek to contribute to the profession's literature and to share their knowledge at professional meetings and conferences.

(e) Social workers should act to prevent the unauthorized and unqualified practice of social work.

5.02 Evaluation and Research

(a) Social workers should monitor and evaluate policies, the implementation of programs, and practice interventions.

(b) Social workers should promote and facilitate evaluation and research in order to contribute to the development of knowledge generally.

(c) Social workers should critically examine and keep current with emerging knowledge relevant to social work and fully utilize evaluation and research evidence in their professional practice.

(d) Social workers engaged in evaluation or research should consider carefully possible consequences and follow guidelines developed for the protection of evaluation and research participants. Appropriate institutional review boards should be consulted.

(e) Social workers engaged in evaluation or research should obtain voluntary and written informed consent from participants, when appropriate, without any implied deprivation or penalty for refusal to participate, and with due regard for participants' privacy and dignity.

(f) Social workers engaged in empirically based evaluation of practice should obtain clients' informed consent, when appropriate.

(g) Social workers should inform participants of their rights to withdraw from evaluation and research at any time.

(h) Social workers should ensure that participants in evaluation and research have access to appropriate supportive services.

(i) Social workers engaged in evaluation or research should protect participants from unwarranted physical or mental distress, harm, danger, or deprivation.

(j) Social workers engaged in the evaluation of services should discuss obtained information only for professional purposes and only with persons directly and professionally concerned with this information.

(k) Social workers who report evaluation and research results should protect participants' confidentiality by omitting identifying information unless proper consent has been obtained authorizing disclosure.

(l) Social workers should inform participants in evaluation and research of any limits of confidentiality.

(m) Social workers should report evaluation and research findings accurately.

(n) Social workers should educate themselves, their students, and colleagues about responsible research practices.

Source Reprinted with permission from *Code of Ethics of the National Association of Social Workers,* as adopted by the 1996 NASW Delegate Assembly.

Research and Practice: The World Wide Web Connection

The Basics   484

Authors' Web Page   486

Internet Glossary   487

Since the first edition of *Applied Social Research* was published, remarkable changes have occurred in computer technology and global communications systems. These changes have had a profound impact on many facets of society, including how we learn, how we conduct research, and how we conduct practice in the human services. Unquestionably, the biggest change has been the advent of the **Internet,** or simply "the Net," as it is called in common parlance. Ubiquitous as it already is, the Internet will only become more important as a source of communication and information exchange, although at the moment, because it is so new, it can seem a little chaotic and unorganized. The Internet can be accessed in many ways, but those most useful for materials related to research and human service practice are electronic mail (or e-mail), the World Wide Web, discussion lists, and Usenet groups. This appendix will provide some of the basics on using the Internet in conjunction with the Exploring the Internet section of each chapter. However, please keep two things in mind. First, addresses and software used to access the Internet change frequently, so addresses that worked when we wrote this edition may have changed by the time you try them. Second, in part because of the first point, be ready to explore and innovate. If some address or procedure described in this appendix doesn't work, use some of the other tools described to search out the desired information or site. Use what is described in this appendix as a platform from which to find other sources of information on social research and human service practice and other ways to use the Internet. We will assume that you know how to operate in a Windows environment and how to access the Internet through your university computer or a commercial computer service. For good introductions to using the

Internet, see McLaren (1996) and Poindexter (1996).

The Basics

One of the most widespread uses of the Net is for electronic mail, or **e-mail,** which involves typing a message on a screen and sending it electronically. Many universities provide their students with an e-mail address, or you can get an e-mail address by subscribing to a commercial service, such as America Online or CompuServe. Contact the computer center on your campus or one of the commercial services to learn exactly how to get your Internet address and how to send e-mail.

The Internet not only helps connect people all over the world, but it is also a world unto itself with its own culture and language. Although our goal is to keep this introduction basic and as free of jargon and acronyms as possible, some "computerese" is inevitable. One important Internet label is Uniform Resource Locator, or URL. A **URL** is basically a code or label that you use to reach an information source, much like you use a phone number to call someone. Just as different area codes, such as 1-800 or 1-900 or 1-616, tell you something about the type of call you're placing, URL designations are assigned according to the kind of Internet source being used. Somewhat like the area code in the phone number, the Uniform Resource Locator utilizes a type specifier to identify different kinds of programs encountered on the Internet. For example, some Internet sites contain graphics and text that you can look at and read, while others consist of computer programs and files that you download and use on your own machine. It is beyond the scope of this appendix to delve into the specifics of using the various protocols, but you are encouraged to expand your Internet proficiency by using the sources mentioned here or by making use of consultants at your school. Here are some common type specifiers that you may encounter in making use of the Internet:

http	Hypertext Transport Protocol for a WWW site	http://[hostname] [pathname]
gopher	Gopher protocol to access a gopher site	gopher://[hostname] [pathname]
ftp	File Transfer Protocol for retrieving remote files	ftp://[hostname] [pathname]
news	Usenet News site	news: [newsgroup name]
telnet	Uses telnet to emulate a terminal session	telnet: [hostname]

The specifer http is the acronym for Hypertext Transport Protocol. It is probably the most common URL that you'll encounter because it's used by sites on the World Wide Web (WWW), a program that allows access to the Internet for a variety of uses. For example, the WWW can be used to access the home pages or other locations that are made available by individuals and organizations. **Hypertext** involves the linking of many documents together, so that clicking on a word or symbol, called a "button," in one document will transfer you to other documents on a similar topic. Buttons are usually set apart on the screen in a different color from the rest of the text. If you move the arrow/cursor on the screen to a button and the arrow/cursor becomes a little fist pointing a finger, this means that this button is a link to other sites; clicking on it will move you to those other sites.

Gopher is another protocol that you may want to learn how to use. It is commonly used for public, campus-wide information services at colleges and universities. You may use it to access data files and information for your own use.

FTP stands for File Transfer Protocol and is used to locate and download files directly to your own computer. For example, you might wish to download the most recent version of a software package, such as a statistics program.

Usenet News is a network of computers that carry discussion groups devoted to almost any subject imaginable. It is primarily text-based and lacks the sophisticated graphics of http sites, but it can still provide a wealth of information.

Telnet is what is known as a terminal emulation tool. It permits you to log on to sources such as library catalogs and other public access information sources. Some Internet services are accessible via telnet or http. Although http is easier for many people to use because of its graphic display format, accessing a source via telnet may prove faster and more trouble-free once you become familiar with it.

Of all the ways of accessing the Internet, the **World Wide Web** with the http protocol is by far the easiest and the most popular. Consequently, we have focused primarily on it in our chapter exercises. A few basic commands need to be described. In our illustrations, we have used a Web browser called Netscape Navigator because it is widely used and is the one that we happen to have available. At the top of the screen is a menu bar with common Windows commands, such as "File" and "Edit." Below that is a toolbar with commands such as "Back" and "Forward." Just below the toolbar is the Location block where you can type in Internet address and hit "enter" to go to that site. For example, if you enter the URL code "http://www.nmu.edu," you'll see the Northern Michigan University Home Page. Below the Location block are Directory buttons, with commands such as "Net Search" and "Newsgroups." If you are a newcomer to the program, the "Handbook" button is a good place to start. It provides a tutorial and many helpful hints that make using the Internet more productive and convenient.

One useful command is the "Back" button on the toolbar. By clicking on that button, you go back to the previous site that you had visited. This is very handy while surfing the Net because sometimes you go down a path that proves unproductive or uninteresting; you can backtrack to the point where you had diverged down that path by clicking on the "Back" button the requisite number of times. If you go too far, the "Forward" button enables you to advance again.

"Bookmarks" is an option on the menu bar that is extremely useful when you have located a Web site to which you'd like to return in the future. To use it, simply click on the Bookmark icon while you are connected to the site of interest. A menu then appears, and one of the options is "Add Bookmark." By clicking on this option, the Web site that you are currently using will be added to your bookmarks. The next time you want to return to this site, click on the bookmark icon and you'll see your selected Web site as an option. Click on it and the Web site will be immediately accessed.

Browsing through the World Wide Web is often done with what are called search engines. Search engines allow you to enter key words in a search box, and then the computer program searches for all materials in its database that contain those key words. Browsing is also done through Subject Guides, which resemble the table of contents to a book: You are presented with a list of topics; selecting one with the mouse pointer produces a list of topics or actual Web sites on those topics. Some search vehicles utilize both search engines and subject guides. The following are addresses of some of the more common search vehicles for the World Wide Web. In addition, there are special search engines for FTP and Gopher sites.

> http://altavista.digital.com
> http://www.yahoo.com
> http://www.lycos.com
> http://www.webcrawler.com
> http://www.infoseek.com

The search vehicle is activated by typing its address in the Location block. In some computer facilities, you can also activate a search vehicle by clicking the "Net Search" button on the Directory line. In addition, some universities and commercial organizations will let you select among search vehicles at their home page. It is often a good idea to use more than one search vehicle in a search because each one uses different criteria and procedures in its searches and each will produce somewhat different materials.

Once you have located material of interest, you have a number of options. By selecting "File" from the menu bar, you may be able to save the information as a file for later use. For example, you might save a file in order to view the material later or to incorporate the data as a quotation in a term paper. You can also print text and graphics for future reference.

In the Exploring the Internet section with each chapter, we have tried to identify a variety of useful Internet sites that will enhance your learning about research, evaluation, and human service practice. But these are only intended as a starting point. We encourage you to explore the wealth of information that the Internet provides by utilizing the search engines and other tools of the Web.

Even though we have attempted to keep a rein on technical terms in this discussion of the Internet, it is obvious that the Information Superhighway is littered with jargon. Understanding some of it is important to negotiating through the system, so we end this section with a brief glossary of common Internet terms.

Authors' Web Page

We have provided many Internet exercises for you to use to learn more about both research methods and the World Wide Web. As your final exercise, visit the home page of this textbook at http://members.aol.com/tsulli3206/research.htm. At that site, you will find more opportunities to learn about research and the Internet. However, addresses on the Internet sometimes change. If the above URL does not work, it may have changed. If this happens, you should now be familiar enough with searching the Internet to find our new address with one of the search engines—start with a search for the title of the textbook or the authors' names.

Internet Glossary

E-mail: electronic mail

FTP (File Transfer Protocol): a network-wide client-server standard that allows users to send files from one computer to another.

Gopher: a tool developed at the University of Minnesota that creates menus for accessing network resources by moving an on-screen pointer.

Hypertext: data that provide links between key elements and enable moving nonsequentially through information. Generally set apart from other text by a distinguishing font and color.

Internet: the worldwide matrix of connecting computers using the TCP/IP protocols.

TCP/IP (Transmission Control Protocol/Internet Protocol): set of protocols that drives the Internet and regulates how data are transferred between computers.

Telnet: an Internet application allowing log-ins to remote computers where you can run programs and browse through information. For many uses, it is being replaced by the World Wide Web.

URL (Uniform Resource Locator): a method for describing the location and the access address of a resource on the Internet.

World Wide Web: an Internet system that lets you move from one document or one computer to another simply by clicking on choices that appear on the screen in the form of hypertext or graphical buttons.

Glossary

Accidental Samples: samples composed of those elements that are readily available or convenient to the researcher.

Alpha Error: the probability of rejecting a null hypothesis when it is actually true.

Alpha Level: the probability at which the null hypothesis will be rejected; the amount of Type I error (probability of rejecting a true null hypothesis) that is acceptable in a research design, typically $p < .05$ or $p < .01$.

Alphanumeric Variables: variables consisting only of type characters, being without the property of quantitative value, and treated as labels or strings by data analysis programs.

Anonymity: a situation in which no one, including the researcher, can link individuals' identities to their responses or behaviors that serve as research data.

Applied Research: research designed with a practical outcome in mind and with the assumption that some group or society as a whole will gain specific benefits from the research.

Area Sampling: a multistage sampling technique that involves moving from larger clusters of units to smaller and smaller ones until the unit of analysis, such as the household or individual, is reached.

Available Data: observations collected by someone other than the investigator for purposes that differ from the investigator's but that are available to be analyzed.

Availability Samples: samples composed of those elements that are readily available or convenient to the researcher.

Bar Graph: a frequency distribution graph for variables treated as nominal or ordinal, in which each value is plotted on the X axis as a separate bar whose height signifies the frequency of the value.

Baseline: a series of measurements of a client's condition prior to treatment that is used as a basis for comparison with the client's condition after treatment is implemented.

Basic Research: research conducted for the purpose of advancing our knowledge about human behavior with little concern for any immediate or practical benefits that might result.

Beta Error: the probability of failing to reject a null hypothesis that is actually false.

Bivariate Statistics: statistics that describe the relationship between two variables.

Blocking: a two-stage system of assigning subjects to experimental and control groups whereby subjects are first aggregated into blocks according to one or more key variables; members of each block are then randomly assigned to experimental and control conditions.

Causality: the situation where an independent variable is the factor—or one of several factors—that produces variation in a dependent variable.

Central Limit Theorem: if random samples are taken from any population with a given mean and standard deviation, the sampling distribution of sample means will be approximately normally distributed and the mean of the sampling distribution will be equal to the population parameter.

Clinical-Research Model: the merger of clinical practice and research through the use of single-subject designs.

Closed-Ended Questions: questions that provide respondents with a fixed set of alternatives from which they are to choose.

Cluster Sampling: a multistage sampling technique that involves moving from larger clusters of units to smaller and smaller ones until the unit of analysis, such as the household or individual, is reached.

Coding: the categorizing of behavior into a limited number of categories.

Coding Scheme: a plan by which the researcher organizes responses to a variable, together with specifications for including the variable in a computer data file.

Common Sense: practical judgments based on the experiences, wisdom, and prejudices of a people.

Concepts: mental constructs or images developed to symbolize ideas, persons, things, or events.

Concurrent Validity: a type of criterion validity in which the results of a newly developed measure are correlated with results of an existing measure.

Confidentiality: ensuring that information or responses will not be publicly linked to specific individuals who participate in research.

Construct Validity: a complex approach to establishing the validity of measures involving relating the measure to a complete theoretical framework, including all the concepts and propositions that the theory comprises.

Content Analysis: a method of transforming the contents of documents from a qualitative, unsystematic form to a quantitative, systematic form.

Content Validity: the extent to which a measuring device covers the full range of meanings or forms that would be included in a variable that is being measured.

Continuous Variables: variables that theoretically have an infinite number of values.

Control Condition: the condition in an experiment that does not receive the experimental stimulus.

Control Group: the subjects in an experiment who are not exposed to the experimental stimulus.

Control Variables: variables whose value is held constant in all conditions of an experiment.

Convenience Samples: samples composed of those elements that are readily available or convenient to the researcher.

Cost-Benefit Analysis: an approach to program evaluation wherein program costs are related to program benefits expressed in dollars.

Cost-Effective Analysis: an approach to program evaluation wherein program costs are related to program effects, with effects measured in the units they naturally occur.

Cover Letter: a letter that accompanies a mailed questionnaire and serves to introduce and explain it to the recipient.

Criterion Validity: a technique for establishing the validity of measures that involves demonstrating a correlation between the measure and some other standard.

Cross-Sectional Research: research based on data collected at one point in time.

Data Analysis: the process of placing observations in numerical form and manipulating them according to their arithmetic properties to derive meaning from them.

Data Archives: a national system of data libraries that lend sets of data, much as ordinary libraries lend books.

Deductive Reasoning: inferring a conclusion from more abstract premises or propositions.

Dependent Variable: the passive variable in a relationship or the one affected by an independent variable.

Descriptive Research: research that attempts to discover facts or describe reality.

Descriptive Statistics: procedures that assist in organizing, summarizing, and interpreting the sample data we have at hand.

Dimensional Sampling: a sampling technique designed to enhance the representativeness of small samples by specifying all important variables and choosing a sample that contains at least one case to represent all possible combinations of variables.

Direct Costs: a proposed program budget or actual program expenditures.

Direct Replication: the repeated application of the same treatment by the same clinician to clients suffering from the same basic problem.

Discrete Variables: variables with a finite number of distinct and separate values.

Discriminatory Power Score: a value calculated during construction of a Likert scale that indicates the degree to which each item discriminates between high scorers and low scorers on the entire scale.

Double-Blind Experiment: an experiment conducted in such a way that neither the subjects nor the experimenters know which groups are in the experimental and which are in the control condition.

Ecological Fallacy: inferring something about individuals from data collected about groups.

Empirical-Practice Model: *see* Clinical-Research Model.

Ethics: the responsibilities that researchers bear toward those who participate in research, those who sponsor research, and those who are potential beneficiaries of research.

Evaluability Assessment: a preliminary investigation into a program prior to its evaluation to determine those aspects of the program that are evaluable.

Evaluation Research: the use of scientific research methods to plan intervention programs, to monitor the implementation of new programs and the operation of existing programs, and to determine how effectively programs or clinical practices achieve their goals.

Experiential Knowledge: knowledge gained through firsthand observation of events and based on the assumption that truth can be achieved through personal experience.

Experimental Condition: the condition in an experiment that receives the experimental stimulus.

Experimental Group: those subjects who are exposed to the experimental stimulus.

Experimental Stimulus: the independent variable in an experiment that is manipulated by the experimenter to assess its effect on behavior.

Experimental Variability: variation in a dependent variable produced by an independent variable.

Experimentation: a controlled method of observation in which the value of one or more independent variables is changed in order to assess its causal effect on one or more dependent variables.

Explanatory Research: research with the goal to determine why or how something occurs.

External Validity: the extent to which causal inferences made in an experiment can be generalized to other times, settings, or people.

Extraneous Variability: variation in a dependent variable from any source other than an experimental stimulus.

Face Validity: the degree to which there is a logical relationship between the variable and the proposed measure.

Field Experiments: experiments conducted in naturally occurring settings as people go about their everyday affairs.

Field Notes: detailed, descriptive accounts of observations made in a given setting.

Focus Group: an interview with a whole group of people at the same time, especially for the purpose of seeking people's subjective reactions and levels of meaning that are important to people's behavior.

Formative Evaluation Research: evaluation research that focuses on the planning, development, and implementation of a program.

Fraud (scientific): the deliberate falsification, misrepresentation, or plagiarizing of data, findings, or the ideas of others.

Frequency Polygon: a frequency distribution graph of an interval or ratio level variable in which interval midpoints are plotted on the X axis, the corresponding frequencies are plotted on the Y axis, and the resulting points are connected by a line.

Grant: the provision of money or other resources to be used for either research or service delivery purposes.

Group Depth Interview: an interview with a whole group of people at the same time, especially for the purpose of seeking people's subjective reactions and levels of meaning that are important to people's behavior.

Guttman Scale: a measurement scale in which the items have a fixed progressive order and that has the characteristic of reproducibility.

Histogram: a graph for depicting the frequency distribution of an interval or ratio level variable in which intervals of the variable are plotted on the X axis and frequencies are depicted as bars on the Y axis.

Human Services: professions with the primary goal of enhancing the relationship between people and societal institutions so that people may maximize their potential.

Hypotheses: testable statements of presumed relationships between two or more concepts.

Independent Variable: the presumed active or causal variable in a relationship.

Index: a measurement technique that combines a number of items into a composite score.

Indicator: an observation assumed to be evidence of the attributes or properties of some phenomenon.

Inductive Reasoning: inferring something about a whole group or class of objects from knowledge of one or a few members of that group or class.

Inferential Statistics: procedures that allow us to make generalizations from sample data to the populations from which the samples were drawn.

Informed Consent: telling potential research participants about all aspects of the research that might reasonably influence their decision to participate.

Internal Validity: an issue in experimentation concerning whether the independent variable actually produces the effect it appears to have on the dependent variable.

Interval Measures: measures that classify observations into mutually exclusive categories with an inherent order and equal spacing between the categories.

Interview: a technique in which an interviewer reads questions to respondents and records their verbal responses.

Interview Schedule: a document, used in interviewing, similar to a questionnaire, that contains instructions for the interviewer, specific questions in a fixed order, and transition phrases for the interviewer.

Item: a single indicator of a variable, such as an answer to a question or an observation of some behavior or characteristic.

Judgmental Sampling: a nonprobability sampling technique in which investigators use their judgment and prior knowledge to choose people for the sample who would best serve the purposes of the study.

Laboratory Experiments: experiments conducted in artificial settings constructed in such a way that selected elements of the natural environment are simulated and features of the investigation are controlled.

Levels of Measurement: rules that define permissible mathematical operations on a given set of numbers produced by a measure.

Likert Scale: a measurement scale consisting of a series of statements followed by five response alternatives, typically: strongly agree, agree, no opinion, disagree, or strongly disagree.

Longitudinal Research: research based on data gathered over an extended time period.

Matching: a process of assigning subjects to experimental and control groups in which each subject is paired with a similar subject in the other group.

Measurement: the process of describing abstract concepts in terms of specific indicators by the assignment of numbers or other symbols to these indicants, in accordance with rules.

Measurement Scale: a measurement device allowing responses to a number of items to be combined to form a composite score on a variable.

Measures of Association: statistics that describe the strength of relationships between variables.

Measures of Central Tendency: statistics, also known as averages, that summarize distributions of data by locating the "typical" or "average" value.

Measures of Dispersion: statistics that indicate how dispersed or spread out the values of a distribution are.

Misconduct (scientific):   scientific fraud, plus such activities as carelessness or bias in recording or reporting data, mishandling data, and incomplete reporting of results.

Missing Data: incomplete data found in available data sets.

Multidimensional Scale: a scale designed to measure complex variables composed of more than one dimension.

Multistage Sampling: a multiple-tiered sampling technique that involves moving from larger clusters of units to smaller and smaller ones until the unit of analysis, such as the household or individual, is reached.

Multitrait-Multimethod Approach: a particularly complex form of construct validity involving the simultaneous assessment of numerous measures and numerous concepts through the computation of intercorrelations.

Multivariate Statistics: statistics that describe the relationships among three or more variables.

Needs Assessment: the collection of data to determine how many people need particular services and to assess the level of services or personnel that already exist to fill that need.

Nominal Definitions: verbal definitions in which one set of words or symbols is used to stand for another set of words or symbols.

Nominal Measures: measures that classify observations into mutually exclusive categories but with no ordering to the categories.

Nonprobability Samples: samples in which the probability of each population element being included in the sample is unknown.

Nonreactive Observation: observation in which those under study are not aware that they are being studied and the investigator does not change their behavior by his or her presence.

Normal Distribution: a symmetrical, unimodal distribution in which the mode, median, and mean are identical and have the same proportion of cases between the same two ordinates.

Null Hypothesis: a statement in statistical hypothesis testing which states that no relationship exists between two variables in the population or that there is no difference between a sample statistic and a population parameter.

Numeric Variable: a variable that has the property of quantitative value; a variable in a computer data file that can be used in computations.

Observational Techniques: the collection of data through direct visual or auditory experience of behavior.

Open-Ended Questions: questions without a fixed set of alternatives, which leaves respondents completely free to formulate their own responses.

Operational Definitions: definitions that indicate the precise procedures or operations to be followed in measuring a concept.

Opportunity Costs: the value of forgone opportunities incurred by funding one program as opposed to some other program.

Ordinal Measures: measures that classify observations into mutually exclusive categories that have an inherent order to them.

Panel Study: research in which data are gathered from the same people at different times.

Participant Observation: a method in which the researcher is a part of, and participates in, the activities of the people, group, or situation that is being studied.

Physical Traces: objects or evidence that result from people's activities that can be used as data to test hypotheses.

Pie Chart: a circular graph depicting the frequency distribution of a variable; the number of degrees of the circle for each section or slice represents the proportionate number of cases for each value of the variable.

Pilot Study: a trial run on a small scale of all procedures planned for a research project.

Population: all possible cases of what we are interested in studying.

Positivism: the perspective that human behavior should be studied only in terms of behavior that can be observed and recorded by means of some objective technique.

Predictive Research: research that attempts to make projections about what will occur in the future or in other settings.

Predictive Validity: a type of criterion validity wherein scores on a measure are used to predict some future state of affairs.

Preexperimental Designs: crude experimental designs that lack the necessary controls of the threats to internal validity.

Pretest: a preliminary application of the data-gathering technique to assess the adequacy of the technique.

Privacy: the ability to control when and under what conditions others will have access to your beliefs, values, or behavior.

Probability Samples: samples in which each element in the population has a known chance of being selected into the sample.

Probes: follow-up questions used during an interview to elicit clearer and more complete responses.

Proportional Reduction in Error (PRE): a property of a measure of association that permits estimation of how much the independent variable contributes to reducing error in predicting values of the dependent variable.

Propositions: statements about the relationship between elements in a theory.

Pure Research: research conducted for the purpose of advancing our knowledge about human behavior with little concern for any immediate or practical benefits that might result.

Purposive Sampling: a nonprobability sampling technique wherein investigators use their judgment and prior knowledge to choose people for the sample who would best serve the purposes of the study.

Qualitative Research: research that focuses on data in the form of words, pictures, descriptions, or narratives.

Quantitative Research: research that uses numbers, counts, and measures of things.

Quasi-Experimental Designs: designs that approximate experimental control in nonexperimental settings.

Questionnaire: a set of written questions that people respond to directly on the form itself without the aid of an interviewer.

Quota Sampling: a type of nonprobability sampling that involves dividing the population into various categories and determining the number of elements to be selected from each category.

Random Assignment: a process for assigning subjects to experimental and control groups that relies on probability theory to equalize the groups.

Random Errors: measurement errors that are neither consistent nor patterned.

Ratio Measures: measures that classify observations into mutually exclusive categories with an inherent order, equal spacing between the categories, and an absolute zero point.

Reactivity: the degree to which the presence of a researcher influences the behavior being observed.

Reliability: the ability of a measure to yield consistent results each time it is applied.

Representative Sample: a sample that accurately reflects the distribution of relevant variables in the target population.

Research Design: a detailed plan outlining how a research project will be conducted.

Research Hypothesis: the alternative statement to the null hypothesis, stating that a relationship is present between variables at the population level, or that there is a difference between a sample statistic and a population parameter.

Response Bias: responses to questions that are shaped by factors other than the person's true feelings, intentions, and beliefs.

Response Rate: the percentage of a sample that completes and returns a questionnaire or agrees to be interviewed.

Sample: one or more elements selected from a population.

Sampling Distribution: a theoretical distribution of all possible values of a sample statistic, which is distinguished by being a normal distribution whose mean is the population parameter.

Sampling Error: the extent to which the values of a sample differ from those of the population from which it was drawn.

Sampling Frame: a listing of all the elements in a population.

Sampling Validity: an approach to establishing validity of measures through determining whether a measuring device covers the full range of meanings that should be included in the variable being measured.

Scale: a measurement technique, similar to an index, that combines a number of items into a composite score.

Science: a method of obtaining objective knowledge about the world through systematic observation.

Secondary Analysis: the reanalysis of data previously collected for some other research project.

Semantic Differential: a scaling technique that involves respondents rating a concept on a scale between a series of polar opposite adjectives.

Simple Random Sampling: a sampling technique wherein the target population is treated as a unitary whole and each element has an equal probability of being selected for the sample.

Single-Subject Designs: quasi-experimental designs featuring continuous or nearly continuous measurement of the dependent variable on a single research subject over a time interval that is divided into a baseline phase and one or more additional phases during which the independent variable is manipulated; experimental effects are inferred by comparisons of the subject's responses across baseline and intervention phases.

Snowball Sampling: a type of nonprobability sampling characterized by a few cases of the type we wish to study leading to more cases, which, in turn, lead to still more cases until a sufficient sample is achieved.

Social Research: a systematic examination (or re-examination) of empirical data collected by someone firsthand, concerning the social or psychological forces operating in a situation.

Statistics: procedures for assembling, classifying, and tabulating numerical data so that some meaning or information is derived.

Stratified Sampling: a sampling technique wherein the population is subdivided into strata with separate subsamples drawn from each strata.

Subjectivism: an approach to understanding phenomena that emphasizes the importance of personal perception and personal meaning in understanding people and what they do.

Summated Rating Scales: scales in which a respondent's score is determined by summing the numbers of questions answered.

Summative Evaluation Research: evaluation research that assesses the effectiveness and efficiency of programs and the extent to which program effects are generalizable to other settings and populations.

Survey: a data collection technique in which information is gathered from individuals, called respondents, by having them respond to questions.

Systematic Errors: measurement errors that are consistent and patterned.

Systematic Replication: an attempt to extend a treatment to different settings, practitioners, or client disorders or any combination of these conditions.

Systematic Sampling: a type of simple random sampling wherein every *n*th element of the sampling frame is selected for the sample.

Theory: a set of interrelated propositions or statements, organized into a deductive system, that offers an explanation of some phenomenon.

Thurstone Scale: a measurement scale consisting of a series of items with a predetermined scale value to which respondents indicate their agreement or disagreement.

Time Sampling: a sampling technique used in observational research in which observations are made only during specified preselected times.

Traditional Knowledge: knowledge based on custom, habit, and repetition.

Trend Study: research in which data are gathered from different people at different times.

True Experimental Designs: experimental designs that utilize randomization, control groups, and other techniques to control threats to internal validity.

Type I Error: the probability of rejecting a null hypothesis when it is actually true.

Type II Error: the probability of failing to reject a null hypothesis that is actually false.

Unidimensional Scale: a multiple-item scale that measures one, and only one, variable.

Units of Analysis: the specific objects or elements whose characteristics we wish to describe or explain and about which data are collected.

Univariate Statistics: statistics that describe the distribution of a single variable.

Unobtrusive Observation: observation in which those under study are not aware that they are being studied and the investigator does not change their behavior by his or her presence.

Validity: the degree to which a measure accurately reflects the theoretical meaning of a variable.

Variables: operationally defined concepts that can take on more than one value.

Verification: the process of subjecting hypotheses to empirical tests to determine whether a theory is supported or refuted.

Verstehen: the effort to view and understand a situation from the perspective of the people actually in that situation.

References

Achen, C. H. *The Statistical Analysis of Quasi-Experiments.* Berkeley, Calif.: University of California Press, 1986.

Adair, J. G., Terrance W. Dushenko, and R. C. L. Lindsay. Ethical Regulations and Their Impact on Research Practice. *American Psychologist,* 40 (January 1985), 59–72.

Adams, S., and M. Orgel. *Through the Mental Health Maze: A Consumer's Guide to Finding a Psychotherapist.* Washington, D.C.: Health Research Group, Public Citizen, 1975.

Adler, P. A. *Wheeling and Dealing: An Ethnography of an Upper-Level Drug Dealing and Smuggling Community.* New York: Columbia University Press, 1985.

Allen, G. J. Case Study: Implementation of Behavior Modification Techniques in Summer Camp Settings. *Behavior Therapy,* 4 (1973), 570–575.

Allen-Meares, P. Content Analysis: It Does Have a Place in Social Work Research. *Journal of Social Service Research,* 7 (Summer 1984), 51–68.

Alreck, P., and R. Settle. *The Survey Research Handbook.* Homewood, Ill.: Irwin, 1985.

Alter, C., and W. Evens. *Evaluating Your Practice: A Guide to Self-Assessment.* New York: Springer, 1990.

Amato, P. R. Family Processes in One-Parent, Stepparent, and Intact Families: The Child's Point of View. *Journal of Marriage and the Family,* 49 (May 1987), 327–337.

———. Children's Adjustment to Divorce: Theories, Hypotheses, and Empirical Support. *Journal of Marriage and the Family,* 55 (February 1993), 23–38.

Amato, P. R., and S. J. Rezac. Contact With Nonresident Parents, Interparental Conflict, and Children's Behavior. *Journal of Family Issues,* 15 (June 1994), 191–207.

Anderson, A. Scientific Misconduct Still an Unknown. *Nature,* 340 (1989), 3.

Anderson, B., B. Silver, and P. Abramson. The Effects of the Race of the Interviewer on Race-Related Attitudes of Black Respondents in SRC/CPS National Election Studies. *Public Opinion Quarterly,* 52 (1988), 289–324.

Annis, R. C., and B. Corenblum. Effect of Test Language and Experimenter Race on Canadian Indian Children's Racial and Self-Identity. *Journal of Social Psychology,* 126 (December 1986), 761–773.

Annual Register of Grant Support: A Directory of Funding Sources, rev. ed. 1997. New Providence, N.J.: Bowker, 1996.

Aquilino, W., and L. LoSciuto. Effects of Interview Mode on Self-Reported Drug Use. *Public Opinion Quarterly,* 54 (1990), 362–395.

Archer, D., B. Iritiani, D. D. Kimes, and M. Barrios. Face-ism: Five Studies of Sex Differences in Facial Prominence. *Journal of Personality and Social Psychology,* 45 (1983), 725–735.

Arches, J. Social Structure, Burnout, and Job Satisfaction. *Social Work,* 36 (May 1991), 202–206.

Armstrong, J. S., and E. J. Luck. Return Postage in Mail Surveys: A Meta-Analysis. *Public Opinion Quarterly,* 51 (Summer 1987), 233–248.

Arnold, D. O. Dimensional Sampling: An Approach for Studying a Small Number of Cases. *The American Sociologist,* 5 (1970), 147–150.

Ashcraft, N., and A. E. Scheflen. *People Space: The Making and Breaking of Human Boundaries.* New York: Doubleday, 1976.

Ayres, I. Fair Driving: Gender and Race Discrimination in Retail Car Negotiations. *Harvard Law Review,* 104 (February 1991), 817–872.

Babbie, E. R. *The Practice of Social Research,* 7th ed. Belmont, Calif.: Wadsworth, 1995.

Bachman, J. G., and P. M. O'Malley. Yea-Saying, Nay-Saying, and Going to Extremes: Black–White Differences in Response Styles. *Public Opinion Quarterly,* 48 (1984), 491–501.

Backstrom, C. H., and G. D. Hursh. *Survey Research,* 2nd ed. New York: Macmillan, 1981.

Bailey, K. *Methods of Social Research,* 3rd ed. New York: Free Press, 1987.

Bailey, R. C., Y. Hser, S. Hsieh, and M. D. Anglin. Influences Affecting Maintenance and Cessation of Narcotics Addiction. *Journal of Drug Issues,* 24 (1994), 249–272.

Bainbridge, W. A., et al. Artificial Social Intelligence. In J. Hagan and K. S. Cook, eds., *Annual Review of Sociology,* vol. 20. Palo Alto, Calif.: Annual Reviews Inc., 1996.

Balassone, M. L. A Research Methodology for the Development of Risk Assessment Tools in Social Work

Practice. *Social Work Research and Abstracts,* 27 (1991), 16–23.

Bales, R. F. *Interaction Process Analysis.* Cambridge, Mass.: Addison-Wesley, 1950.

———. Some Uniformities of Behavior in Small Social Systems. In G. E. Swanson, T. M. Newcomb, and E. L. Hartley, eds., *Readings in Social Psychology,* rev. ed. New York: Henry Holt and Company, 1952, 146–159.

Barlow, D., and M. Hersen. Single-Case Experimental Designs: Uses in Applied Clinical Research. *Archives of General Psychiatry,* 29 (1973), 319–325.

Barlow, D., and M. Hersen. *Single-Case Experimental Designs: Strategies for Studying Behavior Change,* 2nd ed. New York: Pergamon Press, 1984.

Barlow, D. H., M. G. Craske, J. A. Cerny, and J. S. Klosko. Behavioral Treatment of Panic Disorder. *Behavior Therapy,* 20 (1989), 261–282.

Barlow, D. H., S. C. Hayes, and R. O. Nelson. *The Scientist Researcher: Research and Accountability in Clinical and Educational Settings.* Boston: Allyn & Bacon, 1992.

Barlow, H. *Introduction to Criminology,* 7th ed. New York: HarperCollins, 1996.

Bastion, L. Criminal Victimization 1993. *Bureau of Justice Studies Bulletin* (May 1995), 1–6.

Barth, R. P. Education for Practice-Research: Toward a Reorientation. *Journal of Education for Social Work,* 17 (1981), 19–25.

Bassuk, E. L. The Homelessness Problem. *Scientific American,* 251 (July 1984), 40–45.

Bauer, D. G. *The "How To" Grants Manual: Successful Grantseeking Techniques for Obtaining Public and Private Grants.* Phoenix: Oryx, 1995.

Baumrind, D. Research Using Intentional Deception. *American Psychologist,* 40:2 (February 1985), 165–174.

Bean, G. J., Jr., M. E. Stefl, and S. R. Howe. Mental Health and Homelessness: Issues and Findings. *Social Work,* 32 (September/October 1987), 411–416.

Beauchamp, T. L., R. R. Faden, R. J. Wallace, Jr., and L. Walters, eds. *Ethical Issues in Social Science Research.* Baltimore, Md.: Johns Hopkins University Press, 1982.

Becerra, R. M., and R. E. Zambrana. Methodological Approaches to Research on Hispanics. *Social Work Research and Abstracts,* 21 (Summer 1985), 42–49.

Becker, H. S. Becoming a Marijuana User. *American Journal of Sociology,* 59 (1953), 235–242.

———. Whose Side Are We On? *Social Problems,* 14 (1967), 239–247.

Bedell, J. R., J. C. Ward, Jr., R. P. Archer, and M. K. Stokes. An Empirical Evaluation of a Model of Knowledge Utilization. *Evaluation Review,* (9 April 1985), 109–126.

Behavioral Science Institute. *Home Builders Cost Effectiveness With Various Client Populations, 1974–1986.* Federal Way, Wash.: Author, 1987.

Bell, A. P., and M. S. Weinberg. *Homosexualities: A Study of Diversity Among Men and Women.* New York: Simon & Schuster, 1978.

Bell, W. *Contemporary Social Welfare,* 2nd ed. New York: Macmillan, 1987.

Benbenishty, R. Monitoring Practice on the Agency Level: An Application in a Residential Care Facility. *Research on Social Work Practice,* 1 (1991), 371–386.

Benton, T. *Philosophical Foundations of the Three Sociologies.* Boston: Routledge and Kegan Paul, 1977.

Berg, B. *Qualitative Research Methods for the Social Sciences,* 2nd ed. Boston: Allyn & Bacon, 1995.

Berger, R. Nazi Science: The Dachau Hypothermia Experiments. *The New England Journal of Medicine,* 322 (1990), 1435–1440.

Berger, R. L. Ethics in Scientific Communication: Study of a Problem Case. *Journal of Medical Ethics,* 20 (1994), 207–211.

Berk, R., and P. Rossi. *Thinking About Program Evaluation.* Newbury Park, Calif.: Sage, 1990.

Berk, R. A., and D. Rauma. Capitalizing on Nonrandom Assignment to Treatments: A Regression Discontinuity Evaluation of a Crime-Control Program. *Journal of the American Statistical Association,* 78 (1983), 21.

Berk, R. A., et al. Social Policy Experimentation: A Position Paper. *Evaluation Review,* 9 (August 1985), 387–430.

Berman, P., and E. Pauly. *Federal Programs Supporting Educational Change.* Vol. 2: *Factors Affecting Change Agent Projects.* Santa Monica, Calif.: Rand, 1975.

Berry, M. An Evaluation of Family Preservation Services: Fitting Agency Services to Family Needs. *Social Work,* 37 (1992), 314–321.

Berry, S. H., and D. E. Kanouse. Physician Response to a Mailed Survey: An Experiment in Timing of Payment. *Public Opinion Quarterly,* 51 (Spring 1987), 102–114.

Biklen, D. P. Behavior Modification in a State Mental Hospital: A Participant Observer's Critique. *American Journal of Orthopsychiatry,* 46 (1976), 53–61.

Billups, J. O., and M. C. Julia. Changing Profile of Social Work Practice. *Social Work Research and Abstracts,* 23 (Winter 1987), 17–22.

Binder, A., G. Geis, and D. Bruce. *Juvenile Delinquency: Historical, Cultural, and Legal Perspectives.* New York: Macmillan, 1988.

Binder, A., and J. Meeker. Experiments as Reforms. *Journal of Criminal Justice,* 16 (1988), 347–358.

Bloom, M, J. Fischer, and J. G. Orme. *Evaluating Practice: Guidelines for the Accountable Professional,* 2nd ed. Boston: Allyn & Bacon, 1995.

Bogdan, R., and S. J. Taylor. *Introduction to Qualitative Research Methods.* New York: Wiley, 1975.

Bonjean, C. M., R. J. Hill, and S. D. McLemore. *Sociological Measurement: An Inventory of Scales and Indices.* San Francisco: Chandler, 1967.

Borgatta, E., and G. Bohrnstedt. Levels of Measurement: Once Over Again. In G. Bohrnstedt and E. Borgatta, eds., *Social Measurement: Current Issues.* Beverly Hills, Calif.: Sage, 1981.

Bradburn, N. M., and S. Sudman. *Improving Interview Method and Questionnaire Design.* San Francisco: Jossey-Bass, 1979.

Brajuha, M., and L. Hallowell. Legal Intrusion and the Politics of Fieldwork. *Urban Life,* 14 (1986), 454–479.

Brent, E., Jr., and R. Anderson. *Computer Applications in the Social Sciences.* New York: McGraw-Hill, 1990.

Bridge, R. G. *Nonresponse Bias in Mail Surveys.* Defense Advanced Research Projects Agency R-1501. Santa Monica, Calif.: Rand, 1974.

Bronowski, J. *The Origins of Knowledge and Imagination.* New Haven, Conn.: Yale University Press, 1978.

Brown, S. V. The Commitment and Concerns of Black Adolescent Parents. *Social Work Research and Abstracts,* 19 (1983), 27–34.

Brunner, G. A., and S. J. Carroll. Effect of Prior Telephone Appointments on Completion Rates and Response Content. *Public Opinion Quarterly,* 31 (1967), 652–654.

Brunswick-Heineman, M. The Obsolete Scientific Imperative in Social Work Research. *Social Service Review,* 55 (1981), 371–397.

Bryson, M. The Literary Digest Poll: Making of a Statistical Myth. *The American Statistician,* 30 (November 1976), 184–185.

Buckhout, R. Eyewitness Testimony. *Scientific American,* 231 (1974), 23–31.

Buetow, S. A., R. M. Douglas, P. Harris, and C. McCulloch. Computer-Assisted Personal Interviews: Development and Experience of an Approach in Australian General Practice. *Social Science Computer Review,* 14 (1996), 205–212.

Burch, G., and V. Mohr. Evaluating a Child Abuse Intervention Program. *Social Casework,* 61 (1980), 90–99.

Burgess, R., and L. Youngblade. Social Incompetence and the Intergenerational Transmission of Abusive Parental Practices. In G. Hotaling, D. Finkelhor, J. Kirkpatrick, and M. Strauss, eds., *Family Abuse and Its Consequences: New Directions in Research.* Newbury Park, Calif.: Sage, 1988.

Burgess, R. G. *In the Field: An Introduction to Field Research.* London: Allen & Unwin, 1984.

Burnam, M. A., and P. Koegel. Methodology for Obtaining a Representative Sample of Homeless Persons: The Los Angeles Skid Row Study. *Evaluation Review,* 12 (April 1988), 117–152.

Cahalan, D. The Digest Poll Rides Again! *Public Opinion Quarterly,* 53 (1989), 129–133.

Campbell, D. T., and D. W. Fiske. Convergent and Discriminant Validity by the Multitrait-Multimethod Matrix. *Psychological Bulletin,* 56 (1959), 81–105.

Campbell, D. T., and J. C. Stanley. *Experimental and Quasi-Experimental Designs for Research.* Chicago: Rand McNally, 1963.

Campbell, J. A. Client Acceptance of Single-System Evaluation Procedures. *Social Work Research and Abstracts,* 24 (1988), 21–22.

Cannell, C. F., and R. L. Kahn. Interviewing. In G. Lindzey and E. Aronson, eds., *The Handbook of Social Psychology,* 2nd ed. Vol. 2. Reading, Mass.: Addison-Wesley, 1968.

Caplan, L. *An Open Adoption.* New York: Farrar, Straus & Giroux, 1990.

Carlock, C. J., and P. Y. Martin. Sex Composition and the Intensive Group Experience. *Social Work,* 22 (1977), 27–32.

Carpenter, E. H. The Evolving Statistics and Research Process Using Microcomputer Statistical Software, *Social Science Microcomputer Review,* 5 (Winter 1987), 529–545.

Carpenter, J., D. Deloria, and D. Morganstein. Statistical Software for Microcomputers. *Byte* (April 1984), 234–264.

Carroll, L. *Through the Looking Glass.* New York: Random House, 1946.

Cartwright, A., and W. Tucker. An Attempt to Reduce the Number of Calls on an Interview Inquiry. *Public Opinion Quarterly,* 31 (1967), 299–302.

Catlin, G., and S. Ingram. The Effects of CATI on Costs and Data Quality: A Comparison of CATI and Paper Methods. In Centralized Interviewing in R. G. Groves, et al., eds., *Telephone Survey Methodology.* New York: Wiley, 1988.

Cavan, S. *Liquor License.* Chicago: Aldine, 1966.

Ceci, S. J., D. Peters, and J. Plotkin. Human Subjects Review, Personal Values, and the Regulation of Social

Science Research. *American Psychologist,* 40 (September 1985), 994–1002.

Centers for Disease Control. *HIV/AIDS Surveillance Report,* February 1992.

Centers for Disease Control. Reports on HIV/AIDS: January–December 1989. *Morbidity and Mortality Weekly Report,* January 1990.

Chaiken, M. R., and J. M. Chaiken. Offender Types and Public Policy. *Crime and Delinquency,* 30 (April 1984), 195–226.

Champion, D. J. *Basic Statistics for Social Research,* 2nd ed. Scranton, Pa.: Chandler, 1981.

Chen, H., and P. H. Rossi. The Multi-Goal, Theory-Driven Approach to Evaluation. A Model Linking Basic and Applied Social Science. *Social Forces,* 59 (1980), 106–122.

Christie, R., and F. L. Geis. *Studies in Machiavellianism.* New York. Academic Press, 1970.

Chronicle of Higher Education, June 22, 1988, A-22.

———, October 7, 1992, 825.

Chun, K., S. Cobb, and J. French. *Measures for Psychological Assessment.* Ann Arbor, Mich.: Institute for Social Research, University of Michigan, 1975.

Clum, G. A. *Coping With Panic: A Drug-Free Approach to Dealing With Anxiety Attacks.* Belmont, Calif.: Brooks/Cole, 1990.

Coehlo, R. J. *An Experimental Investigation of Two Multi-Component Approaches on Smoking Cessation.* Unpublished doctoral dissertation, Michigan State University, East Lansing, Mich., 1983.

Cohen, J. *Statistical Power Analysis for the Behavioral Sciences,* 2nd ed. Hillsdale, N.J.: Lawrence Erlbaum, 1988.

Cohen, M. R., and E. Nagel. *An Introduction to Logic and Scientific Method.* New York: Harcourt, 1934.

Committee on the Status of Women in Sociology. *The Treatment of Gender in Research.* Washington, D.C.: American Sociological Association, 1986.

Cook, T. D., and D. T. Campbell. *Quasi-Experimentation: Design and Analysis Issues for Field Settings.* Chicago: Rand McNally, 1979.

Cook, T. D., F. L. Cook, and M. M. Mark. Randomized and Quasi-Experimental Designs in Evaluation Research: An Introduction. In L. Rutman, ed., *Evaluation Research Methods.* Beverly Hills, Calif.: Sage, 1977.

Corcoran, K., and J. Fischer. *Measures for Clinical Practice: A Sourcebook.* New York: Free Press, 1987.

Corry, J. Children's TV Found Dominated by White Men. *New York Times,* July 15, 1982, 14.

Cotter, P. R., J. Cohen, and P. B. Coulter. Race-of-Interviewer Effects in Telephone Interviews. *Public Opinion Quarterly,* 46 (1982), 278–284.

Coulton, C. J. Developing an Instrument to Measure Person–Environment Fit. *Journal of Social Service Research,* 3 (1979), 159–174.

Council on Social Work Education. *Handbook of Accreditation Standards and Procedures,* 4th ed. Washington, D.C., 1994.

Cox, D. E., and C. N. Sipprelle. Coercion in Participation as a Research Subject. *American Psychologist,* 26 (1971), 726–728.

Crockenberg, S., and B. Soby. Self-Esteem and Teenage Pregnancy. In A. Mecca, N. Smelser, and J. Vasconcellos, eds., *The Social Importance of Self-Esteem.* Berkeley: University of California Press, 1989.

Cronbach, L. J. Coefficient Alpha and the Internal Structure of Tests. *Psychometrica,* 16 (1951), 197–334.

Cronbach, L. J., and P. Meehl. Construct Validity in Psychological Tests. *Psychological Bulletin,* 52 (1955), 281–302.

Crosby, F., S. Bromley, and L. Saxe. Recent Unobtrusive Studies of Black and White Discrimination and Prejudice. *Psychological Bulletin,* 87 (1980), 546–563.

Davis, L. V. Beliefs of Social Service Providers About Abused Women and Abusing Men. *Social Work,* 29 (May/June 1984), 243–250.

———. A Feminist Approach to Social Work Research. *Affilia* (Spring 1986), 32–47.

Dawson, J. A., and J. J. D'Amico. Involving Program Staff in Evaluation Studies: A Strategy for Increasing Information Use and Enriching the Data Base. *Evaluation Review,* 9 (April 1985), 173–188.

DeMaio, T. J. Social Desirability and Survey Measurement: A Review. In C. F. Turner and E. Martin, eds., *Surveying Subjective Phenomena,* 2. New York: Russell Sage Foundation, 1984.

DeMartini, J. Basic and Applied Sociological Work: Divergence, Convergence, or Peaceful Coexistence? *Journal of Applied Behavioral Science,* 18 (1982), 203–215.

Denzin, N. *The Research Act: A Theoretical Introduction to Sociological Methods,* 3rd ed. Englewood Cliffs, N.J.: Prentice Hall, 1989.

Dignan, M., R. Michielutte, P. Sharp, J. Bahnson, L. Young, and P. Beal. The Role of Focus Groups in Health Education for Cervical Cancer Among Minority Women. *Journal of Community Health,* 15 (1990), 369–375.

Deutch, S. J., and F. B. Alt. The Effect of Massachusetts's Gun Control Law on Gun-Related Crimes in the City of Boston. *Evaluation Quarterly,* 1 (1977), 543–567.

DeVellis, R. *Scale Development: Theories and Applications.* Newbury Park, Calif.: Sage, 1991.

Dillman, D. The Design and Administration of Mail Surveys. *Annual Review of Sociology,* Vol. 17, 1991.

DiVista, F. J. A Developmental Study of the Semantic Structure of Children. *Journal of Verbal Learning and Verbal Behavior,* 5 (1966), 249–259.

Dotson, L. E., and G. F. Summers. Elaboration of Guttman Scaling Techniques. In G. F. Summers, ed., *Attitude Measurement.* Chicago: Rand McNally, 1970.

Dressel, P. L., and D. M. Petersen. Becoming a Male Stripper: Recruitment, Socialization, and Ideological Development. *Work and Occupations,* 9 (August 1982), 387–406.

Duncan, G. J., and S. D. Hoffman. A Reconsideration of the Economic Consequences of Divorce. *Demography,* 22 (1985), 485–497.

Dunford, F., D. Huizinga, and D. Elliott. *The Omaha Domestic Violence Police Experiment.* Washington, D.C.: National Institute of Justice, 1989.

Durkheim, E. *Rules of the Sociological Method.* Trans., S. Solovay and J. Mueller. Chicago: University of Chicago Press, 1938.

Dutton, D. G. *The Domestic Assault of Women,* revised and expanded ed. Vancouver: UBC Press, 1995.

Edlesen, J. L. Rapid Assessment Instruments for Evaluating Practice With Children and Youth. *Journal of Social Service Research,* 8 (1985), 17–31.

Edwards, A. L. *Techniques of Attitude Scale Construction.* New York: Appleton-Century-Crofts, 1957.

Edwards, A. L., and F. P. Kilpatrick. A Technique for the Construction of Attitude Scales. *Journal of Applied Psychology,* 32 (1948), 374–384.

Eichler, M. *Nonsexist Research Methods: A Practical Guide.* Boston: Allen & Unwin, 1988.

Ellickson, P., and R. Bell. Challenges to Social Experiments: A Drug Prevention Example. *Journal of Research in Crime and Delinquency,* 29 (1992), 79–101.

Elliott, D. S., and D. Huizinga. Social Class and Delinquent Behavior in a National Youth Panel: 1976–1980. *Criminology,* 21 (1983), 149–177.

Elms, A. C. Keeping Deception Honest: Justifying Conditions for Social Scientific Research Strategies. In T. L. Beauchamp, R. R. Faden, R. J. Wallace, Jr., and L. Walters, eds., *Ethical Issues in Social Science Research.* Baltimore, Md.: Johns Hopkins University Press, 1982.

Engler, R. L., et al. Misrepresentation and Responsibility in Medical Research. *New England Journal of Medicine,* 17 (November 26, 1987), 1383–1389.

Epstein, I., and T. Tripodi. *Research Techniques for Program Planning, Monitoring, and Evaluation.* New York: Columbia University Press, 1977.

Erdfelder, E., F. Faul, and A. Buchner. GPOWER: A General Power Analysis Program. *Behavior Research Methods, Instruments, and Computers,* 28 (1996), 1–11.

Erikson, K. T. A Comment on Disguised Observation in Sociology. *Social Problems,* 14 (1967), 366–373.

Estroff, S. E. Making It Crazy: Some Paradoxes of Psychiatric Patienthood in an American Community and a Research/Discovery Process to Encounter Them. Paper presented at the Annual Meeting of the American Anthropological Association, Los Angeles, Calif., 1978.

Evans, W. Computer-Supported Content Analysis: Trends, Tools, and Techniques. *Social Science Computer Review,* 14 (Fall 1996), 269–279.

Faludi, S. *Backlash. The Undeclared War Against American Women.* New York: Doubleday, 1991.

———. Statistically Challenged. *The Nation* (April 15, 1996), 10.

Fanshel, D. Status Differentials: Men and Women in Social Work. *Social Work,* 21 (1976), 448–454.

Farley, R. *Blacks and Whites: Narrowing the Gap.* Cambridge, Mass.: Harvard University Press, 1984.

Fay, B. *Critical Social Science: Liberation and Its Limits.* Ithaca, N.Y.: Cornell University Press, 1987.

Federal Bureau of Investigation. *Uniform Crime Reports: Crime in the United States, 1991.* Washington, D.C.: U.S. Government Printing Office, 1992.

Felce, D., U. deKock, and A. Repp. An Eco-Behavioral Analysis of Small Community-Based Houses and Traditional Large Hospitals for Severely and Profoundly Mentally Handicapped Adults. *Applied Research in Mental Retardation,* 7 (1986), 393–408.

Feldman, R. A., and T. E. Caplinger. Social Work Experience and Client Behavioral Change: A Multivariate Analysis of Process and Outcome. *Journal of Social Service Research,* 1 (1977), 5–33.

Ferree, M., and E. Hall. Visual Images of American Society: Gender and Race in Introductory Sociology Textbooks. *Gender and Society,* 4 (1990), 500–533.

Ferrell, J. Urban Graffiti: Crime, Control, and Resistance. *Youth and Society,* 28 (1995), 73–92.

Festinger, L., H. Riecken, and S. Schachter. *When Prophecy Fails.* New York: Harper & Row, 1956.

Fienberg, S., M. Martin, and M. Straf, eds. *Sharing Research Data.* Washington, D.C.: National Academy Press, 1985.

Fischer, J. Is Casework Effective? A Review. *Social Work,* 18 (1973), 5–20.

———. The Social Work Revolution. *Social Work,* 26 (1981), 199–207.

Fischer, J., and K. Corcoran. *Measures for Clinical Practice: A Sourcebook,* 2nd ed. New York: Free Press, 1994.

Fisher, E. Children's Books: The Second Sex, Junior Division. In Judith Stacey, et al., eds., *And Jill Came Tumbling After: Sexism in American Education.* New York: Dell, 1974.

Fortune, A. E. Communication in Task-Centered Treatment. *Social Work,* 24 (1979), 390–397.

Foundation Directory, 18th ed. New York: The Foundation Center, 1996.

Fowler, F., Jr., and T. Mangione. *Standardized Survey Interviewing.* Newbury Park, Calif.: Sage, 1990.

Fredman, N., and R. Sherman. *Handbook of Measurements for Marriage and Family Therapy.* New York: Brunner/Mazel, 1987.

Frey, J. H. An Experiment With a Confidentiality Reminder in a Telephone Survey. *Public Opinion Quarterly,* 50 (Summer 1986), 267–269.

———. *Survey Research by Telephone,* 2nd ed. Newbury Park, Calif.: Sage, 1989.

Fridlund, A. J. Statistics Software. *Infoworld* (September 1, 1986), 31–39.

Frisch, M. B., and R. L. Higgins. Instructional Demand Effects and the Correspondence Among Role-Play, Self-Report, and Naturalistic Measures of Social Skill. *Behavioral Assessment,* 8 (Summer 1986), 221–236.

Fulford, K. W. M., and K. Howse. Ethics of Research With Psychiatric Patients: Principles, Problems, and the Primary Responsibilities of Researchers. *Journal of Medical Ethics,* 19 (1993), 85–91.

Furstenberg, F. F., Jr., and J. O. Teitler. Reconsidering the Effects of Marital Disruption: What Happens to Children in Early Adulthood? *Journal of Family Issues,* 15 (June 1994), 173–190.

Gallagher, B. J., III. *The Sociology of Mental Illness,* 2nd ed. Englewood Cliffs, N.J.: Prentice-Hall, 1987.

Galtung, J. *Theory and Methods of Social Research.* New York: Columbia University Press, 1967.

Gardner, J. E. Behavior Therapy Treatment Approach to a Psychogenic Seizure Case. *Journal of Consulting Psychology,* 31 (1967), 209–212.

Garfield, E., and A. Welljams-Dorof. The Impact of Fraudulent Research on the Scientific Literature. *JAMA,* 263 (1990), 1424–1426.

Garson, G. D. News and Notes. *Social Science Computer Review,* 9 (1991), 684.

Gelles, R. J. Methods for Studying Sensitive Family Topics. *American Journal of Orthopsychiatry,* 48 (1978), 408–424.

———. What to Learn From Cross-Cultural and Historical Research on Child Abuse and Neglect: An Overview. In R. J. Gelles and J. B. Lancaster, eds., *Child Abuse and Neglect: Biosocial Dimensions.* New York: Aldine de Gruyter, 1987.

Gentry, M. E., R. S. Connaway, and M. Morelock. Research Activities of Social Workers in Agencies. *Social Work Research and Abstracts,* 20 (Winter 1984), 3–5.

George, M., and H. Skinner. Using Response Latency to Detect Inaccurate Responses in a Computerized Life-Style Assessment. *Computers in Human Behavior,* 6 (1990), 167–175.

Gibbs, L. *Scientific Reasoning for Social Workers: Bridging the Gap Between Research and Practice.* New York: Macmillan, 1991.

———. Evaluation Researcher: Scientist or Advocate? *Journal of Social Service Research,* 7 (Fall 1983), 81–92.

Gilligan, C. *In a Different Voice: Psychological Theory and Women's Development.* Cambridge, Mass.: Harvard University Press, 1982.

Gingerich, W. Rethinking Single-Case Evaluation. In L. Videka-Sherman and W. Reid, eds., *Advances in Clinical Social Work Research.* Silver Spring, Md.: NASW Press, 1990.

Ginsburg, H., and S. Opper. *Piaget's Theory of Intellectual Development,* 3rd ed. Englewood Cliffs, N.J.: Prentice-Hall, 1988.

Glaser, B., and A. Strauss. *Awareness of Dying.* Chicago: Aldine, 1965.

———. *The Discovery of Grounded Theory.* Chicago: Aldine, 1967.

Gold, R. L. Roles in Sociological Field Observations. *Social Forces,* 36 (1958), 217–223.

Goldberg, G. S., R. Kantrow, E. Kremen, and L. Lauter. Spouseless, Childless Elderly Women and Their Social Supports. *Social Work,* 31 (March/April 1986), 104–112.

Goldfried, M. R., and B. E. Wolfe. Psychotherapy Practice and Research: Repairing a Strained Alliance. *American Psychologist,* 51 (October 1996), 1007–1016.

Goldscheider, F. K., and L. J. Waite. *New Families, No Families? The Transformation of the American Home.* Berkeley: University of California Press, 1991.

Golombok, S., and F. Tasker. Do Parents Influence the Sexual Orientation of Their Children? Findings From a Longitudinal Study of Lesbian Families. *Developmental Psychology,* 32 (1996), 3–11.

Goode, W. J., and P. K. Hatt. *Methods in Social Research.* New York: McGraw-Hill, 1952.

Gorden, R. L. *Interviewing: Strategies, Techniques, and Tactics,* 4th ed. Chicago: Dorsey Press, 1987.

Gordon, M. M. *The Scope of Sociology.* New York: Oxford University Press, 1988.

Gottman, J. M. *Marital Interaction: Experimental Investigations.* New York: Academic Press, 1979.

———. *Time-Series Analysis: A Comprehensive Introduction for Social Scientists.* New York: Cambridge University Press, 1981.

———. Observational Measures of Behavior Therapy Outcome: A Reply to Jacobson. *Behavioral Assessment,* 7 (Fall 1985), 317–321.

Gottschalk, L. A. *Content Analysis of Verbal Behavior: New Findings and Clinical Applications.* Hillsdale, N.J.: Lawrence Erlbaum, 1995.

Gouldner, A. The Dark Side of the Dialectic: Toward a New Objectivity. *Sociological Inquiry,* 46 (1976), 3–16.

Goyder, J. Face-to-Face Interviews and Mailed Questionnaires: The Net Difference in Response Rate. *Public Opinion Quarterly,* 49 (Summer 1985), 234–252.

Graham, K., L. LaRocque, R. Yetman, T. J. Ross, and E. Guistra. Aggression and Barroom Environments. *Journal of Studies on Alcohol,* 41 (1980), 277–292.

Graham, K. R. *Psychological Research: Controlled Interpersonal Research.* Monterey, Calif.: Brooks/Cole, 1977.

Gray, B. H. The Regulatory Context of Social and Behavioral Research. In T. L. Beauchamp, R. R. Faden, R. J. Wallace, Jr., and L. Walters, eds., *Ethical Issues in Social Science Research.* Baltimore, Md.: Johns Hopkins University Press, 1982.

Greenberg, D. S. Probers Charge Top Psychologist Faked Research Results. *Science and Government Report,* 17 (March 15, 1987*a*), 1–5.

———. Researcher Sounds Fraud Alarm—and Loses NIMH Grant. *Science and Government Report,* 17 (April 1, 1987*b*), 1–3.

Greene, J. G. Stakeholder Participation and Utilization of Program Evaluation. *Evaluation Review,* 12 (April 1988), 91–116.

Greenley, J. R., and R. A. Schoenherr. Organization Effects on Client Satisfaction With Humaneness of Service. *Journal of Health and Social Behavior,* 22 (1981), 2–18.

Grichting, W. L. Do Laws Make a Difference? *Journal of Social Service Research,* 2 (1979), 245–265.

Groth-Marnat, G. *Handbook of Psychological Assessment.* New York: Van Nostrand, 1984.

Groves, R. M., P. B. Blemer, L. E. Lyberg, J. T. Massey, W. L. Nicholls, and J. Waksberg, eds. *Telephone Survey Methodology.* Somerset, N.J.: Wiley, 1988.

———. *Survey Errors and Survey Costs.* New York: Wiley, 1989.

———. Theories and Methods of Telephone Surveys. *Annual Review of Sociology,* Vol. 16, 1990.

Groze, V. Adoption and Single Parents: A Review. *Child Welfare,* 70 (1991), 321–332.

Guba, E. G., and Y. S. Lincoln. Competing Paradigms in Qualitative Research. In N. K. Denzin and Y. S. Lincoln, eds., *Handbook of Qualitative Research.* Thousand Oaks, Calif.: Sage, 1994.

Guttman, L. A Basis for Scaling Qualitative Data. *American Sociological Review,* 9 (1944), 139–150.

———. The Basis for Scalogram Analysis. In S. A. Stouffer, et al., eds., *Measurement and Prediction.* Princeton, N.J.: Princeton University Press, 1950.

Halfpenny, P. *Positivism and Sociology: Explaining Social Life.* London: Allen & Unwin, 1982.

Hall, V. R. *Managing Behavior: Behavior Modification in School and Home.* Lawrence, Kans.: H & H Enterprises, 1971.

Hanney, J. *Detection of Faked Responses on a Computer-Administered Questionnaire by Means of Response Latency.* Doctoral dissertation, Illinois Institute of Technology, Chicago, 1989.

Harris, F. N., and W. R. Jenson. Comparisons of Multiple-Baseline Across Persons Designs and *AB* Designs With Replication: Issues and Confusions. *Behavioral Assessment,* 7 (Spring 1985), 121–127.

Harrison, W. D. Role Strain and Burnout in Child-Protective Service Workers. *Social Service Review,* 54 (1980), 31–44.

Hawkins, J. D., and B. R. Salisbury. Delinquency Prevention Programs for Minorities of Color. *Social Work Research and Abstracts,* 19 (1983), 5–12.

Heineman, M. B. The Obsolete Scientific Imperative in Social Work Research. *Social Service Review,* 55 (September 1981), 371–397.

Heise, D. R. The Semantic Differential and Attitude Research. In G. F. Summers, ed., *Attitude Measurement.* Chicago: Rand McNally, 1970.

Henry, G. *Practical Sampling.* Newbury Park, Calif.: Sage, 1990.

Hepworth, D. H., and J. Larsen. *Direct Social Work Practice.* Belmont, Calif.: Wadsworth, 1990.

Higgins, P. C., and J. M. Johnson. *Personal Sociology.* New York: Praeger, 1988.

Hirschel, J., I. Hutchison III, and C. Dean. The Failure of Arrest to Deter Spouse Abuse. *Journal of Research in Crime and Delinquency,* 29 (1992), 7–33.

Holmes, R., and J. De Burger. *Serial Murder.* Newbury Park, Calif.: Sage, 1988.

Holsti, O. R. *Content Analysis for the Social Sciences and Humanities.* Reading, Mass.: Addison-Wesley, 1969.

Homans, G. C. Contemporary Theory in Sociology. In R. E. L. Faris, ed., *Handbook of Modern Sociology.* Chicago: Rand McNally, 1964.

Honey, M. *Creating Rosie the Riveter: Class, Gender, and Propaganda.* Amherst: The University of Massachusetts Press, 1984.

Hooker, E. The Adjustment of the Male Overt Homosexual. *Journal of Projective Techniques,* 21 (1957), 18–31.

Hornung, C. A., B. C. McCullough, and T. Sugimoto. Status Relationships in Marriage: Risk Factors in Spouse Abuse. *Journal of Marriage and the Family,* 43 (1981), 675–692.

Horowitz, R. Community Tolerance of Gang Violence. *Social Problems,* 34 (December 1987), 437–450.

Hoshino, G., and M. M. Lynch. Secondary Analysis of Existing Data. In R. M. Grinnell, Jr., ed., *Social Work Research and Evaluation.* Itasca, Ill.: Peacock, 1981.

Huber, B. New Human Subjects Policies Announced; Exemptions Outlined. *ASA Footnotes,* 9 (1981), 1.

Hudson, W. W. *CAS: The Clinical Assessment System.* Tallahassee, Fla.: WALMYR, 1988.

———. *The Clinical Measurement Package: A Field Manual.* Homewood, Ill.: Dorsey Press, 1982.

———. *Computer-Assisted Social Services.* Tempe, Ariz.: WALMYR, 1996.

Hughes, M., and S. Fancett. The Challenge of IT. *Computers in Human Services,* 13 (1996).

Humphreys, L. *Tearoom Trade: Impersonal Sex in Public Places.* Chicago: Aldine-Atherton, 1970.

Hyman, H. *Interviewing in Social Research.* Chicago: University of Chicago Press, 1954.

ICPSR (Inter-University Consortium for Political and Social Research). *Guide to Resources and Services, 1995–1996.* Ann Arbor, Mich.: ICPSR, 1996.

Irwin, D. M., and M. M. Bushnell. *Observational Strategies for Child Study.* New York: Holt, Rinehart and Winston, 1980.

Ivanoff, A., B. J. Blythe, and S. Briar. The Empirical Clinical Practice Debate. *Social Casework: The Journal of Contemporary Social Work,* 68 (1987), 290–298.

Ivanoff, A., E. A. R. Robinson, and B. J. Blythe. Empirical Clinical Practice From a Feminist Perspective. *Social Work* (September/October, 1987), 417–423.

Jackson, B. O., and L. B. Mohr. Rent Subsidies: An Impact Evaluation and an Application of the Random-Comparison-Group Design. *Evaluation Review,* 10 (August 1986), 483–517.

Jacobson, N. S. Problem Solving and Contingency Contracting in the Treatment of Marital Discord. *Journal of Consulting and Clinical Psychology,* 45 (1977), 92–100.

James, J., and R. Bolstein. The Effect of Monetary Incentives and Follow-up Mailings on the Response Rate and Response Quality in Mail Surveys. *Public Opinion Quarterly,* 54 (1990), 346–361.

Javidi, M., L. Long, M. Vasu, and D. Ivy. Enhancing Focus Group Validity With Computer-Assisted Technology in Social Science Research. *Social Science Computer Review,* 9 (1991), 231–243.

———. Single-Subject and Group Designs in Treatment Evaluation. *Social Work Research and Abstracts,* 13 (1977), 35–42.

Jayaratne, S. Analytic Procedures for Single-Subject Designs. *Social Work Research and Abstracts,* 14 (Fall 1978), 30–40.

Jayaratne, S, and R. Levy. *Empirical Clinical Practice.* New York: Columbia University Press, 1979.

Jeger, A. M., and R. S. Slotnick. Community Mental Health: Toward a Behavioral-Ecological Perspective. In A. M. Jeger and R. S. Slotnick, eds., *Community Mental Health and Behavioral Ecology.* New York: Plenum, 1982.

Jendrek, M. P. *Through the Maze: Statistics With Computer Applications.* Belmont, Calif.: Wadsworth, 1985.

Jenkins-Hall, K., and C. A. Osborn. The Conduct of Socially Sensitive Research: Sex Offenders as Participants. *Criminal Justice and Behavior,* 21 (1994), 325–340.

Johnson, F. C. Practice Versus Research: Issues in Teaching of Single-Subject Research Skills. *Journal of Education for Social Work,* 17 (1981), 62–68.

Johnson, J. M. *Doing Field Research.* New York: Free Press, 1975.

Johnson, S. M., and O. D. Bolstad. Methodological Issues in Naturalistic Observation: Some Problems and Solutions for Field Research. In L. A. Hamerlynck, L. C. Handy, and E. J. Mash, eds., *Behavior Change.* Champaign, Ill.: Research Press, 1973.

Johnson, S. M., and G. White. Self-Observation as an Agent of Behavioral Change. *Behavioral Therapy,* 2 (1971), 488–497.

Jones, J. H. *Bad Blood: The Tuskegee Syphilis Experiment,* exp. edition. New York: Free Press, 1992.

Jones, M. A. *A Second Chance for Families: Five Years Later, Follow-Up of a Program to Prevent Foster Care.* New York: Child Welfare League of America, 1985.

Jorgensen, D. *Participant Observation: A Methodology for Human Studies.* Newbury Park, Calif.: Sage, 1989.

Kadushin, A. *The Social Work Interview.* New York: Columbia University Press, 1972.

Kamerman, J. B. *Death in the Midst of Life: Social and Cultural Influences on Death, Grief, and Mourning.* Englewood Cliffs, N.J.: Prentice-Hall, 1988.

Kassebaum, G., D. Ward, and D. Wilner. *Prison Treatment and Parole Survival.* New York: Wiley, 1971.

Katz, J. *Experimentation With Human Beings.* New York: Russell Sage Foundation, 1972.

Kazdin, A. E. Selection of Target Behaviors: The Relationship of the Treatment Focus to Clinical Dysfunction. *Behavioral Assessment,* 7 (Winter 1985), 33–47.

———. *Single-Case Research Designs.* New York: Oxford University Press, 1982.

Kelle, U., ed. *Computer-Aided Qualitative Data Analysis: Theory, Methods, and Practice.* Thousand Oaks, Calif.: Sage, 1995.

Kelly, J. R., and J. E. McGrath. *On Time and Method.* Beverly Hills, Calif.: Sage, 1988.

Kemeny, J. G. *A Philosopher Looks at Science.* Princeton, N.J.: Van Nostrand, 1959.

Kemper, P., D. Long, and C. Thornton. *The Supported Work Evaluation: Final Benefit-Cost Analysis.* New York: Manpower Demonstration Research Corporation, 1981.

Kenny, G. K. The Metric Properties of Rating Scales Employed in Evaluation of Research: An Empirical Examination. *Evaluation Review,* 10 (June 1986), 397–408.

Kiesler, S., and L. Sproull. Response Effects in the Electronic Survey. *Public Opinion Quarterly,* 50 (1986), 402–413.

Kimmel, A. *Ethics and Values in Applied Social Research.* Newbury Park, Calif.: Sage, 1988.

Kirk, J., and M. L. Miller. *Reliability and Validity in Qualitative Research.* Beverly Hills, Calif.: Sage, 1986.

Kirk, R. E. *Experimental Design: Procedures for the Behavioral Sciences,* 2nd ed. Belmont, Calif.: Brooks/Cole, 1982.

Kirk, S., and H. Kutchins. *The Selling of DSM: The Rhetoric of Science in Psychiatry.* New York: Aldine de Gruyter, 1992.

Kirkham, G. L. *Signal Zero.* Philadelphia: Lippincott, 1976.

Kish, L. *Survey Sampling.* New York: Wiley, 1965.

Kline, D. The Power of the Placebo. *Hippocrates: The Magazine of Health and Medicine,* 2 (May/June 1988), 24–26.

Knudsen, D. D., H. Pope, and D. P. Irish. Response Differences to Questions on Sexual Standards: An Interview–Questionnaire Comparison. *Public Opinion Quarterly,* 31 (1967), 290–297.

Kogan, L. S. Principles of Measurement. In N. A. Polansky, ed., *Social Work Research.* Chicago: University of Chicago Press, 1975.

Kohfeld, C., and L. Leip. Bans on Concurrent Sale of Beer and Gas: A California Case Study. *Sociological Practice Review,* 2 (April 1991), 104–115.

Kolata, G. New Picture of Who Will Get AIDS Is Crammed With Addicts. *New York Times,* February 28, 1995, B6.

Korbin, J. E. Child Maltreatment in Cross-Cultural Perspective: Vulnerable Children and Circumstances. In R. J. Gelles and J. B. Lancaster, eds., *Child Abuse and Neglect: Biosocial Dimensions.* New York: Aldine de Gruyter, 1987.

Kraemer, H. C., and S. Thiemann. *How Many Subjects? Statistical Power Analysis in Research.* Newbury Park, Calif.: Sage, 1987.

Krasnick, J. A., and D. F. Alwin. An Evaluation of a Cognitive Theory of Response-Order Effects in Survey Measurement. *Public Opinion Quarterly,* 51 (Summer 1987), 201–219.

Krathwohl, D. R. *How to Prepare a Research Proposal: Guidelines for Funding and Dissertations in the Social and Behavioral Sciences,* 3rd ed. New York: Distributed by Syracuse University Press, 1988.

Krippendorff, K. *Content Analysis: An Introduction to Its Methodology.* Beverly Hills, Calif.: Sage, 1980.

Krishef, C. *Fundamental Approaches to Single-Subject Design and Analysis.* Malabar, Fla.: Krieger, 1991.

Krueger, R. A. *Focus Groups: A Practical Guide for Applied Research,* 2nd ed. Thousand Oaks, Calif.: Sage, 1994.

Kuo, W. H., and Y. Tsai. Social Networking, Hardiness, and Immigrant's Mental Health. *Journal of Health and Social Behavior,* 27 (June 1986), 133–149.

Lake, D. G., M. B. Miles, and R. B. Earle, eds. *Measuring Human Behavior: Tools for the Assessment of Social Functioning.* New York: Teachers College Press, 1973.

Lally, J. J. Social Determinants of Differential Allocation of Resources to Disease Research: A Comparative Analysis of Crib Death and Cancer Research. *Journal of Health and Social Behavior,* 18 (1977), 125–138.

Landrine, H. Race and Class Stereotypes of Women. *Sex Roles,* 13 (July 1985), 65–75.

Lantz, H. R., R. Schmitt, M. Britton, and E. C. Snyder. Pre-Industrial Patterns in the Colonial Family in America: A Content Analysis of Colonial Magazines. *American Sociological Review,* 33 (1968), 413–426.

Larzelere, R., and G. Patterson. Parental Management: Mediator of the Effect of Socioeconomic Stress on Early Delinquency. *Criminology,* 28 (1990), 301–324.

Lavrakas, P. J. *Telephone Survey Methods: Sampling, Selection, and Supervision.* Beverly Hills, Calif.: Sage, 1987.

Leading Researcher Indicted on Charges of Falsifying Data for U.S. Grant. *New York Times,* April 17, 1988, 18.

Lehman, R. Statistics on the Macintosh. *Byte* (July 1987), 207–214.

Lenihan, K. *Unlocking the Second Gate.* Department of Labor R & D Monograph 45. Washington, D.C.: U.S. Government Printing Office, 1977.

Levin, J., and J. L. Spates. Hippie Values: An Analysis of the Underground Press. *Youth and Society,* 2 (1970), 59–73.

Levitt, J. L., and W. J. Reid. Rapid-Assessment Instruments for Practice. *Social Work Research and Abstracts,* 17 (1981), 13–19.

Lewis, K. G. Children of Lesbians: Their Point of View. *Social Work,* 25 (1980), 198–203.

Liebow, E. *Talley's Corner.* Boston: Little, Brown, 1967.

Likert, R. A. Technique for the Measurement of Attitudes. *Archives of Psychology,* 21 (No. 140, 1932).

Linsk, N., M. W. Howe, and E. M. Pinkston. Behavioral Group Work in a Home for the Aged. *Social Work,* 20 (1975), 454–463.

Lockhart, L. L. Methodological Issues in Comparative Racial Analyses: The Case of Wife Abuse. *Social Work Research and Abstracts,* 21 (Summer 1985), 35–41.

Lofland, J., and L. H. Lofland. *Analyzing Social Settings,* 2nd ed. Belmont, Calif.: Wadsworth, 1984.

Lolley, J. L. *Your Library—What's in It for You?* New York: Wiley, 1974.

Luebke, B. Out of Focus: Images of Women and Men in Newspaper Photographs. *Sex Roles,* 20 (1989), 121–133.

Magnet, M. Behind the Bad-News Census. *Fortune,* 103 (1981), 88–93.

Magura, S., and B. S. Moses. *Outcome Measures for Child Welfare Services: Theory and Applications.* Washington, D.C.: Child Welfare League of America, Inc., 1986.

Malcolm, D. Statistical Navigator Professional. *Social Science Computer Review,* 10 (1992), 121–123.

Manning, P. K. Review of Signal Zero by George L. Kirkham. *Criminology,* 16 (1978), 133–136.

Manson, S. M. Recent Advances in American Indian Mental Health Research: Implications for Clinical Research and Training. In M. R. Miranda and H. H. L. Kitano, eds., *Mental Health Research and Practice in Minority Communities: Development of Culturally Sensitive Training Programs.* Rockville, Md.: U.S. Department of Health and Human Services, DHHS Publication No. (ADM) 86-1466, 1986.

Marascuilo, L., and P. L. Busk. Combining Statistics for Multiple-Baseline *AB* and Replicated *ABAB* Designs Across Subjects. *Behavioral Assessment,* 10 (No. 1, 1988), 1–28.

Margolin, G., B. Burman, and R. John. Home Observations of Married Couples Reenacting Naturalistic Conflicts. *Behavioral Assessment,* 11 (1989), 101–118.

Margolin, J. *Foundation Fundamentals: A Research Guide for Grant Seekers,* 4th ed. New York: The Foundation Center, 1991.

Marin, G., and B. VanOss Marin. *Research With Hispanic Populations.* Newbury Park, Calif.: Sage, 1991.

Marx, K. *Selected Writings in Sociology and Philosophy.* Edited by T. B. Bottomore and M. Rubel. Baltimore, Md.: Penguin, 1964 (originally published 1848).

Maslach, C. Burned-Out. In J. R. Folta and E. S. Deck, eds., *A Sociological Framework for Patient Care,* 2nd ed. New York: Wiley, 1979.

Mayo, J. K., R. C. Hornick, and E. G. McAnany. *Educational Reform With Television: The El Salvador Experience.* Palo Alto, Calif.: Stanford University Press, 1976.

McCord, J. A. Thirty-Year Follow-Up of Treatment Effects. *American Psychologist,* 33 (1978), 284–289.

McDowell, I., and C. Newell. *Measuring Health: A Guide to Rating Scales and Questionnaires,* 2nd ed. New York: Oxford University Press, 1996.

McFall, R. M. Effects of Self-Monitoring on Normal Smoking Behavior. *Journal of Consulting and Clinical Psychology,* 35 (1970), 135–142.

McGranahan, D. V., and I. Wayne. German and American Traits Reflected in Popular Drama. *Human Relations,* 1 (1948), 429–455.

McKillip, J. *Need Analysis: Tools for Human Services and Education.* Beverly Hills, Calif.: Sage, 1987.

McLanahan, S., and G. Sandefur. *Growing Up With a Single Parent: What Hurts, What Helps.* Cambridge, Mass.: Harvard University Press, 1994.

McLaren, B. J. *Understanding and Using the Internet.* Minneapolis/St. Paul: West, 1996.

McLuhan, M. *Understanding Media: The Extensions of Man* (paperback ed.). New York: McGraw-Hill, 1965.

McMahon, M. O. *The General Method of Social Work Practice: A Problem Solving Approach,* 2nd ed. Englewood Cliffs, N.J.: Prentice-Hall, 1990.

McNeely, R. L., and G. Robinson-Simpson. The Truth About Domestic Violence: A Falsely Framed Issue. *Social Work,* 32 (November/December, 1987), 485–490.

Melton, G. B. Certificates of Confidentiality Under the Public Health Service Act: Strong Protection But Not Enough. *Violence and Victims,* 5 (1990), 67–71.

Melton, G. B., and J. N. Gray. *Ethical Dilemmas in AIDS Research: Individual Privacy and Public Health,* 43 (1988), 60–64.

Mendelsohn, H. *An Author's Guide to Social Work Journals.* Annapolis, Md.: NASW Press, 1992.

Mendes, H. A. Single Fatherhood. *Social Work,* 21 (1976), 308–312.

Mertz, W., J. Tsui, J. Judd, S. Reiser, J. Hallfrisch, E. Morris, P. Steele, and E. Lashley. What Are People Really Eating? The Relation Between Energy Intake Derived From Estimated Diet Records and Intake Determined to Maintain Body Weight. *American Journal of Clinical Nutrition,* 54 (1991), 291–295.

Michigan Women's Commission. *Sex Discrimination in an Elementary Reading Program.* Lansing, Mich., 1974.

Miller, D. C. *Handbook of Research Design and Social Measurement,* 5th ed. Newbury Park, Calif.: Sage, 1991.

Miller, L. P. The Application of Research to Practice: A Critique. *American Behavioral Scientist,* 30 (September/October 1987), 70–80.

Miner, L. E. *Directory of Research Grants.* Phoenix: Oryx, 1996.

Mitchell, J., J. Tucker, P. Loftman, and S. Williams. HIV and Women: Current Controversies and Clinical Relevance. *Journal of Women's Health,* 1 (Spring 1992), 35–39.

Mitchell, J. V. *The Ninth Mental Measurements Yearbook.* Lincoln: University of Nebraska Press, 1985.

Mitsos, S. B. Personal Constructs and the Semantic Differential. *Journal of Abnormal and Social Psychology,* 62 (1961), 433–434.

Moe, K. Should the Nazi Research Data Be Cited? *The Hastings Center Report,* 14 (December 1984), 5–7.

Monaghan, P. Sociologist Is Jailed for Refusing to Testify About Research Subject. *Chronicle of Higher Education,* 39 (May 26, 1993), 10.

Moody, E. J. Urban Witches. In J. E. Nash and J. P. Spradley, eds., *Sociology: A Descriptive Approach.* Chicago: Rand McNally, 1976.

Morash, M., and J. R. Greene. Evaluating Women on Patrol: A Critique of Contemporary Wisdom. *Evaluation Review,* 10 (April 1986), 230–255.

Morgan, D. L. *Focus Groups as Qualitative Research,* 2nd ed. Thousand Oaks, Calif.: Sage, 1994.

Morrison, R. S. Disreputable Science: Definition and Detection. *Journal of Advanced Nursing,* 15 (1990), 911–913.

Moser, C. A., and G. Kalton. *Survey Methods in Social Investigation,* 2nd ed. New York: Basic Books, 1972.

Murphy, J., and J. Pardeck. *The Computerization of Human Service Agencies: A Critical Appraisal.* New York: Auburn House, 1991.

Murray, L., R. Donovan, B. L. Kail, and L. J. Medvene. Protecting Human Subjects During Social Work Research: Researchers' Opinions. *Social Work Research and Abstracts,* 16 (1980), 25–30.

Nachmias, C., and D. Nachmias. *Research Methods in the Social Sciences.* New York: St. Martin's Press, 1992.

Nelsen, J. C. Issues in Single-Subject Research for Nonbehaviorists. *Social Work Research and Abstracts,* 17 (1981), 31–37.

Nelson, K. Populations and Outcomes in Five Family Preservation Programs. In K. Wells and D. Biegel, eds., *Family Preservation Services: Research and Evaluation.* Newbury Park, Calif.: Sage, 1991.

Newman, E., and J. Turem. The Crisis of Accountability. *Social Work,* 19 (1974), 5–16.

News and Notes. *Social Science Microcomputer Review,* 5 (1987), 576–577.

New York Office of Mental Health. *Who Are the Homeless? A Study of Randomly Selected Men Who Use the New York City Shelters.* Albany: New York Office of Mental Health, May 1982.

Nielson, J. M., ed. *Feminist Research Methods.* Boulder, Colo.: Westview Press, 1989.

Nigro, G. N., et al. Changes in the Facial Prominence of Women and Men Over the Last Decade. *Psychology of Women Quarterly,* 12 (June 1988), 225–235.

Norland, S. E., J. R. Hepburn, and D. R. Monette. Labeling Positive Differentiation: Effects on the Construction of Deviance. *Sociology and Social Research,* 61 (1976), 83–95.

Nurius, P., and W. Hudson. Computer-Based Practice: Future Dream or Current Technology? *Social Work,* 33 (1988), 351–362.

———. *Human Services: Practice Evaluation and Computers.* Pacific Grove, Calif.: Brooks/Cole, 1993.

Ogilvie, D. M., P. J. Stone, and E. S. Shneidman. Some Characteristics of Genuine Versus Simulated Suicide Notes. In P. J. Stone, D. C. Dunphy, M. S. Smith, and D. M. Ogilvie, eds., *The General Inquirer: A Computer Approach to Content Analysis in the Behavioral Sciences.* Cambridge, Mass.: M.I.T. Press, 1966.

O'Hare, T. Integrating Research and Practice: A Framework for Implementation. *Social Work,* 36 (May 1991), 220–223.

Oksenberg, L., L. Coleman, and C. F. Cannell. Interviewer's Voices and Refusal Rates in Telephone Surveys. *Public Opinion Quarterly,* 50 (Spring 1986), 97–111.

Ollendick, T. H. Cognitive Behavioral Treatment of Panic Disorder With Agoraphobia in Adolescents: A Multiple Baseline Design Analysis. *Behavior Therapy,* 26 (1995), 517–553.

Orcutt, B. *Science and Inquiry in Social Work Practice.* New York: Columbia University Press, 1990.

Orme, J. G., and T. D. Combs-Orme. Statistical Power and Type II Errors in Social Work Research. *Social Work Research and Abstracts,* 22 (1986), 3–10.

Orme, J. G., and W. W. Hudson. The Problem of Sample Size Estimation: Confidence Intervals. *Social Work Research,* 19 (June 1995), 121–127.

Orme, J. G., and R. M. Tolman. The Statistical Power of a Decade of Social Work Education Research. *Social Service Review,* 60 (1986), 619–632.

Orne, M. T. On the Social Psychology of the Psychological Experiment: With Particular Reference to Demand Characteristics and Their Implications. *American Psychologist,* 17 (1962), 776–783.

Osgood, C. E., W. May, and M. Miron. *Crosscultural Universals of Affective Meaning.* Urbana: University of Illinois Press, 1975.

Osgood, C. E., G. J. Suci, and P. H. Tannenbaum. *The Measurement of Meaning.* Urbana: University of Illinois Press, 1957.

Ost, L. G., B. E. Westling, and K. Hellstrom. Applied Relaxation, Exposure in Vivo and Cognitive Methods in the Treatment of Panic Disorder With Agoraphobia. *Behavior Research and Therapy,* 31 (1993), 383–394.

Parker, M. W., G. H. Chynoweth, D. Blankinship, E. R. Zaldo, and M. J. Matthews. A Case for Computer Applications in Social Work. *Journal of Social Work Education,* 23 (Spring/Summer 1987), 57–68.

Patterson, C. J. Children of Lesbian and Gay Parents. *Child Development,* 63 (1992), 1025–1042.

Pepler, D. J., and W. M. Craig. A Peek Behind the Fence: Naturalistic Observations of Aggressive Children With Remote Audiovisual Recording. *Developmental Psychology,* 31 (1995), 548–553.

Perkins, C., and P. Klaus. National Crime Victimization Survey. *Bureau of Justice Statistics Bulletin,* (April 1996), 1–8.

Peterson, R. D. The Anatomy of Cost-Effectiveness Analysis. *Evaluation Research,* 10 (February 1986), 29–44.

Peterson, R. R. A Re-Evaluation of the Economic Consequences of Divorce. *American Sociological Review,* 61 (1996), 528–536.

Peterson, S., and T. Kroner. Gender Biases in Textbooks for Introductory Psychology and Human Development. *Psychology of Women Quarterly,* 16 (1992), 17–36.

Peterson, S., and M. Lach. Gender Stereotypes in Children's Books: Their Prevalence and Influence on Cognitive and Affective Development. *Gender and Education,* 2 (No. 2, 1990), 185–197.

Peyrot, M. Coerced Voluntarism: The Micropolitics of Drug Treatment. *Urban Life,* 13 (January 1985), 343–365.

Phillips, D., and Y. Berman. *Human Services in the Age of New Technology: Harmonising Social Work and Computerisation.* Brookfield, Vt.: Ashgate, 1995.

Phillips, D. P. The Impact of Mass Media Violence on U.S. Homicides. *American Sociological Review,* 48 (August 1983), 560–568.

Piliavin, I., and S. Briar. Police Encounters With Juveniles. *American Journal of Sociology,* 70 (1964), 206–214.

Piliavin, I., S. Masters, and T. Corbett. Factors Influencing Errors in AFDC Payments. *Social Work Research and Abstracts,* 15 (1977), 3–17.

Poindexter, S. E. *The Internet Using Netscape Navigator Software.* Cambridge, Mass.: Course Technology, 1996.

Pollard, W. E. Decision Making and the Use of Evaluation Research. *American Behavioral Scientist,* 30 (July/August 1987), 661–676.

Polsky, N. *Hustlers, Beats, and Others.* Chicago: Aldine, 1967.

Pressman, J., and A. Wildavsky. *Implementation: Or How Great Expectations in Washington Are Dashed in Oakland.* Berkeley: University of California Press, 1973.

Prothro, J. W. Verbal Shifts in the American Presidency: A Content Analysis. *American Political Science Review,* 50 (1956), 726–739.

Punch, M. *The Politics and Ethics of Fieldwork.* Beverly Hills, Calif.: Sage, 1986.

Purcell, P., and L. Stewart. Dick and Jane in 1989. *Sex Roles,* 22 (Nos. 3–4, 1990), 177–185.

Radbill, S. X. Children in a World of Violence: A History of Child Abuse. In C. H. Kempe and R. Helfer, eds., *The Battered Child,* 3rd ed. Chicago: University of Chicago Press, 1980.

Rainwater, L., and D. J. Pittman. Ethical Problems in Studying a Politically Sensitive and Deviant Community. *Social Problems,* 14 (1967), 357–366.

Rank, M. R. Exiting From Welfare: A Life-Table Analysis. *Social Service Review,* 59 (September 1985), 358–376.

Rapee, R. M., M. G. Craske, and D. H. Barlow. Subject-Described Features of Panic Attacks Using Self-Monitoring. *Journal of Anxiety Disorders,* 4 (1990), 171–181.

Rathje, W., and C. Murphy. *Rubbish! The Archaeology of Garbage.* New York: HarperCollins, 1992.

Ratzan, R. M. The Experiment That Wasn't: A Case Report in Clinical Geriatric Research. *The Gerontologist,* 21 (1981), 297–302.

Rea, L., and R. Parker. *Designing and Conducting Survey Research.* San Francisco: Jossey-Bass, 1992.

Reamer, F. G. *Social Work Values and Ethics.* New York: Columbia University Press, 1995.

Reece, R., and H. Siegal. *Studying People: A Primer in the Ethics of Social Research.* Macon, Ga.: Mercer University Press, 1986.

Reese, H. W., and W. J. Fremouw. Normal and Normative Ethics in Behavioral Science. *American Psychologist,* 39 (1984), 863–876.

Register, C. *Are Those Kids Yours?: American Families With Children Adopted From Other Countries.* New York: Free Press, 1991.

Reid, P. N., and J. H. Gundlach. A Scale for the Measurement of Consumer Satisfaction With Social Services. *Journal of Social Service Research,* 7 (1983), 37–54.

Reid, S. *Crime and Criminology,* 6th ed. Fort Worth, Tex.: Holt, Rinehart and Winston, 1991.

Reid, W. The Social Agency as a Research Machine. *Journal of Social Service Research,* 2 (1978), 11–23.

Rein, M. *Social Service Crisis, Social Policy.* New York: Random House, 1970.

Reinharz, S. *Feminist Methods in Social Research.* New York: Oxford University Press, 1992.

Reinherz, H., M. C. Grob, and B. Berkman. Health Agencies and a School of Social Work: Practice and Research in Partnership. *Health and Social Work,* 8 (1983), 40–47.

Reiss, A. K., and L. Rhodes. An Empirical Test of Differential Association Theory. *Journal of Research in Crime and Delinquency,* 4 (1967), 28–42.

Repp, A., M. Harman, D. Felece, R. VanAcker, and K. Karsh. Conducting Behavioral Assessments on Computer-Collected Data. *Behavioral Assessment,* 11 (1989), 249–268.

Reynolds, P. D. *Ethical Dilemmas and Social Science Research.* San Francisco: Jossey-Bass, 1979.

Robinson, J., P. Shaver, and L. Wrightsman, eds. *Measures of Personality and Social Psychological Attitudes.* San Diego, Calif.: Academic Press, 1991.

Robinson, W. S. Ecological Correlations and the Behavior of Individuals. *American Sociological Review,* 15 (1950), 351–357.

Rosen, A. The Scientific Practitioner Revisited: Some Obstacles and Prerequisites for Fuller Implementation in Practice. *Social Work Research,* 20 (June 1996), 105–111.

Rosenberg, P. S. Scope of the AIDS Epidemic in the United States. *Science,* 270 (November 24, 1995), 1372–1375.

Rosenhan, D. L. On Being Sane in Insane Places. *Science,* 179 (1973), 250–258.

Rosenthal, R. Covert Communication in the Psychological Experiment. *Psychological Bulletin,* 67 (1967), 356–367.

———. Replication in Behavioral Research. In J. Neuliep, ed., *Replication Research in the Social Sciences.* Newbury Park, Calif.: Sage, 1991.

Rosenthal, R., and R. Rosnow. *The Volunteer Subject.* New York: Wiley, 1975.

Rossi, P. H., R. A. Berk, and K. J. Lenihan. *Money, Work, and Crime: Experimental Evidence.* New York: Academic Press, 1980.

Rossi, P. H., and H. Freeman. *Evaluation: A Systematic Approach,* 5th ed. Newbury Park, Calif.: Sage, 1993.

Rossi, P. H., J. D. Wright, G. A. Fisher, and G. Willis. The Urban Homeless: Estimating Composition and Size. *Science,* 235 (March 13, 1987), 1336–1341.

Roth, D., J. Bean, N. Lust, and T. Saveanu. *Homelessness in Ohio: A Study of People in Need.* Columbus: Ohio Department of Mental Health, Office of Program Evaluation and Research, February 1985.

Rudd, M. D., M. H. Rajab, and D. T. Orman. Effectiveness of an Outpatient Intervention Targeting Suicidal Young Adults: Preliminary Results. *Journal of Consulting and Clinical Psychology,* 64 (1996), 179–190.

Ruggles, P. *Drawing the Line: Alternative Poverty Measures and Their Implications for Public Policy.* Washington, D.C.: Urban Institute Press, 1990.

Runcie, J. F. *Experiencing Social Research,* rev. ed. Homewood, Ill.: Dorsey Press, 1980.

Russell, B. On the Notion of Cause, With Applications to the Free-Will Problem. In H. Feigel and M. Brodbeck, eds., *Readings in the Philosophy of Science.* New York: Appleton-Century-Crofts, 1953.

Russell, M. *Clinical Social Work: Research and Practice.* Newbury Park, Calif.: Sage, 1990.

Rutman, L. Introduction. In L. Rutman, ed., *Evaluation Research Methods,* 2nd ed. Beverly Hills, Calif.: Sage, 1984.

Saunders, D. G. Other "Truths" About Domestic Violence: A Reply to McNeely and Robinson-Simpson. *Social Work* (March/April 1988), 179–183.

Saxe, L., and M. Fine. *Social Experiments: Methods for Design and Evaluation.* Beverly Hills, Calif.: Sage, 1981.

Schaeffer, N. C. Evaluating Race-of-Interviewer Effects in a National Survey. *Sociological Methods and Research,* 8 (1980), 400–419.

Schafer, A. On Using Nazi Data: The Case Against. *Dialogue,* 25 (Autumn 1986), 413–419.

Scheaffer, R. L., W. Mendenhall, and L. Ott. *Elementary Survey Sampling,* 5th ed. Belmont, Calif.: Wadsworth, 1996.

Schiffman, S., M. Reynolds, and F. Young. *Introduction to Multidimensional Scaling.* New York: Academic Press, 1981.

Schuckit, M. *Drug and Alcohol Abuse,* 3rd ed. New York and London: Plenum, 1989.

Schuman, H., and S. Presser. The Open and Closed Question. *American Sociological Review,* 44 (1979), 692–712.

Schutte, N. S., and J. M. Malouff. *Sourcebook of Adult Assessment Strategies (Applied Clinical Psychology).* New York: Plenum, 1995.

Scott, C. Research on Mail Surveys. *Journal of the Royal Statistical Society,* Series *A,* 124 (1961), 143–195.

Scott, J. *A Matter of Record: Documentary Sources in Social Research.* Oxford, England: Polity Press, 1990.

Scott, R. A. The Selection of Clients by Social Welfare Agencies: The Case of the Blind. In Y. Hasenfeld and R. A. English, eds., *Human Service Organizations.* Ann Arbor: University of Michigan Press, 1975.

Sechrest, L., and J. Belew. Nonreactive Measures of Social Attitudes. *Applied Social Psychology Annual,* 4. Beverly Hills, Calif.: Sage, 1983.

Segal, S. P. Research on the Outcome of Social Work Therapeutic Intervention: A Review of the Literature. *Journal of Health and Social Behavior,* 13 (1972), 3–17.

Seibert, S. M., and N. V. Ramanaiah. On the Convergent and Discriminant Validity of Selected Measures of Aggression in Children. *Child Development,* 49 (1978), 1274–1276.

Seiler, L. H., and R. L. Hough. Empirical Comparisons of the Thurstone and Likert Techniques. In G. F. Summers, ed., *Attitude Measurement.* Chicago. Rand McNally, 1970.

Sellitz, C., L. S. Wrightsman, and S. W. Cook. *Research Methods in Social Relations,* 3rd ed. New York: Holt, Rinehart and Winston, 1976.

Sheafor, B. W., C. R. Horejsi, and G. A. Horejsi. *Techniques and Guidelines for Social Work Practice,* 4th ed. Boston: Allyn & Bacon, 1997.

Shearing, C. D. How to Make Theories Untestable: A Guide to Theorists. *The American Sociologist,* 8 (1973), 33–37.

Sheley, J. F. A Study in Self-Defeat: The Public Health Venereal Disease Clinic. *Journal of Sociology and Social Welfare,* 4 (1976), 114–124.

Shepard, R. N., A. K. Romney, and S. Nerlove, eds. *Multidimensional Scaling: Theory and Applications in the Behavioral Sciences.* New York: Academic Press, 1971.

Sherman, L. *Policing Domestic Violence: Experiments and Dilemmas.* New York: Free Press, 1992.

Sherman, L., and R. A. Berk. The Specific Deterrent Effects of Arrest for Domestic Assault. *American Sociological Review,* 49 (1984), 261–271.

Shilts, R. *And the Band Played On: Politics, People, and the AIDS Epidemic.* New York: St. Martin's Press, 1987.

Shireman, J. F., and P. R. Johnson. A Longitudinal Study of Black Adoptions: Single Parent, Transracial, and Traditional. *Social Work,* 31 (May/June 1986), 172–176.

Shulman, L. A Study of Practice Skills. *Social Work,* 23 (1978), 274–280.

Shupe, A. D., Jr., and D. G. Bromley. Walking a Tightrope: Dilemmas of Participant Observation of Groups in Conflict. *Qualitative Sociology,* 2 (1980), 3–21.

Sieber, J., ed. *Sharing Social Science Data: Advantages and Challenges.* Newbury Park, Calif.: Sage, 1991.

Siegel, D. Defining Empirically Based Practice. *Social Work,* 29 (1984), 325–329.

Siegel, K., and P. Tuckel. The Utilization of Evaluation Research. A Case Analysis. *Evaluation Review,* 9 (June 1985), 307–328.

Singer, E., D. R. VonThurn, and E. R. Miller. Confidentiality and Response: A Quantitative Review of the Experimental Literature. *Public Opinion Quarterly,* 59 (1995), 446–459.

Skinner, H. A. Benefits of Sequential Assessment. *Social Work Research and Abstracts,* 17 (1981), 21–28.

Skipper, J. K. Stripteasers: A Six-Year History of Public Reaction to a Study. In L. Cargan and J. Ballantine, eds., *Sociological Footprints.* Boston: Houghton Mifflin, 1979.

Smart, B. *Sociology, Phenomenology, and Marxian Analysis: A Critical Discussion of the Theory and Practice of a Science of Society.* Boston: Routledge and Kegan Paul, 1976.

Smith, A. Another Look at Content Analysis: An Essay Review. *Social Work Research and Abstracts,* 18 (Winter 1982), 5–10.

Smith, A. W. Problems and Progress in the Measurement of Black Public Opinion. *American Behavioral Scientists,* 30 (March/April 1987), 441–455.

Smith, H. W. *Strategies of Social Research,* 2nd ed. Englewood Cliffs, N.J.: Prentice-Hall, 1981.

Smith, M. F. *Evaluability Assessment: A Practical Approach.* Boston: Kluwer Academic Publishers, 1989.

Smith, S. H., and D. D. McLean. *ABC's of Grantsmanship.* Reston, Va.: American Alliance for Health, Physical Education, Recreation, and Dance, 1988.

Smith, S. S., and D. Richardson. Amelioration of Deception and Harm in Psychological Research: The Important Role of Debriefing. *Journal of Personality and Social Psychology,* 44 (No. 5, 1983), 1075–1082.

Smith, T. W. That Which We Call Welfare by Any Other Name Would Smell Sweeter: An Analysis of the Impact of Question Wording on Response Patterns. *Public Opinion Quarterly,* 51 (Spring 1987), 75–83.

Socolar, M. J. *Greater Use of Exemplary Education Programs Could Improve Education for Disadvantaged Children.*

GAO Report to Congress. Washington, D.C.: U.S. Government Printing Office, 1981.

Spitzer, R. L., J. Endicott, and J. Cohen. The Psychiatric Status Schedule: A Technique for Evaluating Psychopathology and Impairment in Role Functioning. *Archives of General Psychiatry,* 23 (1970), 41–55.

SPSS: SPSS 6.1 Syntax Reference Guide. Chicago: SPSS, p. 67, 1994.

Squire, P. Why the 1936 *Literary Digest* Poll Failed. *Public Opinion Quarterly,* 52 (1988), 125–133.

Stein, J. *Fiddler on the Roof.* New York: Crown, 1964.

Straus, M. Measuring Intrafamily Conflict and Violence: The Conflict Tactics (CT) Scales. In M. Strauss and R. Gelles, *Physical Violence in American Families: Risk Factors and Adaptations to Violence in 8,145 Families.* New Brunswick, N.J.: Transaction Publishers, 1990.

Straus, M., and R. J. Gelles. How Violent Are American Families? Estimates From the National Family Violence Resurvey and Other Studies. In G. Hotaling, D. Finkelhor, J. Kirkpatrick, and M. Straus, eds., *Family Abuse and Its Consequences: New Directions in Research.* Newbury Park, Calif.: Sage, 1988.

Straus, M. A., S. L. Hamby, S. Boney-McCoy, and D. B. Sugarman. The Revised Conflict Tactics Scales (CTS2): Development and Preliminary Data. *Journal of Family Issues,* 17 (May 1996), 283–316.

Street, D., R. D. Vinter, and C. Perrow. *Organizations for Treatment: A Comparative Study of Institutions for Delinquents.* New York: Free Press of Glencoe, 1966.

Strickland, S. P. *Politics, Science, and Dread Disease.* Cambridge, Mass.: Harvard University Press, 1972.

Study Finds Bias in House Hunting. *New York Times,* September 1, 1991, 14.

Sudman, S. Time Allocation on Survey Interviews and Other Field Occupations. *Public Opinion Quarterly,* 29 (1965), 638–648.

———. *Applied Sampling.* New York: Academic Press, 1976.

———. Mail Surveys of Reluctant Professionals. *Evaluation Research,* 9 (June 1985), 349–360.

Sudman, S., and N. M. Bradburn. *Asking Questions.* San Francisco: Jossey-Bass, 1982.

Suen, H. K., and D. Ary. Poisson Cumulative Probabilities of Systematic Errors in Single-Subject and Multiple-Subject Time Sampling. *Behavioral Assessment,* 8 (Spring 1986), 155–169.

Sullivan, C. The Provision of Advocacy Services to Women Leaving Abusive Partners. *Journal of Interpersonal Violence,* 6 (1991), 41–54.

Sullivan, T. J. *Introduction to Social Problems.* Boston: Allyn & Bacon, 1997.

Sulzer-Azaroff, B., and G. Mayer. *Behavior Analysis for Lasting Change.* Fort Worth, Tex: Holt, Rinehart and Winston, 1991.

Sutherland, E. *Criminology.* Philadelphia: Lippincott, 1939.

Taber, M., and I. Shapiro. Social Work and Its Knowledge Base: A Content Analysis of the Periodical Literature. *Social Work,* 10 (October 1965), 100–107.

Teich, A., and M. Frankel. *Good Science and Responsible Scientists: Meeting the Challenge of Fraud and Misconduct in Science.* Washington, D.C.: American Association for the Advancement of Science, 1992.

Thrasher, E., and C. Mowbray. A Strengths Perspective: An Ethnographic Study of Homeless Women With Children. *Health and Social Work,* 20 (1995), 93–101.

Thurstone, L. L., and E. J. Chave. *The Measurement of Attitudes.* Chicago: The University of Chicago Press, 1929.

Timberlake, E. M. Children With No Place to Call Home: Survival in Cars and on the Streets. *Child and Adolescent Social Work Journal,* 5 (No. 4, 1994), 268.

Timms, N., and J. Mayer. *The Client Speaks.* London: Routledge and Kegan Paul, 1971.

Toseland, R. W., and W. J. Reid. Using Rapid Assessment Instruments in a Family Service Agency. *Social Casework,* 66 (1985), 547–555.

Tran, T. V., and L. F. Williams. Effect of Language of Interview on the Validity and Reliability of Psychological Well-Being Scales. *Social Work Research,* 18 (March 1994), 17–25.

Treas, J., and A. VanHilst. Marriage and Remarriage Rates Among Older Americans. *The Gerontologist,* 16 (1976), 132–140.

Tripodi, T. *Uses and Abuses of Social Research in Social Work.* New York: Columbia University Press, 1974.

Turnbull, J. E., and B. Dietz-Uhler. The Boulder Model: Lessons From Clinical Psychology for Social Work Training. *Research on Social Work Practice,* 5 (October 1995), 411–429.

Uchida, C. NIJ Sponsors System to Speed Information to Police on Drug Hotspots. *NIJ Reports,* (1990), 6, 36.

U.S. Bureau of the Census. *Statistical Abstract of the United States: 1991,* 111th ed. Washington, D.C.: U.S. Government Printing Office, 1991.

Vannicelli, M., and G. Hamilton. Sex-Role Values and Bias in Alcohol Treatment Personnel. *Advances in Alcohol and Substance Abuse,* 4 (1984), 57–68.

Verdonik, E., and L. Sherrod. *An Inventory of Longitudinal Research on Childhood and Adolescence.* New York: Social Science Research Council, 1984.

Vinokur, A., L. Oksenberg, and C. Cannell. Effects of Feedback and Reinforcement on the Report of Health Information. In C. Cannell, L. Oksenberg, and C. Converse, eds., *Experiments in Interviewing Techniques.* Ann Arbor: University of Michigan, Institute for Social Research, 1979.

Wagenaar, A. C., and M. B. T. Wiviott. Effects of Mandating Seatbelt Use: A Series of Surveys on Compliance in Michigan. *Public Health Reports,* 101 (September/October 1986), 505–512.

Wakefield, J. C. When an Irresistible Epistemology Meets an Immovable Ontology. *Social Work Research,* 19 (March 1995), 9–17.

Ward, D. A., and G. G. Kassebaum. On Biting the Hand That Feeds: Some Implications of Sociological Evaluations of Correctional Effectiveness. In C. H. Weiss, ed., *Evaluating Social Programs: Readings in Social Action and Education.* Boston: Allyn & Bacon, 1972.

Warwick, D. P., and C. Lininger. *The Sample Survey: Theory and Practice.* New York: McGraw-Hill, 1975.

Webb, E. J., D. T. Campbell, R. D. Schwartz, L. Sechrest, and J. B. Grove. *Nonreactive Measures in the Social Sciences.* Boston: Houghton Mifflin, 1981.

Weber, M. Science as a Vocation. In H. H. Gerth and C. W. Mills, eds., *Max Weber: Essays in Sociology.* New York: Free Press, 1946 (originally published 1922).

———. *The Theory of Social and Economic Organization.* Trans., A. M. Henderson and T. Parsons. New York: Free Press, 1957 (originally published 1925).

Weber, R. P. *Basic Content Analysis,* 2nd ed. Beverly Hills, Calif.: Sage, 1990.

Weeks, M. Call Scheduling With CATI: Current Capabilities and Methods. In R. G. Groves et al., eds., *Telephone Survey Methodology.* New York: Wiley, 1988.

Weinberg, M. Sexual Modesty, Social Meanings, and the Nudist Camp. In M. Truzzi, ed., *Sociology and Everyday Life.* Englewood Cliffs, N.J.: Prentice-Hall, 1968.

Weiss, C. *Evaluation Research: Methods for Assessing Program Effectiveness.* Englewood Cliffs, N.J.: Prentice-Hall, 1972.

Weiss, R. L., and P. E. Frohman. Behavioral Observation as Outcome Measures: Not Through a Glass Darkly. *Behavioral Assessment,* 7 (Fall 1985), 309–315.

Weitzman, E. B., and M. B. Miles. *Computer Programs for Qualitative Data Analysis.* Thousand Oaks, Calif.: Sage, 1995.

Weitzman, L. J. *The Divorce Revolution: The Unexpected Social and Economic Consequences for Women and Children in America.* New York: Free Press, 1985.

Weitzman, L. J. The Economic Consequences of Divorce Are Still Unequal: Comment on Peterson. *American Sociological Review,* 61 (1996), 537–538.

Wells, K., and D. Biegel. *Family Preservation Services: Research and Evaluation.* Newbury Park, Calif.: Sage, 1991.

Wells, W. D., and G. Smith. Four Semantic Rating Scales Compared. *Journal of Applied Psychology,* 44 (1960), 393–397.

Whyte, W. F. Freedom and Responsibility in Research: The Springdale Case. *Human Organization,* 17 (1958), 1–2.

———. *Street Corner Society,* 2nd ed., Chicago: University of Chicago Press, 1955.

Williams, J. A., Jr., J. Vernon, M. Williams, and K. Malecha. Sex Role Socialization in Picture Books: An Update. *Social Science Quarterly,* 68 (March 1987), 148–156.

Williams, T. *The Cocaine Kids: The Inside Story of a Teenage Drug Ring.* Reading, Mass.: Addison-Wesley, 1989.

Wilson, T. Normative and Interpretive Paradigms in Sociology. In J. Douglas, ed., *Understanding Everyday Life: Toward the Reconstruction of Sociological Knowledge.* New York: Aldine, 1970.

Wingard, D. Trends and Characteristics of California Adoptions: 1964–1982. *Child Welfare,* 66 (July/August, 1987), 303–314.

Witkin, B. R. *Assessing Needs in Educational and Social Programs.* San Francisco: Jossey-Bass, 1984.

Witt, K. J., and S. Bernstein. Best Practices in Disk-by-Mail Surveys. *Sawtooth Software Conference Proceedings.* Sawtooth Software, Inc., 1992.

Wolfe, V. V., et al. Negative Affectivity in Children: A Multitrait-Multimethod Investigation. *Journal of Consulting and Clinical Psychology,* 55 (April 1987), 245–250.

Wolfgang, M. E. Confidentiality in Criminological Research and Other Ethical Issues. *Journal of Criminal Law and Criminology,* 72 (1981), 345–361.

Wuebben, P. L., B. C. Straits, and G. I. Schulman. *The Experiment as a Social Occasion.* Berkeley, Calif.: Glendessary Press, 1974.

Yates, B. T. Cost-Effectiveness Analysis and Cost-Benefit Analysis: An Introduction. *Behavioral Assessment,* 7 (Summer 1985), 207–234.

Young, C., K. Savola, and E. Phelps. *Inventory of Longitudinal Studies in the Social Sciences.* Newbury Park, Calif.: Sage, 1991.

Zill, N., and C. W. Nord. *Running in Place: How American Families Are Faring in a Changing Economy and an Individualistic Society.* Washington, D.C.: Child Trends, Inc, 1994.

Name Index

Abramson, P., 179
Achen, C. H., 271, 296, 298, 331
Adair, J., 52, 282
Adams, S., 3
Adler, P. A., 224
Agnew, N., 15
Alkin, M. C., 341
Allen, G. J., 303, 309
Allen-Meares, P., 201, 207
Alreck, P., 179
Alt, F. B., 331
Alter, C., 286
Amato, P. R., 24
Anderson, A., 62
Anderson, B., 179
Anderson, E., 247
Anderson, R., 201
Annis, R. C., 180
Aquilino, W., 165
Archer, D., 212, 213
Arches, J., 34, 35
Armstrong, J. S., 168
Arnold, D. O., 145
Aron, A., 424
Aron, E. N., 424
Ary, D., 240
Ashcraft, N., 55
Austin R., 453
Ayres, I., 243

Babbie, E. R., 39, 169
Bachman, J. G., 179
Backstrom, C. H., 139
Bahnson J., 184
Bailey, K., 57, 136, 224, 242
Bailey, R. C., 87
Bainbridge, W. A., 214
Balassone, M., 6
Bales, R. F., 202, 231, 232
Banfield, J., 398
Barlow, D. H., 2, 15, 24, 287, 294,
   296, 298, 300, 304, 306, 307, 309,
   311
Barth, R. P., 311
Bassuk, E. L., 146
Bastian, L., 202
Bauer, D. G., 428, 430, 436, 437, 438, 446
Baumrind, D., 50, 52
Baxter, P. M., 473
Beal, P., 184
Bean, G. J., 146
Bean J., 147
Beauchamp, T. L., 46, 69
Becerra, R. M., 114, 148
Bech, P., 366
Becker, H. S., 64, 224, 453
Bedell, J. R., 337
Belcher, J. C., 453

Belew, J., 227
Bell, A. P., 128
Bell R., 260
Bell, W., 31
Benbenishty, R., 12
Bensman, J., 53
Benton, T., 221
Berg, B., 86, 96
Berg, B. L., 247
Berger, R., 50
Berk, R. A., 268, 322, 332, 334, 335
Berkman, B., 2
Berman, P., 324
Berman, Y., 14
Bernstein, S., 118
Berry, M., 198
Berry, S. H., 168
Biegel, D., 198
Biklen, D. P., 226, 227
Billups, J., 209
Binder, A., 63, 116
Birkerts, S., 454
Blalock, A. B., 341
Blemer, P. B., 188
Bloom, M., 109, 291, 314, 366
Blythe, B. J., 88, 120
Bogdan, R., 238, 239
Bohrnstedt, G., 107
Bolner, M. S., 472
Bolstad, O. D., 242
Bolstein, R., 168
Boney-McCoy, S., 164
Bonjean, C. M., 109, 291
Borgatta, E., 107
Boruch, R., 341
Bowen, B. D., 191
Bowen, R. W., 398
Bradburn, N., 191
Bradburn, N. M., 159, 177, 179
Brajuha, M., 54
Bransford, J. D., 96
Brent, E. 201
Breuning, S. E., 60, 61
Briar, S., 241
Bridge, R. G., 166
Bromley, D. G., 223, 243, 245
Bronowski, J., 22, 24
Brown, S. V., 78
Bruce, D., 116
Brunner, G. A., 172
Brunswick-Heinemann, M., 64
Bryson, M., 127
Buckhout, R., 240
Buetow, S. A., 118, 188
Burch, G., 267
Burgess, R. G., 77, 120, 220
Burman, B., 236, 237
Burnam, M. A., 146, 147
Bush, G., 140, 273

Bushnell, M. M., 240
Busk, P. L., 298

Cahalan, D., 127
Callanan, P., 69
Camasso, M., 120
Campbell, D. T., 3, 110, 258, 267, 272,
   275, 278
Campbell, J. A., 112
Cannell, C. F., 169, 170, 186
Caplan, L., 23
Caplinger, T. E., 142
Carley, M., 341
Carlock, C. J., 264
Carpenter, E. H., 13
Carpenter, J., 422
Carroll, L., 19, 219
Carroll, S. J., 172
Cartwright A., 172
Catlin, G., 189
Cavan, S., 72, 238
Ceci, S. J., 47
Cerny, J. A., 304
Chaiken, J. M., 109
Chaiken, M. R., 109
Champion, D. J., 136
Chave, E. J., 353, 354, 356
Chen, H., 326
Christie, R., 347
Chun, K., 291
Churchill W., 22
Clum, G. A., 306
Cobb, S., 291
Coelho, R. J., 66
Cohen, J., 147, 179, 418
Cohen, M. R., 31
Coleman, L., 169
Combs-Orme, T. D., 418
Connaway, R. S., 12
Cook, F. L., 330
Cook, T. D., 258, 275, 278, 330, 343
Corbett, T., 197, 210
Corbin, J., 247
Corcoran, K., 109, 117, 291, 292, 366
Corenblum, B., 180
Corey, G., 69
Corey, M., 69
Cormier, L. S., 187
Cormier, W. H., 187
Corry, J., 205
Cotter, P. R., 179
Coulter, P. B., 179
Coulton, C. J., 347, 349
Cox, D. E., 276
Craft, J. L., 398
Craig, W. M., 228
Craske, M. G., 304
Crockenberg, S., 6, 83

Cronbach, L. J., 110, 114
Crosby, F., 243
Crossen, C., 69
Cuba, L., 454, 472
Cuzzort, R. P., 424

D'Amico, J. J., 340
Davidson, W. S., 283
Davies, J. A., 214
Davis, L. V., 20, 88, 89
Dawson, J. A., 340
Dean, C., 269, 270
DeBurger, J., 72
Deloria, D., 422
DeMaio, T. J., 179
DeMartini, J., 320
Denzin, N., 81, 143, 244, 247
Deutch, S. J., 331
DeVellis, R., 347
DeVellis, R. F., 366
Dietz-Uhler, B., 3
Dignan, M., 184
Dillman, D. A., 138, 161, 183, 187
DiVista, F. J., 358
Dotson, L. E., 359
Douglas, R. M., 118, 188
Dressel, P. L., 72
Duncan, G. J., 74
Dunford, F., 269
Durkheim, E., 221
Dushenko, T. W., 52
Dutton, D. G., 103

Earle, R. B., 109, 291
Edleson, J. L., 292
Edwards, A. L., 359, 362
Eichler, M., 180, 279
Ellickson, P., 260
Elliott, D., 269
Ellis, A., 25
Elms, A. C., 50
Endicott, J., 147
Engler, R. L., 62
Epstein, I., 152, 169
Erez, E., 341
Erikson, E., 20
Erikson, K. T., 245
Estroff, S. E., 220
Evans, J. D., 398, 425
Evans, W., 214
Evens, W., 287

Faden, R., 69
Fairweather, G. W., 283
Faludi, S., 74
Fancett, S., 14
Fanshel, D., 212
Farley, R., 210

Fay, B., 64
Felce, D., 248
Feldman, R. A., 142
Ferree, M., 212
Ferrell, J., 229
Festinger, L., 242
Fielding, N., 247
Fienberg, S., 195
Finsterbush, K., 15
Fischer, J., 109, 117, 286, 291, 292, 314, 329, 366
Fisher, E., 212
Fisher, G. A., 147
Fiske, D. W., 110
Fortune, A. E., 205, 206
Fowler, F., 177, 178, 180
Fox, W., 398
Frankel, M., 57
Fredman, N., 109, 291, 368
Freeman, H., 6, 280, 281, 319, 320, 327, 330, 332, 333, 335, 340
Fremouw, W. J., 45
French, J., 291
Freud, S., 20, 101
Frey, J. H., 169, 179
Fridlund, A. J., 422
Friendly, M., 398
Frisch, M. B., 294
Frohman, P. E., 291
Frost, P. J., 16
Fulford, K. W. M., 65
Furstenberg, F. F., Jr., 24

Gabor, P. A., 283, 316
Gallagher, B. J., 162
Galtung, J., 136
Gardner, J. E., 309
Garfield, E., 61
Garrison, D. H., Jr., 68
Garson, G. D., 151
Gates, J. K., 473
Geis, F. L., 347
Geis, G., 116
Geismar, L. L., 120
Gelles, R. J., 33, 78, 100, 103, 143
Gentry, M. E., 12
George, M., 118
Gibbs, L. E., 64, 82, 329
Gilligan, C., 88, 89
Gingerich, W., 287
Ginsburg, H., 101
Glaser, B. G., 39, 77, 221
Glaser, D., 341
Gold, R. L., 223, 224
Goldberg, G., 145
Goldenberg, S., 40
Goldfried, M. R., 3
Goldscheider, F. K., 24
Golombok, S., 27
Goode, W. J., 114

Gorden, R. L., 172, 178, 187
Gordon, M. M., 64
Gottman, J. M., 236, 283, 294, 296, 298
Gottschalk, L. A., 201
Gouldner, A., 64
Goyder, J., 166, 168
Graham, K., 228, 235, 242, 277
Gravetter, F. J., 425
Gray, B. H., 47
Gray, J. N., 54
Greenberg, D. S., 60
Greene, J. G., 340
Greene, J. R., 328
Greenley, J. R., 125
Grichting, W. L., 85
Grinnell, R. M., Jr., 283, 316
Grob, M. C., 2
Gross, R., 96
Groth-Marnat, G., 291
Groves, R. M., 169, 188
Groze, V., 20
Grubrium, J., 69
Guba, E. G., 221, 342
Gundlach, J. H., 354
Guttman, L., 359, 361, 362

Hahn, H., 473
Halfpenny, P., 64, 221
Hall, D., 454
Hall, E., 212
Hallfrisch, J., 165
Hallowell, L., 54
Hamby, S. L., 164
Hamilton, G., 25
Hanney, J., 118
Harris, F. N., 303
Harris, P., 118, 188
Harrison, W. D., 34, 35
Hatt, P. K., 114
Hawkins, J. D., 85
Hayes, S. C., 2, 15, 24, 294
Haynes, S. N., 316
Healey, J. F., 398, 425
Heineman, M. B., 88
Heise, D. R., 358
Hellstrom, K., 304
Henry, G. T., 131, 152, 398
Hepworth, D. H., 30
Hersen, M., 287, 290, 294, 296, 300, 306, 307, 309, 311, 368
Hess, I., 152
Higgins, P. C., 72, 96
Higgins, R. L., 294
Hill, R. J., 109, 291
Hindelag, M. J., 120
Hirschel, J., 269, 270
Hirschi, T., 120
Hoffman, S. D., 74
Holmes, R., 72

Holsti, O. R., 204, 206, 208
Homan, R., 69
Homans, G. C., 26
Honey, M., 205
Hooker, E., 128
Hoover, K., 16, 40
Horejsi, C. R., 3, 7
Horejsi, G. A., 3, 7
Hornick, R. C., 331
Hornung, C. A., 102, 103
Horowitz, R., 72
Hoshino, G., 197, 200
Hough, R. L., 354, 356
Howe, M. W., 233, 234
Howe, S. R., 147
Howse, K., 65
Huber, B., 47
Huberman, A. M., 247
Hudson, W., 15, 189, 292, 293, 314, 363
Hughes, M., 14
Huizinga, D., 269
Hult, C. A., 454
Humphreys, L., 55, 224
Hunt, M., 96
Hursh, G. D., 139
Hutchison, I., 269, 270
Hyman, H., 180

Ingram, S., 189
Irish, D. P., 170
Irwin, D. M., 240
Ivanoff, A., 2, 88
Ivy, D., 119

Jackson, B. O., 331
Jacob, H., 215
Jacobs, F. H., 343
James, J., 168
Javidi, M., 119
Jayaratne, S., 291, 295, 298, 300, 302, 303, 311
Jeger, A. M., 4
Jenkins-Hall, K., 58
Jenson, W. R., 303
John, R., 236, 237
Johnson, F. C., 295, 310
Johnson, J. M., 72, 96, 225
Johnson, P. R., 23
Johnson, S. M., 242, 294
Jones, F., 454
Jones, G. E., 398
Jones, J. H., 46
Jones, M. A., 7
Jorgensen, D., 225
Jorner, U., 399
Judd, J., 165
Julia M., 209

Kachigan, S., 399
Kadushin, A., 186
Kahn, R. L., 170
Kalton, G., 139, 162, 165, 168, 170
Kamerman, J. B., 259
Kamins, M. A., 215
Kanouse, D. E., 168
Kantrow, R., 145
Kaplan, L., 40
Kassebaum, G., 325, 340
Katz, J., 46
Kazdin, A. E., 289, 298, 316
Keisner, R. H., 17
Kelle, U., 214
Kelly, J. R., 90
Kemeny, J. G., 16, 36
Kemper, P., 338
Kenny, G. K., 105
Kettner, P. M., 121
Kiesler, S., 165
Kilpatrick, F. P., 359
Kimmel, A., 46, 50, 54, 69
Kirk, J., 121, 240, 242
Kirk, R. E., 254, 283
Kirk, S., 117
Kirkham, G. L., 223
Kish, L., 125, 134, 139, 152
Klaus, P., 203
Kline, D., 277
Klosko, J. S., 304
Knudsen, D. D., 170
Kock, E., 79
Koegel, P., 146, 147
Kogan, L. S., 362
Kohfeld, C., 211, 274
Kolata, G., 78
Korbin, J. E., 100
Kraemer, H. C., 418
Krathwohl, D. R., 430, 436, 440, 442, 444
Krause, D. R., 342
Kremen, E., 145
Krippendorff, K., 201, 204
Krishef, C., 287
Kroner, T., 212
Krosnick, J. A., 191
Krueger, R. A., 119, 184, 185
Kuo, W. H., 148
Kutchins, H., 117

Lach, M., 85, 212
LaFollette, M., 69
Lake, D. G., 109, 291
Lally, J. J., 78
Landon, A., 127
Landrine, H., 267
Lantz, H. R., 204, 210
Larsen, J. A., 30
Larzelere, R., 23
Lashley, E., 165
Lauter, L., 145

Lavrakas, P. J., 126
Lee, R., 69, 247
Lehman, R., 422
Leip, L., 211, 274
Lenihan, K. J., 322, 334
Levin, J., 207, 209
Levin, W. C., 357
Leviton, L. C., 343
Levitt, J. L., 292
Levy, R. L., 291, 295, 298, 300, 302, 303
Lewis, K. G., 26, 27
Liebow, E., 222, 247
Likert, R., 350, 355
Limback, J., 476
Lincoln, Y. S., 221, 247, 342
Lindsey, R. C. L., 52
Lininger, C., 177
Linsk, N., 233, 234
Lockhart, L. L., 33
Lofland, J., 220, 238
Lofland, L. H., 220, 238
Lolley, J. L., 457
Long, D., 338
Long, L., 119
LoSciuto, L., 165
Luck, E. J., 168
Luebke, B., 212
Lukefeld, C. G., 454
Lust, N., 146
Lyberg, L. E., 188
Lynch, M. M., 197, 200

Machiavelli, N., 347
Magnet, M., 144, 179
Magura, S., 109, 199, 291, 368
Malcolm, D., 422
Malouff, J. M., 109, 368
Mangione, T., 177, 178, 180
Manning, P. K., 223
Manson, S. M., 114
Marascuilo, L., 298
Margolin, G., 236, 237, 436, 440, 442
Marin, B., 115, 180
Marin, G., 115, 180
Mark, M. M., 330
Marshall, C., 247
Martin, L. L., 121
Martin, M., 195
Martin, P. Y., 264
Marx, K., 64
Maslach, C., 34
Massey, J. L., 188
Masters, S., 197, 210
May, W., 358
Mayer, G., 27
Mayer, J., 354
Mayo, J. K., 331
McAnany, E. G., 331

McCord, J., 326
McCulloch, C., 118, 188
McCullough, B. C., 102, 103
McDowell, I., 109, 368
McFall, R. M., 294
McGranahan, D.V., 203
McGrath, J. E., 90
McKie, C., 68
McKillip, J., 6, 322
McLanahan, S., 23
McLaren, B. J., 473, 484
McLean, D. D., 428, 436
McLemore, S. D., 109, 291
McLuhan, M., 118
McMahon, M., 10
McNeely, R. L., 103
Mecca, A. M., 83
Meehl, P., 110
Meeker, J., 63
Melton, G. B., 54
Menard, S., 96
Mencken, H. L., 160
Mendelsohn, H., 448
Mendenhall, W., 128, 134, 139, 152
Mendes, H. A., 142
Merton, R., 40
Mertz, W., 165
Michielutte, R., 184
Miles, M. B., 109, 214, 247, 291
Milgram, S., 69
Miller, A. G., 69
Miller, D. C., 109, 121, 169, 291, 358, 368
Miller, E. R., 52
Miller, L. P., 337
Miller, M. L., 121, 240, 242
Miner, L. E., 436
Miron, M., 358
Mitchell, J., 79, 291
Mitsos, S. B., 358
Moe, K., 50
Mohr, L. B., 331
Mohr, V., 267
Monaghan, P., 54
Moody, E. J., 224
Morash, M., 328
Morelock, M., 12
Morgan, D. L., 184, 230
Morganstein, D., 422
Morris, E., 165
Morrison, R. S., 57
Moser, C. A., 139, 162, 165, 168, 170
Moses, B. S., 109, 199, 291, 368
Motz, A. B., 15
Mowbray, C., 174, 176
Mowrer, H., 25
Mueller, D. J., 368
Murphy, C., 229
Murphy, C. E., 454
Murphy, J., 14, 201
Murray, L., 47

Nachmias, C., 259
Nachmias, D., 259
Nader, R., 3
Nagel, E., 31
Nas, T. F., 342
Nelsen, J. C., 2, 24, 294, 295, 310
Nelson, K., 199
Nelson, R. O., 15, 294
Newell, C., 109, 368
Newman, E., 289
Nicholls, W. L., 188
Nielson, J. M., 88
Nigro, G. N., 213
Nixon, R., 340
Nord, C. W., 23
Norland, S. E., 94
Nurius, P., 15, 293

Ogilvie, D. M., 206, 210
O'Hare, T., 2
Oksenberg, L., 169, 186
Ollendick, T. H., 304, 305, 307, 368
O'Malley, P. M., 179
Opper, S., 101
Orcutt, B., 287
Orgel, M., 3
Orman, D.T., 66
Orme, J. G., 109, 291, 314, 316, 366, 418, 419
Orne, M. T., 276
Orshanksy, M., 31
Osborn, C. A., 58
Osgood, C. E., 356, 358
Ost, L. G., 304
Ott, L., 128, 134, 139, 152

Pardeck, J., 14, 201
Parker, M.W., 201
Parker, R., 158, 166, 169, 181
Patterson, C. J., 27
Patton, M. Q., 343
Pauly, E., 324
Pechman, J., 283
Pepler, D. J., 228
Perkins, C., 203
Perrow, C., 145
Perrson, R., 399
Peters, D., 47
Peterson, D. M., 72
Peterson, R. R., 63, 75
Peterson, S., 85, 212
Peyrot, M., 276
Phelps, E., 195
Phillips, D., 14
Phillips, D. C., 41
Phillips, D. P., 272
Piaget, J., 101
Piliavin, I., 197, 210, 241
Pinkston, E. M., 233, 234
Pittman, D. J., 63

Plotkin, J., 47
Poindexter, S. E., 484
Polsky, N., 72
Pope, H., 170
Presser, S., 159, 187
Pressman, J., 324
Price, J. L., 121, 215
Prothro, J. W., 204
Punch, M., 223
Purcell, P., 85, 212
Pyke, S., 15

Radbill, S. X., 78
Rae, L., 181
Rainwater, L., 63
Rajab, M. H., 66
Ramanaiah, N.V., 364
Rank, M. R., 40
Rapee, R. M., 304
Rathje, W., 229
Ratzan, R. M., 52
Ravizza, R., 283
Ray, W., 283
Rea, L., 158, 166, 169
Reamer, F. G., 25, 69
Reece, R., 54
Reed, J. G., 473
Reese, H. W., 45
Register, C., 23
Reid, P. N., 354
Reid, S., 116
Reid, W., 12, 206, 292, 316
Rein, M., 354
Reinharz, S., 96, 180
Reinherz, H., 2
Reiser, S., 165
Reiss, A. K., 143
Repp, A., 248
Reynolds, M., 363
Reynolds, P. D., 47, 54
Rezac, P. R., 24
Rhodes, L., 143
Richardson, D., 56
Riecken, H., 242
Ries, J. B., 454
Robinson, E. A. R., 88
Robinson, J., 109, 291, 368
Robinson, W. S., 85
Robinson-Simpson, G., 103
Rogers, C., 25
Roosevelt, F. D., 127
Root, M., 41
Rosen, A., 3, 24
Rosenberg, M., 187, 347
Rosenberg, P., 78
Rosenhan, D. L., 117, 223, 239
Rosenthal, R., 22, 276
Rosnow, R., 276
Rossi, P., 6, 147, 280, 281, 319, 320, 322, 326, 327, 330, 332, 333, 334, 335, 340

Rossman, G., 247
Roth, D., 146
Rothman, J., 16
Rudd, M. D., 66
Ruggles, P., 31
Runcie, J. F., 239
Russell, B., 36
Russell, M., 287, 311
Rutman, L., 7, 215, 324
Rygor, R., 144

Sagan, C., 41
Salant, P., 138, 183, 187
Salisbury, B. R., 85
Sandefur, G., 23
Saunders, D. G., 103
Saveanu, T., 146
Savola, K., 195
Saxe, L., 243
Scarce, R., 54
Schachter, S., 242
Schaeffer, N. C., 179
Schafer, A., 50
Scheaffer, R. L., 128, 134, 139, 152
Scheflen, A. E., 55
Schiffman, S., 363
Schoenherr, R. A., 125
Schuckit, M., 31
Schulman, G. I., 276, 281
Schumacher, D., 454
Schuman, H., 159, 187
Schutte, N. S., 109, 368
Schwarz, N., 191
Scott, C., 168
Scott, J., 206, 209
Scott, R. A., 149
Sechrest, L., 227
Segal, S., 320
Seiber, J., 69
Seibert, S. M., 364
Seiler, L. H., 354, 356
Sellitz, C., 239
Settle, R., 179
Shadish, W., 343
Shamdasni, P. N., 191
Shapiro, I., 208
Sharp, P., 184
Shaver, P., 109, 291, 368
Sheafor, B., 3, 7
Shearing, C. D., 81
Sheley, J. F., 225, 242
Sherman, L., 63, 268, 271, 330
Sherman, R., 109, 291, 368
Sherrod, L., 195
Shertzer, M., 454
Shilts, R., 79
Shireman, J. F., 23
Shneidman, E. S., 206, 210
Shulman, L., 109, 112, 113, 114
Shupe, A. D., Jr., 223, 245

Sieber, J., 195
Siegal, H., 54
Siegel, D., 287
Silver, B., 179
Silverman, D., 69, 247
Singer, E., 52
Sipprelle, C. N., 276
Skinner, H., 118, 365
Skipper, J. K., 72
Slotnick, R. S., 4
Slutsky, R., 62
Smart, B., 221
Smelser, M. J., 83
Smith, A. W., 148, 201
Smith, H. W., 47, 54, 176
Smith, K. W., 191
Smith, M., 324
Smith, S. H., 56, 428, 436
Smith, T. W., 159, 214
Soby, B., 6, 83
Socolar, M. J., 337
Spates, J. L., 207, 209
Spitzer, R. L., 147
Sprague, R. L., 60
Sproull, L., 165
Squire, P., 127
Stablein, R. E., 16
Stake, R. E., 343
Stanley, J. C., 112, 258, 267, 272, 275
Steele, P., 165
Stefl, M. E., 147
Stein, B. S., 96
Stein, J., 19
Stewart, D. W., 191, 215
Stewart, L., 85, 212
Stewart, W., 68
Stone, P. J., 206, 210
Straf, M., 195
Straits, B. C., 276, 281
Straus, M., 33, 101, 103, 162, 165, 368
Strauss, A. L., 39, 77, 221, 247
Street, D., 145
Stricker, G., 17
Strickland, S. P., 78
Stuart, A., 152
Suci, G. J., 356, 358
Sudman, S., 127, 131, 152, 157, 159, 167, 171, 177, 179, 191
Suen, H. K., 240
Sugarman, D. B., 164
Sugimoto, T., 102, 103
Sullivan, C., 92
Sullivan, T. J., 17, 31
Sulzer-Azaroff, B., 27
Summers, G. F., 359
Sutherland, E., 26

Taber, M., 208
Tannenbaum, P. H., 356, 358
Tasker, F., 27

Taylor, S. J., 238, 239
Teich, A., 57
Teitler, J. O., 24
Tesch, R., 247
Thiemann, S., 418
Thomas, E. J., 16
Thornton, C., 338
Thrasher, S., 174, 176
Thurstone, L. L., 353, 354, 355, 356
Timberlake, E., 174, 175, 176
Timms, N., 354
Timpane, P. M., 283
Tolman, R., 419
Toseland, R. W., 292
Tran, T. V., 114, 115
Treas, J., 197
Tripodi, T., 56, 120, 152, 169, 316
Tsai, Y., 148
Tsui, J., 165
Tucker, W., 172
Turem, J., 289
Turnbull, J. E., 3

Uchida, C., 91

VanHilst, A., 197
Vannicelli, M., 25
Vasconcellos, J., 83
Vasu, M., 119
Verdonik, E., 195
Vernon, J. A., 212
Videka-Sherman, L., 316
Vidich, A., 53
Vinokur, A., 186
Vinter, R. D., 145
VonThurn, D. R., 52
Vrettos, J. S., 424

Wagenaar, A. C., 133
Wainer, H., 152
Waite, L. J., 24
Wakefield, J. C., 86, 221
Waksberg, J., 188
Walker, J. R., 453
Wallgren, A., 399
Wallgren, B., 399
Wallnau, L. B., 425
Ward, D., 340
Warwick, D. P., 177
Wayne, I., 203
Webb, E. J., 227, 242
Webb, J. D., 215
Weber, M., 63, 217, 221
Weber, R. P., 201, 206
Weeks, M., 189
Weinberg, M., 72
Weinberg, M. S., 128
Weis, J. G., 120
Weisberg, H. F., 191

Weiss, C., 320, 326, 327, 332, 340
Weiss, H. B., 343
Weiss, R. L., 291
Weiss, R. S., 191
Weitzman, E. B., 214
Weitzman, L. J., 74, 75
Welljams-Dorof, A., 61
Wells, K., 198
Wells, W. G., 358
Wentland, E. J., 191
Westling, B. E., 304
White, G., 294
Whyte, W. F., 53, 224, 247
Wildavsky, A., 324

Williams, C., 248
Williams, L. F., 114, 115
Williams, T., 222
Willis, G., 147
Wilson, T., 221
Wingard, D., 194
Witkin, B. R., 6
Witt, K. J., 118
Wiviott, M., 133
Wolfe, B. E., 3
Wolfe, V. V., 110
Wolfgang, M. E., 57
Wright, B., 358
Wright, J. D., 147

Wrightsman, L., 109, 291, 368
Wuebben, P. L., 276, 281

Young, C., 195
Young, F., 363
Young, L., 184
Youngblade, L., 77

Zakour, M. J., 360
Zambrana, R. E., 114, 148
Zeisel, H., 399
Zill, N., 23

Subject Index

AB design, 299
ABAB design, 299
Absolutist, 50–51
Abstracts, 449, 464–466
Accountability, 4
  See also Cost-benefit analysis
Accretion, 229–230
Advocacy
  ethics of, 63–64
  evaluation and, 337–340
Advocates, 440
African Americans. *See* Minorities
Aged
  attitude scale, 357
  studies of, 145, 329
Aggression
  coding, 235
  observational study of, 242
  scales for, 364
AIDS (Acquired Immune Deficiency
  Syndrome), 54, 78–80
Alcohol Use Inventory, 365
Alpha error, 416–417
Alpha level, 416–417, 418–419
Alphanumeric variables, 373–374
America on the Line, 140
American Psychiatric Association, 117
American Psychological Association, 126,
  282, 316
American Society of Criminology,
  126
*American Sociological Association Code of
  Ethics,* 67, 478–480
An Author's Guide to Social Work Journals,
  448
Analysis of data
  preparing for, 370–376
  research steps and, 9–10
  single-subject, 312–314
Analysis of variance (ANOVA), 420
Annual Register of Grant Support,
  436–439
Anonymity
  defined, 56
  observation and, 241
  questionnaires and, 167–168
Applied research, 5–6
  See also Evaluation research
Area sampling, 134–136
Assessment of client functioning
  computers and, 14–15
  as focal area, 6–7, 117, 236–237,
  292–293
Association, 36
Asymmetrical distributions, 380
Attitude Toward Church Scale, 356
Availability sampling, 141–143
Available data
  agencies and, 194–199, 201

assessment, 209–211
  bias in, 211
  coding of, 201–204, 207–208
  described, 194
  longitudinal analysis and, 210–211
  method, 13
  minorities and, 211–213
  reactivity in, 210
  secondary analysis of, 195
  single-subject designs and, 291
  social workers, 212
  sources, 195–197
  validity of, 200–201
Average. *See* Central tendency

Baltimore LIFE Project, 332–335
Bar graphs, 385–386
Bar room behavior, 228–229
Baselines, 7, 289–294
Basic research, 5–6, 320–321
Behavior and social environment, as focal
  area, 6, 88–89, 102–103
Behavioral-ecological approach, 4
Beta error, 416–417
Bias
  available data and, 211
  in quota samples, 144
  nonresponse, 128
  operational definitions and, 33
  response, 162–165, 169
  sampling, 211
Bivariate statistics, 388, 403
Block grants, 429
Blocking, 257–258, 260–263
Bookmarks, 486
Brainstorming, 437
Budgets, 446
Bullets, 443
Burnout, 34–35

Cambridge-Sommerville Youth Study,
  326
Card catalog, 461
Case histories, 287
Case-opening cohort, 41
Casual experiments, 253–254
Catalog of Federal Domestic Assistance,
  432–434, 453
Categorical grants, 429
Causal inference, 36–39
Causality
  defined, 36
  experiments and, 254–256, 279–280
  practice models and, 24
Cause and effect
  defined, 36–39
  evaluation research, 321

CD-ROM
  abstracts on, 466
  data sets on, 471
  grant information on, 432
  library access, 458–459
  sampling use in, 151–152
Census, Bureau of, 85–86, 124, 126, 153,
  197
Census Web site, 216
Center for Applied Research in Educa-
  tion, 250
Center for Mental Health Services Re-
  search Measures Collection, 121
Centers for Disease Control, 79
Central limit theorem, 414–415
Central tendency, 405–406
Certificates of confidentiality, 54–55, 57
Changing criterion design, 307–309
Chi-square, 420–421
Child Well-Being Scales, 199
Children
  aggression scales for, 364
  of lesbians, 26–27
Citation styles
  Harvard method, 450
  Internet, 453
  serial method, 450–451
City directories, 127
Clever Hans, 276–277
Clients
  ethics and, 64–67
  satisfaction scale, 354–355
  See also Assessment of client func-
  tioning
Clinical Measurement Package, 292–293,
  363, 367
Clinical research
  assessment of, 310–311
  ethics and, 64
  model, 286–288
  process, 288–289
  See also Scientific practice
Closed-ended questions, 156–159
Closure, 11
Cluster sampling, 134–136
Codebooks, 375–376, 471
Codes of ethics, 478–482
Coding schemes, 202–204
Coding sheets, 231
Coding
  available data and, 201–204,
  207–208
  edge coding, 376
  exhaustive categories, 372
  missing values, 375
  mutually exclusive categories, 372
  observation and, 231–238
  of aggression, 235
  of marital conflict, 236–237

of social interaction, 231–235
schemes, 371–375
Coefficient of determination, 410
Coefficient of reproducibility, 361–362
Coercion
ethics and, 65
external validity and, 276
See also Ethics
Cohort groups, 331–332
Committee on the Status of Women in Sociology, 33, 148
Common sense, 21–22
Community Oriented Needs Assessment, 6
Community forums, 438
Community foundations, 430
Computer Assisted Qualitative Data Systems, 250
Computer-Assisted Social Services (CASS), 15, 121, 189, 293, 314, 367
Computer reporting network (CRN), 40–41
Computer-assisted telephone interviewing (CATI), 188–189
Computer-assisted survey research (CASR), 118–119
Computers in Human Services, 15
Computers in Mental Health, 15
Computers
agency data and, 40–41
content analysis by, 214–215
data coding, 372–375
journals, 152
libraries and, 458–459
measurement and, 118–119
observational research by, 248–249
sampling and, 151–152
scaling software, 353
single-subject designs and, 312–314
software, 314
surveys and, 188–189
COMSEARCH, 436
Concealment, 223–224
Concepts
definition of, 30–31
development of, 80–81
literature review and, 81–83
minorities and, 33–34
Conclusions, 10, 449–450
See also Hypotheses
Concurrent validity, 109
Confidence interval, 136–138
Confidence limits, 136–138
Confidentiality
certificates of, 54–55, 57
ethics, 50
interviewing and, 169
principles of, 52–57
survey research, 167–168
Conflict Tactics (CT) scale, 100–101, 162–165

Construct validity, 110
Content analysis
defined, 201
reliability in, 206–207
sampling in, 208–209
units of analysis and, 204–205
validity in, 205–206
Web site, 216
Content validity, 108
Contingency control, 394–397
Contingency questions, 164–165
Contingency tables, 388–397
Continuous audience response technology (CART), 119
Continuous variables, 106–107
Control
condition, 255–256
experimental, 254–256, 280
groups, 65–67, 255–256, 260–263
purposive sampling and, 144–145
single-subject designs and, 310
statistical, 332
variables, 255, 310
Control groups, 65–67, 255–256, 260–263
Corporate Foundation Profiles, 435–436
Corporate foundations, 430–432
Correction formula, 139
Correlation coefficient, 409–410
Cost-benefit analysis
described, 332–336
grant writing and, 437
of Supported Work, 338–339
Cost-effective analysis, 336–337
Costs
direct, 333
estimating, 333
experiments, 280
indirect, 93
project feasibility, 91–93
Cover letter, 166–168
Crime
operationalization of, 33
research on, 202–203
systematic error and, 116
theories of, 33
Crime index, 203
Crime Statistics Site, 216
Crime Victimization Survey, 153
Criterion validity, 108, 241
Critical Path Method (CPM), 439
Critical thinking, 471
Cronbach's alpha, 114, 353, 355
Cross-race interviewing, 179–180
Cross-sectional studies, 37, 87–90
Cultural sensitivity, 114–115
Curbing, 179
Current Population Survey, 153
Curvilinear relationship, 407

Data
archives, 195
cleaning, 378–379
collection, 9
distributions, 380, 404, 411–414
missing, 197–199
qualitative and quantitative, 174–176, 221–222
single-subject design analysis, 312–314
sorting, 378
source versus unit of analysis, 85–86
sources, 470–471
statistical properties, 403–404
statistical validity and, 200–201
See also Available data
Data analysis
bivariate, 388, 403
defined, 370
multivariate, 388, 403
preparation for, 370-376
research process, 9–10
single-subject, 312–314
univariate, 380, 403
Web sites, 398
Data distributions
normal, 411–413
sampling, 414
standard normal, 411-413
types, 380
Data entry, 376–378
Debriefing, 58
Deception, 50–52
Deduction, 27–28, 34–36, 198–200
Delinquency
available data and, 202–203
dimensional sampling, 145
sampling and, 142–143
Demand characteristics, 276
Department of Health and Human Services (DHHS), 47, 53, 62, 78
Dependent variable
causality and, 37
defined, 32
Descriptive research, 5
Descriptive statistics, 403, 405–413
Design development, 9
Design Power, 151–152, 418–419
Dewey decimal system, 460–461
Diagnostic and Statistical Manual of Mental Disorders, (DSM), 117
Different group time series design, 273
Differential association theory, 27–28
Dimensional sampling, 145–147
Direct costs, 333
Direct replication, 309
Disclosure of results, 58–59
Discount rate, 334–335
Discrete variables, 106–107
Discrimination (in scaling), 351–352
Discriminatory power score (DP), 351–353, 359

Disguised observation, 50–52, 228–229
Dispersion, measures of, 406–407
Dissemination of results, 337
Distress, 57–58
Distributions, 380
Divorce Revolution, 74–76
Document delivery service, 459
Documentation, 11
Documents division of library, 458
DP score. *See* Discriminatory power
 score

Ecological fallacy, 85
Edge coding, 376
Educational Resources Information Cen-
 ter (ERIC), 459
Effect size, 419
Electric utilities, 127
Empirical data, 4
Empirical practice. *See* Clinical research
Equal-appearing intervals, 353–355
Equivalence, 111
ERIC Clearinghouse on Assessment and
 Evaluation, 342
Erosion, 229–230
Error
 ethics and, 59, 63
 in hypothesis testing, 416–417
 in measurement, 115–117
 proportionate reduction in, 408–410
 random, 115–116, 162
 reanalysis of data and, 74–76
 sampling and, 127–132
 stratified sampling and, 130–132
 systematic, 115–117, 162–165
 Type I, 416–417
 Type II, 416–419
Ethics
 absolutist position, 50–51
 advocacy and, 63–64
 anonymity, 56, 167–168, 241
 clients and, 60–61, 64–67
 clinical research, 64
 codes of, 67–68, 478–482
 coercion, 65
 concealment, 223–224
 confidentiality, 50, 53–55, 167–168
 control groups and, 65–67
 courts and, 53–54
 deception, 50–52
 defined, 45
 error and, 59, 63
 experiments and, 268–271
 evaluation research, 481–482
 harm, 45
 informed consent, 50–53, 56–57, 59,
  65
 Internet sources, 68
 minorities, 46–50
 Nuremberg trials and, 46

participant observation, 223–224
 privacy, 45, 55–56
 risk-benefit doctrine, 52
 self-determination, 45
 survey research and, 167–169
 values, 45
 withholding treatment and, 65–67,
  268–271
Evaluability assessment, 324–325
Evaluation Quarterly, 321
Evaluation research
 barriers to, 337–341
 basic research comparison, 320–321
 cohort groups and, 331–332
 cost-benefit analysis, 332–336
 cost-effective analysis, 336–337
 defined, 319
 designs for, 328–337
 dissemination of, 340
 ethics of, 481–482
 goals of, 5
 in practice, 11
 journals, 340
 minorities and, 328
 priorities, 320
 problem selection and, 73–76
 reasons for, 319–320
 statistical control and, 332
 types, 321–322
 Web sites, 342
Ex ante analysis, 333
Ex post analysis, 333
Ex-sample, 151
Exhaustive categories, 204
Experience, 20–21
Experimental attrition, 263–264
Experimental condition, 254
Experimental design, 420
Experimental effectiveness, 296–298
Experimental effects, 281
Experimental group, 254, 260–263
Experimental stimulus, 254
Experimental variability, 255
Experimentation, 253
Experimenter expectations, 276–277
Experiments
 assessment of, 279–281
 classic, 265
 defined, 253
 double-blind, 277
 factorial, 267
 field, 253
 laboratory, 253
 minorities and, 278–279
 multiple experimental group, 267–268
 posttest-only, 267
 pretest-posttest, 265–266
 single-subject designs and, 287
 Solomon four-group design, 266
 Web sites, 282
Explanatory research, 5

External validity
 defined, 275
 experiments and, 275–278
 threats to, 275–278
Extraneous variability, 255

Face validity, 108, 240–241
Facism, 212–213
Factor analysis, 358
Factorial design, 267
Family foundations, 430
Family preservation, 198–199
Feasibility, 90–94
Federal Assistance Program Retrieval System,
 432
Federal Bureau of Investigation, 116, 201
Federal contracts, 429
Federal Register, 432
Field notes, 238–239
File Transfer Protocol (FTP), 485
First order tables, 395
Flow model, 325
Focal areas
 assessment of client functioning, 6–7,
  117, 236–237, 292–293
 behavior and social environments, 6,
  88–89, 102–103
 defined, 5–6
 needs assessment, 6, 26–27, 146–147,
  162–165, 174–176
 practice effectiveness, 7–8, 12, 34–35,
  304–307
 program evaluation, 6–7, 58–61,
  133–134, 198–199, 202–203,
  226–227, 260–263, 268–270,
  334–335, 338–339, 354–355
Focus groups, 230, 322
Formative evaluation, 321–324
Formula grants, 429
Foundation Directory, 428, 435–436
Foundation Fundamentals, 436
Foundations, 430–436
Fraud, 57–63
Frequency count, 207
Frequency distributions, 380–385
Frequency polygons, 387
Fully ordered data, 409
Funding sources, 336, 439–442
 See also Grants
Funneling, 165

Gallery of Data Visualization, 398
Gamma, 409
Garbology, 229
Gender, 179–180, 279, 328
 See also Women
General purpose foundations, 430
General Services Administration, 453

General Social Survey, 153, 367
Generalization, 275, 281
Goals, 288–289, 325–327
Gopher, 485
Government documents, 467–470
Graffiti, 229–230
Grants
    budget, 446
    components, 444–446
    defined, 428
    planning, 436–437
    submission, 447
    types, 428–430
Grants Database, 432
Graphs, 385–388
Groups
    control, 255–256
    experimental, 254–256
    unit of analysis, 84
Gun control, 331
Guttman scales, 358–362
    See also Scales, Scaling

Harm, 45
Harvard method of referencing, 450
Hispanics, 148
Histograms, 387
History, 259, 299, 332
Homeless, sampling and, 146–147
Homosexuals, 26–27, 55–56, 79
Household, 85–86
Human services
    abstracts for, 464–466
    defined, 2
    evaluation, 320
    journals for, 462–464
    problem source, 76–77
    scaling in, 363–364
    See also Practice
Hypertension Network, 282
Hypertext, 485
Hypotheses
    deduction and, 32, 34–36
    development of, 31–32
    evaluation research, 320
    literature review and, 81–82
    sample size and, 136
    types of, 415

Impact assessment, 319–320
Implementation, 11, 321, 323–324
Independence, 404
Independent variable
    causality and, 37–39
    defined, 32
    experimental design and, 254–256
    literature review and, 81–82
Indexes, 102
Indexes to human service literature,
    464–466

Indicators, 100–101
Indirect costs, 93
Induction, 34–36, 198–200
Inference, 21
Inferential statistics, 403, 413–421
Informants, 225
Information technology, 14–15
Informed consent
    ethics, 50–53
    sex offender research, 56–57
    NASW Code of Ethics and, 480–481
    sponsored research, 59
    study design, 93
    vulnerable clients and, 65–67
Institutional review boards (IRB),
    47–49, 68
Instrumentation, 259
Intensity, 208
Inter-University Consortium of Political
    and Social Research, 195, 216
Interactive sampling, 143
Interlibrary loan, 457
Internal validity, 258–264, 269
Internet
    citation format, 453
    content analysis, 216
    data analysis, 398
    defined, 484
    ethics, 68
    evaluation research, 342
    experiments, 282
    grants, 453
    library sources, 471
    observation, 250
    problem formulation, 95
    sampling, 153
    scaling, 367
    single-subject design, 316
Interquartile range, 359
INTERV, 189
Interval data, statistics for, 409–411
Interval measures, 104–105, 107, 353
Interval width, 384
Interviewers, 177–178
Interviews
    assessment of, 180–181
    control of, 178–179
    defined, 156
    practice and research compared, 186
    probes, 178
    social relationships, 177–180
    structure of, 170–171
Inverse relationship, 32
Items, 102, 346–350

Journal of Applied Behavior Analysis, 316
Journal of Social Service Research, 142
Journals for human services, 462–464
Judges, 348, 354
Judgmental sampling, 144–145

Justice Information Center, 95, 342, 453
Juvenile courts, 202–203

Kendall's tau, 409
Key informants, 438
Knowledge
    common sense, 21–22
    experiential, 20–21
    traditional, 19–20
Kruskal's tau, 408

Labor Statistics, Bureau of, 153, 471
Laboratory experiments, 253
Lambda, 408
Lesbians, 26–27
Levels of measurement, 103–106,
    207–208, 346–347, 401–403, 407
Library divisions, 457–458
Library of Congress, 460–461, 472
Likert scales, 350–353
    See also Scales, Scaling
Literary Digest, 127–128, 141
Literature review, 81–83, 93
Longitudinal research, 37, 87–90,
    210–211

Machiavellianism scale, 348
Main characters, 205
Management Information Report, 196
Marital conflict observation, 236–237
Matching, 256–257, 331
Maturation, 259
Mean, 406
Measurement
    cultural sensitivity and, 114–115
    definition, 99
    error in, 115–117
    indicators, 100–101
    instruments, 109, 291–294
    items, 102
    levels, 103–106, 207–208, 346–347
    minorities and, 114–115
Measures
    of central tendency, 405–406
    of dispersion, 406–407
Measures for Clinical Practice: A Sourcebook,
    292–293
Measures of association, 407–411
Median, 405–407
Mental Health Net, 367
Minnesota Higher Education Center
    Against Violence and Abuse, 95
Minorities
    available data analysis and, 211–213
    concepts and, 33–34
    ethics and, 46–50
    evaluation research and, 328
    experiments and, 278–279
    homosexuals, 26–27, 55–56, 79

institutional review boards, 68
interview relationship and, 179–180
measurement and, 114–115
observational research on, 221, 243
operational definitions, 33–34
problem selection and, 77–80
research issue, 8, 243
research on, 7–8
sampling and, 148
Misconduct, 59–63
Missing data, 197–199
Missing values, 374
Mode, 405
Monetizing benefits, 333
Monthly Catalog of U.S. Government Publications, 459, 467–470
Multidimensional scales, 362–363
Multiple baseline design, 299–307
Multiple-forms reliability, 112–113
Multiple regression, 420
Multiple testing effects, 112
Multiple time series design, 273–275
Multiple treatment design, 306–307
Multiple treatment interference, 277–278
Multistage sampling, 134–136, 209
Multitrait-multimethod validity, 110
Multivariate statistics. *See* Statistics
Mutually exclusive categories, 204

NASW News, 209
National Archive of Computerized Data on Aging, 216
National Archive of Criminal Justice Data, 216
National Association of Social Workers
available data study, 212
code of ethics, 67–68, 480–482
sampling frame, 126
National Center for Health Statistics, 197
National Clearinghouse for Alcohol and Drug Information, 95, 342, 367
National Clearinghouse on Alcohol and Drug Information, 453
National Crime Survey (NCS), 116 202–203
National Criminal Justice Reference Service, 95
National Institute of Child Health and Human Development, 195
National Institute of Justice, 91–92, 195
National Institute of Mental Health, 60–61
National Institutes of Health, 62
National Science Foundation, 78
Native Americans, 114–115, 148
Nazi concentration camps, 46–50
Needs assessment
as focal area, 6, 26–27, 146–147, 162–165, 174–176

formative evaluation and, 322
grants and, 437–438
Negative relationships, 32, 407
Nominal data, statistics for, 408
Nominal measures, 103–104, 107
Nonprobability samples, 140–147
Nonreactive observation, 227–228
Nonresponse bias, 128
Nonschedule-standardized interviews, 171–172
Normal distribution, 404, 411–413
Null hypothesis, 415, 418–419
Numeric variables, 373–374
Nuremberg Code, 47

Objectives, 327
Objectivity, 24–25, 88–89
Observation
aggression and, 242
anonymity and, 241
assessment of, 244–245
coding, 231–238
computers and, 248–249
cooperation, 225
disguised, 50–52, 228–229
hidden, 228
human service practice and, 245–246
marital conflict, 236–237
methods, 11
minorities, 221, 243
nonreactive, 227–228
participant, 223–227
reactivity and, 242–243
recording, 231–239
reliability and validity, 221–222
seat belt study, 132–133
single-subject designs and, 291
steps in, 224–227
structured, 230
techniques, 219
token economy, 226–227
unobtrusive, 227–230
Web sites, 250
Observer expectations, 241
Observer roles, 222–224
Online public access catalog, 459
Open-ended questions, 156–159, 189
Operational definitions
available data and, 201
defined, 31
literature review and, 82
measurement and, 99
minorities and, 33–34
of homelessness, 146
Opportunity costs, 333
Optical scanning, 377–378
Ordinal data
statistics for, 408–409
Guttman scale as, 362

Ordinal measures, 104
Organizations
mission, 438–439
unit of analysis, 84–85

Panel studies, 87–90, 189
Paragraph, unit of analysis, 205
Partial tables, 395
Partially ordered data, 409
Participant observation
ethics of, 223–224
in human services, 245–246
role alternatives, 222–224
steps in, 224–227
Participants
in observation research, 223
payment to, 168
researcher as, 220
Pearson's *r,* 409–410
Peer review, 61–62
Percentage difference, 389
Periodicals, 462–464
Periodicity, 130, 209
Person-environment fit, 348–350
Personal interest, 72
Phi coefficient, 408
PhoneDisc USA Residential, 151–152
Physical trace, 229–230
Pie charts, 387–388, 391
Pilot study, 9, 90, 93
Pittsburgh Survey, 156
Placebos, 277
Point-in-time cohort, 40–41
Population
definition, 125
homogeneity, 138
Pornography, 340
Positive relationship, 32, 407
Positivism, 221
Poverty, 223
Practice
computer use in, 312–314
effectiveness, 7–8, 12, 34–35, 304–307
interviews, 186
reactivity in, 242–243, 246
research parallels and linkages, 2, 10–12
sampling and, 149–150
scientific, 24–25
stages of, 10–12
See also Human services
Practice effectiveness
as focal area, 7–8, 12, 34–35, 304–307
Precision, 136–139
Predictive research, 5
Predictive validity, 109–110
Preexperimental designs, 264–265
Prejudice. *See* Minorities

President's Commission on Pornography, 340
Pretest, 9, 322, 359–360
PREVLINE, 342
Primary sampling units, 133, 153
Privacy, 45, 55–56
Probability sample, 414
Probability theory, 128–129, 413–414
Probes, 178
Problem formulation
 research process, 8–9
 selection, 72–77, 437, 439
 shaping, 80–90
 statistical power and, 419
 Web sites, 95
Program, as unit of analysis, 85
Program evaluation
 confidentiality in, 56–58
 defined, 7
 as focal area, 7, 60–61, 132–133,
  198–199, 202–203, 226–227,
  260–263, 268–271, 334–335,
  338–339, 354–355
Program evaluation review technique
 (PERT), 439
Program inputs, 325
Project ALERT, 260–263
Project for Windows, 439
Project grants, 428–429
Proportional reduction in error (PRE),
 408–410
Proposal Development Workbook
 (PDW), 437
Propositions, 26–27
Proximate goals, 326
Psychiatric Status Schedule, 147
Public catalog, 461
Public Health Service (PHS), 46–47
Pure research, 5–6, 320–321
Purposive sampling, 144–145

QDATA, 377–379
Qualitative data, 174–176, 221
Qualitative Report, 250
Qualitative research, 86–87
Qualitative Research Resources, 250
Quantitative data, 221–222
Quantitative research, 86–87
Quartiles, 407
Quasi-experimental designs, 270–275,
 330–332
Questionnaires
 assessment of, 170
 costs, 92
 cover letter and, 166–168
 defined, 156
 follow-ups, 168
 length, 168–169
 respondent payment, 168

response rate, 165–169
 structure of, 161–165
Questions
 contingency, 164–165
 format, 161
 open-ended, 189
 order, 161
 types, 156–159
 wording, 159–160
Quota sampling, 143–144

Random assignment, 256–257
Random digit dialing, 126–127, 152
Random error, 115–116, 162
Random numbers, 127, 129, 257,
 475–476
Random samples, 129–136
Randomization
 alternatives to, 331–332
 disadvantages, 280
 in evaluation, 329–331
 logic of, 257–258
 monitoring of, 330–331
 rationing services by, 330
Range, 406–407
Rapid assessment instruments (RAI),
 292–293
Rapport, 225–226
Ratio measures, 105–106
Ratio variables, 107
Raw data distributions, 380
Reactivity
 available data and, 210
 control of, 277
 defined, 86
 in human service practice, 242–243,
  246
 in observational research, 242–243
 of self-report, 294
 settings and, 276–277
 testing and, 275
Re-analysis, problem selection, 74–76
References, 450–451
Refusal rate, 171–177
Regression, 420
Regression, internal validity and,
 259–263
Regression discontinuity design, 332
Relationships
 between variables, 407
 bivariate, 388
 spurious, 396
Reliability
 available data and, 204
 Clinical Measurement Package,
  292–293
 content analysis and, 206–207
 defined, 111
 equivalence, 111
 intercoder, 207, 242

language differences, 114–115
 multiple forms, 112–113
 observation research and, 221–222,
  240–242
 scaling and, 346
 Spearman-Brown correction formula,
  113–114
 split-half, 113–114
 stability, 111
 test-retest, 111-112
Replication
 control variables and, 310
 direct, 309
 domestic violence experiments,
  268–271
 external validity and, 278
 fraud detection and, 61–62
 in science, 22
 problem formulation, 74–76
 single-subject, 309–310
 systematic, 309–310
Representative samples, 124–125,
 128–129, 136
Reproducibility, 359–361
Request for Proposals (RFP), 78, 429
Research
 basic, 5–6, 320–321
 costs, 91–93
 cross-sectional, 87–90
 defined, 3
 explanatory, 5
 goals of, 3–5
 longitudinal, 87–90
 parallels to practice, 10–12
 practice effectiveness, 7–8, 34–35,
  304–307
 qualitative, 86–87
 quantitative, 86–87
 service interference, 66–67
 steps in, 8–10
Research hypothesis, 415
Research reports, 447–452
Respondents
 contacting, 171–177
 payment to, 92
Response, bias, 162–165, 169
Response delay, 118
Response pattern anxiety, 351
Response rate, 128, 165–169
Response recording, 178
Response set, 164, 351
Restricted assignment, 260–263
Reversal design, 299
Risk-benefit approach, 52, 57, 66
Role theory, 34–35
Roper Center, 195
Rosenberg Self-Esteem Scale, 347

Salk polio vaccine, 330
Sample size, statistical power and, 419

Samples
  area, 134–136
  availability, 141–143
  defined, 125
  dimensional, 145–147
  disproportionate random, 132–134
  population and, 124–125
  probability, 129–136
  proportionate, 131–132
  purposive, 144–145
  representative, 128–129, 136
  simple random (SRS), 129
  size, 136–139, 211
  snowball, 143, 149
  stratified, 130–134
  systematic, 129–130
  time, 239–240
  unrepresentative, 275–276
Sampling
  bias, 211
  content analysis and, 208–209
  defined, 124
  distribution, 414
  drug abuse prevention and, 260–263
  error, 128–129, 130–132
  fraction, 139
  frame, 126–128
  generalizing, 149
  interactive, 143
  interval, 130
  literature review and, 82
  minority populations, 148
  random digit dialing and, 126–127
  technique, 139
  validity, 108
  Web sites, 153
Scale discrimination technique, 359
Scale items, 102, 346–350
Scales
  Alcohol Use Inventory, 365
  Attitude Toward Church, 356
  Attitudes Toward the Elderly, 357
  Child Well-Being Scales, 199
  childhood aggression, 364
  client satisfaction, 354–355
  Clinical Measurement Package, 292–293
  Conflict Tactics Scale, 100–101, 162–165
  Guttman Volunteering, 360
  Index of Self-Esteem, 292–293
  Machiavellianism Scale, 348
  Michigan Alcohol Screening Test, 365
  Psychiatric Status Schedule, 147
  Rapid assessment instruments, 292–293
  Rosenberg Self-Esteem, 347
Scaling
  advantages of, 346–347
  defined, 346
  development process, 347–350
  discrimination of items in, 351–353

  formats for, 350–363
  Guttman, 358–362
  in human services, 364–365
  judges in, 354
  Likert, 350–353
  measurement and, 102
  multidimensional, 362
  Semantic differential, 356–358
  single-subject design and, 291–294
  summated rating, 350–351
  Thurstone, 353–356
  unidimensional, 349–350
  validity in, 348–349
  Web sites, 367
Scattergrams, 410–411
Schedule-standardized interviews, 171–173
Scheduling grant projects, 439
Schizophrenics, 226–227
Scholastic Aptitude Test, 109
Science, 19, 22–24
Science Citation Index, 61
Scientific advocacy, 63–64
Scientific practice, 3–4, 24–25
  See also Clinical research
Search engines, 16, 42, 486
Seat belt use, 132–133
Secondary analysis, 195
Selection, 263
Self-determination, 45
Self-esteem scales, 347
Self-report, 294
Semantic differential scales, 356–358
Semi-interquartile range, 406–407
Sensitive research, 47, 54–57
Sentence, as unit of analysis, 205
Serial dependence, 404
Serial method of referencing, 450–451
Sexism, 85–86, 212–213
  See also Women
Shade-treeing, 179
Single-subject designs
  AB, 299
  ABAB, 299
  baselines, 289–294
  changing criterion, 307–309
  clinical research and, 286–288
  defined, 286
  effectiveness and, 7–8, 295–298
  ethics and, 53
  generalization from, 309–310
  goals in, 288–289
  multiple-baseline, 299–303
  multiple-treatment, 306–307
  reversal, 299
  statistics in, 296, 312–314
  Web sites, 316
  See also Clinical research
Skew, 406
Small Town in Mass Society, 53
Snowball sampling, 143, 149

Social research, 3
Social Science Citation Index, 61
Social Science Computer Review, 15, 152
Social Security Administration, 31
Social Work Abstracts, 465
Social Worker Networker, 16, 95
Societal perspective, 336
Society for the Study of Social Problems, 73
Sociometrics Corporation, 472
Solomon Four-Group Design, 266
Somer's *D,* 409
Spearman's rho, 409
Spearman-Brown formula, 113–114
Special purpose foundations, 430
Split-half reliability, 113–114
Sponsored research, 58–59
Spouse abuse
  experimental study of, 268–271
  measurement of, 100–101
  research priorities and, 77–78
  status and, 100–101
Spreadsheets
  data entry, 376
  random number generator, 475
  single-subject design, 312–314
Spurious relationships, 37–38, 396
Stability, 111
Stacks, 457
Standard deviation, 406–407
Standard normal distribution, 411–413
Standard scores, 411–413
State government grants, 429–430
Statistical control, 332
Statistical effectiveness, 298
Statistical hypothesis testing, 415–417
Statistical Navigator Professional, 422-423
Statistical power, 418–419
Statistical regression, 259–263
Statistical significance, 298
Statistics
  bivariate, 388
  choosing, 401–404, 422–423
  data properties and, 403–404
  described, 401
  descriptive, 403, 405–413
  inferential, 403, 413–421
  types, 403
  univariate, 388
Statistics Canada, 216
Statistics and Statistical Graphs, 398
Stratified samples, 130–134
Street Corner Society, 222
String variables, 373–374
Structured observation, 230
Student's *t,* 420
Subjectivism, 221
Summated rating scales, 350–351
Summative evaluation, 312, 324–337
Super-Project, 439

Superintendent of Documents (SUDOCS) Number, 470
Supported Work Program, 338–339
Suppressor variables, 396
Survey research, 11
Survey Sampler, 152
Surveys
    computer assisted, 118–119, 188–189
    confidentiality and, 167–168
    cost comparisons, 182–183
    crime victimization, 153
    Current Population Survey, 153
    defined, 156
    General Social Survey, 153, 367
    interview, 156
    National Crime Victimization Survey, 116, 202–203
    Pittsburgh Survey, 156
    telephone and, 181–184
Symmetrical distributions, 380, 404
Syphilis, 46–47
Systematic error, 116–117, 162–165
Systematic replication, 309–310

Table elaboration, 394–397
Table of contents service, 459
Tables
    contingency, 388
    percentage, 388–389, 394
Technical Assistance Center, 42, 367
Teenage pregnancy, 78
Telephone directories, 126–127
Telnet, 485
Temporal order, 36–37
Test-retest reliability, 111–112
Testing, 259, 275
Theme, as unit of analysis, 205
Theory
    concepts and, 30–31, 80–81
    deductive system, 26–28
    defined, 26
    functions of, 28–30
    personal, 28
    problem selection and, 73
Therapeutic effectiveness, 296
Thurstone scale, 353–356
Time sampling, 239–240
Time sequence, for grants, 439
Time series design, 133, 271–274
    See also Single-subject designs

Token economy, observational study of, 226–227
Topic identification, 72–77, 437
Tradition, 19–20
Treatment phase in SSD, 294–295
Trend studies, 87–90
Type I error, 416–417
Type II error, 416–419

Uncover, 472
Uniform Crime Reports, 116–117, 201
Uniform Resource Locator (URL), 484–485
Unit of analysis
    content analysis and, 204–205
    options for, 83–85
    problem formulation, 78
    problem formulation and, 83–85
    sampling and, 125
    versus data source, 85–86
Univariate analysis, 380
Univariate statistics, 388, 403
Unobtrusive observation, 227–230
Unrepresentative samples, 275–276
Unstandardized interviews, 170–172

Validity
    available data and, 200–201
    construct, 110
    content, 108
    content analysis and, 205–206
    criterion, 108–110, 241
    definition of, 107
    external, 275–278
    face, 108
    internal, 258–259, 269
    known groups, 110
    multitrait-multimethod approach, 110
    observation and, 221–222, 240–242
    sampling, 108
    scale items and, 346, 348–349
Value free controversy, 63–64
Values, 24–25, 45, 63–64
Variables
    alphanumeric, 373–374
    evaluation and, 325
    computer format, 372–375
    continuous, 106–107
    control, 255–310

creation of, 379
dependent and independent, 32, 37–39, 254–256
discrete, 106–107
interaction, 396
interval, 104–105, 107
labeling, 374
nature of relationships, 407
nominal, 103–104
numeric, 373–374
ordinal, 104
ratio, 105–107
string, 373–374
suppressor, 396
Verstehen, 221
Videotape, in observation, 236–237
Viking Form Manager, 189
Voluntary consent, 50–53, 65
Volunteering scale, 360

Withholding treatment, 65–67, 268–271
Women
    AIDS and, 79–80
    experimental study and, 268–271
    female voices, 88–89
    gender insensitivity, 279
    interview relationship and, 179–180
    lesbian mothers, 26–27
    observation research, 236–237
    operational definitions and, 34–36
    performance evaluation and, 328
    purposive sampling and, 145
    research on, 7–8
    research priorities and, 77–78
    work and studies of, 33
Women's Bureau, 471
Words, as unit of analysis, 204
World Wide Web, 484–486
Writing
    grants, 442–447
    process of, 451–452
    research reports, 447–452

Yule's Q, 408

Zero order tables, 395
z-scores, 411–413